# A History of Old English Meter

University of Pennsylvania Press
MIDDLE AGES SERIES
Edited by
*Edward Peters*
Henry Charles Lea Professor
of Medieval History
University of Pennsylvania

A listing of available books in the series
appears at the back of this volume

# A History of
# Old English Meter

## R. D. FULK

*upp*

University of Pennsylvania Press

Philadelphia

*This publication has been supported by a grant from the National Endowment for the Humanities, an independent federal agency.*

Library of Congress Cataloging-in-Publication Data

Fulk, R. D. (Robert Dennis)
    A history of Old English meter / R. D. Fulk.
        p.   cm. — (Middle Ages series)
    Includes bibliographical references and index.
    ISBN 0-8122-3157-0
    1. English language—Old English, ca. 450–1100—Versification.
I. Title. II. Series.
PE257.F85 1992
829´. 1—dc20                           92-30918
                                           CIP

*For Al and Linda David*

# PREFACE

The recent early death of Ashley Crandell Amos is a source of profound regret for Anglo-Saxonists of all interests, but particularly metrists and philologists. Her work on the dating of Old English literature is more ambitious and of wider scope than any similar project conceived by Eduard Sievers and his contemporaries, and its effect on the study of Old English verse has been profound. Although the present study lends support to few of her conclusions about metrical history, it should be apparent that the sort of research presented here would not be possible without the background of the questions about Old English philology that she posed, and the framework for discussion that she constructed. The influence of her work is pervasive in the following pages, and it is to the work of Ashley Amos and Eduard Sievers that this study is most indebted.

It is a pleasure to acknowledge two particular debts, to Thomas Cable and Geoffrey R. Russom, who first gave me detailed and perceptive advice about the chapters of this study devoted to resolution and tertiary stress, and subsequently read the entire manuscript carefully and discerningly for the University of Pennsylvania Press. This book has benefited from their suggestions in countless ways. I am indebted to them in a more general sense, as well, since the influence of their published research on Old English meter should be clear throughout.

Some of the conclusions of Chapter 1 were published under the title "West Germanic Parasiting, Sievers' Law, and the Dating of Old English Verse," *SP* 86 (1989), 117–38; and a draft of Chapter 2 appeared as "Contraction as a Criterion for Dating Old English Verse," *JEGP* 89 (1990), 1–16. I am grateful to the editors of *SP* and *JEGP* for permission to incorporate this material here.

While this book was undergoing final revisions I received from Rand Hutcheson portions of his 1991 doctoral dissertation (see below, p. 67, n. 2), in which he reconsiders some of the issues raised in the former of the articles mentioned above, and in a 1989 MLA paper based on the chapters below dealing with resolution. The portions of Hutcheson's dissertation that I have seen contain much interesting and useful material, and I am grateful that I have had the opportunity to read them and discuss them with the author. This book has benefited from his criticisms. It is to be hoped that his dissertation will be published, so that his ideas may be discussed in greater depth.

Much of the initial statistical research for this book was carried out at the University of Copenhagen during the period 1987-88. For their hospitality I wish to thank friends and colleagues who are or were in Denmark, and particularly Graham and Ann Caie, H. James and Susan Jensen, and Steen Schousboe and Jette Holländer.

Many scholars lent their kind advice in matters of detail, and furnished assistance of various sorts. In particular I wish to thank Alfred Bammesberger, Mary Blockley, Joseph P. Crowley, Alfred David, Daniel Donoghue, B. Elan Dresher, Kari Gade, J. R. Hall, Constance Hieatt, Calvin Kendall, Eugene Kintgen, Timothy Long, M. MacMahon, Peter J. Lucas, Donka Minkova, R. I. Page, Herbert Penzl, John C. Pope, Irmengard Rauch, Samuel Rosenberg, Thomas Shippey, Robert P. Stockwell, Mark Taylor, Jun Terasawa, and Joseph F. Tuso.

Indiana University provided a grant for the purchase of the computer software required for the production of this volume, and another small grant defrayed part of the production costs. For their part in securing these funds I owe thanks to Dean Morton Lowengrub, Associate Dean Albert Wertheim, and Professors Patrick Brantlinger, Mary Burgan, and Roger Farr.

Jerome Singerman at the University of Pennsylvania Press has provided invaluable help at every turn, and has shown more than a little courage in taking on such a large and unconventional manuscript. Edward Peters kindly included this volume in the Middle Ages Series. I am deeply indebted also to Mindy Brown, Catherine Gjerdingen, and Carl Gross for the extraordinary care they took with the manuscript, and to Kathleen Moore and others at the Press.

Finally I can only offer thanks to Brian Powell—as if thanks were enough.

R. D. F.

*June 1992*

# CONTENTS

# ABBREVIATIONS

## LANGUAGES AND DIALECTS

| | | | |
|---|---|---|---|
| Angl. | Anglian | OE | Old English |
| IE | Indo-European | OFris. | Old Frisian |
| Gk. | Greek | OHG | Old High German |
| Gmc. | Germanic | OIcel. | Old Icelandic |
| Goth. | Gothic | OSax. | Old Saxon |
| Kent. | Kentish | Skt. | Sanskrit |
| Lat. | Latin | WGmc. | West Germanic |
| MnE | Modern English | WS | West Saxon |

The following are sometimes added before the names of languages:

| | | | |
|---|---|---|---|
| e | early | P | Proto- |
| l | late | Prim. | Primitive |

## PERIODICALS AND SERIES

| | | | |
|---|---|---|---|
| *ANQ* | *American Notes and Queries* | *MP* | *Modern Philology* |
| *Archiv* | *Archiv für das Studium der neueren Sprachen und Literaturen* | *N&Q* | *Notes & Queries* |
| | | *NM* | *Neuphilologische Mitteilungen* |
| *ASE* | *Anglo-Saxon England* | *NTS* | *Norsk Tidsskrift for Sprogvidenskap* |
| *BB* | *Beiträge zur Kunde der indogermanischen Sprachen* | *OEN* | *Old English Newsletter* |
| *EETS* | Early English Text Society | *PBA* | *Proceedings of the British Academy* |
| *ELN* | *English Language Notes* | *PBB* | *Beiträge zur Geschichte der deutschen Sprache und Literatur* |
| *ES* | *English Studies* | | |
| *IF* | *Indogermanische Forschungen* | | |
| | | *PQ* | *Philological Quarterly* |
| *JEGP* | *Journal of English and Germanic Philology* | *RES* | *Review of English Studies* |
| | | *SP* | *Studies in Philology* |
| *KZ* | *Zeitschrift für vergleichende Sprachwissenschaft* | *TPS* | *Transactions of the Philological Society* |
| *MÆ* | *Medium Ævum* | *ZfdA* | *Zeitschrift für deutsches Altertum* |
| *MLN* | *Modern Language Notes* | | |

## TEXTS

| | | | |
|---|---|---|---|
| Cp. | Corpus Glossary, in Sweet and Hoad | Li. | Lindisfarne Gospels, ed. Walter W. Skeat (Cambridge Univ. Press, 1871–87). |
| Ép. | Épinal Glossary, in Pheifer's edition | | |
| Erf. | Erfurt Glossary, in Pheifer's edition. | Rit. | *The Durham Ritual*, facsimile by T. J. Brown (Copenhagen: Rosenkilde & Bagger, 1969). |
| Ld. | Leiden Glossary, in Sweet's *Oldest English Texts*. | | |

Ru.[1]    The Mercian portion of the gloss on the Rushworth Gospels (Matthew, small portions of Mark and John), ed. Skeat.

Ru.[2]    The Northumbrian portion of the gloss on the Rushworth Gospels (most of Mark, Luke, and John), ed. Skeat.

VP    Vespasian Psalter, in Sweet's *Oldest English Texts*.

## GRAMMATICAL TERMS

| | | | |
|---|---|---|---|
| abl. | ablative | midd. | middle |
| acc. | accusative | n. | noun |
| adj. | adjective | neut. | neuter |
| adv. | adverb | nom. | nominative |
| cons. | consonantal | opt. | optative |
| dat. | dative | perf. | perfect |
| fem. | feminine | pl. | plural |
| gen. | genitive | poss. | possessive |
| imp. | imperative | pres. | present |
| ind. | indicative | pret. | preterite |
| inf. | infinitive | pron. | pronoun |
| instr. | instrumental | sg. | singular |
| masc. | masculine | sj. | subjunctive |

In the names of manuscripts, BL designates the British Library, and CCCC refers to Cambridge, Corpus Christi College.

# WORKS FREQUENTLY CITED

Amos
> Ashley Crandell Amos. *Linguistic Means of Determining the Dates of Old English Literary Texts*. Cambridge, Mass.: Medieval Academy of America, 1980.

Arngart (Anderson)
> O. S. Anderson. *Old English Material in the Leningrad Manuscript of Bede's Ecclesiastical History*. Skrifter utgivna av Kungl. Humanistiska Vetenskaps-samfundet i Lund 31. Lund: Gleerup, 1941.

ASPR
> George Philip Krapp and Elliott Van Kirk Dobbie, eds. The Anglo-Saxon Poetic Records. 6 vols. New York: Columbia University Press, 1931–1953. Contents of the individual volumes: 1, *The Junius Manuscript* (Krapp, 1931); 2, *The Vercelli Book* (Krapp, 1932); 3, *The Exeter Book* (Krapp and Dobbie, 1936); 4, *Beowulf and Judith* (Dobbie, 1953); 5, *The Paris Psalter and the Meters of Boethius* (Krapp, 1932); 6, *The Anglo-Saxon Minor Poems* (Dobbie, 1942).

Bammesberger, *Morphologie*
> Alfred Bammesberger. *Die Morphologie des urgermanischen Nomens*. Unter-suchungen zur vergleichenden Grammatik der germanischen Sprachen 2. Heidelberg: Winter, 1990.

Bammesberger, *Runes*
> Alfred Bammesberger, ed. *Old English Runes and their Continental Back-ground*. Anglistische Forschungen 217. Heidelberg: Winter, 1991.

Bartlett
> Helen Bartlett. *The Metrical Division of the Paris Psalter*. Ph.D. dissertation, Bryn Mawr. Baltimore: Friedenwald, 1896.

Behaghel
> Otto Behaghel, ed. *Heliand und Genesis*. 9th ed. rev. by Burkhard Traeger. Halle: Niemeyer, 1984.

Blackburn
> Mark Blackburn. "A Survey of Anglo-Saxon and Frisian Coins with Runic Inscriptions." In Bammesberger, *Runes*, pp. 137–89.

Bliss
> A. J. Bliss. *The Metre of "Beowulf."* Rev. ed. Oxford: Blackwell, 1967.

Bosworth and Toller
> *An Anglo-Saxon Dictionary Based on the Manuscript Collections of the Late Joseph Bosworth*, ed. T. Northcote Toller. Oxford: Clarendon, 1898. Supple-ment by Toller, 1922. Addenda by Alistair Campbell, 1972.

Braune and Eggers
> Wilhelm Braune. *Althochdeutsche Grammatik*. 14th ed. rev. by Hans Eggers. Tübingen: Niemeyer, 1987.

ten Brink
> Bernhard ten Brink. *Beowulf: Untersuchungen*. Quellen und Forschungen 62. Strassburg: Trübner, 1888.

Brooks
    Kenneth Brooks, ed. *Andreas and the Fates of the Apostles*. Oxford: Clarendon, 1961.
Bruckner
    A. Bruckner and R. Marichal. *Chartae latinae antiquiores*. Olten: Graf, 1954–88. Cited by volume and item. English items numbered to 223 are in part 3, the rest in part 4. Commentary on the English charters is by Bruckner.
Brunner
    Karl Brunner. *Altenglische Grammatik nach der angelsächsischen Grammatik von Eduard Sievers*. 3rd ed. Tübingen: Niemeyer, 1965.
Bülbring
    Karl D. Bülbring. *Altenglisches Elemetarbuch, I: Lautlehre*. Heidelberg: Winter, 1902.
Busse
    Wilhelm Busse. *Altenglische Literatur und ihre Geschichte: Zur Kritik des gegenwärtigen Deutungssystems*. Studia humaniora 7. Düsseldorf: Droste, 1987.
Cable, *English Alliterative Tradition*
    Thomas Cable. *The English Alliterative Tradition*. Philadelphia: University of Pennsylvania Press, 1991.
Cable, *Meter and Melody*
    Thomas Cable. *The Meter and Melody of Beowulf*. Illinois Studies in Language and Literature 64. Urbana: University of Illinois Press, 1974.
Cable, "Metrical Style"
    Thomas Cable. "Metrical Style as Evidence for the Date of *Beowulf*." In Chase, pp. 77–82.
Campbell
    A. Campbell. *Old English Grammar*. Oxford: Clarendon, 1959.
Campbell, "The Glosses"
    Alistair Campbell. "The Glosses." In *The Vespasian Psalter*, ed. David H. Wright, pp. 81–92. Early English Manuscripts in Facsimile 14. Copenhagen: Rosenkilde & Bagger, 1967.
J. J. Campbell
    Jackson J. Campbell. "The Dialect Vocabulary of the Old English Bede." *JEGP* 50 (1951), 349–72.
Chadwick
    H. Munro Chadwick. *The Heroic Age*. Cambridge: Cambridge University Press, 1912.
Chase
    Colin Chase, ed. *The Dating of Beowulf*. Toronto: University of Toronto Press, 1981.
Crowley
    Joseph Patrick Crowley. "The Study of Old English Dialects." Ph.D. dissertation, University of North Carolina at Chapel Hill, 1980.
Dahl
    Ivar Dahl. *Substantival Inflexion in Early Old English: Vocal Stems*. Lund Studies in English 7. Lund: Gleerup, 1938.
Doane, *Genesis A*
    A. N. Doane, ed. *Genesis A: A New Edition*. Madison: University of Wisconsin Press, 1978.

Doane, *Saxon Genesis*
A. N. Doane, ed. *The Saxon Genesis: An Edition of the West Saxon Genesis B and the Old Saxon Vatican Genesis*. Madison: University of Wisconsin Press, 1991.
Dobbie
See ASPR.
Donoghue
Daniel Donoghue. *Style in Old English Poetry: The Test of the Auxiliary*. New Haven: Yale University Press, 1987.
Farrell
R. T. Farrell, ed. *Daniel and Azarias*. London: Methuen, 1974.
Fisiak Festschrift
Dieter Kastovsky and Aleksander Szwedek, eds. *Linguistics across Historical and Geographical Boundaries*. 2 vols. Berlin: Mouton de Gruyter, 1986.
Girvan
Ritchie Girvan. *"Beowulf" and the Seventh Century*. Reissued, with a new chapter by Rupert Bruce-Mitford. London: Methuen, 1971.
Gneuss, "Origin"
Helmut Gneuss. "The Origin of Standard Old English and Æthelwold's School at Winchester." *ASE* 1 (1972), 63–83.
Gradon
Pamela Gradon, ed. *Cynewulf's Elene*. London: Methuen, 1958.
Grein, *Sprachschatz*
C. W. M. Grein. *Sprachschatz der angelsächsischen Dichter*. 2nd ed. rev. by J. J. Köhler, with the aid of F. Holthausen. Reprint of the 1912 ed., Heidelberg: Winter, 1974.
Hofmann, *Versstrukturen*
Dietrich Hofmann. *Die Versstrukturen der altsächsischen Stabreimgedichte Heliand und Genesis, I: Textband*. Heidelberg: Winter, 1991.
Holthausen
Ferdinand Holthausen. *Altenglisches etymologisches Wörterbuch*. 3rd ed., unrev. Heidelberg: Winter, 1974.
*Instructions for Christians*
See Rosier.
Jacobs
Nicolas Jacobs. "Anglo-Danish Relations, Poetic Archaism, and the Date of *Beowulf*: A Reconsideration of the Evidence." *Poetica* (Tokyo) 8 (1977), 23–43.
Jordan
Richard Jordan. *Handbook of Middle English Grammar*. Translated and revised by Eugene J. Crook. The Hague: Mouton, 1974.
Jordan, *Eigentümlichkeiten*
Richard Jordan. *Eigentümlichkeiten des anglischen Wortschatzes*. Anglistische Forschungen 17. Heidelberg: Winter, 1906.
Ker
N. R. Ker. *Catalogue of Manuscripts Containing Anglo-Saxon*. Oxford: Clarendon, 1957.
Klaeber
Fr. Klaeber, ed. *Beowulf and the Fight at Finnsburg*. 3rd ed. Lexington, Mass.: Heath, 1950.

Kluge
Friedrich Kluge. *Nominale Stammbildungslehre der altgermanischen Dialekte.* 2nd ed. Halle: Niemeyer, 1899.

Krahe and Meid
Hans Krahe and Wolfgang Meid. *Germanische Sprachwissenschaft.* 2 vols. 7th ed. Berlin: de Gruyter, 1966–69.

Krapp (and Dobbie)
See ASPR.

Krause
Wolfgang Krause. *Handbuch des Gotischen.* 3rd ed. Munich: Beck, 1968.

Kuhn, "Westgermanisches"
Hans Kuhn. "Westgermanisches in der altnordischen Verskunst." *PBB* 63 (1939), 178–236. Reprinted in his *Kleine Schriften,* vol. 1 (Berlin: de Gruyter, 1969), 485–527.

*Learning and Literature*
Michael Lapidge and Helmut Gneuss, eds. *Learning and Literature in Anglo-Saxon England: Studies Presented to Peter Clemoes on the Occasion of His Sixty-Fifth Birthday.* Cambridge: Cambridge University Press, 1985.

Lehmann, "Post-Consonantal *l m n r*"
Winfred P. Lehmann. "Post-Consonantal *l m n r* and Metrical Practice in *Beowulf.*" In *Nordica et Anglica: Studies in Honor of Stefán Einarsson,* edited by Allan H. Orrick, pp. 148–67. The Hague: Mouton, 1968.

Lehmann, *Verse Form*
Winfred P. Lehmann. *The Development of Germanic Verse Form.* Austin: University of Texas Press and Linguistic Society of America, 1956.

*Linguistic Atlas of Late Mediaeval English*
Angus McIntosh, M. L. Samuels, and Michael Benskin. *A Linguistic Atlas of Late Mediaeval English.* 4 vols. Aberdeen: Aberdeen University Press, 1986.

Lowe
E. A. Lowe. *Codices latini antiquiores.* Oxford: Clarendon, 1934–66; Supplement 1971; rev. ed. of pt. 2, 1972. Cited by volume and item.

Lucas
Peter J. Lucas, ed. *Exodus.* London: Methuen, 1977.

Luick
Karl Luick. *Historische Grammatik der englischen Sprache.* Edited by Friedrich Wild and Herbert Koziol. 2 vols. 1914–40. Reprint. Cambridge: Harvard University Press, 1964.

*Luick Revisited*
Dieter Kastovsky and Gero Bauer, eds. *Luick Revisited: Papers Read at the Luick-Symposium at Schloß Liechtenstein, 15.–18.9.1985.* Tübingen: Narr, 1988.

Lyon
Stewart Lyon. "Some Problems in Interpreting Anglo-Saxon Coinage." *ASE* 5 (1976), 173–224.

*Microfiche Concordance*
Richard L. Venezky and Antonette diPaolo Healey. *A Microfiche Concordance to Old English.* Newark: University of Delaware, 1980.

Mitchell
Bruce Mitchell. *Old English Syntax.* Oxford: Clarendon, 1985.

Morsbach
Lorenz Morsbach. "Zur Datierung des Beowulfepos." *Nachrichten der Königlichen Gesellschaft der Wissenschaften zu Göttingen*, Phil.-hist. Klasse, pp. 251–77. Berlin: Weidmann, 1906.

Neckel
Gustav Neckel, ed. *Edda: Die Lieder des Codex Regius nebst verwandten Denkmälern, I: Text*. 5th ed. by Hans Kuhn. Heidelberg: Winter, 1983.

Oakden
J. P. Oakden. *Alliterative Poetry in Middle English*. Vol. 1. Manchester: Manchester University Press, 1930.

*Origins*
R. D. Fulk. *The Origins of Indo-European Quantitative Ablaut*. Innsbrucker Beiträge zur Sprachwissenschaft 49. Innsbruck: Institut für Sprachwissenschaft der Universität Innsbruck, 1986.

Orosius
Janet Bately, ed. *The Old English Orosius*. EETS, s.s. 6 (1980).

Page
R. I. Page. *An Introduction to English Runes*. London: Methuen, 1973.

*Pastoral Care*
Henry Sweet, ed. *King Alfred's West-Saxon Version of Gregory's Pastoral Care*. EETS, o.s. 45, 50 (1871).

Pheifer
J. D. Pheifer, ed. *Old English Glosses in the Épinal-Erfurt Glossary*. Oxford: Clarendon, 1974.

Plummer and Earle
Charles Plummer and John Earle, eds. *Two of the Saxon Chronicles Parallel*. 2 vols. Oxford: Clarendon, 1892–99.

Pope
John Collins Pope. *The Rhythm of "Beowulf."* Rev. ed. New Haven: Yale University Press, 1966.

Prokosch
E. Prokosch. *A Comparative Germanic Grammar*. Baltimore: Linguistic Society of America, 1938.

Ricci
Aldo Ricci. "The Chronology of Anglo-Saxon Poetry." *RES* 5 (1929), 257–66.

Richter
Carl Richter. *Chronologische Studien zur angelsächsischen Literatur auf Grund sprachlich-metrischer Kriterien*. Studien zur englischen Philologie 33. Halle: Niemeyer, 1910.

Roberts
Jane Roberts, ed. *The Guthlac Poems of the Exeter Book*. Oxford: Clarendon, 1979.

Rosier
James L. Rosier, ed. "'Instructions for Christians': A Poem in Old English." *Anglia* 82 (1964), 4–22. See also the addenda, *Anglia* 84 (1966), 74.

Russom
Geoffrey Russom. *Old English Meter and Linguistic Theory*. Cambridge: Cambridge University Press, 1987.

Sarrazin, "Chronologie"
Gregor Sarrazin. "Zur Chronologie und Verfasserfrage angelsächsischer

Dichtungen." *Englische Studien* 38 (1907), 145–95.
Sarrazin, *Kädmon*
    Gregor Sarrazin. *Von Kädmon bis Kynewulf: Eine litterarhistorische Studie.*
    Berlin: Mayer & Müller, 1913.
Sawyer
    P. H. Sawyer. *Anglo-Saxon Charters: An Annotated List and Bibliography.*
    London: Royal Historical Society, 1968.
von Schaubert
    Else von Schaubert. *Vorkommen, gebietsmäßige Verbreitung und Herkunft
    altenglischer absoluter Partizipialkonstruktionen in Nominativ und Akkusativ.*
    Paderborn: F. Schöningh, 1954.
Schücking
    Levin L. Schücking. "Wann entstand der Beowulf?" *PBB* 42 (1917), 347–410.
Scragg
    D. G. Scragg, ed. *The Battle of Maldon.* Manchester: Manchester University
    Press, 1981.
Sedgefield
    Walter John Sedgefield, ed. *King Alfred's Old English Version of Boethius "De
    Consolatio Philosophiae."* Oxford: Clarendon, 1899.
Seiffert
    Friedrich Seiffert. *Die Behandlung der Wörter mit auslautenden ursprünglich
    silbischen Liquiden oder Nasalen und mit Kontraktionsvokalen in der Genesis
    A und im Beowulf.* Dissertation, Halle-Wittenberg. Halle: Hohmann, 1918.
Sievers, *Altgerm. Metrik*
    Eduard Sievers. *Altgermanische Metrik.* Halle: Niemeyer, 1893.
Sievers, "Miscellen"
    Eduard Sievers. "Miscellen zur angelsächsischen Grammatik." *PBB* 9 (1884),
    197–300.
Sievers, "Rhythmik"
    Eduard Sievers. "Zur Rhythmik des germanischen Alliterationsverses." *PBB*
    10 (1885), 209–314 and 451–545.
Sisam
    Kenneth Sisam. *Studies in the History of Old English Literature.* Oxford:
    Clarendon, 1953.
Sleeth
    Charles R. Sleeth. *Studies in "Christ and Satan."* Toronto: University of
    Toronto Press, 1982.
Stanley
    E. G. Stanley. "The Prosaic Vocabulary of Old English Verse." *NM* 72
    (1971), 385–418.
Streitberg
    Wilhelm Streitberg. *Urgermanische Grammatik.* 4th ed., unrev. Heidelberg:
    Winter, 1974.
Sweet
    Henry Sweet. *The Oldest English Texts.* EETS, o.s. 83 (1885).
Sweet and Hoad
    Henry Sweet. *A Second Anglo-Saxon Reader: Archaic and Dialectal.* 2nd ed.
    rev. by T. F. Hoad. Oxford: Clarendon, 1978.
Timmer, *Genesis B*
    B. J. Timmer, ed. *The Later Genesis.* Oxford: Scrivener, 1948.

Timmer, *Judith*
B. J. Timmer, ed. *Judith*. London: Methuen, 1961.
Toller
See Bosworth and Toller.
Toon
Thomas E. Toon. *The Politics of Early Old English Sound Change*. New York: Academic Press, 1983.
Trautmann, *Kynewulf*
Moritz Trautmann. *Kynewulf, der Bischof und Dichter*. Bonner Beiträge zur Anglistik 1. Bonn: P. Hanstein, 1898.
Tupper, "Philological Legend"
Frederick Tupper, Jr. "The Philological Legend of Cynewulf." *PMLA* 26 (1911), 235–79.
Vleeskruyer
R. Vleeskruyer. *The Life of St. Chad: An Old English Homily*. Amsterdam: North-Holland, 1953.
Wenisch
Franz Wenisch. *Spezifisch anglisches Wortgut in den nordhumbrischen Interlinearglossierungen des Lukasevangeliums*. Anglistiche Forschungen 132. Heidelberg: Winter, 1979.
Whitelock, "Anglo-Saxon Poetry"
Dorothy Whitelock. "Anglo-Saxon Poetry and the Historian." *Transactions of the Royal Historical Society*, 4th ser. (1949), 75–94.
Whitelock, *Audience*
Dorothy Whitelock. *The Audience of "Beowulf."* Oxford: Clarendon, 1951.

# INTRODUCTION

## A. The State of Scholarship

§1. The purpose of this study is to identify metrical variation through time and space during the Old English period. Metrical history assumes two forms: (1) It is the study of variation in the metrical value of individual elements in the system. For example, when the negative particle *ne* appears before certain verbs and indefinite pronouns beginning with a vowel, *h*, or *w*, it is usually written as part of the following word; but regardless of how it is written, in many instances it represents a syllable in the meter (see below, Chap. 3). The contraction of *ne* is a historical process in the language, and so might also reflect a pattern of diachronic change in the metrical system. (2) Metrical history is also the study of variation in the set of principles that govern verse construction itself, regardless of the nature of the elements employed in the verse. Such variation may or may not be due to discoverable change in the linguistic system. For example, the significant deviations from classical norms apparent in externally datable verse from the end of the Old English period (as discussed in Chap. 10) are at least in part attributable to the progressive loss of stress on noninitial syllables that has characterized the Germanic languages from prehistoric times, and that was to result in the loss of most inflections in the Middle English period. On the other hand, the appearance of verses like *þæs þe þearf wæs* (*Death of Edward* 34a) and *Is in ðere byri eac* (*Durham* 9a),[1] with two words instead of one in the last two metrical positions, only in datably late verse (see below, §291) is not due to any discoverable linguistic cause; and so if this does represent a historical change it would seem to be the result merely of changing metrical conventions.

§2. The former type of variation has been far more intensively studied than the latter, and the considerably greater part of this study will be devoted to it. Doubtless there is a variety of reasons for its having generated greater interest, but certainly one reason is its relevance to the study of Old English literature and history. If in fact such variation does correlate to diachronic and diatopic change, it possibly furnishes a means of distinguishing, within limits, the relative date and original dialect of

---

[1] In this study the quantity of vowels and diphthongs is everywhere marked except in manuscript spellings and verse quotations. Except where otherwise noted, the latter are derived from the ASPR editions, in which quantities are not marked.

Old English poems. This observation has been the controlling factor in the development of scholarship on the history of meter. The problem of metrical history is a linguistic one, and the groundwork for the study of metrical history was laid in a linguistic context; yet nearly all subsequent discussion has been conducted in literary and historical contexts. The point bears some elaboration.

§3. The study of metrical variation originates in some problems in the development of Old English metrical theory. It has never been possible to construct a reasonably complete and coherent description of Old English meter without recourse to the assumption that a certain amount of scribal change intervenes between the composition of most extant Old English poems and the recorded form in which they survive. When Eduard Sievers first published his findings about the nature of Old English meter it was already clear to him that in some respects the language of the existing manuscripts of verse is at odds with the apparent usage of most Old English poets. An example is the use of inflected infinitives, which, as Sievers points out ("Rhythmik," pp. 255–56, 312, 482), creates metrical anomalies in sixteen verses (e.g. *idese to efnanne* at *Beowulf* 1941a). Since the uninflected infinitive with *tō* is found ten times in verse (e.g. in *freode to friclan* at *Beowulf* 2556a, where the substitution of *friclanne* would spoil the meter), there is no obstacle on this score to assuming that the sixteen inflected forms have been tampered with in the course of scribal transmission. It would not in fact be a very reasonable interpretation to insist otherwise, since the proportion of unmetrical verses containing inflected infinitives is so extraordinarily high that chance is not a plausible explanation. The uninflected infinitive with *tō* is rare in prose (Brunner, §363, n. 3; Mitchell, §921), and so the sort of scribal alteration postulated here has a natural and credible cause: the scribes presumably regarded constructions like *to friclan* as unusual, and altered them to something more familiar.

§4. In several instances Sievers suggested that similar discrepancies evidenced by the meter can be correlated to a poem's original date and dialect of composition ("Rhythmik," pp. 459, 463–64, 465, 478, etc.). Thus the possibility arose of tracing a history of metrical practice in Old English, and in the years following Sievers' first discoveries there appeared a variety of research on metrically detectable variation, as discussed in the following chapters. These were detailed linguistic studies that attempted to glean all relevant examples of particular metrical configurations from a variety of poems, and to compile comparative statistics. Most of these studies drew conclusions about the date of composition and original dialect of Old English poems, and this research contributed to the rise of a presumed chronology of verse and a general assumption that nearly all the surviving longer poems originated north of the Thames. The presumed chronology cannot be regarded as ever having been very definite, since there could be considerable disagreement about the date of individual poems—for example, *Judith*, once regarded as Cædmonian or Cynewulfian, later came to be assigned more usually to the tenth century.[2] But a fairly fluid chronology for the longer poems was nonetheless agreed upon among philologists, placing, for instance, *Genesis A*, *Daniel*, *Beowulf*, and *Exodus* in the early or "Cædmonian" period (the first two perhaps being earliest), with the *Guthlac* poems, *Andreas*, and the signed works of Cynewulf between these and the Alfredian *Meters of Boethius*.[3] As for the relevance of metrics to dialect studies, it was likewise Eduard Sievers who first asserted that the metrical treatment of the second and third person singular indicative endings of long-stemmed strong verbs and weak verbs of the first class, and of the preterite participial ending of weak verbs of the first class with stems ending in an oral dental stop, could serve as an indicator of whether a poem was composed in an Anglian or a Southern dialect.[4] The issue is discussed in Chapter 11 below.

§5. Though Sievers' syncope in verb endings was widely regarded as a reliable dialect indicator until relatively recently, it must not be supposed that the results of the metrically based dating studies were ever accepted wholly and uncritically in Old English scholarship, even though a variety of specious dialect criteria were, and still are, regularly discussed in the introductions to critical editions. It is true that the presumed chronology did come to be commonly considered probable, but largely because of considerations outside the area of metrics. A set of assumptions about the relative dates of Old English poems had in fact arisen long before Lorenz Morsbach, Gregor Sarrazin, Carl Richter, and Friedrich Seiffert attempted to demonstrate the relevance of metrical criteria, though these preconceptions generally go unacknowledged now.[5]

---

[2] B. J. Timmer provides a brief history of thought on the date of the poem in his edition, pp. 6–10.

[3] A list of some earlier scholars' proposed dates is provided by Schücking, pp. 347–49. See also the table constructed by Herbert Pilch and Hildegard Tristram, *Altenglische Literatur* (Heidelberg: Winter, 1979), pp. 199–201.

[4] "Miscellen," p. 273; "Zum Codex Junius XI," *PBB* 10 (1885), 195–99, at 196; "Rhythmik," pp. 464–75.

[5] Modern discussions of the history of opinions about dating verse tend to produce the impression that the rise of chronological assumptions was due primarily to the development of metrical and syntactic tests: see, e.g., Colin Chase, "Opinions on the Date of *Beowulf*, 1815–1980," in his *Dating of Beowulf*, pp. 3–8. That the case is otherwise should be apparent from discussions of dating in the introductions to critical editions, and from early histories of English literature. For example, already in 1877 Bernhard ten Brink regarded *Widsith* as the oldest English poem; *Genesis A* as the work of Cædmon (an attribution originating with Franciscus Junius in the seventeenth century), but not *Daniel* and *Exodus*; *Beowulf* as older than *Genesis* (except perhaps for the "Christian interpolations"); Cynewulf as a poet of the second half of the eighth century; *Guthlac* and *Andreas* as late eighth-century compositions (because attributed to Cynewulf); *Genesis B* as belonging to the ninth century; the *Riming Poem*, *Christ and*

Thus their findings were neither revolutionary nor essential to the maintenance of widespread assumptions about chronology, since they tended to support commonly held opinions. Nor do the editors of any of the above-mentioned poems ever seem to have settled on a probable date of composition on the basis primarily of the metrical evidence. It would be peculiar if one did, since few editors can be credited with greater philological acumen than those who conducted the most thorough studies of these metrical criteria—who, it is shown below, were themselves incapable of attaining accuracy or agreement. Rather, when these metrical matters are mentioned at all it is generally with a note of caution. Typical is the view of Elliott Van Kirk Dobbie: "Of these studies it may be said that the results are often mutually contradictory" (ASPR 4:lvi), and of Friedrich Klaeber that "these criteria are liable to lead to untrustworthy results when applied in a one-sided and mechanical manner and without careful consideration of all the factors involved," though he also concedes, "it cannot be gainsaid that these tests, which are based on undoubted facts of linguistic development, hold good in a general way" (pp. cviii–cix). Even in the heyday of philology these studies seem to have provoked as much skepticism as support.[6] And so it must

---

*Satan*, and *Solomon and Saturn*, along with datable poems such as *Brunanburh* and *Maldon*, as post-Alfredian; and most of the longer poems as Anglian in origin: see the first volume of his *Geschichte der englischen Literatur* (Berlin: R. Oppenheim, 1877), chaps. 3–8 and appendix A. (In his *Beowulf: Untersuchungen* ten Brink sets out his ideas about the composition of *Beowulf* in more detail, arguing that its elements were composed in the seventh century in Northumbria and Mercia, combined in the eighth century, and eventually peppered with Christian sentiments in a final treatment.) Particularly important in assigning dates and dialects before the discovery of metrical, syntactic, and lexical criteria were considerations of style and the influence of one poem on another—the former depending on the credibility of various philologists' *Stilgefühl*, and the latter perhaps as much depending on chronological preconceptions as creating them. Sarrazin provides some references (*Kädmon*, pp. 6–7). Undeniably (as should be evident from ten Brink's history) the single most influential factor in the early development of chronological assumptions was not linguistic: it was the Romantic assumption that verse devoted to early Germanic myth and legend must be very early, at least in conception, and Christian verse must be later, with poems attributable to Cædmon identified as the earliest of these.

[6]This includes a particularly earnest rebuttal by Frederick J. Tupper, Jr., "Philological Legend," along with his "Notes on Old English Poems, I: The Home of the Judith," *JEGP* 11 (1912), 82–89. The skepticism, however, is more frequently mitigated by the concession that the tests are valuable if not interpreted too rigidly—by which is meant, for example, that while we may not conclude that *Beowulf* was composed in the period 720–30, we may infer that it is a relatively early poem, and that it antedates the signed works of Cynewulf. For some negative or cautionary comments see R. W. Chambers, *Beowulf: An Introduction to the Study of the Poem*, 3rd ed. (Cambridge: Cambridge Univ. Press, 1959), pp. 104–12; Schücking, pp. 357–59; Ricci, pp. 259–60; ten Brink, pp. 211–17; Rudolf Imelmann, *Forschungen zur altenglischen Poesie* (Berlin: Weidmann, 1920), pp. 284–85 and passim; Girvan, pp. 15–25; reviews of Richter's *Chronologische Studien* by Gustav Binz in *Anglia Beiblatt* 22 (1911), 79, by

not be supposed that the fairly broad consensus about the dates of Old English poems prevailing until a little over a decade ago was founded primarily on the widespread and credulous acceptance of the conclusions of metrical studies.

§6. With the decline of the position of philology within medieval studies over the course of this century, and with the concomitant refinement of literary and historical research, these metrical indicators of date and dialect, though frequently mentioned in Anglo-Saxon scholarship, have rarely been discussed in any detail, and almost never with a linguistic aim. Consequently, when these issues are discussed it is not generally in the context of addressing the data, but with the premise that statistical regularities in the data and the assumptions underlying the interpretation of the data are separable issues, and it is only the latter that are addressed. The most substantial and most frequently cited discussions are those of Dorothy Whitelock and Kenneth Sisam.[7] Both again advise caution. Whitelock points out uncertainties in the metrical variables and finds that they might be lax enough to permit *Beowulf* to be assigned to the second rather than the first half of the eighth century. Her purpose in doing so is to facilitate the process of characterizing the culture out of which the poem grew, mainly on historical grounds. Sisam, warning that only structural, that is, metrically confirmable, linguistic criteria are reliable, argues that although it must be ruled out later, Wessex in the pre-Alfredian era is as likely a place of composition for classical Old English verse as anywhere else. His thesis also has its basis ultimately in historical considerations, since his intent is to demonstrate that the cultural preeminence accorded Northumbria and Mercia by modern historians is insufficiently justified, and Wessex should not be assumed to have been a cultural backwater (pp. 132–39). Whitelock's and Sisam's arguments are discussed in detail in this and the following chapters.

§7. The one noteworthy exception to the general inattention to the problem by linguists in this half of the century is represented by the work of Ashley Crandell Amos, whose recent death represents a severe blow to Old English studies. Her Yale University doctoral dissertation, revised and published in 1980, adopts a revolutionary position: there is almost no metrical or other linguistic evidence for assigning dates to poetic texts, and what little evidence there is may for the most part be dismissed, since its genuine value cannot be proved. Amos' book commands considerable

---

Rudolf Imelmann in *Deutsche Literaturzeitung* 31 (1910), 2986–87, and by H. Hecht in *Archiv* 130 (1913), 430–32; and reviews of Sarrazin's *Von Kädmon bis Kynewulf* by O. Funke in *Anglia Beiblatt* 31 (1920), 121–34, esp. 121–22, and by Max Kaluza in *Literarisches Zentralblatt* 66 (1915), 666–68, with a final comment on Richter's book.

[7]Whitelock, "Anglo-Saxon Poetry," p. 81, and *Audience*, pp. 26–28; and Sisam, *Studies*, pp. 119–39.

attention in the present context, not only because it is the only critique of metrical dating studies to address the data with any methodicalness, but also because it offers more detailed counterarguments to the linguistic support for the presumed chronology than any prior study. This book represents the first very thorough synthesis of a wide variety of linguistic evidence for the dating of Old English verse. Although Amos' position represents an extreme departure from earlier conclusions of most metrists, philologists, and editors from Sievers onward, many of her criticisms are valuable, and even those that prove ill-founded are built on reasoning worthy of serious discussion. Of particular importance in this respect are questions of linguistic methodology that the book raises, since many of these have not been addressed before in this context. And so a general discussion here of the methodological issues raised by this book will obviate the necessity of continually raising such questions in the chapters that follow.

## B. Probability, Proof, and the Nature of Linguistic Argumentation

§8. Chief among the methodological issues to which Amos' study draws needed attention are those centering on the nature of proof in historical linguistics. One of these is the matter of objectivity. She regards linguistics as an empirical science in which theories, relying on inviolable natural laws, may be proved or disproved absolutely by the application of thoroughly objective experiments. For instance, after considering Klaeber's plea that chronological linguistic criteria not be applied in a mechanical manner, as quoted in part above, she argues the opposite position: "But if the tests are to have an authority that is more than subjective, they must be, in a sense, 'mechanical'; critics have too often condemned in them a quality to which they aspired. The designers of the tests, 'these mechanical appraisers of verse,' as Tupper calls them, tried to find criteria that were reliable, objective, and independent of the minds applying them" (p. 8). It is true that Sarrazin considered his dating criteria objective (*Kädmon*, p. 7), and compared the metrical detection of earlier linguistic forms to the application of a chemical reagent (pp. 3–4). But in actuality he was aware of the limits of linguistic objectivity, since he attributed earlier wrong conclusions to the mechanical application of individual criteria (p. 7), and warned that the metrical criteria leave room for some doubt (p. 2), on account of such factors as the possibility that not all poets adhered to the rules of metrics equally well (p. 3). The other chief proponent of constructing metrical history, Carl Richter, is even more doubtful about the rigidness with which his metrical variables may be applied:

Es ist nicht zu leugnen, daß der Wert unserer Kriterien oft überschätzt und übertrieben worden ist. Auf Grund dieser Kriterien allein feste Daten zu geben und eine sichere Chronologie festzusetzen, ist unmöglich, zumal für manche, namentlich kürzere Denkmäler nur wenig Beweismaterial vorliegt. Aber wir können doch mit ihrer Hilfe gewisse Wahrscheinlichkeiten aussprechen, frühere Annahmen und Datierungen stützen oder widerlegen. (p. 83)

Because subjectivity informs the values prized most in the humanities, such as ambiguities of poetic structure and the open-endedness of literary interpretation, it is perhaps not surprising that some humanists who are not linguists should entertain the idea that a field such as linguistics has, or ought to have, nothing to do with subjectivity.[8] Nor have linguists always been innocent of promoting such a view. For example, the neo-grammarians at one time believed that language change might be shown to conform to regular and exceptionless laws on the order of physical laws in the natural sciences. This doubtless is the impulse behind Sarrazin's chemical analogy. Whether the experimental method as used in any of the empirical sciences can be called thoroughly objective has in fact become a widely disputed issue in recent years.[9] But the status of logical positivism is actually beside the point, since the truth of course is that historical linguistics, to the extent that it can be called a science, is not a natural one but a social or behavioral one.[10] The most empirical evidence it employs is therefore statistical, that is, relative rather than absolute. But even statistical evidence is relatively infrequent in philological argumentation, which instead relies primarily on plain inductive logic. Methodologists thus distinguish between the deductive logic of the "exact" sciences and the probabilistic logic that characterizes most scientific inquiry.[11] The former is "mechanical" in the sense that

[8]On the same topic, in his *Desire for Origins* (New Brunswick, N.J.: Rutgers Univ. Press, 1990), pp. xii, 25, and passim, Allen Frantzen's thesis is, in part, that Anglo-Saxonists too readily regard philology and textual criticism as objective. But his aim seems to be not to affirm the value of probabilistic logic, but to demonstrate that modern philology is debased by its origins in Romantic positivism.

[9]For general discussion and references see, e.g., Harold I. Brown, *Perception, Theory and Commitment: The New Philosophy of Science* (Chicago: Univ. of Chicago Press, 1977); Rom Harré, *Varieties of Realism: A Rationale for the Natural Sciences* (Oxford: Blackwell, 1986); and Helen E. Longino, *Science as Social Knowledge: Values and Objectivity in Scientific Inquiry* (Princeton: Princeton Univ. Press, 1990). It is of course no accident that at the same time the presumed "objective" bases of literary criticism have been undermined by postmodernist hermeneutics, and, ultimately, that so much received knowledge in Anglo-Saxon studies has been cast adrift.

[10]For a brief history of the changeable fortunes of scientism in language study see Konrad Koerner, "Positivism in Linguistics," in *The Eighth LACUS Forum, 1981*, ed. Waldemar Gutwinski and Grace Jolly (Columbia, S.C.: Hornbeam Press, 1982), pp. 82–99.

[11]On the difference between the two, and their different uses in the sciences, see, e.g., Nicholas Rescher, *Scientific Explanation* (London: Collier-Macmillan, 1970), p. 37;

conclusions follow inevitably from its premises, and a conclusion, for example in a mathematical proof, based on true premises is indisputably true, once the efficacy of deductive logic and of numbers (and the mathematical axioms they entail) are granted.[12] This is what is meant by logical positivism, which is defined as rejecting induction and all reasoning that is subjective, and insisting on deduction.[13] Commoner in scientific inquiry is the use of probabilistic logic. In such reasoning proof is not absolute—it is to a greater or lesser extent, but always to some extent, subjective.[14] Yet there is nothing unscientific about such subjective reasoning.[15] On the contrary, most science is built on hypothesis formation, and hypotheses can never be proved in the mathematical sense, but can only be rendered extremely probable.[16]

---

and Carl G. Hempel, "Scientific Explanation," in *Philosophy of Science Today*, ed. Sidney Morgenbesser (New York: Basic Books, 1967), pp. 79–88, at pp. 80–84. Deduction is usually opposed to induction, though Charles S. Peirce proposed a third category, abduction, that in many ways more accurately describes the sort of argumentation discussed here: see Henning Andersen, "Abductive and Deductive Change," *Language* 49 (1973), 765–93, esp. 775–76, with the references there.

[12]Cf. Ernest R. House, *Evaluating with Validity* (Beverly Hills: Sage, 1980), p. 72: "Logical certainty is achievable only within a closed, totally defined system like a game." Esa Itkonen discusses the error of replacing the concept of causality with deductive proof, especially in the "intuitive" sciences, in *Causality in Linguistic Theory* (London: Croom Helm, 1983), remarking, e.g., that in confusing mathematical and probabilistic reasoning, "first, positivism gives an inaccurate picture of natural science; second, it transfers this picture *tel quel* into social science, raising its inaccuracy to the second degree" (p. 17). The virtual identity of causality and probabilistic reasoning in Itkonen's discussion seems a sufficient response to Roger Lass's charge that causality in current diachronic linguistics is incapable of proof (see below, n. 20): what is required is not proof of causality, but sufficient evidence to establish probability.

[13]See, e.g., the analysis by Charles S. Peirce quoted in Cable's *English Alliterative Tradition*, p. 110.

[14]Richard Rudner, "Value Judgments in the Acceptance of Theories," in Frank (see n. 17 below), pp. 24–28, makes the subjective nature of hypothesis formation explicit: "I assume that no analysis of what constitutes the method of science would be satisfactory unless it comprised some assertion to the effect that the scientist validates—that is, accepts or rejects—hypotheses. But if this is so, then clearly the scientist does make value judgments. Since no scientific hypothesis is ever completely verified, in accepting a hypothesis on the basis of evidence, the scientist must make the decision that the evidence is *sufficiently* strong or that the probability is *sufficiently* high to warrant the acceptance of the hypothesis" (p. 26).

[15]The scientific nature of the deductive method was first demonstrated, and the principles of logical proof in the social sciences formulated, by John Stuart Mill, *A System of Logic, Ratiocinative and Inductive* (London: John W. Parker, 1843), book 6.

[16]Cf. William J. Goode and Paul K. Hatt, *Methods in Social Research* (New York: McGraw-Hill, 1952), p. 87: "It is impossible not to come to the conclusion that certainty can never be reached by any design of proof. This is no cause for despair, however, for uncertainty can be diminished, and the *probable* accuracy of observation increased, with every addition to knowledge. . . . It is clear, then, that by whatever design the hypothesis

Unless our very understanding of numbers is itself denied, it can be proved (and has been proved in a variety of ways) that the square of the hypotenuse of a right triangle is equal to the sum of the squares of the other two sides. On the other hand, the existence of subatomic particles cannot be proved, since we have no way of observing them directly. Yet by probabilistic reasoning their existence is rendered so likely that reasonable observers cannot doubt it, since it explains a wide variety of observable facts, such as changes of energy, mass, and momentum in the process of radioactive decay.

§9. Most science is of this sort, constructing and testing hypotheses, rendering probable (that is, *validating*) what cannot be proved. Validation almost never depends upon a single, irrefutable piece of evidence: such usually carries less weight than a variety of probabilistic evidence. Theories, then, are evaluated not according to how easily they are validated, but how much they are capable of explaining.[17]

§10. The point can be illustrated with a concrete linguistic example. In 1879 Ferdinand de Saussure proposed that there had existed in the Indo-European protolanguage a number of consonants that had been lost in all the Indo-European languages, and these are referred to now as *laryngeal* consonants.[18] Since they had all been lost, their existence could only be posited on the basis of a number of peculiar phenomena they are capable of explaining. For example, loss of a laryngeal consonant, with compensatory lengthening, explains why there is a long vowel in the second syllable of Vedic Sanskrit *pánthām* (acc. sg.) 'path', as well as why the *t* is aspirated (cf. Old Prussian *pintis*), and why there is an *i* before the desinence in the instrumental plural *pathíbhis*.[19] This sort of reasoning is fundamentally circular: the laryngeal must have existed because it explains three otherwise peculiar phenomena in the Vedic paradigm; and the three phenomena must be related to one another, since they are

---

is tested the results are never certain but *are approximations stated in terms of probability.*"

[17]Philipp G. Frank, "The Variety of Reasons for the Acceptance of Scientific Theories," in *The Validation of Scientific Theories*, ed. Philipp G. Frank (Boston: Beacon Press, 1956), pp. 3–17, puts this another way: "The scientific community has accepted theories only when a vast number of facts has been derived from few and simple principles. A familiar example is the derivation of the immensely complex motions of celestial bodies from the simple Newtonian formula of gravitation, or the large variety of electromagnetic phenomena from Maxwell's field equations" (p. 3).

[18]*Mémoire sur le système primitif des voyelles dans les langues indo-européennes* (rpt., Hildesheim: Georg Olms, 1968). Much has been written about laryngeals in the intervening years. For a general introduction to the hypothesis see Frederik Otto Lindeman, *Introduction to the "Laryngeal Theory"* (Oslo: Norwegian University Press, 1987), and for a survey of the evidence for laryngeal consonants see *Evidence for Laryngeals*, ed. Werner Winter (The Hague: Mouton, 1965).

[19]For a more detailed discussion see *Origins*, pp. 74–78.

explained so well by the laryngeal. But there is nothing inherently vicious in such circularity, and no one would deny that the laryngeal consonant is an elegant explanation of these phenomena that would otherwise simply be unexplained anomalies. And one of the primary purposes of historical linguistics (and other fields employing the inductive method) is to locate apparent anomalies and determine their causes, demonstrating that they are neither random nor accidental. The same charge of circularity could be leveled at any widely held scientific hypothesis, since a hypothesis derives its strength mainly from its ability to relate a wide variety of phenomena under one explanation; and yet the assumption of relatedness for any group of phenomena is not entirely independent of one's choice of hypothesis. In other words, scientific method is based on the mutual support that epistemology and ontology lend each other in the testing of hypotheses.[20] And so circular reasoning in linguistic argumentation is vicious only if the number of concentric circles—that is, the amount of evidence adduced, and therefore the explanatory power of the proposed explanation—is too small, as would certainly be the case in this instance if the evidence for laryngeal consonants rested solely on this Vedic paradigm.[21] But when the vast array of similar phenomena in a

---

[20]The scientific and philosophical necessity of such circular reasoning is explored by Paul Weiss, *Reality* (Princeton: Princeton Univ. Press, 1938), chap. 1. Roger Lass mounts a valiant assault on the validity of probabilistic reasoning in *On Explaining Language Change*, Cambridge Studies in Linguistics 27 (Cambridge: Cambridge Univ. Press, 1980), 20ff., where he argues that the statistical basis of probabilistic reasoning leads to its vicious circularity. Taking the example of the assimilation of nasal consonants to the place of articulation of a following stop consonant, he remarks that the naturalness of the process is gauged only by its frequency in the world's languages; and so this naturalness, being identical with statistical frequency, cannot actually explain that frequency, as is widely assumed. But naturalness consists more properly in the interaction of related phonological features in the direction of ease of articulation: though linguistic theory would of course somehow have to cope with it, it would be surprising if nasal consonants were dissimilated rather than assimilated before stops. Our surprise at encountering such a situation would stem not so much from its statistical infrequency as its promotion of difficulty of articulation. That probability is not merely statistical in nature is an important consideration in metrical history. For example, increasing incidence of parasiting may be credible as an indicator of chronology, since it it known that parasiting did affect the language over the course of time, while the syntactic position of auxiliaries is not as compelling an indicator of chronology, since there is no independent evidence that this changed over time, except, eventually, in the direction of SVO order. In other words, naturalness does not and cannot reside solely in statistics, since some statistics seem more significant than others.

[21]Lass rejects the conclusions of the functional approach to explanation, on the basis of the argument that functionalism can make no predictions that are not based on circular reasoning. This seems a misperception of the aims of the "intuitive" sciences, since the predictive requirement in the rigid sense that Lass employs is proper only to deductive reasoning. That is why the most reliable predictions of historical linguistics are those based on the linguistic entities most nearly comparable to natural laws, i.e. neogrammarian-style sound changes—e.g., phonologists can predict with considerable

variety of Indo-European languages is added to the evidence, the explanatory power of laryngeals becomes so great that their existence is virtually proved. To be sure, Saussure's hypothesis enjoyed little currency until after the decipherment of Hittite and its identification as an Indo-European language, when Jerzy Kuryłowicz, in 1927, demonstrated that some laryngeals are actually preserved in the language.[22] But despite its instrumentality in convincing the linguistic community, the apparently irrefutable evidence of Hittite is actually less consequential than the combined value of all the other, circumstantial evidence: if there were no other evidence, the mysterious consonants encountered in Hittite would most plausibly and logically be explained by other means as an Anatolian innovation (as in fact some earlier opponents of the laryngeal hypothesis tried to explain them), not an inheritance from Proto-Indo-European. This is the course that linguistic methodology demands.[23] Dramatic discoveries like Kuryłowicz' may serve to confirm a hypothesis for which there is already a variety of evidence, but it will never serve as proof by itself. The point is that it is vain to demand a "mechanical" proof with "nonsubjective" results, since convincing proof in historical lingustics usually depends instead on a variety of circumstantial evidence. As one methodologist remarks,

Any single test does not prove the proposition is true—it merely adds one more piece of evidence that the proposition has not yet been disconfirmed. Although theoretically the process of escaping disconfirmation is never-ending, in effect what is happening is that each piece of evidence lowers the uncertainty about the relationship until it crosses the knowledge threshold. The amount of evidence required is a personal decision. Even after the relationship has crossed that threshold, there might still be some as yet untested instance in which it

---

accuracy the reflex of a proto-form in any daughter language, as discussed by Christian Peeters, "On Prediction in Comparative Linguistics," *General Linguistics* 21 (1981), 17–18. Lass seems to do what Itkonen warns against (see n. 12 above)—i.e., he applies deductive standards of reasoning to nondeductive argumentation. For a different set of objections to Lass's rejection of functionalism see M. L. Samuels, "The Status of the Functional Approach," in *Explanation and Linguistic Change*, ed. Willem Koopman et al., Current Issues in Linguistic Theory 45 (Amsterdam: Benjamins, 1987), 239–50, followed by Lass's reply (251–55) and Samuels' final rejoinder (257–58).

[22]"ə indo-européen et ḫ hittite," in *Symbolae grammaticae in honorem Ioannis Rozwadowski* (Cracow: Gebethner & Wolff, 1927), pp. 95–104.

[23]The methodological principle is formulated succinctly by Oswald Szemerényi in a discussion of reconstructive methodology in historical linguistics: "Anomale Erscheinungen, die nur in einer Sprachgruppe anzutreffen sind, dürfen bei der Rekonstruktion nicht verwendet werden bzw. müssen sehr sorgfältig auf ihre Tragfähigkeit untersucht werden"; see "Rekonstruktion in der indogermanischen Flexion—Prinzipien und Probleme," in *Flexion und Wortbildung: Akten der V. Fachtagung der Indogermanischen Gesellschaft, Regensburg, 9.-14. September 1973*, ed. Helmut Rix (Wiesbaden: Reichert, 1975), pp. 325–45, at p. 343.

would be disconfirmed. That is why all scientific knowledge is held as tentatively true.[24]

§11. Why this is so can be illustrated with reference to metrical dating criteria themselves. What would be proved by a single, irrefutable, "mechanical" criterion? First would have to be settled the question of what would amount to clear results: An absolute distinction between poems with and without parasiting? A gradual increase in parasited forms along the presumed continuum? (Amos argues for the former.) But then the evidence of such clear results could never be considered indisputable, since (as in the analogy of Kuryłowicz' discovery) it would always be subject to alternative explanations. For example, Dorothy Whitelock objects, "the arranging of the various poems in a relative chronology is completely valid only if there is reason to suppose that they come from approximately the same part of the country. The rate of development need not have been uniform in the various dialects" (*Audience*, pp. 26–27). If the objection has any validity for a relative chronology of verse, then perforce it would have the same validity if a supposedly irrefutable proof turned out to arrange Old English verse into two groups rather than along a continuum. For most proposed dating criteria it is indeed true that there is no evidence as to the rate of change in different dialects. Thus a variety of circumstantial evidence is of considerably more importance than one such clear distribution: several discrete criteria vaguely indicative of the same chronology are far more persuasive, since the probability is negligible that several randomly selected sound changes should have followed the same geographical path from dialect to dialect. The only safeguard against the form of linguistic interference that Whitelock warns against, and others like it, is in the variety of criteria applied.

§12. Another error inherent in a positivist, mechanistic approach to the history of meter is the supposition that because probabilistic evidence is not proof, it can be ignored. It would not be fair to single out Amos for ignoring probabilities, since it is dubitable whether much or any Anglo-Saxon scholarship could be found that is free of this weakness. Nonetheless, her objections are the ones that must be met. One instance arises from her rejection of the chronological significance of Kaluza's law (p. 100). As discussed below (§181), the *Wanderer* is metrically less conservative (and therefore, if objections to the assumption of a connection between metrical conservatism and relative date can be answered effectively, probably later) than *Beowulf* because the verse *ferðloca freorig* (33a, and others like it) demands resolution in -*loca*. The *Beowulf* poet clearly avoids such verses, since they violate Kaluza's law. Amos objects that

---

[24]David R. Krathwohl, *Social and Behavioral Science Research* (San Francisco: Jossey-Bass, 1985), p. 60.

perhaps -*loca* is unresolved: although the metrical pattern of a verse such as *\*gūðrēowe gāras* is not found in *Beowulf* (cf. *gealorand to guþe* 438a, and see Bliss, §4), perhaps it was acceptable to the *Wanderer* poet; if so, -*loca* need not be resolved. Then it need not violate Kaluza's law, and so the poem need not postdate *Beowulf*. Such reasoning cannot be admitted. Relatively general counterarguments such as "metrical practice may have been governed by personal style rather than chronology" (as discussed below, §§35ff.) must be given careful consideration because under most circumstances they are difficult to prove or disprove effectively. This is not the case with Amos' objection, which can readily be tested. In fact, verses like *\*gūðrēowe gāras* occur neither in the representative group of poems examined in this study (as defined below, §§70ff.) nor in the *Wanderer* itself. And so it is implausible that the type could have been acceptable to the *Wanderer* poet. This is especially true because such verses are intrinsically unlikely even in the late tenth century. They require five underlying metrical positions, when even the faulty meter of *Maldon* does not violate the rule that a verse has four underlying positions.[25]

§13. Another example of this observation about probabilistic reasoning can be drawn from H. L. Rogers' attempt to overturn the consensus that the rhymes in *Elene* demonstrate that Cynewulf wrote in an Anglian dialect.[26] As first observed by Sievers, these imperfect rhymes—for example *riht : geþeaht* and *miht : þeaht*—can be rendered regular by the substitution of the corresponding Anglian forms for these West-Saxon ones (as discussed below, §§389ff.). Rogers, on the other hand, argues that the substitution of Anglian forms is unjustified because it cannot be proved that Cynewulf intended full rhyme. He concludes, "In matters like this, the burden of proof rests upon those who wish to depart from the MS readings, to suppose that the poetry was composed long before the MS was written, and to argue that the original dialect of composition was different from that in which the poetry is now known. In short, I do not have to prove Sievers wrong; it is sufficient to show that he has not proved himself right" (p. 52). The methodological assumption behind this claim, and behind Amos' objection to the evidence of Kaluza's law, is that credence in a hypothesis is invalidated by the mere existence of an alternative hypothesis: Sievers has not "proved himself right," and so the existence of an alternative explanation relieves Rogers of the obligation to disprove Sievers' explanation. This is clearly wrong. As we have seen, a hypothesis is unlike a mathematical theorem in that it cannot be proved under any circumstances; and so because Rogers' reasoning is that an

---

[25]For an explanation of the significance of the four positions see Cable, *Meter and Melody*, esp. pp. 84–93.

[26]"Rhymes in the Epilogue to *Elene*: A Reconsideration," *Leeds Studies in English*, n.s. 5 (1971), 47–52.

unproved explanation merits no credence, it follows that no explanation short of mathematical reasoning ever merits credence.[27] In our daily lives we naturally, necessarily, and constantly assume otherwise, since humans cannot abandon all beliefs. The methodological error underlying the great many arguments exemplified by Amos' and Rogers' reasoning is the assumption that there is such a thing as a hypothesis to which there is no alternative. But a hypothesis with no alternative is a logical discontinuity: such a hypothesis would lose its hypothetical character and cease to be a hypothesis. As George Gale remarks, "In any scientific area there is a series of alternative theories which must be decided among. I cannot overemphasize this logical point. *Every* set of observable data has at least two possible explanations."[28] In linguistics, as in all fields of research employing probabilistic reasoning—including, for instance, literary criticism—no explanation is to be considered disproved, or even uncertain enough to be held in abeyance, simply because an alternative explanation has been offered. Rather, Gale continues, "we must believe that not both explanations are true. Consequently, the scientist is every time forced into making a decision between alternative explanations" (p. 68). This decision that must be made in every instance always involves the determination of probability. To be precise, it rests largely upon the relative implausibility of all competing explanations. Because Sievers' argument is reasonable and self-consistent, its probability is affected only if one or more competing explanations is shown to be equally probable, or nearly so. As Roger Lass remarks, "I can't legitimately criticize a claim about the nature of scientific explanation . . . on the grounds that I can think of other kinds of explanation that someone sufficiently muddled or uninterested would find acceptable."[29] Rogers' alternative explanation is not in fact very plausible (see §§389ff.); but that is of little consequence, because the issue here is not whether Cynewulf was an Anglian, but whether the mere existence of Rogers' explanation,

---

[27]Rogers' assertion that "the burden of proof rests with those who wish to depart from the MS readings" would provide a criterion for preferring one explanation to another; but it is false, at least in the sense he intends. If it were true, no editor would be justified in altering a manuscript reading, since all emendations are hypotheses, and anyone might object, with Rogers, that the emendation is unproved. Because no hypothesis can be proved, the claim turns a reasonable principle of editorial practice (emendations require compelling justification) into an indefensible absolute. If it were true it would lead to self-contradiction, since the assumption that manuscript readings are "correct" (assuming that correctness can somehow be defined) is also a hypothesis, and thus cannot be proved. Self-contradiction is the inevitable result whenever absolutes are assumed within systems depending on inductive logic.

[28]*Theory of Science: An Introduction to the History, Logic, and Philosophy of Science* (New York: McGraw-Hill, 1979), p. 68. Cf. Frank (n. 17 above): "We never have one theory that is in full agreement [with 'observed facts'] but several theories that are in partial agreement, and we have to determine the final theory by a compromise" (p. 14).

[29]See p. 6 of the book cited above, n. 20.

regardless of whether or not it is plausible, invalidates credence in Sievers' position, as Rogers claims. It is not necessary to appeal to scientific literature to locate examples demonstrating that we do not abandon, or even diminish our trust in, widely held assumptions simply because contrary possibilities cannot all be disproved. The mere existence of alternative explanations implies nothing about the validity of a hypothesis, and any reference to alternative explanations that does not take into account relative probability has no persuasive value.

§14. Accordingly, the analogy that Hans Henrich Hock draws to a court of law is not entirely appropriate.[30] The subjective nature of a jury's decision is apposite: jurors are advised that they may convict at the point at which they are able to decide "beyond a reasonable doubt." However, since theories always retain some of their hypotheticism, "guilt" or "innocence" cannot be established once for all, but is organic, and must continually be reevaluated.[31] Nor is a hypothesis "innocent" until proved "guilty": under such an assumption scientific inquiry would come to a standstill, since research cannot proceed under the assumption that all possible explanations are of equal probability. Rather, scientists *must* decide which is the most likely hypothesis (as Gale says, above) and proceed under its assumptions, waiting to see whether it produces internal inconsistencies. An important consequence of this method is that if the attempt to disprove the hypothesis produces no inconsistencies it almost inevitably leads to further evidence for the hypothesis, since the plausibility of an explanation frequently depends upon the number of disparate phenomena it accounts for or agrees with. The linguist who begins with the assumption that consonant gemination in Old English and Old Saxon is the result of the same historical event, rather than an independent development, is then enabled to account for other linguistic affinities between the two languages, as well as for the fact that some speakers of Old English referred to themselves as Saxons, claimed that their forebears came from the Continent, wore personal ornaments like those found in Lower Germany, and so forth. As remarked above (§10), such reasoning is circular, but the circularity is not inherently vicious: the linguistic and historical materials are mutually supportive, and yet the fact that the body of evidence is a closed one does not diminish the probability of the explanation. Rather, such reasoning is thoroughly convincing as long as the circle is not too small: the larger the number of facts accounted for, the more reasonable the hypothesis seems.[32] Thus a likely hypothesis will participate in "circular" or holistic systems of reasoning, supporting and being supported by related evidence and

[30]*Principles of Historical Linguistics* (Berlin: Mouton de Gruyter, 1986), p. 567.

[31]*Hypotheticism* is the term used by the master critic of induction, Sir Karl Popper: see *The Logic of Scientific Discovery* (New York: Basic Books, 1959), esp. §§79–85.

[32]Cf. Frank's reference to "a vast number of facts . . . derived from few and simple principles" (above, n. 17).

related theories, to produce a more coherent overall picture. As William J. Goode and Paul K. Hatt remark, "*Scientific experimentation is set against an existing body of generalizations.* . . . Not only does the scientist seek generalizations, but he also wishes to extend their utility by relating them to other generalizations; in short, he wishes to create a system of theory."[33] One gauge of the relative validity of a hypothesis is thus its explanatory power.

§15. The corollary to this method of building probability by accounting for a wide variety of phenomena is that one may begin with a less probable hypothesis and demonstrate how little it explains, or what internal inconsistencies or outright improbabilities it leads to. Accordingly, much recent worthwhile reassessment of the linguistic and metrical evidence for dating and localizing Old English verse is vitiated by the limitedness of its aims. It attempts merely to disprove older views, without demonstrating that the alternative proposals participate in such holistic systems of reasoning, and thus that they have any explanatory power beyond the particular case under consideration—that is, that they are not simply ad hoc. For example, when Rogers objects that Cynewulf may be using consonance rather than rhyme in pairing *riht* with *gepeaht* and *miht* with *peaht* in the epilogue to *Elene*, he is not providing an explanation for any phenomenon but the imperfect rhymes themselves. His purpose is solely to discredit the standard view, a point he makes explicit: "I am not putting forward the hypothesis that Cynewulf wrote in Canterbury, many though the attractions of it are, but merely observing that the substitution of -*eht* forms in the Epilogue to *Elene* would be consistent with Kentish provenance no less than with West Mercian" (p. 49). There is a methodological error here. We have seen (as Gale says, p. 14 above) that one must always choose among hypotheses, from which it follows that it is not an acceptable procedure to attempt to discredit one hypothesis without supporting another. Either the idea that Cynewulf was Kentish is at least as credible as the idea that he was Anglian (in which case there is no justification for proposing the idea without seriously championing it) or it is not. Discrediting one hypothesis while refusing to explain the merits of the other effectively puts an end to scholarship, since research has reached an impasse when the relative merits of competing explanations cannot be weighed against each other.

§16. But the more immediate point is that while Rogers' explanation is ad hoc, accounting only for the imperfect rhymes, Sievers' argument that Anglian forms ought to be substituted accounts for a variety of other facts: for example, that although there are several instances of imperfect rhymes in *Elene* and *Christ II* (as well as the *Riming Poem*) that could be

---

[33]Goode and Hatt, p. 33 (as above, n. 16). Cf. Gale: "Theory acceptability grows as . . . the new hypothesis provides a growing conceptual unity within and/or between different sets of notions" (p. 261).

corrected by the substitution of Anglian forms (*contra* Macrae-Gibson: see p. 365, n. 42 below), there are no Southern rhymes that would be spoilt by Anglian substitutions; that consonance does not substitute for rhyme in the one indubitable rhyming passage outside of Cynewulf's works; that Cynewulf uses no contracted forms of the second and third person singular indicative of strong verbs, though indubitably Southern verse does (see §§318ff. below); that certain characteristically Anglian spellings other than conventional poetic spellings appear in Cynewulf's verse (see §§340ff. below); that items of Anglian vocabulary other than conventionally poetic ones characterize his works (§§356ff.); and that his works are widely regarded as being linguistically and stylistically close to *Guthlac B*.[34] Nearly all these other criteria for placing Cynewulf north of the Thames have of course been questioned in other contexts. The objections are considered in the sections cited. But the situation is the same in each instance: the objections are not raised to defend alternative proposals with holistic aims, but simply to argue that these criteria are inconclusive. Thus each of these objections is another instance of the general point expressed by the example of Rogers, that the assumption that Cynewulf was an Anglian explains a variety of peculiarities in his verse, while the alternative proposal neither supports nor is supported by a comparable body of related facts about the texts.

§17. The subjective requirements of the inductive method are more than a matter of theoretical interest, since they have practical implications in regard to how metrical criteria for dating and localizing verse are to be tested. The construction of Amos' study is predicated on the assumption that objectivity is attainable. "Subjective criteria for dating the literature," she says, "exist in plenty." What she calls for instead is "a good, operator-blind, mechanical linguistic test" (p. 8). But no linguistic evidence can be objective in this sense of the word, since it demands reasonable and informed observers to evaluate it. Unlike mathematical proof, its truth value cannot be derived by the mechanical application of pure logic, but always depends upon human judgment.[35] "Operator-blind" objectivity in such a study is not simply unattainable but undesirable, since attempts at objectivity produce untenable results. Examples of this point are offered in several places below, where it is shown that Alan Bliss's findings about the meter of *Beowulf* are not always predictions about what is metrically possible. For instance, his observation that no more than six syllables appear in the first thesis of verses of type a1 in *Beowulf* does not constitute a claim about the acceptability of a verse with seven syllables in this position, as explained

---

[34]See Sisam, *Studies*, pp. 13n and 134; and Roberts, p. 61.

[35]This is what Krathwohl means by his remark (§10 above) that "the amount of evidence required [to validate a hypothesis] is a personal decision."

below (§140).[36] Such verses do appear outside *Beowulf*. Yet Amos treats Bliss's findings as uniformly absolute, rejecting any metrical type that does not appear in his analysis of *Beowulf*. The error is small, but the point it illustrates is significant, since it leads to wrong conclusions about the data. Many of Bliss's findings about what metrical types appear in *Beowulf* do constitute claims about what is or is not metrically acceptable; but this is not consistently the case. To apply Bliss's conclusions as a seamless measure of metrical acceptability, as if every one of his findings represented a prediction equal in firmness to every other, is to use his analysis of *Beowulf* in a way no metrist could condone, and one that Bliss himself certainly did not intend. His metrical system is not an "operator-blind" tool that can be applied without any value judgments about its components. This, then, is an example of why attempts to achieve complete objectivity actually impede the attainment of fair and credible results.

§18. To resort to Amos' book for another example, in an attempt at objectivity she rejects all editorial emendations. Her statistics are based solely on what the manuscripts themselves say. It would not be reasonable to suppose she means by this that the manuscripts do not need to be emended: Kenneth Sisam's essay "The Authority of Old English Poetical Manuscripts," for instance, is too well known a demonstration of scribes' unreliability.[37] Rather, presumably the intention is to avoid the subjectivity inherent in choosing whether or not to accept a particular editor's emendations. The result is, instead of a set of data that might be correct, a set that is certainly incorrect, treating several impossibilities (e.g. MS *weorc feos* at *Genesis A* 2721a: see below, p. 95, n. 3) as if they were chronological evidence. Because of the way poetic texts are freely altered by scribes, Sisam advises, with some justice, "To support a bad manuscript reading is in no way more meritorious than to support a bad conjecture, and so far from being safer, it is more insidious as a source of error" (p. 39). Well-intended as it might be to eliminate the temptation to bias, it cannot be done without sacrificing the plausibility of the conclusions. It is precisely because the validation of hypotheses is a subjective process that it is a scholar's responsibility not to cede the use of his or her own reason. One is instead obliged to evaluate the probability of individual emendations. This is a subjective process, and admittedly can be abused, but it is also the only possible way to attain fair results. The scholar's obligation, then, is to set aside as much bias as human nature will permit, and if this is responsibly done it will merit the respect of reasonable observers.

[36]Yet in some other instances there may be a certain amount of probability attached to questions about the number of syllables permissible in the first drop of light verses: see p. 77, n. 29 below, in reference to verses like *sette friðotacen* (*Genesis A* 2371a).

[37]*RES* 22 (1946), 257–68; rpt. in his *Studies*, pp. 29–44.

§19. But even if objectivity were desirable it would not be possible, since a thoroughly objective proof is a chimera. The process of designing chronological experiments inevitably demands subjective choices that affect the results. For example, in considering contraction (see below, Chap. 2) Amos presents the evidence for the four types separately. This choice makes a considerable difference in the statistical results. The choice is a good one, since the different types of contraction apparently did not take place at the same time; but it is not an inevitable choice, since, as Amos notes (p. 44), Carl Richter does not distinguish them. Amos makes the same subjective choice in deciding to treat all the negative compounds as separate contractions (p. 65). In this instance the choice is not a good one, since the contractions apparently took place at the same time—or, if not that, at most in two groups (see below, §§134ff.). The result is that examples of each contraction are too few to provide Amos with any conclusions, while if they had been combined their purport would have been clear. The point is not that these particular experiments are incapable of objectification, but that all are.[38] Philological proof does not rest on the avoidance of subjectivity, but on demonstration of the most probable circumstances of a linguistic change, a demonstration that demands persuasion by means of subjective argumentation.

§20. A final misapprehension about linguistic proof is that subjective argumentation is not convincing. The conviction that a linguistic argument carries of course depends on the degree of probability that can be established, but with sufficient evidence it is not difficult to establish such a degree of probability that doubts are rendered unreasonable. In this regard improbability perhaps plays an even more important role than probability, since a proposition can be considered more or less proved when to reject it would demand acceptance of an extreme linguistic coincidence. As Werner Winter remarks in a study of reconstructive methodology in historical linguistics, "We have to be content with the preliminary formulation that chance agreement does indeed occur, but that the probability of its occurring is extremely small, so that for all practical purposes an agreement not limited to just a very few items in a large inventory should be interpreted as resulting not from chance, but from other causes."[39] For example, for a variety of reasons Old High German is classified as a West Germanic language, and thus as more closely related to English than to Norse or Gothic. One reason is that

[38]For another example illustrating why subjectivity is unavoidable in metrical argumentation see the discussion of Hoyt N. Duggan's recent article, §31 below. For references to studies arguing the impossibility of complete objectivity in the experimental method see n. 9 above.

[39]"Basic Principles of the Comparative Method," in *Method and Theory in Linguistics*, ed. Paul L. Garvin (The Hague: Mouton, 1970), pp. 147–56, at 147–48.

gemination of consonants before *j* is general in Old High German and in the Ingvaeonic languages, while it is missing from Gothic and restricted to velar consonants in Norse. It is of course possible that precisely the same sound change arose independently in High German and the Ingvaeonic languages, and thus an alternative explanation does exist. But this is improbable—it is too much of a coincidence to be readily reconciled with what we know about the randomness of sound change. The position of Old High German is not proved at this point, since one feature is not sufficient evidence, even if to reject it would be to embrace an improbability. But there are several other features that High German shares with the Ingvaeonic languages and not with Norse and Gothic, for example gemination before *r* and *l*, development of *ð* to a stop consonant, and agreement in root vocalism of the second person singular preterite of strong verbs with the plural rather than with the first and third person singular. The variety of agreement reinforces the initial impression that coincidence is not an acceptable explanation—too many coincidences are involved here.

§21. Similar would be a hypothetical situation in which there are six unrelated archaisms serving as signs of metrical change in Old English verse. Each shows a wide distribution in poems presumed to be very early, with generally decreasing incidence through the corpus, until it is virtually unattested in poems presumed to be very late. None of these criteria could serve as proof on its own, since factors such as dialect, style, and scribal interference might create additional variations that would disrupt those governed by chronological development. But when six separate criteria show more or less the same distribution, this cannot be chance. The chronology is not proved in the mathematical sense of proof, but still, to attribute the agreement of six unrelated criteria to chance is unreasonable. Thus, by the accumulation of probabilistic evidence a probability roughly equivalent in force to absolute proof can be developed. Aldo Ricci captures the essence of this idea when he remarks, "Only when all these tests, taken together (and especially the *h*-tests), point to the same conclusion in a fairly long poem, will it be really safe to rely upon them" (p. 260). Amos also recognizes the validity of the point, adding that agreement among the results need not be rigid: "When for a given text the results of all the linguistic tests point independently to a certain date, however, even mixed evidence is likely to be meaningful. The consistency of the results makes it less likely that the mixture of early and late forms represents the chance choice of the author and more likely that it represents the actual linguistic usage of a given period" (p. 12).

§22. It may be further remarked that even if "subjective criteria for dating the literature exist in plenty," the linguistic evidence, even though subjective, differs in essential ways from other types of evidence. Dorothy Whitelock's observation that *Beowulf*, a poem that honors Danes, must have been composed before the Danish attacks on England became severe, about 835, is also a probabilistic argument.[40] And as with the linguistic arguments, this argument could be (and has been) combined with other probabilistic arguments in support of a fairly early date. But still this evidence is essentially different from linguistic evidence. To return to the example just mentioned, because it is the conclusion that methodology demands, it is more than a matter of linguistic opinion that Old High German is a West Germanic language. Although, in accordance with Popper's dictum, the hypothesis cannot finally be proved, nonetheless it is virtually proved because any other assumption is unreasonable. Such certainty is attainable because language changes in predictable ways. For example, West Germanic gemination before -j- is a natural change paralleled in other natural languages, with an identifiable cause (unstable syllable structure in consonant clusters ending in -j-), while a change such as the conversion of the cluster -dj- to -m- is unnatural: it has no discernible phonological motive, and is probably not to be found in the history of any of the world's languages. Thus, linguistic conclusions are verifiable on the basis of comparison with a large body of detailed information, garnered over more than two centuries of Western linguistics, about what is natural and possible in language change, and what is not. Philological conclusions are supported by an enormous data base unparalleled in any other area of dating research. There is less reason for assurance in reconstructing the feelings of ninth-century Anglo-Saxons about Danes, an essential part of Whitelock's argument. Linguistic evidence also affords the opportunity for fairly precise dating, since language change can often be dated with significantly more accuracy than such evidence as Whitelock's. But most important, nonlinguistic evidence does not offer the same opportunities for firm conclusions based on the rejection of coincidence. For these reasons linguistic evidence must take precedence over other types of

[40]*Audience*, pp. 24–25. That is, the argument is of a probabilistic nature, regardless of how probable or improbable it might be. Whitelock's argument—originally advanced by N. F. S. Grundtvig, and espoused by Klaeber, p. cvii—has faced considerable opposition in studies arguing that more or less peaceable relations were possible with Danes in the Viking age. "It is astonishing how often this [argument] has been picked out for reproof in recent years," remarks Thomas Shippey in an article titled "Old English Poetry: The Prospects for Literary History," to appear in *Sociedad Española para Lengua y Literatura Inglés Medieval*. Counterarguments to Whitelock's view are presented in three essays in Chase's *Dating of Beowulf:* see Alexander Callander Murray, "*Beowulf*, the Danish Invasions, and Royal Genealogy," pp. 101–11; Raymond Page, "The Audience of *Beowulf* and the Vikings," pp. 113–22; and Roberta Frank, "Skaldic Verse and the Date of *Beowulf*," pp. 123–39, at p. 123. See also Norman Blake, "The Dating of Old English Poetry," in *An English Miscellany Presented to W. S. Mackie*, ed. Brian Lee (Cape Town: Oxford Univ. Press, 1977), pp. 14–27, at 25, as well as Jacobs, pp. 35–41, and Busse, pp. 74 and 86ff.; and Chase and Stanley in the Chase volume, pp. 6 and 197. That relations with the Danes were not consistently hostile was perhaps first suggested by Schücking, pp. 364–66.

evidence, lacking such firm external indicators as allow *Cædmon's Hymn* to be dated to the seventh century. Amos reaches a similar conclusion (p. 166).

§23. A regrettable aspect of recent discussions of dating has been the frequency of the charge of bias against studies that tend to support the presumed chronology. Amos, for example, finds that Sarrazin tailors the evidence for parasiting to suit his "foregone conclusion," and she concludes that Seiffert is doctoring the evidence when he argues that *gedōn* is a scribal alteration of *dōn* in *Beowulf.*[41] More direct is the criticism of Wilhelm Busse, who sees the aims of earlier dating studies as entirely jaundiced:

> Wo hingegen die linguistische Analyse von Texten zum Zwecke ihrer Datierung auf der Basis eines Vorverständnisses vom archaischen Charakter der poetischen Sprache nicht einmal davon absieht, sprachliche Daten nur in diesem vorverständigten Sinne und mit Blick auf das gewünschte Datierungsergebnis zu deuten, dabei vergleichbare Daten aus der Überlieferungszeit und später stillschweigend zu übersehen: da enthüllen sich schlaglichtartig die Absicht und das Interesse solcher Interpretation. (p. 60)

These accusations raise another methodological point, concerning the relationship between hypotheses and proof. In the natural as in the social sciences, proof begins with the formation of a hypothesis, followed by the generation of data that will confirm or disprove the hypothesis. The point is that the scientific method requires the very thing that Busse condemns as bias—the formation of a hypothesis, a preconception, to be tested against the facts. As Joseph Weizenbaum remarks, "The scientist must believe his working hypothesis, together with its vast underlying structure of theories and assumptions, even if only for the sake of argument."[42] Sir Karl Popper explains in more detail:

> (*a*) I do not believe that we ever make inductive generalizations in the sense that we start with observations and try to derive our theories from them. I believe that the prejudice that we proceed in this way is a kind of optical illusion, and that at no stage of scientific development do we begin without something in the nature of a theory, such as a hypothesis, or a prejudice, or a problem—often a technological one—which in some way *guides* our observations, and helps us to select from the innumerable objects of observation those which may be of interest. But if this is so, then the method of elimination—which is nothing but that of trial and error . . . —can always be applied. However, I do not think that it is necessary for our present discussion to insist upon this point. For we can say (*b*) that it is irrelevant from the point of view of science whether we have obtained our theories by jumping to

---

[41]For explanations why these charges are unfair see below, §§82f. and 110.
[42]*Computer Power and Human Reason* (San Francisco: W. H. Freeman, 1976), quoted by House (as above, n. 12), p. 71.

unwarranted conclusions or merely by stumbling over them (that is, by "intuition"), or else by some inductive procedure. The question, "How did you first *find* your theory?" relates, as it were, to an entirely private matter, as opposed to the question, "How did you *test* your theory?" which alone is scientifically relevant.[43]

A violation of the scientific method would occur if the data were interpreted in an unusual way in order to support the hypothesis, without any independent motivation for that interpretation. But this is not what Busse is criticizing, since what he objects to is the very formation and testing of the hypothesis that Old English verse should have been composed in a form other than that in which it is attested. To many scholars his hypothesis of a tenth-century origin for all but a few lines of Old English verse will perhaps seem no less tendentious than the usual assumption that it was composed over several centuries. This is fairly obvious: if, for example, no Northumbrian version of the *Leiden Riddle* survived, there would be nothing to prove that such a poem existed before the tenth-century West-Saxon version recorded in the Exeter Book. Conversely, since no earlier recension of *Genesis A* exists, it cannot be proved by the same means that it was composed before the tenth century, and yet the case of the *Leiden Riddle* proves that no probability attaches to this fact. If it is a form of bias that earlier philologists attempted to explain linguistic and metrical variation in verse by means of a single, unified theory of dating and dialect origins, it is a bias that the inductive method demands—and one that Busse, too, must engage in in order to defend his own hypothesis. Moreover, it is difficult to imagine how scholars like Richter and Sarrazin could have begun with any hypothesis other than the presumed chronology they did begin with, since the subjective evaluations of scholars like C. W. M. Grein, Bernhard ten Brink, Karl Müllenhoff, and Sievers had already created the presumption that, for instance, *Genesis A* and *Beowulf* are early, while *Genesis B* and *Christ and Satan* late.[44] If the mere formation of a hypothesis were a reprehensible form of bias, no scholarship would pass the test of impartiality.[45] This is not to say that bias does not exist in scholarship —examples are too familiar, especially when industry has an interest in the results. Yet biased reasoning is never defeated by exposure of the bias, but by demonstration of the improbabilities that it produces. Thus

[43]Karl R. Popper, *The Poverty of Historicism* (London: Routledge, 1957), pp. 134–35.

[44]See n. 5 above on the factors giving rise to chronological assumptions before the discovery of metrical criteria.

[45]For example, Amos' decision to use only the data of prior studies leads to a methodological cul-de-sac. A study that reached the same conclusions as earlier studies would not be a reasonable contribution to scholarship if it used the same data, and so a study that sets out with the intention of using the same data will be obliged to reject earlier conclusions. This observation is not intended to discredit Amos' book, but to demonstrate the larger point, that charges of bias are of no benefit to scholarship.

it is not bias but antiprobabilistic reasoning that requires correction; and when such faulty reasoning is discovered and corrected, that is all that is required, since the causes of bad reasoning are, as Popper says, a "private matter." Charges of bias thus serve no rational purpose. Rather, they carry only emotional weight, and so however they are intended, they are in substance personal attacks, and thus have no place in scholarship.

## C. The Causes of Inconsistency in Chronological Findings

§24. It was pointed out above (§§2ff.) that the objections raised to the attribution of metrical variation to chronological and dialectal causes have in general addressed not the data, but the assumptions underlying the interpretation of the data. An example is Dorothy Whitelock's observation that unless the linguistic change traced by a metrical study took place at the same time in all dialects, a chronology constructed on the basis of this criterion might be inaccurate. In the discussion of this objection it was pointed out (§11 above) that obstacles like this to the construction of a chronology can be considered obviated if the distribution of several different metrical variables points to roughly the same chronology. The present study demonstrates that the data for several criteria do conform generally to a single chronology, and so objections such as Whitelock's may be regarded as excessively cautious, at least to the extent that they reflect on the validity of metrical chronology in general. What objections like Whitelock's amount to are claims that there exist reasons not to expect regular results from such experiments; yet it has been remarked in another context that the existence of a pattern in a body of data will be all the more convincing *because* of the reasons adduced not to expect a pattern.[46] Though such objections are intended as counterevidence to metrical history, in practice they have the opposite effect: because such arguments explain why inconsistencies should be expected in the data, agreement among a variety of criteria in regard to chronology need not be precise. If one test places *Genesis A* before *Beowulf* and another after it, objections such as Whitelock's explain why this is to be expected. Thus, all that is required of the various types of metrical evidence in order to validate them is that they evince a high degree of approximate agreement (as Amos remarks: see §21 above). Since the metrical criteria examined in the following chapters are not in complete agreement about all details of the chronology that they suggest, it will be worthwhile to rehearse the objections of this sort, distinguishing the most from the least valid, and thus determining which are likeliest to account for the inconsistencies in the results.

[46]See "Dating Beowulf to the Viking Age," *PQ* 61 (1982), 341–59, at 352–53.

§25. A number of scholars have remarked that our understanding of Old English meter is not reliable enough to support the application of rigid metrical rules in developing chronological evidence. Thus, for instance, a verse such as *Ðær wæs hæleþa hleahtor* (*Beowulf* 611a) might simply represent a rare metrical type rather than evidence of monosyllabic *hleahtor*.[47] It is true that much remains to be explained in Old English metrics, and Ritchie Girvan correctly points out that "abnormal metrical types consequential on change could be and were regarded as admissible licence and imitated later" (p. 15; also p. 18; for examples see below, p. 88, n. 49). In other words, although originally *hleahtor* had to be monosyllabic, the development to a dissyllable in normal speech might eventually have changed the scansion of *Ðær wæs hæleþa hleahtor* and afforded metrical admissibility to a previously unacceptable type. But this question, too, must be viewed in terms of probability, and on that basis there are ways of testing the hypothesis. If *Ðær wæs hæleþa hleahtor*, with dissyllabic *hleahtor*, was an acceptable metrical type, then several other verses may be of the same sort, for example *þa mec sinca baldor* (*Beowulf* 2428b) and *sete sigores tacn* (*Genesis A* 2313a). The fact is, however, that verses like *\*þæt wæs Grendles hēafod* are nowhere found—that is, the peculiar metrical type is encountered only when the extra syllable is the result of parasiting. The coincidence is too great to be credible. Thus the aberrant metrical type must be considered so improbable that *hleahtor* may with some confidence be regarded as monosyllabic.

§26. But there are varying degrees of argumentative value to this objection, depending on the degree of specificity appealed to. Norman Blake's position typifies the argument in its most general and uncompromising form, contrasting contemporary conceptions of Old English meter with the Anglo-Saxon audience's own conception:

We should not forget that we know nothing about the Anglo-Saxons' attitude towards English alliterative style or metre. We cannot tell whether they regarded things in the same light as we do or what movements of style motivated their approach. We may think that the style of *The Battle of Maldon* is decadent and so base our dating on that view—but there is no evidence that they saw the poem in this way. Their understanding of the metre is also something that eludes us. We can try to decide when they used hypermetric lines, for example, but we cannot tell whether people then approved of them or not. In the same way most attempts to date the poetry by metrical tests are inconclusive, precisely because we can argue only from our understanding of the metre, not theirs.[48]

This view presents scholarship, in most science as in the humanities, not as an act of persuasion, but as a medium that somehow can put one

---

[47]See, for example, Sarrazin, *Kädmon*, p. 3; Klaeber, p. cix; Dobbie, ASPR 4:lvi; Whitelock, "Anglo-Saxon Poetry," p. 81; Amos, pp. 8, 43–44; Lehmann, "Post-Consonantal *l m n r*," pp. 165–66; and Jacobs, p. 25.

[48]"The Dating of Old English Poetry" (as above, n. 40), pp. 15–16.

directly in touch with truth and reality. If it were of any significance that modern theories of Old English versification cannot be tested against "reality," meaning the opinions of Dark Age Anglo-Saxons,[49] the objection would be all the more relevant as applied to nonlinguistic types of evidence, which are even less capable of proof.[50] The very broad objection that metrical theory *in general* may have nothing to do with metrical realities not only rejects the significance of probabilistic reasoning but also violates the inductive requirement that one hypothesis cannot be discredited without the presentation of a counterproposal accounting for the same facts (see above, §15). If we discredit modern metrical analyses altogether it will prove impossible to explain a great many regularities for which there does not seem to be any reasonable alternative explanation, such as the fact that verses like *\*þæt wæs Grendles hēafod* do not occur, while several like *Ðær wæs hæleþa hleahtor* do. To take an example with wider implications, Chapter 6 below concludes that the *Beowulf* poet demonstrates a clear acquaintance with the etymological distinction between long and short vowels in final syllables by observing Kaluza's law with almost complete fidelity. The distinction is maintained in the text with such a high degree of accuracy—98 percent—that the conclusion cannot be doubted, and there is no possibility that such a degree of conformity could have been achieved by chance. Yet this figure could not have been arrived at without access to a system of general metrical assumptions underlying it—roughly, all the basic assumptions attached to the acceptance of Sievers' five metrical types. There is no feature of Sievers' assumptions that could have influenced the statistical results in such a dramatic way—after all, other poets do not show a regard for Kaluza's law even vaguely resembling the *Beowulf* poet's. And so the only way to account for the statistical regularity in *Beowulf*, short of accepting the unacceptable supposition that the *Beowulf* poet's observance of

[49]It is not out of place to wonder what would be real about such corroboration, since there is nothing like a consensus about the nature of contemporary speakers' perceptions of Modern English metrics. Helpful as it would be to have the opinion of a native speaker of Old English, this would not end metrical debate. The error is, I think, analogous to both the New Critical intentional fallacy and the essentialism deplored by postmodernist literary theory. It at any rate sweeps aside not just the field of historical linguistics (since native informants are almost never available to it), but also most scientific and humanistic inquiry, along with many practical everyday assumptions, which we cannot dispense with, and yet which cannot be proved by reference to this elusive concept "reality."

[50]For example, a primary consideration in Blake's argument is the assignment of most Old English manuscripts to the late ninth century and later, and yet the dating of manuscripts surely has no more basis in reality as he means it than the observation of metrical regularities. And so undermining the linguistic evidence in this way does not render any likelier Blake's own hypothesis that most Old English verse was composed in the late ninth and early tenth centuries, since it relies on assumptions that similarly cannot be confirmed by reference to "reality."

Kaluza's law in 106 of 108 instances is pure coincidence, is to conclude that Sievers' system of analysis is correct in essence, if not in fine. This is an example of the sort of holistic reasoning described above (§§14f.) as desirable in the validation of hypotheses: Sievers' hypothesis of five types makes possible the compilation of statistics on Kaluza's law, and the statistics validate Sievers' hypothesis with unambiguous evidence based on probability. Thus it is hardly possible to suppose that our understanding of Old English metrics is so completely wrong as to invalidate metrical evidence in principle, since this supposition leads to gross violations of probability. Blake's objection is untenable because it is too general to offer an alternative explanation.

§27. This not to say that metrical theory is seamless and must be accepted wholesale. But even if the objection has the more specific sense of doubting the reliability of a *particular* system of metrical analysis it is too general. No theory of Old English meter is monolithic and independent of all others: all are based ultimately on the observation of regularities in the poetic corpus. And so, for instance, it does not matter whether one applies Sievers' analysis or Geoffrey Russom's or Pope's or Bliss's to the verse *ealne utanweardne* (*Beowulf* 2297a). In no instance will it be possible to regard this as a normal verse, since there is no other normal verse like it. And the normal verses that do occur in the poetic corpus contain stressed and unstressed syllables in distributions suggesting underlying principles that exclude the possibility of a pattern like *ealne utanweardne*—even though these four systems of analysis disagree about what exactly those principles are. Metrical analysis thus is not pure theory. That verses like *Ðær wæs hæleþa hleahtor* occur only when the final word is one that was monosyllabic in West Germanic is a linguistic fact independent of any particular metrical system, and a regularity that must still be accounted for even if all systems of metrical analysis can be shown to be flawed. Moreover, objections to an entire system of metrical analysis are subject to some of the same criticisms applied above to the more general objection to metrical theory per se, especially the requirement that a hypothesis cannot compete with no hypothesis.

§28. The alternative to employing a system of metrical analysis such as Sievers' or Bliss's is to suppose that "Old English verse is really the spoken language rather tidied up," a view advanced by Marjorie Daunt and taken up more recently by Johan Kerling.[51] Put this way, the point

---

[51]Daunt, "Old English Verse and English Speech Rhythm," *TPS* 1946, pp. 56–72, at 64; Kerling, "Sievers and Scops: A Revaluation of Old English Poetic Techniques," *Dutch Quarterly Review of Anglo-American Letters* 12 (1982), 125–40. In a similar vein, Herbert Pilch argues that because lifts and drops in Old English verse may appear in any combination that will produce four metrical positions, Laȝamon's verse is not metrically freer than classical Old English verse: see *Layamons "Brut": Eine literarische Studie*, Anglistische Forschungen 91 (Heidelberg: Winter, 1960), 141–42.

of course is untenable, since verse is characterized, for example, by diction and syntax that differ widely from prose usage. But the point that seems actually to be intended pertains only to the patterns of stressed and unstressed syllables in prose and verse: these are not as dissimilar as they might at first seem. Put this way, the point hardly needs to be made, since it is one with which no metrist could disagree. Recent work in particular, such as Russom's, has emphasized the basis for many metrical regularities in the structure of the language rather than in an autonomous metrical system; and Sievers himself, who based his assumptions about stress in large part on the patterns observable in the modern Germanic languages, certainly never claimed that the patterns he observed in verse were not grounded in the patterns of prose. And the meagerness, for instance, of the changes necessary to turn the prose *metra* of Alfred's translation of Boethius into verse is remarkable.[52] This is not, however, to say that metrical study may be dispensed with because verse is really no different from prose. Daunt and Kerling analyze passages of prose in order to demonstrate the point. But even if their analyses were correct, the experiment would not be very relevant, since it still fails to explain why some of the metrical types they identify in prose are extremely rare in verse (e.g. *Ælfrede cyninge* and *on þæm lande norþweardum*), why other types found in prose appear not to be admissible in verse (e.g. *\*grondorleas geong* and *\*þæs folces dryhten*), and why some types may appear in the on-verse while others may not. And regardless of whether the regularities observable in the distribution of stressed and unstressed syllables are due to the prosodic contours of the language itself or to special rules for verse, the regularities are nonetheless real, and must be accounted for. They cannot be ignored by discarding the principle of resolution (as Kerling does, p. 135), which would imply, for example, that clause-initial verses like *\*hē cleopade* are acceptable. The structured nature of Old English meter is particularly demonstrable from the differences between the meter of *Genesis B* and most Old English verse, and from the differences between classical verse such as Cynewulf's and late and transitional poems such as *Maldon*, *Durham*, and the *Grave* (see Chap. 10 below).

§29. Rather, the only tenable objections to metrical analysis on this score are to the specific claims of individual analytical systems. One may prefer one metrical theory to another, but that preference is always based on individual features of the theories—for example, Pope allows verses of the D* type in the off-verse while Bliss does not, and one or the other theory might be preferable on that basis. As an objection to metrical evidence it might be argued that the provisions of the metrical theory employed are faulty; but this is an objection to the statistics produced by

[52]See, e.g., Larry D. Benson, "The Literary Character of Anglo-Saxon Formulaic Poetry," *PMLA* 81 (1966), 334–41.

specific experiments, not to the principle of metrical change. At any rate, this most specific sense of the claim that our understanding of Old English meter is too insecure is not the form that the objection has taken, since, as pointed out above, all the objections to metrical history before the appearance of Amos' study addressed the assumptions underlying metrical criteria rather than the data themselves. And even Amos does not address this issue directly, since she makes no attempt to criticize the metrical assumptions of earlier researchers. She assumes instead the correctness of Bliss's system and substitutes it for theirs.

§30. In sum, it should be recognized that while the objection about our understanding of Old English metrics might have some validity, that is so only in the specific sense that certain assumptions about the scansion of individual verses might be wrong. It should be said now, though, that the respects in which the most widely approved metrical systems differ, however important they may seem to metrists, are actually relatively minor—as must be the case, since they must account for many of the same regularities, whatever their theoretical underpinnings. By drawing attention to the most controversial aspects of the metrical system employed in the following chapters (that of A. J. Bliss, now indisputably the most widely used) and treating statistics based on the least reliable of his claims as ambiguous, this study attempts to temper the impact of the idiosyncrasies of any particular metrical system on the statistical results. By this reasoning it can also be seen why there is no particular virtue in adhering slavishly to the dictates of a single analytical system.[53] And so in those instances in which I believe Bliss's reasoning is wrong I have not hesitated to abandon his analysis—though always with an explanation of the reasons for doing so and an indication of the extent of the changes entailed, so that the final statistics may be adjusted by the unconvinced. But these divergences from Bliss's system are relatively few and unimportant, and in the following chapters it will be apparent that even if, for instance, Sievers' and Pope's scansions of individual verses might differ from Bliss's, still their systems would produce roughly the same overall results—for example, many instances of parasiting in *Genesis A* and *Beowulf*, and few in the *Meters of Boethius*.

§31. Hoyt N. Duggan has recently reminded us of another source of uncertainty in the construction of metrical systems—the basis of such systems in unreliable texts.[54] He demonstrates that Middle English

---

[53]For a discussion of the dangers inherent in employing Bliss's system without reference to other systems, particularly Pope's, see the preface to Jeffrey Vickman's *Metrical Concordance to "Beowulf,"* Old English Newsletter Subsidia 16 (Binghamton, N.Y.: Center for Medieval and Early Renaissance Studies, State University of New York, 1990), ii–iii.

[54]"The Evidential Basis for Old English Metrics," *Studies in Philology* 85 (1988), 145–63. Chadwick adduces the same caveat (p. 108), referring the point to George Saintsbury, *A Short History of English Literature* (London: Macmillan, 1898), 1:3.

manuscripts are so unreliable that if their testimony were accepted with half the credence lent Old English manuscripts, our conception of Middle English metrics would be badly confused. In the case of Middle English it is possible to detect metrical corruptions in the manuscripts because in so many instances faulty verses can be compared with variant readings in other manuscripts. In Old English, on the other hand, no poem of significant length is preserved in more than one manuscript. It follows that conclusions about what is or is not an acceptable metrical type are intrinsically less firm in Anglo-Saxon studies. The point is an important one, and has significant implications for dating studies. In Old English studies, proof and disproof of metrical arguments must be grounded more firmly in probability than might normally be required, making the demand for absolute, nonprobabilistic evidence especially unreasonable. This is all the more reason, then, that the data for any criterion ought not to be interpreted "mechanically": it must continually be reiterated that the evidence of rare metrical types is of poor value, since such verses may be due to scribal changes. This uncertainty is an unavoidably subjective factor in the interpretation of the evidence.

§32. Another objection of a textual sort, concerning the effects of scribal alteration, pertains to the application of metrical criteria rather than the construction of metrical systems. Wilhelm Busse presents the argument in its least moderated form when he says that it is erroneous to speak of any poem preserved only in a late tenth-century copy as an eighth- or ninth-century composition: because Kenneth Sisam has demonstrated so clearly that some poems existing in more than one copy, such as *Soul and Body*, have undergone profound transformations in transmission ("The Authority of Old English Poetical Manuscripts," in *Studies*, pp. 29–44), Busse asserts that preserved poems could not resemble the originals of a century or more earlier on which they are assumed to be based. Thus, for instance, *Beowulf* must be regarded as a poem of about the year 1000, even if it could be demonstrated that it was first written down in the eighth century (*Altenglische Literatur*, pp. 22–26 and passim; see also Ricci, pp. 261–64). One objection to Busse's point is that it cannot be assumed that no verse has been transmitted relatively faithfully: John C. Pope replies that some poems, such as *Cædmon's Hymn* and *Riddle 35*, do demonstrate faithful transmission.[55] But while this objection is sufficient response to Busse's overall hypothesis that nearly all Old English verse must be dated to the tenth century, it does not dispose of the problem that some verse might very well be so changed in the course of transmission that it can no longer be considered even roughly equivalent to the form it had when originally composed. This is the more usual form of the objection, as represented by Dorothy Whitelock's view: "The possibility of a different textual history must be

---

[55]See Pope's review of Busse's book in *Speculum* 64 (1989), 135–43, at 136–37.

reckoned with, for some works may have been exposed to greater modernization than others" ("Anglo-Saxon Poetry," p. 81).

§33. This latter contingency is not unrealistic, since there is indisputable evidence for the scribal modernization of texts. There is some evidence that *Genesis A*, for example, in accordance with the findings of A. N. Doane, underwent an unusually thorough modernization at the time it was combined with *Genesis B* (see below, §362). But when Klaeber makes the same point he specifically limits the objection to the syntactic criteria of A. Lichtenheld (p. cix). The reason for this limitation should be apparent from Kenneth Sisam's claim that only structural—that is, metrically verifiable—features can be considered reliable dialect indicators (*Studies*, p. 123). Thus Whitelock's objection cannot be applied very reliably to metrical variations, since they are structural: conceivably, a scribe might manage a variety of cosmetic changes, and even a few structural alterations, without being detected, but to make enough structural alterations to change significantly the proportions of a metrical criterion would be to write a new poem—in which case it might with some justice be regarded as a later composition. The only danger involved, at any rate, is that because of modernizing scribal tendencies an early poem might be mistaken for a late one, not the reverse; and since it has never been the aim of objectors to metrical history to date poems earlier than is usually supposed, but consistently later, this danger seems of small consequence. The data of the following chapters support this conclusion: for example, though *Genesis A* seems to have undergone extensive modernization, its metrical features are still clearly rather archaic. Or to advert again to the evidence of Kaluza's law, it is clear that the effects of scribal corruption must be minimal in *Beowulf* for such an archaic feature to be preserved so well. The same can be said of some other dating criteria. This is not to say that the text of *Beowulf* has not been much corrupted by scribes, but that the effects of such corruption on the meter cannot be extensive—that is, *Beowulf* cannot under any circumstances be thought of as a thorough tenth-century reworking of an earlier work. Rather, the demonstrable corruptions of the text are mostly at the level of mere orthography, and the metrics of the poem do not conform to specifically tenth-century practices as identified in the following chapters. The objection is thus excessively cautious as applied to the validity of metrical history in general, though it might account for some few inconsistencies in the data. It should be noted, however, that Sisam's complete exclusion of nonstructural evidence is also unwarrantedly conservative (see Chap. 11 below). Amos, for example, finds that scribal transmission seems fairly reliable in regard to certain items of Anglian vocabulary (p. 155).

§34. Nicolas Jacobs objects to contraction and parasiting as chronological variables because both "show some signs of association with formulaic patterns" (p. 25). He offers some examples: for instance, *metodsceaft seon* (*Beowulf* 1180a) is identical to *Genesis A* 1743b. Yet not all his examples correspond to what we normally think of as formulae, such as *feorhseoc fleon* (*Beowulf* 820a) next to *mandream fleon* (1264b). Together these form neither a syntactic nor a semantic formula, and to call this a metrical formula will not do, either, since *flēon* is the only fixed part of the formula: the supposed formula then affords the poet no mnemonic aid that is not already inherent in the word itself. That is to say, the formula contains no useful metrical information except that the word may be dissyllabic, and thus the information contained in the formula could be associated in a less complicated fashion with the word itself rather than the formula. The objection has some validity in regard to the matter of compensatory lengthening upon loss of postvocalic *h*, since so many of the relevant instances are examples of the formula *(tō) wīdan fĕore* (see Chap. 3 below). But an examination of the verses listed below (§§88 and 103) that display uncontracted vowel groups and nonsyllabic resonants reveals how infrequent genuine formulae are in the data. A wide variety of metrical types is also represented. In fact, there is, for example, much greater variety of metrical types among verses without parasiting than among those with it, which tend to be dominated by the type 2A1a(i). Even if this were not true, the objection would not affect the value of such archaic forms, given that the dating value of metrical criteria is almost exclusively relative rather than absolute. Since the assumption is that the incidence of archaisms should decrease with time, the same decrease in archaic types found only in formulae should lead to the same conclusion, since archaic, unmetrical formulae also ought to disappear in the course of time. It is true that the restriction of metrical archaisms to formulae would affect the results for the *Meters of Boethius*, since Alfred's language is certainly less formulaic than the language of the other poems in the chronology. But this would leave unexplained the wide divergences among, for instance, *Genesis A*, *Andreas*, and *Judith*. Formulism seems less likely than some other considerations to have produced inconsistencies in the statistics.

§35. A particularly telling objection to chronological studies is that alternations assumed to be the result of dating differences may be governed instead by stylistic variation that obscures real chronological development. There are two discrete conceptions of style that must be considered in this regard. One is contextual: primarily the subject matter, but perhaps also other factors, such as knowledge of the intended audience, might influence metrical variables. If this is true, one ought to expect, for instance, that the *Battle of Maldon* would display proportionately more metrical archaisms than the *Meters of Boethius*, since its subject, diction, and sentiments are characteristic of conventions dating to prehistoric times, while the *Meters*, being philosophical, represent something new in Germanic verse. The other conception of style is personal: the poet is aware of a wide variety of archaisms, but chooses not to use them consistently—not because of any external consideration, such as the relative conservatism of his subject, but on the basis of what can only be called personal aesthetics or whim.[56] It seems to be the latter type of style that Dorothy Whitelock has in mind, though perhaps not to the exclusion of the former, when she remarks that "if a poet feels himself able to use two pronunciations of a word, the extent to which he avails himself of the opportunity may be a matter of personal choice."[57]

§36. The second type of style does exist. For example, the *Beowulf* poet uses *aldor-* 'life' as a monosyllable in *aldorbealu eorlum* (1676a), but as a dissyllable in *aldorleasne* (1587a). C. L. Wrenn points out the analogue in Shakespeare's use of the suffixes *-ion* and *-ience* as either monosyllables or the more archaic dissyllables (as always in Chaucer), as the meter requires.[58] But personal style must not be construed as anything like a conscious form of self-expression. The *Beowulf* poet must not be imagined to have made such metrical decisions on the basis of some conception of himself as the innovative sort of poet who might use *aldor-* as a dissyllable, in the way Wordsworth could consciously avoid Latinate poeticisms like apostrophe and substantivization of adjectives on the grounds that such decadent clichés do not suit an enlightened innovator. This would be to engage in a historical fallacy, attributing to the Dark Ages an essentially post-Romantic view of the poet as Genius, and of innovations in verse as self-conscious reactions against tradition. This is the point with which Daniel Calder begins his survey of studies of poetic style in Old English: "The Old English poetic tradition remained intact for centuries. While some minor changes did occur, the basic principles of this strongly conservative style scarcely altered. Thus Romantic notions of 'The Poet' offer no help in explicating these largely anonymous and formulaic poems, because their impersonality and remoteness call attention to style without reference to biography."[59] Opinion seems fairly unanimous on this point.[60] Everything we know about Old English

---

[56]Levin Schücking recognizes the difference between these two types of style, distinguishing "individuelle" and "stylistische" factors (p. 359).

[57]"Anglo-Saxon Poetry," p. 81; see also Ricci, p. 259; Cable, "Metrical Style," p. 77; and Amos, p. 10.

[58]*Beowulf, with the Finnsburg Fragment*, 2nd ed. (London: Harrap, 1953), p. 31.

[59]"The Study of Style in Old English Poetry: A Historical Introduction," in *Old English Poetry: Essays on Style*, ed. Daniel G. Calder (Berkeley: Univ. of California Press, 1979), pp. 1–65, at p. 1.

[60]F. P. Magoun, Jr., also remarks on the uniformity of Old English poetic style, and its basis in extreme conservatism, in "The Oral-Formulaic Character of Anglo-Saxon Narrative Poetry," *Speculum* 28 (1953), 446–67, at 458; rpt. in *Interpreting "Beowulf"* (Bloomington: Indiana Univ. Press, 1991), at p. 57. See also Lehmann, *Verse Form*, pp. 13, 201; Barbara C. Raw, *The Art and Background of Old English Poetry* (New York: St. Martin's Press, 1978), p. 65; and Calvin Kendall, *The Metrical Grammar of "Beowulf"* (Cambridge: Cambridge Univ. Press, 1991), chap. 1, esp. p. 11. I am grateful to Professor Kendall for providing me with a copy of the manuscript before publication.

verse suggests that poets attempted to be as conservative as possible, so that, for instance, the *Maldon* poet clings to the most conservative style (see below, §39), and attempts classical meters even though they are clearly beyond his capabilities, owing perhaps to the degeneration of tertiary stress (Chap. 10 below). That poets should have striven to be as conservative as possible is to be expected in a culture as saturated as this with veneration for old things and a firm belief in the degeneracy of the present age in comparison to the past. Other evidence for scops' conservatism is their ability to transmit old Germanic lore orally from one generation to another with surprising accuracy: the parallels between *Beowulf* and *Grettis saga*, between the Hæthcyn/Herebeald story and the Baldr myth, and between the Scyld Scefing story and the Bergelmir myth, are truly remarkable examples of this sort.[61]

§37. The accuracy of this observation about Old English poets' conservatism is illustrated by metrical anomalies such as nonparasited and uncontracted forms, which, though clearly archaisms, disappear slowly rather than at once, with a few instances even in very late verse. Thus there is no recognizable avoidance of archaisms in any known instance—rather, the poets seem to have tried to retain them as long as they could. This is also the expectation raised by the linguistic facts. For example, the slow disappearance of forms without parasiting accords with the fact that in the course of the seventh century at the latest it became impossible to distinguish whether or not a form had undergone parasiting—for instance, there was no way of knowing that *ealdor* 'elder, prince' was originally dissyllabic and *ealdor* 'life' monosyllabic, except that the former was not generally monosyllabic in the conservative language of verse. Thus the disappearance of nonparasiting was slow because it was a matter of the gradual loss of purely poetic knowledge, moving through the lexicon: for each succeeding generation of poets, fewer such exceptional poetic values for these words were remembered, in much the way the loss of strong preterites in English has been gradual since the Old English period. Therefore in late verse we might expect parasiting to be not only less frequent, but also less various. This is the case: in the demonstrably late *Meters of Boethius* all six instances of nonparasiting are of a single word, *tungol*, five of them in a single metrical type (§§91f.).

§38. And so the personal style involved in the *Beowulf* poet's

[61]On these three parallels see, respectively, Chambers, *Beowulf*, pp. 48–54 (as above, p. 4, n. 6); Gustav Neckel, *Die Überlieferungen vom Gotte Balder dargestellt und vergleichend untersucht* (Dortmund: Ruhfus, 1920), pp. 141ff.; and "An Eddic Analogue to the Scyld Scefing Story," *RES*, n.s. 40 (1989), 313–22. In a review of the last of these in *OEN* 24.2 (1991), 31, the view is attributed to me that the connection between Bergelmir and Beow evidences an early date for the composition of *Beowulf*. To prevent similar misunderstandings I should say that the view actually expressed in the article is that the connection attests to the antiquity of the legendary material out of which the poem was created.

employment of both monosyllabic and dissyllabic *aldor-* must not be personal in the sense that another poet might choose to have a different style. It is only personal in the sense that it is unpredictable, apparently dictated solely by whim. It follows that the amount of such variation ought to be roughly the same for all poets, the important difference among poets residing not so much in the number of instances of nonparasiting as in the variety of words without parasiting. But since this personal variation ought to be roughly the same for all poets, the simple statistics for frequency of parasiting may also be significant, since the same amount of "stylistic" variability in this sense should be found in all poems.

§39. Thus, the interference of personal style does not seem one of the more likely sources of inconsistency in the data. But even supposing there did exist such a thing as a personal style in the sense that one poet might choose to use parasiting more frequently than another, such a choice could hardly have remained uninfluenced by considerations of subject— that is, high style for heroic verse, lower for other subjects. Thus, if personal style is understood in this sense it is to some extent inseparable from the other type of style mentioned above, the contextual. And variation in contextual style can be shown to contradict the distribution of metrical archaisms. For example, the *Battle of Brunanburh* is generally said to be composed in the fine old high style,[62] while the *Meters of Boethius*, written about forty years earlier (see below, §72), are low and prosaic. Kenneth Sisam, for instance, refers to their "prosy and often feeble expression."[63] The stylistic difference is at least partly due to the difference in subject, since the opportunities for poetic compounds are fewer in the *Meters*; but Sisam's opinion that Alfred's talent was at fault is nonetheless very likely justified.[64] The dearth of compounds perhaps in part explains one of the metrical peculiarities of the *Meters*, that normally unstressed words are frequently obliged to take stress, as in *Gif þæt nære, þonne hio wære* (20.103). *Brunanburh* contains just one metrically anomalous verse, *grædigne guðhafoc* (64a).[65] Thus, though the *Meters* show some idiosyncrasies, neither composition diverges widely from the patterns of stressed and unstressed syllables found in classical verse, and at least in this instance metrical variation seems to have little to do

---

[62]See, e.g., Dobbie, ASPR 6:xl: "In style and diction the *Battle of Brunanburh* follows the older poetry rather closely."

[63]*Studies*, p. 297. Allan A. Metcalf collects similar appraisals in *Poetic Diction in the Old English "Meters of Boethius"* (The Hague: Mouton, 1973), p. 2.

[64]"Alfred was a prose-writer, whose natural prose would be both diluted and distorted by the effort to make verse" (*Studies*, p. 297). Metcalf (see n. 63) provides figures on the incidence of poetic vocabulary in the *Meters*, pp. v–vii, 11, and passim.

[65]The verse *beforan þissum* (67b, with alliteration on *f*; cf. *beforan ðære sunnan* at *Meters* 28.47a, with alliteration on *s*) is not actually anomalous, as the low stress of a following pronoun may permit metrical ictus on a preceding preposition: cf. the discussion below (§206) of verses like *Raþe æfter þon* (*Beowulf* 724b).

with either the wide divergence of style in the two poems or of general competence in the two poets. On the other hand, the poet of the *Battle of Maldon*, whose style "clearly belongs to the traditional heroic poetry," was "evidently unable to understand, or at least to follow perfectly, the metrical conventions of his predecessors" (Dobbie, ASPR 6:xxxi–xxxii). The difference of about fifty-five years between *Brunanburh* and *Maldon* has made an enormous metrical difference (see Chap. 10) that cannot be correlated to style. The point can also be demonstrated for dialect indicators: it is shown below (Chap. 11) that a body of linguistic features can be associated with fifteen Southern poems, though the poems range in style from the heroic to the prosaic. A similar point may be raised in regard to *Andreas*, since this is the longer Old English poem that is frequently said to be closest to *Beowulf* in style. And yet metrically *Beowulf* is more like *Genesis A* than *Andreas*, according to the results of this study.

§40. But finally there is a decisive piece of counterevidence to the stylistic objection, in the form of Kaluza's law. As demonstrated in Chapter 6, the *Beowulf* poet carefully observes a metrical distinction between etymologically long and short final vowels under secondary stress. Such a length distinction cannot have been preserved phonologically into the latter part of the Anglo-Saxon period, nor readily learned by later poets from older verse, and so *Beowulf* must derive its linguistic conservatism not from the poet's stylistic choice (or at least not from that alone), but from the fact that it must really be a relatively early poem. The probability, then, that poems with the same conservative features as *Beowulf* are not also early but just stylistically conservative seems low.

§41. None of this proves that stylistic influence on metrical variation did not occur, but it establishes a sufficient counterprobability that evidence may justly be demanded before stylistic variation is lent much credence, even if there were no other reason to discount the objection. What does prove the point is the fact that several different metrical variables pattern in accordance with the presumed chronology. It might be believable that the gradual decrease in the incidence of nonparasited forms along the chronological continuum is only accidentally chronological, and actually due to the poet's choice of which forms to use; or that the same was true of any other metrical variable. But it is not plausible that the poet's choice should have resulted in the same configuration in several different variables at once. In view of the counterprobabilities discussed here, it is at any rate not surprising that the statistical results of the metrical studies evidence no great stylistic interference.

§42. The abovementioned gradual decrease in the incidence of nonparasited forms within the framework of the presumed chronology is the occasion of another objection. Schücking compares the use of forms like *er singet* and *er schwärmet* in German verse, and concludes:

Wo ältere und jüngere formen dieser art in der ags. poesie überhaupt nebeneinander vorkommen, ist mit den mitteln der statistik keine folgerung möglich.
Schlüsse können nur gezogen werden, wo in einem der beiden vergleichsstücke
*ausschließlich* die einen oder die andern erschienen, und auch da nur, wo es sich
um so viele formen auf so lange strecken handelt, daß ein zufall ausgeschlossen
erscheint und ferner nach berücksichtigung anderer erklärungsmöglichkeiten, wie
z.b. dialektischer oder individueller oder stilistischer. (p. 359)

Amos reaches the same conclusion on the basis of the observation,
"There is no reason to assume, once forms have become archaic, that
poets will use gradually fewer and fewer of them in a smooth progression
as time passes" (p. 10). Amos' point about gradualness is well taken. It
seems unlikely, for instance, that a study of monosyllabicity in words like
*stolen, fallen,* and *swollen* would reveal that Pope uses fewer monosyllabic
forms than Dryden, Gray fewer than Pope, and so forth, even though
there is a general development from absolute monosyllabicity in the
Renaissance to absolute dissyllabicity in the modern age. But again it
must be kept in mind that the analogy is not entirely apposite, since the
verse of Dryden, Pope, and Gray is subject to many of the variables—for
example, poetic innovation, personal style, and the liberty to stray from
recognized metrical types—that have now been shown unlikely to have
affected Old English metrical practice. In at least this respect the
language of Old English verse is more like everyday speech, which is
unaffected by these factors. A more appropriate analogy, then, is the one
already mentioned, the slow and steady loss of strong preterites through
the history of English, or the continuing loss of voicing alternations in the
plural-formation of nouns with stems ending in fricatives (cf. the current
restricted status of *clothes, staves,* and so forth, prophesying the fate of
words such as *knives, thieves*). Ultimately, whether change was gradual in
verse is an issue that cannot be settled without recourse to the data, and
so this is perhaps the one objection to linguistic certainty that is
independently valid. It does not follow, however, that for a metrical
feature to be genuinely convincing as an indicator of chronology it must
therefore be consistently present or absent, not governed by statistical
frequency. Among other reasons, it has been shown above (§31) that such
a clear distribution might never be encountered simply because scribal
transmission is too unreliable to provide such "objective" results. Rather,
the proper conclusion is that the evidence of a single criterion is not
usually significant by itself. What is required is agreement among a
number of criteria, regardless of whether their results reveal absolute
distinctions or gradations in usage.

§43. A related obstacle to linguistic certainty is the impossibility of
determining the lifetime of an archaism. Few types of nonparasiting can
have been normal in the Old English that the *Beowulf* poet spoke: linguistic history demands the assumption that nonparasited forms be

regarded as archaisms preserved only in verse.[66] And so it is with justice that Dorothy Whitelock remarks that she would "not care to dogmatize on the length of time a usage may continue in verse after it has ceased to be normal otherwise."[67] In this instance as in others, linguistic conclusions can only be probabilistic; but linguistic conclusions can nonetheless be drawn. It should not be supposed that metrical developments can date poems very narrowly: though the dating criteria might point to a particular span of time as the likeliest for the composition of a given poem, it would be foolhardy to claim that the evidence is of a nature to preclude absolutely a date outside such a circumscribed period. On the other hand, the uncertainty must not be exaggerated. In most cases it cannot be proved on such a basis that the same poem was not composed a century later than the metrical evidence suggests, but there is such a degree of linguistic improbability attached to the proposition that strong evidence for a date a century later would have to be adduced to justify ignoring the linguistic probability. Whitelock was well aware of the limits of doubt, as her argument is not that the approximate date of *Beowulf* is not determinable, but that there is enough uncertainty in the linguistic criteria to permit the poem to be dated half a century later than the linguistically most probable date ("Anglo-Saxon Poetry," p. 81; *Audience*, pp. 26–29). The problem at any rate applies only to absolute dating, not relative chronology, and as will become apparent in the Conclusion, the decay of archaisms is neither the only nor the most effective way of dating absolutely.

§44. In the same vein Amos offers a more detailed objection to Richter's account of the gradual loss of archaisms:

> It surpasses credibility, however, to assume that centuries could pass before a sound change already complete in the spoken language, like contraction or the syllabification of the liquids and nasals, made itself felt in a primarily oral poetic medium. Moreover, if poets are truly using metrical forms of words that have not been spoken for decades, even centuries, why have they made no mistakes? There are no unetymological archaisms (analogous, somewhat, to hyperurbanisms). We do not find, for example, words that could never have had an "uncontracted" dissyllabic form occupying two syllables in the meter. Not all words of archaic form occur in formulas, where they might be preserved long after their current pronunciation no longer satisfied metrical rules. . . .
>
> I believe it is far more likely that Old English poetry was composed in the spoken language of the time, with contemporary pronunciation, syllabification, and accent, although with a traditional vocabulary and a number of traditional

---

[66]For example, it is improbable that Cynewulf should have lived as early as the seventh century, and yet that is the period to which Luick (§320) dates parasiting. Magoun raises a similar point in regard to contraction (pp. 60–61 in *Interpretations of "Beowulf,"* as above, n. 60).

[67]"Anglo-Saxon Poetry," p. 81; see also Klaeber, p. cix.

formulas that might "sound all right" to poets without meeting the metrical norms otherwise applied. (p. 11)

The point of the observation that the preservation of archaic forms is not restricted to formulae seems to be that their genuineness would be more plausible if the case were otherwise. But whether or not such archaisms might be better preserved in formulae than elsewhere, it can hardly be said that the nonformulaic preservation of archaic forms is unusual in the verse of other times and cultures. Winfred Lehmann mentions two analogous instances: "A general example is Chinese verse, which until recently was based on rimes current in the language more than a millennium ago and determinable only with the help of a dictionary. A restricted example is the poetic use of English *wind* to rhyme with *kind*, in contrast with its every-day pronunciation" ("Post-Consonantal *l m n r*," p. 150). Archaisms are to be found in poetry of all ages, and some particularly apposite analogues in Finnish and Vedic Sanskrit have been studied in detail by Paul Kiparsky, who casts his account of archaisms in a generative framework.[68] And in English, for example, since John Clare could usually employ *heaven* as a monosyllable, without the aid of formulaic diction, more than two centuries after the monosyllabic form had passed out of common speech, it would be rash to suppose that poets of a culture more conservative of its traditions could not do the same. Greater feats of preservation in Old English verse are recorded—the example of close parallels, particularly linguistic ones, between Norse myth and legend and various incidents in *Beowulf*, was mentioned above (§36). The conclusion that "Old English poetry was composed in the spoken language of the time" means in effect that aside from some poetic vocabulary and formulae, the language of verse is no more conservative than that of prose. It is not necessary to resort to the analogy of other times and cultures to justify dissent: *Beowulf*, for instance, also displays archaisms of orthography, morphology, and syntax, in addition to its archaic subject.[69]

---

[68]See "Metrics and Morphophonemics in the Kalevala," in *Linguistics and Literary Style*, ed. D. C. Freeman (New York: Holt, 1968), pp. 165–81; also published in *Studies Presented to Professor Roman Jakobson by His Students*, ed. C. Gribble (Cambridge, Mass.: Slavica, 1968), pp. 137–48; and "Metrics and Morphophonemics in the Rigveda," in *Contributions to Generative Phonology*, ed. M. Brame (Austin: Univ. of Texas Press, 1972), pp. 171–200. His method of accounting for metrical variation is to posit underlying metrical forms, in the tradition of generative phonology, and to assume that some of the prosodic rules that apply to them are optional. He specifically applies this analysis to metrical variables in Old English in an article written with W. O'Neil, "The Phonology of Old English Inflections," *Linguistic Inquiry* 7 (1976), 527–57. See also Russom's discussion, pp. 39–44.

[69]For examples of orthographic archaisms see Janet Bately, "Linguistic Evidence as a Guide to the Authorship of Old English Verse: A Reappraisal, with Special Reference to *Beowulf*," in *Learning and Literature*, pp. 409–31, at 411–15. For examples of

§45. As for the objection that there ought to be examples of hypercorrection evident in Old English verse, the data below contradict the point. It is true that there is no evidence of hypercorrection in the type of word Amos mentions—contracted forms—but there could not be any, since the language affords no opportunities. There would be no analogical inducement to introduce noncontraction into forms like *cēosan* and *stān*, because with just one significant exception (*wordbēot*, §127 below), in the poetic records noncontraction occurs only across a morpheme boundary after a morpheme ending in a vowel or a disappearing consonant. And there are no structures of that sort that could gain noncontraction by analogy, since all are etymologically subject to contraction themselves. When it comes to metrical criteria that do afford opportunities, hypercorrection is in fact in evidence: examples like *eðelðrym onhof* (*Genesis A* 1634b) are discussed below (§§95f.).

§46. Kenneth Sisam questions whether it is possible to determine a poem's original dialect of composition, since Old English dialects are defined by groups of texts, not geographical areas. For example, Mercian may be the dialect of the Midlands, but since the features of the dialect can be traced only in a certain limited number of texts, it cannot be established that those features were characteristic of the entire Midland area. Moreover, dialect areas need not have been geographically stable in the Old English period (*Studies*, pp. 120–21). These objections are estimable ones, and the former point is a source of broad uncertainty in the study of Old English dialects (see, e.g., Campbell, §19). But the relevance of this point to the discovery of dialect features in verse is fairly limited. Though it is usually impossible to localize prose texts with assurance, certain kinds of evidence frequently suggest probabilities—for example, Middle English evidence suggests that the Vespasian Psalter and (less precisely) the *Royal Glosses* represent the language of the Southwest Midlands, and a small amount of nonlinguistic evidence points to the probability that the latter is a Worcester manuscript.[70] But it is

---

morphological and syntactic archaisms see Klaeber's edition, pp. lxxxv–xciv. The highly artificial nature of Old English poetic language is demonstrated below in Chap. 10. It is because poetic language differs so widely from prose that experiments like Albert S. Cook's, "translating" *Judith* into tenth-century Northumbrian, are of little value. See his "Metrical Observations on a Northumbrianized Version of the Old English *Judith*," *Transactions of the American Philological Association* 20 (1889), 172–74, and cf. David N. Dumville's informative "*Beowulf* and the Celtic World: The Uses of Evidence," *Traditio* 37 (1981), 109–60, at 125. Aside from the variations studied in the following chapters, all the metrical alterations that Cook discovers are due to developments in late Northumbrian prose, and such forms need not be assumed ever to have been used in verse.

[70]See Ivor Atkins and Neil R. Ker, eds. *Catalogus Librorum Manuscriptorum Bibliothecae Wigorniensis* (Cambridge: Cambridge Univ. Press, 1944), pp. 18 (with n. 3) and 67. Another formulation has it that the second fronting dialect is conterminous with

almost never possible to define the original dialect of a poetic text more closely than to call it Northumbrian, Mercian, Saxon, or Kentish, and more usually the evidence permits no finer distinction than between Anglian and Southern texts.[71]

---

the dioceses of Hereford and Lichfield: see below, p. 284, n. 38. R. M. Wilson argues that VP may as well be early Kentish as Mercian: see "The Provenance of the Vespasian Psalter Gloss: The Linguistic Evidence," in *The Anglo-Saxons: Studies in Some Aspects of Their History and Culture, Presented to Bruce Dickins*, ed. P. Clemoes (London: Bowes & Bowes, 1959), pp. 292–310. This argument requires that the Middle English evidence be ignored, since Wilson concedes its apparent reliability (p. 308). And it is difficult to see how the assumption of Mercian influence on early Kentish orthography (see, e.g., Campbell, §207, and see below, §§337ff.) can be discarded, as Wilson demands. For example, whatever sound *ea*, the back mutation of *æ*, may represent, it is clear that *ea* from other sources remains separate from the reflex of *æ* in later Kentish, so that the supposed disappearance of the back mutation of *æ* is not to be explained easily. The evidence that Wilson considers is almost entirely phonological: that the gloss on VP could reflect the early Kentish dialect cannot be easily reconciled with the evidence of the morphological, syntactic, and lexical Anglian features considered below in Chap. 11. There is also now the evidence of the *Linguistic Atlas of England*, ed. Harold Orton, Stewart Sanderson, and John Widdowson (London: Croom Helm, 1978), which finds that the reflex of OE *æppel* (*eappul-* in the Vespasian Psalter) has a rounded vowel only in an area of the Southwest Midlands with Worcester near its center (map Ph1). So also the *Linguistic Atlas of Late Mediaeval English* reveals *e* for OE *æ* in *wes* only in Kent and in the Southwest Midlands, aside from a very few scattered instances elsewhere (map 139), indicating that the second fronting, if not Kentish, is likelier to be a Southwest Mercian feature than anything else. K. Cameron finds reflexes of the second fronting in place-names as far north as northwest Derbyshire: see "An Early Mercian Boundary in Derbyshire: The Place-Name Evidence," in the same volume as Wilson's study, pp. 13–34. For a further response to Wilson's position see Toon, p. 201, and also his "Old English Dialects: What's to Explain; What's an Explanation?" in *Explanation and Linguistic Change*, ed. Willem Koopman et al. (Amsterdam: Benjamins, 1987), pp. 275–93, at 290–91; and specifically in response to Wilson's treatment of the charter evidence, which is the basis for his argument, see Campbell, "The Glosses," pp. 87–88.

[71]Richard Hogg objects that the idea of "four more or less homogeneous and discrete speech-communities" is delusive, and suggests that all texts should be regarded as potentially mixed in their dialect: see "On the Impossibility of Old English Dialectology," in *Luick Revisited*, pp. 183–203, at 189–90. In support of the point he argues that certain variations in early West-Saxon texts reflect phonological rather than merely orthographic mixture, and that they can be correlated to speech differences based on social class. In particular, WS *æ* is not generally confused with *ē* because the phonemic distinction between them is an important one in early West Saxon, while that between *a* and *ea* before covered *l* is not, with the result that they vary freely. But even if this is true, it is not clear why the orthographic contrast between *æ* and *e* need be assumed any less significant than the phonological one. See also below, n. 77. Those accustomed to looking at Old English dialects from the perspective of verse rather than of specifically prose texts must find it difficult to credit the view that Mercian features in early West-Saxon texts should be regarded as evidence of actual dialect mixture rather than *Schriftsprache*, given the wealth of evidence for the existence of a poetic koine: see in particular the discussion of *Christ and Satan* in Appendix A. Hogg's paper is nonetheless an invaluable discussion of the dangers inherent in a pre-Labovian approach to Old English dialectology. But caution is desirable, since sociolinguistic

§47. Ideally, then, concluding from its language that a poem is Mercian or Northumbrian in origin should mean nothing more than that certain features of its language most closely resemble the language of a particular small group of prose texts. Yet in actuality the linguistic evidence is almost never regarded as bearing purely textual implications. Rather, the assignment of a poem to a particular dialect (or date) is widely believed to imply cultural and political affinities, licensing or limiting a variety of historical and literary speculations, for example that Cynewulf, whose rhymes show him to have been an Anglian, was a priest of the diocese of Dunwich who attended the synod of Clovesho in 803; and that the allusions to Offa, king of the Angles, at *Beowulf* 1949b and 1957b—a poem with some Mercian dialect features—imply that the poem was composed at the court of the Mercian Offa.[72] Sisam himself, though he warns against the equation of textual and geographical dialect mapping, mixes the textual and nonlinguistic senses of "West Saxon," for example when he suggests that the *Ruin*, because it appears to describe the ruins of Bath, is likely to be a West-Saxon poem (*Studies*, p. 137). Nor, of course, would the linguistic evidence for the dialect origins of various poems be a matter of much interest to historians and literary scholars if it had no cultural significance beyond correlation with a particular group of texts. And in practice it is not always possible to separate linguistic and nonlinguistic considerations. For example, the earlier the date of the *Battle of Maldon*, the likelier it is that the few Southeastern dialect features that it contains have authorial significance; and the date assigned to the poem depends largely upon its historical accuracy and the purpose of its composition (see Appendix B below).

§48. If the linguistic and geographical/cultural meanings of the dialect designations cannot be separated consistently even in the work of linguists, instead of discrediting the linguistic evidence altogether for drawing broader conclusions than are strictly justified, it would be best to gauge the relative probability of the linguistic evidence, both in terms of its internal consistency and in comparison to other types of evidence. For example, the metrical indications that Cynewulf spoke a Mercian

---

models based on urban societies may not be applicable to Anglo-Saxon England. If the Mercian features in early West-Saxon texts are phonological, they represent linguistic variation as great as any between social classes in present-day Norwich, though the by no means comparable size of ninth- and tenth-century Winchester leads one to expect considerably less linguistic stratification. Although there are of course considerable differences between the two, perhaps a better comparison is to present-day Iceland, a country urbanized in relatively recent times, which, with a population better comparable to Alfred's Wessex, has a small amount of regional linguistic variation, but no class-based social dialects.

[72]Vain as such conjectures seem, they are not the least plausible of their kind. Dorothy Whitelock very sensibly addresses the issue in "Anglo-Saxon Poetry," providing a variety of examples.

dialect suggest that he lived somewhere between the Thames and the Humber, though the conclusion can hardly be called a certainty, given the very real limits of Old English dialectological study. Yet the probability of that conclusion is infinitely greater than the probability of any known nonlinguistic piece of evidence, for example the similarity of Cynewulf's interests to those expressed in certain other Old English texts. Linguistic conclusions, again, are only statements of probability; and yet it would be irresponsible to suppose that the uncertainties of Old English dialect studies are so great that a poem with Mercian dialect features was no more probably composed in the Midlands than in the South or the North.

§49. As for Sisam's objection that dialect areas need not have been geographically stable in the Old English period, the point is on the whole correct, though it must be qualified. To be sure, in regard to some dialect features there is no independent evidence, but for a surprising number there is the evidence of both Middle English texts and the modern dialects, the tools for the study of which have been improved dramatically since the time when Sisam raised his objection. For example, in modern surveys, rounding of /a/ before nasal consonants is still evident in an area of the West Midlands associated with this feature in Middle English.[73] With the dramatic developments in the field of dialectology since the 1950s, it can be said now that although change in the geographical position of phonological isoglosses does occur, more striking is how stable such boundaries tend to be over time.[74] Phonological dialect features are more likely to fade or disappear altogether than to change their locational distribution once a sound change is completed. Changes of this sort are almost always demonstrably associated with important political developments. So, also, isoglosses that continue to follow obsolete political boundaries very probably have remained stable.

§50. A related problem is the tendency of Old English dialectologists to regard dialects as linguistic sytems of a homogeneous nature. Yet the evidence of living languages demonstrates that regional dialects are not so much isolable entities as fluid stages in a continuum of variation.[75]

---

[73]See, for example, *The Linguistic Atlas of England* (as above, n. 70), map Ph5; and for the Middle English distribution cf. *A Linguistic Atlas of Late Mediaeval English* 2:57–62, showing also such an incidence in northern Northumbria as one is led to expect by the evidence of the gloss on the Lindisfarne Gospels.

[74]See, for example, the discussion of changes in the position of isoglosses for the High German sound shift in Theodora Bynon's *Historical Linguistics* (Cambridge: Cambridge Univ. Press, 1977), pp. 173–83. Martyn Wakelin demonstrates the geographical immobility of a variety of English dialect features in "The Stability of English Dialect Boundaries," *English World-Wide* 4 (1983), 1–15. An example of change is the incorporation of many late West-Saxon features into the orthography, if not the phonology, of the Southwest Midlands, mentioned below.

[75]See, for example, the *Linguistic Atlas of Late Mediaeval English* 1:4. The tendency to regard dialect areas as more or less uniform was given a careful critique as early as 1903 by L. Gauchat, "Gibt es Mundartgrenzen?" *Archiv* 111 (1903), 365–403; for a

The former view entails the assumption that dialect boundaries are formed by thick bundles of isoglosses, as if we should not expect the sort of broad diffusion of isoglossic bands across the countryside that is encountered, for example, in regional German and Middle English dialectology. Rather, calling Farman's gloss on the Rushworth Gospels "Mercian" perhaps disguises the fact that it is in many ways as close linguistically to texts called Northumbrian as to the *Royal Glosses* or the gloss on the Vespasian Psalter. And because of the undeniable transcription of Anglian texts into West-Saxon form, the unevenness of dialect forms in a given text is almost always attributed to the mixture of "pure" dialects, without regard to the possibility that the dialects involved were never quite so pure. It is particularly because of this uncertainty that it is hazardous to speculate about the geographical distribution of some dialect features.

§51. Yet the problem is not so insistent in regard to verse, since, once again, it is almost never possible to distinguish more than four dialects in poetry. Certainly there are Old English dialect features that are not conterminous with any of the four main dialect groups, for example the second fronting and the appearance of *æ* for umlauted *a* before nasal consonants. But regardless of whether they are evenly distributed across the geographical areas associated with the four main dialects, there happens to be a large number of features distinguishing the Anglian, Kentish, and Saxon groups. As linguistic categories, then, the four dialects are valid at least to the extent that they differentiate groups of texts. Nor should it, after all, be so surprising if a large number of isoglosses happened to bundle in the general area of the Thames. Though isoglosses may fan across regions, it is not uncommon to encounter dialect areas set off by a considerable variety of features with much the same geographical distribution.[76] Bede tells us that the East, South, and West Saxons were descended from the continental Saxons, and that the English nations to the north of them—the East and Middle Angles, the Mercians, and the Northumbrians—were settled by the Angles. Doubtless this is a considerable oversimplification, yet the very fact that the Southerners called themselves *Seaxan* speaks for the significance of the Thames as a dividing line. And even if Bede's account could be proved an outright fabrication, it is still significant that he regarded the nations on opposite shores of the Thames as having separate origins. The reality of the Saxon dialect boundary is further suggested by later dialect evidence, for example, the

discussion based on modern theoretical principles see C.-J. N. Bailey, "Conceptualizing 'Dialects' as Implicational Constellations rather than as Entities Bounded by Isoglossic Bundles," in *Dialekt und Dialektologie*, ed. Joachim Göschel (Wiesbaden: Steiner, 1980), pp. 234–72.

[76]See, e.g., the discussion by Jacek Fisiak, "Old East Anglian: A Problem in Old English Dialectology," *AUMLA* 70 (1988), 336–65, esp. 337–39.

distribution of forms of "live" and "have" in the *Linguistic Atlas of Late Mediaeval English*, and the reflexes of Gmc. *a* in "calf" and "half" (maps Ph9 and 10) in the *Linguistic Atlas of England* (as above, n. 70). Hogg suggests that dialectologists are unduly influenced by notions of the Anglo-Saxon heptarchy, and ought instead to think of the political make-up of the island in the early period as "a set of hegemonies, which have only a poorly-defined center, which fluctuate in strength incessantly, and which overlap and intermingle with one another in a confusion which we can scarcely disentangle" (p. 188; as above, n. 71). Yet the rapidity with which political allegiances shifted is all the more reason to doubt their linguistic effect. Possibly the national divisions that the Anglo-Saxons recognized among themselves are linguistically misleading; but since they reckoned nations as peoples rather than as geographical areas, their own cultural divisions, especially when corroborated by later evidence, do seem the likeliest guide to dialect distribution, and ought not to be abandoned without recourse to an equally plausible alternative account.

§52. A more formidable obstacle to dialect studies in verse is the influence of one orthographic system on another. Such influence is undeniable: for example, in the later Old English period, good West Saxon was written as far from Winchester as Yorkshire (see below, p. 286, n. 43), and there is a large number of prose texts that represent either an attempt by a West-Saxon scribe to copy a non-West-Saxon text into the standard language, or an attempt by a non-West-Saxon scribe to write the standard dialect. The respects in which the Middle English "AB dialect" of the West Midlands differs from the expected reflex of that of the Vespasian Psalter (if the differences are mainly orthographic rather than phonological) are generally matters of Saxonization, paralleled by the especially close political ties between Winchester and Worcester in the later period (see the references below, §353.2). In like fashion, at an earlier date, when Mercia was the dominant political force in the affairs of the South, the orthography of both Kentish and West-Saxon texts shows a remarkable admixture of superficial Mercian habits of orthography.[77] But most important for the study of dialects in verse, it is clear that Old English poetry is for the most part preserved in a

---

[77]See below, §§337ff. That such influence is merely orthographic is suggested by the sudden disappearance of these features in the later tenth century with the rise of a new orthographic standard under the influence of Æthelwold at Winchester, and by the virtual restriction of the influence to apparently phonological features, when in fact the evidence of natural languages suggests that lexical borrowing is much more likely. To the contrary, there was a concerted effort on the part of West-Saxon scribes, even before Æthelwold's reforms, to eliminate Mercian vocabulary from manuscripts of the Old English translation of Bede's *History*: see J. J. Campbell's study, and particularly his findings about BL MS Cotton Otto B xi. There is in any case considerable evidence for the employment of orthographic standards in Anglo-Saxon manuscripts, so that the more drastic assumption of actual phonological change in most such instances of apparent phonological borrowing is not required.

particular poetic language, or koine, mainly West-Saxon in character, but incorporating many archaic or Anglian features.[78] The discovery of non-West-Saxon dialect features in a poetic text then need not actually imply non-West-Saxon origins, since the koine could have been written anywhere. Without question, West-Saxon poets did use certain apparently Anglian features in their verse, such as retraction in forms like *waldend* (see §335.1 below). But these features almost exclusively express phonological differences between West Saxon and the other dialects. An examination of morphological, syntactic, and lexical features, many of which would affect the meter if altered, demonstrates that there are clear and regular linguistic differences between verse known to have been composed in the South and verse suspected to be of Anglian provenance. This issue is addressed in detail in Chapter 11.

§53. A related difficulty is the ease with which orthographic and phonological evidence can be confused. It is convenient, for example, to say that West Saxon differs from Mercian in having diphthongized front vowels after palatal consonants, but whether the West-Saxon digraphs represent diphthongs is a matter of dispute (see Campbell, §248, n. 4). The editors of the *Linguistic Atlas of Late Mediaeval English* have resolved this difficulty by advancing no claims regarding the phonological significance of their findings about graphetic variation.[79] Yet this is not an entirely satisfactory solution for Old English dialectology, since the sources and variety of graphetic evidence are so limited, and need to be supported by other types of evidence. Moreover, the interpretation of the orthographic evidence may depend vitally on phonological probabilities. For example, the assumption that scribes of early West Saxon followed certain Mercian spelling habits depends to a large extent on the

---

[78]See Chap. 11 below. Norman Blake (as above, n. 40) objects to the assumption of a literary koine, arguing that the mixture of forms in poetic texts "arose because the poems were also either written or composed in the late ninth or early tenth century before the regularity was again established [i.e. after the Viking invasions] in what we call late West Saxon" (p. 17). But the existence of a poetic koine seems indisputable: see, e.g., the discussion in §335.5 and Appendix A of how the Kentish and Anglian scribes of the *Kentish Hymn*, *Psalm 50*, and *Christ and Satan* have attempted, often unsuccessfully, to make their work conform to a poetic standard that included both West-Saxon and non-West-Saxon features. So also there is much evidence, the most convincing of it involving scribal errors, that certain poetic texts have been Saxonized, many of their originally Anglian features having been altered to conform to the mainly West-Saxon standards of the koine—a process that is at any rate assured by the existence of Anglian and West-Saxon versions of such texts as *Cædmon's Hymn*, *Bede's Death Song*, the *Leiden Riddle*, and the *Dream of the Rood*. The koine is also paralleled in prose, as mentioned above.

[79]Vol. 1, pp. 5–7. But Gero Bauer points out that Angus McIntosh nonetheless concedes that the graphetic evidence is not without phonological significance, and offers supporting evidence, along with a bibliographical survey of the controversy: see "Medieval English Scribal Practice: Some Questions and Some Assumptions," in the Fisiak Festschrift, 1:199–210.

improbability of the notion that changes like that from early -*ald*- to late -*eald*- represent actual phonological developments. The assumption of a certain amount of phonological significance to spelling is inevitable, since most conditioned variations have no reasonable orthographic explanation for their conditioning. Thus, for example, the appearance of *ē* in some Anglian texts as the front mutation of *ā* in the word *clēne* would not be of much value as a dialect indicator without the added evidence of words like *lēreð, gebrēded, hēlend*, and so forth. Yet the justification for regarding these words as a group can only be phonological: in each instance a dental consonant follows. Occasionally, apparent dialectal variation may have no phonological significance, as with the alternation of -*ig*- and -*i*- in the present system of weak verbs of the second class (Campbell, §756). But such instances are few. And so while it is safest to base conclusions only on orthographic variation, a certain amount of phonological interpretation is inevitable. In verse the problem is perhaps less troublesome, as the phonological dialect indicators are the features most subject to scribal alteration, and are thus for the most part the weakest sort of evidence.

§54. Wilhelm Busse hypothesizes that variation taken for chronological change is actually synchronic:

Die sprachwissenschaftliche Forschung hat gezeigt, daß es für die Prämisse des "reinen Dialektes" keine empirische oder theoretisch begründbare Basis gibt, wo nicht zugleich gezeigt werden kann, daß Sprechergruppen sich fast hermetisch abschließen. . . . Die sprachlichen Merkmale liefern also keine Rückschlüsse auf die Entstehungszeit der überlieferten Versdichtung; sie lassen allenfalls eine (vage) regionale Einordnung zu. Sprachmischung in den Texten sollte demnach nicht länger gedeutet werden als Ausweis für einen zu hypostasierenden Übermittlungsprozeß: sie sollte vielmehr verstanden werden als Beleg für eine *synchron* auftretende Sprachvarietät in Gebieten, die den Einflüssen verschiedener Kulturzentren unterlagen. (pp. 67–68)

He offers a parallel from New High German:

Näherliegender ist selbstverständlich, daß Bewahrung und Innovation gleichzeitig nebeneinander existieren: wir selbst erfahren gegenwärtig in unserer Sprache den Abbau der Verwendung einiger weniger Präpositionen mit Genitiv zugunsten der größeren Dativ-Klasse: bis dieser Wandel endgültig durchgesetzt ist, kommen beide Verwendungen (sogar bei gleichen Sprachern!) nebeneinander vor. Es wäre widersinnig, in späterer Zeit den Text eines Sprechers wegen dessen konservativen Sprachverhaltens für älter anzusehen als den, in dem sich diese Neuerung schon heute niederschlägt. (p. 49)

In support of the latter claim he cites two studies by William Labov. This is an interesting hypothesis, and whatever objections might be raised to its interpretation of the principles of sociolinguistics, at least one of the uncertainties it raises is genuine. For example, Kenneth Sisam has argued that the syncope in verbs that Sievers associates with dialect distribution can as readily be correlated to the date of a poem's composition (see Chap. 11 below); and there is some evidence that negative contraction in verbs may indicate place rather than time of composition.[80] But there are obstacles to turning all dating criteria into dialect criteria. Nonparasiting, for example, is not a regular feature of any Old English dialect. Luick (§320) dates the appearance of the parasitic vowels to the seventh century, and no dialect was immune to this development. The evidence thus is not indifferent: if nonparasiting were a dialect feature it would have to be explained why it is not associated with any particular dialect in any text, prose or verse. And so it would contravene probability to accept Busse's position.

§55. Similarly, the rejection of "pure" dialects seems also an instance of a reasonable principle overgeneralized.[81] Certainly, it must not be assumed that Northumbrian, Mercian, West Saxon, and Kentish were of a uniform nature across the areas in which they were spoken. Within these dialect areas there must have been both regional and social variation. Yet this does not mean that regional dialect features do not have a relatively well defined geographical distribution. Every speaker of English knows otherwise, since accents associate speakers with particular geographical regions. Busse's example of German prepositions taking the genitive or the dative illustrates some of the difficulties facing his idea of language variation in cultural centers as the real cause of apparently diachronic linguistic variation in verse. This is a syntactic change, which may be relatively slow, while all but a minuscule amount of the sort of phonological change that underlies metrical variation is accomplished relatively quickly—in the space of about a generation, according to the best-known studies of the problem.[82] And yet, although nearly all the sound changes associated with metrical variation must have been initiated in the prehistoric period (since they are attested in the earliest surviving manuscripts), Busse's hypothesis demands that they should have continued uncompleted, in a state of flux, in certain cultural centers through the end of the tenth century.

§56. If Busse's hypothesis were tenable it would serve the inductive requirement mentioned above (§15) that objections to a hypothesis must not propose to replace that hypothesis with no hypothesis, but must account for the same facts, and more plausibly. On that score it is

[80]See §§147ff. below. Richard Hogg (see n. 71 above) also rightly criticizes "the classic muddle between diatopic and diachronic diversity" in Old English dialectology (p. 185). It is occasionally impossible to determine whether a particular variation is geographical or chronological, or whether it has another cause altogether. As always, probabilities must be weighed.

[81]For an examination of the historical response to just such a position in the development of dialect geography see Bynon (as above, n. 74), pp. 190–97.

[82]See the references in §417 below.

superior to most of the objections that have been raised to metrical history. But clearly it faces some significant obstacles even before it is measured against the data. And the data present an especial difficulty in that the variation of historically conservative forms is not random. The balance of metrical variables in, for example, *Genesis A* is consistently toward conservative forms (such as monosyllabic *wuldor* and dissyllabic *sēon*), while in the signed works of Cynewulf it is consistently toward more innovative ones (such as dissyllabic *wuldor* and monosyllabic *sēon*). Such consistencies across the spectrum cannot be explained convincingly as accidental, as Busse's hypothesis demands.

§57. In sum, about these objections to the assumption of the influence of dialectal and phonological change on metrical variation it may be said that the dangers in relying on the linguistic evidence clearly have been overstated. The dating capabilities of metrical variants have certainly been sometimes exaggerated, and it is salutary to keep this in mind, since skepticism is indispensable to the operation of inductive logic, as long as it is coupled with respect for probability. Still, the limitations of metrical evidence have also been exaggerated, and to at least an equal degree. No doubt one reason for the currency of such overcautiousness about metrical history is the widespread assumption that linguistic explanations for metrical variation are not intrinsically more probable than any other. Otherwise it is difficult to imagine how so many alternative explanations, such as stylistic interference and formulism, could be proposed without reference to their holistic value in constructing hypotheses (as explained above, §§14f.). Yet the efficacy of linguistic means of drawing conclusions about the history of Old English texts has already been demonstrated in other contexts. A familiar instance is Eduard Sievers' conclusion, on the basis of similarities of vocabulary and meter, and of entire individual verses, that *Genesis B* must be a translation from Old Saxon—a point left beyond dispute by the discovery nineteen years later of a fragment of the Old Saxon source, which *Genesis B* turns out to follow closely.[83] So, also, externally datable texts conform to the patterns derivable from metrical criteria. For example, on the basis of metrical evidence one would be obliged to conclude that the *Meters of Boethius* are a late Southern composition, even if the author were unknown. Similar reasoning applies to the *Battle of Maldon*.

§58. But the unequal initial probabilities of metrical criteria and competing explanations can also be illustrated on more subjective grounds. It is not surprising that until relatively recently there was wide concurrence with Klaeber's opinion that these dating studies are reliable

---

[83]Sievers, *Der Heliand und die angelsächsische Genesis* (Halle: Lippert, 1875), pp. 6–17. Stylistic differences between *Genesis A* and *B* had been noticed earlier by John Conybeare, who suggested that *Genesis B* "formed originally a distinct composition": see his *Illustrations of Anglo-Saxon Poetry*, ed. William D. Conybeare (1826; rpt., New York: Haskell House, 1964), p. 188.

if interpreted a general way to corroborate the widely held belief that *Beowulf* and the scriptural narratives are early (i.e. composed before the middle of the eighth century) and Cynewulf's works somewhat later (before ca. 825). These are not actually very bold claims, and yet the context of recent scholarship makes even such general assertions seem bold. They are not bold because it does not require careful study of the linguistic features of these poems to see the general differences among them. Even without the statistical corroboration of Moritz Trautmann, Richter, and others, any reader may observe that the *Beowulf* poet's language seems less ordinary, and requires more editorial explanation, than Cynewulf's. For example, in Klaeber's edition one is continually confronted with a mark of circumflexion over uncontracted vowels, many unstressed vowels are underdotted, and recourse to Klaeber's notes is frequently required to explain unfamiliar, archaic forms like instr. *dōgor* and acc. sg. *dǣd*, while such linguistic aberrations are so infrequent in Cynewulf's verse that editions generally do not require these editorial aids. The assumption that *Beowulf* is older than the works of Cynewulf might by careful examination of the evidence be proved incorrect, but it could never fairly be claimed that it is not at least initially the most reasonable assumption, since it is what a cursory examination of such textual features suggests to any alert reader. Busse's charge that preconceived notions about dating invalidate much linguistic work does not seem reasonable in view of these facts, and even those who, like Eric Stanley, ultimately reject all the linguistic evidence are nonetheless likely for these reasons to share his feeling when he remarks that he "sense[s] in everything that *Beowulf* is relatively early."[84] And so we begin not with a *tabula rasa*, but, like natural and social scientists, with a hypothesis more likely than any other, which, if not disproved by counterevidence in the course of experimentation, will emerge with a degree of probability more or less equivalent to proof if it accounts for a considerably wider variety of facts than any other explanation.

## D. Postulates of the Present Study

§59. The objections to the evidence for metrical history examined in the preceding paragraphs are of two types: these are objections to the supposed ways of determining how the origins of the extant verse are distributed across Anglo-Saxon geography and history (exemplified by Whitelock's arguments) and objections to the very assumption that the verse was so distributed, rather than confined to the South, and roughly to the period of the existing manuscripts themselves (exemplified by Blake's, Busse's, and, to a lesser extent, Amos' arguments). The data of

[84]See the Chase volume, p. 209.

the following chapters provide counterevidence to both sorts, and yet the second objection, which is ultimately the more disturbing, can be more effectively countered by a wider consideration of initial probabilities. The discussion of the preceding paragraph introduces the necessary context for considering the problem.

§60. Although almost all Old English verse is recorded only in manuscripts of the late Anglo-Saxon period, and is therefore strongly colored by the West-Saxon dialect that dominated the manuscript culture of the time, probability favors the assumption that not all of this verse was composed in that dialect. Aside from the *Kentish Hymn* and *Psalm 50*, the only unmistakably non-West-Saxon verse is a handful of early Anglian poems, all either verifiably or presumably Northumbrian: they are *Cædmon's Hymn*, *Bede's Death Song*, the *Leiden Riddle*, the *Proverb from Winfred's Time*, and the inscriptions on the Ruthwell Cross and Franks Casket. Four of these six also survive in West-Saxon form, and so because this would otherwise be an extraordinary coincidence, it should be assumed that dialect translation was not rare during the period. It would be a peculiar coincidence, then, if no Old English poem existing only in a unique West-Saxon recension was originally composed in a different dialect. This would require the improbable assumption that the accidents governing the preservation of manuscripts into modern times, dictating that just one copy of most Old English poems should survive, happened to coincide with the dialect origins of these poems, given the probability established by this group of six poems that dialect translation of verse was common. The point is corroborated by the rhymes at *Elene* 1236–50 and *Christ II* 591–96, which show Cynewulf to have been an Anglian, since they are spoilt by translation into the West-Saxon dialect; and a similar conclusion may be drawn about the *Riming Poem*. Since all the testable instances of dialect origins, the Northumbrian poems and the rhymes, turn out to be Anglian, the pure, "objective" statistics favor Anglian composition for the remainder of untestable verse. This does not amount to evidence that the remainder is Anglian, but it means that if one were obliged to make a rash guess without the benefit of any evidence, Anglian composition would be the more probable choice. Probability tells especially against West-Saxon composition for those poems particularly associated with places outside Wessex: the *Guthlac* poems, *Durham*, *Maldon*, and, if the poem is early and refers to Bath, the *Ruin*.[85] If a poem was not first composed in West Saxon, despite later Saxonization it might preserve some linguistic features of its original dialect. Doubt has been cast on the reliability of the features of this sort that have been identified as dialect indicators in verse, and in many cases

---

[85]Despite Sisam's remarks (*Studies*, p. 137), R. F. Leslie points out in his edition that in the first half of the eighth century Bath was in Mercian territory: see *Three Old English Elegies* (Manchester: Manchester Univ. Press, 1961), p. 34.

this doubt can be justified on a linguistic basis (see §335). Nonetheless, that some poems—*Cædmon's Hymn*, for example—were translated into West Saxon is undeniable; and that dialect translation could be imperfect is also undeniable, as demonstrated by the *Kentish Hymn* and *Psalm 50*.[86] The point is demonstrable also from *Genesis B*, which is clearly a poem based on an Old Saxon original, and which contains many Saxonisms. It thus demonstrates how aspects of the original text can remain embedded in a translation from one dialect to another.[87] And so even if many supposed dialect indicators can be shown to be specious, the existence of reliable indicators remains probable. Their existence in fact cannot be doubted: for example, as Kenneth Sisam points out, certain types of syncope in verbs are a reliable indicator of Southern composition, even if poems without such syncope cannot be proved to be Anglian (see below, §§318ff.).

§61. Metrical history, because it cannot begin without some cognizance of initial probabilities, is thus necessarily at odds with some hypotheses, such as Busse's. But are all chronological assumptions like his necessarily at odds with the concept of metrical history? It might be argued, for instance, that clear evidence of a chronology should be interpreted to mean only that the poems were composed in a specific order within a shorter period of time, perhaps a single century. But even before methods of dating verse absolutely are considered, there is an initial probability telling against so narrow a chronology. Much of the reasoning applied to dialect markers applies here as well. For example, once again, in just four instances are there Northumbrian poems corresponding to West-Saxon translations, and yet in two of these instances the Northumbrian original can be shown to date to the seventh or eighth century (see Appendix D below), and in the other two the language of the poems appears to date to the eighth century, and at any rate cannot be later than the middle of the ninth (see §72 below), while the West-Saxon versions are generally preserved in tenth-century form. The two untranslated Northumbrian poems have the same early dating. As a testable sample, then, the Northumbrian poems create a more than adequate statistical probability that some verse existing uniquely in West-Saxon form was composed much earlier. And so it would be a violation of probability to suppose, once again, that the accidents of manuscript preservation coincide with the chronological distribution of the manuscripts' contents. It follows that there is no probability of late composition

---

[86]The point is not significantly weakened if these poems were simply composed in Kent by a poet with limited skill at writing the poetic koine. After all, a West-Saxon poet translating into the koine would also not be writing his native dialect.

[87]As Doane remarks, (*Saxon Genesis*, pp. 49–50), the relationship between West Saxon and Old Saxon is analogous to that between West Saxon and, say, Northumbrian, since the two were mutually intelligible in the ninth and tenth centuries. And so the analogy to dialect translation is appropriate.

attached to the fact that almost all Old English verse is preserved only in late form; rather, it is an improbability that all verse preserved late should actually have been composed late. The historical considerations also suggest that if all or nearly all Old English verse is not roughly contemporary with the manuscripts in which it is preserved, some of it is probably fairly early. Manuscripts were exclusively the product of religious establishments (or perhaps nearly so: see §374 below), mainly monasteries. And yet Thomas Shippey points out that monasticism was so severely curtailed in the ninth century that if a poem is not to be dated to the later tenth century or after, rather early composition seems likeliest.[88]

§62. If the extant Old English verse was composed over a considerable span of time, as probability suggests, then this ought to be linguistically detectable. The time period from Cædmon to the Conquest is too great for Old English meter not to have been affected by some language change. Some important sound changes can be dated to this period, or shortly before, and so it would be surprising if such changes were not attested. For example, on the basis of manuscript evidence the loss of intervocalic *h*, with subsequent vowel contraction, is usually dated to the beginning of the eighth century at the latest (see Luick, §§249, 291; but see below, §§395ff.). If the longer poems were not all composed at once, it would be surprising if this sound change could not be detected in verse, since the language of verse is conservative, and the disappearance of the older forms ought not to be rapid. The distribution of uncontracted forms does vary considerably over the corpus of Old English verse: they predominate in presumably eighth-century verse, they are in the minority throughout the next century, and they are unknown in the tenth century (§105). And so, admittedly, although any of the factors discussed above, such as stylistic preference, dialect interference, and formulism, might have skewed the statistics of this distribution (and it is by no means necessary that they should have), it cannot be said that this distribution is linguistically surprising or improbable.

[88]See the article mentioned above, n. 40. Shippey's argument is based on the conclusion of David Knowles's standard work, *The Monastic Order in England*, 2nd ed. (Cambridge: Cambridge Univ. Press, 1963), that "Anglo-Saxon monasteries had ceased to live by the time of Alfred" (p. 24); that there was "a complete collapse of monasticism by the end of the ninth century" (p. 33); and that "we are justified in regarding England in the reign of Athelstan as being wholly without any organised monastic life" (p. 36). Perhaps Knowles's conclusion is too absolute: he presents some counterevidence himself (pp. 35–36), and Sisam offers some other evidence for undisturbed scholastic activity in the monasteries fairly late in the ninth century (*Studies*, p. 7; see also Amos, pp. 162–64). And as Sisam remarks, it is not at all improbable that Cynewulf belongs to the first half of the ninth century. Yet, as he also concedes, there undeniably was a dwindling of literature and learning in the first three quarters of the century—from which it may be concluded that for poems composed before the monastic revival of the tenth century, the recording of such verse in the eighth century is still, on the whole, likelier than in the ninth.

§63. Accordingly, in sum, there is an initial probability that the surviving Old English verse was composed in several different parts of England, that it was first recorded at widely separated dates within the Old English period, and that certain types of linguistic variation in verse ought to be due at least in part to place and date of composition. Because of the possible interference of other factors, there is no initial probability in regard to whether or not the distribution of those variations should fall into consistent patterns, and thus whether or not it will be possible to date and localize verse on this basis. But of course there is no way to settle that question but by moving beyond the discussion of theoretical underpinnings and examining the data. The point is that regardless of whether or not the data furnish any likely conclusions, the assumptions underlying prior studies of metrical variation are justified by probability, and in that respect are better designed than those underlying any competing hypothesis about the nature and causes of metrical variation.

§64. As pointed out above, prior studies of metrical change have always been defective. Part of the problem is philological, stemming from insufficient regard for etymological and other concerns, but other aspects of the problem have now been remedied by the appearance of some valuable research tools. Chief among these are the concordance to the Anglo-Saxon poetic records and the *Microfiche Concordance to Old English*. The former simplifies the task of locating metrical variables, since it provides complete verse lines, while C. W. M. Grein's *Sprachschatz* does not.[89] The varied uses of the microfiche concordance are evident throughout this study. As mentioned above, the *Linguistic Atlas of Late Mediaeval English* helps to identify more precisely the probable distribution of some Old English dialect features. But of greater consequence is the development of Alan Bliss's system of metrical scansion, and widespread recognition of it as a sort of standard. It is also the system used by Amos. Of course, that the considerable majority of recent metrical studies have employed this system does not mean that it is correct, or even the most appropriate system for uses such as this. But certainly the use of any other system would require more detailed justification. Perhaps the most convenient of its advantages is its allowance of very little ambiguity of classification, coupled with great subtlety and variety of classificatory types. This latter quality is at points taken to extremes, so that the system is in some respects hyperanalytic.[90]

---

[89] *A Concordance to the Anglo-Saxon Poetic Records*, ed. by J. B. Bessinger, Jr., programmed by Philip H. Smith, Jr., with an index of compounds compiled by Michael W. Twomey (Ithaca: Cornell Univ. Press, 1978). On the other hand, the *Sprachschatz* is useful for locating spelling variants, since the ASPR concordance is unlemmatized. Useful as these tools are as correctives, they should not be used to the exclusion of reading through the texts themselves.

[90] In other respects, it should be noted, Bliss's system makes fewer distinctions than Pope's, for example in regarding *þurh sidne sefan* (*Beowulf* 1726a) as belonging to the

But of course it is easier to ignore distinctions with no significance than to employ a system that makes insufficient differentiations. It was demonstrated above (§17) that attempts to apply Bliss's system "objectively"—that is, without examining its claims—have led to errors and misunderstandings about its implications. In addition, at several places in this study it is demonstrated that not all of Bliss's theories are tenable, and in these respects his system will not be followed slavishly here. But on the whole his rules are nonetheless impartial with respect to metrical dating criteria, and so if, with or without these few corrections, they are applied consistently and accurately, metrical change ought to become apparent in spite of any shortcomings in the classificatory system itself.[91] A point of departure that ought particularly to be mentioned is that Bliss does not hesitate to apply Kaluza's law to disambiguate verses that may or may not have resolution. Since this is itself a dating criterion (see Bliss, §40; Amos, pp. 98–100; and below, Chaps. 6 and 8), it cannot be applied fairly in a chronological study, and is not applied here for this purpose.

§65. But some more detailed justification for using Bliss's analysis can be offered here. Few would disagree that it is necessary to begin with Sievers' five metrical types as an analytic axiom. If this choice requires justification, it may be pointed out once again (cf. §26 above) that the evidence of Kaluza's law in *Beowulf* creates a probability virtually equivalent to proof in regard to fundamental aspects of Sievers' types: if and only if Sievers is right that resolution is essential in verses like *sincfato sealde* (*Beowulf* 622a), and inadmissible in verses like *deorc deaþscua* (160a), does it follow that the *Beowulf* poet observes Kaluza's law in a remarkable 106 of 108 instances—a proportion that stands outside the range of coincidence, especially when these figures are compared with those for other poems. Sievers' assumptions about resolution in these environments must then be correct, since it is inconceivable that they could produce such a statistical regularity by accident. In turn it seems hardly possible to accept these conclusions about the environments to which resolution is proper without accepting the correctness of the five types—simply as a descriptive tool, regardless of what theoretical basis

---

same type as *on sidne sæ* (507a). The two systems complement each other, and the user of one has much to gain from consulting the other.

[91]This is not to say that Bliss's system is impartial in all respects. Probably no useful system could be. For example, Bliss emends or otherwise explains a few verses that seem to contradict his conclusion that double alliteration is compulsory in type D*1 (§64). (Whether or not these exclusions are justified is not as important an issue as it might at first seem, since the fact remains that single alliteration in this environment is so rare that all such verses must remain suspect.) Rather, Bliss's system is generally impartial to chronological issues because he does not posit any metrical types specifically in order to account for anomalous patterns containing such features as parasite vowels and contract verbs. A system that admits rare metrical types paralleled only by verses containing such chronological features is useless for the purpose of tracing metrical change.

is used to explain their validity.[92] Once Sievers' types are allowed, certainly *some* system of analysis based on it must be chosen, and this is why it is not a valid criticism of a metrical study that it relies on a particular system. Rather, although individual aspects of that system may be faulted, along with any conclusions based on such faulty assumptions, to reject the whole system as unproven is to reject Sievers' findings altogether—an unbalanced argument, in view of facts like Kaluza's law. In other words, such a criticism rejects the field of metrics altogether, and so is subject to the objections offered above (§§25ff.). Once Sievers' findings are recognized as correct in essence, if not in fine, the choice of an analytical system is effectively limited by current usage and practical applicability to the analyses of Pope, Bliss, and Sievers himself;[93] and since the last is considerably less detailed than the others, the choice actually rests between the theories of Pope and Bliss. As remarked above (§30), although the theoretical differences between the two systems are profound, in practice they are not actually as different as they might at first appear, and so the choice of one or the other should have little effect on the statistical results of studies such as this. Neither system seems to me entirely correct in its postulates. But without judging the theoretical bases of the two systems it can be said that Bliss's is more useful for this purpose because it is more rigid. A limitation of Pope's system is that it does not carefully distinguish secondary from tertiary stress—for example, *folcstede frætwan* (76a) and *þreatedon þearle* (560a)

---

[92]In his *English Alliterative Tradition* Thomas Cable argues that the difference in resolution between verses like *sincfato sealde* and *deorc deaþscua* is due not to the patterns dictated by Sievers' five types, nor to the metrical contours he proposed in 1974, but to a rule of syllable count in the coda of the verse. Sievers' five types then can be dispensed with, and, it might be objected, the facts of Kaluza's law can still be accounted for. But this hypothesis does not actually change matters in the present argument, since Cable's point is not that Sievers' types are observationally wrong, but that a limited set of rules will produce the same results. As Cable observes, Sievers' five types stand at an intermediate level between pure description and theory. My point is that Sievers' types are descriptively accurate, and an adequate theory must begin with the facts they describe, even if it rejects some of Sievers' theoretical apparatus—as, for instance, Bliss rejects the concept of stress at the tertiary level, and Pope rejects the concept of the foot.

[93]This is not to slight Russom's analysis, which is more of a theoretical explanation for the metrical types encountered than a system of analysis, and is thus less apposite to this purpose. Its usefulness in the present circumstances, at any rate, is of a different order from Pope's and Bliss's, since Russom's is less prescriptive, and his book includes no detailed tables of scansion like those in the other books. Another recent and innovative approach is that of Wolfgang Obst, *Der Rhythmus des Beowulf: Eine Akzent- und Takttheorie*, Anglistische Forschungen 187 (Heidelberg: Winter, 1987). Obst's system cannot be used for the purpose of tracing metrical history, since it treats most parasited and contracted forms as authorial, ignoring the regularity with which metrically unique or unusual verses can be rendered normal by the substitution of archaic forms. For a critique of Obst's analysis, in the context of a survey of recent metrical theories, see Hofmann, *Versstrukturen*, pp. 25–8.

are regarded as belonging to the same type, while it is demonstrated in Chapter 6 below that the accentual distinction between them is essential to the workings of Kaluza's law. On purely practical grounds, then, Pope's system could not be employed as effectively in this study. The other differences between the two analyses that are the most significant for the purposes of this study may be examined briefly here.

§66. Bliss limits most varieties of type D to the on-verse with double alliteration, while Pope does not. The difference is clearest in regard to the expanded type. Pope lists eighteen examples of type D* in the off-verse (pp. 365–66). Of these, four must be excluded because the thesis of the first foot is the reflex of a syllabic resonant (e.g. in *wæpen hafenade*, 1573; also 840, 2020, 3032): to assume beforehand that *wæpen* is dissyllabic would prejudice the dating criterion of parasiting. Another six Pope himself regards as dubitable (53, 1125, 1724, 2432, 2671, 2863). This leaves eight examples in the off-verse, as opposed to the 211 examples Pope finds in the on-verse, of which seven may be eliminated for the same reasons as in the off-verse. Instances in the off-verse thus comprise 3.7 percent of the total incidence of type D*. This is a statistically insignificant proportion, especially when the probability of scribal error is taken into account—for example, even a relatively conservative edition of *Beowulf*, such as the ASPR one, settles on a great many more emendations than 3.7 per hundred lines.[94] Moreover, even the figure 3.7 is probably inflated, since several of the eight remaining examples in the off-verse are hardly secure. Three might be explained as requiring elision (e.g. *ðolode ær fela*, 1525; also 1869, 1997),[95] and two as requiring resolution in the coda, and thus belonging to type A (*Dead is Æschere* 1323, and *him on andsware* 1840).[96] And given that Pope's method is to give every possible syllabic resonant full syllabic value as long as this renders an acceptable type, the number of verses that may be excluded on the grounds of Pope's own doubts is itself evidence for Bliss's view: if type D* were permissible in the off-verse, it would be an extreme statistical coincidence that the number of verses with possibly nonsyllabic resonants, possible examples of inflected for uninflected infinitives, and such, is roughly the same in the on-verse and the off-verse, even though the total incidence of D* in the off-verse is a minuscule fraction of that in the

---

[94]That the ASPR texts are conservatively edited is the opinion of J. R. Hall, who justly characterizes himself as a textual conservative: see his "Old English Editing," in *Scholarly Editing: An Introduction to Research*, to be published by the MLA. Thanks are due to Professor Hall for sharing his work with me before publication.

[95]Bliss (§64) explains one other, *ðeodne Heaðobeardne* (2032), as requiring elision, but elision before *h* seems unlikely. The verse is emended from MS *ðeoden heaðo beardna*, which, if correct, might be explained as an example of hypercorrection, with etymologically incorrect monosyllabic *ðeoden*, as perhaps in 1675a and 1871a, and like *eþel Scyldinga* (913a: see §§95f. below).

[96]"Resolution" is perhaps not actually the correct term in regard to the latter: see p. 86, n. 45, and §262 below; but also §234.

on-verse. Moreover, it can now be seen that there is a reason type 1D1 may appear in the off-verse, while types with secondary stress may not. Calvin Kendall has pointed out that an "intially stressed compound in which the second element is semantically significant is marked for alliteration."[97] Thus, because compounds with secondary stress must alliterate in type D, they may not appear in the off-verse, where alliteration on the second lift is forbidden. And so Bliss's views on this verse type seem more persuasive than Pope's. But even if Pope's views were to be adopted, it would hardly be logical to conclude that all verses like *wæpen hafenade* are ambiguous in respect to parasiting. Even if type D* were permitted in the off-verse, the probability of dissyllabic *wæpen* at (maximally) 3.7 percent is so low that to call the verse ambiguous would be an unfair assessment, if calling a verse ambiguous means in practice to treat it as bearing no probabilistic significance in regard to chronology. On the other hand, if due consideration of their probabilistic value were accorded such verses, in practice the difference between Pope's and Bliss's analyses in this regard would be too slight to bear any statistical meaning.

§67. Bliss allows anacrusis in exceedingly few instances: he admits just 47 examples in the 6,364 verses of *Beowulf*, of which 3 instances are dissyllabic, the rest monosyllabic. Pope also limits anacrusis to two syllables, but finds 344 examples in the poem. The difference is largely due to Pope's assumption of anacrusis in certain subtypes of B and C (e.g. *on Grendles gryre* 478a and *ofer Biowulfe* 2907a, respectively), an analysis peculiar to his system. Perceptive and coherent as Pope's system is, this seems one of its less plausible claims. Perhaps the chief source of doubt is that it contradicts Cable's compelling explanation of Sievers' five types as governed in part by the condition that every verse must comprise four metrical positions (see n. 25 above); and under Sievers' principles *Biowulfe* in 2907a must fill three positions, while anacrustic *ofer* would demand that it fill four. Pope's analysis of types B and C also leads him to the conclusion that anacrusis may precede a series of unstressed syllables: for example, in *mæg þonne on þæm golde ongitan* (1484a, type B2) only the first syllable is anacrustic. While there is perhaps no valid theoretical objection to this analysis, the distinction between anacrusis and initial thesis in Pope's system does seem sufficiently arbitrary to excuse a preference for the straightforwardness of Sievers' and Bliss's analysis. When verses of types B and C are eliminated there remain 120

---

[97]"The Prefix *un-* and the Metrical Grammar of *Beowulf*," *ASE* 10 (1982), 39–52. The accuracy of Kendall's point is corroborated by Geoffrey Russom's observation (see esp. pp. 84–86 and 96–97) that double alliteration is compulsory in verses like *þryðlic þegna heap* (400a), with a final fully stressed noun, but not in *secg weorce gefeh* (1569b; Bliss scans this as type 3E*2: cf. Bliss's own explanation in his *Introduction to Old English Metre* [Oxford: Blackwell, 1962], p. 20), with a final particle. Once again, the relative stress of a following syllable is clearly related to the requirements of alliteration.

examples of anacrusis in Pope's tables. Much of the remaining statistical difference is due to Bliss's argument that many finite verbs in verses that Sievers and Pope would classify as type A should not be stressed, and that instead these are light verses, in accordance with his interpretation of Kuhn's first law. So, for example, Pope classifies *Gewat him ða se goda* (2949a) as a type of A3 verse, while Bliss makes it a light a1e. Bliss's position is more difficult to justify when the verb alliterates, as in *ne gefeah he þære fæhðe* (109a), which he calls a light a1f. This is perhaps the most controversial aspect of Bliss's system, and it is hardly possible to settle the question here. There is further discussion in Chapter 7. Since the question cannot be settled, note is made in the following chapters whenever acceptance or rejection of Bliss's idea of light verses would have a significant effect on the analysis of the data. If Bliss is right, the comparatively small number of verses with anacrusis that Sievers' system locates in *Beowulf* must be diminished further. But regardless of whether or not Bliss is right on this score, he is certainly right that anacrusis appears in a sharply delimited subset of the variety of verse types he identifies in *Beowulf*. In particular, it is exceedingly rare or nonexistent in type A when the caesura falls immediately before the second lift—for example, though *ahæfen of horde* (1108a) is the commonest sort of verse with anacrusis, *tō Hrǣdles lēodum* would be unusual. Moreover, anacrusis is found in the off-verse only in type A, and a particular subtype at that, 1A1a(i); and in the on-verse it appears only in verses with double alliteration (i.e. alliteration on both lifts).[98] (Pope finds just one example of type D with anacrusis in the off-verse—*þa secg wisode* 402b—though he thinks *þa* should be omitted; and this is a point he has now argued at length.)[99] Neither Pope nor Bliss locates any examples of anacrusis in type E. In sum, Pope's and Bliss's conclusions about anacrusis are not as dissimilar as they might at first seem. Like Bliss, Pope identifies certain types of anacrusis as unlikely (as evidenced, for instance, by the article mentioned in n. 99), and the types they consider unlikely frequently coincide.

§68. Another claim of Bliss's is that the position of the caesura is of some significance. This, admittedly, is perhaps the least reliable of the unique features of his system, and counterevidence is offered below (see

[98]These requirements seem to be due not to any separate constraints on anacrusis, but on the distribution of the verse types with which anacrusis appears. There is no verse type in *Beowulf* attested more than twice with anacrusis for which the incidence of single alliteration in the on-verse is not minuscule in comparison to the incidence of double alliteration. Likewise the incidence of all these types in the off-verse is small in comparison to the incidence in the on-verse, except in three types: 1A1a(i), 1A1b(i), and 1A*1a(i). The first of these is the only type for which Bliss finds evidence of anacrusis in the off-verse.

[99]See "The Irregular Anacrusis in *Beowulf* 9 and 402: Two Hitherto Untried Remedies, with Help from Cynewulf," *Speculum* 63 (1988), 104–13.

Chap. 7). Yet although the significance of the caesura cannot be supported on theoretical grounds, observationally it still remains true that, for instance, anacrusis is exceedingly rare or nonexistent in type A in *Beowulf* when the caesura immediately follows the second lift. Thus, adherence to Bliss's system may still prove informative in discerning probabilities, even when its postulates cannot be justified—for example, even if Bliss's theory of the caesura is incorrect, a correct analysis must still account for many of the regularities that the caesura explains. At any rate, the weakness of Bliss's theory of the caesura should be borne in mind in the following pages, and no conclusion depending vitally on it should be accorded much credence without corroboration, for instance in Pope's system.

§69. Although it was demonstrated above (§§25ff.) that our limited understanding of the principles governing Old English verse does not pose a great obstacle to tracing metrical history, it should nonetheless be obvious that such a history would be considerably more secure if there were a wider consensus about the nature of Old English meter. In one sense, then, there must be a degree of provisionality to any attempt to trace metrical history. But as pointed out above, it is not so much the descriptive part of Old English metrical study that is incomplete as the theoretical. And so while it is still impossible to say with assurance why certain metrical patterns are allowed or disallowed, it is not actually very difficult to separate common from uncommon types. And that is all that is required for most of the purposes of metrical history. Yet because of the limitations of metrical theory, a study such as this cannot pretend to much completeness or authoritativeness. It is perhaps like many of those medieval productions that are also called metrical histories—a necessary early step in the process of turning a subject fraught with myth and hearsay into a field of study constructed on estimable scholarly principles. If it has no better justification, a study of metrical history may at least serve the purpose of countering the widespread impression that such a thing is impossible: a more reliable study than this will not be attempted as long as the belief prevails that metrical variation does not and cannot have any historical consequences. In any case the writing of metrical history itself contributes to a better understanding of meter and its theoretical underpinnings, and so is to that extent self-validating. The best example is the significance for Sievers' five types of the findings about Kaluza's law, as mentioned above (§26).

§70. Under the methodological principles set forth above, firm evidence of metrical change will depend on the general conformity of more than one variable to a given chronological continuum. It might be that that continuum will differ from the chronology suggested by linguistic dating studies like Richter's and Sarrazin's: the evidence will be discussed in the final summary. But it is necessary to begin with some chronology against which the evidence of each variable may be tested. As noted above, there never has been a single, firm chronology agreed upon. For the most part, however, the major points of disagreement until relatively recently were in regard to the precise dates of individual poems rather than their relative position with respect to one another. It is possible, then, to present a chronology that reflects near consensus on relative values. For this purpose it will be useful to adopt the list of poems provided by Thomas Cable in a 1981 study of a metrical dating criterion ("Metrical Style," p. 80), retaining his order and his impression of the presumed dates. This list has the virtue of being impartial and representative, in addition to being the most recent listing of this sort available. It also limits the corpus to those poems for which a date is either independently determinable or has been widely assumed:[100]

| | |
|---|---|
| 657–80 | *Cædmon's Hymn* |
| 735 | *Bede's Death Song* |
| 8th c. | *Leiden Riddle* |
| 8th c. | *Genesis A (I and II)* |
| 8th c. | *Daniel* |
| — | *Beowulf* |
| 8th–9th c. | *Exodus* |
| 9th c. | *Elene* |
| 9th c. | *Fates of the Apostles* |
| 9th c. | *Juliana* |
| 9th c. | *Andreas* |
| 890–99 | *Preface* and *Epilogue, Pastoral Care* |
| 897 | *Meters of Boethius* |
| 937 | *The Battle of Brunanburh* |
| 942 | *Capture of the Five Boroughs* |
| 10th c. | *Judith* |
| 973 | *Coronation of Edgar* |
| 991 | *The Battle of Maldon* |
| 1066 | *Death of Edward* |
| 1110 | *Durham* |

§71. There are certain disadvantages to employing such a list. It includes a number of rather short poems, which frequently yield no evidence; and when they do contain relevant forms, the evidence is too meager to be of any statistical significance. But this is merely an inconvenience. A more substantive problem is that it excludes some important evidence. To be sure, there are few poems of sufficient length to be statistically significant that are not included on the list. But if, say, *Christ and Satan* seemed to belong to the tenth century by the evidence

---

[100]Since Cable compiled this list, Peter Kitson has uncovered a few lines of good Old English verse in the bounds of a Rochester charter dated 868 (Sawyer's no. 339): see "Some Unrecognized Old English and Anglo-Latin Verse," *N&Q* 232, n.s. 34 (1987), 147–51. The sample is too brief to afford metrical dating evidence of any sort, except that its metrical defects are fewer than might be expected in such a context.

of one dating criteron, and to the eighth by that of another, this would be important evidence against the dating criteria, and ought not to be ignored. To remedy this problem, all the remaining poems of sufficient length are examined separately in Appendix A (pp. 393–414 below). This seems the best solution because some chronology must be adopted: it is not possible to evaluate Amos' charge that the criteria do not support any chronology, or to gauge the accuracy of the metrical dating criteria at all, without comparing the results to some preconceived chronological frame- work. And though the choice of framework has no actual importance (since the framework may be corrected in the end on the basis of the results of this study), it does have some argumentative importance, in that it is best to strive for as much impartiality as possible in determining what has or has not been the general consensus. And of course the longer poems omitted from Cable's list are those about which there has been the least agreement on dating, so that these would be the most difficult to locate impartially in the chronology.

§72. The list should be regarded with caution, since it is only a subjective balancing of a variety of opinions. But once again its exact terms are ultimately of no great importance, since the purpose of this study is to test the chronology, and to correct it where that is possible. More important is the general division of works into "Cædmonian," "Cynewulfian," and late groups. But some of the list's most debatable aspects may be noted: (1) Cable's assignment of the *Meters of Boethius* to the year 897 is based on the assumption that they are the composition of King Alfred himself. Sisam[101] has shown the counterarguments to be so improbable that Cable's assumption will freely be regarded here as correct and the *Meters* assigned to Alfred. Still, only metrically confirm- able features of his works should be attributed to Alfred himself—not only because of the possibility of scribal corruption, but also because it is dubitable whether Alfred himself knew how to write,[102] or, if he did, whether in fact he would have written rather than dictated his composi- tions. (2) The dates on the list that cannot be independently verified are perhaps somewhat later than those generally assumed by philologists—as should be apparent, for instance, from Schücking's survey of dating schol- arship, and Pilch and Tristram's (see n. 3 above). Thus, for example, even after the supposition that *Genesis A* is Cædmon's work fell out of favor, the poem continued to be assigned a very early date. In summarizing views on dating the poem G. P. Krapp, by averaging, settles on a date "about the year 700" (ASPR 1:xxvii; this is also Klaeber's date, p. cxiii). (3) Cable suggests that *Beowulf* and *Exodus* should be bracketed together

---

[101]*Studies*, pp. 124, 293–97. See also Allan A. Metcalf, "On the Authorship and Originality of the *Meters of Boethius*," *NM* 71 (1970), 185–87.

[102]Katherine O'Brien O'Keeffe argues that the evidence for Alfred's ability to write is unreliable: see *Visible Song: Transitional Literacy in Old English Verse* (Cambridge: Cambridge Univ. Press, 1990), pp. 77–84.

(p. 80), that is, under "8th–9th c."; but until recently the two were generally dated to the first half of the eighth century. For instance, in summarizing the evidence, Klaeber assigns *Beowulf* to this period (p. cxiii), and Dorothy Whitelock acknowledges this consensus when she argues that the linguistic evidence is not so firm that a date in the second half of the century can be excluded (*Audience*, pp. 22–33). (4) As Schücking's list of dating studies reveals, in his day it was generally thought that Cynewulf lived in the latter half of the eighth century. Since Schücking's time, scholarship has generally favored the earliest part of the ninth century. The evidence is discussed below in the Conclusion. (5) There is room for doubt about the dates of the Chronicle poems and *Maldon*, since there is the possibility that some time elapsed between the events they describe and the composition of the poems. The point has been urged particularly for *Maldon*. See Appendix B (pp. 415–18 below) for a discussion of why Cable's dating of *Maldon* is preferable. (6) The date "8th c." assigned to the *Leiden Riddle* appears to be based on the assumption that the language of the poem, copied by a continental scribe, is earlier than the manuscript in which it appears—a manuscript that is generally dated to the earlier ninth century. Malcolm Parkes has offered cogent reasons for regarding the text of the *Leiden Riddle* as a tenth-century addition to the manuscript, though the issue is still debated.[103] The dating of Northumbrian texts is notoriously difficult, but the linguistic evidence suggests that no matter what the date of manuscript, the language of the poem, copied by a Continental scribe, is likely to belong to the eighth century; in any case it is certainly no later than the middle of the ninth (cf. below, p. 342, n. 155, and the discussion under the heading of the *Riddles* in Appendix A). In addition, the manuscripts containing *Cædmon's Hymn* and *Bede's Death Song* are certainly later than the dates given above, and this is an important consideration for phonological purposes; but for metrical purposes the manuscript dates are not of much importance. On the date of *Cædmon's Hymn* see also below, Appendix D (pp. 426–28). For the purposes of this study, the precise date of the *Leiden Riddle* is not important, as it is too short a text to yield much metrical evidence. Still, it should be borne in mind that the dating given here ought not to be regarded as reliable.

§73. Ultimately it is the relative chronology rather than the absolute dates on the list that is important for this study. Since this list is merely a convenience, to facilitate comparing the results of the various dating criteria to one another, and the question of absolute dates will not be considered until the Conclusion, the dates provided in this list serve no

---

[103]Parkes, "The Manuscript of the Leiden Riddle," *ASE* 1 (1972), 207–17; but compare Johan Gerritsen, "Leiden Revisited: Further Thoughts on the Text of the Leiden Riddle," *Medieval Studies Conference, Aachen 1983*, ed. Dietrich Bald and Horst Weinstock, Bamberger Beiträge zur englischen Sprachwissenschaft 15 (Frankfurt: P. Lang, 1984), 51–59.

very useful purpose, and hold only relative value for this study. Although the question whether the composition of poems can be located in time and space by metrical means is of fundamental importance to the construction of metrical history, the date and original dialect of individual poems is not, except insofar as these reflect on the larger question. It matters little whether, for instance, *Beowulf* was composed in the North or the South, in the seventh century or the eleventh. What matters is whether or not the linguistic evidence is worthy of study—that is, whether it points with any consistency to a particular time and place.

§74. Despite uncertainties about the absolute dates of the poems, the relative position of the poems in the chronology agrees well with conventional thought on the subject. The most debatable issues in this respect are the relative position of *Bede's Death Song* and the *Leiden Riddle* with regard to the next four poems on the list (given that *Genesis A* and *Daniel* are generally dated ca. 700); the question whether *Exodus* should precede or follow *Beowulf*; the question whether *Andreas* should be positioned before or after the signed works of Cynewulf (or even be considered one of Cynewulf's own works); and the relative position of *Judith*. But Cable's choices may be regarded as a fair assessment of dating scholarship, and so his list will be adopted here and referred to as the "presumed chronology." Hypotheses about metrical change will be tested against this set of poems, which will be referred to as the "test group" of poems.

§75. Three minor alterations have been made to the list for use in this study: (1) It seemed permissible to add *Christ II*, since Cynewulf's authorship is not generally doubted,[104] and the poem's inclusion does

---

[104]Daniel Donoghue (pp. 107–16) has suggested that Cynewulf merely added his runic signature to *Christ II* and the *Fates of the Apostles*, on the basis of his statistics on the use of auxiliaries in these two poems, which are different from those for *Elene* and *Juliana*, in terms of the overall incidence of auxiliaries, percentage of auxiliaries that are initial, and three other categories. But the question remains whether the incidence of auxiliaries and initial auxiliaries is an accurate gauge of authorial differences—an issue separate from that of style, especially since *Elene* and *Juliana* are hagiographies, while *Christ II* is homiletic. More particularly it may be doubted whether the amount of statistical variation encountered is significant. For example, the average number of auxiliaries per 100 lines in *Juliana* is 19.2; in *Elene* 18.9; and in *Christ II* 18.5. The percentage of auxiliaries that are initial in *Elene* is 21; in *Juliana* 19; in *Christ II* 25, and so forth. Without statistics on the deviation from the mean incidence within individual poems, it is impossible to say whether these statistical differences are significant. But a difference of .4 in overall incidence between *Christ II* and *Elene* seems small, and is only slightly higher than the .3 difference between *Elene* and *Juliana*; and much the same may be said about the incidence of initial auxiliaries. The statistical differences among poems that are examined in the following chapters are of a different order, as the truly significant ones are too large to be accidental. On the significance of the margin of error in such statistics see the review of Hiroshi Ogawa, *Old English Modal Verbs*, in *JEGP* 90 (1991), 546–49. Peculiarities of auxiliary usage may indeed define stylistic differences between texts, but whether they do in any given case, let alone whether a stylistic difference implies an authorial one, remains to be demonstrated. Thus it is more difficult, in one respect at least, to establish the probability of a stylistic difference than

not significantly alter any of the relevant statistics for the various criteria studied below, while it does broaden the base on which conclusions may be drawn, thereby strengthening them. (2) Cable does not provide a date for *Beowulf* because the particular purpose of his study is to date that poem. As noted above, dating on a philological basis has generally been to the eighth century (most commonly the first half), a practice that will be adopted for the purposes of this test chronology. (3) Cable distinguishes the portion of *Genesis A* preceding *Genesis B* from the rest—that is, he assumes that they are different compositions. While it remains to be proved that the two parts are one poem, A. N. Doane offers persuasive reasons to regard to the two as parts of a single composition (*Genesis A*, pp. 35–36; *Saxon Genesis*, p. 48). Aside from the matters Doane treats, nowhere in the following data are there any striking statistical differences between the two portions with regard to any of the features studied, even though the first portion is so much shorter, and sparsely attested features may therefore produce unrealistic percentages for it. It was thus of no practical use to keep the statistics separate. The statistics are presented in such a way, however, that those who are convinced that the two portions are the work of different poets may readily separate the evidence of the two. The same may be said of other some poems, including *Beowulf*, the unity of which has sometimes been questioned. The one longer poem in regard to which such claims seem to me likely is *Daniel*.[105] Yet because separating lines 279–361 or 279–408 from the remainder of the poem would have little effect on the results offered in the following chapters, it has not seemed worthwhile to divide the poem. At any rate, the features studied in the following chapters provide no very good evidence for the views of dissectors of this or other poems.

---

a chronological one: language change is independently discernible, so that if it is known that the language changed in a particular way, and there is corresponding variation in verse, a dating criterion is probable. On the whole, stylistic criteria cannot be independently confirmed this way.

[105]Sir Israel Gollancz was the first to propose a composite origin, in *The Caedmon Manuscript of Old English Poetry* (London: Oxford Univ. Press, 1927), pp. lxxxv–xcvii. For other references see R. T. Farrell, "The Unity of Old English *Daniel*," *RES*, n.s. 18 (1967), 117–35, who would explain the suspicious repetitions as due to the poet's thematic concerns. Still, this requires the assumption of more than one considerable coincidence. One reason to think that the Prayer of Azariah and the Song of the Three Boys are later additions is that they contain no hypermetric verses, which are very common in the rest of *Daniel*. Earl R. Anderson regards *hwæt, þu eart mihtum swið* (283b, in Farrell's edition) and *Bletsige þec, soðfæst cyning* (*Azarias* 77a) as hypermetric, but there seems no good reason not to regard them as belonging to normal type 3B1c, nor does Bliss regard them as hypermetric (pp. 162–68): see Anderson, "Style and Theme in the Old English *Daniel*," *ES* 68 (1987), 1–23, at 3. So also, the meter of the version in *Daniel* is looser than in *Azarias*, containing more unstressed words, just as in the rest of *Daniel*. It may be that the *Azarias* poet streamlined his source, but it seems likelier that the *Daniel* poet expanded his. This matter requires more careful study before any firm conclusions can be reached.

# I

# WEST GERMANIC PARASITING

§76. In the course of developing his theory of Germanic meter, Sievers discovered that many abnormal verses in Old English can be regularized by dropping vowels before resonants when they are of West Germanic origin.[1] For instance, *hleahtor* must be monosyllabic in the verse *Ðær wæs hæleþa hleahtor* (*Beowulf* 611a), and this is explicable by reason of the assumption that *hleahtor* derives from early West Germanic *\*hlahtr* after the loss of the nominative singular ending *\*-az*: the second vowel in *hleahtor* is due to parasiting in later West Germanic. Moritz Trautmann then postulated that Sievers' observation might be used as a dating criterion, since monosyllabic forms should be commoner in early verse, reflecting earlier Germanic poetic tradition (*Kynewulf*, pp. 120–21). Trautmann's position was substantiated in subsequent studies by Gregor Sarrazin, Carl Richter, and Friedrich Seiffert, and until recently, most have considered West Germanic parasiting a sure sign of chronological development in Old English meter.

§77. What exactly parasiting amounts to is an issue clouded by some ambiguous terminology. The usual assumption is that *r* in WGmc. *\*hlahtr* is "syllabic" or "silbenbildend," and parasiting consists in the development of syllabic *r* to a sequence of two phonemes, vowel plus *r*. This assumption obscures the metrical issues, since *\*hlahtr* with a syllabic *r* is dissyllabic by definition of the terms *syllabic* and *silbenbildend*, and thus *\*hlahtr* is metrically no different from OE *hleahtor* when it must be scanned as two syllables. The difficulty arises from widespread *phonological* generalization of Sievers' view that nonsyllabic *r* was *phonetically* impossible in a form like *\*hlahtr*.[2] Winfred Lehmann is certainly right to criticize this procedure.[3] The best counterevidence is the treatment of

---

[1]See "Rhythmik," pp. 480–82, and *Altgerm. Metrik*, §§79.4b and 156.4.

[2]See Sievers, *Grundzüge der Phonetik*, 5th ed. (Leipzig: Breitkopf & Härtel, 1901), §814. See also his *Altenglische Grammatik* (Halle: Niemeyer, 1882), §138, where he indicates that in words like *wæstm* the *m* must be syllabic "nach einem allgemeinen phonetischen Gesetze." Cf. §85 below, where it is demonstrated that *wæstm* in verse is never treated *phonologically* as a dissyllable. In his 1991 Columbia Univ. dissertation, "Old English Poetry: A Metrical Study" (pp. 416ff.), B. R. Hutcheson responds to some of the views offered in the earlier published version of this chapter. He expresses doubt that a West Germanic form such as *\*wuldrz* could have contained a consonantal *r*. In his generous correspondence with me he has subsequently abandoned his objection.

[3]"Post-Consonantal *l m n r*," pp. 166-67. Wilhelm Schulze argues for the monosyllabicity of words like Gothic *maiþms* in "Gotica," *KZ* 55 (1928), 113–15 (§10).

these resonants in some modern West Scandinavian areas, where they are for the most part still nonsyllabic. For example, in Modern Icelandic the words *vatn, býsn, segl,* and *gísl* are all monosyllables, even in compounds, and thus *vatnsberi* contains three syllables. The resonant *m* is not reflected as such in this position in Icelandic, and *r* in this environment developed an *u* before it in the course of the fourteenth century, for instance in *hestr > hestur,* though the monosyllabicity of the former is assured by eddic and skaldic meters, and by the monosyllabic reflexes of similar words in some Norwegian dialects: for instance, Old Norse *okr* 'usury', *otr* 'otter', and *slátr* 'meat' have monosyllabic reflexes in the Gyland dialect, and *akr* 'field' has a monosyllabic one in the Åsdalen dialect.[4] Similarly, the Gothic form *þwalh* for *þwahl* 'bath' seems to suggest that *l* is nonsyllabic here, unless the metathesis is mere scribal blunder; but opinion now seems to favor the assumption of nonsyllabicity here.[5] And the metathesis in forms of OE *ādl, setl, mæþl,* and *botl* cited by Campbell (§425) seems to require nonsyllabic *l,* as does the loss of *þ* with compensatory lengthening in *mæl* and *sæl* (§421), if the change occurred originally in uninflected forms.

§78. It should be understood that assigning a specific number of syllables to a word is a matter of native speakers' perceptions rather than absolute physiological facts—that is, the determining factor is phonemics rather than phonetics. For example, no native speaker of English would deny that *asks* is a monosyllable, even though *k* has smaller aperture than *s* (see below, §22); but Bernard Bloch notes that if the word is "pronounced with a long vowel and distinctly released consonants, a Japanese will hear five syllables."[6] The difference between Japanese and English speakers' analyses of the word is in part due to the fact that there are no

---

[4]See P. Kydland, *Gylands-målet: eit yversyn yver ljodverket,* Bidrag til nordisk filologi 11 (Oslo: Aschehoug, 1940), pp. 48–50; and Didrik Arup Seip, *Lydverket i Åsdølmålet,* Bidrag til nordisk filologi 2 (Oslo: Aschehoug, 1915), pp. 15, 32–34. The situation in Faroese is like that in Icelandic: see William B. Lockwood, *An Introduction to Modern Faroese* (Copenhagen: Munksgaard, 1955), pp. 18–19. For these references I am indebted to B. Richard Page, who kindly gave me a copy of his paper "Multi-Linear Phonology and the Development of Post-Consonantal Resonants in Word-Final Position in West Scandinavian and Germanic," presented at the University of California, Berkeley, April 11, 1992, at the Berkeley-Michigan Germanic Linguistics Roundtable. The proceedings of this conference will be published.

[5]The point was first made by Schulze (n. 3 above), and opposed by Sievers, "Gotisch *þwahl,*" *PBB* 52 (1928), 148–50. Now in opposition to Sievers' view see Trygve Sagan, "Zur Aussprache der gotischen Liquiden und Nasale zwischen Konsonanten und nach Konsonanten im Auslaut," in *Gedenkschrift für Trygve Sagen,* pp. 11–15a, Osloer Beiträge zur Germanistik 3 (Oslo: Veröffentlichungen des Germanistischen Instituts der Universität Oslo, 1979); Ernst A. Ebbinghaus, "Gothic ḷ, ṛ, ṃ, ṇ? The Evidence Reviewed," *JEGP* 69 (1970), 580–83; and Page's paper, as above. So also Krause (§§91.1, 94.2) argues that only *r* may be syllabic in Gothic; see also his "Zu den lautlichen Typen got. *fugls, akrs,*" *KZ* 55 (1927–28), 312–13.

[6]"Studies in Colloquial Japanese IV: Phonemics," *Language* 26 (1950), 92, n. 14.

voiceless vowels in the Germanic languages, as there are in Japanese—which is also in part why dissyllabicity in *vatn*, *býsn*, etc., is impossible for an Icelander. The Japanese analysis of *asks* is partially analogous to English speakers' difficulty with forms like monosyllabic Russian [fpskof] 'to Pskov'. Accordingly, some phonologists distinguish between phonetic and phonological syllables. But since the phonetic status of metrically nonsyllabic resonants is debatable, and at any rate irrelevant in the present context, "syllabic" will be used here only as a phonological term, and metrical monosyllables like *eaxl* and *māþm* will be said to contain nonsyllabic resonants.

§79. Lehmann challenges the usual analysis of West Germanic para-siting when he argues that after heavy syllables the resonants had been syllabic all along, since Proto-Indo-European times, and monosyllabic after light syllables. This then is the distribution that should be expected in the most conservative Old English verse, and he sets out to demon-strate that it is the distribution to be found in *Beowulf*. Lehmann's aim is not to demonstrate the dating value of postconsonantal resonants—indeed, he takes for granted the accuracy of the chronology suggested by prior dating studies—but to show that their scansion supports the hypo-thesis he had presented in an earlier study, that Sievers' law was an active phonological process in Proto-Germanic.[7] Sievers' law, in Franklin Edgerton's formulation of it (see n. 12 below), states that antevocalically the PIE resonants /y, w, r, l, m, n/ should be syllabic after a heavy syllable and nonsyllabic after a light. So, for example, the PIE phoneme /y/ should have the allophone [iy] in *\*ḱerdh-iy-es(y)o* > Gothic *hairdeis* 'shepherd's', but [y] in *\*kor-y-es(y)o* > Gothic *harjis* 'army's'. Although these examples demonstrate that Gmc. /j/ did alternate in the manner of Sievers' law at some point in the development of Gothic, Lehmann's hypothesis has met considerable opposition, and the consensus now appears to be that the government of the syllabicity of Gmc. /j/ by the weight of the preceding syllable can only have arisen dialectally in Germanic, and cannot reflect Sievers' law inherited intact from Proto-Indo-European.[8] One strong piece of evidence against the assumption that Sievers' law was inherited in Germanic from Proto-Indo-European is the development of early Germanic loanwords in Finnish, since these demand nonsyllabic *y* after a long syllable.[9] Another obstacle to Lehmann's hypothesis with regard

---

[7]"The Proto-Indo-European Resonants in Germanic," *Language* 31 (1955), 355–66.

[8]This, for instance, is the view of Elmar Seebold, who offers a particularly extensive examination of the Germanic evidence in *Das System der indogermanischen Halbvokale* (Heidelberg: Winter, 1972), pp. 64-98. It appears that as recently as 1982 Lehmann's views were unchanged: see his "Drink Deep!" in *Approaches to Beowulfian Scansion*, ed. Alan Renoir and Ann Hernandez (Berkeley: Old English Colloquium, Dept. of English, University of California, 1982), p. 21.

[9]This is the conclusion of Jorma Koivulehto, "Die Sieverssche Regel im Lichte der germanisch-finnischen Lehnbeziehungen," in *Germanic Dialects: Linguistic and Philo-*

to *j* is his support of the so-called converse to Sievers' law—that is, not only does -*j*- become -*ij*- after a heavy syllable, but -*ij*- becomes -*j*- after a light. Considerable counterevidence has been offered for Germanic, and now it appears that the Rigvedic evidence for a converse (verb forms like 3. pl. perf. midd. *cakre* and *dadhre*, next to *cakrire* and *dadhrire*) actually lends itself better to the assumption that there was no converse.[10] The Rigveda in fact provides telling counterevidence to a converse, in the declension of *ī*-stems like *vr̥kī́ḥ*. With just three exceptions in approximately 150 instances, stem-final *y* in such words is syllabic (*iy*) before a vocalic ending, regardless of whether the stem is long or short. The Rigveda even casts doubt on the antiquity of Sievers' law itself, because in *ī*-stems of the other type (or *yā*-stems), like *devī́*, after a heavy syllable the stem-final *y* is nonsyllabic approximately one instance in four. There are also undeniable exceptions to Sievers' law in Germanic with regard to -*(i)j*-.[11] But even if it were a tenable hypothesis that PGmc. /j/ conformed to Sievers' law, the other resonants could not be made to conform.[12] So for instance if the hypothesis were correct we should expect /n/ to take the form [n̥n] (to use the commonest notation) in PGmc. *\*wǣpn̥nam*. And yet if Sievers' law were inherited from Proto-Indo-European we should expect this form to become *\*wǣpunam*, which is not reflected in any Germanic language.[13] A form such as *\*wǣpn̥nam*

---

*logical Investigations*, ed. Bela Brogyanyi and Thomas Krömmelbein (Amsterdam: Benjamins, 1986), pp. 249–94. See also Jens Elmgård Rasmussen, "Two Phonological Issues in Germanic," *Acta Linguistica Hafniensia*, 18 (1983), 201–19, with the references at p. 214. Rasmussen argues that the divergent developments of PIE *\*gʷʰ* in Germanic are best explained under the assumption that the phonological changes affecting it occurred before the rise of the specifically Germanic form of Sievers' law.

[10]For evidence against a Germanic converse see James W. Marchand, "The 'Converse' of Sievers' Law and the Germanic First-Class Weak Verbs," *Language* 32 (1956), 285–87 (with Lehmann's reply in "A Definition of Proto-Germanic: A Study in the Chronological Delimitation of Languages," *Language* 37 [1961], 71–73); and Werner H. Will, "The Resonant System in Proto-Germanic," *JEGP* 69 (1970), 216–17. On the Vedic evidence see *Origins*, pp. 8–13 and 142–51. Seebold (as above, n. 8) also concludes that there is no converse. N. E. Collinge provides other references in a succinct discussion of scholarship on Sievers' law, in *The Laws of Indo-European* (Amsterdam: Benjamins, 1985), pp. 159–74.

[11]For examples in Germanic see Wilhelm Streitberg, *Urgermanische Grammatik* (Heidelberg: Winter, 1896), §75; and Alois Walde, *Die germanischen Auslautgesetze* (Halle: Niemeyer, 1900), pp. 136–37. For Old English examples see Dahl, pp. 74–81, and Campbell, §417, n. 2.

[12]Sievers himself, it should be noted, formulated his law to apply only to /y,w/, but Lehmann's analysis of course relies on Franklin Edgerton's reformulation—which represented something of a consensus until the 1970s—in including other resonants. For Edgerton's views see especially "The Indo-European Semivowels," *Language* 19 (1943), 83–124.

[13]Admittedly, the point is difficult to prove because there do not seem to be any indisputable examples of the development of *n̥n* to *un*: e.g., although OE *numen* has

cannot be assumed to have been altered by any very straightforward analogy, since *n* should have been syllabic in all case-forms, by Lehmann's reasoning; and the same may be said of exceptions to Sievers' own formulation of the law, for example Gothic *waurstwa* 'laborer'.

§80. Another impediment to Lehmann's analysis is that it requires scansions that are disallowed in most metrical systems based on Sievers' five types. For example, his hypothesis demands that *aldor-* and *maðþum-* be dissyllabic, and yet this produces a metrical type in *aldorbealu eorlum* (1676a) and *maðþumfæt mære* (2405a) that Sievers rejects as nonexistent (*Altgerm. Metrik*, §85, n. 3). Sievers observes that the only evidence for such a type is in verses where a resonant may be assumed to show parasiting. Moreover, Lehmann's scansion would render these five-position verses. Accordingly, Pope and Bliss (and Klaeber) also assume nonsyllabic resonants here. Similarly, Lehmann's views on Sievers' law demand syllabic resonants in *oncerbendum fæst* (1918a), *morgenlongne dæg* (2894a), and four others that he classifies as "E verses of a little favored metrical sub-type" (p. 165). But Sievers calls such a type "zweifelhaft" (§85.7), finding just two unambiguous examples in Old English verse, both of which are perhaps otherwise explicable.[14] In *winter yþe beleac* (1132b)

---

antevocalic weak grade of the root in all Germanic languages, still it is possible that this vocalism arose analogically in Proto-Germanic after the normal changes in the Proto-Indo-European syllabic consonants; and although Gothic *lauhmuni* 'lightning' has *-un-* from an antevocalic syllabic resonant, this is probably by analogy to a weak case such as PIE gen. sg. *\*louk(s)mn̥ās*. For the reason see *Origins*, §3.4 and p. 117. Nonetheless, if all such examples are to be eliminated, it still appears that there is no indisputable evidence for any development other than simply *n* from antevocalic *n̥n*, while all other forms of syllabic *n* give *un* in Germanic. In that event it would seem that there was no antevocalic syllabic *n* in Proto-Germanic, and therefore no converse of Sievers' law.

[14]Pope (p. 318) is uncertain about these verses because of doubts about whether *oncer-* and *morgen-* could be etymologically monosyllabic. His doubts are well founded, but they do not render it likelier that type E* has any antiquity: see below, §95. The two unambiguous examples that Sievers points out are *Ungelice wæs* (*Juliana* 688b) and *middangeardes weard* (*Daniel* 596a). In the latter instance it should be pointed out that the word *middangeardes* creates metrical problems in several poems: cf. *Andreas* 82a, 227a, *Judgment Day I* 65a, *Meters of Boethius* 21.22a and *Solomon and Saturn II* 180b. In all but the last instance the substitution of *midgeardes* would correct the problem; and *midgeard* is an actual Old English form, attested once in Rit. (see the *Microfiche Concordance*). Note, however, that although *a* cannot be excrescent in *middan-*, there does appear to be a Northumbrianism with an excrescent vowel: cf. *middin-* and *middun-* in the two Northumbrian texts of *Cædmon's Hymn*, and *midden-* in Ru.². Forms in *middel-* also occur in early Middle English, e.g. in the *Ormulum*. Similarly, *ungelic(e)* creates metrical problems at *Genesis B* 356b, *Daniel* 112a, *Wulf and Eadwacer* 3, 8, and *Meters of Boethius* 31.4b. Substitution of forms without *-ge-* would resolve these difficulties, but such forms are not attested in prose. On the other hand, comparison may be offered to the analogous instances of unmetrical verses with *ungemet-*: nearly all the thirty-seven instances require *unmet-*, instead, and none would be rendered unmetrical by the substitution. *Unmet-* as a simplex (cf. OSax. *unmet*, OHG *unmez*, *ungamez*) is attested twice in Bede's *Ecclesiastical History*, and even once in verse, at

and *Frofor eft gelamp* (2941b) the first word must be monosyllabic because Bliss finds that type D* appears only in the on-verse, and then must have double alliteration. Pope agrees on monosyllabic *winter* and *frōfor* (pp. 363–64). Other recalcitrant verses Lehmann assumes are later interpolations in the poem (p. 166). Thus Amos doubts these conclusions because of "Lehmann's willingness to revise metrical criteria in order to obtain consistent linguistic results" (p. 76; see also Russom, p. 44).

§81. Studies of parasiting have produced widely different results. Sarrazin initially found thirty-seven examples of nonsyllabic resonants after long syllables in *Genesis A* ("Chronologie," p. 174—a number he later reduced in *Kädmon*, p. 27), while Richter found sixteen, Seiffert twenty-five, and Amos just four. The disparities are due in part to different interpretations of the limits imposed by the metrical system employed. Only Amos employs Bliss's method of scansion, and yet her findings are different from those offered below. The differences are due in part to some misunderstandings about the requirements of Bliss's system. The most general of these are: (1) Bliss distinguishes normal and light verses, the latter type taking its first stress on the last word of the verse. Thus, a verse like *oðþæt aldorgedal* (*Genesis A* 1071b) is not an ambiguous type 2B1b or 3B*1b, but a light d4b (on which see below, n. 36). (2) Bliss's caesura differs from Sievers' foot-division in that it must coincide with a word boundary. Thus, a verse such as *wuldorspedum welig* (87a) cannot belong to type 1D*5, but only 3E2. Bliss's findings also demand restrictions on where the caesura may fall, so that, for example, in type D* it must fall immediately before the second lift; otherwise the verse must be reckoned type A. So also the place of the caesura distinguishes types 1A and 2A, and anacrusis is forbidden in the latter. (3) Most subtypes of the D variety are restricted to the on-verse, where they take only double alliteration.[15] Therefore *seofon winter her* (1139a) cannot belong to type 1D5, but only 3E2; and *sundor anra gehwilc* (*Daniel* 369b) is neither type 1D6 nor 1D*6, but 3E*2.[16] These generalities account for many of the differences between Amos' findings and those given below. Other, more detailed differences are explained in the notes below, in reference to the scansion of particular verses.

§82. In addition, studies of parasiting have failed to distinguish properly between etymologically monosyllabic stems like *tāc(e)n* and

---

*Instructions for Christians* 136b, if these are not simply variant spellings of *unmæt*. Bliss's position (§86) that in verses like *wyrd ungemete neah* the word must be unstressed because it is an adverb of degree is untenable: cf., e.g., the treatment of *swīðe* in *swīðe werig* (*Genesis A* 1469b) and *ðæt he swīðe oft* (*Andreas* 618b).

[15]Bliss was not the first to notice these requirements: see Sievers, *Altgerm. Metrik*, §20.3; and Seiffert, p. 33.

[16]Bliss's practice in this regard is based on statistics of incidence rather than syntactic considerations: see Bliss, §§80–82.

*bēac(e)n*, and dissyllabic stems like *ēþel*, *candel*, and *sāwel*. Sarrazin noticed the difference and pointed out that because of this error both he, in his earlier study, and Richter had counted several irrelevant verses in their statistics (*Kädmon*, p. 27). But Sarrazin's warning has gone largely unheeded. Amos dismisses the distinction, referring to Sarrazin's "manipulation of statistics" and "doctor[ing] the results" (pp. 71–72); yet she does adopt the principle in regard to words with light first syllables when Lehmann invokes it in order to exclude words like *micel* from his study (Lehmann, "Post-Consonantal *l m n r*," p. 161; Amos, p. 73).

§83. The distinction is genuine and significant. West Germanic parasiting applied to forms like *\*hlahtr-az* after they lost the inflection, but not to forms like *\*angil-*, in which the resonant was preceded by a vowel; and indeed, *hleahtor* may be monosyllabic in Old English verse, while *engel* never is. The etymological difference can sometimes be determined by spelling: for example, *wolcen* is frequently spelt *wolcn*, while *þēoden* is never *\*þeodn*. Yet many parasited forms are rarely if ever spelt without the parasite vowel when uninflected, particularly those in *-r*; and reverse spellings do occur, and at least in the instance of the word *sāwl* (see below, §98) may even be commoner than the etymological spelling. And so the only sure method of distinguishing parasited forms is by reference to cognates in East and North Germanic: in regard to the examples *hleahtor* and *engel*, OIcel. *hlátr* (not *\*hlátarr* or *\*hláttarr*) may be contrasted with *engill* (Gothic *aggilus*, Lat. *angelus*). Although Lehmann acknowledges the distinction, his lists include a variety of etymologically dissyllabic stems that are irrelevant to parasiting, which then are adopted by Amos, due to the influence of his study on hers. Thus he includes *eodor* (OIcel. *jaðarr*), *eofor* (OIcel. *jǫfurr*), *fetel* (OIcel. *fetill*), *gomel* (OIcel. *gamall*), *gomen* (OIcel. *gaman*), *gehwæðer* (Gothic *hvaþar*), *mægen* (OIcel. *megin* beside *magn*), *open* (OIcel. *opinn*), *seofon* (Gothic *sibun*), and *sigel* (cf. Gothic *sauil*). The dissyllabicity of these words is evident in Old English verse: for instance, *sweotol* (*-ul, swu-, su-*), which appears thirteen times uninflected in verse, is three times dissyllabic, and ambiguous in the other instances, while *fugol* (*-ul, -l, -el* < PGmc. *\*fugla-*) appears thirty-seven times, and is never demonstrably dissyllabic, though it is three times monosyllabic in *Solomon and Saturn*.[17] Among the originally dissyllabic forms with long first syllables that should be excluded from Lehmann's lists are *āþum*,[18] *æfen* (dat. *æfenne*), *collen*,[19] *dōgor* (*es*-stem),

---

[17] The verse *wildne fugol* in the same text (299a) is anomalous regardless of whether or not *fugol* is dissyllabic.

[18] From *\*aiþuma-*: cf. OHG *eidum*, and see Friedrich Kluge, *Etymologisches Wörterbuch der deutschen Sprache*, 20th ed. rev. by Walther Mitzka (Berlin: de Gruyter, 1967), s.v. *Eidam*.

[19] As *coll-* derives from *\*koln-*, the suffix *-en-* cannot result from syllabic *n*. The fact that the suffix always has the form *-en-* rather than *-on-* is not definitive proof of its status, since *-en-* came to stand for syllabic *n* generally, and could appear after back

*ēagor* (*es*-stem: cf. OIcel. *ægir*), *ealdor* 'elder, prince',[20] *hǣðen* (OIcel. *heiðinn*), *īren* (gen. pl. *īrenna*), *morgen* (Gothic *maurgins*), *oncer* (Lat. *ancora*), and *sāwel* (Gothic *saiwala*: see n. 55 below). To these may be added some included by Amos: *condel* (Lat. *candela*), *ēðel* (OSax. *ōdil*, OIcel. *ōðal*), *fīfel-* (OIcel. *fimbul-*), and *wēsten* (dat. *wēstenne*, OSax. *wōstunnia*, OHG *wuostinna*). These words with long roots are almost always dissyllabic in Old English verse; the exceptions are discussed below (§95). It may be noted, as well, that the cognates of words that become dissyllabic by parasiting in Old English are always treated as monosyllables in the scansion of Old Icelandic verse.

§84. Studies of parasiting have also suffered from the practice of including forms with a resonant after a short syllable in the results— words like *swef(e)n* and *seg(e)l*, for instance. Monosyllabic scansions of these have been detected by applying the criterion that a short lift or half-lift may not stand for a long one except after a single long syllable— an assumption that is largely true, but not consistently reliable (see below, §249). And so *hrefn*, for example, must be monosyllabic in *oþþæt hrefn blaca* (*Beowulf* 1801a). But these forms can be of no value in dating because in fact there is almost no metrical evidence that such words are ever dissyllabic. Once the etymologically dissyllabic forms like *gomel* and *open* are excluded, there seem to be just four unambiguously dissyllabic scansions in all of Old English verse, though the number of morphemes involved is large, exceeding thirty.[21] By contrast, after long syllables the resonants are frequently syllabic, as demonstrated below. If it cannot be shown that the words with short first syllables were normally dissyllabic, then monosyllabicity can be of no value as a dating criterion; and with just four examples, dissyllabicity can hardly be correlated to lateness.

---

vowels (Campbell, §363). It could in fact become the exclusive form after back vowels, as in the instance of *bēacen, tācen,* and *wolcen* outside of Anglian texts.

[20]Comparative: cf. OSax. pl. *aldiron, eldiron,* the latter with umlaut, proving the status of the *i*. On the other hand, *ealdor* 'life' is originally monosyllabic: cf. OIcel. *aldr,* gen. *aldrs*.

[21]The four are at *Phoenix* 18a and 56b, *Order of the World* 73b, and *Meters of Boethius* 26.28b. Here and throughout, the metrical Psalms are excluded from such statistics, since these are characterized by "very general metrical irregularity" (Krapp, ASPR 5:xvii); see also Benno Tschischwitz, *Die Metrik der angelsächsischen Psalmen- übersetzung* (Greifswald diss.; Breslau: H. Fleischmann, 1908), p. 32; and this is a point on which Amos agrees (p. 75). Also excluded are words like *bit(t)er* and *snot(t)or*, which may or do show long first syllables after leveling of the geminate from the inflected cases, though the number of these also is not large. Amos' examples of dissyllabic stems with short roots are not reliable: *and ymb þæt hehsetl* (*Christ and Satan* 219a) cannot belong to type 2C2c, because under Bliss's analysis (which Amos employs) it is light, and so it must be called either type a2c or d3c; *þyrel* at *Finnsburh* 45b has a long root vowel; and the lines with *wæter* must be excluded because etymologically the word is at least partially dissyllabic. (It is a heteroclitic stem, with a vowel before the resonant in the *r*-cases, but not the *n*-cases, in Proto-Indo-European.) Amos correctly identifies the word as etymologically dissyllabic (p. 73), but still includes such verses in her results.

§85. Another factor that has not been taken into consideration is the difference in parasiting among the resonants involved. Karl Luick observes that generally no parasiting occurs before *l* after *d* or *t*, and that forms without parasiting before *l* are especially common when the preceding consonant is *g* or *s*. Parasiting is frequent after long syllables before nasal consonants, he says, but there are also forms without it.[22] Like many of Luick's findings, these claims are based on purely orthographic evidence; but the metrical evidence indicates that they are not far from the truth. After a long syllable *l* is never syllabic after *d*, *t*, *s*, or *f*, though it is frequently distinctively nonsyllabic.[23] The same is true of all stems in *m*, for which *þ* may be added to the list (there are no long-stemmed examples of *l* after *þ*).[24] With both of the groups there is

[22]Luick, "Zur altenglischen Grammatik," *Festschrift Wilhelm Viëtor*, Die neueren Sprachen, Ergänzungsband (Marburg: N. G. Elwert, 1910), pp. 260–62; and *Historische Grammatik*, §318.

[23]The relevant morphemes are *gebrastl*, *eaxl*, *gīsl*, *hūsl*, *spātl*, *sūsl*, and *(ge)wrixl*. The phonological rule thus appears to be that *l* is nonsyllabic after fricatives and alveolar consonants. A probable exception is *ādl*, which is twice dissyllabic in *Guthlac*, but the word has no known cognates. F. A. Wood reconstructs PIE *\*oitlo-* (cf. Gk. οἶτος 'fate, doom') and draws a connection with OE *īdel* (OSax. *īdal*, OHG *ītel*; and also with OIcel. *illr*, which he derives from *\*iðlaR*), presumably under the assumption that these reflect the PIE *e*-grade of the root: see "Etymological Notes," *MLN* 13 (1898), 3. Yet considering the consistency with which *īdel* is spelt thus, an originally dissyllabic stem seems to be required. Less convincing is F. Holthausen's proposed connection with the Greek interjection αἴ (better οἴ, exclamation of pity, grief, astonishment), leading to his reconstruction PGmc. *\*aiþlō*: see "Beiträge zur englischen Wortkunde," *Anglia Beiblatt* 29 (1918), 254. In his later dictionary he rightly expresses doubt about C. Uhlenbeck's idea of a connection with Lithuanian *aitrùs*: see "Etymologien," *PBB* 26 (1901), 568. Aside from the examples in *Guthlac*, the only unambiguous instances in verse are at *Beowulf* 1763a and *Judgment Day II* 259a.

[24]The relevant words are *ǣþm*, *bearhtm*, *bōsm*, *māþm*, and *wæstm*. Note that although the words are frequently attested, the variety is small, and the phonological rule here is not necessarily any different from that for *l*. Here and throughout, *Genesis B* is excluded from consideration, since it is a translation from Old Saxon, and shows some divergences from normal Old English metrical practice. This exclusion is in accordance with the views of most metrists, who consider the poem unreliable as metrical evidence: for discussion see, e.g., Bliss, §106; Pope, p. 99; E. G. Stanley, "Verbal Stress in Old English Verse," *Anglia* 93 (1975), 307–34, at 328; Patricia Bethel, "Notes on the Incidence and Type of Anacrusis in *Genesis B*: Some Similarities to and Differences from Anacrusis Elsewhere in Old English and Old Saxon," *Parergon*, n.s. 2 (1984), 1–24; David J. G. Lewis, "The Metre of *Genesis B*," *ASE* 16 (1987), 67–125; and Doane, *Saxon Genesis*, pp. 65–88. Like most of these scholars, Peter J. Lucas argues that the meter of the poem, though unusual, conforms to normal Old English standards to a considerably greater extent than is usually acknowledged: see "Some Aspects of *Genesis B* as Old English Verse," *Proceedings of the Royal Irish Academy* 88, sec. C (1988), 143–78. But the sorts of divergences from normal standards that he finds— anomalous verses of the type *heofonrices hehðe*, which he labels type 3A; unusual anacrusis; breaches of Kuhn's first law; frequent linking of normal and hypermetric verses in a line; exceptionally long initial theses, and other peculiarities—seem sufficient to justify excluding the poem from a survey whose conclusions rest on fairly subtle

parasiting in neither compounds nor simplices, and the body of evidence is large enough to leave no doubt. It might also be true that *n* is nonsyllabic after fricatives, but this cannot be proved, since the only evidence one way or the other is *ðios oðru bysen* (*Meters of Boethius* 12.7a).[25] These facts about *l* and *m* indicate that such words must be excluded from consideration in evaluating the chronological implications of parasiting, since these words show no variation at all. They are thus irrelevant to chronology, and would distort any patterns discernible in resonants that do show variation. The facts about *l* and *m* also provide fairly firm evidence against Lehmann's views on Sievers' law.[26]

§86. The facts about *l* after consonants other than alveolar stops and fricatives are not as clear. It is difficult to draw firm conclusions because of etymological difficulties: the relevant words attested unambiguously in verse are few—just six—and most of these contain a suffix in *-l-* that could appear with or without a vowel in front of it in Proto-Germanic. As Friedrich Kluge remarks (§189), it is impossible to tell without Gothic cognates. *Symbel* is exceptionally obscure. Seiffert's reconstruction *\*sumbil-* (p. 30) is unlikely, since this leaves OIcel. *sumbl* unexplained. The Icelandic word could be one of those rare exceptions in which the suffix vowel is syncopated, as with OIcel. *eldr* = OE *æled*; but it still lacks umlaut. Also improbable is P. A. Erades' reconstruction *\*sumil-*.[27] Dissyllabic stems in Norse usually remain dissyllabic—*gaman* and *hǫfuð*, for instance—and when syncopated forms are extended from the inflected cases, as with *magn/megn* and *rǫgn*, these are generally found beside unsyncopated forms—compare *megen* and *regen*. In the one exceptional

---

metrical variations. Moreover, the fact that initial theses are exceptionally long in the poem indicates more important underlying metrical differences. For example, an attempt to apply Calvin Kendall's rules of metrical grammar for *Beowulf* to *Genesis B* would reveal some significant differences in the relationship between particles and naturally stressed elements. There is an apparently dissyllabic *wæstm* in the poem at 643b. The Old Saxon cognate *wastum* is metrically dissyllabic (as should be expected, since there is no nonparasiting in Old Saxon), e.g. in *uueriat im thena uuastom* at *Heliand* 2523a (Behaghel's edition).

[25] Although fricatives are "stronger" than nasals and liquids in the universal strength scales of Natural Generative Phonology (see below, §97), this does not prevent the retention of monosyllabicity in words like *māðm* until fairly late. Since the strength hierarchy in *bȳsn* is identical to that in *māðm*, it would be rash to assume different treatment without further evidence.

[26] To maintain Lehmann's position one would have to assume that *l* and *m* were originally syllabic here, and lost their syllabicity in prehistoric Old English. But since these resonants are nonsyllabic in East and North Germanic (by Lehmann's own reasoning), it is less complicated to assume that they were nonsyllabic in Proto-Germanic, and remained as such in West Germanic while *r* and *n* were syllabified. Old English orthography supports this view, since the existence of spellings like *susel* and *wæstem* surely indicates that Old English verse preserves a conservative pronunciation rather than an innovation.

[27] "A Romance Congener of O.E. *symbel*," *English Studies* 48 (1967), 25–27.

instance, *gagn*, there is still an umlauted form, *gegn*, attested. Moreover, OSax. *sumbal* tells against both of these reconstructions, since it demands a suffix *-al-* or *-l-* rather than *-il-*; and yet suffix ablaut cannot be ruled out altogether. More likely is PGmc. *\*sumli-*, since the long-stemmed neuter *i*-stems have gone over to other classes throughout Germanic. This also explains the umlaut difference: in Old English, umlaut is all that distinguishes the long-stemmed neuter *i*-stems from *a*-stems, while umlaut is not found in the cognates of these words—for example, compare OE *gehygd*, *geþyld*, and *gehlȳd* to OSax. *gihugd*, *githuld*, and OIcel. *hljóð*. Even the two words with clear etymologies in this group of words ending in *-l* are nonetheless also somewhat ambiguous: *tempel* (Lat. *templum*) is almost always dissyllabic, while *tungol* (Gothic dat. pl. *tugglam*, OIcel. *tungl*) is more often monosyllabic than dissyllabic—though under peculiar circumstances, as explained below. Because of uncertainties it seems best to reserve these words in *-l* for separate treatment below.

§87. Another group that must be segregated is the kinship terms in *-r*, *brōþor*, *dohtor*, *mōdor*, and *sweostor*. The reason is that etymologically, in the singular, the nominative and accusative had the dissyllabic stem *\*brōþar-*, and similar, in Proto-Germanic, while the genitive and dative had the stem *\*brōþr-*. A word such as *hleahtor*, on the other hand, had a monosyllabic stem throughout the paradigm, *\*hlahtr-*. Thus the kinship terms will perhaps be more inclined to dissyllabicity, and should be examined separately in order to determine whether they need to be discarded altogether, as Sarrazin suggests (*Kädmon*, p. 27). In the process it will be worthwhile to determine whether monosyllabicity is commoner in the cases with an originally monosyllabic stem.

§88. In regard to the other stems in *-r*, and those in *-n*, difficulties of these sorts are minimal, and there is a wealth of evidence to show that both monosyllabic and dissyllabic scansions of these words are common. Below are listed all the unambiguous instances of monosyllabic scansion in the test group of poems. The approximate dates suggested for each poem are explained above in the Introduction, §§70ff.

> *Cædmon's Hymn* (657-80)
>     No unambiguous verses with or without parasiting.
> *Bede's Death Song* (735)
>     No unambiguous verses with or without parasiting.
> *Leiden Riddle* (8th c.)[28]
>     No unambiguous verses with or without parasiting.

---

[28]*Hrisil* 'shuttle' is probably relevant in *hrisil scelfath* (7b), but the word is etymologically obscure. Campbell (§574.4) assumes a short root-vowel, as does Bülbring (§444), though the meter demands a long one in this poem. Karl Kärre supports the assumption of a short vowel on the basis of the observation that the word is spelt with an intrusive *t* in the form *hristle* in a glossary, but this appears to be a ghost entry: see *Nomina agentis in Old English*, pt. 1 (Uppsala, 1915), 65–66. Moreover, the principle

Genesis A (8th c.)[29]
Without parasiting:
    27a    wuldorfæstan wic (3E1)
    87a    wuldorspedum welig (3E2)
    979a   tiber sceawian (1D1)
    2193a  wuldorfæstne wlite (3E1)
    2313a  Sete sigores tacn (1D5 or 3B1b)
    2389a  hihtleasne hleahtor (3E1)
    2514b  aldornere mine (2A3a)
    2694a  Ac ic me, gumena baldor (3B1c)
    2753b  tuddorsped onleac (2E2a)
    2770a  wuldortorht ymb wucan (2E2a)
    2913a  wuldorgast godes (2A3b)[30]
With parasiting:
    119b   Þa wæs wuldortorht (d5b)
    988a   tregena tuddor (2A1a)
    1044b  tacen sette (2A1a)

---

seems dubitable: other intrusive consonants are unaffected by vowel length (cf. *bræmbel* beside *brēmel*, *æmptig* beside *æmtig*), and very probably the root vowel in OE *hwistlian* was originally long: otherwise it is difficult to explain OIcel. *hvísla*. Presumably this derives from the PIE *e*-grade of the root, as in OIcel. *hvína* (*o*-grade in OHG *hwaijōn*, OE *āhwǽnan*). That the second syllable of *hrisil* is parasitic is demonstrated by the form *hrisl* in Erf.

[29]At 2389a, *hihtleasne hleahtor* cannot belong to type 2A1a (cf. Amos, p. 85) because resolution is not possible in the second position. On verses like *wuldorcyninges* see below, n. 33. At 979a, *tiber sceawian* must be called type 1D1 rather than 2A1a(ii), if just on probabilistic grounds, since the probability is overwhelming: the former type appears in the off-verse in *Beowulf* 220 times, and the latter just once. But in fact the one exception is very probably misclassified, and the type is thus unknown in the off-verse, or even outside formulae like *Beowulf maþelode* in the on-verse: see the discussion below, n. 45, and in Chap. 7, §249. At 2720b, *and glæd seolfor* is ambiguous (as remarked by Seiffert, p. 34) because *seolfor* may stand for earlier *silofr* (and similar), as attested in early West Saxon (see Campbell, p. 91, n. 1). Technically the verse *sette friðotacen* (2371a) could belong to either type d2b or a2b. Although the latter does not occur in *Beowulf*, there is no convincing reason that it should not. But since type d2b occurs 96 times in *Beowulf*, the probability that this is type a2b may be considered negligible. The verse *frecenra siða* (1427b) probably belongs here, but cf. OIcel. *frœkinn* beside *frœkn* 'valiant'. At 2278b, *hunger oððe wulf* is ambiguous: the types 2B2– and 2E1b are both suspect—see §§205ff. below. Here *oððe* might be stressed—cf. *Genesis A* 2323b, *Meters of Boethius* 28.23b, and similar—but more likely another *oððe* has dropped out from before *hunger* in the course of scribal transmission: cf. *oððe hunger oþþe þurst* (*Judgment Day II* 258a). In accordance with remarks in n. 36 below, *oð his ealdorgedal* (1959a) must be ambiguous. Some other problematic verses in *Genesis A* are discussed below, n. 49.

[30]There is the possibility that this verse should be considered analogous to a few peculiar verses of a type that appears only in this poem: cf. *Neorxnawong stod* (208b), *eþelstol heold* (1129b), and *dreorigmod tu* (2805b). Presumably, then, *wuldor*- would be considered a dissyllable: whatever the difficulties involved in analyzing these verses, they must at least conform to the requirement that they contain four metrical positions. Thus it is also probable (though inadmissible evidence under Bliss's analysis) that *þancolmod wer* (1705a) is an example of parasiting.

1139a   seofon winter her (3E2)
1402b   eorðan tuddor (2A1a)
1539b   andgiettacen (2A1)
2371a   sette friðotacen (d2b)
2769a   beacen sette (2A1a)
2875b   oðþæt wuldortorht  (d5b)
*Daniel* (8th c.)[31]
    Without parasiting:
        369b    sundor anra gehwilc (3E*2)
        378a    winterbiter weder (3E3 or 2A3b)[32]
        633a    wundorlic wræcca (2A1a)
    With parasiting:
        178b    þa hleoðor cwom (3B1a)
        577a    oðþæt þu ymb seofon winter (2C1d)
        717a    Him þæt tacen wearð (3B1b)
*Beowulf* (8th–9th c.)[33]
    Without parasiting:
        611a    Ðær wæs hæleþa hleahtor (3B1b)
        667b    sundornytte beheold (3E*2)

---

[31]Although Bliss (p. 167) regards it as hypermetric, *bereafodon þa receda wuldor* (59a) might belong to type 3B1e, with monosyllabic *wuldor* and no stress on the finite verb. The off-verse is not hypermetric, nor any other verse near it. Verbs bearing tertiary stress at the beginning of the verse seem always to alliterate, suggesting that they do bear stress, and so it would, admittedly, be unusual if the verb were unstressed here. But since it is also peculiar that a hypermetric half-line should appear alone, with none other near it, the verse is best regarded as ambiguous.

[32]Type 3E3 does not occur in the on-verse in *Beowulf*, but there is no reason it could not, since all others of the E type that Bliss finds in *Beowulf* do. Nonattestation is probably due to infrequency: there are just five verses of this type in *Beowulf*.

[33]The verse *Þæt wæs geocor sið* (765b) may be another instance of parasiting, but the etymology of *geocor* is obscure. James Dishington not improbably suggests a connection with Gothic *jiukan* 'contend', but the suffix still need not be simply *-r-*: see "Functions of the Germanic *ē*-Verbs: A Clue to Their Formal Prehistory," *Language* 52 (1976), 851–65. Bliss scans *wæpen hafenade* (1573b) as type 2A1a(ii), but see above, n. 29; verses 840b and 3032b are thus also included among those without parasiting. Though emended, the verse *hroden hildecumbor* (1022a) is probably an example of nonparasiting; yet the etymology of *cumbor* is uncertain. At 768a, *ceasterbuendum* appears to be an example of nonparasiting, but it is actually ambiguous if *bu-* may be short before another vowel, as argued below (§108). *Hæfde kyningwuldor* at 665b is like *sette friðotacen* at *Genesis A* 2371a (see above, n. 29). Lehmann (pp. 163–64) asserts that in verses like *wuldurcyninge* the first syllable is not actually to be regarded as long, since *-ul-* derives from PIE *-l̥-*; but he is arguing under the assumption that the syllabicity in Old English stem-final resonants is due to Sievers' law rather than West Germanic parasiting. Amos' conclusions about *Beowulf* are exceptionally different from those given here because, it appears, in regard to this one poem she relies on Lehmann's survey rather than Bliss's index to the scansion. Some ambiguous verses, e.g. *to aldorceare* (906b), are probably to be regarded as lacking parasiting, given Jun Terasawa's conclusion that constructions like *hildefrecan* (2205a) are infrequent in *Beowulf*, and in verse in general. Rather, before a resolvable sequence the connecting vowel is more usually lost: cf. *hildfrecan* (2366a). See "Metrical Constraints on Old English Compounds," *Poetica* (Tokyo) 31 (1989), 1–16. Terasawa's findings would disambiguate several other verses

840b    wundor sceawian (1D1)
995b    wundorsiona fela (3E2)
1079a   morþorbealo maga (2A3a)
1128a   wælfagne winter (3E2)
1132b   winter yþe beleac (3E*2)
1136a   wuldortorhtan weder (3E2)
1187a   umborwesendum ær (3E2)
1440a   wundorlic wægbora (1D*3)
1459b   atertanum fah (3E2)
1676a   aldorbealu eorlum (2A3a)
1681a   wundorsmiþa geweorc (3E*3)
1863a   lac ond luftacen (1A2a: see Bliss, §44)
2428b   þa mec sinca baldor (3B1b)
2436b   morþorbed stred (2A3b)
2742a   morðorbealo maga (2A3a)
2941b   Frofor eft gelamp (2E2a)
3032b   wundur sceawian (1D1)
3037b   wundordeaðe swealt (3E2)
3062b   Wundur hwar þonne (2A3a)
3160a   beadurofes becn (3E2)

With parasiting:
665b    Hæfde kyningwuldor (d2b)
685a    wig ofer wæpen (1A1b)
1587a   aldorleasne (2A1)
2567a   winia bealdor (2A1a)
3003a   ealdorleasne (2A1)

*Exodus* (8th–9th c.)
Without parasiting:[34]
390a    wuldorfæst cyning (2A1b)
With parasiting:
75a     Hæfde wederwolcen (d2b)
90a     lyftwundor leoht (3E2)
93b     fyr and wolcen (1A1a)
108b    oðer wundor (2A1a)
146b    morðor fremedon (2A1a)
416a    halig tiber (2A1a)
418a    wuldres hleoðor (2A1a)

*Elene* (9th c.)
Without parasiting:
966a    wuldorfæste gife (3E1)

---

in *Beowulf:* 46b, 718a, 757a, 1018b, 1105a, 1162a, 1301a, 1979a, 2750a, 2795a, 2839a. But it is unnecessary to advert to this probabilistic evidence in order to illustrate the considerable statistical difference between *Beowulf* and presumably later poems.

[34]At 390a, *wuldorfæst cyning* cannot belong to type 2A2 (cf. Amos, p. 84). At 372a, *tuddorteondra* may be scanned as either type 2A1 or 1D1 (like *cnihtwesende*, without contraction). The verse *morðor fremedon* (146b) cannot have the metrical contour of *cnihtwesende* because of the short third syllable: see Chap. 8. On the classification of *Hæfde wederwolcen* (75a) as type d2b and not a2b, cf. the discussion of *Genesis A* 2371a above, n. 29.

With parasiting:

| | |
|---|---|
| 5b | cyninga wuldor (2A1a) |
| 16b | mannum to hroðer (1A*1a) |
| 85a | sigores tacen (2A1a) |
| 162b | þe þis his beacen wæs (3B1c) |
| 171a | tacen wære (2A1a) |
| 178b | cyninga wuldor (2A1a) |
| 184b | sigores tacen (2A1a) |
| 186b | beorna wuldor (2A1a) |
| 344b | wigona baldor (2A1a) |
| 650b | morðorslehtes (2A1) |
| 783b | forð beacen þin (3E2) |
| 887a | sigebeacen soð (3E2) |
| 984b | þæt ðæt sigorbeacen (2C1b) |
| 1070a | ymb wundorwyrd (d5a) |
| 1104a | Leort ða tacen forð (3B1b) |
| 1111b | wundor cyðan (2A1a) |
| 1120b | sigores tacen (2A1a) |
| 1159a | dugoðum to hroðer (1A*1a) |
| 1208a | leahtorlease (2A1) |

*Fates of the Apostles* (9th c.)

No unambiguous verses without parasiting.

With parasiting:

| | |
|---|---|
| 55b | wundorcræfte (2A1) |

*Juliana* (9th c.)

No unambiguous verses without parasiting.

With parasiting:

| | |
|---|---|
| 279b | cyninga wuldor (2A1a) |
| 416b | wyrme to hroþor (1A*1a) |
| 568a | mægþa bealdor (2A1a) |
| 575b | wundorcræfte (2A1) |

*Christ II* (9th c.)[35]

No unambiguous verses without parasiting.

With parasiting:

| | |
|---|---|
| 508a | cyninga wuldor (2A1a) |
| 623a | feondum to hroþor (1A*1a) |
| 688a | eorþan tuddor (2A1a) |

*Andreas* (9th c.)[36]

Without parasiting:

| | |
|---|---|
| 428a | wuldorspedige weras (3E2) |
| 1181b | ealdorgeard sceoran (2A3b) |

---

[35]For their relevance to the question of authorship the figures for *Christ I* and *III* may be compared with these. The former (439 lines) has two verses with parasiting (220a, 285a) and two without (54b, 310a); the latter (798 lines) has one verse with parasiting (905a) and eight without (1010a, 1079a, 1139a, 1416a, 1565a, 1611b, 1615a, 1624a).

[36]In the ASPR edition, *com* is mistakenly put into the off-verse at 88b, where it ruins the alliteration under Kuhn's first law. In the on-verse, where, for example, Brooks has it in his edition, it would provide a normal 3B1d scansion. A possible example of nonparasiting is *wuldorcyninges word* (801a), but the off-verse is hypermetric. The

1265a   wintercealdan niht (3E2)
1457a   wuldortorht gewat (2E2a)
With parasiting:
   13b     wundorcræfte (2A1)
   29b     freaðoleas tacen (2A1a)
   88b     com wuldres tacen (2A1a: see n. 36)
  166b     galdorcræftum (2A1)
  171b     cininga wuldor (2A1a)
  177a     morðorcræftum (2A1)
  214a     treowe tacen (2A1a)
  325b     wuldorþrymmes (2A1)
  547b     þeoda baldor (2A1a)
  555b     cyninga wuldor (2A1a)
  645b     wundorcræfte (2A1)
  702b     wuldorþrymmes (2A1)
  705a     wundorworca (2A1)
  739b     hleoðor dynede (2A1a)
  854b     cyninga wuldor (2A1a)
  899a     cyninga wuldur (2A1a)
1317b     Hwæt is wuldor þin (3B1b)
1338b     mære tacen (2A1a)
1411a     cininga wuldor (2A1a)
1463b     hæleða wuldor (2A1a)
1551b     hleoðor gryrelic (2A1a)
1599b     morðorscyldige (2A1)
*Preface* and *Epilogue, Pastoral Care* (890-99)
No unambiguous instances.

---

etymology of *corðor* in *corðor oðrum getang* (138b) is unknown; the verse is like *sundor anra gehwilc* (*Daniel* 369b: see above, §81). The verse *ealdorgeard sceoran* (1181b) is emended, but the emendation can hardly be doubted. At 1599b, *morðorscyldige* cannot be type 1D1 (cf. Amos, p. 80; for 1D1?), as this would require syllabic -*ig*- in a poem in which it is consistently nonsyllabic: see below, §216. Bliss (§72) regards verses like *wintergeworpum* (1256a) as unambiguous, and this could be regarded as probable if K. Stevens were right that the first element always involves a syllabic resonant: see "Some Aspects of the Metre of the Old English Poem *Andreas*," *Proceedings of the Royal Irish Academy* 81, sec. C (1981), 1–27, at 21–22. In that event, verses like *oð his ealdorgedal* (*Genesis A* 1959a) should be included. In general Stevens' point is indeed true, and it is remarkable how regularly *ge*- is used as a metrical filler in verses like *heahgesceafta* (*Genesis A* 4b). There are more than seventy such verses in *Beowulf*, while verses like *earfoþsiþas* (*Daniel* 656a) do not take internal *ge*-. But there are exceptions—e.g. *dogorgerimes* (*Beowulf* 2728a; cf. *Elene* 779a, but also 705a and hypermetric *deað æfter dogorrime* at *Meters* 10.67a) and *þær he sawulgedal* (*Andreas* 1701b)—which are probably to be explained under the principle established below (§§95ff.). But it is also probable that parasiting in verses like *wintergeworpum* licensed a new metrical type, since *heafodgerimes* (*Judith* 308b) is the only verse of its type in the test group of poems. Suffice it to say that conclusions about all these verses must be less firm, and that they appear in both early and late verse: cf. also *Genesis A* 64b, *Exodus* 589a, *Daniel* 599b, *Beowulf* 2903b, *Andreas* 1256a, 1686b, *Meters* 28.27a, *Brunanburh* 51a, and *Coronation of Edgar* 14a (cf. *Death of Edward* 21a).

*Meters of Boethius* (897)[37]
 No unambiguous verses without parasiting.
 With parasiting:
  5.4b  wolcen hangað (2A1a)
  5.13b  col and hlutor (1A1a)
  9.7a  *man* and morðor (1A1a)
  11.59a Winter bringeð (2A1a)
  13.5a  *w*undorlice (2A1)
  15.3b  *wund*orlice (2A1)
  20.3a  and wundorlic (d5a)
  20.5a  wun*dorlice* (2A1)
  20.101b wundorlicra (2A1)
  20.162b wundorlice (2A1)
  20.203b sun*dor*cræfte (2A1)
  21.16b and sio frofor an (3B1b)
  26.17a tyn winter ful (3E2)
  28.68b wundor ðince (2A1a)
  28.83a wæfðo and wunder (1A*1a)[38]
  29.56b æghwylc tudor (2A1a)
*Battle of Brunanburh* (937)
 Without parasiting:
  3b  ealdorlangne tir (3E2)
 No unambiguous verses with parasiting.
*Capture of the Five Boroughs* (942)
 No unambiguous instances without parasiting.
 With parasiting:
  6a  Ligoraceaster (2A1)
*Judith* (10th c.)
 No unambiguous instances without parasiting.
 With parasiting:
  49b  wigena baldor (2A1a)
  155a  cyninga wuldor (2A1a)
  156b ˋ þæt eow ys wuldorblæd (d5c)
  257a  egesfull ond afor (1A*1a)
*Coronation of Edgar* (973)
 No unambiguous instances.
*Death of Edgar* (975)
 No unambiguous instances.
*Battle of Maldon* (991)
 Without parasiting:
  130b  wæpen up ahof (2E2a)
 No unambiguous verses with parasiting.
*Death of Edward* (1066)
 No relevant instances.

---

[37]A possible example of significant nonparasiting is *ðios oðru bysen* (12.7a); but see above, §85.

[38]Under Bliss's system this verse might be considered ambiguous, either 1A*1a(i) or 2E1a. But it is demonstrated below (§§210ff.) that the assumption of type 2E1, lacking tertiary ictus, is untenable.

Durham (1110)
No relevant instances.

§89. The results may be tabulated as follows, where the proportion is of nonparasited to parasited forms, and the incidence is based on the ratio of unambiguous instances to the total number of verses in the poem or group of poems (consistently less than 1 percent):[39]

| POEM | PROPORTION | INCIDENCE |
|---|---|---|
| Early Northumbrian poems (28 lines) | 0:0 | |
| Genesis A (2,319 lines) | 11:9 | .43 |
| Daniel (774 lines) | 3:3 | .39 |
| Beowulf (3,182 lines) | 22:5 | .42 |
| Exodus (590 lines) | 1:7 | .68 |
| The Cynewulf canon (2,601 lines) | 1:27 | .54 |
| Andreas (1,722) | 4:22 | .75 |
| Poems by Alfred (1,796 lines) | 0:16 | .45 |
| Chronicle poems (178 lines) | 1:1 | .56 |
| Judith (349 lines) | 0:4 | .57 |
| Battle of Maldon (325 lines) | 1:0 | .15 |
| Durham (21 lines) | 0:0 | |

§90. There is clearly a pattern here, and it is one that corresponds relatively well to Cable's presumed chronology of these poems. The poems assumed to be earliest show a comparatively low or even proportion of forms with parasiting to forms without it. Beowulf is by far the most conservative poem with respect to parasiting, with nonparasited forms outnumbering parasited more than four to one. In Genesis A and Daniel the numbers of conservative and innovative forms are about even. In poems presumed to date to the ninth century and later, the proportions are more than reversed, as forms without parasiting are rare. Thus there is just one such form in the entire Cynewulf canon, though the number of parasited forms is greater than in any poem in the test group. In Andreas the proportion is a little higher, at 4:22, while in the later-dated Boethian Meters and Judith there are no such forms at all, even though parasited forms are well attested. Exodus, generally dated between Beowulf and Cynewulf, also falls statistically into that range, with Andreas, at 1:7. The only exceptions to the pattern are the single instances in Brunanburh and Maldon, and the evidence of the latter is not

---

[39]Janet Duthie Collins is certainly right that the incidence of a set of forms in proportion to the incidence of a directly competing set is a more significant statistic than the incidence in proportion to the length, in verse lines, of the source text: see "A Technique for Dating Old English Poetic Texts," in The Eighth LACUS Forum, 1981, ed. Waldemar Gutwinski and Grace Jolly (Columbia, S.C.: Hornbeam Press, 1982), pp. 273–85, at 273.

particularly persuasive, since the scansion of line 130b as type 2E2a rather than 1D*4 depends upon the assumption that, as in *Beowulf*, type D* still demanded double alliteration, when in fact Bliss has shown that there are less subtle differences between the metrics of *Beowulf* and *Maldon* (chap. 16; see also n. 49 below). Moreover, the distribution of the evidence is remarkably even. Variation in the incidence of unambiguous instances is negligible: they occur approximately once in every 200 verses, except in *Maldon*, where there is just one instance in 650 verses. It is surprising how well the list supports the presumed chronology.

§91. The stems in *-l*, which were reserved above for separate treatment, may now be considered. They do not substantially contradict the pattern already established:[40]

> *Genesis A*
>    Without parasiting:
>       1564a  swæf symbelwerig (1D2)
>       2641b  Him symbelwerig (d2a)
>    With parasiting:
>       2192a  rodores tungel (2A1a)
> *Beowulf*
>    Without parasiting:
>       1782b  symbelwynne dreoh (3E2)
>       2431a  geaf me sinc ond symbel (2B1b)
>    With parasiting:
>       1010b  symbel þicgan (2A1a)
> *Exodus*
>    Without parasiting:
>       528a    wile meagollice (d1b)
>    With parasiting:
>       175b    cumbol lixton (2A1a)
>       391b    tempel gode (2A1b)[41]
> *Elene*
>    No unambiguous verses without parasiting.
>    With parasiting:
>       1009b  tempel dryhtnes (2A1a)
>       1092b  deogol bideð (2A1a)

---

[40]*Salomones templ* (*Daniel* 60b) is probably an example of nonparasiting (cf. *Salomanes seld* 711a), but biblical names are metrically unreliable: e.g., to *frumbearn Caines* (*Genesis A* 1056a) compare *on Caines* (1095a). Here and throughout, verses containing biblical names are excluded from consideration unless the name is positioned in the verse in such a way as to afford no doubt about the criterion being tested. The diphthong in *meagollice* (*Exodus* 528a) is long: see Holthausen's dictionary, s.v.; and Alistair Campbell's addenda to Bosworth and Toller's dictionary. In *Christ I* and *III* there are no unambiguous verses without parasiting, and two with it (206b, 1150b).

[41]The verse is unusual in having a short syllable before the short second lift: see Sievers, *Altgerm. Metrik*, §85.1. Amos scans this verse as type 2C2–, but see below, §205.

*Christ II*
No unambiguous verses without parasiting.
With parasiting:
 699a gæstlic tungol (2A1a)
 707b ac hi godes tempel (2C1b)
*Andreas*
Without parasiting:
 4b þonne cumbol hneotan (2C1b)
 621a swylce deogollice (d1b)
With parasiting:
 667b tempel dryhtnes (2A1a)
*Meters of Boethius*[42]
Without parasiting:
 24.23a eallisig tungl (3E2)
 28.6b ymb þas wlitegan tungl (3B1b)
 28.12b ðonne oðru tungl (3B1b)
 29.9b Hwæt, ða mæran tungl (3B1b)
 29.34a Habbað æðele tungol (3B1b)
 29.38b þæt ða wlitegan tungl (3B1b)
With parasiting:
 11.94b forð on sym*bel* (1A1a)
 19.14a þoncolmode (2A1)
*Battle of Brunanburh*
No unambiguous verses without parasiting.
With parasiting:
 14b mære tungol (2A1a)
*Judith*
No unambiguous verses without parasiting.
With parasiting:
 44b reste on symbel (1A*1a)
 145a searoðoncol mægð (3E2)
 172b þancolmode (2A1)

§92. On the whole these data confirm the pattern in the preceding list, showing a few forms without parasiting in the poems usually presumed to be early, and none in the Cynewulf canon or in *Judith*. *Andreas* again has a higher number of forms with parasiting than the Cynewulf poems. The one divergence from the pattern is the very large number of verses without parasiting in the Boethian *Meters*. But this is probably not as significant as it seems at first. All these monosyllabic forms are instances of a single word, *tungl*, and so the bare numbers conceal the fact that Alfred had a single monosyllabic word of this sort in his poetic vocabulary, in opposition to the ten different morphemes he consistently used with parasiting in all the other lines cited from the *Meters*. This is different from the practice of the poets of *Genesis A* and *Beowulf*,

[42]A probable example of parasiting is *þætte mænig tungul* (28.20a); but this might be classified as type a2: see §291.

suggesting, as John Pope remarks, that here it is something of an anti-quarianism.[43] That this is not an unstudied archaism on Alfred's part is further suggested by the observation that all but one of these verses with *tungl* are of the same metrical type. It was pointed out above (§37) that, given the assumption that nonparasited forms are preserved archaisms, the loss of such forms over the course of the period should have proceeded word by word through the lexicon, so that the actual variety of archaisms preserved in verse is more significant than the sheer numbers. The *Meters* thus confirm the prediction that the variety of archaic forms should be smaller in later verse than in earlier. These verses with monosyllabic *tungol* should not of course be disregarded, but it would probably be unwise to accord them much emphasis. Thus, to answer the question posed above about the treatment of -*l* after consonants other than *d*, *t*, *f*, and *s*, it seems likeliest that it normally forms a syllable in these circumstances, except in poetic archaisms, and the strongest counterevidence, these verses from the *Meters of Boethius*, does not bear much weight.

§93. The kinship terms in -*r*, also reserved above for separate treatment, may now be considered. These words usually are unambiguously dissyllabic, and in just five instances are they monosyllabic:[44]

> ussum fæder and meder (*Genesis A* 1575a: dat. sg.)
> modor oðerne (*Genesis A* 2610a: nom. sg.)
> dohtor Hroðgares (*Beowulf* 2020b: nom. sg.)
> broðor oðerne (*Beowulf* 2440a: nom. sg.)
> Sibyrhtes broðor (*Maldon* 282a: nom. sg.)

The first example has an etymologically nonsyllabic resonant, while the others do not. The last instance is inconclusive, since the metrical treatment of Germanic personal names in *Maldon* is peculiar: see below (§235), and compare *Swa hi Æþelgares bearn* (320a), and also *ær him Wig-elines bearn* (300a), if this is Casley's mistranscription of *Wig(h)elmes*, as most editors agree. And Bliss's evidence for monosyllabic scansion in the second and fourth instances is not entirely indisputable.[45] The evidence

---

[43]"On the Date of Composition of *Beowulf*," in Chase, pp. 187–95, at 192 and 193.

[44]There is another instance at *Christ III* 1499b (accusative plural, and so with an etymologically nonsyllabic *r*). One other instance is probable, *agene broðor* (*Meters of Boethius* 9.28b: acc. sg.), but inconclusive because of Sievers' (*Altgerm. Metrik*, §78.4) and Campbell's (§457) observation that by the time the *Meters* were composed geminates in medial syllables were simplified (*agene* = *āgenne*). Thus, the metrical status of the second syllable is in doubt. Cf. *opra* for *ōperra* at 24.36a and 26.90a.

[45]The assumption that type 1D*1 demands double alliteration (it appears only in the on-verse in *Beowulf*) depends upon the classification of verses like *Beowulf maþelode* (631a) as type 2A1a(ii). This seems improbable, not only because resolution is irrelevant to syllables under tertiary stress, but also because if in such verses the last two syllables are "resolved," these are the only instances in the poem in which resolution applies to the final syllables of a weak verb of the second class at the end of the verse—even

is too scant for firm conclusions, but in view of the large proportion of dissyllabic instances it seems likely that these words should be treated no differently from those that were originally dissyllabic, as Sarrazin advises (*Kädmon*, p. 27).

§94. It remains to consider why monosyllabic forms are common in poetry presumed to be early, and not in late poetry. The premise in other studies of metrical history (including Lehmann's) has been that the language of Old English verse, being conservative, preserves archaisms. What this means in this instance is that Old English verse preserves a metrical practice current before the rise of West Germanic parasiting. This need not be as remarkable a feat of conservation as it seems at first, since parasiting need not be thought of as a sound change of Proto-West-Germanic, but may represent an areal change affecting more than one dialect, such as linguists have found so much evidence for in this century.[46] This must be Luick's view, since he dates the change to the seventh century (§320): it must antedate smoothing, or the result would be Anglian *bēcen* rather than the attested *bēcun*; and it must follow the loss of unstressed *æ*, *i*, and *u*. There is further evidence for this view in the observation that -*l* after a long syllable is syllabic after *t*, *d*, *f*, and *s* in the other West Germanic languages, but not in Old English: this, then, appears to be an areal change.

---

though such verbs appear at the end of the verse more than a hundred times. The distinction is an important one: see below, Chap. 7, esp. §249. Moreover, as pointed out above (§66 and n. 97), the reason for the restriction of most verses of type D to the on-verse is that most contain compounds with secondary stress, and under Kendall's principle that these must alliterate, they are barred from the second foot in the off-verse. Under this principle we should expect type 1D*1 to behave like the unexpanded type—i.e., it should be permitted in the off-verse. But even if this were not so, there is sufficient explanation for the appearance of verses like *Beowulf maþelode* in the off-verse, considering their formulaic nature. Bliss himself excuses some formulaic exceptions in *Maldon* to the rule that types 1A and 1A* in the on-verse must have double alliteration, saying that "it would be unreasonable to restrict the useful verb *gemælde* to proper nouns beginning with *M-*" (§117); and elsewhere he excuses the *maþelode* formula itself on the same grounds, in order to classify *weard maþelode* (*Beowulf* 286a) as (oddly) type 1D3—see his *Introduction to Old English Metre* (Oxford: Blackwell, 1962), p. 23. The excuse is particularly appropriate in regard to the *maþelode* formula, since all but one of the twenty-six examples of Bliss's type 2A1a(ii) are instances of this formula, the one exception being also the only example in the off-verse, excluded above (n. 29). Compare also the metrical liberties taken with other formulas, for example *ageaf andsware*, which almost always violates Kuhn's first law. O. D. Macrae-Gibson also argues that type 2A1a(ii) should be abolished: see "The Metrical Entities of Old English," *NM* 87 (1986), 59–91, at 63. Yet in the end there is still room for doubt about this objection to the classification of verses like *brōðor ōðerne* as type 1D1, because if verses like *Beowulf maþelode* are reclassified as type 1D*1, still single alliteration is confined to these formulaic instances (provided, once again, that the single instance in the off-verse is excluded).

[46]For a general discussion see T. Bynon's book (as above, n. 74 to the Introduction), pp. 193–95 and 244–53.

§95. The alternative view espoused by Luick, Campbell, and Amos, and to a lesser extent by Karl Brunner, is that monosyllabic forms with heavy root syllables arose by analogy to inflected forms: for example, *wǣpen* by analogy to gen. *wǣpnes* was reformed to *wǣpn*.[47] Initially this does not seem improbable, as Old English is a language particularly prone to paradigm regularization.[48] Under this hypothesis we should expect that nonparasited forms would be particularly frequent in verse known to be late; yet the data above show that forms without parasiting are almost entirely absent from verifiably late poetry. And the direction of the change in the history of the language tells against the assumption, since it was the syllabic resonants that were generalized in English, not the nonsyllabic ones. The direction of change in the prehistory of the language also raises difficulties, since nonparasited forms did exist in early West Germanic, as proved by their existence in Norse, and probably Gothic; and parasited forms replaced them in West Germanic, as the comparative evidence shows. Most significantly, the suggestion is dubitable because of the improbability of analogically creating forms that are difficult to pronounce (as discussed below). But the issue may be resolved by examining originally dissyllabic stems like *ēþel*. These can only have monosyllabic uninflected forms by analogy, and so an incidence of monosyllabicity in these words comparable to that in the originally monosyllabic stems would prove that nonparasiting in Old English verse is entirely analogical. The evidence for monosyllabicity is as follows:

*Genesis A*[49]
    1197b   ealdordom ahof (2E2a)
    1634b   eðelðrym onhof (2E2a)
    1875a   hie ellenrofe (d2a)

---

[47]Luick, §§318–21; Campbell, §363; Amos, p. 70; Brunner, §152. B. R. Hutcheson (pp. 416ff.; as above, n. 2), points out that unambiguous examples of nonparasiting are commoner in compounds than in simplices. He argues on this evidence that nonparasited forms arose in compounds, and spread to simplices by analogy. But his chief motive for rejecting the assumption of forms like *wuldrz is untenable (see above, §77 and n. 2). Moreover, the higher incidence of nonparasiting in compounds is very likely due in part to the high proportion of ambiguous examples in simplices: a form without parasiting is generally less capable of appearing ambiguous as the first element of a compound than as a simplex. It may well also be true that the perceived poetic nature of compounds was seen to call for specifically poetic, i.e. nonparasited, treatment of the relevant forms: cf. the observations below (§348) about the higher incidence of Anglian back mutation in compounds. Hutcheson's analysis also leads him to the conclusion that parasiting may be correlated to date of composition.

[48]See "Paradigm Regularization and the Verschärfung," to appear in *Essays in Linguistics in Honor of Oswald Szemerényi*, ed. Bela Brogyanyi and Reiner Lipp.

[49]As remarked above, "abnormal metrical types consequential on [language] change could be and were regarded as admissible licence and imitated later" (Girvan, p. 15; see also p. 18). Thus, in *Genesis A* the analogical process under consideration here is extended beyond the realm of words ending in resonants to create a new metrical type:

*Daniel*[50]
   54a     herige hæðencyninga (1D*2)
*Beowulf*[51]
   913a    (eþel) Scyldinga (1D1)
   998b    irenbendum fæst (3E2)
   1675a   þeoden Scyldinga (1D1)
   1871a   þeoden Scyldinga (1D1)
   1918a   oncerbendum fæst (3E2)
   2387b   Ongenðioes bearn (3E1)
   2894a   morgenlongne dæg (3E2)
*Andreas*[52]
   1688a   deofulgild todraf (2E2a)

§96. Clearly analogy does affect originally dissyllabic stems. Yet even though this is a fairly generous list, and some of these verses ought perhaps to be excluded,[53] still the incidence of monosyllabism is so small

---

cf. *earfoðsiða bot* (1476a) and *yrfestole weold* (1629b). This license seems to be an idiosyncrasy of the *Genesis A* poet: superficially similar verses like *middangeardes weard* (*Daniel* 596a; cf. Sievers, *Altgerm. Metrik*, §85.7) have been explained otherwise above (n. 14). So, also, problematic verses with *missenlice* (e.g. *manige missenlice* at *Andreas* 583a) seem to require the substitution of *mislice* (Sievers, *Altgerm. Metrik*, §85, n. 8), as in *þætte mislice* (*Meters* 31.2a; see also *Guthlac B* 898a, *Juliana* 406a, and similar). Verses like *earfoðsiða bot* suggest that the poet of *Genesis A* must have used a syllabic resonant in at least some verses like *wuldorfæstan wic* (27a), since this presumably is the model for the new metrical type. This illustrates the point that the determination of parasiting is not a measure of the poet's pronunciation, but of his knowledge of archaic metrical rules, as explained below. The verse *þæs folces ealdor* (*Maldon* 202b) is not an unambiguous example of analogical influence, since anacrusis in this poem is irregular (see Amos, pp. 75–76, n. 15, in reference to John C. Pope's findings). In addition it may be noted that *mines eþelrices* (*Christ III* 1461a) is probably not an instance: Bliss scans the preceding verse as hypermetric, and in fact if *mines* were appended to that verse it would render a type a(2A), by far the commonest type of hypermetric verse in Old English poetry, with two hundred instances in the off-verse.

[50]At *Daniel* 621a, *wildeora westen* is ambiguous because *wildeora* probably stands for *wildra*: cf. *wildra wærgenga* (662a), in comparison to metrically defective *þe he mid wilddeorum ateah* (649b) and *butan wildeora þeaw* (571b), where *wildrum/wildra* would again mend the meter. The verse *heahheort and hæþen* (539a) is admittedly problematic, but there is no need to assume monosyllabic *hæðen*: the type is paralleled by *gealorand to guþe* (*Beowulf* 438a; cf. also 608a, 1698a).

[51]Though verse 1918a is emended, the emendation can hardly be doubted. On verses 414a and 2032b see Bliss, §§46–47 and 64, respectively, and Pope, pp. xxx and xxxi.

[52]Aside from its being like *eþel Scyldinga* and *Beowulf maþelode* (see the next note and n. 45 above), *þeoden leofesta* (*Andreas* 288a) is ambiguous because *leofesta* may perhaps stand for a syncopated form: cf. *Genesis A* 1055a and 1063a, and see Luick, §306, n. 2. In *geomorgidd wrecen* (1548a) there is no good reason the first word must be considered a compound, and dividing it in fact improves the alliteration. (Although the comparative evidence is inconclusive, *geōmor* must have been dissyllabic in Proto-Germanic. Otherwise *-mr-* would have given *-mbr-*.)

[53]The one example in *Daniel* is dubitable because *-cyning-* is not normally resolved in this position in this poem or others presumed to antedate Cynewulf (see below,

that it seems most improbable that analogy can account for all the instances of monosyllabism in the originally monosyllabic stems listed in §88 above. This becomes particularly clear when one takes into account the large number of relevant words (see the partial listing above, §83), and more especially the enormous incidence of words like *ellen*, *ēþel*, *dēofol*, and *þēoden*, and of others that are never monosyllabic, such as *dryhten* and *engel*. It is not credible that these should be consistently dissyllabic by mere accident, while etymologically monosyllabic stems like *wuldor*- and *wundor*- are so frequently monosyllabic in verse. And, after all, although doubtless the chief analogical influence on the rise of monosyllabism in the above instances was reduction of paradigm allomorphy, the existence of the other type may also be assumed to have been a contributing analogical influence. For instance, since the stem of gen. *wuldres* can be monosyllabic *wuldr* in uninflected forms and in compounds, the stem of *ēþles* may also conform to this pattern. This helps to explain why *ēþel* is monosyllabic less frequently than *wuldr* (one or two instances versus ten). Thus it appears that monosyllabicity in forms like *wuldr* is indeed an archaism rather than an analogical innovation, and in this respect Old English metrical practice antedates West Germanic parasiting.

§97. Old English orthography supports this conclusion. Although words like *sūsl* and *māþm* are often written *susel* and *maþþum*, they are never to be scanned this way. There is no very convincing way to account for this fact but to assume that the language of Old English poetry is conservative, and preserves pronunciations that either had passed out of use or were in the process of changing at the time the extant manuscripts were written. Regardless of when the change took place, the result was that English acquired the morpheme structure constraint characteristic of the language to this day, and characteristic of all the West Germanic languages, though not characteristic of the other early Germanic languages, that monosyllabicity is for the most part disallowed when two segments are separated by a segment of smaller aperture, on a "strength" scale like those employed in Natural Generative Phonology.[54] That is, most native speakers of modern West Germanic languages cannot pronounce *māþm* as a single syllable, because *þ* is "stronger" on an aperture scale than *ā* and *m*. *Wyrm*, on the other hand, presents no difficulties, because nasals are stronger than liquids. If this constraint

---

Chap. 8). One suspects that *hæðencyninga* has been altered from *hæðenra*. Whether the three verses in *Beowulf* of type 1D1 (913a, 1675a, and 1871a; perhaps also 2032b) should be included here is dubitable: see n. 45 above. If they are valid, two of these contain the only examples of monosyllabic *þēoden* in Old English verse.

[54]For an example see Joan B. Hooper, *An Introduction to Natural Generative Phonology* (New York: Academic Press, 1976), p. 206. For more recent studies see Theo Vennemann, *Preference Laws for Syllable Structure and the Explanation of Sound Change* (Berlin: Mouton de Gruyter, 1988), esp. pp. 8–9; and Robert W. Murray, *Phonological Strength and Early Germanic Syllable Structure* (Munich: Fink, 1988).

developed in the course of the Old English period, as the orthographic
evidence suggests (though earlier for *r* and *n* than for *l* and *m*, in most
environments), then this explains why the analogical process that created
monosyllabic *ēþel* and the like should have applied only in poetry
presumed to be early. Indeed, the last group of verses cited conforms to
the pattern supporting the presumed chronology, since *ēþel* and the like
are monosyllabic only in supposedly early poems (with *Andreas* on the
borderline).

§98. There is a further piece of evidence for this analysis. Even if *ēþel*
could not be pronounced as a monosyllable by the time of Cynewulf, still
there should have been no obstacle to forming an analogical monosyllabic
form of originally dissyllabic *sāwul*, since liquids are stronger than glides.
The facts about *sāwul* were withheld above, though the word belongs with
the *ēþel* group. The orthographic evidence is that while the spelling *eþel*
appears perhaps two hundred times in Old English texts, *eþl* occurs just
once. Spellings like *sawl* and *saul*, however, are considerably commoner
than *sawel*, *sawol*, and the like (see the *Microfiche Concordance*). As for
the metrical evidence, the only unambiguously monosyllabic scansions are
in the verifiably late *Meters of Boethius*: *þæt sio sawl wære* (20.182b) and
*Swa dēð monnes saul* (20.210b).[55] Thus, *sāwul* confirms what phonology
predicts if the language of Old English verse is conservative, and the
presumed chronology more or less correct.

---

[55]Campbell (§§345, in reliance on Luick) argues that *sāwl* shows loss of medial *a* in
\**saiwalō*, followed by loss of the inflection. If Luick and Campbell were right it would
be extraordinary that the word is consistently dissyllabic (or ambiguous) in presumably
early verse: e.g., in *Beowulf*, relevant forms of the morpheme are metrically unambiguous in four instances (1406b, 2693a, 2820a, 3033b), in all of which they are
dissyllabic. Since there are in *Beowulf* just five unambiguous verses with parasiting, while
there are twenty-two without it (see the first list above), it is not credible that *sāwul*,
without parasiting in four out of four instances, should have been reduced to a
monosyllable early. More important, etymologically nonsyllabic *l* is never parasited
metrically in the test group of poems, and so *sāwul* simply cannot have been rendered
monosyllabic at an early date. And orthographic evidence for the chronology of the
change is the reverse of Campbell's position, at least in the Anglian dialects, since the
word is written almost exclusively *sawul* in VP, while there are several instances of *saul*
in late Northumbrian texts, beside more usual *sauel*. And so, as the metrical evidence
indicates, the creation of nom. *sāwl* is likely no earlier than the ninth century. This also
explains why forms with a medial vowel appear in apparently early texts, e.g. *sowhula*
on the Bewcastle Column. The syncope of medial vowels had of course occurred long
before this, and so if the nominative form were monosyllabic at this time, there would
have been no model for the analogical restoration of the medial vowel. Nor can
monosyllabic *sāwl* be regarded as a dialect feature rather than a chronological indicator,
in view of the Northumbrian evidence cited above.

# II

# CONTRACTION

## A. Varieties of Contraction
## and the Conclusions of Prior Studies

§99. The most trusted evidence of metrical change in Old English verse has always been the occurrence of vowel contraction. Words that were originally dissyllabic but became monosyllabic through contraction must frequently be scanned as dissyllables in verse, as in *nēan bīdan* (*Beowulf* 528b), where *nēan* derives from *\*nēahan*. Several studies of the phenomenon start from the hypothesis that since dissyllabicity in such words is an archaism, a higher proportion of dissyllabic scansions ought to be found in early verse than in late.[1]

§100. Contraction has been said to have four sources, the commonest of which is the loss of intervocalic *h*, as with *nēan*. Another source is the loss of *w*, which occurred already in West Germanic before *u*, and perhaps that early also before *i*, as in *clēa* < *\*klawu* < *\*klawō*, and *strēd* (at *Beowulf* 2436b), from *\*strawid*. Also in West Germanic, *j* was lost in the sequence *\*-iju-*, as in OE *frēond* < *\*frijund-*; and the process was repeated later, when WGmc. *ij* combined with any back vowel in Old English to give a diphthong, as in WS *sīe* 'be'. Finally, a sequence of two vowels with no intervening consonant contracted in Old English, as in *gān*, from *\*gā-an*. The usual source of such bivocalic sequences was the Germanic thematization of Proto-Indo-European athematic verbs, an analogical development; but they could also occur in borrowings, such as OE *drȳ*, from Celtic *drui*. As in all but one of the previous studies, in the data below the four different types of contraction will be treated separately, starting with loss of *h*. The advisability of this procedure will become apparent in the following discussion.

§101. As with parasiting, there is considerable divergence in the results of studies of contraction. There are various reasons for these discrepancies, including misunderstandings and misapplications of Sievers' and Bliss's systems of scansion, as well as incompleteness of data. A problem of a more theoretical sort is that assumptions about vowel quantities under contraction differ in these studies. A few scholars assume that

---

[1]See the dating studies by Richter, Sarrazin, and Seiffert; also Trautmann, *Kynewulf*, pp. 23–42 and 120–21; and Morsbach, pp. 262–68.

when two syllables are decontracted, the first must be long. Thus, for example, Richter supposes that verses like *geseon mihte* (*Beowulf* 961b) cannot be uncontracted, and Amos scans verses like *fea þingian* (*Beowulf* 156b) as either type 1D1 (with contraction) or 2A1a (without contraction, i.e. like *Hroðgar maþelode* 925a rather than *sele fælsode* 2352b).[2] Bliss himself proceeds under the same assumption, scanning, for instance, verses like *swa hy næfre man lyhð* (*Beowulf* 1048b) as type 2C1d rather than 2C2d—that is, like *swa he hyra ma wolde* (1055b) rather than *þæt he hæfde mod micel* (1167a). The usual assumption, however, is that etymologically short syllables should be counted as short when decontracted. So for example in *fea þingian* the first word is dative singular of *feoh*, and derives from *\*feohæ*, with a short diphthong resulting from breaking. Such words are to be distinguished from those with originally long first syllables, such as *hēan* in *hean huses* (116a), which derives from *\*hēahan*. This is the standard position of current handbooks of Old English phonology. The metrical distinction is confirmed by the observation that words like *fēa* with a short first syllable before contraction are never found in a metrical position that requires an uncontracted form with a long first syllable, such as *hēan* occupies here—for instance, there are no verses of the sort *\*fēa hlēotan* or *\*sēon mihte* (cf. *geseon meahte* at *Beowulf* 1078b, and similar). Bliss does recognize the standard position, since he mentions the possibility of expanding *sēon* to *\*se(o)han* rather than *\*sēoan* (§53), though he consistently chooses the latter type. His assumption then seems to be that when *h* was lost intervocalically, contraction was not immediate, and in compensation for the lost consonant the preceding diphthong was lengthened, just as loss of *h* in *\*mearhes* produced *mēares*. Linguistically Bliss's position must be regarded as improbable, since the phonological motivation for compensatory lengthening upon loss of *h* is the preservation of syllable quantities. If *h* were lost in *mearhes* without compensatory lengthening, the first syllable would be shortened, changing the word's metrical value and creating a paradigm with irregular alternations in the quantity of the root syllable. There is no motivation for such compensatory lengthening in words like *\*feohæ* and *\*seohan*. Moreover, it seems unlikely that the archaic language of verse should reflect this relatively brief supposed intermediate stage *\*sēoan* rather than the older metrical value *\*seohan*: to assume this is to suppose that poems like *Beowulf*, which are metrically resistant to a change such

---

[2]Holthausen's position is by and large the standard one. Richter (p. 14) notes that in Holthausen's edition of *Beowulf*, *sēon* is restored to *sē[h]on* in verses like *metodsceaft seon* (1180a). In fact there is no macron in Holthausen's text, though he carefully distinguishes long and short vowels throughout: see *Beowulf nebst dem Finnsburg-Bruchstück*, 2 vols. (Heidelberg: Winter, 1905–6). Holthausen does decontract *slēa* to *slāe*, perhaps following the same line of reasoning offered below in regard to the Northumbrian treatment of this verb (§126); but there it is also demonstrated that this is a later development in Northumbrian, irreconcilable with other scansions in *Beowulf*.

as contraction itself, are strangely unresistant to this brief-lived compensatory lengthening. But the point does not need further corroboration, since the absence of verses like *fēa hlēotan* is sufficient evidence that forms like *sēoan* do not need to be reckoned with. There is no metrical evidence for such forms, while there is abundant evidence for *seohan*.

§102. The guide to contraction provided by Campbell (§§234–39) is particularly useful because he distinguishes quantities in uncontracted forms, though certain of his views must be modified or interpreted with caution. For example, although uninflected forms like *nēar* may show contraction, inflected ones like Anglian *hēra* 'higher' (from *hēhir-*, §237.1) cannot, because the loss of *i* in open medial syllables after a long syllable antedates the loss of intervocalic *h* and contraction. On the other hand, the superlative may show contraction, since the suffix *-ist-* is a closed syllable (but cf. below, n. 3). The same reasoning applies to forms like *hēane* (accusative singular of *hēah*) and *fāra* (genitive plural of *fāh*). Campbell is certainly right that Northumbrian *betuīen* must derive from *betwīhen* (§237.3), and *bitwīon* from *bitwīhun* (§238.2), but it must be understood that the vowel before *n* is due to West Germanic parasiting, and does not extend to inflected *bitwīonum*. Moreover, since parasiting is a dating criterion, apparently contracted forms like *bitwīon* may actually show nonparasiting, and so they are useless as a test of contraction.

## B.  Loss of Intervocalic *h*

§103. The data for the commonest type of contraction are presented in the following list. Clearly unstressed examples, for instance *Geseoð þæt me of bryde* (*Genesis A* 2186a), are excluded, since they are all inconclusive. The relevant verse type according to Bliss's system is given after each verse.

> *Cædmon's Hymn* (657–80)
>    One relevant form: 8b (ambiguous: 2A1a[i] both ways).
> *Bede's Death Song* (735)
>    No relevant forms.
> *Leiden Riddle* (8th c.)
>    No relevant forms.
> *Genesis A* (8th c.)[3]
>    Uncontracted forms:
>    8b　　Heagum þrymmum (2A1a)
>    62a　　faum folmum (2A1a)

---

[3]Verse 1513a must show contraction because, as pointed out in Chap. 1, under Bliss's system (and others) "a short syllable can only replace a long syllable when it is preceded by a single long syllable" (§54, n. 3). The same is true of *Beowulf* 3159b and the *Meters of Boethius* 23.2b. The verse *Fleonde wæron* (2080b) must show contraction

904b    fagum wyrme (2A1a)
953b    arna ofteon (1A*1a[i])
1017b    forþon heo þe hroðra oftihð (a1d[1A*1a])
1047a    feorran oððe nean (1A*1b)
1103b    þonne ic forð scio (2C2c)
1267a    and on deað slean (2C2b)
1387b    hea beorgas (2A1a)
1401b    on þa hean lyft (3B1b)
1743b    metodsceaft seon (2A3b)
1759b    ealle onfoð (1A*1a[i])
1789a    wæstmum gewlo (1a*1a[i])
2040a    wæpna onfon (1A*1a[i])
2084b    wiðertrod seon (2A3b)
2091b    oðle nior (2A1a)
2260a    mennen ateon (1A*1a[i])
2332b    He onfon sceal (3B1b)
2486a    faum folmum (2A1a)

under Bliss's system because this must belong to type 2A1a(i) rather than (iii): the latter requires resolution of the first thesis (§§4 and 38), while *fléonde* derives from a form with a long root diphthong before contraction. The same is true of *Beowulf* 1203b, 2511a and *Judith* 73a; it is also true, by extension, of *Judith* 4a and 94b. The verse *hehste wið þam herge* (51a) cannot be scanned as type 1A*1a(ii) because Bliss requires resolution in the first thesis of this type; and at any rate Bliss's assumption of that type is based on a single verse in *Beowulf* (534a), a verse that is shown below to have a different explanation (§240). But these verses still ought to be regarded as ambiguous because verses like *Se æresta wæs* (1055a), *se yldesta wæs* (1134a), and others suggest syncope in the superlative suffix, as in WS *wiersta, læsta*, etc.: see Luick, §306, n. 2, with the discussion below, §240. As remarked above (p. 84, n. 40), verses with biblical names must be disregarded, and this applies to *Loth onfon* (1938b). Amos includes in her *Genesis A* data verses 911b and 2260b, but unlike second-class weak verbs like *sméaþ* 'thinks', the verbs *féoð* 'hates' and *fréoð* 'loves' do not derive from forms with medial *h*: they have bare stems in *-ī, to which the class sign *-ō- was added (see Campbell, §761.4–5). It was mentioned above (§18) that for *weorcþeos* at 2721a the manuscript reads *weorc feos*. But the manuscript reading is nonsensical (and the scribal tampering readily explained by the context): *feos* could only be genitive, and if *s* is altered from *h* (see the apparatus in the ASPR edition) the form is not contracted, anyway. It should also be pointed out here that one of the most controversial aspects of Bliss's system is his disregard of the distinction between tertiary and no stress. The issue is examined in detail below, in Chapter 7, where it is demonstrated that verses like *ic me mid Hruntinge* (*Beowulf* 1490b) must contain four metrical positions, and therefore ictus must be assumed at the tertiary level, regardless of whether or not there was phonological stress at this level. Consequently, Bliss's theory of the existence of three-position verses of type 2E1—perhaps the most widely rejected aspect of his system of scansion—must be disallowed. As a result, several verses that Bliss would classify as type 2E1 are disambiguated as showing noncontraction. These are at *Genesis A* 953b, 1017b, 1047a, 1759b, 1789a, 2040a, 2260a, 2669b, 2919b; *Daniel* 111b, and perhaps 561b (on both of which see n. 5 below); *Beowulf* 839b; *Exodus* 241b; perhaps *Elene* 674a; and *Andreas* 782a. The distribution of these verses is itself evidence for the correctness of the assumption of tertiary stress, since in a general way it mirrors the facts demonstrable from the larger list: *Genesis A* has many such forms, while examples are few in the middle range, and entirely missing from late verse such as the *Meters of Boethius*.

2508b   and þas folc slean (2C2b)
2519a   Ic wat hea burh (3B1b)
2669b   egesan geðread (1A*1a[i])[4]
2762b   hæfde wordbeot (d3b)
2855a   hrincg þæs hean landes (1A1a[2A1a])
2878b   hea dune (2A1a)
2899b   hean landes (2A1a)
2919b   selfa onfon (1A*1a[i])
Contracted forms:
1513a   mid gefean fryðo (2C2b)
1572b   mid hrægle wryon (3B1a[i])
1865b   egesum geþreadne (1A*1a[i])
2080b   Fleonde wæron (2A1a).
Ambiguous forms (21): 51a (see p. 95, n. 3), 57b
    (2C1b both ways), 70a (1A1a[i] both ways), 225b
    (1A*1a[i] or 1A1a[i]), 232a (1D1 both ways),
    867a (3B*1a or 2B1a), 875b (2C1b both ways),
    876b (3B1a[i] or 2C2a), 877a (2C1a both ways),
    1400a (d1b or a1b), 1489a (3B1b or 2C2b),
    1523b (a1d[3E*1] both ways), 1821b (3B1a[i] or
    2C2a: see n. 5 below), 1912a (1A*1c or 1A1c),
    2122a (3B1b both ways), 2171b (1A*1a[i] or
    1A1a[i]), 2264b (3B*1b or 2B1b), 2458a (3B1b
    or 2C2b), 2473a (1A*1a[i] or 1A1a[i]), 2659a
    (1D3 both ways), 2660a (1A1b[i] both ways).
Daniel (8th c.)[5]
Uncontracted forms:
235b   sende him of hean rodore (a1d[2A1a])
410b   wið þam nehstum (d1b)

---

[4]H. M. Flasdieck derives the verb *þreagan* from *\*þrauhōjan*, and this seems now to be the consensus: see Flasdieck's "Untersuchungen über die germanischen schwachen Verben III. Klasse (unter besonderer Berücksichtigung des Altenglischen)," *Anglia* 59 (1935), 1–192 at 40; and cf. Campbell, §235.2, and Brunner, §415d. This position is debatable because there is no *h* in closely related forms, and Flasdieck must go as far afield as OIcel. *þrúga* (presumably with voicing under Verner's law) to find evidence of a form with *h*. Still, otherwise it would be difficult to account for the fact that *þreagan* resembles *smēagan* rather than *þrōwigean*. There is an exact cognate in OSax. *githrōon*, but this furnishes no help, since intervocalic *h* is also lost in that language. This verse in *Genesis A* constitutes evidence for Flasdieck's position, since *geðrēad* here would give a metrically peculiar type if it were derived from *\*giþrawōd-*. Disregarding forms of this verb would not alter the support of the statistics for the presumed chronology. Note that in the infinitive *þrēagan* (as at *Juliana* 142b) the *g* reflects Gmc. *j*.

[5]Amos' classification of verse 410b as either type d1b or a1b must not be allowed, since the latter type is not permitted in the off-verse. Verse 166b is unambiguous because Bliss finds no anacrusis with type 1A*1a in the off-verse in *Beowulf*, and there do not appear to be any exceptions in the remainder of the test group before basic changes in anacrusis that take place in the tenth century (see Chap. 10 below). It is best not to include *wundrum geteod* (111b) among the unambiguously uncontracted verses, since it must have a short second lift: the verb (to be distinguished from strong *tēon* 'draw') is like *smēagan*, but with a short root. The verse *to þære heahbyrig* (698b) is not

511b    on weg fleon (2C1a)
665b    and þa hean burh (3B1b)
670b    hea rice (2A1a)
721b    in þæt hea seld (3B1b)
Contracted forms:
166b    onfon ne meahte (1A1a[i])
382b    and hea beorgas (2C1a)
Ambiguous forms (14): 38b (3B1c[i] or 2C2c), 54b
(3B1c[i] or 2C2c), 111b (see n. 5), 198b (3B1c[i]
or 2C2c), 204b (a1d[1A1a] both ways), 206b
(3B1c[i] or 2C2c), 208b (2A1a[i] both ways),
216b (2C1d both ways), 235a (1A*1b[1A1a] both
ways), 264b (a1c[2A1a] both ways), 308b (2C1d
both ways), 415a (1A1a[i] both ways), 561b (see
n. 5), 730b (3B1b both ways, or 2C2b).
*Beowulf* (8th-9th c.)[6]
Uncontracted forms:
25b    man geþeon (1A1a)
116a    hean huses (2A1a)

---

relevant, since loss of the connecting vowel antedates loss of *h* when the first element of a compound is an *a*-stem (Luick, §§249, 303). In these poems there are no relevant compounds of the sort that ought to have preserved the connecting vowel (Luick, §305), and no first elements of compounds that require decontraction. Still, this verse is exceptional, being the only instance of unambiguously dissyllabic *byrig* in Old English verse, though the word is etymologically monosyllabic (see Campbell, §§361, 365), and is never elsewhere metrically dissyllabic, though it is found in verse often (more than fifty times). Moreover, the change of *byrg* to *byrig* begins only in the ninth century, and is restricted perhaps entirely to West Saxon (Luick, §348; it also does not affect cases without a final palatal consonant, such as the accusative singular: cf. 665b). And so perhaps more likely the verse is a scribal corruption of *to þære hean byrig*, a formula that appears twice elsewhere in *Daniel* (at 38b and 54b; so also *in þisse hean byrig* at 206b, and *and hea byrig* at *Genesis A* 1821b), with an uncontracted scansion like the metrical pattern of *in þære widan byrig* (672b), *on þæs þeodnes byrig* (188b), etc. Scribal confusion of *n* and *h* would not be unusual. Thus, the probability of monosyllabic scansion of *hea(n)* at *Daniel* 38b, 54b, and 206b (also *Genesis A* 1821b) is rather low. The strength of the improbability of dissyllabic *byrig* in these instances is such that these verses ought to be regarded as examples of noncontraction, but because this conclusion requires an emendation at 698b, and because there is sufficient evidence for noncontraction in *Daniel* without these examples, they may be listed among the ambiguous verses without detriment to the overall conclusions about contraction. (Amos is inconsistent in respect to these instances, regarding the verse in *Genesis* as showing noncontraction, and those in *Daniel* as ambiguous.) As for *sæde eft onfon* (561b), this must be counted among the ambiguous verses because neither 1A*1b (type 2E1b having been eliminated: see n. 3 above) nor 1D*4 (or 1D4 with elision) is probable. The former scansion offends against Kuhn's first law, but if *eft* is stressed, the verse is of an exceedingly rare type, since type D* is never found in the off-verse in *Beowulf* (nor is 1D4), and rarely in other poems: see below, p. 142, n. 5. By comparison, type D* appears in the on-verse 146 times in *Beowulf* alone, according to Bliss.

[6]There may be nonparasiting in *wolde on heolster fleon* (755b); so also in 920a and 1365b. Although both Klaeber and Dobbie emend the verse, the manuscript reading *hea healle* (1926a) is not impossible, and Amos is perhaps right to retain it. But her

528b    nean bidan (2A1a)
681b    þæt he me ongean slea (2C2d)
820a    feorhseoc fleon (2A3a)
839b    feorran ond nean (1A*1a[i])
1036b   on flet teon (2C1a)
1048b   swa hy næfre man lyhð (2C2d)
1180a   metodsceaft seon (2A3b)
1264b   mandream fleon (2A3a)
1275b   deaþwic seon (2A3b)
1926a   hea healle (manuscript, 2A1a: see n. 6)
2317a   nearofages nið (3E2)
2736a   egesan ðeon (2A1a)
3097b   beorh þone hean (1A1b)
Contracted forms:
910b    geþeon scolde (2C1a)
911a    fæderæþelum onfon (3E*2)
1140b   þurhteon mihte (2C1a)
1307b   on hreon mode (2C1a)
1504b   ðurhfon ne mihte (1A1a)
1755b   fehð oþer to (3E2)
2581b   on hreoum mode (2C1a)
3104b   neon sceawiað (1D1)
3159b   on tyn dagum (2C2a)
Ambiguous forms (49): 43b (2A1a[i] both ways),
        80a (2B2a both ways), 84b (2A1 both ways),
        156b (1D1 both ways), 387a (1D6 both ways),
        396b (2E2a both ways: see §210 below), 439a
        (1A*1a[i] or 1A1a[i]), 470b (1D1 both ways),
        480a (d1c both ways), 511b (2C1a both ways),
        523b (2E2a both ways), 536a (d1b both ways),

---

classification of *þæt he me ongean slea* (681b) as type a2d must not be allowed, since the type does not occur in the off-verse; and at any rate the verse is not light. Similarly, *neon sceawiað* (3104b) must belong to type 1D1 because 1D*1 does not appear in the off-verse (but cf. p. 86, n. 45), and *fehð oþer to* (1755b) cannot belong to type 1D*5 because this type is also disallowed in the off-verse. Verse 1504b is included among the contracted verses because, once again, type 1A*1a does not appear in *Beowulf* with anacrusis in the off-verse (see the preceding note). Because type 2E1a has been excluded (see above, n. 3), *eam his nefan* (881a) must be considered ambiguous, and somewhat anomalous. It perhaps shows unusual tertiary stress on the second, uncontracted syllable of *eam*, as with *Beowulf geþah* (1024b), *dreamleas gebad* (1720b), and sixteen other verses in *Beowulf* listed below (§210); or perhaps there is unusual stress on *his* (not required by Kuhn's laws: cf., e.g., *Genesis A* 57a); or perhaps it simply has an anomalous short second lift, as with *Hreðel cyning* (2430b) and eight others in *Beowulf* listed by Sievers ("Rhythmik," p. 231). Actually, the verse does not fit conveniently into this last group, since it would be the only such verse that is not of type 2A; but since an anomaly is involved regardless, it is safer not to classify the verse as unambiguously noncontracted. Verses containing *gebēotedon* (480a, 536a), from *gi-bi-hāt-*, are to be regarded as ambiguous because the rule that a short (half-)lift must not follow a resolved lift does not apply to syllables at the level of tertiary ictus: cf. *gold glitinian* (2758a) and *hord openian* (3056b), and see below, §249.

548b (1A*1b or 1A1b[i]), 562b (2C1a both ways), 571b (2C1a both ways), 648b (1A1a[i] both ways), 713b (1A1a[i] or 2B1a), 745b (3E*2 or 2E2a), 755b (2C1c or 3B1c[i]), 764a (1A2a[ii] or 1A*2a[ii]), 881a (see n. 6), 919b (1A1a[i] or 2B1a), 920a (3E2 both ways, or 2A3b), 961b (2C1a both ways), 1003a (d1b or a1b), 1016b (1A1a[i] or 2B1a), 1078b (2C1a both ways), 1126b (2E2a both ways; see above, n. 3), 1174a (1A*1a[i] or 1A1a[i]), 1203b (2A1a[i]; see n. 3), 1365b (3E2 both ways, or 2A3b), 1380b (1D1 both ways), 1452b (2A1a[i] both ways), 1485a (1D2 both ways), 1628b (2C1a both ways), 1875b (2C1a both ways), 1984b (1A1a[i] or 2B1a), 1998b (2C1a both ways), 2041b (2B1b both ways), 2076a (d1b or a1b), 2295b (1A*1a[i] both ways), 2317b (1A*1a[i] or 1A1a[i]), 2455a (1D3 both ways), 2510b (3E2 both ways), 2511a (2A1a[i]; see n. 3), 2525a (1D*5 or 1D5), 2526b (2B1b both ways), 2740b (2C1a both ways), 3102a (1A1a[i] both ways).

*Exodus* (8th-9th c.)

Uncontracted forms:

    241b   hilde onþeon (1A*1a[i])

    308b   læste near (2A1a)

Contracted forms:

    220a   sweot sande near (1D5)

    530b   He us ma onlyhð (2B1b)

Ambiguous forms (4): 83b (2C1a both ways), 207a (1A1a[i] both ways), 232a (2E2a both ways), 394a (1A*1a[i] or 1A1a[i]).

*Elene* (9th c.)[7]

Uncontracted forms:

    197a   ond hyht nihst (manuscript, 2C1a)

    674a   wisdom onwreon (1A*1a[i])

Contracted forms:

    321b   egesan geþreade (1A*1a[i])

    413b   georne smeadon (2A1a)

    657b   nean myndgiaþ (1D1)

    1296b  in ðam midle þread (3B1b)

Ambiguous forms (11): 171b (2C1b both ways), 174a (1A1a[i] both ways), 195b (3B*1b both ways), 243a (e1d both ways), 668a (2C1b both

---

[7]This list is generous, as both examples of uncontracted forms are insecure. The manuscript reading *ond hyht nihst* (197a) is perhaps not impossible, but it is improbable, and is emended by all recent editors. At 674a, *wisdom onwreon* may belong to type E, as explained below (§§210ff.). The possibility that verse 657b could be classified as type 2A1a(ii) is too remote to consider seriously: as noted above (p. 77, n. 29), in the off-verse this type appears once in *Beowulf*, while type 1D1 appears 220 times.

ways), 869b (3B\*1b both ways), 948a (3B\*1b
both ways), 979a (3E\*1 both ways), 990a
(1A1a[i] both ways), 1120a (3B\*1b both ways),
1308a (1D5 both ways).

*Fates of the Apostles* (9th c.)
  One relevant form: 81b (ambiguous: 3B\*1c both ways).
*Juliana* (9th c.)
  No uncontracted forms.
  Contracted forms:
      142b   susle þreagan (2A1a)
      344a   þragmælum geþread (3E\*2)
      482b   on hean galgan (2C1a)
      546b   Hwæt, þu mec þreades (2C1b)
  Eight ambiguous forms: 65b (1A1a[i] both ways),
      78b (1A1b[i] both ways), 137b (2C1a both
      ways), 176b (2A1a[i] both ways), 185a (3E2 both
      ways), 446b (3B1b),[8] 670b (3B\*1b both ways),
      716b (3B1c[i]: see n. 8).
*Christ II* (9th c.)
  One uncontracted form:
      535b   þonan hy god nyhst (2C1c)
  Contracted forms:
      717a   gehleapeð hea dune (1D\*2)
      829a   lifdon leahtrum fa (1D\*5)
      830a   ferðwerige onfon (3E\*2)
  Ambiguous forms (12): 451a (3B\*1b both ways),
      476a (1A1b[i] both ways), 502a (1A1b[i] both
      ways), 512a (3B\*1b both ways), 522a (3B\*1b
      both ways), 542b (2E2a both ways), 585b (3B\*1c
      both ways), 743a (1D\*6 both ways), 749a (d1d
      or a1d), 757a (3E\*2 both ways), 757b (3B\*1b
      both ways), 794a (1D3 both ways).
*Andreas* (9th c.)
  One uncontracted form:
      782a   gaste onfon (1A\*1a[i])
  Contracted forms:
      327a   swa he ealle befehð (3B\*1b)
      452b   Windas þreade (2A1a)
      748b   ond hreo wægas (2C1a)
      1230a  ðragmælum teon (3E2)
      1599a  syððan mane faa (3B1b)
      1687b  herigeas þreade (2A1a)

---

[8]This verse, along with 716b, may show syncope rather than contraction: see above,
p. 95, n. 3. Bliss would admit an uncontracted type 3B2 here with a long syllable bearing
tertiary stress in the second thesis, and Sievers allows such verses in later poetry
(*Altgerm. Metrik* §78.4: cf. *Meters of Boethius* 24.29a, 26.44b, 29.73a, and *Judith* 308a).
But the question is examined below in Chap. 7, where it is demonstrated that the type
is of dubitable validity when the medial syllable is long: see esp. §§238ff. It should be
noted in regard to *se hyhsta dæl* (*Judith* 308a) that type 3B2a does not occur in *Beowulf*.

Ambiguous forms (25): 14b (1A1a[i] both ways), 274a (1D*3 or 1D3), 347a (e1f both ways),[9] 391a (d1c or a1c), 436a (1A*1b or 1A1b[i]), 520a (1A*1a[i] or 1A1a[i]), 598a (3B*1b both ways), 760a (1D5 both ways), 771b (3E1 both ways), 797b (2A1a[i] both ways), 866a (2C1b both ways), 890a (3B1d both ways), 987a (3E*1 both ways), 1013a (1A1b[i] both ways), 1176b (3B*1b or 2B1b), 1225a (1D2 both ways), 1300a (1D1 both ways), 1500b (2B1c both ways), 1504a (1D2 both ways), 1512b (2C1a both ways), 1538a (1D*5 or 1D5), 1593a (1D*3 or 1D3), 1670a (3B*1b both ways), 1693a (3B*1a both ways), 1714b (2C1a both ways).

*Preface* and *Epilogue, Pastoral Care* (890–99)
One relevant form: *Ep.* 6b (ambiguous: 3B1b both ways).
*Meters of Boethius* (897)[10]
Uncontracted forms:

    20.218b   mid gescead smeað (2C1b)
    21.30b    a fleondu (1D1)

Contracted forms:

    13.74b    swa *swa hweol deð* (2C2b: see n. 10)
    20.212a   oft smeagende (1D1)
    20.214b   secende smeað (3E1)
    20.221b   secende smeað (3E1)
    23.2b     gif he gesion mæge (2C2c)
    25.24a    and him þonne oftion (3B*1b)
    25.59a    ne magon æfre þurhtion (3B*1c)
    28.38a    merestreame þe near (3E*2)
    29.64a    Forðæm eorðe onfehð (3B*1b)

Ambiguous forms (32): Proem 9a (1A*1a[i] or 1A1a[i]), 3.6b (3B*1b both ways), 4.51b (2A3a[i] both ways), 5.27b (3E*1 both ways), 5.37a (1D*1[i] or 2A1a[i]), 5.42b (1A1a[i] both ways),

---

[9]Type e1f is not actually attested in *Beowulf.*

[10]There must be contraction in *swa swa hweol deð* (13.74b) because it is demonstrated below (§§107ff.) that the first syllable of uncontracted *dēð* is short; and therefore it may not serve as a lift after a resolved lift. In *þonne eow fon lysteð* (19.11b) the finite verb may stand for a syncopated form: see Chap. 11. Amos' scansion of *nean ymbcerreð* (28.14b) as either type 1D*2 or 1D2 must not be allowed, since this would require stress on *ymb-*. Moreover, Bliss will not allow type 1D*2 in the off-verse. The verse *secende smeað* (20.214b; so also 20.221b) cannot belong to type 2A1a: see Bliss, §4. Note also the aberrant alliteration. There must be contraction in *oft smeagende* (20.212a) because of the rule of the coda discussed in Chap 7. Here ictus is at the tertiary level, and so the rules of resolution discussed in Chap. 8 do not apply. The verse *hwilum eft smeað* (20.215a) must be regarded as ambiguous because it is shown below (§291) that in the *Meters* the half-lift of type a2 may be a separate word, while this is never permitted in presumably earlier verse. It should be pointed out, however, that type a2 does not occur in *Beowulf* with just two unstressed syllables before the lift, though there is no reason it should not. Type a1, for instance, does: see the discussion below, §140.

9.4a (1A*1b or 1A1b[i]), 11.38b (1A1a[i] both
ways), 11.89a (3B1b or 2C2b), 13.13b (1A*1a[i]
both ways), 13.52b (1A*1a[i] or 1A1a[i]), 19.11b
(3B1c or 2C1c), 20.139b (1A*1c or 1A1c),
20.211a (1A*1a[i] both ways), 20.215a (2C1b or
a2b: see n. 10), 20.217a (1a*1a[i] both ways),
20.231b (2B1b both ways), 20.259a (2E2a both
ways), 20.273b (2C1a both ways), 24.14b (1A1a[i]
both ways), 24.29a (3B1c[i]: see p. 95, n. 3),
24.57b (3B*1b both ways), 25.26a (e1e both
ways), 26.17a (1D5 both ways), 26.38a (1A*1a[i]
or 1A1a[i]), 26.44b (3B1c[i]: see p. 100, n. 8),
27.9a (e1e both ways), 28.14b (1A*1a[i] or
1A1a[i]), 28.65b (2B1b both ways), 28.67a
(3B*1b both ways), 28.72a (3B*1b both ways),
29.73a (3B1b: see p. 100, n. 8).

*Battle of Brunanburh* (937)
No relevant forms.
*Capture of the Five Boroughs* (942)
One relevant form: 4b (ambiguous: 3B1a[i] both ways)
*Judith* (10th c.)[11]
No uncontracted forms.
One contracted form:
     53b    him þe near hete (2C1b)
Ambiguous forms (7): 4a (see nn. 3 and 11), 43b
     (1A1a[i] or 2B1a), 73a and 94b (see p. 100,
     n. 8), 136b (2C1a both ways), 308a (3B1a[i]: see
     p. 100, n. 8), 345b (a1d[1A*1a] both ways).
*Coronation of Edgar* (973)
One relevant form: 11a (ambiguous: 2A3a[i] both ways).
*Death of Edgar* (975)
One relevant form: 13b (ambiguous: 3E2 both ways).
*Battle of Maldon* (991)
Five ambiguous forms: 15b (1A1b[i] both ways),
     27a (2B1b both ways), 213b (1A1a[i] both ways),
     247a (1D*5 or 1D5), 290a (3B2b both ways).
*Death of Edward* (1066)
No relevant forms.
*Durham* (1110)
One relevant form: 4a (ambiguous).[12]

§104. The results may be tabulated as follows, where the proportion
is of uncontracted to contracted forms, and the incidence, once again, is

[11]Verse 4a may belong to type 1A*1a(2A1a), as Bliss has it, but type 1A*1a(3A1)
is also possible: cf. verse 10a. In 43b, *træfe* has a short root vowel.

[12]This line is unmetrical as it stands. If the readings of Hickes's edition are adopted
(see Dobbie's apparatus), the verse will be metrical but still ambiguous, belonging to
type 1D5 both ways.

based on the ratio of unambiguous instances to the total number of verses in the poem or group of poems (consistently less than 1 percent):

| POEM | PROPORTION | INCIDENCE |
|---|---|---|
| Early Northumbrian poems (28 lines) | 0:0 | |
| *Genesis A* (2,319 lines) | 27:4 | .63 |
| *Daniel* (774 lines) | 6:2 | .57 |
| *Beowulf* (3,182 lines) | 15:9 | .38 |
| *Exodus* (590 lines) | 2:2 | .34 |
| The Cynewulf canon (2,601 lines) | 3:11 | .27 |
| *Andreas* (1,722) | 1:6 | .20 |
| Poems by Alfred (1,796 lines) | 2:9 | .31 |
| Chronicle poems (178 lines) | 0:0 | |
| *Judith* (349 lines) | 0:1 | .14 |
| *Battle of Maldon* (325 lines) | 0:0 | |
| *Durham* (21 lines) | 0:0 | |

§105. The data conform to a pattern that supports the presumed chronology. The poems thought to belong to the eighth century and earlier show a significantly higher number of uncontracted forms than contracted. *Exodus*, the one poem dated to the turn of the eighth century, occupies a middle position, with equal numbers of contracted and uncontracted forms; and then in poems dated to the ninth century the contracted forms predominate. In the tenth century, uncontracted forms are missing altogether, though the incidence of relevant forms is too small to be of any real significance. The proportion of uncontracted to contracted forms in fact steadily decreases from top to bottom of the table, except that the proportion for the works of Alfred is slightly higher than that for *Andreas*. The incidence also steadily decreases, with the same exception. The decreasing incidence may be insignificant, or it may reflect increasing reluctance on the part of the poets to use the relevant forms because of uncertainty about their metrical value. When the number of unambiguous forms is small, as for instance in *Exodus*, minor aberrations make a considerable difference, and so the evidence in such cases must be viewed with especial caution. So, also, the notes reveal how much honest uncertainty there must be about some verses, which might with reason be classified otherwise. But still, no amount of reasonable alteration to these debatable classifications would change the general trend in the data, that uncontracted forms are common in presumably early verse, and rare in later verse. And the probabilistic evidence of verses excluded because of uncertainty seems to strengthen rather than weaken the trend in the data. Given the uncertainties, it is all the more surprising how well these results conform to the presumed chronology.

§106. On the basis of the single verse *Þone heahan dæg* at *Gloria I* 27a (since this is clearly a late and West-Saxon poem) it has been said that contraction cannot be correlated to chronology.[13] John Pope explains this form as the result of a late and specifically West-Saxon development; and this development did occur in Wessex at the end of the tenth century, at least orthographically, as discussed below (§124).[14] But regardless of whether or not such an explanation is accurate, the data above show that the occurrence of a single uncontracted form in late verse is of no great significance. As demonstrated in the preceding chapter, isolated instances of nonparasiting also occur in late verse, and yet they do not refute the conclusion that nonparasiting is common in the first part of the chronology and rare in the latter part. And as the evidence of *tung(o)l* in the *Meters of Boethius* demonstrates, there is no reason to suppose that a late poet could not have used an occasional archaism of this sort. It is not likely, on the other hand, that the profusion of nonparasited forms in *Genesis A* and *Beowulf* could be the work of a late poet. The same reasoning applies to the data on contraction: given the wealth of contracted forms in other identifiably late verse, a single uncontracted form in the *Gloria I* would be of little significance even if it were certainly a poetic archaism rather than a West-Saxon innovation. It merely reinforces the point that the results of statistical analysis of metrical features must be regarded as approximate correlates of chronology rather than firm indicators of specific dates.

## C. The Verba Pura

§107. The type of contraction affecting vowels already adjacent in Proto-Germanic, with no intervening consonant, is attested in verse almost solely by forms of *dōn* and *gān*, though the incidence is relatively high. The evidence is as follows. The numbers of verses containing unambiguously unstressed examples (all ambiguous) are italicized.

> *Genesis A*
> Uncontracted (7): 870b (2C1c), 1206b (2C1b), 1789b (2C1b), 1918b (2C1c), 2236a (2C1a), 2356b (1D2), 2413b (2C1b).
> Contracted (4): 1970b (3E1), 2326b (2B1c or 3B*1c), 2801b (2B1b), 2821b (2C1a).
> Ambiguous (5): 190a, 993b,[15] *2182b*, 2325b, 2467b.

---

[13]See E. G. Stanley, "The Date of *Beowulf*: Some Doubts and No Conclusions," in Chase, pp. 197–211, at 209.

[14]See "On the Date of Composition of *Beowulf*" in Chase, pp. 187–95, at 191–92. As Pope notes, and as discussed below, this change is restricted to this one word, and so does not suggest the possibility of late composition for poems with noncontraction of other words.

[15]Neither type 1D5 nor 1D*5 appears in the off-verse in *Beowulf*, but cf. *Him an wuldres god* (*Genesis A* 2916b).

*Daniel*
    Uncontracted (2): 23b (2A1a), 520b (2C1a).
    Contracted (2): 168b (2C1a), 493b (3B1b).
*Beowulf*
    Uncontracted (11): see below.
    Contracted (7): see below.
    Ambiguous (6): *455b*, 1163a, 1231b, 1394b, *1732a, 2470b*.
*Exodus*
    Uncontracted (1): 526b (1D2).
*Elene*
    Contracted (2): 1158b (2C1a), 1174b (3B1b).
    Ambiguous (1): *783a*.
*Juliana*
    Contracted (3): 138a (3B*1b), 301b (2C1c), 330a (2C1a).
*Andreas*
    Uncontracted (1): 775a (2C1a).
    Contracted (4): 342b (2C1a), 365b (3B1b), 765b (2C1a), 1444b
      (2C1a).
    Ambiguous (3): *1182b, 1332b*, 1665a.
*Meters of Boethius*
    Uncontracted (4): 13.74b (2C1b), 13.79a (2C1b), 19.26b (2C1b),
      20.207b (2C1b).
    Contracted (13): 8.17a (2B1b), 9.62a (3B*1b), 10.32a (3E*2),
      11.23b (3B*1b), 18.1b (3E*1), 20.130b (3E*1), 20.272b
      (3B*1b), 21.27b (3B*1d), 26.102b (2C1c), 28.35b (3B1b),
      28.47b (3B1b), 29.40b (3E2),[16] 31.16a (3E2).
    Ambiguous (8): *4.26b, 7.14b, 13.35a, 13.56a*, 15.13b, 19.39b,[17]
      *20.210b, 29.65a*.
*Judith*
    Contracted (3): 140b (2C1a), 149b (3B1c), 219b (2C1a).

§108. The pattern emerges again that poems presumably of the eighth century and earlier show more uncontracted forms than contracted, while the proportions are reversed in the ninth century, and uncontracted forms are missing altogether in the tenth. But this evidence is not altogether reliable, because there is no trustworthy evidence that the first syllable of any dissyllabic scansion of these words need ever be long. The only evidence at all is *soð forð gan* (*Genesis A* 2356b) and *ræd forð gæð* (*Exodus* 526b), which under Bliss's system might be classified as type 1D2 rather than 1D3 because the latter type does not occur in the off-verse in *Beowulf*. But in fact the former appears just twice, and it is not clear why type 1D2 should appear in the off-verse, but not type 1D3 (the only difference being in the length of the third position). There are a few examples of type 1D3 in the off-verse in the test group of poems: cf. *godes*

---

[16]At 29.40b, *deð siððan ymbe* will not scan under Bliss's system, but *ymbe* in the *Meters* consistently may stand for *ymb*, and sometimes must, as at 1.59b and 28.24b.
[17]Here *lysteð* may stand for *lyst*.

*spelbodan* (*Daniel* 229b, 464b) and *godes heahmægen* (*Elene* 464b). Certainly the incidence of dissyllabic *dōn* and *gān* is large enough that the complete absence of unambiguous verses like \**gān hæfdon* (cf. *gegan hæfdon* at *Judith* 140b and elsewhere), comparable to *hean huses*, is surprising. That the modern reflexes of these verbs require an etymological long vowel is no impediment to assuming a short vowel in Old English, since contraction of course would have produced lengthening. This analysis also has the advantage that it is the one that verbs like *bēon* and *fēoð* (§115 below) lead one to expect. It is possible that the vowel was not originally long in Germanic: under the laryngeal hypothesis the Proto-Indo-European stem of *dōn* was \**dheH-*, which could develop to *dō-* only before a consonant; before a vowel the *H* would simply be lost. Comparative evidence, presented below, does suggest that the short vowel is at least as old as Ingvaeonic, and the Old High German evidence does not preclude a short vowel at the West Germanic stage of development. (The word is not found in East or North Germanic.) Another possibility is that all such athematic vocalic stems were thematized in Proto-Germanic, using the anteconsonantal form of the stem, with long vowel, as the base form, with thematic endings added analogically; and in West Germanic or later, all antevocalic long vowels were shortened. (The shortening, at any rate, must antedate the loss of intervocalic *h* in prehistoric Old English, since *hēan* when uncontracted has a long first syllable). The evidence for this latter possibility is scant and inconclusive. The participle *buend-* seems to require a short vowel in *þurh þe eorð-buende* (*Genesis A* 1759a), while *buendra leas* (89b) demands a long one. But in the former instance *-buend-* could stand for *-būnd-* (Campbell, §236.1; cf. *gebun hæfdon* at *Beowulf* 117b), and probably does, since resolution is almost unknown in such an environment in verse before Cynewulf (see below, Chap. 8). Still, this evidence is inconclusive, because shortening of *ō* and *ā* need not have affected *ū*, due to the greater tendency of antevocalic high vowels to develop a following glide. And a lone instance of *ū* in *-buend-* does not carry much conviction, since the long vowel may be restored from the preterite *būde*, while there is no corresponding opportunity for analogical replacement in *dōn* and *gān*.

§109. The alternative is to suppose that *gāan* is metrically equivalent to *wesan*, and so *gā* to *wes*, and so forth. This is the situation in Norse: compare *beits stafni búa* (ljóðaháttr: *Helgakviða Hjǫrvarðssonar* 14.6), *þótt róa kynni* (*Hymiskviða* 28.6), and the like. This possibility seems less likely. Forms like dissyllabic *hēan* seem to be counterevidence, although, after all, their scansion is artifical and archaic, merely a poetic retention of the original, uncontracted scansion. Verses like *buendra leas* would then be more difficult to account for; but as mentioned above, high vowels have a greater tendency than mid or low vowels to develop an antevocalic glide after them, and such a development seems to be what is indicated by spellings of *būan* with *g* after the root vowel, which occur several times in verse, though instances are found almost exclusively in the Exeter Book, for example in *beorgseþel bugan* (*Guthlac A* 102a).[18] The Norse scansion of words like *róa* and *búa* at any rate is peculiar, and apparently reflects the anomaly of words of this sort in a set of languages in which syllable division dictates that an intervocalic consonant belongs to the following syllable, as in *sci-pes*. This anomaly is sufficient to explain the shortening of the first syllable of *\*dōan* and *\*gāan* in West Germanic.

§110. But there is other evidence for a short first syllable in uncontracted *dōn* and *gān*. The distribution of unambiguous verses in *Beowulf* forms a remarkable pattern:[19]

Uncontracted:
386b    hat in gan (2C1a)
1058b   swa he nu git deð (2C1c)
1116b   ond on bæl don (2C1b)
1134b   swa nu gyt deð (2C1b)
1172b   swa sceal man don (2C1b)
1534b   Swa sceal man don (2C1b)
1644a   Ða com in gan (2C1b)
2034b   on flett gæð (2C1a)
2054b   on flet gæð (2C1a)
2166b   Swa sceal mæg don (2C1b)
2859b   swa he nu gen deð (2C1c)
Contracted:
603b    Gæþ eft se þe mot (2E2b)
1277b   gegan wolde (2C1a)
1462b   gegan dorste (2C1a)
1535b   gegan þenceð (2C1a)
2090b   gedon wolde (2C1a)
2186b   gedon wolde (2C1a)
2630b   gegan hæfdon (2C1a)

In the latter group only the first verse is fairly individual, while the rest fit a narrow mold. It is not simply that they all have the same metrical classification, and the same syntactic structure, and the same *ge-* prefix,

---

[18]Other instances are at *Guthlac A* 298b, *Guthlac B* 1240b, *Azarias* 38a, *Phoenix* 157b, *Riddles* 7.2a, 15.8b, 67.12b, *Husband's Message* 18b, and *Metrical Charms* 2.35b. The participle *būgend-* appears in a few prose texts, but this is to the weak verb of the second class. And yet, that this spelling of the (originally) strong verb is found only in verse suggests the possibility that it is metrically rather than phonologically motivated.

[19]In *doð swa ic bidde* (1231b) the verb is monosyllabic according to Angus Cameron, Ashley Crandell Amos, and Gregory Waite, with the assistance of Sharon Butler and Antonette diPaolo Healey, "A Reconsideration of the Language of *Beowulf*," in the Chase volume, pp. 33–75, at p. 45. But with a long, uncontracted first syllable there is no reason this verse could not belong to type 1A*1b. They omit *ga þær he wille* (1394b) from consideration, though the form is optative, and so shows orthographic contraction of the root with the optative ending. The verse thus is ambiguous, either type 1A*1a(i) or 1A1a(i). By contrast, *gā* at 1782a is imperative, and thus endingless and irrelevant.

but also that the verb always appears in the first foot. With equal regularity, in the former group every verse is some form of type 2C1, has no *ge-* prefix, and has the verb in the second foot. Thus, excluding verse 603b, the forms with and without *ge-* are in perfect complementary distribution in a number of ways.[20] Seiffert (pp. 54-56) argues that apparently contracted forms in *Beowulf* with the prefix *ge-* can be explained as due to the substitution of forms with *ge-* for originally dissyllabic forms without *ge-*. Amos objects to this argument as "special pleading" (p. 46), and it is true that this would amount to doctoring the evidence if *Beowulf*'s place in the earlier part of the chronology depended on it. But since Seiffert added this idea at the end of his analysis of *Beowulf*, after he had already reached his conclusion that, according to his data, there is no contraction in *Genesis A*, while there is much contraction in *Beowulf*—a conclusion that this afterthought does not alter—his suggestion cannot be called biased. On the contrary, Seiffert's is the conclusion that linguistic methodology demands if *gān* and *dōn* are to be scanned as trochees, since linguists are constrained to accept coincidence only when there is no reasonable alternative (see the Introduction, §20). Complementary distributions thus always demand an explanation, and it is a dictum of structural analysis that morphs in complementary distribution at any level of analysis must be regarded as allomorphs, in the absence of counterevidence. At least in regard to *(ge)dōn* one is thus not free simply to decide for oneself whether or not to believe Seiffert's argument: linguistic methodology offers no choice until counterevidence is produced.

§111. But the problem is obviated if dissyllabic *dōn* and *gān* have short first syllables, and that is the conclusion that these verses in *Beowulf* must lead to. For it remains to consider why a scribe should have substituted forms with *ge-* for forms without it in all these instances of *gedōn*. Amos argues that the substitution could as easily have been the opposite: "For if *gedōn* could be [i.e. could stand for] *dōan*, there is no reason *dōan* could not also, in almost any occurrence, become *gedōn*" (p. 47). But this argument is not tenable, because in at least two of the eleven instances (2034b, 2054b; and perhaps 386b, though anacrustic *hāt* would be unparalleled), substitution of the form without *ge-* is metrically unnecessary no matter what the scansion of the unprefixed verb. And so while there is a consistent metrical reason for forms with *ge-* to be substituted for forms without it, the reverse is not true. But then why should this hypothetical scribe who pronounced *dōn* as a monosyllable have consistently introduced *ge-* into the latter group but never the former, when it would have marked an improvement there, as well? This cannot be mere oversight, because the structural differences between the two groups in complementary distribution are too regular for it to be

---

[20]The complementary distribution is metrical, morphological, and syntactic, but not consistently semantic, since *gān* and *gegān* usually do not have the same meaning.

mere chance that one group was changed and the other was not. Nor is it likely to be due to the supposed revisor's ignorance: it is difficult to believe that he could have known that *gān wolde with monosyllabic gān is unmetrical and *not* known that the same is true of *hat in gan*. This reasoning leads inevitably back to the assumption that there is no scribal alteration here, but that the poet in fact pronounced *dōn* as two short syllables. This explanation is advantageous relative to the others in regard to both of the problems raised by these verses: it accounts adequately for the scansion of all the verses, while the alternative demands the inconsistent uncontraction of forms; and it accounts also for the complementary distribution of types with and without *ge-*, since *ge-* appears everywhere it must, and only there, if it precedes a short syllable.

§112. This explanation also provides a solution to the vexed problem of the origin of the Old English preterite *dyde*. This is thought to derive from *dudī-*, the preterite optative, whence the root vocalism was leveled into the indicative. Yet the root vowel *u* is unparalleled in the other Germanic languages, and is difficult to explain. Sievers and Wilhelm Streitberg supposed that it could be derived from PIE *ə, but there is no precedent for this development, since *ə otherwise gives Gmc. *a* in stressed syllables.[21] Eduard Prokosch's suggestion (p. 222) that the vocalism here is analogical to the optatives of preterite-present verbs like *dyge*, *þyrfe*, and *scyle* is more reasonable, but still unpersuasive: *dōn* is not a preterite-present verb, *y* in *dyde* is not restricted to the optative as it is in the preterite-present verbs, and there is no very good motivation for the analogical change, especially considering that *dyde* has completely supplanted the earlier form (presumably *dedæ: cf. OSax. *deda*, OHG *teta*), when without a strong motivation for the change we might expect some relic forms to survive. On the other hand, if the prehistoric form was *doan rather than *dōan, there would have been a strong motivation for the leveling of *o* into the preterite: regardless of whether *dedæ actually reflects a reduplicated form, it would certainly have been perceived as a weak preterite; and since present and preterite root vocalism were identical in other weak verbs in West Germanic, the pressure for analogical extension would have been strong. In prehistoric Old English there was no *o* in stressed syllables. This is why, for example, when the name *Vortigern* was borrowed into the language the *o* of the root was identified with *u* before umlaut applied, giving OE *Wyrtgeorn*. Thus, *dodī

[21]Sievers, "Germanisch *u* as Vertreter von indogerm. ə," *PBB* 16 (1892), 235–37; Streitberg, review of Friedrich Kluge, *Vorgeschichte der altgermanischen Dialekte*, in *Anzeiger für indogermanische Sprach- und Altertumskunde* 2 (1893), 44–52, at 48. Nor is the problem obviated by the supposition that the reflexes of *ə were determined before the Germanic accent shift, since there remain exceptions, and at any rate there is counterevidence to this assumption: see "PIE *ə in Germanic Unstressed Syllables," in *Die Laryngaltheorie und die Rekonstruktion des indogermanischen Laut- und Formensystems*, ed. Alfred Bammesberger (Heidelberg: Winter, 1988), pp. 153–77.

should give *dyde*. Presumably in *\*doan*, too, the shortened *o* was identified with *u*, giving *\*duan*, but was soon lowered by the following low vowel (Campbell, §115). The existence of this *\*duan* is suggested by the cognates OFris. and OSax. *duan* (the latter beside *don, duon, doen,* and *duoan*). These are explained by the standard handbooks as due to raising of *ō* before *a*. But it is less likely that the same development should have occurred in the two languages than that the form is a common inheritance, especially when *\*duan* also explains both the metrical problem in Old English and the origin of OE *dyde*. OHG *tuan* is less anomalous than the Ingvaeonic forms, but it is compatible with the assumption that *\*duan* had a short root vowel in West Germanic that could be lowered to *o*.[22]

§113. This solution provides an alternative to the supposition that the front mutation in *dyde* is due to analogical extension from the optative *\*dudī-*. This has always seemed improbable, because unprecedented and unmotivated: the optative is not normally a source for analogical remodeling, nor is there a reason it should be. If the preterite of *dōn* was reformed from the present stem as a weak verb, the preterite suffix that was added should not have been simply *-d-*, but *-id-*, since the connecting vowel in parallel short-stemmed forms like *\*hazidæ* must have been analyzed as part of the suffix rather than the stem, by comparison to pres. *\*hazjō, \*hazis, haziþ*, and so forth.[23] It is perhaps peculiar that *\*duidæ* should have produced the short root vowel required by the verses *swa ic gio wið Grendle dyde* (*Beowulf* 2521b) and *swa he ær on ðam beame dyde* (*Dream of the Rood* 114b). But as *ui* was not a Germanic diphthong, it need not have developed to a long vowel; and in the parallel instance, *ui* in Celtic *drui* has developed to short *y* in OE *dry*, as demonstrated by the verse *sægde hy dryas wæron* (*Juliana* 301b).[24]

---

[22]The co-occurence of variants with *u* and *o* in Old Saxon and Old High German may be compared to the facultative nature of lowering in Old English (Campbell, §115), which may be the result of analogical extension of one or the other variant. Forms like OHG *tuan* are inconclusive because *ua* may be the normal diphthongization of *ō*. Braune and Eggers (§380) remark that the most archaic forms of the verb have *ō*, with diphthongization following shortly thereafter. But in fact diphthongs are found alongside *o* in the earliest attestations, e.g. inf. *tuan, toan,* and 1. sg. *tuam, toam* in Kero's gloss on the *Benedictine Rule* (ca. 800), beside 1. sg. *tom* in the glosses of Pseudo-Hrabanus (contemporary or later), though this latter text also uses a geminate spelling in 2. sg. *toos* (suggesting that *tom* may also stand for a geminate), and a purely analogical 3. sg. *toit*. Moreover, although this verb is not attested until later, diphthongized spellings of WGmc. *ō* appear already in the very earliest High German texts, some attributable to the first half of the eighth century: see Irmengard Rauch, *The Old High German Diphthongization* (The Hague: Mouton, 1967).

[23]On the long-stemmed equivalents cf. below, §229.

[24]It might be objected that any rule producing shortening in *\*dōan* would also have affected verba pura such as the etyma of *sāwan, grōwan,* etc. But it is now frequently assumed that these verbs no longer had stems with final vowels even in Proto-Germanic, if not earlier, as proposed by Fredrik Otto Lindeman, "Bemerkungen zu den germanischen Verbalstämmen auf *-ē, -ō*," *NTS* 22 (1968), 48–71. As this matter requires

§114. If dissyllabic *dōn* and *gān* had short first syllables, then all the forms listed above as contracted are actually ambiguous, and there is no unambiguous evidence for contraction in these verbs in verse. Without contracted forms for comparison, the figures for uncontracted forms alone are unremarkable.[25] In the parallel instance of forms like *sēon*, with a short root vowel before loss of intervocalic *h*, the evidence of uncontracted forms is still significant, even though very few forms can be shown to have been contracted. This is because there are no examples of uncontracted forms of such words in verse later than *Beowulf* in the presumed chronology. The situation is different with *dōn*, of which there are four uncontracted examples in the *Meters of Boethius*. Thus, the contrast with earlier verse is not so impressive. Yet there may still be some chronological significance to the data. The proportion of uncontracted to ambiguous forms (including now those listed as contracted) in the *Meters* is remarkable, especially given that the *Meters* furnish much more evidence than any other composition, including much longer poems. The extreme proportion would make better sense if it were assumed that Alfred used both the uncontracted form preserved in the koine and the contracted, West-Saxon form in much the way he uses both the unsyncopated verb forms of the koine (*bringeð*, *grōweð*, etc.) and the West-Saxon syncopated equivalents (*drīfð*, *stent*, etc.: see Chap. 11 below). Such evidence is certainly meager, and so conclusions based on the verba pura cannot be considered very firm.

## D. Loss of Intervocalic *j*

§115. The third type of contraction results from the loss of intervocalic *j*. Luick (§247; so also Campbell, §238) includes here *bēo* 'bee', as well as some forms of the verb *bēon*, since he derives the latter from PGmc. *\*bi-* plus inflections beginning with back vowels. By this reasoning also stem-final *\*-ij-* developed to *-ī-* in prehistoric Old English, and so forms like *fēoð* 'hates', *frēoð* 'loves', and *sīe* 'be' underwent the same development as *bēon*. On the other hand, *-iju-* had already lost its *j* and undergone contraction in West Germanic, as in OE *fēond* < *\*fijund-*. But the metrical evidence suggests otherwise. It is true that *frēond* and *fēond* are never dissyllabic in the test group of poems, while *sīe* is frequently so;

---

a detailed consideration of the verba pura in Germanic, it is treated separately in an article, "Old English *dōn, dyde*, and the Verba Pura in Germanic," forthcoming in *Indogermanische Forschungen*. Sievers, it should be noted, emends *dryas* to *drȳs*, with contraction, in the verse from *Juliana* ("Rhythmik," p. 480).

[25]In the earlier version of this chapter published under the title "Contraction as a Criterion for Dating Old English Verse," *JEGP* 89 (1990), 1–16, it was concluded that these verbs furnish no evidence for metrical change. This view should be moderated, for the reasons offered in this paragraph.

and, for instance, *frēoð* is dissyllabic in *swa þin mod freoð* (*Genesis A* 2260b), as is *feoð* in *þe þæt wif feoð* (*Genesis A* 911b). But there is no evidence that a dissyllabic scansion of *sīe* ever requires a long first syllable, as demanded by the assumption that *-ij-* developed to *-ī-* in prehistoric Old English.[26] The lack of such instances when *sīe* is so common in verse cannot be attributed to accident, in view of the frequency of verses like *hean huses*, when *hēan* is considerably less common in verse, and in view of the corresponding complete absence of dissyllabic scansions of words like *fēa* and *sēon* with a long first syllable, as pointed out above (§101). Thus it may be that, for instance, verse preserves the prehistoric scansion of *\*sijai-* (with a short vowel, as in the cognate Gothic *sijai*). But it is more likely that this form lost the *j* in prehistoric Old English and remained uncontracted (or was analogically decontracted), since there is much evidence for noncontraction of words like this even in verse presumed or known to be late, but no reliable evidence for contraction. Such words then offer no evidence for metrical change.

§116. Once forms like *sīe* and *frēond* are eliminated, the only remaining word relevant to contraction upon loss of *j* is *frēa*. Sievers was the first to point out the metrical necessity of decontraction in this word ("Rhythmik," p. 479). Under the heading "Nach ausfall von *j*" he remarks, "Hier kommt nur das wort *freá* in betracht. Eine zweisilbige form ws. *frîga* (= kent. angl. *\*frêga*) ist in einigen prosatexten mehrfach erhalten: *se frîgea* L. Ine 74, E, *mid þŷ frîgean* L. Ine 74, E, *sê âgena frîgea* L. Aeth. 3, 4, *âgenfrîgea* L. Ine 42. 49 Park., und wird durch das metrum an folgendum stellen gefordert." There follows a list of twenty-three relevant verses. Elsewhere he explains that the word is to be derived from *\*frêga* (i.e. *\*frêja*), presumably by comparison to Gothic *frauja* (*Altgerm. Metrik*, §76.4f.). In subsequent dating studies Sievers' position was widely misunderstood, and his error thus compounded.[27] There could be no loss of *j* in *\*frau(w)jan-*, as illustrated by forms like Anglian *strēgan* (Gothic *straujan*) and WS *cīegan* < *\*kau(w)jan*. Rather, the correct cognate of Gothic *frauja* is OE *frīgea*, and *frēa* is to be derived from a simple *an*-stem *\*frawan-*, as the standard handbooks have it. The point is demonstrated, for example, by the co-occurrence of Old Saxon *frō(ho)* or *fraho* with *frōio*.[28] As with *fēond* above, the stem of the form without *j*

---

[26]The verse *irsung sie* (*Meters* 20.186a) may be mentioned, though it is not decisive. Girvan (pp. 15–16) notes that *Beowulf* has both contracted and uncontracted forms of *sīe*, and compares *than him tharf sie* (*Bede's Death Song* 2b). But if the first syllable of the uncontracted form is short, there are no unambiguously contracted forms in *Beowulf*.

[27]For instance, Girvan classes this with words that have lost *h* (p. 17). Edwin Duncan's reconstruction of the word without a root vowel perhaps involves a typographical error: see "Chronological Testing and the Scansion of *Frea* in Old English Poetry," *NM* 87 (1986), 92–101, at 92.

[28]On these see Ferdinand Holthausen, *Altsächsisches Elementarbuch* (Heidelberg: Winter, 1900), §311 and n.

should have been *frawun- in half the case-forms in early West Germanic (Luick, §294.3; Campbell, §331.6, n. 4), which should have lost the *w* and undergone contraction already in West Germanic itself (Luick, §100; Campbell, §120.3). Since *feond* and *freond*, which also underwent contraction in West Germanic itself, are never dissyllabic in Old English verse, it is less likely that *frēa* preserves a West Germanic scansion than that it is an orthographic substitution for *frīgea* in these instances, motivated by the rarity of the latter. That at least some of the dissyllabic instances of *frēa* are due to replacement of *frīgea* is rendered fairly certain by ten or so verses like *Deniga frean* (*Beowulf* 271a) and *sinum frean* (*Daniel* 159b), which demand a long first syllable in the uncontracted form. *Frēa*, on the other hand, never had a long first syllable before contraction.

§117. Conversely, while it is clear that not all instances of *frēa* in verse can actually reflect *frawan- rather than *frau(w)jan-, it is also clear that not all instances of *frēa* should be read as *frīgea*. For instance, the word appears uncompounded forty-two times in *Genesis A*, as in *He frean hyrde* (1951b), and in no instance must it be scanned as a dissyllable with a long first syllable. By comparison, relevant forms of *hēah* appear eleven times in the poem, and in five of those instances it has an unambiguously long first syllable when decontracted. On the contrary, *frēa* when uncompounded must be scanned as monosyllabic thirty-five of the forty-two times it appears, if as a dissyllable it would have a long first syllable.[29] From these facts it should be concluded either that *frēa* should generally be contracted in this poem or that when decontracted its first syllable is short. The former possibility is shown to be improbable by the six instances in which *frēa* appears in the poem as the second element of a compound, since here it is always dissyllabic. It is not likely that the uncontracted form should have been restricted to use in compounds and the contracted one to simplices.[30] And so it seems likeliest that at least in the majority of instances *frēa* stands for the reflex of WGmc. *frawan- rather than *frau(w)jan-. Although *frēa* cannot be an example of contraction upon loss of *j*, it may show loss of *w*: see below, §119.

§118. There is a genuine environment for the loss of *j* that has not been considered: *j* is lost in West Germanic before *i* (Campbell, §405).

---

[29]Verse 2231 is not a counterexample because *hwæðer* belongs in the off-verse: as a conjunction it is never stressed. This, for instance, is how Ferdinand Holthausen has it in his edition, *Die ältere Genesis* (Heidelberg: Winter, 1914), p. 60.

[30]This is in fact the position of Edwin Duncan (see n. 27 above). He explains some of these facts about *Genesis A* with the conclusion, "*Frea* was monosyllabic unless it occurred as the second element of a compound or as a separate word following a possessive pronoun" (p. 101). But several verses contradict the rule (e.g. *frean mihtum* at *Daniel* 350b), and to arrive at the rule he is obliged to posit unlikely compounds such as *swæs-frēa* (*Genesis A* 2784a) and *hold-frēa* (*Exodus* 19b). The conditioning of morphophonemic rules need not be very natural, but this example does seem to be a type unparalleled in the history of English.

The only relevant instances are examples of the third person singular of some weak verbs, WS *cīegan*, Angl. *strēgan, hēgan*. Analogical WS *cīegð* corresponds to Angl. *cēð < \*kau(w)jiþ*. The only relevant instance in the test group of poems is *cleopað and cigeð* (*Genesis A* 1013a), with an uncontracted form. Elsewhere in the poetic records only contracted forms appear: compare *glom ofer cigð* (*Order of the World* 71b) and *ond him dryhten gecygð* (*Phoenix* 454b).[31] Aside from forms with root-final *h* in the third person, these latter two are also the only instances in these poems of syncopated spellings in the third person singular, indicating perhaps that the scribe (or perhaps several scribes) was aware of the metrical difficulty of writing such a form as that found in *Genesis*, which is a hybrid, neither Anglian nor etymologically normal West Saxon. In the older view, the Anglian development of the word should have been from *\*kau(w)iþ* to *\*cēþ* by front mutation and syncope, with subsequent analogical restoration of *-eþ* in the ending, as usual in the Anglian dialects (but cf. §§320ff. below). And so possibly this might better be regarded as exemplifying loss of *w* before *i*: see §120 below.

E.  Loss of Intervocalic *w*

§119. Again, in regard to the final type of contraction, loss of *w* before *u* was followed by contraction in West Germanic itself, as with loss of *j* in *frēond, sīe*, and such, and there is no evidence for uncontracted forms of *clēa < \*klawu* and such, except where there has clearly been analogical change. Etymologically, most oblique cases should have no contraction, since *w* did not precede *u*—for example, dat. sg. *clawe*—and spellings of this sort are in fact found in prose. But paradigm regularization has blurred the original distinctions: see the discussion in Chapter 5. *Rēon* 'rowed' (inf. *rōwan*) is dissyllabic at the two places it appears in *Beowulf*, and it is unclear whether this is an archaism or the result of analogical change. It is difficult to believe that the scansion of the poem should be linguistically more innovative than the orthography of the manuscript; and yet it is also difficult to believe that this form was not contracted in West Germanic itself, especially since cognates like Sanskrit *arí-tra-* and Greek *ἐρέ-της* demonstrate that the *w* of the present stem is, as most comparatists assume, a post-Ingvaeonic innovation, as in *blōwan, hlōwan*, and the like. In Psalm 138, *sæwum* (7.2b, next to unambiguous *sǣm* eight times in other verse) is certainly analogical. It has already been remarked (§117 above) that it is unlikely that all instances of dissyllabic *frēa* are for original *frīgea*; rather, some may represent *\*frawan-* instead

---

[31]In *swa hine wide cigað* (*Menologium* 184a) the manuscript has *cigð*, but the sense requires a plural form. It is true, however, that the plural form does not render a metrical verse.

of *frawun-. And so, in sum, there is no unambiguous evidence in Old English meter for nonanalogical uncontracted forms in which *w* was lost before *u* in West Germanic.

§120. On the other hand it is uncertain whether the loss of *w* before *i* is to be dated as far back as West Germanic (Campbell, §406, n. 4). But aside from *cigeð* at *Genesis A* 1013a, which is at least partly analogical (as explained above), the only evidence of noncontraction is *strēd* in *morþorbed stred* (*Beowulf* 2436b). Nominative singular *sǣ* < *\*saiwiz*, for instance, is never dissyllabic, but then presumably even after the loss of *w* the *i* shared the general fate of the nominative singular *i*-stem inflection after long stems. Dative singular *sǣwe*, again, is correct.

§121. At least orthographically there seems to be a tendency to lose *w* in connection with relatively low stress, in *ond orcneas* (*Beowulf* 112b), *bonan Ongenþeoes* (1968a), and the like. On this problem see p. 150, n. 10.

F.  Summary and Analysis

§122. The last two types of contraction either have no real historical basis or offer too meager evidence to suggest metrical change. The verba pura perhaps offer a small amount of evidence, since the very large number of ambiguous forms in the *Meters of Boethius* might best be interpreted as concealing some contracted forms. But forms that have lost intervocalic *h* are the only very reliable source of evidence for metrical change. The pattern into which these forms fall is the one prescribed by the presumed chronology assigned to Old English verse, whereby among the longer poems, the scriptural paraphrases and *Beowulf* would appear to be the earliest compositions, followed by the Cynewulf canon and *Andreas*, then the *Meters of Boethius*, and finally *Judith*.

§123. Some doubts have been expressed as to how such evidence is to be interpreted. Amos discards her evidence that leads broadly to the same conclusion. She finds that her data suggest an approximate dating value with regard to the figures for *Genesis A*, *Beowulf*, and the Cynewulf canon (pp. 46, 49), and yet she rejects the evidence because of the suggestion of Randolph Quirk that uncontracted forms are as likely to be due to analogy as to the preservation of archaic forms:

Outside of West Saxon no form of Old English was without "at least a sporadic tendency to preserve uncontracted forms." Morphological suture, the analogical addition of the normal endings to the contracted forms, simply restores the uncontracted state: *dōað* becomes, by contraction, *dōð*, which, by analogy to all third person endings in *-að*, becomes *dōað* again. . . . Dissyllabic forms then need not be "uncontracted" or necessarily early; they may occur long after contraction. The metrically attested presence of dissyllabic forms in a poem therefore need not testify to its date, and if a poet felt himself free to alternate between monosyllabic and dissyllabic forms of a word, the actual proportion of one to another attested by his meter will be merely a matter of chance or temperament.[32]

Because the questions raised here cannot be isolated from the context of dialect variation, the issue poses different problems according to whether most of the longer poems are believed to be of Anglian origin, as has usually been assumed, or whether they are West-Saxon compositions, as argued for example by Wilhelm Busse. The latter possibility may be considered first.

§124. If the poems were composed in Wessex, the objection is improbable because the spelling *doað* does not occur in the poetic records, and forms like *heagan* for *hēan* are exceedingly rare. It would be necessary to suppose that after contraction took place, and after the endings were analogically restored, in nearly every instance the scribes of the various manuscripts have replaced the restored forms with contracted spellings. This is implausible if the longer poems of the first half of the chronology are not Anglian in origin, because forms like *doað*, though common in late Anglian prose, are unattested in genuine West Saxon: the only forms of this sort at all in West Saxon are two instances of *doan* in the Old English translation of Bede's *Ecclesiastical History*, a work of Mercian origin.[33] In late West Saxon there are a few instances of decontraction of inflected forms of *hēah* spelt *heag-*. These are restricted almost exclusively to the works of Ælfric (written in the period 989–1012), and the gloss on the *Liber Scintillarum* (eleventh century). Such spellings do suggest an analogical development in late West Saxon, as remarked above in regard to John Pope's treatment of *heahan* in the *Gloria I* (§106). But Pope points out that only *hēah* seems to have been affected, and he suggests that the development may be an attempt to avoid confusion with *hēan* 'low'. Even if the change were not restricted to this one word, it occurs at such a late date that in order for the change to have produced any effect in verse, all the poems in the chronology except the early Northumbrian ones would have to be dated to the eleventh century at the earliest—an unlikely proposition if for no other reasons than that some of the poetic manuscripts seem to be earlier, and that it is implausible that a change just beginning to be evidenced in prose in the last decade of the tenth century should be widely evidenced in the more conservative

---

[32]Pp. 44–45. The quotation is from Quirk's "On the Problem of Morphological Suture in Old English," *Modern Language Review* 45 (1950), 1–5, at 2.

[33]See Campbell, §17, and for more detailed discussion of the work's Mercian origin, Dorothy Whitelock, "The OE Bede," *PBA* 48 (1962), 57–90; Elizabeth M. Liggins, "The Authorship of the OE Orosius," *Anglia* 88 (1970), 289–322 (with material on Bede), and Sherman M. Kuhn, "The Authorship of the Old English Bede Revisited," *NM* 73 (1972), 172–80. *Doað* itself does not appear in West Saxon at all: it is attested only in three late Anglian texts, Rit., Li., and Ru.², all from the tenth century.

language of verse composed at the same time. And supposing *Genesis A*, *Daniel*, and *Beowulf* to be West-Saxon in origin, if the analogical development were widespread enough in West Saxon to have affected most of the relevant forms in these poems (since there are many more uncontracted forms in these works than contracted), there would have been no motivation for the restoration of contracted spellings. It would also have to be assumed that West-Saxon uncontracted spellings conceal dissyllabic pronunciation. This in fact is the position of Quirk, who says that dissyllabic forms of *fōn, sēon*, and *dōn* occurred beside the monosyllabic ones in West Saxon (see above, n. 32). But this is implausible. Even the orthographically most aberrant texts do not reveal errors on this score,[34] while late texts in dialects other than West Saxon attest to uncontracted forms like *doan*. The evidence that Quirk offers for West-Saxon is actually from a manuscript whose main dialect features are Kentish (Cambridge Univ. Libr. MS. II.1.33), with typically Kentish spellings such as *ya* for *ea* and *e* for *æ*, whatever other admixture of features it might display.[35] Indeed, in many West-Saxon forms there is little motivation for analogical restoration: as explained below (§320), West Saxon generalized the syncope in constructions like *\*bindistū < \*bindis þū*, while the Anglian dialects did not. And so when *\*dē-iþ* contracted to *\*dēþ* in Anglian, the form was especially anomalous because there were no monosyllabic forms to compare to this. In West Saxon, on the other hand, monosyllabism was the norm in the third person singular indicative, and so there was no very strong analogical pressure to restore the syllabic ending in the standard dialect.

§125. Matters are less straightforward if most verse is Anglian in origin, but it is still an implausible assumption that noncontraction in verse could be due to an Anglian innovation. The analogical restoration of contracted syllables is widespread in Anglian prose texts. For example, Alan S. C. Ross points out that although geminate vowels are used sparingly to represent long vowels in Li., spellings like *gesiið* 'videt' are so usual that these must represent dissyllabic pronunciation.[36] So also although *doð* 'facite' is regular in VP (Mercian, ninth-century), there also

---

[34]Thomas Cable similarly objects on the basis of the regularity of spelling: "To assume that contractions could be reformed a century or a century and a half later in ways that exactly recapitulate the pre-history of *þēon, flēon, tēon, fēon*, and *slēan* is less plausible than to assume that these disyllabic forms are early. (One would expect, for example, aberrant analogical reformation such as Quirk cites from Ritchie Girvan: infinitive *wrigan* instead of *wrion*, with an unhistorical *g* from the third principal part of the verb.)" See his review of Amos' book, *JEGP* 85 (1986), 93–95.

[35]See the discussion by S. J. Crawford, *The Old English Version of the Heptateuch*, EETS, o.s. 160 (1922), appendix 2. Crawford would locate the language of the manuscript in some area bordering Kent.

[36]*Studies in the Accidence of the Lindisfarne Gospels*, Leeds School of English Language Texts and Monographs 2 (Leeds: Titus Wilson, 1937), 162–63.

appear forms like *doa* 'fecerim' and *befoo* 'compraehendam'.[37] The significance of geminates in forms like *seende* in Li. is made clear by parallel forms like *gesegende* and *slægendo*, even if these are influenced by the preterite plural and past participle, as Brunner supposes (§374, n. 5). Forms like sj. pl. *foen* and inf. *gedoan* are also found in Kentish charters as early as the first half of the ninth century. Nor is the analogical process restricted to verbs, as other forms, though rarely attested, also show the change, as in gen. sg. *fæes* (to *feh*, WS *feoh*) in Li. and pl. *heae* (to *hēh*, WS *hēah*) in VP. The analogical change cannot be dated with any precision because of the scarcity of Anglian prose texts dated before the ninth century. There are uncontracted forms in the early glossaries—Amos provides a partial list, p. 42—for example, *faehit* 'paints' (Ép. 785 in Pheifer's edition), where *h* is almost certainly an indication of hiatus rather than a consonant (see below, §395). But these are genuinely uncontracted forms rather than analogical restorations, as demonstrated by *suehoras* (Ép. 1062a), in which there is no juncture, and so no model for restoration. The glossaries cannot be dated with any accuracy: the dates of the manuscripts are disputed, and the material in them may be considerably earlier, some of it perhaps based on texts compiled before ca. 650 (see below, §400). Thus the analogical restoration of contracted syllables in the Anglian dialects may have occurred at any time between ca. 650 and when VP was glossed in the ninth century.[38] The question to be decided, then, is whether the state of contraction in poems like *Genesis A*, *Daniel*, and *Beowulf* is more like that in the early glossaries, in which there are some forms that clearly were never contracted and some that appear only recently to have undergone contraction, or whether it is like that in VP, in which some vowels appear still to be contracted and some contracted syllables have clearly been restored by analogy.

§126. The latter possibility seems unlikely because the vowels that were lengthened by contraction should have remained long even after analogy set in—for example, *\*sihiþ* by loss of *h* and contraction became *\*sīþ*, and then by analogical restoration became not *\*siiþ* but *sīþ*.[39] The long vowel was retained because there was no model for restoration of a short vowel. Contraction affected all forms of the present paradigm, indicative and optative, giving a long vowel or diphthong everywhere. Only in the imperative singular was the original short vowel of the

---

[37]Early Middle English evidence concerning analogically uncontracted forms, it should be noted, is mostly rather negative as regards the Midlands, including the evidence of the *Ormulum* and texts in the AB dialect.

[38]One example of noncontraction in the names in Bede's *Historia Ecclesiastica* is dubitable: see below, p. 371, n. 51.

[39]Such a form would not have been subject to the much earlier shortening of antevocalic long vowels described above in §§108ff. It was pointed out there that the rule had ceased to apply by the time intervocalic *h* was lost, as evidenced by the scansion of verses like *hean huses* (*Beowulf* 116a).

present stem preserved, and it is clear that the imperative did not serve as a model for restoration of the original vowel. For example, Li. has 2. and 3. sg. *gesiist* and *gesiiþ* to *sēa*, and the root vowel in these forms is clearly unaffected by analogy, since it is mutated, even though mutation is usually removed analogically in such verb forms in the Anglian dialects. On the contrary, it is the imperative that has suffered analogy, for beside etymological *geseh* there is *gesih* (Mk. 1:44, etc.), which is analogical to the contracted present stem.[40] The failure to remove front mutation in forms like *gesiist* is itself evidence of the larger point. In verbs other than contract verbs, only the second and third singular have anomalous vocalism in the present system, and so the mutated vowels are easily removed by the analogical pressure of the vowel found in the rest of the present system. In contract verbs, on the other hand, contraction produced a variety of types of vocalism in the present system. For example, in the paradigm of *sēa* there should have been contraction of *e* and *o* in the first person singular, *e* and *a* in the plural, and *e* and *e* in the subjunctive. Analogical restoration failed because there was no consistent model for the root vowel in such verbs. The point is corroborated by forms like 1. sg. *geseom* (Mk. 8:24, etc.) and VP *fleom*. The -*m*, which is by analogy to verbs with the PIE -*mi* ending, such as Anglian *eam*, *bīom*, and *dōm*, was added only to monosyllabic verbs. The only very likely reason is that after contraction, only *mi*-verbs and contracted verbs were monosyllabic in the first person singular. Likewise contraction seems to be the reason that the ending 2. pers. -*st* in VP appears only in forms made monosyllabic by contraction, like *sīst*, and that the ending is encountered chiefly in monosyllabic forms in other Anglian texts. As discussed below (§§320ff.), apparently syncope originally occurred only in forms with a suffixed pronoun, like *\*bindistū*. In such forms there would be stress on *ū* because an unstressed syllable preceded it (cf. the discussion of forms like *rūmedlīce* below, §203), but not after a monosyllabic form like *sīstu*; and under low stress the *t* was reanalyzed as part of the inflectional ending. Thus it is not surprising that the -*st* appears earliest in contract verbs and *mi*-verbs (Brunner, §356, n. 1). That lengthening did take place in these verbs and was retained is also suggested by a form like gen. sg. *fǣes* (Lk. 15:12, to *feh*): the *ǣ* is explained by the assumption that it is long, since the Anglian dialects had no long open *e* to correspond to the short vowel.[41] And so the short vowel, when lengthened, was identified with *ǣ*, the umlaut of *ā*. The assumption that the first vowel is long in forms like *gesiist* and *fǣes* precludes the possibility that noncontraction in verse is

---

[40]The vocalism of *gesūst, gesūþ* has also been extended occasionally to the first person singular: cf. *sium* appearing in Ru.[2], Li., and Rit.

[41]That Anglian OE *ē* < WGmc. *ǣ* was a close vowel is demonstrable from Middle English verse in which it rhymes neither with the reflex of OE *ǣ*, the umlaut of *ā*, nor with lengthened OE *e*. For the geographical distribution see Jordan, pp. 78 and 80.

not original but due to the analogical restoration of endings, since it was demonstrated above that such words when uncontracted in verse must be scanned with short first syllables.[42]

§127. Another piece of counterevidence to the supposition that non-contraction in verse is analogical is a form that cannot have undergone analogical restoration. In the verse *hæfde wordbeot* (*Genesis A* 2762b) the element *bēot* derives from *\*bi-hāt-*. Although *\*bi-hāt-* represents two original morphemes, *bēot* is only analyzable as one, and so there is no morphological juncture to provoke analogical restoration of the second syllable. And yet it is still dissyllabic. There are very few words of this sort in verse, especially verse presumed to antedate Cynewulf, and so its evidence is of some importance.

§128. A further reason that the analogical explanation seems implausible is that four uncontracted forms do occur in a verifiably West-Saxon composition, the *Meters of Boethius*. As remarked above, analogical restoration in West Saxon seems to have been restricted to the one word *hēah*, and it does not appear in prose texts until the last decade of the tenth century. Thus there is no convincing way to account for uncontracted forms in Alfred's verse but to assume that they are part of the archaic koine of verse, not a recent Anglian innovation that has somehow found its way into West-Saxon verse at the end of the ninth century.

§129. Other problems with the assumption that these poems are Anglian and have their uncontracted forms from Anglian analogical processes rather than poetic archaism are of a more probabilistic sort. Under this reasoning the poems must be presumed to be late. For instance, the evidence would then suggest that the poems usually presumed to be early are actually later than the works of Cynewulf, which are undeniably Anglian, and in which (under this line of reasoning) the analogical replacement of endings is still nascent, since contracted forms are still considerably in the majority. But the evidence for noncontraction must be viewed in the context of the evidence for nonparasiting, and other dating criteria considered in the following chapters, several of which support the presumed chronology. In the context of these other criteria

---

[42]The status of the Anglian cognate of WS *slēan* is ambiguous with respect to the developments discussed in this paragraph. In VP there are 2. and 3. sg. *sles*, *sleþ*, probably representing *\*slēes* and *\*slēeþ*, the analogical forms expected to develop from WGmc. *\*slahis*, *\*slahiþ*. In Northumbrian, on the other hand, the usual forms are of the sort 1. sg. *slæ*, 2. sg. *slæs*, 3. sg. *slaeþ*, etc. Spellings with *ae* instead of *æ* are frequent enough to suggest dissyllabic pronunciation. Co-occurrence of dissyllabic and monosyllabic forms then seems less probable than that spellings with *æ* conceal uncontracted pronunciation, e.g. either *slæeþ* or *slǣeþ*. (Spellings with *æe* would be awkward and unusual enough to explain the use of simple *æ* and *ae*.) The former would show normal fronting of borrowed *a* (for an explanation see Campbell, §145, n. 2). In the latter, *ǣ* may have developed from either the contraction of *æi* (where *æ* is again the result of borrowing) or of *ei* (as in Mercian), with identification of lengthened *e* with *ǣ* once again as in *fǣes*.

it is difficult to explain noncontraction as an innovation rather than an archaism. For example, if these poems are late Anglian compositions, the incidence of nonparasiting in them is extraordinary. This is not a feature of the late Anglian dialects: for instance, in Li. and Ru.[2] the spellings *becon* and *becun* are frequent, while *becn* does not occur. Thus, the supposition that noncontraction is analogical leads to insoluble linguistic contradictions, and a coherent picture of the lingustic history of these texts cannot then be built on this analysis, while the assumption that uncontracted forms are archaic affords a unified explanation for the most salient linguistic aberrations of these works, as attested by the meter.

§130. These considerations suggest some dating limitations upon the earliest poems. If noncontraction in these poems is an archaism rather than an Anglian innovation, these poems ought to be assumed to antedate the analogical change in the Anglian dialects, which probably belongs to the first half of the ninth century: see §421 below. With the rise of this analogical change, uncontracted forms can no longer have seemed archaic, and thus poetic; this, rather, is how the contracted forms must now have seemed. The result is the steep decline in the incidence of uncontracted forms in the Cynewulfian group.

# III

# CONTRACTION IN NEGATED VERBS AND INDEFINITE PRONOUNS

§131. In 1907 Sarrazin argued that two types of contraction restricted to specific morphological categories can be correlated to metrical change across the chronology: (1) Early poetry should evince few or no examples of the contraction of the unstressed adverbial particle *ne* with certain verbs bearing relatively low stress, as in *næs* < *ne wæs*, and *nylle* < *ne wille*. (2) Contractions of the sort *(n)āht* < *(n)āwiht* and *(n)āwðer* < *(n)āhwæðer* should not be evident in early verse.[1]

§132. Amos (pp. 64–69) discusses a variety of reasons the evidence for such change might be misleading. She is right to point out that a poem with only uncontracted forms is not thereby proved to be early, since these may appear in a text of any date. Only the presence of contracted forms might furnish reliable chronological evidence. But the objection really is convincing only in regard to relatively short poems, in which the proportion of contracted to uncontracted forms may be unrepresentative. Given the relative frequency of contracted forms in verse, in a longer poem the complete exclusion of contracted forms cannot reasonably be regarded as accidental. If there are many such forms in the *Meters of Boethius* and none in *Genesis A* (as turns out to be the case), it would be methodologically wrong to regard this as chance, in the absence of counterevidence.

§133. Amos is also right to point out that most of Sarrazin's examples are inconclusive—for example, *ne wæs hit lenge þa gen* (*Beowulf* 83b), where the substitution of *næs* for *ne wæs* would be metrically acceptable. To afford certainty, contractions must be metrically verifiable (or "structural," to use Kenneth Sisam's term), not merely orthographic. Yet this requirement is not actually so very important, since the table below demonstrates that spelling is generally a good guide to contraction: among the sixty-two metrically unambiguous verses listed, there are no examples of uncontracted spelling in which a contracted form is required. Indeed, for the reasons given below (§§47ff.), we should expect scribes writing the West-Saxon standard to have altered uncontracted forms, but not the reverse. Yet in the test group of poems there is just one example

---

[1]Sarrazin, "Chronologie," pp. 159, 175–76; *Kädmon*, pp. 3, 72–73, 103, 134–35, 145. In verbs, Old English has negative contraction in common with Old Frisian: see Samuel R. Levin, "An Anglo-Frisian Morphological Correspondence," *Orbis* 9 (1960), 73–78.

of this kind, *ne bið auht* (*Meters of Boethius* 6.6b, alliteration on *b*), where *auht* is metrically dissyllabic, though in the nine other metrically unambiguous examples of the word in this work a metrical distinction between *awuht* (or *awiht*) and *auht* is maintained. And it is true, as Amos says, that Sarrazin restricts his survey to a circumscribed set of poems, excluding those generally dated late. If these contractions are capable of singling out early poems, that cannot be proved without a demonstration of consistency with the results for poems thought to be late.

§134. Amos' other objections are less persuasive:

In general it seems that the contraction of each compound or negated verb should be considered independently, since contraction occurred at different times in the different words. As Luick confesses, "the more precise conditions of this process cannot be clearly understood from the available texts" [§311]. Certain of the contractions, like *nāht* < *nāwiht*, may indeed have occurred rather late. But "in all dialects at an early date the negative adverb *ni* contracted with a following accented *ụi-* to produce *ny-*" (Campbell, §265). Luick dates the contraction "at the latest at the beginning of the ninth century" (§283). And in fact *Genesis A*, a poem often considered early, has the metrically attested contracted form *nelle* (for *nylle*). So if Sarrazin's test is to have any consistency, it must be applied with respect to individual word groups alone: *næs, nǣre, nǣron; nolde, noldon; nāh, nāhton; āht, nōht; āðere, nāðere; nysse, nyston, nylle, nyllon*; etc. Of these, the last group contracted so early that it is virtually useless as a test. (p. 65)

Several issues need to be considered here. The objection that there is a metrically attested contracted form *nelle* in *Genesis A* cannot be credited, since her data for the poem (pp. 67, 68–69) and those given below are in agreement that there are no metrically confirmable contracted forms of any kind in the poem.[2] The error is an important one, since it is apparently on this basis that she concludes that *nylle, nyllon* "contracted so early that it is virtually useless as a test," Luick remarking, as she notes, that the change may have occurred as late as the beginning of the ninth century. And the general question of dating the various contractions is not as complex as it would seem from this account, since Luick's views do not actually support her position when examined in context. The sentence that she translates here from §311 of Luick's grammar does not in reality suggest that Luick believed the contraction of *\*ni* with such words as *wæs, wille*, and *habban*, and of *\*bi* with *innan, ufan*, and the like, took place at different historical periods. The sentence means that the precise conditions for the loss of *i* in these contractions are unknown—why, for example, do *næs* and *ne wæs* often appear side by side in the same text?[3]

---

[2]The objection seems to be the result of some clerical error. The only instance of *nelle* in the poem is in *Nelle ic þa rincas* (2153a), which may belong to type a1d or a1e.

[3]That this is the real import of Luick's admission of doubt is made clear by the immediately following note, which concerns the conditions for the change, and ends with

§135. Actually, if the negated verbs like *næs* and the indefinite pronouns like *āht* are treated as separate groups, as Sarrazin intended, phonologically it is improbable that the contractions within either group did not take place at the same time. It is not improbable that *\*ni* should have contracted with *habban* at a different time from the very different sort of contraction in *āht*, etc.; nor is it improbable (though it turns out not to be the case: see below, §148) that the former contraction should have occurred later than the contraction of *\*ni* with *ǽnig*, since *habban* and *ǽnig* are different parts of speech, and so did not necessarily have the same sentence stress. But Sarrazin's first test applies only to verbs, and moreover only to verbs of high frequency and relatively low sentence stress, as demonstrated by the fact, pointed out by Bliss (§§27–29), that this group of verbs (without the negative element) almost never alliterates in *Beowulf*. It would be phonologically unnatural if the syncope of *i* in these instances were an unrelated series of accidents: to assume that these contractions took place at different times is to assume that the same rule, applying to the same morphological category, was recapitulated at several different times over the course of the history of Old English. This is not what happens in natural languages.[4] It should be borne in mind, too, that such a change could not be conditioned on a morphological basis—that is, for no other reason than simply that *willan* and *wesan* are different verbs. This is not possible because phonological change is always initiated on the basis of phonological conditioning, and is only later morphologized. The only imaginable phonological difference between *willan* and *wesan* that could account for their contracting at different times is a difference in stress, and Bliss's point renders the assumption of such a difference implausible. Luick is doubtless right that all these instances of pretonic syncope are results of the same process that resulted in the loss of *i* in medial syllables (§311)—and thus, it should be added, ought to be dated to the same period, that is to say, the beginning of the seventh century. Therefore it is not necessary to divide the negated verbs into so many different categories.

---

the remark, "So mochten zunächst Doppelformen entstehen, die synkopierten aber dann verallgemeinert werden, wenn sie häufig waren und nicht etwa sonst unübliche Anlautverbindungen entstanden." In this note he offers what is perhaps the only plausible explanation, that the proclitic particles *\*ni* and *\*bi*, in the position of low sentence stress, could undergo the same *i*-syncope that applied in noninitial syllables. The only other reason I can imagine for Amos' advancing the claim that contraction affected different words at different times is that Campbell discusses the *nylle* group (§265) at a place removed from his discussion of the rest (§354). Yet the reason for this is clear from the fact that the former passage begins a chapter headed "Changes of Accented Vowels from About 700 to 1000" (since *iwi* becomes *y*), while the latter appears in the chapter "The Vowels of Unaccented Syllables" (since here pretonic *i* is simply lost).

[4]So also slow lexical diffusion of the change is unlikely for the same reasons offered in the Conclusion, §386.

§136. But even supposing these contractions occurred at different times, it would not follow that the evidence of each group must be considered separately. If some contractions occurred before others, the likely result of examining them as a whole rather than in small groups would still be a greater number of contractions in later than in early verse. The difference is that in addition to greater numbers, there should be greater variety of contracted types in later verse. This in fact is not an unlikely situation, because even if the contractions all occurred at the same time, it does not follow that they all became acceptable in the conservative language of verse at the same time. But this situation is not essentially different from that of parasiting and contraction upon loss of intervocalic *h*: as demonstrated in the preceding chapters, most texts show a mixture of conservative and innovative forms with regard to these phonological developments, sometimes revealing uneven degrees of conservatism with respect to individual words, for example *aldor(-)* in *Beowulf.* Treating each parasited or contracted word as a separate category thus seems unjustified; yet it is because Amos treats each type of contraction separately that she finds insufficient evidence in any category to indicate any direction of change. The same indeterminacy would result if words undergoing parasiting and contraction upon loss of *h* were so divided. The table below demonstrates that when contracted forms are examined as a whole, or divided at most into two groups, verbs and pronouns, the evidence is sufficient to indicate unambiguous change. Since there is the possibility that the contracted forms became acceptable in verse at different times, the data should be examined to determine whether relevant forms found in early poetry belong to just one or two of the subgroups, while later verse evinces examples from all the subgroups—for instance, whether a presumably early poem like *Beowulf* shows contraction only in forms of *ne + willan*, while the Boethian *Meters* show contraction of *ne* with *willan*, *witan*, *habban*, and the like.

§137. In cautioning that the absence of contractions does not prove a text early, Amos remarks that Brunner's grammar

places the contraction *nāht* not before the Vespasian Psalter and Alfred (§172, n.), and in fact there are no instances among those Sarrazin cites of a metrically attested *nāht* or *āht*. But, even if Sievers-Brunner is to be trusted as to the date, the absence of the contracted form in these texts merely allows the possibility of their being earlier than the mid-ninth century (the date of the Vespasian Psalter; Campbell, §11, n. 1); it does not prove them early. Poems with the metrically attested forms *āht* and *nāht*, however, can be dated mid-ninth century (if Anglian) or later—unless their evidence is itself used to shake the statement in Sievers-Brunner. (p. 65)

This argument would seem to furnish an important, independently datable criterion, for although in the test group of poems there is just one example of a pronominal contracted form in the data that Amos adopts from Sarrazin's work, a more extensive survey of the poetic records turns up others of some importance, as shown below. But the argument is not tenable, and in fairness to Brunner it should be said that these remarks are an interpretation, since his statement need not be taken to mean anything other than that orthographically contracted forms of *nāuht* are not attested in texts earlier than Alfred's works and the Vespasian Psalter.[5] The relative lateness of the first attestations is in fact of no great significance, since there is hardly an earlier text of such a nature and length that the nonappearance of contracted forms in it should be surprising. In Sweet's charters the only example of a relevant indefinite pronoun is uncontracted *owihte* in Mercian charter 48, line 19, dated ca. 840. This is slim evidence, but it may be compared with the evidence for negative contraction, which begins in the charters with *næbbe* in Æðelnoð's endorsement to Sweet's no. 34 (Kentish, dated 805), line 13. Among Sweet's authentic charters this is in fact the earliest in English—that is, it is the first that does not simply contain English names in a Latin text—and so negative contraction is thus attested in the earliest source in which evidence might be expected. And if *nænig* is classed with the group of negated verbs, the evidence for contraction begins with *Bede's Death Song* (see below, §148). Moreover, the co-occurrence of contracted and uncontracted negated verbs in late texts is not significant for chronology, since uncontracted forms continually arose again by analogy. On the other hand, there was no analogical motivation for restoration of uncontracted forms in the indefinite pronouns, and in fact uncontracted forms are rare in late texts of all periods. And so the co-occurrence of contracted and uncontracted indefinite pronouns in VP does suggest that the change was relatively recent when this text was glossed in the ninth century. It is not unlikely that contraction in indefinite pronouns did occur later than in negated verbs.

§138. The evidence for Sarrazin's conclusions about contraction is listed below.[6] As in earlier chapters, the data cover only the poems of the test group, though in this instance only poems containing unambiguous examples are included in the table, since most of the poems provide no evidence: *Judith*, *Christ II*, and all the short poems contain no examples at all, while *Exodus* and the *Fates of the Apostles* have only ambiguous instances (three and one, respectively). Except at *Beowulf* 2124a and *Maldon* 224a (discussed below), unstressed examples are self-evidently of no interest, because in no instance does the decontraction of

[5] What he actually says is, "Abfall eines anlautenden *w* findet sich vor *u* (vgl. §173) in *uton* neben *wuton* und ebenso im Anlaut nebentoniger Silben in *nāuht* (urspr. wohl zweisilbig *nā-uht*, dann und zwar zuerst bei Ælfred *nāht*; ebenso *nōht*, zuerst Vesp. Ps. und Ælfred aus *nōwuht, nōwiht* . . .)."

[6] The results differ from Amos' results, largely because she adopts Sarrazin's data rather than surveying the poetic records themselves.

an unstressed example affect the metrical acceptability of a verse. Discarding these irrelevant examples reduces the data considerably: of the twenty-three examples that Amos lists from *Beowulf*, for example, sixteen are unstressed. In the table, A = *ne* + preterite forms of *wesan*, B = *ne* + preterite forms of *willan*, C = *ne* + present forms of *willan* or preterite forms of *witan* 'know', D = *ne* + present forms of *witan*, or forms of *āgan*, E = *ne* + forms of *habban*, F = *(n)āwiht* and related forms, G = *(n)āhwæðer* and related forms, and H = *æghwæðer* and related forms. These are the same groups that Amos distinguishes, except that she does not include *habban* or *æghwæðer*, and she does list *ōhwær/ōwer*, excluded here. Sarrazin should not have listed these last forms, since they do not and cannot show contraction under any circumstances. One other contraction, not previously noted, is omitted because of its extreme rarity: *swæðer* occurs nowhere in the test group (and otherwise only at *Finnsburh* 27a, where it is unstressed and ambiguous), and *swā hwæðer* just once (at *Beowulf* 686a). The varieties of contraction are listed separately in the table below because of the observation offered above that not all of the contractions within either of the two main groups need have become acceptable in verse at the same time. But the the division between groups A–E and F–H is perhaps the only relevant subcategorical distinction, if any is relevant. The scansion of the verse under Bliss's system is provided in parentheses after each verse number.

| UNCONTRACTED | CONTRACTED | AMBIGUOUS |
| --- | --- | --- |

*Genesis A*  (2,319 lines)

| | | |
| --- | --- | --- |
| A: 901b (2B1b) | | A: 978b (1A*1a or 2A1a) |
| 1482b (2B1c) | | 1565b (3B*1b or 3B1b) |
| 1994b (2B1b) | | 2364b (see below) |
| 2824b (2B1c) | | B: 1448b (1A*1a or 2A1a) |
| B: 1979b (1A1a) | | 1580b (1A*1a or 2A1a) |
| 2423b (1A1a) | | 1590b (see below) |
| C: 179b (1A1a) | | 1937b (1A*1a or 2A1a) |
| D: 1686b (1A1a) | | 2241b (1A*1a or 2A1a) |
| F: 1905a (2A1a) | | 2265b (1A*1a or 2A1a) |
| | | 2571a (1A*1a or 2A1a) |
| | | G: 2468b (2A1a[iii] or [i]) |

*Daniel*  (764 lines)

| | | |
| --- | --- | --- |
| A: 16b (2B1d) | B: 189b (2C1b) | A: 342b (3B*1c or 3B1c) |
| 102b (1A1a) | | 668b (3E*1 or 3E1) |
| 176a (2B1c) | | B: 197b (1A1a or 2C1a) |
| C: 125a (a1c) | | F: 273b (1A*1a or 1A1a) |
| | | 343a (1A*1a or 1A1a) |
| | | 428b (3B2b or 3B1b) |

| UNCONTRACTED | CONTRACTED | AMBIGUOUS |
| --- | --- | --- |

*Beowulf* (3,182 lines)

A: 2467b (2B1c)
C: 798a (a1c)
D: 1331b (2C2b)
F: 1822b (3E1)
H: 287b (3E1)
   1636b (d1b)
   2564b (3E1)

A: 860b (1A*1a or 2A1a)
   1167b (see below)
   2332b (3B*1c or 3B1c)
   2682b (3B*1b or 3B1b)
B: 154b (1A*1a or 2A1a)
   706b (1A1a or 2C1a)
   803b (1A*1a or 2A1a)
   812b (1A*1a or 2A1a)
   967b (1A1a or 2C1a)
   1523b (1A*1a or 2A1a)
   2476b (1A*1a or 2A1a)
C: 246b (1A*1a or 2A1a)
   679b (1A*1a or 2A1a)
   878b (1A*1a or 2A1a)
E: 1850b (1A*1a or 2A1a)
F: 2314b (3B1b or 2C2b)
H: 2844a (d1b or a1b)

*Elene* (1,321 lines)

A: 782b (1A1a)
B: 394b (3B1b)
F: 571b (2A1a)

A: 171b (2C1b)
   776b (2C1b)
C: 719b (2C1c)
   1239b (1A*1a)
D: 640b (2B2b)

B: 219b (1A*1a or 2A1a)
   361b (1A*1a or 2A1a)

*Juliana* (731 lines)

A: 258b (2B1b)

E: 77b (2C1b)
F: 329b (3B1b)

C: 126a (3B*1c or 3B1c)
   174a (3B*1c or 3B1c)
   251b (3B*1c or 3B1c)

*Andreas* (1,722 lines)

A: 898b (1A1a)
B: 1660b (1A1a)
C: 261a (a1c)
F: 800b (1D1)

H: 1051a (1A*1b)

B: 402b (1A*1a or 2A1a)
C: 178b (1A*1a or 2A1a)
   745b (2B1b or 2C2b)
H: 1015a (1D*1[ii] or [i])

*Meters of Boethius* (1,750 lines)

A: 8.15b (1A1a)
F: 6.6b (2C1a)
   9.62b (2A1a)
   11.9b (2A1a)
   18.7b (2A1a)
   20.107b (2A1a)

A: 8.12b (1A1a)
   20.20b (3E2)
   31.21b (1A1b)
C: 25.67b (3B1b)
D: 19.37a (2B2a)
E: 20.195b (2C1b)

A: 20.37a (see below)
   20.103a (1A1a or 2C1a)
   26.92b (3B*1c or 3B1c)
   28.36a (3B*1b or 3B1b)
   28.71b (1A*1a or 2A1a)
C: 9.63a (2B1b or 2C2b)

| UNCONTRACTED | CONTRACTED | AMBIGUOUS |
|---|---|---|
| 25.59b (2A1a) | 25.71a (3B1b) | 11.10b (3B*1b or 3B1b, etc.) |
| H: 20.12b (d1b) | F: 6.16b (1D1) | 26.66b (1A*1a or 2A1a, etc.) |
| | 11.87b (1A*1a) | D: 16.21a (3B*1b or 3B1b) |
| | 16.20b (1A*1a) | E: 22.46b (3B*1b or 3B1b, etc.) |
| | 29.87b (1A*1a) | 27.5b (2B1c or 2C2c) |
| | | F: 11.10b (3B1b or 2C2b, etc.) |
| | | 13.26b (1A*1b or 1A1b) |
| | | 20.30b (3B*1b or 2B1b) |
| | | 20.42a (*auht*: 1A*1b or 2B2a) |
| | | 20.42a (*nauht*: 1A*1b or 2B2a) |
| | | 20.166b (1A*1a or 1A1a) |
| | | 21.23b (1A*1b or 1A1b) |
| | | 22.46b (3B1b or 2C2b, etc.) |
| | | G: 20.42b (2A1a[iii] or [i]) |
| | | 29.10a (1D*5[ii] or [i]) |
| *Maldon* (325 lines) | | |
| A: 190b (2B1b) | B: 6a (2C1b) | B: 201b (1A*1a or 2A1a) |
| | 9b (2C1b) | C: 317b (1A1b or 1A1a) |
| | 185b (2C1b) | |
| | C: 246b (2C1b) | |
| | H: 133a (1A*1b) | |

§139. Several of these verses merit comment. The verse *þeah þe he his magum nære* (*Beowulf* 1167b) is hypermetric, either type a1d(1A*1a) or type a1d(2A1a). In a few places the scansion given here differs from Amos'. She indicates that *to gode noldon* (*Daniel* 197b) may be read with either a long or a short vowel in *gode*, but the context makes it clear that a short vowel is required:

> Cnihtas cynegode    cuð gedydon,
> þæt hie him þæt gold    to gode noldon
> habban ne healdan,    ac þone hean cyning,
> gasta hyrde,    ðe him gife sealde. (196–99)

The point is confirmed a few lines later, where Nebuchadnezzar is said not to have been able to persuade the three young Hebrews to turn *to þam gyldnan gylde, þe him to gode geteode* (204). Moreover, Bliss would not allow *tō gōde ne woldon* because he finds no anacrusis with type 1A*1a in the off-verse. The verse *þa þis hegan ne willaþ* (207a) cannot belong to type 1A*1a, since there ought not to be anacrusis in the on-verse, and dissyllabic anacrusis at that, without double alliteration. And when double alliteration does occur, it usually consists of a dissyllabic prefix or a monosyllabic prefix and a negative particle. Moreover, Bliss insists on alliteration on the first lift of every verse, and the alliteration here is on *w*. The line is corrupt—there is also double alliteration on the off-verse, which will not scan—and *hegan* is usually emended.[7]

§140. The verse *laðra owihte* (*Beowulf* 2432b) does not belong ambiguously either to type 2A1a(ii) or (i), since the former type requires resolution in the second thesis (Bliss, §54), which is impossible here. Bliss would emend *ōwihte* to *ōhte* (§64), but instead most editors have preferred *wihte* (see Klaeber's apparatus). This is more likely because adverbial *wiht(e)* appears thirteen times in the poem, with no instances of adverbial *ōhte* or *āhte*.[8] It was mentioned above that examples of relevant forms in unstressed position have been disregarded, since they are all ambiguous. In one instance, however, Amos scans an unstressed form as unambiguously contracted: *Nōðer hy hine ne moston* (*Beowulf* 2124a) belongs to type a1f.[9] The problem here is that Bliss finds no more than six unstressed syllables in the first thesis of type a1 in *Beowulf*. It is sufficient to note that the type does occur outside of *Beowulf*, as in *Ne sceolon me on þære þeode* (*Maldon* 220a; also *Dream of the Rood* 83a, 122a, etc.). But the general methodological principle here is also worthy of remark. Bliss clearly did not intend his findings on the number of

---

[7]Toller, however, suggests that this may stand for *hīgan*, and compares *hēan* 'exalt'. Emendation to *wegan* 'submit to' seems not to have been suggested, though this reading makes sense of the passage and is metrically acceptable. This in turn perhaps explains how the off-verse *ne þysne wig wurðigean* was corrupted. If originally the verb was not *wurðigean* but another of the same meaning, *herian*, this would give acceptable scansion and proper alliteration. But the alteration of *wegan* to *hegan* would then have changed the alliteration from *w* to *h*, putting alliteration into the final arsis, and thus inviting further scribal change.

[8]As a pronoun, though, *āht* does appear once in the poem, at 2314b. And *ōwihte* also appears once, at 1822b:

> Gif ic þonne on eorþan　　owihte mæg
> þinre modlufan　　maran tilian,
> gumena dryhten,　　ðonne ic gyt dyde,
> guðgeweorca,　　ic beo gearo sona. (1822–25)

Klaeber presumably considered the word adverbial, parsing it as dative singular; but the meaning 'any' or 'at all' with the comparative (see his note to line 1825) seems to require the use of *þy/þon*. And so *ōwihte* here is more likely pronominal, i.e. it is the genitive object of *tilian*, modified by the adjective *māran*, this phrase in turn being modified by the genitive phrase *þīnre mōdlufan*, lit. 'any(thing) more of your affection'. This explains *gūðgeweorca* at 1825a, which Klaeber finds puzzling. He seems reluctant to connect it with *ōwihte* because they are widely separated; but the two constructions are not actually so far apart if *māran* modifies *ōwihte*.

[9]The same reasoning applies to a verse for which she does not offer a scansion, *he wæs ægðer min mæg* (*Maldon* 224a). But here, as her doubts about the scansion of this verse imply, it might be that *min* is stressed, as it is in the off-verse. In classical verse this would not be possible, but it is demonstrated below (§291) that in later verse, beginning with the *Meters of Boethius*, the lift and half-lift in type a2 may be separate words.

pretonic syllables found in light verses in *Beowulf* as a guide to what is possible in verse. This is a different sort of finding from, for instance, his conclusion that type D* is restricted to the on-verse with double alliteration. This latter finding he advances as an inviolable rule (see, e.g., §§65, 77, and 78). And it is not surprising that the pretonic patterns of light verses in *Beowulf* are not offered as the absolute limits of acceptable types, since this is an instance in which a metrical limitation has a clear nonmetrical motivation. There is no discernible reason to insist that six unstressed syllables may appear in the first thesis of type a1, but not seven. Rather, that no more than six appear in *Beowulf* is attributable to the fact that Old English syntax can rarely accommodate this many particles in pretonic position. In other words, there is no metrical reason to exclude eight or nine unstressed syllables before the arsis; but such verses probably do not exist, given the limitations of syntax. The point is demonstrated by the fact that seven syllables do occur once in the first thesis of type a2 in *Beowulf*.

§141. A few other instances are similar, since they might be scanned as types that are not improbable, though Bliss does not find such types in *Beowulf*. Amos concludes, not unreasonably, that *andsaca ne wæs* (*Daniel* 668b) may belong to either type 3E*3 or 3E3, though the former does not appear in the off-verse in *Beowulf* (it in fact appears just once in the poem), and the latter appears only in the off-verse (five times).[10] The distribution of E subtypes in *Beowulf* offers no reason to think either 3E*3 or 3E3 should be restricted to the on-verse or the off-verse, respectively. No other E subtype is so restricted. Similarly, *auðer oðres rene* (*Meters* 29.10a) should be considered ambiguous: even though type 1D*5(ii) is not attested in *Beowulf*, its acceptability is probable, since it is partially paralleled by *sellice sædracan* (*Beowulf* 1426a) and *eahtodan eorlscipe* (3173a). On the other hand, it would be unwise to consider *Ægðer þara eorla* (*Andreas* 1051a) and *ægþer hyra oðrum* (*Maldon* 133a) ambiguous under the same reasoning. In just one instance does Bliss find resolution immediately following the first lift in type 1A* in *Beowulf*, in *earfeþo on yþum* (534a). But this is a different matter, as here the second syllable is etymologically long; and in any case this verse is shown below to be dubitable on a variety of grounds (§241), as it ought to seem, at any rate, since it is the only such verse among 604 of type 1A* in the poem.

§142. In a similar vein, a certain amount of guesswork is involved in scanning the Boethian *Meters* and *Maldon*, as there are some metrical differences between these poems and *Beowulf*—the reason being, it is usually assumed, that these poems are later, and the verse tradition has undergone development (see esp. Chap. 10). An example is the verse *Nis*

---

[10]In deference to convention the verse is scanned above as either type 3E*1 or 3E1, since *andsaca* is usually assumed to bear tertiary stress. But Amos may well be right: see below, §234.

*þæt gedafenlic* (*Meters* 31.21b), where the alliteration is on *n*. Bliss (§§19–21) argues at length that finite verbs should not be stressed in this position in *Beowulf*, and even those who are unconvinced by his reasoning would undoubtedly agree that the verse seems odd, since stressed forms of the copula are rare in *Beowulf*. But the *Meters* contain many anomalies of this sort. In this instance there can at any rate be no doubt of contraction, because of the alliteration. The alliteration is decisive in some other instances, as well, for example in *gif we yfles noht* (*Juliana* 329b) and *þæt he winnan nyle* (*Meters* 25.67b), where noncontraction would put alliteration into the final lift of the line. The verse *forðam þe nan þing nis* (*Meters* 20.37a, with alliteration on *þ*) is ambiguous because, once again, it is demonstrated below (§291) that in the *Meters* and other verifiably late poetry the lift and half-lift in type a2 may be separate words, while in poetry that presumably antedates the *Meters* this is not permitted.

§143. In accordance with the principle set forth above (Chap. 1, n. 40), *Cham ne wolde* (*Genesis A* 1590b) must be considered ambiguous, since the scansion of biblical names is unreliable: *Cham* might be dissyllabic. On the other hand, the ambiguity inherent in *Genesis A* 978b and *Elene* 219b has nothing to do with the proper names they contain. At *Genesis A* 2364b, *þam þe gen nis* must in all fairness be regarded as ambiguous, since Sievers ("Rhythmik," p. 484) suggests emending *gēn* to *gēna*. But there seems little scribal motivation for this. The verse *Nis hit owihtes god* (*Daniel* 428b), though counted here as ambiguous, despite the spelling is perhaps more likely to represent a contracted form, since Bliss's type 3B2 is dubitable: see below, §238 in Chap. 7.

§144. Two verses have been omitted in desperation. Bliss (§79) argues that a scribe has expanded the pronoun *nāthwylc* to a clause in *sceaðona ic nat hwylc* (*Beowulf* 274b), since verses of this type ought not to appear in the off-verse. Bliss is most likely right, not primarily for the metrical reason, but because the construction is peculiar, and unique in verse. And if the phrase represents a separate clause, and thus does not offend against Kuhn's first law, the stress on *nāt* is troublesome: compare *Fates of the Apostles* 111b, *Juliana* 700b, and the like. If Bliss is right, the verse is irrelevant to the issue at hand; and even if he is not, the uncontracted scansion hardly seems less metrically anomalous than the contracted one. Also omitted is *We ðæt æbylgð nyton* (*Elene* 401b), since secondary stress in the second thesis of type B is paralleled in the test group only in *þæt ðu mildheort me* (*Andreas* 1285a). There seems no remedy for the problem, and at any rate the omission is not significant, since the verse is ambiguous, regardless.

§145. The data contained in the table would be more valuable if there were more unambiguous verses involved, but on the other hand there are certainly enough examples here to afford the conclusion that these contractions show development in accordance with the presumed chronology.

It is to be expected that uncontracted forms should be found in the verse of all periods, since contracted and uncontracted forms both occurred until the end of the Old English period, and uncontracted forms, if they occurred by no other means, could be recreated by analogy. Contracted forms, however, should be commoner in the later verse than in the earlier, and this in general is what the table indicates. Uncontracted forms are missing altogether from *Genesis A* and *Beowulf*. There is just one contracted form in *Daniel*, but the number increases considerably in the Cynewulf canon, and dramatically in the *Meters of Boethius* and *Maldon*, in proportion to the length of these poems. Moreover, it was pointed out above that if the contracted forms did not all become acceptable at the same time (and there seems no good reason to insist that they should have), then it should be expected that the variety of contracted types should widen with the passage of time. This is what the table suggests, since *Daniel* shows contraction only in the *nolde* type, while Cynewulf's signed poems and the Boethian *Meters* show a variety of types. The two types attested in *Maldon* are also remarkable for a poem this short. As for *Andreas*, a strict count of the verbs reveals fewer contractions than in *Daniel*, but of course it cannot reasonably be argued that this means *Andreas* is earlier, since the statistical difference is too small. On the other hand, the difference between *Andreas* and both the Cynewulfian poems and the *Meters* is more extreme, and so is considerably less likely to be due to accident.

§146. It was remarked above (§133) that orthography is generally a good guide to contraction, because spelling disagrees with scansion in just one of the sixty-two metrically unambiguous forms relevant to this type of contraction in the test group. Among the ambiguous verses in the table above, spelling indicates the following scansions:

|  | UNCONTRACTED | CONTRACTED |
|---|---|---|
| *Genesis A* | 8 | 3 |
| *Daniel* | 5 | 1 |
| *Beowulf* | 7 | 10 |
| *Elene* | 2 | 0 |
| *Juliana* | 0 | 3 |
| *Andreas* | 3 | 1 |
| *Meters* | 3 | 18 |
| *Maldon* | 1 | 1 |

For the most part these figures are congruent with the results for metrically unambiguous verses, for example, many uncontracted forms in *Genesis A* and many contracted ones in the *Meters of Boethius*. Only the figures for *Beowulf* are very surprising. They suggest the possibility that the nonoccurrence of metrically contracted forms in this poem is accidental, for while the seven metrically uncontracted forms seem an estimable number, they are actually few in comparison to the total of relevant forms in the poem, since ambiguous verses are numerous. Yet it is also fairly certain that at least some scribes were aware of the meter as they copied, and although they altered spellings at will, they tended not to modernize spellings required by the meter: see Appendix A below in regard to scribal practice in the Psalms of the Paris Psalter. In the present instance, the latter possibility derives some support from the fact that three ambiguous verses in *Genesis A* are spelt with contracted forms, though the metrically unambiguous verses are numerous enough to render it fairly certain that contracted forms are not to be expected at all in this poem.

§147. A study by Samuel R. Levin sheds some light on this question, and suggests a different interpretation of the data for the verbs.[11] Levin finds that in West-Saxon prose texts of all periods the incidence of uncontracted verb forms is so small as to be negligible. For instance, in the texts and portions of texts from before ca. 1000 that he examined (The Hatton MS of the *Pastoral Care*, the Tollemache Orosius, and the West-Saxon Gospel According to St. Matthew), the proportion of contracted to uncontracted forms was 306:9. On the other hand, in Anglian prose texts (limited necessarily to the ninth and tenth centuries), uncontracted forms are not infrequent: the combined figures for the Mercian texts he examined (Ru.[1] and VP, with the Hymns) were 127:56, and for the Northumbrian (Li. and Rit.), 66:43. Moreover, the distinction can be traced in both prose and verse in Middle English. Texts from the South and the West Midlands use almost exclusively contracted forms (the total proportion is 495:2), while those from the East Midlands and the North evince both types (107:210). In this latter category, however, there are not in fact any negative contractions in the Northern texts studied (prose treatises of Richard Rolle, *Cursor Mundi*, songs of Laurence Minot, and Barbour's *Bruce*), though they contain a rather low number of uncontracted forms (twenty-one in all).[12] Levin's findings are confirmed by the *Linguistic Atlas of Late Mediaeval English*.[13]

---

[11]"Negative Contraction: An Old and Middle English Dialect Criterion," *JEGP* 57 (1958), 492–501.

[12]The forms *nart* and *nere* do in fact appear in portions of the *Cursor Mundi* that Levin did not examine: see the glossary by R. Morris, EETS, o.s. 99 (1892). But since the work is translated from a southern dialect, these are not firm evidence.

[13]In dot maps 1048–55, restricted to the South (which in the *Atlas* includes East Anglia and the southern portion of the West Midlands, extending in a line between them as far north as Warwickshire and Cambridgeshire), reflexes of OE *ne* + *wesan*, *willan*, *habban*, and *witan* are distributed throughout the area. The four Northern texts that Levin studied are from the fourteenth century, and so are rather later than most of the Southern texts. But they are the earliest Middle English texts of any significance from the North, for reasons explained in the *Linguistic Atlas*, 1:3. Although the atlas does not survey the Northwest Midlands for this feature, it is found in the poems of the *Pearl* manuscript.

§148. If it is true that negative contractions are not a feature of the Northern dialects in the fourteenth and fifteenth centuries (see nn. 12 and 13), they must have been discarded in the course of the early Middle English period, since they are found in all the longer Northumbrian texts of the tenth century, Li., Rit., and Ru.[2], where they are common enough that it seems implausible that they should have disappeared altogether before the end of the Old English period. There is no Old English dialect attested that does not evince examples of these negative contractions, and so it is not plausible that the absence of such forms from *Genesis A* should be a dialect feature rather than an archaism. The point is corroborated by forms of *nænig*, a word that does not fit conveniently into either of the two main categories treated above, since it has contraction of *ne*, but with a pronoun rather than a verb. The word is missing altogether from *Genesis A*, though *ænig* is used in negative constructions eight of the twelve times it appears in the poem.[14] It is found, however, in all the other poems in the table above, except *Maldon*,[15] with instances confirmed by the alliteration in *Beowulf*, *Elene*, *Andreas*, and the *Meters of Boethius*.[16] But the word is found in all the longer Northumbrian texts of the tenth century, and is also confirmed for early eighth-century Northumbrian by the alliteration in *naenig uuiurthit* (*Bede's Death Song* 1b). Yet *nænig* is especially important because it is in fact a dialect indicator—but it is an Anglianism, not a West-Saxonism.[17] And there is a wealth of evidence to show that *Genesis A* must originally have been composed in an Anglian dialect (see Chap. 11 below). And so at least in this instance the absence of negative contraction seems more likely a sign of antiquity than of dialect origins. The evidence in regard to *Genesis A*, then, is strong, as it involves negative contraction in verbs both metrically and orthographically, contraction in indefinite pronouns, and the word *ænig*. *Beowulf* would appear to be less conservative, since it has *nænig*, as well as orthographic contraction, while all other poems show metrical contraction in the negated verbs. The evidence of *Genesis A* thus suggests that *ne* did contract with *ænig* at about the same time it did with verbs.

§149. While negative contraction is distributed at least in part on a dialectal basis in Old English, contraction in indefinite pronouns is

---

[14]See verses 180b, 948b, 1023a, 1591b, 1690a, 2178a, 2217b, 2652a. Nor does *nænig* appear in *Genesis B*, but then there is no equivalent to the word in Old Saxon.

[15]In *Maldon* the word *ænig* appears twice, once in a negative construction (70a).

[16]Cf. *Beowulf* 598b, *Elene* 505b, *Andreas* 1037b, and *Meters* 20.25a (a partial list).

[17]Sisam (*Studies*, p. 294, n. 1) points to an instance of *nænig* in the Prologue to Ine's laws as evidence that the word was not merely an Anglianism in the earlier period. But Wenisch (p. 199) counters that the Old English laws show considerable Anglian influence—e.g., Ine's laws contain examples of *hafað* and *bebycgan*; and in the Prologue to Alfred's laws, those of Offa are cited as a source. He lists and examines all instances of the word in prose, and concludes that the few times the word appears in West-Saxon texts it is always due to dialect interference.

common in the prose of all dialects, and uncontracted forms are rare in late texts of all dialects. And so the complete absence of this type of contraction in verse presumed to antedate Cynewulf reinforces the conclusions of the preceding chapters. Reasons were offered above (§137) to suppose that this contraction occurred later than negative contraction, and that it was still relatively new when VP was glossed. These probabilities are consonant with the assumption that *Genesis A*, *Daniel*, and *Beowulf* are to be dated before the ninth century. This evidence is not as strong as that presented in the preceding chapters. The implications are questionable for the early part of the chronology (though least so for *Beowulf*) because the overall incidence of relevant types in the indefinite category is low. But they are corroborated by the evidence of orthography, since just one (*Beowulf* 2314b) of the six instances of metrically ambiguous forms in the group through *Beowulf* is spelt with contraction. This may be compared with the situation in the *Meters of Boethius*, in which just one of the ten instances is spelt without contraction.[18]

§150. Recently Mary Blockley has proposed that the co-occurrence of contracted and uncontracted negated verbs in verse is not random, but is governed on a syntactic basis.[19] This is argued by analogy to Modern English, where deletion and movement transformations affecting elements immediately after the verb block contractions like *she's*, *I'd*, and (in American English) *wanna*. To use one of Blockley's examples, the meaning of *He's interested in the car and she is in the truck* is ambiguous, as the second clause may mean either that she is sitting in the truck or that she is interested in it. On the other hand, if *she is* is contracted to *she's* the clause is disambiguated, since contraction is blocked under the second interpretation. The reason, according to trace theory, is that when *interested* is deleted by transformation it leaves a trace, which in turn prevents the morphophonological component from applying the contraction rule. The assumption that a trace really is involved receives support from instances in which material is not deleted, but simply extraposed from its normal position in the deep structure, as in *How interested do you think she is in the truck?* in which *wh*-movement has shifted *how interested* to the beginning of the sentence.[20] Blockley attempts to demonstrate that a similar constraint governs the distribution of contracted and uncontracted

---

[18]The only other relevant ambiguous verse in the test group of poems is at *Andreas* 1015a, with an uncontracted form. The high incidence of these pronouns in the *Meters* is presumably due to the prosaic nature of the work.

[19]See "Constraints on Negative Contraction with the Finite Verb and the Syntax of Old English Poetry," *SP* 85 (1988), 428–50; and "Uncontracted Negation as a Cue to Sentence Structure in Old English Verse," *JEGP* 89 (1990), 475–90. These articles are cited as "Constraints" and "Cue" in the remainder of the chapter. I wish to thank Professor Blockley, who heard out my doubts and graciously sent me off-prints.

[20]The example is based on one of Andrew Radford's in *Transformational Syntax* (Cambridge: Cambridge Univ. Press, 1981), p. 164.

negated verbs in Old English verse. For example, as remarked by Bruce Mitchell (§1131), the following two passages from *Genesis A* do not seem sufficiently different in their syntax to support the supposition that the difference in contraction between 1448b and 2571a is anything but random:

>                        Eft him seo wen geleah,
>      ac se feonde gespearn        fleotende hreaw;
>      salwigfeðera        secan nolde. (1446a–48)

>                        Æfre siððan
>      se monlica,        þæt is mære spell,
>      stille wunode,        þær hie strang begeat
>      wite, þæs heo wordum        wuldres þegna
>      hyran ne wolde. (2567b–71a)

Blockley explains that in the latter it is the movement of *wordum* (the "indirect object"—the quotation marks are hers, "Constraints," p. 437) to its position in front of the verb that blocks contraction. Movement of the direct object, as in the former passage, does not constrain contraction. Another minimal pair of passages, illustrating the effects of deletion, derives from the Psalms of the Paris Psalter:

>      fore ænigre        egesan næfde,
>      ne him fultum þær        fæstne gelyfde;
>      ac he on his welan spede        wræste getruwode,
>      and on idel gylp        ealra geornost. (51.6.1–4)

>      Hi hine samnuncga        scearpum strelum
>      on scotiað,        egsan ne habbað,
>      ac hi mid wraðum        wordum trymmað
>      and sare sprecað:        Hwa gesyhð usic? (63.4.1–4)

In the former instance the "indirect object, the recipient of the direct object *egesan*," is expressed, and is positioned before the verb; in the latter instance it is unexpressed. The first instance resembles the second passage from *Genesis A* above, but the difference is that the latter has a preposition before the direct object. Blockley thus refines her proposal, arguing that it is not simply the position of the indirect object, but the deletion of a preposition before the indirect object that blocks contraction in the passage from *Genesis A*.

§151. Blockley's is a valuable and interesting hypothesis, not least of all for its innovative application of generative theory to a morphological problem of Old English. Yet her conclusion cannot be considered so firm as to undercut the evidence of a chronological distribution for negative contraction. While the constraint on contraction in Modern English has a clear motivation, this cannot be said of the Old English constraint. In

Modern English, contraction is blocked at the morphophonological level by stress on the verb, that stress being the phonological interpretation of the trace left by the transformation affecting the moved or deleted material. A more impressionistic but less abstract way of saying the same thing is that the speaker has a sense that *is* means something more in *He's paid by the council and she is by the directorate* than it does in *She is on the telephone*. That is, in the former instance *is* means *is paid*, and because of that added meaning the word has greater stress. As a result of that stress, it cannot be contracted.[21] No such motivation is observable in the Old English examples. It is *ne*, not the verb, that loses its vowel in contraction, and yet preventing contraction by this means is problematic, since meter demonstrates that *ne* is never stressed. More important, *ne* is on the wrong side of the verb to acquire a stress-providing trace from an extraposed direct object, and it is frequently at a considerable distance from a direct object with no preposition.

§152. Equally important is the problem of specifying the precise conditions for the constraint. From the examples above it was concluded that contraction is blocked by deleting a preposition in front of a direct object placed before the verb; and yet this formulation seems to be contradicted by the clause *þæt hie him þæt gold to gode noldon / habban ne healdan* (*Daniel* 197–98a), where *him* lacks a preposition. (The assumption, incidentally, that a preposition in the deep structure has been deleted before these "indirect objects" is unlikely, given the history of case relations and the use of prepositions from Proto-Indo-European times to the present.) At any rate, from the example *forþan ic hine sweorde swebban nelle* (*Beowulf* 679) it is necessary to conclude that neither movement of the indirect object to a position in front of the verb nor the deletion of a preposition in addition to that movement is sufficient to block contraction: the preposition can be deleted without blocking contraction if the direct object is also expressed ("Constraints," p. 437). At this point the qualifications have become sufficiently complex that the problem of whether and how a grammar could specify such an intricate set of restrictions becomes urgent; and the clause from *Daniel* remains recalcitrant. The differences in the conditions for contraction among the relevant verbs also suggest some difficulties specifying the constraint in the grammar: clause-initially, *willan* contracts "when its complement is an intransitive infinitive or a transitive infinitive with its objects expressed"; *habban* "when its complement includes an expressed

---

[21]This account in terms of "added meaning" is admittedly oversimplified, as it does not account very straightforwardly for the prohibition against contraction in constructions like *I wonder where Gerard's today. Description in terms of deleted and moved elements is certainly more accurate. The example is Harold V. King's in "On Blocking the Rules for Contraction in English," *Linguistic Inquiry* 1 (1970), 134–36, at 135; see also C. L. Baker, "Stress Level and Auxiliary Behavior in English," *Linguistic Inquiry* 2 (1971), 167–81, at 170–71.

direct object (accusative case)"; and *witan* "when its complement is a clause that is *not* anticipated by a demonstrative *þæt*" ("Constraints," p. 436). This is a complex set of rules to be learned in the course of language acquisition.

§153. Similar rule complexity arises in regard to another minimal pair, in *Beowulf*:

> Wod under wolcnum      to þæs þe he winreced,
> goldsele gumena,      gearwost wisse,
> fættum fahne.  Ne wæs þæt forma sið
> þæt he Hroþgares      ham gesohte;
> næfre he on aldordagum      ær *ne* siþðan
> heardran hæle,      healðegnas fand. (714–19)

>                 næfre hit æt hilde ne swac
> manna ængum      þara þe hit mid mundum bewand,
> se ðe gryresiðas      gegan dorste,
> folcstede fara;      næs þæt forma sið
> þæt hit ellenweorc      æfnan scolde.
> Huru ne gemunde      mago Ecglafes,
> eafoþes cræftig,      þæt he ær gespræc
> wine druncen,      þa he þæs wæpnes onlah
> selran sweordfrecan. (1460b–68a)

Here in both instances the relevant clause is followed by an independent clause. Again the hypothesis must be augmented: the relationship between the independent clauses is causal, assuming that ll. 718–19 explain why Grendel has been able to visit Heorot so often (the litotic implication of ll. 716–17); and causal relationships between clauses block contraction ("Constraints," pp. 439–40; "Cue," pp. 480–82). But it has frequently been remarked that the governing theme in the description of Grendel's approach to Heorot is the ironic contrast between his expectations and the actual fate that awaits him.[22] Yet, granting the causal relationship, it would be difficult to find a linguistic parallel to such an instance of morphophonological influence between independent clauses, or a single morphophonological alternation that is governed by a variety of syntactic and semantic phenomena as diverse as preposition deletion, the movement of noun phrases, and causal relationships among clauses. Contraction is made to do much. If the sort of syntactic and semantic information conveyed by noncontraction is useful, it is peculiar that it is overtly expressed only in negative clauses, which comprise a relatively small proportion of all clauses, and that this should be so only in verse.

[22]R. E. Kaske was the first to point this out, in "*Sapientia et Fortitudo* as the Controlling Theme in *Beowulf*," *SP* 55 (1958), 423–57, at 439. The idea was subsequently elaborated independently by Richard N. Ringler, "*Him sēo wēn gelēah*: The Design for Irony in Grendel's Last Visit to Heorot," *Speculum* 41 (1966), 49–67, and Edward B. Irving, Jr., *A Reading of "Beowulf"* (New Haven: Yale Univ. Press, 1968), pp. 22–31.

§154. Clause-final contraction is also difficult to analyze. Here existential *be* (e.g. *is* in the sense 'exists') always contracts—the opposite of the situation in Modern English, where existential *be* is always stressed. That it should always be unstressed in Old English, while other forms of *wesan* may presumably be stressed, seems counterintuitive, since existential *be* has greater semantic force than the copula, which is simply a connector between subject and complement, and in Modern English is thus usually unstressed. A specific problem arises with the appearance of *þe* (or *swa*) *hit riht ne wæs* at *Maldon* 190b and *Vainglory* 63b (cf. also *swa hit gedefe ne wæs* at *Meters* 26.92b and *Psalms* 105.22.2b). Since contraction is understood not to be constrained when the subject complement is expressed, it is necessary to assume that some material has been deleted before the verb: "While Godric and Lucifer are clearly the particular persons whose behavior is being condemned, the poets stop short of saying that such conduct was not right *for them*, in order to imply that to do so is wrong for anyone" ("Constraints," p. 444). The virtue of accounting for all instances in verse is balanced by the unrestrictedness of the power that must be accorded the hypothesis, allowing the absolute neutralization of major elements in the deep structure. At this point, governance of the phenomenon is transferred from the hypothesis itself to an unpredictable factor, the deletion of elements like this *for them*. The explanatory power of the hypothesis is thus undercut, since an extratheoretical factor takes over, explaining the unknown by the unknown.

§155. In sum, then, the obstacles to accounting for the distribution of contracted and uncontracted verbs on the basis of syntactic environment are sufficient to prevent this from standing as an impediment to the chronological analysis of contraction in negated verbs. On the other hand, it must be true that variation in the incidence of contracted verbs has a dialectal distribution. Yet even this will not account for the complete absence of contracted, negated verbs in *Genesis A* (less certainly *Beowulf*), though it will account for the near absence in the *Meters of Boethius*. Contraction in verbs then does appear to correlate at least partially to the presumed chronology, and contraction in indefinite pronouns certainly does, as this is unaffected by peculiarities of dialectal distribution. This evidence is not as strong as that of the preceding chapters, for the reasons given above, and also because so many poems are wholly unrepresented. But the evidence is nonetheless fairly definite, and all of it is consistent with the evidence of the preceding chapters. It would of course be rash to build a chronology on this evidence alone, but as supporting evidence for the presumed pattern of metrical change it is of some significance.

# IV

# COMPENSATORY LENGTHENING
# UPON LOSS OF *h*

§156. One of the sources of metrical change first suggested to have dating value is an alternation arising from the loss of *h* between a resonant consonant and a vowel (Morsbach, pp. 264–68). In such instances a vowel before the consonant was lengthened: *\*feorhes*, for example, became *fēores*. The result was an irregular paradigm, with a short diphthong in uninflected *feorh*, and with a long diphthong and no *h* in the inflected cases. Since Old English is a language that tolerates very little of this sort of allomorphy, the paradigm was eventually regularized by leveling the short diphthong into the inflected cases. Thus, compensatory lengthening is usually obscured by later analogy; but that the lengthening did take place is proved by forms in which there was no opportunity for restoration of the short vowel or diphthong by analogy to alternants within the paradigm, for example *þȳrel* < *\*þurh-il-*, and *ōnettan* < *\*on-haitjan*. The date of the original lengthening is not metrically discernible, as there is no metrical difference between *fēores* and earlier *\*feorhes*, and the former could in fact stand for the latter if there were any poems without short forms. Rather, the only metrically significant change is the analogically induced shortening. Yet the date of the lengthening is significant, since it sets a *terminus a quo* for the analogical change. If *h* was lost in this environment at the same time that it was lost between vowels, the standard view would suggest that *h* was lost at about the same time that the earliest glossary manuscripts (Ép., Erf.) were written. But it is demonstrated in the Conclusion (§§395ff.) that the change actually took place before this, and thus may have occurred at any time before the close of the seventh century.

§157. The form *fīras* 'men' never has a short vowel, though it is generally assumed that etymologically it belongs to the paradigm of *feorh* 'life', and so should have suffered the analogical change. The most likely reason, according to the standard view, is that it is an Anglian form that failed to be recognized as belonging to the paradigm of *feorh* after it had passed into the poetic vocabulary, and so appeared to show no alternation in the root vowel.[1] In other words, it is a petrified, nonalternating

---

[1]Luick (§§139.2, 239, n. 1) explains the failure of breaking in *fīras* as due to *i* in the following syllable, though Campbell (§154 n. 3) indicates that smoothing is also possible. Luick's claim at first seems odd, since clearly there was no following *i* in *fīras*, according

relic found only in verse. Yet perhaps a more likely explanation is Wilhelm Schulze's: the word reflects a different construction with the same stem, bearing the suffix -ija-, as suggested by the form *Alaferhviae* in an inscription from Altdorf, near Jülich.[2] This does seem to be the best explanation of the root vocalism of *fīras* and its cognates, OIcel. *fīrar*, OSax. *firiho, firihon*, OHG *uiriho, firahim*. In *\*ferhwija-* there was no case-form in which *h* should have been preserved, and so no alternation between long and short root vowels in the paradigm to induce the analogical change.

§158. If some Old English verse shows only forms with long root vowels in the oblique cases, and in sufficient number, then very likely that verse was composed before the shortened analogical forms became acceptable in verse. Thus the length of the vowel may serve as a dating criterion. The material has been treated frequently, and the list of relevant verses provided by Amos is complete for the test group, as far as unambiguous verses are concerned—though quite a few ambiguous examples may be added.[3] A few small alterations to her list should be made.[4] She scans *feores orwena* (*Andreas* 1107b) as ambiguous, either type 1D*2 or 1D2. But the former classification is unlikely, since Bliss will not allow this type in the off-verse in *Beowulf*;[5] and the latter is not possible, since *orwena* is generally assumed to bear tertiary rather than secondary

---

to the standard interpretation. His assumption must be that the word was originally an *u*-stem, like the Gothic cognate *fairhus*—and cf. OIcel. *fjǫr*, a *wa*-stem that very probably was originally an *u*-stem. In that event there would indeed have been a following *i* in the original *u*-stem nominative plural ending *\*-iwiz*, before the word went over to the *a*-stems. If this is Luick's reasoning, then his explanation seems preferable to Campbell's, since Campbell's cannot explain the high vowel in *fīras*, while Luick's leads us to expect raising of *e* in the root of the nominative and dative plural of *u*-stems (see Luick, §73).

[2]See "Alaferhviae," *ZfdA* 54 (1913), 172–74. Schulze's position has the support of Alfred Bammesberger, *Beiträge zu einem etymologischen Wörterbuch des Altenglischen: Berichtigungen und Nachträge zum Altenglischen etymologischen Wörterbuch von Ferdinand Holthausen* (Heidelberg: Winter, 1979), p. 52.

[3]In the test group the additional ambiguous examples are at *Genesis A* 1162b, 1831b, 1838a; *Daniel* 15b; *Beowulf* 578b, 1048a, 1433b, 1548b, 1898a, 1942b, 2166a; *Exodus* 361a; *Elene* 498a, 1175a; *Juliana* 679b; *Andreas* 133b, 179b, 1101b; *Meters of Boethius* 25.16b; and *Maldon* 317a. Sievers ("Miscellen," p. 232; "Rhythmik," p. 485) regards *horu* as instrumental, from *horh*, in *Ge mid horu speowdon* (*Elene* 297b); but Campbell (§574.2, n. 2) is surely right that this is an Anglian accusative after *mid* (see below, §355), to the analogical stem *horw-*.

[4]One such alteration is hardly worth notice, since it appears to be an oversight: she points out the irrelevance of *Cædmon's Hymn* 9a, containing the word *fīrum* (p. 34), but still includes it in her tables.

[5]Yet a few examples of the D* type do occur in the off-verse in the test group of poems: cf. *gode orfeorme* and similar at *Andreas* 406b, 1617b, and *Judith* 271b. At least at *Andreas* 406b it is clear that *gode* has a long root vowel, since it corresponds to τῶν ἀγαθῶν in the Greek. And so it is necessary to correct my remarks in "An Eddic Analogue to the Scyld Scefing Story," *RES*, n.s. 40 (1989), 313–22, at 314 n. 4.

stress.[6] If *feores* has a short root syllable the verse is a normal type 1D1, while if the syllable is long the only possibility is type 2A1a(ii). But it was shown above (p. 77, n. 29) that since there are 220 instances of type 1D1 in the off-verse in *Beowulf*, and just one of type 2A1a(ii), itself a suspect instance, the probability of the latter scansion is insignificant, and the verse should be considered unambiguously type 1D1. Another alteration affects verses containing the formula *widan feore*. This is in variation with *to widan feore* (once with *on* for *to*, at *Elene* 1288b), and as Amos remarks, the *to* might easily be added by a scribe after the analogical shortening was complete. That formulae of this sort were in fact subject to scribal alteration is suggested by some metrical peculiarities: for example, the metrically objectionable formula *to widan aldre* appears twice in *Andreas* beside three instances of *to widan feore*. This is not to say that the evidence of this formula is thus utterly negligible, but that its evidence is not as strong as nonformulaic evidence, and so should be considered separately. The point bears emphasis because, for instance, three of the four unambiguous instances in *Elene* are examples of this formula, and this makes a considerable difference in terms of the force of the evidence of *Elene*. It is true that in the poems of the test group the distribution of the two versions of the formula for the most part supports the presumed chronology, since, as Amos observes,

what is particularly striking is that late, short forms of the formula abound. . . . It is possible, of course, that some of these instances involve scribal alteration rather than authorial innovation, but the large number of occurrences makes it likely that at least some poets recast the formula to fit a later pronunciation. H. M. Chadwick even argues that such refashioning of formulas to accommodate linguistic change was the rule: "Poems which are preserved by oral tradition alone are manifestly liable to small verbal changes, especially in a metre so flexible as that of the Teutonic alliterative verse."[7]

The formula *(to) widan feore* appears in eight instances in the test group of poems, once with a long vowel, at *Juliana* 508b, and seven times with

---

[6]The evidence presented below (Chap. 7, esp. §234) is inconclusive. In any case in *Beowulf* type 1D2 appears in the off-verse twice, while type 1D1 appears there 220 times.

[7]P. 36. The reference to Chadwick is to *The Heroic Age* (Cambridge: Cambridge Univ. Press, 1912), p. 46. She adds, "This is heartening evidence that perhaps practice did reflect contemporary usage." The remark refers to her position, "I believe it is far more likely that Old English poetry was composed in the spoken language of the time, with contemporary pronunciation, syllabification, and accent," as discussed above (§44). But the evidence of the Paris Psalter tends to cast doubt on this line of reasoning, since it has nineteen instances of the formula *awa to feore* as a complete verse, which must belong to type 1A*1a, with a long root syllable in *feore*. Yet this is generally regarded as a fairly late text. Of course the metrics of the Psalms are corrupt, so this evidence is not firm. But other doubts are offered in the Introduction, and the evidence of the preceding chapters demonstrates the preservation of some archaisms (e.g. *tungl* in the *Meters*) late into the period.

a short one, at *Beowulf* 933b, *Exodus* 548b, *Elene* 211a, 1288b, 1321b, and *Andreas* 106a and 1452a. Although it is true that most short forms occur in verse presumably later than *Beowulf*, there is just one example in verse up to *Beowulf*, and so the evidence is clearly rather meager and inconclusive. The evidence of instances aside from this formula are of more interest:[8]

> *Genesis A:* 2 long, 1 short, 3 ambiguous
> *Daniel:* 1 long, 1 short, 1 ambiguous
> *Beowulf:* 11 long, 2 short, 9 ambiguous
> *Exodus:* 3 long
> *Elene:* 1 short, 2 ambiguous
> *Juliana:* 1 long, 1 ambiguous
> *Andreas:* 6 short, 3 ambiguous
> *Meters of Boethius:* 1 ambiguous
> *Brunanburh:* 1 ambiguous
> *Maldon:* 1 long, 2 short, 2 ambiguous

§159. The data for individual poems are for the most part unremarkable. For example, little can be deduced from the fact that *Maldon* has one long instance and two short, since the difference between this poem and *Genesis A*, for instance, in this respect is so small as to be statistically negligible. Similarly, even if the instances of *(to) widan feore* are added to the statistics for the signed works of Cynewulf, the result is still just four short forms for the entire corpus. The proportion this makes with the two long instances in *Juliana* is the same as that for *Maldon*, and while this proportion is different, for instance, from that for *Exodus*, and might have some significance if based on a large number of instances, no ratio derived from so few examples can carry much conviction. This is especially true in view of the fact that clearly at no time were either long or short forms entirely unacceptable in verse.

[8]Amos identifies the verse types, and so it is sufficient to list the numbers of unambiguous verses here: *Genesis A* 1184b, 1330a, 1342b; *Daniel* 101b, 225a; *Beowulf* 73b, 537a, 855b, 865b, 917a, 1035b, 1152a, 1293a, 1306a, 1843a, 2163b, 2664a, 3013b; *Exodus* 171b, 384b, 404a, *Elene* 134b; *Juliana* 191b, *Andreas* 284b, 810a, 1096a, 1107b, 1130b, 1538b; *Maldon* 194b, 239b, 259b. The ambiguous verses not mentioned in n. 3 above are at *Elene* 680b, *Brunanburh* 72b, and *Maldon* 260b. The verse *feores ingeþanc* (*Elene* 680b) must belong to type 1D(*)4 rather than 1D(*)5, though neither type appears in the off-verse in *Beowulf*. The form *inþoncæ* appears once in the literary records, in a late Old English or early Middle English homily (see the *Microfiche Concordance*), but *ingeþanc* is metrically confirmed several times in verse, though never elsewhere in the Cynewulf canon. Outside the test group, several unambiguous verses may be added to Amos' collection: there are short forms at *Guthlac A* 627b, *Riming Poem* 45b, *Lord's Prayer I* 11b, *Fortunes of Men* 40b, *Psalm 50* 20b, and *Maxims I* 141b; and there are long forms at *Fragments of Psalms* 50.12.2b and *Descent into Hell* 20a. Thus, most of these additional forms are short, but some of these poems are not metrically very reliable. There are three more examples of *to widan feore* at *Christ III* 1543a, *Guthlac B* 840a, and *Whale* 88a.

§160. Although the statistics for most poems are too scant to be conclusive, there are two poems on the list with sufficient instances to furnish significant statistics, *Beowulf* and *Andreas*. The figures are consistent with the view that *Beowulf* is earlier. This is a particularly appropriate comparison, since, as has been remarked, of the surviving longer poems in Old English, *Andreas* is the one closest to *Beowulf* in spirit, style and diction. Thus the wide statistical difference here cannot as readily be attributed to a stylistic difference as with some other poems.

§161. The figures for the two halves of the chronology *in toto* perhaps also are of some small significance. Excluding *Beowulf* and *Andreas*, which would have a disproportionate effect on the figures because the evidence is so scant, in poems up to and including *Exodus* there are six long instances and three short; or six long and four short, including the formulaic instances. In the rest of the poems there are two long and three short; or three long and six short, including the formulae. On this basis, Amos may be right to conclude that the data are "reasonably consistent with the dates of the externally datable poems that have relevant forms," and "overall the test of vowel length after loss of post-consonantal *h*, although it does not lead to particularly fine-structured datings, has not been invalidated" (p. 35). In sum, then, the evidence here is weaker than in any of the preceding chapters, and yet in a general way it does support the supposition that the analogical substitution of short root vowels is reflected in metrical change that correlates broadly to the presumed chronology of Old English verse.

# V

# ANALOGICAL LENGTHENING IN
# DIPHTHONGAL STEMS

§162. The standard handbooks of Old English phonology assert that short front vowels are broken before *w* when there is no *i* in the next syllable.[1] Thus, for example, *niowol* is said to derive from *\*niwal*, while the variant *niwel* derives from *\*niwil*.[2] In declensional categories like the *wa*-stems the result was an irregular paradigm, for instance gen. *þeowes* < *\*þewas(a)*, next to nom. *þēo* < *\*þeu* < *\*þewaz*. To regularize the paradigm, the *w* of the inflected cases could be leveled into the nominative singular, giving *þēow*; and the long diphthong of the nominative could be extended to the oblique cases, giving gen. *þēowes*. This sort of paradigm regularization is characteristic of Old English, as demonstrated for instance in the preceding chapter, and in the paradigmatic leveling of affricate alternations (Campbell, §437), and the wholesale transferral of weak verbs of the third class to the more regular second class. Old English was a language that tolerated very little paradigm allomorphy that was not phonologically conditioned, unless it uniquely conveyed grammatical information, the way, for example, the alternation of *bōc* with *bēc* did. In the present instance, the analogical origin of the *w* in nominatives like *þēow* is demonstrable from the fact that a prosaic word

[1] See Luick, §134; Campbell, §§146, 583; Brunner, §§87–89.

[2] Elsewhere I have suggested that there never was breaking before *w*, since exceptions like pret. part. *gesewen* argue against it, and forms like *hweowol* and *niowol* can consistently be explained as due to velar umlaut. If this is the case, it could be that manuscript spellings like *þeowes* represent contemporary pronunciation (i.e. *þĕowes*), metrically no different from the original form, *\*þewæs*, in the same way that, for instance, the manuscripts usually have medial *-ig-* for metrical *-g-* in words like *mihtigum* (§216 below). This explanation seems phonologically more natural on two counts: it accords better with the fact that there is no breaking of low front vowels before *w*, but retraction; and it obviates the objection that there is no good phonological reason for front vowels to be broken before *w* when a back vowel follows, but not a front vowel. It is true that there is a parallel in the treatment of breaking before *r* (Campbell, §154.3) Since breaking is the product of velarity in consonants, however, it does not make sense that the process before *w* should be hindered by a following front vowel: the velarity of *w* cannot have been variable under such conditions. A third advantage of this explanation is that it obviates the necessity of an extra rule, relying instead on a phonological development (back mutation) already required to explain other phenomena. It thus simplifies the grammar of Old English. But even if this explanation is incorrect, the possible dating value of the forms metrically attested as long is not altered. See n. 7 of the article mentioned above, p. 88, n. 48.

like *strēaw* 'straw' always has the *w*, except in the compound *strēaberige*, while *hlēo* 'protection', found almost exclusively in the more conservative language of verse, is almost never *hlēow*. Similarly, in prose texts *cnēow* 'knee' is commoner than *cnēo*, while the reverse is true in verse.

§163. Although the analogical change of *þeowes* to *þēowes*, and the like, cannot be dated with any accuracy, it is probable that the change was not particularly early, since the long root vocalism was for the most part unacceptable in verse, as first recognized by Sievers.[3] And it may be added that although long forms are sometimes found in late Old English verse (as demonstrated below), the short forms could still be used in the early Middle English period: Orm uses the spellings *þeowwess* and *þewwess*, indicating short root vocalism. But long forms do nonetheless appear occasionally in Old English verse, and studying these, Moritz Trautmann came to the conclusion that long forms do not appear in verse composed before the conclusion of the ninth century.[4] Trautmann's hypothesis seems not to have been noticed in subsequent studies of dating criteria.

§164. The evidence is exceptionally meager. The relevant words are rare, being inflected forms of *cnēow*, *trēow* 'tree' (but not *trēow* 'faith'), *þeow* 'servant' (including its derivatives *lāreow* and *lātteow*),[5] and *hlēo*. *Strēaw* is not attested in verse. On *fēa* 'few' and *þrēa* 'affliction' see below, §166. Compounds of which these form the second element are also relevant, though they are never unambiguous; but compounds of which these form the first element are not relevant, since, for instance, West Germanic *\*þewa-dōmaz* should have lost the connecting *a*, giving rise to a diphthong in *þēo(w)dom*. Since analogy not only regularizes paradigms but also affects transparently related forms, these must also be taken into consideration. For example, although there is no phonological reason for a long diphthong to have developed in any case-form of *þeowen* 'female servant', analogy to *þēow* has induced lengthening in the first syllable in *þeowen þrymful* (*Judith* 74a: cf. *earmre þeowenan*, with a short vowel, at Psalm 122.3.1b). Analogy has also affected some forms of *clēa* 'claw' and *þrēa* 'affliction', if spelling is to be trusted, though it cannot be proved metrically whether most of the oblique forms attested in verse are long monosyllables or short dissyllables. Nominative forms of these must at any rate be carefully excluded, for example *þrea ormǣte* (nom., *Andreas* 1166a), since these contracted in West Germanic (see above, §119). Campbell (§584) includes *þēaw* 'custom' in the group of forms originally

---

[3]"Rhythmik," pp. 490–91. But Alfred Bammesberger has recently suggested an interpretation of the runic inscription on the Lovedon Hill urn that would require the change to have occurred perhaps as early as the sixth century: see "Three Old English Runic Inscriptions," in his *Runes*, pp. 125–36, at 127–28.

[4]"Zum altenglischen Versbau," *Englische Studien* 44 (1912), 329–39.

[5]Presumably these still had secondary stress on the second element: the latter, at any rate, is frequently spelt *ladteow*.

without a diphthong in the oblique cases (*cnēow* and the like). But the word is usually assumed to have been subject to the Germanic Verschärfung, as suggested by the cognates OSax. *thau* (not *\*thao* or *\*thā*) and OHG *dau-, ka-thau, ungadouwīg*.[6] The assumption is corroborated by Old English meter, since the root is always metrically long in unequivocal verses, such as *halige þeawas* (*Genesis A* 1531b) and *sido and þeawas* (*Meters of Boethius* 11.12b).

§165. Trautmann (pp. 330–31, 334) reaches the conclusion that long forms are attested only in the following verses:

> þeodum to þrea  (*Christ III* 1091a)
> monge, nales fea  (*Christ III* 1170a)
> Ic þe feawe dagas  (*Metrical Psalms* 101.21.3b)
> þeowas sindon  (*Meters of Boethius* 11.11b)
> þenað and ðiowað  (*Meters of Boethius* 29.75a)
> þæt hi þiowien  (*Meters of Boethius* 29.91a)
> ne þiowoden  (*Meters of Boethius* 29.96a)
> þeowen þrymful  (*Judith* 74a)
> gleawra godes ðeowa  (*Death of Edgar* 19a)

He then eliminates the verse from *Judith* on the basis of the observation that *þeowen* here could stand for *þeowena*; but this of course is not a strong objection to the verse. There are two other instances of *feawe* in the metrical Psalms, *feawe wæran ænige* (104.11.2b) and *and dimme and feawe* (108.8.1b). The former is ambiguous, and although the latter would have to be considered type 3B*1a if it appeared in classical verse, the meter of the Psalms is such that anacrusis cannot be ruled out here (see Chap. 10, passim, and Appendix A). Under Bliss's principles, verse 29.91a of the Boethian *Meters* is light, and therefore ambiguous—that is, it is either type a1 (with resolution) or d1. This objection does not, however, apply to verse 29.96a, since resolution would reduce the number of metrical positions in the verse to three, when four is the minimum. But the evidence of all verses containing *þiowian* is merely orthographic, since this apparently was originally a verb of the third weak class (Campbell, §764). To these examples perhaps should be added *Ðu þæm treowum selest* (*Meters of Boethius* 4.21b), since a short lift does not usually follow a resolved lift. But the principle seems dubitable in this instance (as in some others: see §249 below), since the four other examples of *treowum* in the *Meters* listed below all require a short first syllable. The two verses from *Christ III* might be scanned as type 2E1 under Bliss's system, but, once again, the type is demonstrated below to be specious (§§210ff.).

§166. For these examples of analogical lengthening to have any significance they must be compared with the figures for attested instances of

---

[6]See, e.g., Winfred P. Lehmann, *Proto-Indo-European Phonology* (Austin: Univ. of Texas Press, 1952), p. 43.

short forms. The number of such forms is relatively small, but sufficiently well distributed. There are twenty-three examples in the test group of poems. A certain amount of ambiguity arises in some instances because of alternative analogical developments: Campbell indicates that *feawe* (or *fēawa*) is the normal nominative form of this adjective that appears only in the plural (§653.2), meaning that the root vocalism has been lengthened; but *þrēa* can extend the nominative form through most of the paradigm (§598.2). The difference means that *fēa* may stand for itself, the monosyllabic reflex of neut. *\*fawō* (with loss of *w*); or for *\*fawe*, the dissyllabic reflex of masc. or fem. *\*fawōs, -ōz*, with no loss of *w*; or for analogical *fēawe*. Dative singular *þrēa*, on the other hand, can stand either for itself or for earlier *\*þrawe*, but not for *\*þrēawe*. Campbell's assumptions are guided purely by orthography: the spellings *feawe* and *feawa* are much more frequent than *fea*, and yet the stem *\*þreaw-* does not occur at all. In that event *þrēa* ought to be disregarded altogether as a nonalternating form. Yet the example of *þeodum to þrea* (*Christ III* 1091a, as above) suggests that orthography may not be an entirely reliable guide, and perhaps it should be supposed that the preference for *þrea-* rather than *þreaw-* is mere spelling tradition. So also *nymðe fea ane* (*Genesis A* 2134b) is unambiguous in regard to the analogical development in question, since *fea* requires a nominative plural ending, and although conceivably a neuter form has been substituted for an original masculine one, the meter will not allow it to stand for *\*fēawe*. It can be added that the spelling *feawa* does not occur in verse, and *feawe* appears only in the Paris Psalter (three times, as cited above), while *fea* appears fourteen times in verse. Conversely, *fea* is rare in prose, appearing almost exclusively in Anglian or Anglian-influenced texts. Therefore even ambiguous verses with *fea* are unlikely to be examples of *fēawe*.

§167. The evidence for short forms in the test group is as follows:

> Genesis A[7]
>      Short (4):
>          892a    on treowes telgum (2C1a)
>          1470a   on treowes telgum (2C1a)
>          2134b   nymðe fea ane (2C1b)
>          2747b   Ne meahton freo ne þeowe (2B1c)
>      Ambiguous (7):
>          1458b   ne on leaf treowes (2C2b or 2C1b)
>          1813b   oððæt brohþrea (d3b or d2b)
>          2262a   hire worcþeowe (d3b or d2b)
>          2265a   þrea and þeowdom (1A1a[i] or 1A*1a[i])

---

[7]Most editors of *Genesis A* do not have *þe ic wægþrea on* at 1490b, as Krapp does, but put *on* into the next verse. Krapp's reading seems unlikely in view of the metrical treatment of -*þrēa* in all its other occurrences in this list, and in view of the fact that in the test group of poems there are just two other verses of type B with secondary stress in the second thesis: see §144 above.

2509b   mid cwealmþrea (d3a or d2a)
2547b   Grap heahþrea (1D3 or 1D2)[8]
2721a   and weorcþeos (d3a or d2a)[9]

*Daniel*

Short (3):
180b   on cneowum sæton (2C1a)
325b   ðeah heora fea lifigen (2C1c)
690a   under wealla hleo (3B1b)

Ambiguous (2):
74b   to weorcþeowum (2C2a or 2C1a)
293a   nu we þec for þreaum (e1d or a1d)

*Beowulf*[10]

Short (4):
156b   fea þingian (1D1)
1081b   nemne feaum anum (2C1b)
2246b   fea worda cwæð (3E2)
2662b   fea worda cwæð (3E2)

Ambiguous (2):
178a   wið þeodþreaum (d3a or d2a)
2940b   sum on galgtreowum (d3b or d2b)

*Elene*

Short (5):
174b   þeah hira fea wæron (2C1c)
706b   be ðam lifes treo (3B1b)
817b   nalles feam siðum (2C1b)
855a   on rode treo (3B1a[i])
1251b   Ic þæs wuldres treowes (3B1b)

Ambiguous (1):
1209a   ond þæs latteowes (d3b or d2b)

---

[8]Bliss finds two examples of type 1D2 and none of 1D3 in the off-verse in *Beowulf*, and Kendall's principle that compounds with secondary stress normally alliterate implies that 1D3 should not be found in the off-verse: see above, §66. But as mentioned above (§108), type 1D3 does appear in the off-verse unambiguously in a few other places. An examination of the *Microfiche Concordance* reveals that *þréa* has a peculiar distribution in prose—e.g., Ælfric avoids it altogether—and so perhaps this is an instance like *ealo-wǽge* at 495b, on which see Russom, pp. 96–97.

[9]See p. 95, n. 3 to Chap. 2.

[10]*Wealhþeo secan* (664b) appears to be an example of a short form, but the spelling is peculiar: there is some small evidence in such forms for the loss of intervocalic *w* under relatively low stress (see §121), and contraction would follow. Some similar verses appear to have short (or contracted?) forms, e.g. *bonan Ongenþeoes* (1968a; see also 2475a and 2986a); but in view of *Ongenðioes bearn* (2387b) it is clear that the metrical rules once again could be modified to accommodate formulae, as in the case of the formula *Beowulf maðelode* (see p. 77, n. 29). Unavoidably, Klaeber underdots the second vowel in *Ongenðioes*, though etymologically it is not parasitic. Supposing the vowel should be ignored in scansion in every instance, the implication of verses like *bonan Ongenþeoes* is that the *Beowulf* poet did use uncontracted forms, and in fact there is no instance in which an uncontracted form is unlikely. But since all of this is conjectural, it is best not to count any of these verses as evidence. So also the numerous examples of the ambiguous formula *bearn Ecgþeowes*, and the like, are omitted here.

*Juliana*
Short (1):
    354b     nalæs feam siðum (2C1b)
Ambiguous (1):
    678a     þurh þearlic þrea (3B1a[i]; neuter)
*Christ II*
Ambiguous (1):
    458b     Hy þæs lareowes (d3b or d2b)
*Andreas*
Short (1):
    605b     nalas feam siðum (2C1b)
Ambiguous (2):
    107a     Geþola þeoda þrea (1D5)
    111a     to hleo ond to hroðre (1A1b[i] or 1A*1b)
*Meters of Boethius*
Short (5):
    4.52b    buton fea ane (2C1b)
    13.36b   gif hi on treowum *weorðað* (2C1c)
    13.39b   Hi on treowum *wilde* (2C1b)
    13.51a   *Swa bið e*allum treowum (3B1b)
    19.6b    *on* grenum triow*um* (3B1a[i])
Ambiguous (3):
    10.55b   swel*cra* lariowa (d3b or d2b)
    13.38a   heora lareowas (d3b or d2b)
    13.42a   *h*eora *lareowa* (d3b or d2b)

§168. In sum, the only poems with undeniable analogical lengthening are *Judith* and the *Meters of Boethius*, the former presumed and the latter known to be late. The evidence is scant, but it does conform to the assumption that these and *Maldon* (for which there is no evidence of any sort) are the latest of the longer poems. The incidence of short forms, while having no apparent significance of its own, is sufficient to indicate that the absence of long forms in poems presumably earlier than the *Meters* is difficult to explain as mere chance. This becomes especially clear when it is pointed out that the total number of lines of verse making up the poetic texts in the test group of poems from *Cædmon's Hymn* to *Andreas* is several times the total from the *Meters* to *Durham* (the numbers are 11,206 and 2,623, respectively). Moreover, the *Meters, Judith*, and the *Death of Edgar* are the only poems in the latter group that contain any relevant forms at all, ambiguous or otherwise, and so it is not likely to be an accident that two of them contain forms unambiguously affected by the analogical process in question. It is reasonable to conclude that while this evidence is certainly not of the first importance, it is hardly negligible, either, as supporting evidence.

§169. Appended is a list of all the possibly relevant verses in poems outside the test group. The list is entirely uncritical, including many dubitable forms and metrically irregular poems:

*Azarias* 42b, 150a; *Christ I* 151a, 361a; *Christ III* 946a, 1063b, 1320b, 1364a; *Dream of the Rood* 115b, 146a; *Guthlac A* 59b, 69a, 80a, 359b, 364a, 502a, 547a; *Guthlac B* 922a, 1041a: *Instructions for Christians* 237b; *Judgment Day I* 57b; *Lord's Prayer II* 98b; *Phoenix* 76a, 175a, 277a; *Precepts* 13a; *Psalms* 57.8.1a, 68.31.3b, 75.5.1a, 85.15.4a, 93.9.6a, 95.9.3a, 99.1.3b, 103.8.1a, 104.11.2b, 104.12.2b, 104.24.1b, 106.38.1a, 108.8.1b, 108.10.3b, 108.13.2a, 108.24.1a, 115.6.3a, 118.49.2b, 122.3.1b, 149.7.2a; *Psalm 50* 9a; *Resignation* 66a; *Riddles* 3.50a, 3.57b, 12.15b, 60.3b; *Solomon and Saturn II* 400b; *Vainglory* 47a.

A verse that does not belong here is *æþele treowe* (*Rune Poem* 80b). Although the verse puns on 'wood', the primary meaning is 'fidelity', since the word must be feminine (plural, which frequently appears for the singular in this sense).

# VI

# KALUZA'S LAW

§170. In 1896 Max Kaluza made the remarkable discovery that in some metrical positions resolution is governed in part by etymological considerations.[1] His discovery is predicated on the distinction between "long" and "short" inflectional endings. The former are those that end in a consonant, for example masc. *a*-stem gen. sg. *-es*; or in a vowel that, according to the older view of Germanic philologists, carried the *Schleifton* ("circumflex" or "abnormal intonation") in Proto-Germanic,[2] such as *ō*-stem nom. pl. *-a* < *-ô(z)* < PIE *-âs*. Final noninflectional syllables must also be included here, for instance *-ig* in *monig* < *manag* < PGmc. *managaz*, but not *-er* in *æcer* (cf. Gothic *akrs* < PGmc. *akraz*). The short endings are all the rest, such as neut. *a*-stem nom. pl. *-u* < PIE *-ā*, and masc. *i*-stem nom. sg. *-e* < PIE *-is* (preserved after short stems only). The phonological distinction between long and short endings in Proto-Germanic is not Kaluza's discovery, but was noticed by several scholars in the 1880s. It is invoked to explain divergent developments like the

---

[1]"Zur Betonungs- and Verslehre des Altenglischen," in *Festschrift zum siebzigsten Geburtstage Oskar Schade* (Königsberg: Hartung, 1896), pp. 101–34, at 120–31.

[2]Such vowels were also at one time widely believed to be trimoric, and the circumflex was justified etymologically by comparison to the Greek circumflex and the Lithuanian *Schleifton*. A series of articles by Jerzy Kuryłowicz, culminating in his book *L'accentuation des langues indo-européennes* (Wrocław: Polska Akademia Nauk, 1958), pp. 106–368, demonstrated that the Greek and Baltic phenomena are almost certainly dialectal innovations, not inheritances from the Indo-European protolanguage, with the result that the assumption of trimoric vowels (and, to a lesser extent, broken accents) in Proto-Germanic has largely been abandoned by comparatists. Yet this change of theory is of limited relevance to Kaluza's law. Whatever the precise reason, there is undeniably an etymological distinction between, e.g., the PGmc. *a*-stem gen. pl. inflection *-ôm* ( > Gothic *-o*, OE *-a*, etc.) and *ō*-stem acc. sg. *-ôm* ( > Gothic *-a*, OE *-e*, etc.). The sign of the broken accent may be regarded as an abstraction, standing not necessarily for an intonational difference, but for whatever the actual etymological distinction between the two types of vowels might be. George Lane's suggestion that the circumflected vowels are to be identified etymologically with sequences of uncontracted vowels has the partial support of Vedic verse, in which certain vowels corresponding to Hellenic and Baltic circumflected ones must frequently be scanned as two syllables: see his "Bimoric and Trimoric Vowels and Diphthongs: Laws of Germanic Finals Again," *JEGP* 62 (1963), 155–70, at 169. See also the discussion in *Origins*, pp. 56–57 and 139ff., and particularly the rather thorough treatment of the problem by P. H. Hollifield, "The Phonological Development of Final Syllables in Germanic," *Die Sprache* 26 (1980), 19–53 and 145–78, at 20ff. Under standard assumptions about Ingvaeonic phonology Lane's explanation seems particularly promising because the result of the Germanic

difference between PGmc. *ō*-stem fem. nom. sg. *-ō* (from PIE *-ā*) > Gothic *-a*, and PGmc. *a*-stem abl. sg. *-ô* (from PIE *-ôd*) > Gothic *-o* (*jainþro, galeiko, undaro*, etc.).[3] A table of long and short endings is provided in Appendix C (pp. 419–25), with a discussion of some important details.

§171. Sievers' classificatory system requires that a dissyllabic word (or element of a compound) with a short first syllable be resolved at the end of the verse in his types B and E, where it follows a weakly stressed syllable—for example in *on nicera mere* (*Beowulf* 845b) and *uncuþes fela* (876b)—but that it be unresolved in Sievers' types C, D1, and A2k, where it follows a long, stressed syllable—for example in *ac þæt wæs god cyning* (863b), *heard hondlocen* (322a), and *guðrinc monig* (838b). Kaluza finds that the unresolved word takes a long ending in the latter group, but usually a short one in the former group.[4] More important, he remarks that the distinction is observed in the first foot of types A and E, as well, since only short endings are found in verses of type A, like *gilpcwide Geates* (640a), while long endings are used in type E, like *beaghroden cwen* (623b; "Verslehre," p. 126; as above, n. 1). He thought that eleven verses like *fleon on fenhopu* (764a) were exceptions to his rule (p. 129), but

---

contraction of the PIE *i*-stem desinence nom. pl. *-eyes* is a vowel treated in Old Saxon and Old High German like an etymologically circumflected one—an identification that Campbell otherwise found puzzling (p. 242, n. 1; but cf. the following note). Of course under this analysis some analogical explanation is required, since, e.g., the nominative singular of masculine *n*-stems ought etymologically to involve no sequence of uncontracted vowels.

[3]On the discovery of the distinction, and for an extensive list of such phonological oppositions, see the article by Lane mentioned in the preceding note. The distinction is also usually assumed to explain the preservation of the nom.-acc. pl. *i*-stem ending *-i* < PIE *-eyes* after long stems in Old Saxon and Old High German, where short *-i* ought to have been lost. But possibly this ending is analogical to the corresponding case-forms of the short stems. This assumption obviates the difficulty that the Old High German ending is unquestionably short (see Braune and Eggers, §215, n. 4), a situation that Prokosch (p. 246) explains as due to analogical extension of the accusative ending (from *-ins*) into the nominative. This leaves unexplained why short *-i* < *-ins* should not have been lost. Yet the possibility remains that circumflected high vowels were shortened earlier than other high vowels in Old Saxon and Old High German: see the discussion in Appendix C.

[4]Kaluza's own formulation is as follows: "Bei näherer Untersuchung ergibt es sich auch, dass in der älteren Dichtung, z.B. im Beowulf, überall da, wo ein derartiges Wort am Versschluss zwei Hebungen bezw. zwei Glieder des Verses in sich aufnehmen muss, die zweite Silbe in der Regel eine in älterer Zeit betonte oder lange Flexions- oder Ableitungssilbe war, die vielleicht noch etwas von ihrem alten Eigenton bewahrt hatte, wie z.B. *scipes, selē* D. Sg., *dagum, frumā, cuman, cumen, stigon, micel, monig, fæder* u.ä., während bei 'Auflösung' einer Hebung oder eines Gliedes am Ende der Typen B, D², E und ebenso bei Auflösung der Nebenhebung im ersten Fusse des gesteigerten Typus A² immer nur zwei sprachlich ganz kurze Silben stehen dürfen, wie z.B. Nom. oder Akk. von *i*- und *u*-Stämmen." See his *Englische Metrik in historischer Entwicklung*, Normannia: Germanische-romanische Bücherei, 1 (Berlin: Felber, 1909), §52 (pp. 57–59, at p. 58).

under Bliss's system of scansion this is not necessarily the case: in this instance Bliss would place the caesura after the first word, so that this verse belongs to type A, and thus correctly has resolution.

§172. Kaluza's conclusions cannot be supported in their entirety. For example, in type B there are too many exceptions to the conclusion that a dissyllable at the end of the verse must bear a short ending: compare *þurh rumne sefan* (*Beowulf* 278a), *þæt wæs geomuru ides* (1075b), *on swa geongum feore* (1843a), and *him Beowulf þanan* (1880b).[5] And although the proportion of verses of type C with a long syllable at the end of the verse is admittedly large, there are quite a few exceptions here, too (see below, §174). Bliss recognized some of these difficulties and attempted to put Kaluza's law on a sounder footing. He analyzed all of *Beowulf* (Kaluza had only demonstrated the point for the first thousand lines, and for no other poem), and found that all verses of type 2A3a(ii) have short endings in the first foot (e.g. *bengeato burston*, 1121a), and all of type 1D3 have long endings in the second foot (e.g. *leof landfruma*, 31a; see Bliss, §§34–37); the length of the ending is variable after an unstressed syllable at the end of type 3B1b (e.g. *syððan Geata cyning* 2356a, beside *wið his sylfes sunu* 2013a; see §40); and, as Kaluza also claims, the law in its strictest form applies only to dissyllables, including dissyllabic elements of compounds, and thus is not relevant to words with tertiary stress (e.g. *þreatedon þearle*, 560a, and *secg wisade*, 208b; see §§38–39). But Bliss's treatment of the problem is not entirely satisfactory. In order to avoid classifying them as type D, he says of verses like *win of wunderfatum* (1162a) and *deorc ofer dryhtgumum* (1790a), "In every instance the final syllable consists either of a short vocalic ending or of a consonantal ending; as we have seen in §40, both these endings are ambivalent, and there is no reason why these verses should not belong to Type A2b, with resolution of the secondary stress" (§45; see also §54). But what he had actually demonstrated in §§38–40 was that consonantal, short vocalic, and long vocalic endings all may be resolved at the end of verse type 3B1b; and only consonantal and short vocalic endings may be "resolved" under *tertiary* stress. Even this latter conclusion is questionable, being based only on observations about types 2A1a(iii) and 2A2(iii), and not taking into account *sellice sædracan* (1426a). And so if *win of wunderfatum* and *deorc ofer dryhtgumum* belong to type A rather than D, as his ideas about the caesura demand, it cannot be claimed that they conform to Bliss's findings about resolution. In a similar vein, he disambiguates verses like *Þæt wæs tacen sweotol* (833b) and *Ða wæs winter scacen* (1136b), reading monosyllabic *tacen* and *winter* on the basis of the observation, "A

[5]Since Kaluza's formulation is based on stress rather than vowel or syllable length, he is able to explain exceptions like *hwæt me Grendel hafað* (474b) and *Þanon eft gewiton* (853a) as due to the lower stress borne by finite verbs: thus the suffix bears no "Nebenton" ("Verslehre," p. 127). Certainly Kaluza's law does not apply to syllables under tertiary stress, as demonstrated in the next chapter.

comparison with the conditions described in §40 shows that resolution here is improbable" (§58).[6] But if *tacen* and *winter* are dissyllabic, then *sweotol* and *scacen* follow unstressed syllables, and under the reasoning of Bliss's §40 they may thus be resolved. Bliss's assertion appears to be based on his conclusion about resolution at the end of type 3B1b: "Out of twenty-two endings, four are consonantal (one with two consonants), three are long vocalic endings (*hreþe, feore, scyle*); the remaining 15 are short vocalic endings. This proportion is representative" (§40). But this is no reliable basis on which to conclude that resolution in *Þæt wæs tacen sweotol* is improbable. And at any rate the given figures are debatable: among his 22 verses are two masculine *i*-stem datives (*hryre* and *bite*) and six examples of *fela* (see Campbell's grammar, §§666 and 612). Thus, the proportion for vocalic endings might better be called eleven long to seven short (granting him the benefit of the doubt in regard to the ending of *scyle* and *wile*). Yet it is on these conclusions in his §§38–40 that Bliss bases his claims about resolution as a dating criterion. The rules of resolution "were most fully preserved in *Beowulf* in the second element of full compounds, less fully in disyllabic formative and derivative endings, less fully still in isolated disyllables. . . . The degree to which the equivalences are preserved might provide a new criterion of the relative chronology of Old English verse" (§40). There does not in fact appear to be any reliable evidence for observance of Kaluza's law under primary or tertiary stress.

§173. Kaluza's own formulation of his law advances no chronological claims about the distribution of long and short final syllables in words with tertiary stress. Rather, with the exception of his untenable claims about types B and E, it applies only to dissyllables after stressed syllables. About these he finds that his law operates "in der älteren Dichtung, z.B. im Beowulf" (*Englische Metrik*, §52; as above, n. 4). To test this hypothesis it is necessary to clarify some of the finer points of Kaluza's law. His assumption (again excluding the claims about types B and E) is that the rule applies only when the resolvable syllables and the immediately preceding lift stand in the same foot. For example, he remarks that two short syllables can only be unresolved at the end of a verse "*wenn demselben eine lange starktonige Silbe . . . unmittelbar vorhergeht*, so dass ein

---

[6]See also §72, where he argues that, for instance, *aldor-* must be monosyllabic in *næfre he on aldordagum* (718a) because resolution of *-dagum* is improbable. This claim is consistent with his reasoning because technically *-dagum* does carry secondary stress in his system of scansion, regardless of whether *aldor-* is dissyllabic. It will become apparent below, however, that the relevant criterion here is not absolute stress value but relative: the law applies to syllables whose stress is subordinated to an immediately preceding stress, under the requirement established by Thomas Cable that the second of two adjacent stresses must be subordinated (*Meter and Melody*, esp. pp. 65–74). That it could be otherwise is implausible, since the existence of a stress-based metrical system governed by absolute rather than relative stress is a linguistic improbability: see, e.g., §266 below.

dreigliedriger Fuss mit absteigender Betonung entsteht" (*Englische Metrik*, §52). This must also be Bliss's assumption, since he believes that by dividing the compounds in *þeod ealgearo* (*Beowulf* 1230b) and *Beorh eallgearo* (2241b) he obviates the problem of the anomalous nonresolution, turning these into type 2A3b, with caesura after the second syllable (§§62, 77). Kaluza's belief that his law applied to verses like *guðrinc monig* and *on bearm scipes* was based on assumptions about the caesura or foot division different from Bliss's. But adherence to Bliss's ideas about the caesura eliminates consideration of many verses in *Beowulf* that would otherwise be exceptions—a number that would be surprising in view of the great regularity of Kaluza's law otherwise in the poem, as demonstrated by Bliss. Examples are *uhthlem þone* (2007b) and *wæs on bæl gearu* (1109b), for respective comparison.[7]

§174. Thus, given Bliss's assumptions about placement of the caesura, we should not expect Kaluza's law to apply to verses of type 2C2 (*on bearm scipes*). The figures for this type might at first appear to support Kaluza's position rather than Bliss's, but they are misleading. Type 2C2 appears 216 times in the off-verse, with 18 instances of unambiguously short vocalic endings.[8] The proportion is small enough to be suggestive, until it is realized that, for instance, in type D the forms subject to Kaluza's law are consistently nouns and adjectives, while in type 2C2 they are mostly verbs and adverbs: nouns and adjectives account for just 32 of the instances, or 15 percent.[9] But an examination of Appendix C below reveals that almost all the short vocalic endings in Old English occur among the nouns and adjectives: there are none among the adverbs, and among the finite verbs the only unambiguously short vocalic ending that can appear after a fully stressed syllable is the preterite optative singular inflection (in the main, represented in *Beowulf* by the present optative of preterite-present verbs). And even in this instance there is room for doubt, as discussed in Appendix C. Thus, 18 violations of Kaluza's law represent in fact a rather high proportion—too high a number to permit

[7]On the possibility that verses like the former actually do not violate the law, see below, p. 239, n. 4.

[8]Bliss's statistics in his appendix C are frequently at variance with those derivable from his "Index to the Scansion." They are are corrected, as in this instance, by Vickman's metrical concordance (as above, p. 29, n. 53). The eighteen instances with short vocalic endings are at 489b, 507b, 589b, 676b, 680b, 966b, 1109b, 1179b, 1250b, 1367b, 1660b, 2031b, 2530b, 2749b, 2818b, 2976b, 3105b, and 3176b. The search is restricted to the off-verse for appropriate comparison with type d3, below. As pointed out in the appendix, the quantity in *dyde* and *hafa* is uncertain. Bliss's claim (§58) that *Grendel* is monosyllabic in *þonne Grendel hine* (678b) is unjustified, since the name can only derive from *\*Grandilaz*, demanding a dissyllabic uninflected form under the principles set forth in §§81f. above. There is no exceptional treatment of a noun, except in the on-verse, at 2047a.

[9]To be sure, in the on-verse the proportion is considerably higher, at 26 out of 48 instances.

the assumption that type 2C2 generally conforms to the law, especially in view of how faithful the poet is to it in other metrical types.

§175. An informative comparison is to type d3 (e.g. *in geardagum* 1b), the light equivalent of 2C2. This type appears in the off-verse sixty-one times in *Beowulf*, according to Bliss, and in nine instances the last syllable is an unambiguously short vocalic ending.[10] Thus, the proportion of exceptions is even higher than in type 2C2. If the foot division may fall between the two elements of a compound, as Russom suggests,[11] then the behavior of type d3 with respect to Kaluza's law is further evidence that d3 is not actually a light type, but is metrically identical to 2C2, an assumption supported by the observation that d is the only light type permitted in the off-verse (see §202 below). In most metrical analyses of Old English, for example Sievers' and Pope's, d is in fact regarded as indistinguishable from type C. And so it does appear to be true that Kaluza's law applies only when the resolvable syllables immediately follow a lift in the same foot.[12] Yet there is room for doubt here, especially if

---

[10]Most instances in the on-verse are ambiguous, since they might be interpreted as type a2 with resolution. The nine exceptions mentioned are at 77b, 116b, 771b, 820b, 1192b, 1279b, 1992b, 2884b, and 3112b. Bliss's classification of *Ic him þenode* (560b) as type d3b is in error, since this bears tertiary stress.

[11]See p. 26 and passim. The foot division that Russom employs is distinct from Bliss's concept of the caesura, however—a point that Russom elaborated in a paper presented at the 1990 meeting of the Modern Language Association of North America. Moreover, I do not wish to imply that Russom would in fact scan this verse with the foot division between the elements of the compound. But his bracketing rules do not exclude this scansion, since his metrical feet are based on two-word patterns, and the pattern of *ongean gramum* (1034a) of course is common.

[12]Why this should be so is not clear, nor how such a limitation on the operation of the rule can be incorporated into metrical theory, since the concept of the foot is doubted by many, and Bliss's theory of the caesura is probably incorrect (see §§246ff below). One method of accounting for this limitation perhaps may be derived from Russom's observation that verses like *\*oþþe þæt heard sweord* are disallowed (p. 54; the restriction does not apply to later verse: see §291 below). One principle governing Russom's system of scansion is that metrical rules aim to reduce ambiguity of scansion. Because resolution in a verse like *wæs on bæl gearu* would give a pattern with a single final half-lift, as in the disallowed *\*oþþe þæt heard sweord*, resolution is impossible. Nor could the verse be regarded as incomplete, with another word to follow, as secondary stress is disallowed in the second thesis of type B, and there are no verses like *\*on bæl gearu gestōd* (or *stōdon*) in type D. Thus there can be no ambiguity about such verses, and because Kaluza's law is not required to disambiguate the scansion, it simply does not apply in type C. Another possible explanation derives from the observation that in very few instances of type 2C2 in *Beowulf* is the final word in the verse not a verb. It might then be supposed that the final word does not bear secondary stress, and so is not subject to Kaluza's law. (Cf. the similar possibility entertained below, p. 239 n. 4, in regard to verses like *uhthlem þone* 2007b. Cf. also the implications of Thomas Cable's observation in *English Alliterative Tradition*, p. 145, that verses like *hlyn swynsode* 611b are confined to the off-verse.) But this still leaves unexplained why verses of type d3 are unaffected. On B. R. Hutcheson's formulaic explanation for the nonapplication of the law in verses of type C, see below, p. 386 n. 74.

secondary stress is defined as merely a positional variant of primary stress (see p. 240, n. 6 below), or if Kaluza is right to exclude verses with a final finite verb, due to the lower stress.[13]

§176. This restriction on the operation of the law leaves a small number of relevant verse types. Bliss demonstrates the regularity of the law in types 2A3a(ii), 2A4, and 1D3 (§§35–37).[14] There is one example of type 2A3a(iv) in *Beowulf* (*fyrdsearu fuslicu* 232a). The requisite pattern for nonresolution is also found in type 3E3 (e.g. *beaghroden cwen*, 623b), but type 3E*3 (one instance in *Beowulf*, *wundorsmiþa geweorc* 1681a) is ambiguous, because with resolution it could be scanned as type 2E2a. Similarly, type 1D*3 (e.g. *mære mearcstapa*, 103a) is usually ambiguous, because with resolution it could be scanned as type 2A2(ii), like *mearcað morhopu* (450a).[15] But the type is disambiguated when it carries anacrusis (e.g. *alætan lændagas*, 2591a), since anacrusis is not permitted in type 2A. The type is also disambiguated when there is more than one unstressed syllable after the first lift—except when the caesura immediately precedes the second lift, as in *sellice sædracan* (*Beowulf* 1426a). Several varieties of type 1A are relevant here, for example *fleon on fenhopu* (764a). In practice it is convenient to divide all these types into two groups, depending on whether the resolvable syllables fall before or after the caesura. This is useful because although exceptions to Kaluza's law are not common in the latter type, nonexceptional verses are considerably more numerous. The disparity is explained below. There are in fact too many verses of the latter type to be quoted in full, and so the lists below provide all instances of type I verses, while only the exceptions in type II are cited in full, with figures and line numbers for the nonexceptional verses. Ambiguous verses are omitted. It may be noted that type I comprises verses of types A and E, and that consonantal and vocalic endings are exceptional in the former, but unexceptional in the latter.

TYPE I

*Genesis A*
    Exceptional: none.
    Unexceptional (2):
        1821a  hornsele hwite (acc. sg. masc. *i*-stem)
        2514b  aldornere mine (acc. sg. fem. *ō*-stem)

---

[13]See above, n. 5, and the preceding note; and for evidence that the stress on such verbs is weaker, see Campbell, §93, and Russom, pp. 84–86.

[14]There are a few discrepancies between the lists in §§35–36 and the figures in his appendix C because of arguments he adduces after §§35–36. E.g., in §80 the heavy verses 90a, 376a, and 570a are added to the list of type 1D3, and in the errata (p. vii) the scansion of 1069a is altered to 1D3.

[15]It should be noted that Bliss disregards his own findings in this respect, scanning this and four other verses like it—596a, 986a, 1358a, and 2800a—as type 1D*3. This of

*Daniel*
Exceptional (1):
    407a     heahcyning heofones (cons. ending)
Unexceptional (4):
    462a     færgryre fyres (acc. sg. masc. *i*-stem)
    689a     alhstede eorla (acc. sg. masc. *i*-stem)
    704a, 748a  huslfatu halegu (acc. pl. neut. *a*-stem)
*Beowulf*
Exceptional: none.
Unexceptional (65): Bliss lists 61 unambiguous verses of this type
(§35; 1534a is ambiguous). The following may be added:
    232a     fyrdsearu fuslicu (acc. pl. neut. *wa*-stem; cf. 2618a)
    623b     beaghroden cwen (cons. ending)
    783b     Norðdenum stod (cons. ending)
    2779b    mundbora wæs (nom. sg. masc. *n*-stem)
*Exodus*
Exceptional (1):
    240a     gylpplegan gares (cons. ending)
Unexceptional (6):
    61a      mearchofu morheald (acc. pl. neut. *a*-stem)
    137a     wælgryre weroda (see below, §177)
    290a     bæðweges blæst (gen. sg. masc. *a*-stem)
    325b     garwudu rærdon (acc. sg. masc. *u*-stem)
    329a     bilswaðu blodige (nom. sg. fem. *ō*-stem)
    573b     þurh þa heora beadosearo wægon (acc. pl. neut. *wa*-stem)
*Elene*
Exceptional (2):
    62a, 129b  Romwara cyning (gen. pl. fem. *ō*-stem)
Unexceptional (3):
    51a      campwudu clynede (nom. sg. masc. *u*-stem)
    201a     goldwine gumena (nom. sg. masc. *i*-stem)
    244b     brimwudu snyrgan (acc. sg. masc. *u*-stem)
*Fates of the Apostles*
Exceptional (1):
    49a      lifwela leofra (nom. sg. masc. *n*-stem)
Unexceptional: none.
*Juliana*
Exceptional: none.
Unexceptional (1):
    573a     feorhcwale findan (acc. sg. fem. *ō*-stem)
*Christ II*
Exceptional (2):
    636a     freonoman cende (cons. ending)
    827b     beorht cyning leanað (cons. ending)

---

course refers only to type D* in the on-verse, since it may not appear in the off-verse—which is why *bæron ut hræðe* (*Andreas* 1221b) violates Kaluza's law. Similarly, Bliss scans *modges merefaran* (502a) as type 2A2(ii)—the only example of the type in the poem—on the basis of the assumption that a short lift may not immediately follow a resolved lift; but cf. below, §249.

Unexceptional (4):
    673a    wordcwide writan (acc. sg. or pl. masc. *i*-stem)
    677b    sundwudu drifan (acc. sg. masc. *u*-stem)
    708b    blodgyte worhtan (acc. sg. masc. *i*-stem)
    853a    flodwudu fergen (acc. pl. or sg. masc. *u*-stem)

*Andreas*
Exceptional (2):
    103b    boldwela fægrost (nom. sg. masc. *n*-stem)
    1509a    sincgife, sylla (dat. sg. fem *ō*-stem)
Unexceptional (6):
    20b    folcstede gumena (nom. sg. masc. *i*-stem)
    127a    guðsearo gullon (nom. pl. neut. *wa*-stem)
    1136a    þeodbealo þearlic (nom. sg. neut. *wa*-stem)
    1158b    Hornsalu wunedon (nom. pl. neut. *a*-stem)
    1316b    hidercyme þinne (acc. sg. masc. *i*-stem)
    1576a    streamfare stillan (acc. sg. fem. *ō*-stem)

*Metrical Preface to the Pastoral Care*
Exceptional: none.
Unexceptional (1):
    9b    Romwara betest (gen. pl. fem. *ō*-stem)

*Meters of Boethius*
Exceptional (1):
    1.50a    sincgeofa sella (nom. sg. masc. *n*-stem)
Unexceptional (2):
    1.34a    Romwara bearn (gen. pl. fem. *ō*-stem)
    28.63a    ismere ænlic (nom. sg. masc. *i*-stem)

*Judith*
Exceptional (1):
    29a    dryhtguman sine (cons. ending)
Unexceptional (1):
    22a    goldwine gumena (nom. sg. masc. *i*-stem)

*Maldon*
Exceptional: none.
Unexceptional (1):
    322a    wælspere windan (acc. sg. neut. *i*-stem)

## TYPE II

*Genesis A*
Exceptional: none.
Unexceptional (7): 55a, 917a, 1154a, 2496a, 2512a, 2659a, 2874a.

*Daniel*
Exceptional (1):
    754a    godes goldfatu (acc. pl. neut. *a*-stem)
Unexceptional (5): 56a, 229b, 464b, 532a, 742a.

*Beowulf*
Exceptional (2):
    1409a    steap stanhliðo (acc. pl. neut. *a*-stem)
    1790a    deorc ofer dryhtgumum (cons. ending)

Unexceptional (41): 31a, 54a, 90a, 160a, 288a, 322a, 376a, 551a, 554a, 692a, 742a, 764a, 868a, 936a, 1069a, 1554a, 1622a, 1641a, 1845a, 1895a, 1948a, 1954a, 2025a, 2042a, 2090a, 2112a, 2118a, 2226a, 2271a, 2273a, 2315a, 2368a, 2414a, 2455a, 2462a, 2476a, 2517a, 2563a, 2642a, 2827a, 3152a.

*Exodus*

Exceptional (2):
    76a     eorðan and uprodor (cons. ending)
    219a    beran beorht searo (acc. pl. neut. *wa*-stem)
Unexceptional (14): 14a, 15a, 40a, 125a, 159a, 248a, 253a, 282a, 298a, 327a, 354a, 399a, 475a, 515a.

*Elene*

Exceptional (2):
    252a    ald yðhofu (acc. pl. neut. *a*-stem)
    673a    godes gastsunu (nom. sg. masc. *u*-stem)
Unexceptional (10): 10a, 94a, 246a, 343a, 438a, 464b, 475a, 841a, 1045a, 1299a.

*Fates of the Apostles*

Exceptional: none.
Unexceptional (1): 12a.

*Juliana*

Exceptional: none.
Unexceptional (4): 211a, 245a, 529a, 603a.

*Christ II*

Exceptional (4):
    660a, 860a  godes gæstsunu (nom. sg. masc. *u*-stem)
    697a    englum ond eorðwarum (cons. ending)
    794a    geseon synwræce (acc. sg. fem. *ō*-stem)
Unexceptional (3): 458a, 540a, 751a.

*Andreas*

Exceptional (6):
    370a    onhrered hwælmere (nom. sg. masc. *i*-stem)
    467a    hreoh holmþracu (nom. sg. fem. *ō*-stem)
    561a    ahof hearmcwide (acc. sg. or pl. masc. *i*-stem)
    803a    open eorðscræfu (acc. pl. neut. *a*-stem)
    1221b   bæron ut hræðe (adverb)
    1657a   beorht beagselu (acc. pl. neut. *a*-stem)
Unexceptional (9): 84a, 656a, 917a, 1202a, 1297a, 1346a, 1507a, 1519a, 1673a.

*Meters of Boethius*

Exceptional (1):
    5.10a   onhrerað hronmere (acc. sg. masc. *i*-stem)
Unexceptional (5): 1.47a, 7.3a, 22.54a, 29.74a, 31.7a.

*Judith*

Exceptional: none.
Unexceptional (2): 163a, 224a.

*Maldon*
    Exceptional (2):
        102a    wyrcan þone wihagan (cons. ending)
        286a    Offa þone sælidan (cons. ending)
    Unexceptional (2): 61a, 262a.

§177. Some of the verses included and excluded in the formulation of these lists merit comment. For type I, a probable exceptional verse in *Genesis A* is *ordbanan Abeles* (1097a), but as pointed out above (p. 84, n. 40), because the scansion of biblical names is sometimes capricious, such verses must be considered ambiguous. In *Daniel*, the verse *folctogan feran* (527a) is an emendation (*feran* is not in the manuscript); and *ealhstede eorla* (673a, dat. sg.) is uncertain, but is probably unexceptional, and an archaism, as explained in the appendix. The same is true of *mundgripe mægenes* (*Beowulf* 1534a), which Bliss scans as unexceptional (§35). In *Beowulf* also, *Suðdena folc* (463b) appears to be unexceptional, but may not be relevant, because the earlier form is *-deniga*: see below, Chap. 9. The verse *Beowulf is min nama* (343b) is ambiguous, either type 2E1b, as Bliss has it (but with stress on *-wulf*: see §210 below), or 1A\*1b (but with a short second lift), or 1A\*2a, with stress on *mīn*: compare *Meaht ðu, min wine* (2047a, with alliteration on *m*). In *Exodus*, the first word in the verse *wælgryre weroda* (137a) could be either singular or plural, as pointed out in the appendix, though it is probably singular here; and *beorselas beorna* (564a) may stand for earlier *-sele* (so also *-cwide* in *sang soðcwidas* at *Meters* 6.2a; cf. 2.4a). Compare how *hleoðorcwyde* at *Daniel* 315b corresponds to *hleoþorcwidas* in the equivalent verse at *Azarias* 32b. *Dægsceades hleo* (79b) and *spelbodan eac* (514a) are both emended, though the former emendation is rather probable. The verse *burgwaru bannan* (*Andreas* 1094a) must be considered ambiguous because as a feminine accusative singular, *burgwaru* would be peculiar: see Kenneth Brooks's emendation (p. 100).

§178. In regard to type II, there is a significant number of "heavy" verses like *leoht forð cuman* (*Genesis A* 122b) that appear to belong to type 1D3, though Bliss would classify them as 2A3b (§§77, 80), requiring elision at some places in *Beowulf*. At first glance this may seem an unreasonable classification, since syntactically the adverb is part of the verb phrase, and so the caesura ought to fall after the first word. Bliss's objection, however, is weighty: type 1D3 does not occur in the off-verse in *Beowulf*, and it would therefore be an odd coincidence if all examples happened to be of this type. There are three instances of type 1D3 in the off-verse in other poems of the test group (see §108), but this is hardly a sufficient number in view of the frequency of the heavy type; thus these verses must be regarded as ambiguous. Also in regard to type II, *æðele ærendracan* (*Genesis A* 2436a) must bear tertiary stress, since *-raca* occurs neither as a simplex nor in any other compound. The verse *frea on* *forðwegas* (2814a) appears to be exceptional because the caesura must fall before *on*; but in fact *on* is not in the manuscript. A better emendation is *forðwege*: compare *feorh foldwege* (2512a) and *forð foldwege* (2874a). The same unlikely emendation is to be found in *mara on modsefan* (*Daniel* 491a). The verse *witegena wordcwyde* (*Daniel* 646a) is ambiguous, as it may be like *sellice sædracan* (*Beowulf* 1426a), which Bliss classifies as type 1D*3. In regard to the data for *Beowulf*, Bliss (§37) argues that the vowel may be long in the second-to-last syllable of *steap stanhliðo* (1409a), and Amos agrees (p. 99, n. 16). But this is not possible, since then the plural would be *stānhlīþ*. Two verses that Bliss scans with exceptional resolution (§54) are to be explained otherwise: *-byrig* is etymologically monosyllabic in *lond ond leodbyrig* (2471a: see Campbell, §365, and p. 97, n. 5 above); and *win of wunderfatum* (1162a) is ambiguous, since *wunder-* may be dissyllabic. At the same place he requires resolution in *modges merefaran* (502a), but see note 15 above. He scans *bær on bearm scipes* (896a) with resolution (§79), but his findings (§14) indicate that *bær* here may be unstressed, though exceptionally. The verse *forbærned burhhleoðu* (*Exodus* 70a, nom. pl. neut. *a*-stem) is dubitable because anacrusis with type 2A2 does occur in this poem: compare *alyfed laðsið* (44a). In *biter beorþegu* (*Andreas* 1533a), *biter* may stand for *bitter*: compare, for example, *Phoenix* 404b. The verse *hwæt þis folc segeð* (*Maldon* 45b) may have *segeð* for *sægþ*.[16] Its companion in the line, *Gehyrst þu, sælida* (45a) is ambiguous, given the high incidence of exceptional anacrusis in the poem. If not corrupt, this line is alliteratively inept. But as always with *Maldon*, the data are less secure, since the metrical rules are clearly laxer, and it may be that the two exceptional verses of type II listed above belong to type D.

§179. The most salient point to emerge from this survey is that *Beowulf* is unique in respect to the great ease and regularity of the poet's ability to distinguish long and short endings. The facts about Kaluza's law in *Beowulf* are impressive, as Amos remarks (p. 99): out of 108 unambiguous instances there are just 2 exceptions. Such a proportion is unquestionably outside the statistical range of coincidence, and the exceptions are few enough that they are within the statistical range of being due possibly to scribal corruption.[17] No other poem approaches *Beowulf* in this regard, though most demonstrate some observance of the distinction. Yet exceptions are frequent enough, especially after this point in the chronology, that it is hardly necessary to assume that any of these poets

---

[16]Other examples of this inflection in *Maldon* are metrically ambiguous; but the spelling is commonly contracted (see 45a, 51a, 237b, and cf. 55b, which is metrically ambiguous, given the license of the *Maldon* poet in regard to anacrusis), and it is demonstrated in Chap. 7 that orthographic contraction after long syllables is a fairly reliable correlate of metrical contraction.

[17]On the relative likelihood of scribal corruption in Old English manuscripts see the Introduction, §§31ff. At *Beowulf* 1790a, *deorc* could be deleted without impairing the syntax or the sense.

but the *Beowulf* poet was clearly aware of the distinction. Possibly the amount of conformity to the law encountered outside *Beowulf* is attributable to the formulaic character of the relevant verses: because the law applies only under secondary stress, it is restricted almost entirely to poetic compounds. This supposition is corroborated by the observation that verses of the relevant types are exceptionally frequent in *Beowulf*. For example, while there are 108 relevant verses in *Beowulf*, in *Genesis A* there are just 9, even though the latter poem is nearly three-quarters the length of the former, and is rich in poetic compounds.[18] The difference is especially extreme in type I, where *Beowulf* furnishes 65 examples and *Genesis A* just 2. While it is difficult to explain why the *Beowulf* poet might have used verses of the relevant type with such extraordinary frequency, it is not difficult to explain other poets' avoidance of such verses, since it may be supposed that the metrical value of the vocalic endings was no longer obvious when they composed. The only noteworthy exception to the pattern is *Exodus*, as illustrated by the following figures, representing the proportion of relevant verses to the total number of verses in each poem:

| | | |
|---|---|---|
| *Genesis A*, 9 instances | = | .2 percent |
| *Daniel*, 11 instances | = | .7 percent |
| *Beowulf*, 108 instances | = | 1.7 percent |
| *Exodus*, 23 instances | = | 1.9 percent |
| *Cynewulf*, 37 instances | = | .7 percent |
| *Andreas*, 23 instances | = | .7 percent |
| *Metrical Preface*, 1 instance | = | 3.1 percent |
| *Meters*, 9 instances | = | .3 percent |
| *Judith*, 4 instances | = | .6 percent |
| *Maldon*, 5 instances | = | .8 percent |

The particularly high incidence in *Exodus* accords with the general view that this is the Old English poem with the highest incidence of compounds (see Amos, pp. 160–61). In regard to the proportions of exceptional to unexceptional verses, it may be said that those for Cynewulf, 5:8 in type I and 6:18 in type II, are in the same general range as the proportions for *Andreas*. Strictly speaking, *Daniel* and *Exodus* fall statistically between these poems and *Beowulf*, though the significance of the statistical difference is dubitable. As for the *Meters of Boethius*, *Judith*, and *Maldon*, none has enough examples for the proportions to have any statistical significance with respect to the earlier poems, but all three at any rate do show exceptions to Kaluza's law. *Genesis A* shows no exceptions to the law, but the number of instances is far too low for this fact to bear much weight. Moreover, although the verse *ordbanan Abeles* (1097a) was excluded above, it still carries a certain degree of probability.

---

[18]Conversely, the low incidence of relevant verses in the *Meters* (evidenced below) is perhaps due to the small number of poetic compounds in the poem.

§180. Given the evidence that only the *Beowulf* poet was fully aware of the etymological quantities of final vowels, it is noteworthy how frequently unexceptional verses of type II are encountered in other verse, especially up to and including *Elene*. Most of the endings involved are consonantal, suggesting some limited observance of the law even after the shortening of final circumflected vowels. That the law was not immediately lost altogether when these vowels coalesced is also suggested by the evidence of Chapter 8. Yet it is also remarkable that when a vocalic ending appears in such verses, it is almost consistently -*a* < *-ô*, in the genitive plural and in the nominative singular of masculine *n*-stems. Possibly -*ô* was shortened slightly later than -*ǣ*. It appears to have been lowered before shortening: see below, §418.

§181. Amos (p. 100) objects to the evidence of Kaluza's law because of the possibility that certain metrical types not permitted in *Beowulf* may have been acceptable in other verse. Taking a specific example, she argues that although the metrical pattern of a verse such as *\*gūðrēowe gāras* is not found in *Beowulf* (Bliss, §34), it may have been acceptable in the *Wanderer*, in which *ferðloca freorig* (33a) then need not violate Kaluza's law. And so the *Wanderer* need not postdate *Beowulf*. As pointed out in the Introduction (§12), this reasoning is antiprobabilistic because it assumes that a proposition is of no force if alternative explanations are merely possible rather than plausible. In fact verses like *\*gūðrēowe gāras* are not found in the test group of poems, and it would be peculiar if they were found, since they violate the basic rule that a verse must comprise no more than four metrical positions. It is only in very late and metrically defective poems that five-position verses are found with any regularity. Thus if *ferðloca freorig* did not show resolution, the *Wanderer* would require even more degenerate metrics than *Maldon*, which does not violate the four-position rule. In fact the meter of the *Wanderer* is much superior to that of *Maldon*.

§182. In sum, *Beowulf* is the most conservative poem of the test group with regard to Kaluza's law. Cynewulf and the *Andreas* poet violate it with considerable frequency. Poems known or presumed to date to Alfred's reign or later, to the extent that they provide any evidence at all, contain few instances to offer any statistical significance, but they clearly do not conform to the law. Violations in *Genesis A*, *Daniel*, and *Exodus* are few, but so are the relevant instances, at least in verses of type I. The difference between *Beowulf* and the rest of the test group, in respect both to regularity of application and to overall incidence of relevant verse types, is so profound that it can hardly be dissociated from the elimination of the phonological distinction between long and short vocalic endings. *Beowulf*, at least, must have been composed before the shortening of the long endings. It may also be noted that the pattern of conformity to Kaluza's law is found throughout the poem, and this is true of no other poem of sufficient length to provide credible statistics. This seems especially likely evidence against the view that the poem is of composite origin.

§183. The dating evidence of Kaluza's law is of particular interest for several reasons. First, the facts about *Beowulf* with regard to the law are significant in their own right, outside of any context of comparison. In the preceding chapters, each metrical variation studied has suggested the relative antiquity of *Beowulf* only by comparative statistics: for example, forms with parasiting are not missing altogether from *Beowulf*, but proportionally they are considerably rarer there than in all other verse of any considerable length. In the instance of Kaluza's law, however, exceptions are so rare in *Beowulf* as to be negligible, and so conformity to the law may be regarded as absolute rather than relative. And the contrast between *Beowulf* and other verse is such that this is a particularly forceful criterion. More significantly, the metrical changes studied in prior chapters have been difficult to date absolutely because they involve the slow loss of archaisms. Observance of Kaluza's law, on the other hand, depends upon the maintenance of the original distinctions in vowel quantities. The fidelity of *Beowulf* to the law demonstrates that the poem can only have been composed before the quantitative distinction was lost. The law thus provides a fairly precise *terminus ad quem* for the composition of the poem: see the Conclusion, §§406ff. This form of metrical change also provides particularly good evidence against the claim that metrical differences among Old English poems are as likely to be due to stylistic preferences as to linguistic change (§§35ff. above). An examination of Appendix C demonstrates that the distribution of long and short vocalic endings is irregular, and too complex to have been preserved as consciously archaic language: there must have been a phonological difference between the two types of endings at the time *Beowulf* was composed.[19] Thus it is conceivable that, for instance, *Andreas* is an earlier poem than the evidence of Kaluza's law suggests—that is, the poet was aware of the law but chose not to observe it—but it is not conceivable

---

[19]A consideration of the circumstances under which the Old English scop must have learned his craft makes the point particularly clear, since the process cannot have been essentially different from child language acquisition (as pointed out by Donoghue, p. 13). Although children's grammar is occasionally corrected by elders, such correction rarely has any effect, and grammar is instead learned by the child's own observation. Similarly, anyone who speaks a highly inflected language like Modern Icelandic knows the absurdity of supposing that Old English scops were instructed, "The ending of the nominative singular feminine ō-stem is short," etc. Old English did not even have such grammatical terminology, as Ælfric's grammar illustrates; and in Modern Icelandic, which does have such terminology, even some of the simplest terms are incomprehensible to all but linguists. Similarly, A. B. Lord found that the illiterate Yugoslavian singers whose performances he studied had no understanding of basic concepts such as the verse line: see *The Singer of Tales* (Cambridge: Harvard Univ. Press, 1960), p. 25. The only way a scop can have learned the quantities of final vowels by mere observation is if there was a phonological difference.

that the *Beowulf* poet's observance of the law is a conscious archaism, since the complexity of the distribution of long and short vocalic endings rendered it impossible to observe the law very effectively after the shortening of all remaining final long vowels.

# VII

# CHANGES IN ICTUS
# AT THE TERTIARY LEVEL

A. The Nature of Tertiary Stress and
Its Relation to Chronology

§184. It has sometimes been supposed that changes in the metrical treatment of tertiary stress can be correlated to a poem's date of composition. Thus Sarrazin remarks about *Genesis A*, "Ganz archaische Längen der Ableitungssilben sind erkennbar in V. 180 *earfōða dǣl*, 1476 *earfōða bōt*, 1413 *lȳtlīgan eft*, 2357 *blētsīan nū*, 2273 *hlǣfdīgan hete*, welche schon im Beow. kaum Parallelen haben, denn *egsode eorl* Beow. 6 ist mit Sievers sicher in *egsode eorlas* zu bessern. Zu vergleichen ist Beow. 534 *earfeðo on ȳðum*" (*Kädmon*, p. 26). Roughly, Sarrazin's idea is that vowels under tertiary stress are sometimes shortened in *Beowulf*, while they are not in *Genesis A*. As it turns out, this is not an accurate assessment, since the apparent shortening also occurs in *Genesis A*, for example in *þancode swiðe* (1888b) and *cunnode georne* (2847b). Moreover, to be set against Sarrazin's one example of shortening are many examples in *Beowulf* of the preservation of length under tertiary stress, as in *wisdome heold* (1959b) and *XVna sum* (207b). Nonetheless, it is true that the metrical treatment of syllables under tertiary stress is not uniform over the corpus of Old English verse, and the detectable variations are worthy of study, since they may correlate to historical change in the Old English language.

§185. Alistair Campbell suggests more comprehensive developments involving tertiary stress in verse when he summarizes the standard view of Old English word stress (§§87–92), derived in the main from Sievers' observations about stress and meter (*Altgerm. Metrik*, §78). It should be understood from the start that Campbell does not distinguish between secondary and tertiary stress, referring to both as "half-stress," since "tertiary stress" is a term of Bliss's coinage. The difference in behavior between the two is attributed instead to the property of semantic force. True compounds never lose the half-stress assigned to their second element because the semantic force of the second element always remains intact—that is, the second elements of true compounds are lexical rather than derivational morphemes. For example, it is clear that the second element of *sǣmearh* 'sea-steed' (i.e. 'ship') is identical to the noun *mearh* 'horse'. When the semantic force of a second element was reduced

—when it was no longer identified as a word unto itself, at least with the same meaning it had in the compound—half-stress was not retained where the second element constituted a monosyllable. For example, the name-element *-ferþ* was no longer associated with the noun *friþ*, and shows the effects of reduced stress, through metathesis and lowering of *i* to *e*.[1] But half-stress was retained when the word carried an inflectional syllable, or when the second element was itself dissyllabic. For example, *ārlīcor*, *Ælfrēdes*, *hlāfordes*, and *eorlscipe* all carry half-stress, according to Campbell, but not *ārlic*, *Ælfred*, *hlāford*, or *eorlisc*. In *ārlic* and *Ælfred* there was also shortening of the vowel in the unstressed syllable: "Such syllables are clearly shown to be short by the prosody of the OE Latin poets who scan them short finally but long when an inflexion is added, e.g. *Ælfstan*, *Ælfheah* but *Ælfstānus*, *Ælfhēgus*" (p. 34, n. 4; but cf. below, §212). There are inconsistencies, but, says Campbell, they are primarily to be found in late verse: "Such a system leaves scope for analogy, and especially in late poems (e.g. *Metres*) syllables of [this type] . . . can discard their half-stress when internal if metre so demands" (p. 35, n. 1). This is especially true of syllables ending in a single consonant, such as *-od-* in the preterite of weak verbs of the second class: such stresses "are often neglected in verse, and in late Old English syllables bearing them are frequently subject to change and loss, like fully unaccented syllables" (§92). But shortening could also apply to closed syllables: as Sievers explains (*Altgerm. Metrik*, §78.4), and Campbell reiterates (§457 and n. 2), long middle syllables without secondary stress (e.g. in *ehtende wæs* at *Beowulf* 159b) and syllables made long by the addition of a suffix beginning with a consonant (e.g. in *oðerne bæd* at *Genesis A* 1662b) normally bear half-stress; but in later verse, including the *Meters of Boethius*, this half-stress is frequently disregarded, as in *nænigne metað* (*Meters* 17.18b). Under these conditions single consonants can also be written for geminates, for example in *opera* for *operra* at *Exhortation to Christian Living* 12.[2]

§186. It is not possible to test these claims under Bliss's system of scansion, since an important aspect of his classificatory system, and one of the two most controversial, is his rejection of the distinction between tertiary stress and lack of stress. "Tertiary" is Bliss's term for the stress assigned by Sievers' analysis to all syllables that are neither inflectional nor found in compounds whose elements have retained their semantic force. Thus, included are some final syllables without secondary stress, such as the second syllable of uninflected *hlāford*, though Campbell's explanation above indicates that such syllables do not bear stress. For the purposes of this discussion Campbell's account will be preferred, and tertiary stress will be restricted to exclude all final syllables. Thus

---

[1]The example is discussed in detail in "Unferth and His Name," *Modern Philology* 85 (1987), 113–27.

[2]It should be kept in mind that forms like fem. acc. sg. *ōþ(e)re* should be dissyllabic, while dat. *ōþerre* should be trisyllabic.

Campbell's half-stress comprises all and only instances of secondary and tertiary stress.[3] If Bliss is right that tertiary stress may be ignored, then verses like *earfeþo on yþum* (*Beowulf* 534a) need not be considered anomalous—indeed, Bliss scans this as type 1A\*1a(i), with an expansion comparable to that in *sellice sædracan* (1426a) and *eahtodan eorlscipe* (3173a). If this is so, the chronological significance of variation in the treatment of tertiary stress may be rejected out of hand. It will be necessary to examine Bliss's views in detail.

### B. Phonological Evidence for Tertiary Stress

§187. Bliss rejects Sievers' assumption of stress at the tertiary level simply because he finds no metrical evidence for the distinction. But in an appendix (pp. 113–17) he also offers reasons to disregard the phonological motives for positing tertiary stress, and before turning to the metrical issues it is worth examining the purely phonological ones. He finds two phonological changes that seem to require the assumption of tertiary stress as they are described in Luick's grammar. First, as Bliss explains (p. 113),

> In medial syllables, prehistoric *æ* and *e* are always lost, irrespective of the quantity of the stem syllable (Luick §303); prehistoric *i* and *u* are lost after a long stem syllable but retained after a short stem syllable (Luick §306). Prehistoric long vowels other than *ī* and *ū* were shortened and retained, but prehistoric *ī* and *ū* were shortened and subsequently lost (Luick §§312.5, 314). The retention of the shortened long vowels is explained as due to the survival of a *Nebenakzent* after a long stem syllable, the loss of shortened *ī* and *ū* as due to the loss of the *Nebenakzent* (Luick §314).

Bliss objects that stress is irrelevant to the changes described, and proposes to account for the facts by assuming that *ī* and *ū* were shortened before the other long vowels. In fact they were shortened before originally short *i* and *u* were syncopated, and thus shared their fate. He adds, "it is impossible to understand how the quality of a vowel can affect the survival of *Nebenakzent*; in other words, although there is plenty of analogy for the earlier shortening of the close vowels *ī* and *ū*, there is none for the earlier loss of *Nebenakzent*" (p. 114). The latter point is incorrect, since there is a wealth of evidence in many languages for the

---

[3]The assumption of some stress difference between inflected and uninflected forms seems to be necessary. The verse *æþeling on elne* (2506a), for example, appears to be acceptable, while \**æþelinges ellen* is not (cf. *æþelinges bearn* 888a; but see §§255ff. below). Bliss explains the difference as due to rules for the placement of the caesura. Since it is a matter of convenience to have a term distinguishing secondary stress from Campbell's other instances of half-stress, and since Bliss's conception of tertiary stress is readily identifiable by other means (in his system it is indistinguishable from lack of stress), the term "tertiary stress" will be employed here in the former sense.

syncope of high vowels while mid and low vowels are preserved.[4] And since absence of stress is a precondition for syncope in languages with stress accent, vowel quality in some cases is clearly related to degree of stress. At least in this respect there is nothing intrinsically improbable in Luick's analysis.

§188. The former point, however, does indeed draw attention to an improbability in the standard view. Luick expressly states that $\bar{\iota}$ and $\bar{u}$ in open medial syllables were not syncopated at the same time as originally short $i$ and $u$ (§§306, 315), but were widely syncopated later, after shortening (§314.2). His reason for assuming two separate syncopes of high vowels, apparently, is the observation that in a particular set of instances the originally long high vowels were not lost in medial syllables (§314.2):

Wenn aber mittleres $\bar{\iota}$ and $\bar{u}$ Verkürzung erfuhren, schwand der Nebenakzent vielfach und dann fielen die neuentstandenen $i$ und $u$ dem schon besprochenen Schwund anheim; so regelmäßig im Psalter: *gyldnum* dat. pl. 'den goldnen', *mōnðes* 'des Monats', vorwiegend auch in den übrigen anglischen Dialekten: *nētna* 'der Rinder', *mægdnes* 'des Mädchens', während das Westsächsische in der Regel keinen Schwund aufweist: *mædenes, gyldene*, aber auch *mōnðe*. In den Formen auf *-u* wurde überall der Nebenakzent und daher der Mittelvokal bewahrt: *\*stǽnìnu > stǽnènu* fem. sing. und plur. neutr. und ähnlich *ticcenu* plur. 'Zicklein', *cī(e)cenu* 'Küchlein', *lendenu* 'Lenden', ws. *nīetenu*, angl. *nētenu* 'Rinder', *miehtigu* fem. sing. und plur. neutr. 'mächtige' (nur vereinzelt *nētnu* Ri.).

It is easy to imagine how Luick reached his conclusion. In the records of West Saxon, forms like *hēafdu* and *hēafdum*, in which a short medial high vowel has been syncopated, are standard, and forms like *hēafodu* are rare. By contrast, forms like *nīetenu*, with medial $e < \bar{\iota}$, are standard, and those like *nīetnu* rare. But it can now be seen that there is a credible phonological motivation other than the length of the medial vowel for the peculiar pattern of loss in the Anglian dialects, where the long medial vowel was preserved before the ending *-u*, but not before any other ending, such as *-um*, *-a*, and *-es*. Given the evidence of the preceding chapter that final *-u* was metrically short when *Beowulf* was composed, and these other endings were long, it is possible that final quantity affected the loss or preservation of medial vowels, and thus very likely the degree of stress they assumed. Compare Campbell's remarks on the influence of the relative weight of the second element in determining whether the connecting vowel in compounds was syncopated, for example in *hildewīsa : hildfruma* (§349).[5]

---

[4]For evidence see Alan Bell, "Syllabic Consonants," in *Universals of Human Language*, vol. 2, ed. Joseph H. Greenberg (Stanford: Stanford Univ. Press, 1978), p. 178; and see *Origins*, p. 33, n. 8.

[5]See also Alfred Bammesberger, "Altenglische Komposita mit *hild(e)-*," *Münchener Studien zur Sprachwissenschaft* 39 (1980), 5–10; but cf. the article by Terasawa mentioned above, p. 78, n. 33.

§189. Moreover, the evidence of forms like *nīetenu* is not reliable. Regardless of the behavior of originally long medial high vowels in West Saxon, the major Anglian records do not actually show any difference of treatment between these and their originally short equivalents. Just as with the opposition between *nīetnum* and *nīetenu*, so also in Anglian texts syncope in the paradigm of *hēafod* is excluded only before the inflection *-u*: inflected forms with consonantal and long vocalic endings (*heafde*, *heafdes*, *heafda*) are common in Li., VP, and Rit.; and *heafdum* appears on the Ruthwell Cross.[6] In these texts there are no forms like *\*heafude*, and *\*heafudes*. Conversely, *heafudu* appears twice in VP, while *\*heafdu* does not occur at all in the major Anglian texts. Precise morphological parallels to *hēafod* are few, since a parallel requires a fairly unique structure, with a long root syllable and a second stem syllable with an originally short high vowel, in a word that must take both short and long inflections. But the few parallels tend to confirm this observation. Hans Füchsel, for example, finds that in the Li. gloss to the Gospel According to St. Matthew, the inflected past participle of long-stemmed weak verbs of the first class has syncope before all endings except *-u/-o* (e.g. *ge-begdum*); and, conversely, there is no syncope under these circumstances before *-u/-o* (e.g. *gelæredo*), with just two exceptions.[7] M. D. Kellum's findings for the Luke gloss are identical.[8] There is a clear reason for the divergence of the most prominent exception to this pattern, the feminine abstract nouns in *\*-iþu* (to which the nouns in *-īn-* are analogical: see Campbell, §589.7), for example VP *ebylgðu*: if these retained the *-i-* in the nominative, the stem there would be *æbylgiþ-* or *æbylgeþ-*, but *æbylgþ-* everywhere else in the paradigm—an alternation unparalleled in the language. That this irregularity did at one time exist is suggested by the fact that already in early texts the singular can have *-u* throughout, a paradigm regularization for which there is no other good motivation, since there is no apparent reason for these not to be inflected like other *ō*-stems. The only other exception is the nominative and accusative plural of neuter *ja*-stems, for example *rīcu* < *\*rīkijō*.[9] But such forms with *j*

---

[6]The reading on the cross requires the restoration of some letters, but at any rate there is not space enough for the extra rune required to spell *heafudum*.

[7]"Die Sprache der northumbrischen Interlinearversion zum Johannes-Evangelium," *Anglia* 24 (1901), 1–99, at 78. The form *timbredes* is no exception, since *-re-* here represents a syllabic consonant (Campbell, §364).

[8]*The Language of the Northumbrian Gloss to the Gospel of St. Luke*, Yale Studies in English 30 (New York: Henry Holt, 1906), 88–89.

[9]Campbell (§353, paraphrasing Luick, §309) concludes on the basis of such forms that *i* and *u* (and implicitly he means in both medial and final syllables) were lost at precisely the same time: "otherwise, if *i* were lost first, *\*rīkiu* would have become *\*rīku* and then *\*rīk*; while, if *u* were lost first, the development would have been *\*rīkiu* > *\*rīki* > *\*rīk*." That the loss of *i* and *u* represents a single, unified phonological development is no doubt correct. And yet very possibly there never was syncope of *i* here: it is easier to account for the anomaly of *rīcu* than to explain why *hēafdu* should have been

between the last two syllables are inconclusive, since *j* between unstressed vowels was very probably lost in Proto-Germanic.[10] Thereupon a diphthong would have developed, and since a diphthong *iu* would have been unparalleled as an inflectional ending, its development is unpredictable: it might have been replaced analogically by the ending of the corresponding short-stemmed nouns, or the first element might have been absorbed by the preceding consonant, or the diphthong might have developed naturally to *u*.[11] Because of the uncertainty involved, it is safer to rely on the evidence of words like *hēafudu* with a consonant preserved between the last two syllables.

§190. As for the West-Saxon evidence, Luick's position demands the assumption that this dialect is actually more conservative in this regard than the Anglian dialects. This is improbable, in part because the situation in West Saxon is so irregular, with otherwise identical syncopated and unsyncopated forms existing side by side: *ænigum*, for example, is about as frequent as *ængum*.[12] This sort of distribution is not the result of a regular phonological change, but reflects the sort of irregularity that frequently attends analogical processes. If it is necessary to explain the situation in West Saxon as at least disrupted by analogy, there is no real advantage to supposing it is not due entirely to analogy, or that the original situation was not identical to that in the Anglian texts, which is regular, and so may well result from normal phonological change.

§191. And so neither in the pure Anglian texts nor in any other is there actually a difference between the treatment of originally long and

---

replaced by analogical *hēafudu* (but no *hēafudum*, etc.) in VP (though that is Campbell's position, §353), and *gelǣrdo* by *gelǣredo* in Li., etc.

[10]See the discussion in William H. Bennett's "Parent Suffix in Germanic Weak Verbs of Class III," *Language* 38 (1962), 135–41.

[11]Possibly a similar development took place in Ép. *aetgaeru* if, as Campbell argues, this is the nominative singular of a *jō*-stem (§590, n. 2). Normally the *jō*-stems are endingless in the nominative singular, since the ending *-ī* derived from the IE *ī-/yā*-stems was shortened and lost; but presumably *-u* reflects the IE ending *\*-(i)yā* of the purely thematic *yā*-stems: cf. Skt. *dūtyā* 'message' and Gk. οἰκία 'household'.

[12]The adjective *hālig* appears to be a special case (as Luick recognizes, §314, n. 3). Although Ælfric freely uses forms like *ænigum*, John Pope remarks that in his homilies, forms with an immediately following back vowel lack the medial *i* (as in *halga, halgan*), while aside from forms with a consonantal ending (e.g. *haligre, haligne*) the medial *i* appears only when *e* follows (as in *halige, haliges*). Pope's explanation that the *i* merely indicates palatal articulation of the *g* is surely right: see *Homilies of Ælfric: A Supplementary Collection*, vol. 1, EETS, o.s. 259 (1967), 185. That such a distinction is maintained in a variety of manuscripts, when it is not a general practice among West-Saxon scribes (see the *Microfiche Concordance*), is testimony to the general conservatism of the scribes that Pope details (pp. 177ff.), and for which further evidence is presented below (Chap. 11). Similarly, Orm distinguishes between *haliʒ* and inflected *hallʒhe*, but maintains such a distinction for no other adjective in *-iʒ*. Indeed, alternations due to syncope seem otherwise to have been abandoned altogether in the *Ormulum*, so that, e.g., OE *heofon* has become *he(o)ffne*.

short high vowels in medial syllables. Yet there is positive evidence against Luick's position. The remainder of the evidence he offers for different treatment of medial long and short high vowels is the observation that *eln* < *\*alinō* 'ell' is monosyllabic, while *selen* < *\*salīni-* 'gift' is dissyllabic, because *i* was syncopated in this environment while *ī* was not (§341, n. 3). This cannot be correct. He himself points out that forms such as *swelc* and *hwelc* (see below, §193), along with other forms like *cyln* and *myln* (beside *cylen* and *mylen*), from Latin *culīna* and *molīna*, contradict his rule. An obstacle he does not mention is that in other words like *eln* with an originally short first syllable and an originally short medial high vowel there is free variation like that in *cylen* and *mylen*, for example in *fir(e)n*, *meol(o)c*, and *heor(o)t*. Thus the anomaly to be explained is not why *eln* is not like *selen*, but why it is never *\*elen*, like nearly all other words of this type, regardless of whether their medial vowel was originally long or short. The likeliest reason is that paradigm regularization affected the word differently, as in the case of *hēafod*. As Campbell remarks, "It is, of course, not possible to decide how far the vowel-losses . . . arose first in trisyllabic forms" (§390). And the effects of analogy are not governed by the same regularity of application as phonetic developments.

§192. Certainly, forms like *nīetenu* are not recent innovations—compare *men and netenu* (*Meters* 28.52a), *oð þa nytenu* (*Psalms* 134.8.4b), and *ful cyrtenu* (*Riddle 25* 6a), but also *deor ond nyten* (*Azarias* 145b). Disregarding this last, exceptional instance, they are different from nouns like *hēafod*, which take either the form *hēafud* or *hēafudu* in the plural in Anglian texts, but never *\*hēafdu*.[13] Yet, in the paradigm of *nīeten* there are three instances of *nētno* in Rit. But retention of stress is not the only possible explanation for the difference, since words that behave like *nīeten* all carry the suffix *-en-*, and so a different phonological explanation is possible, given the acknowledged influence of nasal consonants on neighboring high vowels in Old English. At any rate, Luick's explanation faces the difficulty that *-ī-* in the etymon of *nīetenu* must have been shortened in order for *-u* to have been preserved, and yet shortening in Old English noninitial syllables is associated with reduction in stress.

§193. For most purposes it makes little difference whether or not Bliss's contention about the shortening of high vowels is convincing, because even if there were two separate syncopes of high vowels, Luick himself indicates that the shortening must have taken place already in prehistoric times:

---

[13]B. Elan Dresher has studied this variation in VP, and concludes that there is no phonological explanation for it: see *Old English and the Theory of Phonology* (New York: Garland, 1985), chap. 3. This is Dresher's unrevised doctoral dissertation (Univ. of Massachusetts, 1978). Cf. Samuel Jay Keyser and Wayne O'Neil, "Exceptions to High Vowel Deletion in the Vespasian Psalter and Their Explanation," in *Current Topics in English Historical Linguistics*, ed. Michael Davenport et al. (Odense: Odense Univ. Press, 1983), pp. 137–64.

Diese Kürzungen sind wohl ungefähr gleichzeitig mit dem *i*- und *u*-Schwund erfolgt [i.e. the first syncope], doch so, daß ihr Endergebnis, völlige Kürze, mindestens im Auslaut erst erreicht wurde, als jener bereits vollzogen war. In Mittelsilben mögen sie etwas früher eingetreten sein, da hier nur der Nebenton die neue Kürze vor der Synkope zu schützen scheint. (§315)

This assumption about dating is necessary because such shortened high vowels are already missing in the earliest Old English texts. For example, *swelc*, *hwelc*, *ælc*, and *ilca* never have a vowel between the *l* and the *c*, though they all reflect *-līk-*: compare Gothic *swaleiks*, OHG *sulīh*, OSax. *sulīk*, and so forth. Campbell too remarks (§356, n. 1; see also §642, n. 1) that the adjective suffix *-līc-* must have been shortened early: otherwise the inflection *-u* would have been lost in the nominative singular feminine and nominative and accusative plural neuter, a loss that Luick dates to the beginning of the seventh century (§309).[14] Thus, *ī* must have been shortened before the non-high long vowels, which do cause the loss of *-u*, for example after the neuter suffix *-lāc-* (cf. *swa ða witelac* at *Genesis A* 2556b) and the adjective suffix *-lēas-*, and in isolated forms, for example *sēo ēorod* (< *eoh-rād-u*) in Ælfric.[15] So also *wedlac* must be plural in the glosses *bryda lice vel wedlac* and *wedlac, bryda on sponsalia* in two glosses on Aldhelm's *De laude virginitatis* (see the *Microfiche Concordance*). In addition, it is shown below (§§222, 238ff., and 258f.) that while original medial *ī* and *ū* metrically are generally short, short metrical treatment of originally long non-high vowels is uncommon. And the evidence of *-lic-* must be granted wider significance: it would be an extraordinary phonological development for *ī* to have been shortened in this before it was shortened in other environments, as Campbell seems to imply. Such a change would require morphological conditioning of the process, when it is a fundamental principle of historical phonology that initially sound changes are governed solely by phonological conditioning, with morphological factors taking effect only subsequently. It follows that Bliss must be right that the high vowels as a group were shortened before the other

---

[14]The reason that the shortened *i* is lost in *swelc*, etc., but not in adjectives like *frēolicu*, presumably is that there was a stress difference. Particles like West Germanic *\*swa* and *\*hwa* (the first elements of *swelc* and *hwelc*) carry less stress than major class words like *frēo* (the first element of *frēolic*), which naturally have greater semantic content. The greater stress of the latter type permits relatively high stress on the suffix (which of course can be no greater than the stress on the root syllable), though this is excluded in the former type by the low level of stress that begins the word. This principle explains the fact that whether the element of a compound receives secondary or tertiary stress frequently depends on the nature of the first element, as explained by Bliss (§32). For example, *-þanc-* has tertiary stress in *smiþes orþancum* (*Beowulf* 406b), type 1D1 according to Bliss, a type excluded from the off-verse when it carries secondary rather than tertiary stress), but secondary in *mid his heteþancum* (475b, type d2b).

[15]*Ælfric's Lives of the Saints*, vol. 2, ed. Walter W. Skeat, EETS, o.s. 94 (1890), 160.30.

long vowels—though, once again, for our purposes it is sufficient that the change should simply be prehistoric, as Luick demonstrates. The precise chronology of these sound changes does make a difference for Bliss's argument for rejecting tertiary stress, but it is of less significance for other purposes, since Bliss's argument does not prove that there was no tertiary stress—it merely obviates one piece of evidence for the existence of tertiary stress.

§194. The other phonological evidence for tertiary stress that Bliss wishes to refute is the matter of lengthening in later Latin borrowings of the sort *mägister, gīgantas* < Lat. *mägíster, gīgántes*. Luick (§218) proposes that the Latin musical accent was preserved as half-stress in Old English, and since Old English had no words with half-stress after a short initial syllable (cf. *cyningas*, without half-stress), the first vowel in the Latin word was consequently lengthened.[16] Luick's opposition to assuming half-stress in *cyningas* is perhaps ad hoc (and therefore weak), as Bliss charges (p. 115, n. 1), but this does not disqualify the explanation unless there is a more convincing one. It does not appear that any better explanation has been proposed, and so at least in this instance the phonological evidence for tertiary stress has not been disposed of.

§195. David L. Hoover offers evidence against tertiary stress when he points out that compounds without tertiary stress are not distributed like those with secondary stress in respect to alliteration.[17] Verses with double-alliterating compounds bearing secondary stress, such as *wig-weorþunga* (*Beowulf* 176a) and *heardhicgende* (394a), are confined to the on-verse, with the implication that it is the second alliterating position that bans them from the off-verse. By contrast, similar verses bearing tertiary stress like *Swa þu laðlice* (*Genesis A* 910b) occur freely in either half of the line. He draws the conclusion that verses of the latter type bear just one linguistic stress. Bliss argues that the incidence of the double-alliterating compounds with secondary stress is so small that it must be due to chance (§74), and it may be added that one-word verses are commoner in the on-verse than in the off-verse in *Beowulf*. Thus Hoover's demonstration of the restriction of the double-alliterating type to the on-verse, while remarkable, cannot be called decisive. Yet even if this evidence is to be admitted, it cannot be said that it proves the absence of linguistic stress. No one doubts that if tertiary stress existed it must have been less emphatic than secondary. And so while this evidence, if reliable, would help to prove lower stress on the second element of words

---

[16]See also Alois Pogatscher, *Zur Lautlehre der griechischen lateinischen und romanischen Lehnworte in Altenglischen*, Quellen und Forschungen 64 (Strassburg, 1888), §§56–60; Alfred Wollmann, *Untersuchungen zu den frühen lateinischen Lehnwörtern im Altenglischen* (Munich: Fink, 1990), §4.3.4.2; and Campbell, §548.

[17]"Evidence for Primacy of Alliteration in Old English Metre," *ASE* 14 (1985), 75–96. The point is made more succinctly in chap. 2 of his *New Theory of Old English Meter* (New York: Peter Lang, 1985).

like *lāðlīce*, it would not prove that the second syllable is unstressed. The distinction is not a quibble, since most metrists assume that the nonalliterating finite verb in a verse like *ne hyrde ic cymlicor* (*Beowulf* 38a) bears a higher degree of stress than the following particle (given that finite verbs do alliterate in many other verses), but that its stress is less prominent than that of the following adverb. And so it is possible that just as *hyrde* does not disrupt the alliteration in this verse from *Beowulf*, the second syllable of *lāðlīce* bears stress, but not enough for the alliteration of its initial consonant to disrupt the alliterative pattern of the verse. The distinction is of especial significance in the light of the association of alliteration with secondary rather than tertiary stress in compounds (see above, §66, in regard to Kendall's findings). Moreover, even if it could be proved that the second syllable of *lāðlīce* is unstressed, this could not be taken as proof that the syllable does not bear ictus (see below, §§204, 255ff.).

§196. Thus, Hoover's evidence is metrical rather than phonological, and Bliss's treatment of the purely phonological evidence is not complete, since the most important indication of the existence of tertiary stress remains—the difference between the phonological developments of unstressed vowels and those with tertiary stress. For example, after the time of the very earliest texts *u* becomes *o* in unstressed syllables, as in the preterite plural conjugational ending *-on* < *-un* (cf. *scylun* in *Cædmon's Hymn* in the eighth-century Moore MS: on the date see Appendix D below, pp. 426-28). Without tertiary stress there is no way to explain why we find, for instance, *-full* rather than *\*-foll*, and *-dom* rather than *\*-dam*. Moreover, the alternation between stressed and unstressed forms of such suffixes is evidence for the preservation of tertiary stress in inflected forms, with loss in uninflected ones. For example, Luick explains (§113, n. 2) that the co-occurrence of *toward* and *andward* with *wiðerweard* in Ru.[1] is attributable to the stress difference: the latter may be stressed on the last syllable because an unstressed syllable intervenes (see Brunner, §43, n. 2, and cf. the discussion of *rūmedlīce* and such below, §203). And since breaking does not apply to unstressed syllables, the co-occurrence of *-fald*, *-wald* with *-feald*, *-weald*, and the like, is due originally to retention of stress in inflected forms (*-fealdes*, etc.), whence the stressed vowels were extended to the uninflected cases.[18] Leveling in the opposite direction is also found, as in *Gūþferþes* and *Ælfredes*, for *-friðes* and WS

---

[18]The suffix *-fæst* (rarely *-fest*, though this would be the unstressed form) belongs here, though Bliss seems to regard this as bearing secondary stress, as indicated by his scansion of *tryddode tirfæst* (*Beowulf* 922a) as type 2A2. But clearly it cannot bear secondary stress in *And him tirfæst hæleð* (*Death of Edgar* 13a), *sopfæste sawle* (*Death of Edward* 28a), and others. The verse *staðolfæst gereaht* (*Meters* 11.99a), which, it is shown below, ought to bear secondary stress, is a type the *Meters* have in common with *Beowulf*: cf. *Meters* 20.142a, 20.183a, *Beowulf* 874b, 1720b, and similar (as discussed below, §§210ff.).

*-rǣdes*. But in suffixes that were never monosyllabic there was no opportunity for an unstressed form to arise, and so although *-fald* alternates
with *-feald*, we find (at least in West-Saxon texts, where WGmc. *ǣ* remains as such) *-bǣre* rather than *-bere* (*wæstmbǣre*, *hornbǣre*, etc.) and
*-rǣden* rather than *-reden* (*hīwrǣden*, *manrǣden*, etc.). Clearly, then, there
was a phonological distinction between syllables with tertiary stress and
those with no stress at the time of these changes in unstressed vocalism.
And these changes took place in the historical period, after the composition of the earliest poems, such as *Cædmon's Hymn*, since the phonology
of the early Northumbrian texts of this poem illustrates that changes in
unstressed vocalism in Northumbrian were not yet complete at the beginning of the eighth century (see Luick, §§322ff., 350). South of the
Humber, these changes occurred in the course of the eighth century (see
the Conclusion below). It might be argued that tertiary stress was lost
soon after this, but the phonological evidence is rather negative—for
example, *æ* in *-fæst* is not regularly confused with *e*, except in dialects
where *e* and *æ* were confused in all environments, until the time of the
transition to Middle English. More important, the metrical treatment of
tertiary stress in the earliest Old English verse is hardly distinguishable
from that in the vast remainder of the corpus, including even some poems
composed in the tenth century. If tertiary stress was lost soon after the
composition of the earliest surviving Northumbrian poems, it is difficult
to imagine how Old English meter escaped any fundamental changes, and
in particular the incorporation of many unambiguous three-position
verses (on which see below, §§205ff.).

§197. And so there does seem to be good phonological evidence for
tertiary stress. Whether this means that there was a level of stress acoustically intermediate between secondary stress and no stress is difficult to
say; the evidence is examined in greater detail below (§§255ff.). But in
the present context the important question instead is whether there are
four levels of metrical ictus in Old English verse, as opposed to the three
that Bliss ascribes to it. That is, is the metrical treatment of unambiguously unstressed syllables different from that of syllables to which the
phonological evidence suggests we should assign tertiary stress? On the
basis of the metrical evidence considered in the following pages, the
answer is certainly yes.


## C.  Light Verses


§198. The wide use of Bliss's classificatory system in Old English
scholarship is testimony to the fact that his rejection of tertiary stress is
not lightly motivated. It is difficult to prove or disprove the metrical significance of tertiary stress conclusively. One reason for this is that even if
there was a phonetic distinction between tertiary and no stress, under

Campbell's analysis of half-stress there was no phonemic distinction—they are allophonic. Simply, once syllables that begin either a word or an element of a compound are excluded, tertiary and no stress are in predictable, complementary distribution: final syllables are unstressed, and all others have tertiary stress.[19] This is true for purely historical reasons, since originally short medial syllables without tertiary stress were all syncopated, while originally long medial syllables by definition have tertiary stress. Thus in *Beowulf*, as in most Old English verse, the second *i* in *mistige moras* (162a) is purely orthographic, representing later pronunciation resulting from analogical leveling (Campbell, §343). Because of the complementary distribution of tertiary and no stress in Bliss's system, it is difficult to prove any difference in metrical treatment. For example, in a verse such as *Hygelace wæs* (*Beowulf* 2169b) it cannot be proved that the third syllable bears any stress, because different metrical treatment of a completely unstressed syllable cannot be proved, all etymologically unstressed vowels in this position having been syncopated. It is only when short syllables are reintroduced analogically, or later become unstressed, that disruptions in the pattern result, as discussed below. Moreover, Bliss's theories about light verses obviate most of the evidence for tertiary stress. Under Sievers' system a verse such as *oþþæt semninga* (*Beowulf* 644b) demands some sort of stress on the fourth syllable because the verse must be scanned as type C. But if, as Bliss argues, one-stress verses are possible in the off-verse as well as the on-verse, tertiary stress is unnecessary here.

§199. Accordingly, an evaluation of Bliss's views on the metrical treatment of verses with tertiary stress ought to begin with a discussion of light verses. "Light verses are those which contain only one stressed element (§10), and therefore (apparently, at least), only one full stress" (Bliss, §67). In practice this amounts to considering any verse a light verse if the first stress falls on the last word, no matter how long that word. This last-word criterion is valid to the extent that no light verse can contain two stressed words. For example, though a verse such as *\*siþþan him Hnæf wearð* superficially resembles light verses of the type *Me þone wælræs* (*Beowulf* 2101a), it is not actually permissible, at least in classical verse, because there is no metrical type like this among the normal verses, and light verses cannot contain two stressed words.[20] This criterion in fact points up some editorial errors, since nearly all the

---

[19]The exception is in words like *aldorlēasne* (discussed below, §203), in which the second syllable bears no stress. While the allophonic nature of tertiary stress under the standard definition of it is disturbing, it is not in itself counterevidence to the existence or metrical significance of such stress: there is no linguistic reason there could not have been a rule assigning stress to all nonfinal syllables, and of course it remains to be seen whether ictus is assigned to all stressed syllables at the metrical level.

[20]Cf. *seopðan Grendel wearð* (1775b); at 1261b, *siþðan Cain wearð* is generally assumed to have dissyllabic *Cain* (emended from MS *camp*).

apparent exceptions are verses like *Heht þa ymb twa niht* (*Exodus* 63a) and *Nu bið fore þreo niht* (*Andreas* 185a). Here apparently the last two words in each verse must form a compound, as with MnE *sennight* (already written *seoueniht* in Laȝamon, ca. 1205) and *fortnight*: compare *þreonihta fæc* (*Panther* 38b) and *andægne fyrst* (*Exodus* 304a).[21] In another relevant verse, *Ic þe, ead mæg* (*Juliana* 352a), the last two words may again be a compound: compare *ēadfruma, ēadgiefu*, and the like. Pamela Gradon emends *swa him sio cwen bead* (*Elene* 378b), substituting *bebead* in her edition, and this is a likely sort of scribal corruption, though of course there is no motivation for the alteration but the meter. Also in *Elene*, the verse *Ðus mec fæder min* (528a) is peculiar; but elsewhere in the poem *fæder* seems to be treated as a trochee (e.g. *fæder minum* 438b and 454b), perhaps suggesting an underlying form with consonant gemination, like VP *feddras, feddra*.[22] There is one other peculiar verse of this type in *Genesis A, þara an wæs* (1645a). The rule, however, is disregarded in the *Meters of Boethius* (e.g. *Ne synt þa word soð*, 2.18b), and in some other datably late verse: see below, §291.

§200. But the important question about the last-word criterion is not whether every light verse will contain just one stressed word, but whether every verse with just one stressed word must be a light verse. Bliss's answer is yes, with the result that light verses must now be permitted in the off-verse. For example, Sievers would classify *in geardagum* (*Beowulf* 1b) as a normal type C, while for Bliss it is type d3a. Bliss's evidence for his classification is statistical: he finds that normal verses of types B and C are three times commoner in the off-verse than in the on-verse, while the verses of types B and C that he would classify as light are three times commoner in the on-verse. Moreover, double alliteration is relatively frequent in the normal verses, while it is rare in the light verses. He concludes that there really is a metrical difference—that is, that the latter verses really are light (§70).

§201. This evidence is initially impressive, but on closer examination it does not prove the point intended. As regards the latter argument, double alliteration ought to be more frequent in normal verses, since the resources of the language are such that it is easier to find two words that alliterate than to select or create a compound whose two elements alliterate. This is largely because in constructing a normal verse the poet may

---

[21]So also verses like *ymb þreo niht þæs* (*Menologium* 174a) will not scan without the assumption of a compound. This might also be an explanation preferable to the assumption of a short first lift in *nu ofor seofon niht* (*Genesis A* 1349a), but the same explanation would render *ymb seofon niht* (2322a) a three-position verse.

[22]Such gemination, though it began in inflected forms, spread by analogy to uninflected ones (Campbell, §453, n. 4). Sievers ("Rhythmik," p. 483) instead assumes a dative form *fædere* in the latter two verses, as in Li. and the *Dream of the Rood*. The reading *fædder* was first suggested by Trautmann, *Kynewulf*, p. 77; for other references see Pope, *Rhythm*, pp. 273–74.

choose from the entire range of stressable words, while in constructing compounds the choices are limited to a smaller set of grammatical categories. Bliss's first point is the more telling; but while his evidence almost certainly means that there is a difference of some sort between normal and light verses, it does not prove that (to take one example) *þæt ðæs ahlæcan* (989b; type d1b) is a one-stress verse, while *oððe gripe meces* (1765a; type 2C1b) bears two stresses. For instance, the distributional difference might have its basis in syntax: the syntax of the on-verse and the off-verse is not identical (e.g., sentences more frequently begin in the on-verse), and since light verses of type d1b always end with a compound noun, whereas verses of type 2C1b admit a variety of syntactic types, perhaps it was syntactically convenient to limit the former type mainly to the on-verse. Perhaps, too, the difference in degree of stress is relevant: not many are likely to dispute the assumption that *mēc-* bears greater phonological stress than *-læc-* in these verses, and that assumption is sufficient to account for the distributional difference Bliss points out, regardless of what the relationship between the stress difference and the distributional difference might be.[23]

§202. There is in fact what seems to be solid counterevidence to Bliss's position. A distributional peculiarity of light verses as Bliss defines them is that verses with one primary stress and no other stress are disallowed in the off-verse—except for the one type d1 (e.g. *ic me mid Hruntinge* at *Beowulf* 1490b). The off-verse in *Beowulf*, and throughout the test group, consistently requires two stresses (including secondary stress), and excludes one-stress verses like type a (e.g. *Næs ic him to life*, 2432a) and the rare and questionable type e (e.g. *þenden he wið wulf*, 3027a). The likeliest conclusion to be drawn is that verses like *ic me mid Hruntinge* must bear more than one stress—or, at any rate, more than one position of ictus. The point is corroborated by the fact that the restriction of

---

[23]For example, the reason that different stress results in a different distribution might be that the last lift of the poetic line was relatively weak. Thomas Cable (*English Alliterative Tradition*, p. 145) points out that verses like *hlyn swynsode* (*Beowulf* 611b) are confined to the off-verse; and Geoffrey Russom has pointed out to me that verses like *gefaran wolde* (*Beowulf* 738b) show a marked preference for the off-verse. This is in accordance with Sievers' so-called *rule of precedence* (*Altgerm. Metrik*, §§22–29; succinctly stated by Campbell, §93), which dictates that a finite verb need not alliterate if it precedes a noun in a verse, and must not if the noun does not participate in the alliteration; nor may it alliterate if it follows the noun and the noun does not alliterate. Russom discusses the Old English material , pp. 101–6; see also Daniel Donoghue, "Old English Meter," *ANQ*, n.s. 3 (1990), 69–74, at 71. A good discussion of analogous weak stress on verbs in New High German can be found in an article by Paul Kiparsky, "Über den deutschen Akzent," in *Untersuchungen über Akzent und Intonation im Deutschen* ( = *Studia Grammatica* 7), ed. M. Bierwisch (Berlin: Akademie-Verlag, 1966), pp. 69–98. The distributional difference that Bliss points out merely proves a linguistic difference between the two types, not a metrical one. For exceptions to Sievers' rule of precedence see F. Holthausen, "Studien zur altenglischen Dichtung," *Anglia* 46, n.s. 34 (1922), 52–62, at 52–4.

verses of types a and e to the on-verse is certainly related to the requirements of alliteration in the off-verse: the off-verse must contain two arses, since the first must alliterate and the second must not. Appealing as Bliss's theory of one-stress verses might be, it is not so basic to our understanding of Old English meter as to justify abrogating a principle so fundamental and of such great regularity: the off-verse must contain an alliterating lift followed by a nonalliterating one. If we must choose between the two accounts—and there does not seem to be any way to avoid the choice—the latter is certainly a more compelling observation, since Bliss cannot provide an explanation why d1 should be the only light type permitted in the off-verse.

§203. Finally it must be noted that even with his light verses Bliss is obliged to rely on the assumption of tertiary stress. He tacitly admits its existence when he scans a verse such as *aldorleasne* (*Beowulf* 1587a) as type 2A1, which on the third syllable requires some sort of stress, and certainly not secondary stress under his definition (§32). The alternative of assigning no stress to any of the last three syllables of the verse is implausible on both phonological and metrical grounds. The phonological reduction of the second syllable of words like *līcumlic* and *rūmedlīce* demonstrates the accentual prominence of the flanking syllables (cf. *līc-homa* and *rūm-mōd*, and see Brunner's grammar, §43, n. 3). And so Bliss must be right to assign stress to the third syllable: the metrical analysis of the word would clash with its stress contour if it were analyzed as a verse with a continuously descending metrical contour, like type D, within Cable's requirement of four metrical positions to the verse. If tertiary stress is required in *aldorleasne*, it is difficult to see how it can be dispensed with in other verse types.

## D. Metrical Evidence for Tertiary Stress

§204. From the preceding discussion it should already be apparent that the standard accounts of Old English meter, being stress-based, render it virtually impossible to discuss ictus without equating it with stress. So when Campbell outlines the distribution of half-stress, his account is actually based on Sievers' conclusions about the distribution of ictus in meter (as remarked above, §185), and the result is circular argumentation: all medial syllables must be stressed because Sievers finds that they bear ictus, and ictus must be equated with stress because all medial syllables are supposedly stressed. The term *tertiary stress* is thus ambiguous, referring alternately to phonological stress and metrical ictus. That ambiguity is itself useful, perhaps indispensable, to a discussion of ictus within a Sieversian framework, and so in the present context it should be understood that the term is used ambiguously, and that it remains to be proved that the ictus we refer to as tertiary stress actually has anything to do with phonological stress—all that has been proved so far is that phonological stress did fall on some ictus-bearing syllables (*-dōm-*, *-fæst-*, etc.). The exact relationship between ictus and stress will be examined below (§§255ff.), after the distribution of ictus has been more clearly defined.

§205. One reason Bliss's rejection of tertiary stress seems implausible is that it reduces verses of type 1D1 (e.g. *fea þingian* 156b) and 3E1 (e.g. *æþelinges fær* 33b) to three metrical positions, since two contiguous unstressed syllables can only amount to a single metrical position.[24] But four is the minimal number of metrical positions for a normal verse: aside from verses with tertiary stress there are no normal types with fewer than four positions. The best evidence for three-position verses is the five examples that Bliss finds in *Beowulf* with no possibility of tertiary stress:[25]

> 2C1–: secg betsta (947a, 1759a)
> ðegn betstan (1871b)
> 2B2–: Raþe æfter þon (724b)
> 2C2–: Hreðel cyning (2430b)

But even disregarding the rarity of such verses, it raises suspicions that more than half of these contain the word *betsta(n)*. Most editors emend to *secga betsta* and *þegna betstan*, and Klaeber, too, remarks that this was the "original reading, most likely" (p. 167), though John Pope objects that "the weak adjective ought not to take a partitive genitive unless it is accompanied with the definite article" (p. 320). Thus Trautmann's emendation to *secg se betsta* is perhaps superior.[26] But comparison with *Nu is ofost betost* (3007b) raises the possibility that *betsta* should be trisyllabic here, and the verses *feorh cyninges* (1210b) and *fyll cyninges* (2912b) suggest that *secg bet(o)sta* is an acceptable metrical type. Sievers accepts the type (*Altgerm. Metrik*, §85.5), and this position is supported with evidence below (§276).

§206. The fourth verse above seems anomalous to Bliss because he apparently assumes that only the first and last words can be stressed. But this is not true. The phrase *æfter þon/þy/þæm* occurs at twelve other places in the Old English poetic records, and in all but one instance either the situation is metrically identical to the one in *Beowulf* or *æfter* is unambiguously stressed, as in *and æfter þon* (*Phoenix* 238b) and *and æfter*

---

[24]This point is made by Sievers, *Altgerm. Metrik*, §10.1. Bliss responds that two unstressed syllables might count as two positions if they are divided by the caesura (§84), but that is not the case here.

[25]A sixth example, Klaeber's *bord wið rond* (2673a; see Bliss, §85) is corrected in the second supplement (p. 470) to *Born bord wið rond*, which is also Dobbie's reading: see Pope, pp. xxix, 320.

[26]"Berichtungen, Vermutungen und Erklärungen zum Beowulf: Erste Hälfte," *BB* 2 (1899), 175.

*þæm* (*Meters* 21.33b), both with vocalic alliteration.[27] Thus *Raþe æfter þon* is a normal four-position verse, with stress on *æfter*. Parallels abound in the *Heliand*, for instance *bigan imu aftar thiu* (2395b) and *that ik thi than aftar thiu* (2755a); and compare *nis under me* at *Riddle 40* 86a.[28]

§207. The fifth verse is admittedly unique in *Beowulf*,[29] but it is not apparent how regarding it as a three-position verse makes it less anomalous than supposing it shows substitution of a short lift (*cyn-*) for a long one, as Sievers assumes ("Rhythmik," p. 231). At any rate the verse type does appear in other poems, for example *tempel godes* (*Exodus* 391b) and *bil(e)wit fæder* (*Genesis A* 856a, *Meters* 20.69b, 20.255b, 20.269b, etc). So, too, in *Beowulf* there are a few verses like *Hiorogar cyning* (2158b), which Bliss scans as type 2A1b—with a short second lift following a long, unstressed drop. But in fact if *-gar* is unstressed it must be short, since vowel length is neutralized in unstressed syllables (Campbell, p. 34 and n. 4). To suppose that *-gar* may be long in final position is thus to concede that the syllable bears stress, and therefore, in Bliss's system, ought to bear ictus.

§208. None of these examples carries conviction, therefore, and so it can at the very least be said that if types 1D1 and 3E1 (amounting to 414 verses in *Beowulf*) are three-position verses, it is remarkable that there is virtually no evidence for three-position verses in *Beowulf* that do not involve tertiary stress. There is in fact no verse in *Beowulf* that can be said unambiguously to contain just three syllables. It is thus difficult to dispense with tertiary stress in types 1D1 and 3E1. Moreover, three-position verses must seem intrinsically improbable to the many metrists for whom Thomas Cable's explanation of the four-position pattern underlying all Old English normal verse types has become indispensable to an understanding of how Old English meter works (*Meter and Melody*, esp. chap. 7). Laying aside the questionable instances above, in spite of superficial changes such as contraction and parasiting, the underlying four-position pattern remains unchanged over the history of Old English verse, from *Cædmon's Hymn* to *Durham*. Even poems like *Maldon* that differ widely from the standard of *Beowulf* in numerous details do not violate the four-position pattern.

§209. Perhaps the reason it seemed necessary to Bliss to reject tertiary stress is that, like other scholars, he chose *Beowulf* as the basis for

---

[27]See also *Genesis A* 1005a, *Genesis B* 471a, *Guthlac B* 1178b, *Metrical Psalms* 144.18.2b (but cf. 118.116.2a), *Meters* 29.61b, *Solomon and Saturn I* 298b, *Menologium* 128a, and *Instructions for Christians* 15b and 198a. Stress may also fall on *æfter* before *him* and *þissum*.

[28]This scansion was first suggested by Max Rieger, "Die alt- und angelsächsische Verskunst," *Zeitschrift für deutsche Philologie* 7 (1876), 1–64, at 32 and 61; see also Sievers, *Altgerm. Metrik*, §28.

[29]In the only parallel, *hwilum dydon* (1828b), of course *dydon* may stand for Anglian *dēdon* or poetic *dǣdon*: cf. *Genesis B* 722b, *Genesis A* 142a, 2600a, and the like.

his metrical system, when in fact *Beowulf* is metrically, in some respects, the most anomalous poem in the corpus. One of the clearest pieces of evidence for a metrical distinction between tertiary and no stress is that derivational suffixes like *-lic* and *-leas* may bear ictus, while inflectional suffixes like *-um* and *-es* may not. The example *aldorleasne* (*Beowulf* 1587a) was offered above as illustration of Bliss's tacit concession that *-lēas-* may bear ictus, but examples may be multiplied. For example, *geong grondorleas* (*Juliana* 271a) must be stressed on the last syllable, for phonological reasons (the examples *līcumlic* and *rūmedlīce* were given above) and metrical ones: *-leas* must bear ictus because verses like *\*grondorleas geong* are strictly avoided, while the pattern represented by *arlease cyn* (*Genesis A* 2477a) is common.[30] Clearly, then, *-leas* is not metrically interchangeable with an inflectional syllable. Yet Bliss would indeed ignore the stress on the derivational suffix, as illustrated by his treatment of parallel instances in *Beowulf*: for instance, he scans *eal inneweard* (998a) as type 1D1, like *flod fæðmian* (3133a). *Beowulf*, however, is peculiar, inasmuch as it seems to violate the general rule. Here inflectional endings do in four instances appear to receive stress:

> 747b     ræhte ongean
> 845a     niða ofercumen
> 954a     dædum gefremed
> 2150a    lissa gelong

But only the first and last of these are unambiguous, since the others may have a short second lift, as suggested by Pope (p. 272) and Russom (p. 117). This would admittedly be an unusual metrical situation, but no more anomalous than the assumption of three-position verses. And in any case parallel examples are to be found in other poems (see below, n. 34). Of the remaining two, the first must be considered unlikely because Pope has pointed out that the erasure in the manuscript before *ræhte* cannot be deliberate: letters are obscured at the same place on the preceding leaf, indicating that something was spilt on the vellum (p. 372). Therefore *ræhte* was in all likelihood preceded by one or more particles. Pope suggests *him swā* as paleographically and metrically the most likely reading.[31] The last verse, *lissa gelong*, is not so obviously an error, though

---

[30]There are four apparent exceptions in *Genesis A*, e.g. *þancolmod wer* (1705a; see also 208b, 1129b, and 2805b, and see above, nn. 30 and 49 to Chap. 1), but in each of these instances the odd stress is secondary, and so the examples are irrelevant, since there is no question whether the stress could be dropped, as Bliss would argue that tertiary stress could. And at any rate this is clearly a peculiarity of the metrics of *Genesis A*, and no other poem.

[31]Klaeber rejects Pope's emendation, remarking that the emended text "hardly makes acceptable sense" (p. 466). Pope in turn, with characteristic graciousness, concedes the conjectural nature of the emendation, on the grounds that "too many

several alternative readings have been proposed.[32] It is in any case the only one of the four verses that suggests unambiguously the existence of three-position verses. And so the type is too infrequent in *Beowulf* to justify fundamental changes in our understanding of Old English meter: scribal transmission is too uncertain to permit a single example of a metrical type to carry much weight.

§210. Bliss apparently felt justified in making fundamental changes in metrical theory because otherwise it must be assumed that the *Beowulf* poet was in the habit of assigning tertiary stress to final syllables when it ought to have been lost. This happens in the type Bliss labels 2E1, which occurs twenty-two times in *Beowulf*, by his reckoning. In addition to the four verses above, the instances are the following:[33]

| | | | |
|---|---|---|---|
| 343b | Beowulf is min nama | 1127b | Hengest ða gyt |
| 396b | Hroðgar geseon | 1410b | uncuð gelad |
| 759b | uplang astod | 1541b | andlean forgeald |
| 874b | Welhwylc gecwæð | 1720b | dreamleas gebad |
| 881a | eam his nefan | 1983b | Higelac ongan |
| 987b | Æghwylc gecwæð | 2092b | uppriht astod |
| 1024b | Beowulf geþah | 2094b | ondlean forgeald |
| 1044b | onweald geteah | 2680b | Nægling forbærst |
| 1126b | Frysland geseon | 2929b | ondslyht ageaf |

The rejection of tertiary stress in these verses appears to provide a solution to the problem with the first group, because although that group is not large enough to justify such an anomalous type as 2E1, these additional eighteen verses seem to provide sufficient support. The problem with Bliss's solution is that type 2E1 is in fact rather rare outside *Beowulf*. In the poems of the test group, the only unambiguous instances are the following:[34]

---

traces have been obliterated for anything like assurance," but he declines to withdraw it: see the preface to the 1966 edition of his book, p. xxxi. Regardless of precisely how the text is emended, it is clear from Pope's observations that something has dropped out before *ræhte*. This is also apparent in the facsimiles.

[32]See, e.g., Pope, p. 321, and Russom, pp. 117–19.

[33]The manuscript confusion of *and* and *hand* in 1541b and 2094b is paralleled by the opposite substitution at *Riddle 5* 8b. That *hand-* could be correct is implausible: see the references on the phonological treatment of initial *h-* in "Unferth and His Name," *MP* 85 (1987), 113–27, at 119.

[34]Several exclusions should be pointed out. Verses like *eorlum bedroren* (*Genesis A* 2099a) are like *dædum gefremed* (above, §209), and so must be regarded as ambiguous for the same reason. Sievers ("Rhythmik," p. 458) lists twelve such verses, mostly in *Genesis A* and *Daniel*. To these should be added *scriðe and færelt* (*Meters* 28.11b), and there may be others. The verse *drugon and dydon* (*Genesis A* 142a) of course may have *dydon* for *dēdon* or *dædon*. It is significant that most such verses appear in *Genesis A*, since a short second lift in type A seems to be permitted in that poem: cf. *on genimeð* (1209a; also 2085b, 2191a, and *Elene* 578b). Verses with biblical names (see n. 40 to

> ænig ne wearð  (*Genesis A* 2217b)
> lare gebearh  (*Genesis A* 2695b)
> alet gehwearf  (*Daniel* 253b)
> uncuð gelad  (*Exodus* 58b)
> wræcmon gebad  (*Exodus* 137b)
> frigneð ymb ðæt treo  (*Elene* 534a)
> hyhtful gewearð  (*Elene* 922a)
> wisdom onwreah  (*Elene* 1242a)
> unforht oncwæð  (*Juliana* 209b)
> wiðerweard ge*sceaft*  (*Meters* 11.41b, 11.49a)
> *sta*ðolfæst gereaht  (*Meters* 11.99a)
> *Æghwi*lc gesceaft  (*Meters* 20.142a)
> þriefeald gesceaft  (*Meters* 20.183a)
> edlean on riht  (*Meters* 27.26b)
> wisdom and æ  (*Meters* 29.81a)

In other words, there are about as many examples of the type in *Beowulf* as in the rest of the test group as a whole (and nearly half of those in the Alfredian *Meters*), and so at least in this respect, basing a system of scansion for all Old English verse on the meter of *Beowulf* creates improbabilities.

§211. These data suggest that the type *lissa gelong* is not genuine— and indeed, that is the conclusion of most metrical studies. There are just three comparable instances in the preceding list, outside *Beowulf*—that is, instances in which the second syllable could never take tertiary stress, even if an inflectional syllable could be added—and these are the two verses from *Genesis A*, along with *Elene* 534a. If no stress were required in this position, it would be extraordinary that there are just three instances in the nearly eleven thousand lines of the test group excluding *Beowulf*. The type *Hygelac ongan* is a different matter, since -*lāc*- takes tertiary stress when an inflection is added, according to the standard view. And there is a peculiarity in the lists of type 2E1 above, in *Beowulf*

---

Chap. 1) must again be excluded, since the metrical treatment of such names is irregular, e.g. *Abrahame þa gyt* (1727a) beside *Abrahame* (1785a). The verse *dema mid unc twih* (*Genesis A* 2255b) requires stress on *unc* under Kuhn's first law; and those like *Lyfað me þær* (2520b) and *cwic þenden her wunað* (*Christ II* 590a) are inconclusive because stress is possible on *me* and *her*: cf. *Genesis A* 2437b, 2675b, 2882b, and the like. *Wilt ðu, gif þu most* (*Genesis A* 2482b) and others like it are a similar case, where the first *þu* may be stressed without demanding stress on the second under Kuhn's first law because *gif* begins a new clause: cf. *Meters* 13.67b, *Beowulf* 455b, and similar. The verse *lædan mid hie* (*Genesis A* 2786a; see also *Meters* 1.62a) perhaps shows noncontraction of *hīe* (see Luick, §247b), in which case it would be yet another verse of type A in *Genesis A* with a short second lift; but possibly also there is stress on *mid*, as with *Rape æfter þon* above. On *hunger oððe wulf* (*Genesis A* 2278b) see n. 29 to Chap. 1. On *ænegu gesceaft* (*Meters* 13.68b, 73b) see below, §216. In *þegnas on ða tid* (*Judith* 306a) there is stress on *ðā*: cf. *Beowulf* 736a and *Meters* 26.43a. Under these criteria it is also necessary to set aside six of the examples listed for *Beowulf*, 343b, 396b, 845a, 881a, 954a, and 1126b.

and elsewhere, that tells strongly against the assumption that verses like *lissa gelong* are genuine: the lists include almost exclusively instances in which the disputed stress falls on the second element of a personal name or on a suffix of some identifiable semantic force. For example, in *Beowulf* the second element of *uplang* (759b) shares some of the semantic force of the adjective *lang*; the second element of *welhwylc* (874b) is clearly identifiable with the pronoun *hwylc*, close in meaning to *welhwylc*; *-lēas* in *drēamlēas* (1720b) has the same meaning as the adjective *lēas* in *siððan dreama leas* (850b), and so forth. Missing from the lists are compounds with second elements of entirely obscured meaning, such as *gārsecg*, *earfeþ*, and *hlāford*, with the sole exception of *ālet* in *Daniel* (discussed below), since *eam his nefan* may have a short second lift.[35] Presumably, uninflected elements like *-lang*, *-lēas*, and *-dōm* bore more stress than these second elements of obscured meaning, since the latter show vowel developments characteristic of unstressed syllables, while the former do not. Even if the former are analogical to the inflected cases, certainly some amount of heightened stress was still necessary to preserve the vowel quantities. The point is corroborated by the orthographic treatment of such words in the manuscripts: as with words bearing secondary stress, compound words of this sort are frequently written with a space between the two elements, as if they were separate words. This is the case, for instance, with *Hroðgar* at *Beowulf* 396b, *uplang* at 759b, *welhwylc* at 874b, and others. These morphemes with intermediate and variable metrical treatment may be called *semi-lexical* to distinguish them from, on the one hand, fully lexical morphemes like the second elements of compounds with secondary stress (like *feorhcynn* and *healsittende*), and on the other from purely derivative suffixes like *-end-* and *-est-*. If in fact these suffixes did carry an amount of stress lower than in inflected forms, but higher than in unstressed syllables, it is reasonable to suppose that the *Beowulf* poet might treat such syllables as ambiguous.[36] This is essentially Sievers'

---

[35]See n. 34. Hofmann, *Versstrukturen*, pp. 70–72, also concludes that there is ictus in the second position of verses of type 2E1. As for the suffix *-ing* attached to personal names, there is some independent evidence that it may bear ictus, since Cable finds that *Scyldinga* in *Beowulf* behaves metrically like compounds with secondary stress rather than words bearing tertiary stress: see *English Alliterative Tradition*, pp. 15 and 148.

[36]The point remains valid even if there were just two levels of phonological stress in Old English, a possibility examined below (§266). For example, Thomas Cable reports on the acoustic experiments of Philip Lieberman, "In the ubiquitous *light housekeeper*, a good candidate for a C or D verse, the peak fundamental frequency and peak amplitude of *house* and *keep* were the same in one recording, although *house* has stress level 1 and *keep* stress level 3 (pp. 151–52). (The only relevant acoustic cue in the recorded phrase was the extra duration between the syllables *light* and *house* to distinguish it from *lighthouse keeper*; Lieberman found that even this cue disappears in unambiguous phrases" (*Meter and Melody*, p. 98, in reference to Philip Lieberman's *Intonation, Perception, and Language*, Research Monograph 38 [Cambridge, Mass.: MIT Press, 1967]). Thus the acoustic correlates of stress may differ widely from their mental representation, and stress at the secondary and tertiary level need not be acoustically different in order

position ("Rhythmik," p. 265; *Altgerm. Metrik*, §78.2). It is not unnatural to suppose that there was some flexibility in both the classification of suffixes (and therefore the relative amount of stress assigned to them) and their metrical treatment, since this situation is paralleled in living languages, including Modern English. For example, the second syllable of the word *Icelander* may have either the vowel of *man* or a central, unstressed vowel; and in America even educated speakers may give un-suffixed *Iceland*, *Thailand*, and the like, the stressed, low front vowel, though not *England* or *Holland*, since *Eng-* and *Hol-* are bound mor-phemes. Note that most of the first elements of the Old English words in question here are free morphemes. There seems to be no way to avoid the conclusion that the *Beowulf* poet intended stress on these derivational suffixes, since the number of verses like *lissa gelong* is so much smaller than that of verses like *dreamleas gebad*, when in fact words that are metrically like *lissa* are so much more frequent than those like *drēamlēas* —implying that lack of stress in this position is extraordinary. It may be noted that verses comparable to *dreamleas gebad* are encountered occa-sionally in other Germanic languages—for example *dǫglingr at því* and *Hiǫrleif at því* at *Helgakviða Hundingsbana I* 16.3 and 23.6, *Slagfiðr ok Egill* at *Vǫlundarkviða* 4.3, and *uualdand gisprak* and *Hêleand gestôd* at *Heliand* 39a and 3570b—while parallels to *lissa gelong* are no commoner than in Old English.[37] That words like *ondslyht* and personal names did carry some amount of stress on their second element is corroborated by the metrical treatment of second elements with short syllables, like *ondwlita*, under the rule of the coda (§234 below). It is also corroborated by the fact that vowel qualities in the relevant syllables are preserved as in syllables under stress, while in many syllables to which Sievers assigns half-stress, vowel qualities are not preserved. This observation furnishes a fairly objective criterion for distinguishing syllables that may take this excep-tional stress from those that may not: see the discussion below, §§240ff.

§212. Perhaps then the only serious obstacle to assuming that the *Beowulf* poet could stress these uninflected suffixes at will, and the

---

for there to be a metrical difference. The difference may be purely morphophonemic and lexically based: i.e., secondary stress is invariable, while tertiary stress is lost from final syllables. We should expect such a morphophonemic difference to be less secure precisely in those syllables that lost stress late, such as uninflected suffixes like *-lang*, *-lēas*, *-hwylc*, and the second elements of personal names.

[37]Sievers (*Altgerm. Metrik*, §38.1) says that in eddic verse, words like *Hundings* and *ǫflugr* have half-stress on the second syllable as long as the syllable is long; but verses like *Hiǫrvarð ok Hávarð* (*Helgakviða Hundingsbana I* 14.5; cf. verses like *Herebeald ond Hæðcyn* in Old English) suggest otherwise, unless five-position verses are admitted. Sievers was no doubt thinking primarily of verses like *Hundings sono* (14.6); but in regard to comparable instances in Old English, Bliss (§31) objects that the promotion of the third, short syllable to the status of a lift may as well be attributed to the length as to the stress of the preceding syllable. The eddic verses are cited from Neckel's edition; those from the *Heliand* are in Behaghel's edition.

uninflected second elements of personal names, is Alistair Campbell's remark, quoted above (§185), that in Latin verse composed by Anglo-Saxons, Old English names like *Ælfstan* and *Ælfheah* are to be scanned with a short second syllable, but with a long one if a Latin inflection is added, as in *Ælfstānus* and *Ælfhēgus* (Campbell, §90, n. 4). But the conclusion about the shortness of the second element of *Ælfstan* and *Ælfheah* seems to be based on a single text, and a late one at that— Wulfstan of Winchester's metrical life of St. Swithun, written between 992 and 994.[38] This is as late as the *Battle of Maldon*, which differs metrically from the rest of Old English verse in a variety of ways (see Bliss, chap. 16, and see below, §235 and Chap. 10). But there is counterevidence to Campbell's findings. The metrical life of St. Swithun aside, there seems to be just one metrically unambiguous example of an uninflected Old English personal name in Latin verse, and that is in Æthelwulf's *De abbatibus*, definitely datable to the period 803–821.[39] The poem is composed in hexameters, and at line 756 we find *Hyglac, indutus nimium qui uestibus albis*, in which the second syllable is clearly long. Nor can Campbell's observation be wholly confirmed in regard to Old English names with Latin inflections. In Bede's metrical life of St. Cuthbert the name *Ælfflæd* is a dactyl when a Latin inflection is added: compare *Aelffleda, conloquium perpes reticere memento* (534) and *Aelffleda perquirit, quae forte adsederat illi* (664).[40] Yet the second element of the name is etymologically long: cf. OHG *flāt* 'cleanliness, fineness', Middle Dutch *vlēdich* 'clean, pretty', etc. And so Campbell's conclusions cannot be so firm as to exclude the possibility that the *Beowulf* poet could lend ictus to the second elements of uninflected personal names at will.

§213. Further reason to doubt the evidence of the *Life of St. Swithun* comes from the treatment of Old English personal names in early Middle English texts. Here OE *ā* (including *a* lengthened before homorganic consonant clusters: Campbell, §§283–84) in second elements is proved still to have been long at the time of the change *ā* > *ō*: cf. *Aþelwold* in *Havelok* (beside -*wald* once), and *Oswold, Dunston, Aþelston,* and *Wolston* in the *South English Legendary* (beside *Edgar*). So also King Alfred's name rhymes with *red* < OE *ræd* in the *Owl and the Nightingale*, and the reflexes of OE *Æþelmær* and stressed *þær* are made to rhyme in *King Horn*. For the most part, early Middle English texts also show long vowels in uninflected derivational suffixes, though there is considerable variability: for example, *wisdom* is spelt *wissdom* by Orm, and is made to rhyme with pret. *com* in the *Owl and the Nightingale* (though later there is evidence

[38]*Frithegodi monachi breuiloquium vitæ beati Wilfredi et Wulfstani cantoris narratio metrica de sancto Swithuno*, ed. A. Campbell (Zürich: Thesaurus Mundi, 1950), p. x, n. 14.

[39]Ed. A. Campbell (Oxford: Clarendon, 1967), p. xxiii. Campbell did not edit *De abbatibus* until after the publication of his *Old English Grammar*.

[40]Werner Jaager, *Bedas metrische Vita sancti Cuthberti*, Palaestra 198 (Leipzig: Mayer & Müller, 1935).

of -*dōm*: see Luick, §443; Jordan, §137), although in the same poem there must be shortening in *fihtlac* (OE *feohtlāc-*), as there is no development to *ō*. In view of the general avoidance of paradigm allomorphy in Old English, it does not seem unlikely that the analogical processes assumed to be responsible for the appearance of such long vowels in final syllables were already at work in the Old English period. Analogy at any rate seems the best explanation of the fact that most uninflected second elements of personal names in Old English do not suffer the vowel changes characteristic of unstressed syllables, for example -*bearn*, -*burg*, and -*hild*. In some instances, on the other hand, the unstressed form is generalized, as in -*ferþ*, -*red*, and -*elf* beside -*friþ*, -*rǣd*, and -*ælf*.

§214. Finally it may be remarked that Bliss's rejection of tertiary stress depends on a variety of other assumptions, some of them among the most widely doubted aspects of his method of scansion. One of these is his insistence on the metrical significance of the caesura. For example, he points out (§4) that *\*wīgendes egesan* is not an acceptable type. But verses like *eldum swa unnyt* (3168a), *æþeling to yppan* (1815a), and *Herebeald ond Hæðcyn* (2434a) do occur (and the latter two show the same syllable length in the relevant position). As remarked above (p. 171, n. 3), since Bliss assigns no ictus to the second syllable of *wīgendes*, the disallowed *\*wīgendes egesan* would be metrically identical to these others were it not for his assumption of different placement of the caesura. And so unless one is prepared to accept Bliss's theory of the caesura there seems no alternative to the assumption of ictus for tertiary stress to account for the fact that *wīgendes egesan* is unmetrical.[41] The consequences of excluding caesura from an account of Old English meter are considered below (§55). Bliss's rejection of tertiary stress also depends on his acceptance of three-position verses, since verses of type 3E1 in *Beowulf* (e.g. *hæþenra hyht* 179a) can have only three metrical positions under Bliss's assumptions. Both the second and third syllables are unstressed in his system, and in this instance there is no device like caesura to divide those two syllables into separate metrical positions. And clearly they cannot be declared separate positions simply by fiat, since this would leave unexplained why series of unstressed syllables in other contexts always comprise a single metrical position (often in disregard of the caesura), for instance in *wyrce se þe mote* (1387b), *Gæð a wyrd swa hio scel* (455b), and *þara þe he him mid hæfde* (1625b). It was demonstrated above (§205) that the evidence for three-position verses in *Beowulf* amounts to

---

[41]Cable makes a similar point, and objects, "since the caesura as Bliss uses it is simply a syntactic boundary . . . he has only stated the problem in different terms, and the caesura itself becomes a fact that requires explanation" (*Meter and Melody*, p. 50). The verses *æþeling to yppan* and *Herebeald ond Hæðcyn*, with a long syllable after the first lift, are demonstrated below (§264) to be rare and probably marginal. The rarity of the type, then, argues that it is not simply the placement of the caesura that disallows *\*wīgendes egesan*.

five or six verses, all of which can be explained otherwise. And since both Klaeber (in his second supplement) and Dobbie read *Born bord wið rond* (2673a) for Bliss's *bord wið rond*, there are no three-position verses in Beowulf with the metrical pattern he assigns to *hæþenra hyht*, but with a single unstressed syllable in the middle position. There are, however, 118 verses like *hæþenra hyht*. If the word *hæþenra* does represent three metrical positions, it is difficult to see how the last two syllables of the word can fill two positions unless one of them bears metrical ictus: in Old English meter, at least, what is ictus but the perception of a difference between two metrical positions? To be sure, even in a stress-based system it is possible to differentiate between two positions without ictus, as in the thesis of a Modern English dactyl. But this is true only when there is a one-to-one correspondence between syllables and metrical positions. When a position may comprise a variable number of unstressed syllables, as in Old English, to differentiate among positions there must be one or more added features, such as ictus (which may correlate to stress or length at the phonological level) or caesura.[42] Thus Cable is certainly right to remark, "for a syllable to have metrical stress, it must have greater linguistic prominence than at least one adjacent syllable. If at the same time it has *less* prominence than its other adjacent syllable, it does not cease to bear metrical stress, because ictus is established relative to *either* syllable that it stands next to" (*Meter and Melody*, p. 47).

## E.  Chronological Implications

§215. Given that there is evidence for the significance of tertiary stress at both the phonological and metrical levels, claims about chronological change in the metrical value of tertiary stress, such as those mentioned at the beginning of this chapter, may be given serious consideration. Sievers, once again, concludes that, in late poems, long middle syllables without secondary stress, and middle syllables made long by the addition of a suffix beginning with a consonant, frequently lose their half-stress.[43] The evidence seems inconclusive. There are counterexamples: Campbell points out the exception *wæs him Beowulfes sið* (*Beowulf* 501b), and others are listed below (§§49ff.), though it is shown there that many are of dubitable authenticity. And the exceptions in the *Meters* are not particularly numerous—the only indisputable examples of the latter type are *nænigne metað* (17.18b) and *Nis nan mihtigra* (20.18a, with alliteration on *n*)—and counterexamples are more numerous: compare *ælcræftigre*

---

[42]Hofmann (*Versstrukturen*, pp. 14–15) similarly remarks this fundamental difference between early and contemporary Germanic meters.

[43]*Altgerm. Metrik*, §78.4; Campbell, pp. 35, n. 1, and 183, n. 2. See also Jakob Schipper, *A History of English Versification* (Oxford: Clarendon, 1910), p. 28.

(20.38b), *agenne stede* (20.64b), and *dreorigne sefan* (22.33b). In *Judith* there are no verses of this type with loss of tertiary stress; compare, however, *elðeodigra* (215a), *hæðenra hosp* (216a), and *mægð modigre* (334a).

§216. Some other aspects of the distribution of tertiary stress have been offered as evidence of historical change discernible in verse. One of these aspects is the metrical treatment of medial syllables that arose in the course of the Old English period by paradigm regularization. For example, historically the first word in *mistige moras* (*Beowulf* 162a) should be a dissyllable, *mistge*, since short vowels were syncopated in medial syllables in the pre-literary period—at the latest, at the beginning of the seventh century, in Luick's judgment (§§309, 350). And in this instance a dissyllable is what the meter demands, as with most instances of the adjective suffix *-ig-*. But *mistge* is written *mistige* because by the time the existing poetic manuscripts were compiled, paradigm regularization had set in, extending the extra syllable of *mistig* (where *i* was not lost, being internal in a final syllable) to inflected cases (Luick, §303; Campbell, §343). Therefore, any poem ought to be relatively late if it contains forms like *mistige* in which *-ig-* cannot be disregarded metrically, but must form a syllable. The same is true of the preterite participial endings *-en-* and *-ed-*, and other analogically induced medial syllables (e.g., in *Beowulf*, *geōmore* 151a, *dōgores* 219b, and *hæþenes* 986a). Sievers ("Rhythmik," p. 461) lists twenty such verses, and concludes that this feature correlates to lateness of composition (p. 459):

> ealdwerige  (*Exodus* 50a)
> modcwanige  (*Elene* 377b)
> *unscyldegum*  (*Meters* 4.36b)
> his *agenum*  (*Meters* 7.47b)
> þæt hio *æniges*  (*Meters* 13.22b)
> hire agenes  (*Meters* 13.30b)
> hi heora ag*n*e  (*Meters* 13.48b)
> and his agene  (*Meters* 17.26a)
> þinum agenum  (*Meters* 20.23b)
> þæt hit ænige  (*Meters* 20.130a)
> þæt hio on ænige  (*Meters* 20.163b)
> unmehtige  (*Meters* 24.62a)
> for his agenum  (*Meters* 25.57a)
> medowerige  (*Judith* 229a)
> medowerigum  (*Judith* 245a)
> gegrundene  (*Maldon* 109a)
> tireadige  (*Menologium* 13b)
> halige dagas  (*Menologium* 68a)
> þristhydigum  (*Menologium* 223a)
> wuldores stæf  (*Solomon and Saturn I* 112a)

Three of these (*Meters* 17.26a, 20.130a, and 25.57a) must be omitted because under Bliss's system they are light verses, and so they are ambiguous.[44] Sievers rejects two other verses for reasons that are no longer admissible: *ænegu gesceaft* (*Meters* 13.68b, 73b).[45] This list is virtually complete: the only other example in the test group is another instance of *ænegu gesceaft* at *Meters* 20.41b. There is also an example at *Summons to Prayer* 30a, and there are perhaps some in other apparently late verse.

§217. Clearly, this analogical development is evidenced relatively frequently in poetry known or supposed to date to Alfred's reign or later, while it is almost unknown in the first four-fifths of the test group.[46] One of the first two instances, that in *Exodus*, is in fact dubitable on independent grounds, since it is morphologically anomalous:

> Swa þæs fæsten dreah      fela missera
> ealdwerige,      Egypta folc. (49–50)

The word *ealdwerige* is the only example in Old English of *eald-* used as the first element of a compound adjective. Indeed, the use of two adjectives to form a compound is extraordinary, and improbable in the Germanic languages.[47] Several emendations have been proposed, the most widely regarded of which is Sievers' suggestion that the original reading was *ealdwērigra*, in agreement with *Egypta* ("Rhythmik," p. 461). But the only one that accounts for the peculiar compound is Edward B. Irving's emendation to *ealdorwērige*, semantically parallel to *ferðwērig-* (*Guthlac B*

---

[44]Verses like *fiftiges wid* (*Genesis A* 1307b) are not exceptions, since *-tig-* is etymologically distinct from *-ig-*, and inflected cardinal numbers of this sort cannot be demonstrated to have lost the stress on *-tig-* in verse before A.D. 973, for reasons discussed below (§231). On the other hand, *eahtoþa* is dissyllabic, comparable to preterites of the second class of weak verbs (cf. Gothic *ahtuda*); and *fēower* is treated like *ēþel*.

[45]He reasons: "Diese formen machen keine ausnahme, sondern stimmen ganz zu der zuerst von Zeuner, Die sprache des kent. psalters s. 65ff. beobachteten regel, dass die ältesten texte jene *u*-formen der langsilbigen nomina ohne synkope bilden" ("Rhythmik," p. 461). Compare the discussion of the adjective suffix *-lic-* below, where it is shown that when inflected with *-u* the suffix *-lic-* does not normally make position in the onset of the verse, though certainly *-i-* was not syncopated here, either. It would at any rate be peculiar if such a supposed archaism were preserved only in the datably late *Meters*, which is also the Old English poetic work that provides the most evidence for the analogical development of the adjective suffix *-ig-* to a metrical syllable. Although it is shown below that *ū* must have been shortened early, it is also shown there that analogical leveling in weak verbs of the second class set in early, as well, and so *gemicledu* (*Riddle 20* 20b) is not in the same class as the other verses on this list.

[46]*Solomon and Saturn* and the *Menologium* are both generally thought to date to Alfred's reign or later: see Dobbie, ASPR 6:lix–lx and lxv. For the purposes of alliteration, palatal and velar *g* are separate phonemes in the *Menologium* (§302 below), though not in *Solomon and Saturn*: cf. *I* 48, 63, 65; *II* 265, 352, and so forth.

[47]Genuine exceptions are few, and belong to particular categories, for example OIcel. *bláhvítr* 'bluish white'. The remaining exceptions are like *gōdfremmend* and *gōdspēdig*, in which one element or the whole is derived from a different part of speech.

1157a, *Christ II* 830a).[48] The scribal omission is more credible if *Exodus* was first committed to parchment fairly early, when syllabic *r* was still sometimes written simply *r*, as occasionally in the early glossaries.

§218. There is no motive but the metrical one for emending the exception in *Elene*, and so it must be allowed to stand. Campbell's explanation of these two verses, at any rate, is untenable: he suggests that *-ig-* bears half-stress in these two instances because it derives from *-īg-* rather than *-æg-* (§89, n. 3). But while *wērig* does derive from *wōrīg* (cf. OSax. *wōrig*), *cwānig* cannot contain *-īg-*, having no umlaut. Moreover, *ǣnig* does reflect *-īg-*, and yet presumably early verse never gives ictus to the second syllable of *ǣnige* and the like. Rather, since *ī* was almost certainly shortened early in unstressed medial syllables, before the syncope of high vowels (see above, §§187ff.), it was also lost in this suffix, giving the same result as original *-æg-*. The supposition that *ī* was shortened early renders it unnecessary to resort to Luick's unconvincing arguments about confusion of *-īg-* and *-æg-* (§314, n. 3). It might well be that the analogical change of adj. *-g-* to *-ig-* was in the process of establishing itself by the time of Cynewulf—who, after all, need not have lived much earlier than Alfred, according to the presumed chronology. But since this is the only such instance in the 2,601 lines of the Cynewulf canon, it must nonetheless be considered suspect.

§219. Amos (pp. 27–28) suggests that this exceptional treatment of the suffix *-ig-* is an indicator of dialect rather than date. It is in fact true that the Anglian dialects are much more conservative than West Saxon and Kentish in preserving the etymological difference between syncopated and unsyncopated forms of the suffix. This point was demonstrated above in regard to forms like *nēt(e)nu* (§§188ff.), and it holds true of adjectives in *-ig-*, as well.[49] Analogical formations do occur in Anglian texts—for example, Li. has *halige, haligum, eadege, ǣnige,* and *ǣniges,* all once each, and several instances of *ǣnigum,* which is actually more frequent than *ǣngum,* though the situation is the reverse in Ru.[2]. But these forms are exceptional. The gloss on Li. is from the tenth century, and since the analogical change has made so little headway in the prose of this text, it seems unlikely that the analogical forms should have invaded verse in this dialect by that time.

---

[48]*The Old English Exodus,* Yale Studies in English 122 (New Haven: Yale Univ. Press, 1953). Peter J. Lucas' objection that this "does not make good sense since the Egyptians do not die on account of being tired" (*Exodus,* p. 83) does not take into account the more metaphorical uses of *wērig,* as when *dēaðwērig* is applied to Æschere at *Beowulf* 2125a. The most recent discussion of this passage is by Nina Boyd, "A Note on the Old English *Exodus,* Lines 41b-53," *ELN* 18 (1981), 243–47.

[49]For West Saxon the point can be demonstrated by an examination of inflected forms of *ēadig, ǣnig,* etc., in the *Microfiche Concordance.* For Kentish the point can be established by reference to the *Kentish Glosses* in Sweet and Hoad's edition: see, for example, lines 174, 403, 446, 571, 596, 737, and 1042.

§220. On the other hand, even if dialect does play a role in the distribution of these analogical forms, dialect cannot be the sole determinant, since some demonstrably Southern texts show no metrical trace of the analogical change.[50] And in the *Meters of Boethius* the change is still inchoate, though it is widespread in purely West-Saxon prose texts of the same period. Presumably, then, although the analogical change was indeed limited on a dialectal basis, it also did not appear in verse before a relatively late date, as one should expect of an analogical change that was still incomplete in the historical period. Thus, this forms a parallel to Kenneth Sisam's analysis of the dating and dialectal value of syncope in verbs (§§318ff. below). The dialectal distribution of the change, however, cannot have been as simple as the opposition between Anglian and Southern dialects: although *Judith* and *Solomon and Saturn* do evince analogical forms, they do not display typical Southern features, while they do show some Anglian ones (Chap. 11 below).[51] As either a dating or a dialect criterion this is not a particularly fine tool. It cannot distinguish degrees of antiquity, though it does confirm that *Judith* belongs with the *Meters* and *Maldon* in the latter part of the chronology.

## F. The Rule of the Coda

§221. The assignment of ictus to analogically restored medial *-ig-* is in agreement with Campbell's account of half-stress, according to which tertiary stress may be assigned to a medial syllable regardless of its length: *scēotendes* and *wynsume*, for example, should receive identical metrical treatment. It can now be shown that the case is not always so, and that variation in the treatment of some short medial syllables can be correlated in a general way to chronological development. Such is the variation in the metrical treatment of the adjective suffix *-lic-*. Campbell includes this suffix in the group of those that ought to be long and stress-bearing when medial, but short and unstressed when final (§88). Other of his conclusions suggest a different analysis, since he observes that in adj. *-lic-* "the short vowel developed early and extended to the inflected forms, so that final *-u* was retained after the medial syllable, which had

---

[50]See, for example, *Psalm 50* 17a, 54b, 91b, 137b, and *Genesis B* 237a, 245a, 260b. On the features identifying *Genesis B* as Southern see Chap. 11.

[51]The evidence from early Middle English manuscripts is too meager to shed much light on the problem. Orm consistently distinguishes between unsyncopated, uninflected forms and syncopated, inflected forms of *haliʒ*, but gives syncopated forms of no other adjective. This evidence is not very significant, since the word was shown above (p. 174, n. 12) to be an exception already in Old English. The word also is frequently exceptional in the same way in the late Old English or early Middle English homilies edited by A. O. Belfour from MS Bodley 343, EETS, o.s. 137 (1909), though the dialect of these is very late West Saxon.

half-stress before the inflexion, . . . e.g. *heardlicu* like *wynsumu"* (§356, n. 1; see also §642, n. 1). It is certainly true that the vowel was shortened: otherwise, for instance, forms like *freolucu* and *freolecu* would not appear in *Genesis A* (examples below) and in other texts (Campbell, §371). Shortening is a prerequisite to such qualitative changes. On the other hand, it is not categorically true that adj. *-lic-* had half-stress when inflected. This is true of those poems that follow *Exodus* in the chronology of the test group, but forms without ictus are common, and in fact predominate, in the earliest part of the chronology. The instances are the following:[52]

| *Genesis A* | | | *Daniel* | |
|---|---|---|---|---|
| 184a | freolice fæmnan | | 554a | yrre and egeslicu |
| 884a | freolucu fæmne | | *Beowulf* | |
| 895b | Him þa freolecu mæg | | 232a | fyrdsearu fuslicu |
| 998a | freolecu fæmne | | 641a | freolicu folccwen |
| 1053b | þær him freolecu mæg | | 1426a | sellice sædracan |
| 1618a | ful freolice feorh | | 1941b | þeah ðe hio ænlicu sy |
| 1849b | him drihtlicu mæg | | *Exodus* | |
| 2782b | Þa cwæð drihtlecu mæg | | 3a | wræclico wordriht |
| | | | 298a | wrætlicu wægfaru |

Verses in which adj. *-lic-* bears ictus are also to be found in these poems: typical are *freolicu twa* (*Genesis A* 968a) and *se monlica* (2568a). But such verses are less common in these poems, while on the other hand this is the only treatment in the rest of the test group.[53] From *Elene* onward only forms of adj. *-lic-* with ictus are found, although the examples in the Cynewulf canon and *Andreas* are few, and mostly insignificant in view of the rule of the coda introduced below (§226). But just as with the inflected, analogically desyncopated forms of the adjective suffix *-ig-* treated above, it is only in the latter part of the chronology that the short medial syllable in the onset of the verse is granted ictus with any consistency.

§222. The significance of these regularities becomes clear when they are compared with the facts for non-high vowels in the same position, for example in the suffixes *-lēas-*, *-dōm-*, and *-hād-*. These consistently bear ictus, and are undoubtedly long—as evidenced by the retention of their original vowel quality, and by Orm's spellings *ellennlæs*, *wittlæs*,

---

[52]*Judgment Day II* seems to contradict the pattern, and frequently. Closer examination reveals that the metrical faults of the poem are sufficient to account for the exceptions, however. Thus, although verses such as *þas unhyrlican fers* (11a) and *þa ænlican geatu* (63b) at first appear to be counterevidence, they are paralleled by others such as *and synfulra gehwam* (18a) and *nu þu forgifnesse hæfst* (68a); and verses such as *uplicum læce* (46a) and *scearplice bysne* (53b) are paralleled by *ættrenum lige* (146b) and *blissiendum modum* (286a), etc.

[53]The other examples are at *Genesis A* 1708a, 2228b, *Beowulf* 585a, 1158a, 1584a, 2869b, *Elene* 431b, *Juliana* 263b, *Christ II* 644a, *Andreas* 119b, 245a, and *Meters of Boethius* Proem 5b, 7.42b, 8.9a, 11.92a, 20.127a, 20.212b, 20.224a, 20.226b, 21.11a, 21.30a, 25.3b.

*laferrddom, haligdom, widdweshad,* and so forth: the final nongeminate consonant indicates a long preceding vowel, and the vowel *æ* is itself necessarily long, since the short equivalent in the *Ormulum* is written *a,* as in *fasst, sopfasst,* and the like. The suffix *-dōm-,* when inflected, is never found in Old English verse in a position in which it clearly does not bear ictus. Typical are *of cyningdome* (*Daniel* 567b) and *wisdome heold* (*Beowulf* 1959b).[54] The same is true of compounds with second elements of obscured meaning. For example, the following are all the examples of *missēre* 'half-year' in the test group:

| Genesis A | | Beowulf | |
|---|---|---|---|
| 1168b | missera worn | 153b, 2620b | fela missera |
| 1743a | misserum frod | 1498b, 1769b | hund missera |
| 2347b | missarum frod | Exodus | |
| | | 49b | fela missera |

§223. The distribution of adj. *-lic-* agrees well with the historical facts about the suffix. As shown above, although the suffix was originally *-līc-,* it must have been shortened early, as otherwise it is difficult to explain the retention of the inflection *-u* in the nominative singular feminine and nominative and accusative plural neuter (just as with forms like *nēt(e)nu,* §188 above), as well as the occasional development to *-lec-* and *-luc-.* It is also true because, as pointed out above, even if one accepts the unlikely proposition that there were two separate syncopes of high vowels, Luick himself assumes that long high vowels were shortened early, at the same time as the first syncope, since the second syncope was also prehistoric (Luick, §315). There is one environment in which *-līc-* was not shortened, however—in words like *earfoðlīcum,* where it clearly bore more stress than in words like *frēolicum* (as discussed above, §203). And so the likeliest explanation of the consistent length of *-līc-* in presumably later verse is that the long form was extended analogically, in keeping with the very low tolerance of Old English for morphophonemic variation of this sort. That the suffix actually was long in later verse, and not merely the object of changing metrical treatment, is demonstrated by Orm's spelling *-lic* (not *\*-licc*), for instance in *flæshlic, efennlic,* and *e(o)rþlic.*[55]

§224. It is also linguistically natural that *-lic-* should have been ambiguous in the first part of the chronology, before the analogical change set in. The reason for this is that unstressed high vowels had been syncopated everywhere, except after a short stressed syllable, where of

[54]The other examples in the test group are at *Elene* 357a, 543b, 552b, 596b, 938b, 1143a, 1190a, *Juliana* 516b, *Andreas* 645a, the *Metrical Epilogue to the Pastoral Care* 14a, and *Meters of Boethius* 29.39a.

[55]See *The Ormulum,* ed. Robert Holt (Oxford: Clarendon, 1878). Spellings like *eorþlike* are inconclusive, since Orm does not double consonants after short vowels in open syllables: to *mikell* cf. inflected *miccle;* to *gladdshipe* cf. *herrsumm;* but to *-lic* cf. *icc, acc.*

course they could not serve as a lift, anyway. High vowels with suffixal stress were not syncopated (cf. the suffixes *-sum-* and *-scipe*), though they had undergone shortening with the unstressed vowels.[56] This left them in an anomalous position, being the only short vowels bearing tertiary stress. All other, non-high vowels bearing tertiary stress had remained unshortened, and exceptions to the pattern *wisdome heold* (*Beowulf* 1959b) are probably inauthentic, as discussed below (§§238ff.). Thus adj. *-lic-* had systematic affinities with both unstressed syllables and syllables with tertiary stress, and might be treated metrically like either. This is all the truer because high vowels in open syllables with tertiary stress were of exceedingly limited distribution, appearing only in the suffixes *-lic-*, *-sum-*, *-scipe*, and *-ian* (*-ie*, *-ienne*, etc.).

§225. Evidence for this analysis of *-lic-* can be derived from the study of how *-lic-* and *-lec-* are distributed in prose texts. If the suffix with a short vowel was analogically replaced by the suffix with the long vowel beginning in the ninth century, as the data above suggest, then the form *-lec-* ought not to occur in late prose texts, since this must have a short vowel. It is in fact true that in prose *-lec-* seems to be confined to texts composed before the tenth century.[57] Thus, for instance, although spellings of other words with the same lowering of high vowels (e.g. *dysega*) are common in the works of Ælfric, *-lic-* is never spelt *-lec-* there.[58] On the other hand, *-lec-* is common in some Alfredian works, especially the translation of Bede's *History* and of the *Pastoral Care.*[59]

---

[56]The assumption here is that since tertiary stress is no longer required to explain forms like *nētenu*, it may be supposed that suffixes of some recognizable semantic import, such as *-līc-*, *-sum-* and *-scipe*, carried sufficient stress to escape syncope, while suffixes without such semantic import, such as *-īn-* and *-iþ-*, did not carry the requisite stress. This assumption allows the prehistoric distribution of secondary stress more closely to parallel the actual historical situation described by Campbell. The vowel in the present tense of weak verbs of the second class was raised to *i* only later.

[57]It is of course necessary to confine the inquiry to date of composition rather than to the dates of the manuscripts themselves, since scribal corruption may have changed the original features of a text. Thus *-lec-* in a text appears to be evidence against late composition, though its absence implies nothing.

[58]It is true that *-ig-* is not lowered to *-eg-* after a long syllable in Ælfric (e.g. *ēadiga*, never *\*ēadega*), but the reason for this is that here medial *-ig-* is always analogical to uninflected forms, in which there was no motivation for lowering, since a following back vowel is required for the change.

[59]Given the metrical evidence of the *Meters*, Alfred's own practice in this regard must have been less innovative than that of the scribes and translators working for him, at least some of whom of course were Mercian. Another text with *-lec-* is the glossary in MS Cotton Cleopatra A.iii (ed. W. G. Stryker, Stanford Univ. diss., 1951). The manuscript itself is from the middle of the tenth century, but the material itself may be older. It is sometimes assumed that this variation in unstressed vocalism is an exclusively West-Saxon feature: see, e.g., B. J. Timmer's edition of *Genesis B*, p. 23. But while the phenomenon admittedly is considerably less frequent in Anglian texts, it does nonetheless occur: cf., e.g., Li. *monege* (Mt. 6.26), *eadege* (Mt. 11:8), *hefege* (Mt. 11:28), *oferhygdego* (Lk. 1:51); Rit. *hydego*; Ru.[1] *monegra* (8.30 and 24.12), *monegu* (25.21 and

Thus it appears that analogical *-līc-* was in the process of being extended into all positions in the ninth century, and the paucity of relevant forms in Cynewulf's works and *Andreas* is perhaps an expression of uncertainty about the metrical value of the suffix. The appearance of *-lec-* several times in a verse text, even without metrical corroboration of shortness, then implies a textual tradition dating at least to the Alfredian period.

§226. One should expect some corroboration from an examination of the suffixes *-sum-*, *-scipe*, and *-ian*, and indeed there is some. The general rule is that half-stress on such short syllables is applied with any regularity only in the coda of the verse.[60] In the onset, words like *eorl-scipe* and *wynsume* are instead metrically equivalent to *eorlas* and *wynsum*. A more precise way to put this is that suffixes like *-scipe* and *-sume*, with an etymologically short high vowel in the penultimate syllable, count as two metrical positions in the coda of a verse; otherwise they count as one. Since this rule has wider application, and will be referred to frequently below, it will be convenient to give it a name and refer to it as the *rule of the coda*.[61] The effect of the rule is to demand more rigid structure in the latter part of the verse than in the former, since, essentially, each syllable in the coda corresponds to a metrical position, while the number of syllables allowable in the onset is freer. This is in accordance with the general nature of meters in Indo-European languages, which tend to demand more fixed structures toward the end of the verse.[62] Typical verses showing the treatment of *-scipe* and *-sum* are *eard ond eorlscipe* (*Beowulf* 1727a), *eorlscipe efnan* (2622a), *wudu wynsuman* (1919a), and *Feondscype rærdon* (*Juliana* 14b).[63] The only poems here that violate the

---

25.23); VP *geweolegað* (Hymn 4); and there are undoubtedly more examples in these and other texts. The smaller incidence of the variation is no doubt in part due to the fact that Anglian texts preserve the syncopated form in inflected cases after long roots with much greater regularity than West-Saxon texts.

[60] By *coda* is meant the last full lift and all subsequent syllables. The preceding portion of the verse is the *onset*.

[61] After the first draft of this chapter had been completed I received from Thomas Cable drafts of portions of his *English Alliterative Tradition*, which has since appeared in print. In the book he describes an "Antepenultimate Rule for Resolution" that I believe has the same practical effect as the rule of the coda. It is gratifying to find that a rule that I was prompted to posit on purely observational grounds now has the support of his independent discovery of the same principle on primarily theoretical grounds. I am fortunate to have had the opportunity to benefit from his findings in revising this chapter—see below, p. 217, n. 88.

[62] This point is made by John Miles Foley, "The Scansion of *Beowulf* in its Indo-European Context," in *Approaches to Beowulfian Scansion*, ed. Alan Renoir and Ann Hernández (Old English Colloquium, Department of English, University of California, Berkeley, 1982), pp. 7–17, at p. 12. He provides references in n. 17.

[63] Other examples in the test group are at *Genesis A* 231b, 1672b, 1760b, 1906a, 1942b, 2048b, 2324a, 2517a, 2692b, *Daniel* 388a, *Beowulf* 612a, 1470a, 2069a, 2133a, 2535a, 2751a, 2999b, 3007b, *Exodus* 529b, *Elene* 498b, 1166a, *Juliana* 208a, 695a, *Christ II* 486b, *Andreas* 478b, and *Meters of Boethius* 11.93a, 13.19a, 19.44a. A few exclusions

rule of the coda are *Beowulf*, with its three exceptions—*word wæron wynsuman* (612a; type 1A1b), *eard ond eorlscipe* (1727a; 1A1a), and *lif ond leodscipe* (2751a; 1A1a)—and the *Meters*, with one—*wynsume wiht* (13.19a; 3E1). Even these few exceptions can perhaps otherwise be explained.[64]

§227. It is generally assumed that the adverb suffix *-līce* consistently has a long vowel.[65] The metrical evidence in the onset is scant, but tends to support this assumption, at least in verse presumably composed before the tenth century:

> niudlicae ob cocrum  (*Leiden Riddle* 14b)
> drihtlice spræc  (*Genesis A* 2138b)
> healice upp  (*Christ II* 693b)
> *lustlice geo*  (*Meters* 2.1b)
> *wislice astyrest*  (*Meters* 20.15b)

All but the first demand ictus on *-līc-*, and this pattern is sufficiently different from the pattern of adj. *-lic-* to suggest that adv. *-līce* does not have a short vowel. The manuscript reading of the first example is not certain, and so this is not strong corroboration of the earliness of the *Leiden Riddle*. Adverbial *-līce* never forms a single metrical position at the end of a verse in supposedly early poems, where it is not infrequent (twenty-four relevant examples in *Genesis A*, fourteen in *Beowulf*), though it was shown above that adj. *-lic-* plus inflection sometimes does, if Bliss's scansions are correct. And so it ought to be assumed that analogical restoration of the long vowel in the adverb suffix was earlier than in the adjective suffix—not an improbable development, since, once again, analogical developments are not characterized by the same relative universality and regularity of application as phonological developments. What is most interesting here is that except perhaps for the instance in the *Leiden Riddle*, only very late verse contains examples of adv. *-līce* without ictus:

---

should be mentioned. Probability is in favor of regarding *feodon þurh feondscipe* (*Elene* 356a) as belonging to type 1A*1a rather than d1c, since Bliss finds that in *Beowulf*, out of eighty-three instances in which a finite verb is the only particle before the first undeniably stressed element of the verse, the verb alliterates sixty-four times (§15). Still, since he finds that in similar instances the alliteration is frequently ornamental, a proportion 64:83 does not afford certainty. Similar ambiguity is found at 1.68a and 11.91a in the Boethian *Meters*.

[64]If Bliss's ideas about the caesura are discarded (a possibility discussed below, §246), the three *Beowulf* verses may be scanned as type D, and are thus unexceptional. The exception in the *Meters* possibly results from scribal change: Alfred may well have written *wihte* (fem.); and note that *wuhte* is feminine at 11.78b, though *wuht* must be neuter at 13.33b and 20.159a. Nonetheless, since the *Meters* violate the rule of the coda in regard to weak verbs of the second class, too (as demonstrated below), *wynsume wiht* is not unlikely.

[65]For instance, in Sweet's reader, where adjective *-lic-* is consistently left short, in agreement with the conclusion reached above, still *-līce* is always marked long: see *Sweet's Anglo-Saxon Reader*, ed. C. T. Onions, 14th ed. (Oxford: Clarendon, 1959).

> stiðlice clypode (*Maldon* 25b)
> heardlice feohtan (*Maldon* 261b)
> geornlice fylstan (*Maldon* 265b)
> freolice in geatwum (*Death of Edward* 22b)

The Worcester Chronicle (D) has the adjective *freolic* instead, and so this instance in the *Death of Edward* is less certain, but the examples in *Maldon* are clear.[66] Whether Orm's *-like* represents a suffix with a long vowel cannot be determined with certainty, since he does not double consonants after short vowels in open syllables; but shortening seems unlikely in view of the parallel of the adjective suffix. There are no examples of the inflected adjective suffix in these late poems.

§228. Fairly regular in regard to the rule of the coda are weak verbs of the second class. The data are given below. In the preterite these contained *-ōd- in Proto-Germanic, and this normally developed to -ad- in Old English. But when *-ōd- appeared before an inflection containing *u* (-on < *-unð is the only one that survives in Old English) it changed to *-ūd- (Campbell, §331.6), which was shortened to -ud- > -od- at the same time that -līc- was shortened. Thus, at the time of high-vowel syncope the preterite suffix should have alternated between *-ōd- and *-ud-. (The alternant -ed- arose in the plural by the same process that produced forms like *ēadega*.) In the latter form, *u* might or might not appear in a position to be syncopated, depending on the weight of the preceding syllable: for example, it should have been lost in *cwānudun > *cwāndun, but not in *swicudun > swicodon. Since forms like *cwāndon do not occur, and since Old English, once again, is a language that tolerates very little allomorphy of this sort, presumably *u* was retained or restored in the former type by analogy to the latter. (It should be remembered that the allomorphy would not have been simply between paradigms, but within paradigms, since, for instance, *ō* would not have been raised to *ū* in *cwānōdæ, and so would not have been syncopated there; and therefore the motivation for paradigm regularization would have been strong.) The alternation between -ōd- > -ād- and -ud- perhaps remained regular longer, but, nonetheless, already in the earliest records -ode and -ade alternate freely, and the meter of presumably early verse does not indicate a short vowel before -on and a long one elsewhere. Rather, by the time the extant verse was composed the alternation was governed not by the inflectional ending, but by the rule of the coda.[67]

---

[66]But cf. *ofstlice sceat* (143b) and *wurðlice wrec* (279a) in *Maldon*. The high incidence of *-lice* in the onset in *Maldon* is itself an anomaly.

[67]It seems likely that the shortening of *-ōd- took place earlier than that of *ā* (from *ai), as in *earfoþ- < *arðaiþ-, since it is hardly possible that the two vowels crossed paths in the process of shortening without falling together. Some such assumption at any rate seems necessary in order to account for the fact that *earfoþ-* almost consistently bears tertiary stress, even in the onset of the verse. There is in fact some glossary evidence that the shortening of *ā* did not occur until the beginning of the historical

Failure to distinguish -*ad*- and -*ud*- metrically in verse is to be expected, since their distribution is already disturbed in the earliest glossaries, for example in Erf., which has *suarnadun* (198), *meldadum* (for -*un*, 342), *aslacudae* (491), *suicudae* (932), and others.

§229. The rule also applies to nonpreterite forms with -*i*- after the root, such as inf. *þancian* and 3. pl. *þanciaþ*. The etymology of such forms is much disputed, though now it seems the most widely accepted explanation is Warren Cowgill's: the present endings *-jō*, *-s(t)*, *-þ*, *-jāþ*, inf. *-jan*, and so forth, were abstracted by means of morphological reanalysis from long-stemmed verbs of the first weak class, for example *dōm-ijō* > *dōmi-jō*, and *dōm-īþ* > *dōm-iþ* > *dōmi-þ*, with -*i*- analyzed as belonging to the root, in part because of pret. *dōm-i-dæ*. These endings were added to a stem in -*ō*- parallel to the -*i*- of the long-stemmed verbs of the first class.[68] If this is correct, we should expect preterites of the second class to have played much the same role as first-class forms like *dōm-i-dæ*, meaning that the metrical treatment of second-class presents should be like that of the preterites. A different and somewhat simpler explanation is to suppose that -*j*- in *-ō-jan* and the like was lost relatively soon after *i*-umlaut, leaving such forms subject to the shortening of antevocalic long vowels postulated in §108. But neither the date nor the precise environments for the loss of -*j*- can be determined with much certainty: on the former see Luick, §643, and on the latter, Campbell, §757. Regardless of what the correct solution is, it is undeniable that *i* in forms like *þancian* is short. This is clear not only from the conformity of such words to the rule of the coda, but also from the fact that this *i* never forms a metrical syllable in present participles, as in *þa þu gitsiende* (*Genesis A* 890b).[69]

§230. Verbs of the relevant type—those with a long or resolved root and a monosyllabic inflection—appear hundreds of times in the test group. In *Genesis A* alone, for example, there are nearly one hundred examples. In the vast majority of instances the verb falls at the end of the

---

period: see below, §§258f. See also the discussion below (§§241 and 258) of the exceptional verse *earfeþo on yþum* (*Beowulf* 534a).

[68]"The Inflection of the Germanic *ō*-Presents," *Language* 35 (1959), 1–15.

[69]It has been argued that -*iende* in such verses stands for -*ende*, the Anglian form, as in fact it is spelt in several instances, e.g. *ofgiefan gnornende* (*Guthlac A* 232a). This is the position of Sievers ("Rhythmik," p. 482, and *Altgerm. Metrik*, §76.7; see also Campbell, §757, and Brunner, §410, n. 10), who provides other examples. But if this is so, then West-Saxon verse has adopted the Anglian scansion, to judge by verse that can be verified as Southern on the basis of syncope in verbs and other criteria (Chap. 11 below). The relevant instances are at *Judgment Day II* 25a, 44a, 112a, 215a, 286a, and *Genesis B* 347b. Another possible example is *to begrornianne* (*Genesis B* 243a), since -*enne* is the Anglian form of the inflected infinitive; but this may be an example of an inflected infinitive standing for an uninflected one (§3 above). Still, it must be admitted that both of these poems containing exceptions are metrically irregular, and the *Genesis B* poet may be slavishly following the Old Saxon original in allowing verses of this type.

verse, and the *-i(g)-* of the present or *-od-/-ad-* of the preterite bears ictus. Infrequently it comes before the end of the verse, and then the formative syllable generally bears no ictus, as in *þancode swiðe* (*Genesis A* 1888b) and *þanciað þrymmes* (*Daniel* 424a). There are forty-three verses of this sort in the test group.[70] Thus, although the incidence of relevant forms of weak verbs of the second class in the onset of the verse is not great in comparison to their overall incidence, it is large enough to confirm the applicability of the rule of the coda. Sure exceptions to the rule among these verbs are infrequent:[71]

| *Genesis A* | | *Andreas* | |
|---|---|---|---|
| 1413a | lytligan eft | 1090a | deade gefeormedon |
| 2177b | eaforan bytlian | *Meters* | |
| 2293b | folc awæcniað | 1.84b | gyddode þus |
| 2359a | bletsian nu | 21.2b | fundie to |
| 2518b | tiðiað me | 25.13b | þreatiað gehwider |
| | | 29.37b | fæder getiohhode |

Undeniably, *Genesis A* and the *Meters* violate the rule of the coda in this category more frequently than they observe it. This is in contrast, for instance, to the pattern in *Daniel* and *Beowulf*. The frequency of violations

---

[70]The others are at *Genesis A* 2847b, *Daniel* 52a, 215a, 280a, 403a, 549a, *Beowulf* 105b, 560a, 922a, 1105b, 1118a, 1137b, 1161a, 1699b, 2085a, 2096a, 2119a, 2132a, 2702a, 3173a, *Exodus* 117a, 265a, *Elene* 494a, *Fates of the Apostles* 2b, *Juliana* 598a, *Andreas* 55a, 1268a, 1526a, *Meters of Boethius* 1.33b, 20.266a, 27.30a, 28.78a, *Maldon* 10a, 21b, 86a, 91a, 173a, 177b, 268a, 290a, and *Durham* 18a. Given Luick's suggestion that *yldsta* and *lengsta* might actually be old (§306, n. 2; and see further below, §240), *wyrrestan* at *Daniel* 215a might stand for *wyrstan*. Sievers would emend to *wyrsan* ("Rhythmik," p. 486). Some exclusions should be mentioned. *Ic wille fandigan nu* (*Genesis A* 2412b) is the companion to a hypermetric verse. The verse *drohtigen dæghwæmlice* (*Andreas* 682a) seems to conform, but is nonetheless difficult. Note that most of the examples from *Maldon* are less certain than the others because of the *Maldon* poet's treatment of anacrusis (see §303 below). At *Beowulf* 6a the manuscript reads *egsode eorl*, but the emendation is not purely metrical: e.g., Klaeber finds the manuscript reading metrically acceptable, but not stylistically (p. 124). And as Dobbie points out, all recent editions but von Schaubert's adopt the emendation. Kevin Kiernan argues that the "desired meter for the phrase can be achieved . . . without resorting to emendation by pronouncing *eorl* in two syllables—*eor-el*": see "The Legacy of Wiglaf: Saving a Wounded Beowulf," *Kentucky Review* 6.2 (1986), 27–44, at 37–38. Even if there were any orthographic evidence for such anaptyxis in *eorl* (the case is in fact the opposite: cf. lWS *world* < *woruld*, etc.), this would not resolve the metrical difficulty, since *"eor-el"* would of course have a short first syllable.

[71]Sievers ("Rhythmik," p. 484) would substitute *bytlan* for *bytlian* at *Genesis A* 2177b, and *āwæcnað* for *āwæcniað* at 2293b. He would also substitute a verb of the first class for one of the third in *blode spiowedan* (*Juliana* 476b): cf. *speowdon* at *Elene* 297b. Pope (p. 237) advocates returning to the reading of Klaeber's second edition by eliminating the first word of *þa secg wisode* (*Beowulf* 402b), and he is supported by Bliss (§49); see also Pope's article cited above, n. 99 to the Introduction. *Cam in siðian* (*Genesis A* 1577b) is not an exception, since it has already been pointed out elsewhere

in the onset should not be surprising in view of the remark above that Indo-European meters tend to be stricter toward the end. Excluded from the exceptions in the footnote are the twenty-six verses in *Beowulf* that Bliss classifies as type 2A1a(ii), all but one of which end in the word *maðelode* (e.g. *Beowulf maðelode* 405a), the remaining verse (and the only one in the off-verse) being *wæpen hafenade* (1573b). It was pointed out above (n. 29 to Chap. 1; see also below, §57) that Bliss's reasoning here is unpersuasive, for a variety of reasons. To these reasons can now be added that the classification of these verses as type 2A1a(ii) violates the rule of the coda, even though the treatment of weak verbs of the second class in *Beowulf* otherwise conforms entirely to the rule.

§231. There are a few relevant numerals in this category, all carrying the suffix *-tig-*, which retained its stress until after syncope because it was a separate word until relatively late: compare Gothic *twai tigjus, þrins tiguns*, OIcel. *þrír tigir*, and so forth. Examples are few:

> fiftiges wid  (*Genesis A* 1307b)
> ðrittiges heah  (*Genesis A* 1308a)
> þæt he XXXtiges  (*Beowulf* 379b)
> Se wæs fiftiges  (*Beowulf* 3042a)
> þæt he on XX  (*Elene* 829b, dat. pl.)
> and þa on ðam XXX wæs  (*Coronation of Edgar* 20a)

The last example requires *þrītegoþan* (the numeral is written *þrittigæþan* in the B Chronicle, *ðrittigeþan* in C), which would demand loss of stress from a long (resolved) position; but the by-form *þrītegan* is also possible (see Campbell, §694), and this would not only be less anomalous, but would conform to the rule of the coda. And so once again only *Genesis A* clearly violates the rule. Possibly, however, these are no exceptions, if the suffix retained stress later than *-lic-*: see below, §257. By comparison, *eahtoþa* 'eighth' has an etymologically short vowel, as indicated by the cognates (Gothic *ahtuda*, OIcel. *átti*, OS OHG *ahtodo*),[72] and it conforms to the rule of the coda the few times it appears in verse:

---

that *Cam* belongs in the on-verse, as observed by Donoghue (p. 197). Nor is *æpplede gold* (*Juliana* 688a) pertinent: there is no evidence that *\*æpplian* was ever inflected as a finite verb, since *-ede* is from *\*-ōdi-*, as in Old Saxon (see Holthausen's etymological dictionary)—e.g., Kluge remarks that these formations "freilich ihrer bedeutung nach [*sic*] nicht aus verben, sondern vielmehr aus nominibus weiter gebildet sind und die bedeutung 'versehen mit' haben" (§234; see also Campbell, §§339 and 355.5). The verse *ne þysne wig wurðigean* (*Daniel* 207b) was discussed above (§139). *Meters* 21.2b is suspect, but cf. *Genesis A* 1032b and 1856b. Of a different order are verses like *ond gristbitade* (*Juliana* 596b), where perhaps secondary stress (and thus resolution) should fall on the second syllable of the verb.

[72]If the slight evidence for a long vowel in the Old High German word is reliable (see Braune and Eggers, §278, n. 1), this must be a dialectal development, since the cognates are unambiguous.

on þisse eahteþan　(*Guthlac B* 1037a)
Eahtoþan siþe　(*Precepts* 59a)
on þone eahteðan dæg　(*Death of Edgar* 9a)
on þy eahteoðan dæg　(*Menologium* 3b)

§232. Indefinite pronouns and adverbs, when uncontracted, furnish a variety of forms that are subject to the rule, and conform to it consistently:

þara æghwæðer　(*Exodus* 95a)
Æghwæðer oðerne　(*Andreas* 1015a)
ac þær æghwæþer　(*Christ III* 1576b)
se wæs æghwonan　(*Juliana* 580b)
hæfde æghwæðer　(*Beowulf* 2844a; MS *æg hwæðre*)
hine þonne *æghwonan*　(*Meters* 7.45a)
*þæt he hine æghwonon* utan　(*Meters* 10.4a)[73]
þæt hi æghwæðer　(*Meters* 20.12b)
æghwider wolde　(*Meters* 20.92b)
æghwæðer brengeð　(*Solomon and Saturn I* 108b)
æghwanum cumene　(*Judgment Day II* 120a)

§233. Of the twenty verses listed above (§216) like *ænegu gesceaft*, with ictus on an analogically restored short syllable, five violate the rule of the coda. These are of course all in late verse. As with *ænegu*, the middle vowel ought to have been lost in forms like *hindema* (< *\*hindumjō*) and *ȳtemest* (< *\*ūtumistaz*). Its retention must be analogical (cf. *hindeweard* and *ūteweard*), and so like other analogical vowels it ought to be ignored in scansion, as in *hindeman siðe* (*Beowulf* 2049b, 2517b). Alternative forms are encountered in verse: beside *ytemest-* (*Christ II* 879a, *Guthlac B* 1167a), for example, there is the form *ytmestan* (*Guthlac A* 443a, *Meters* 10.25a). In prose, the latter is mainly Anglian.

§234. It was observed above (§§210ff.) that "semi-lexical" morphemes like *-dōm* and *-lēas* occupy an ambiguous position metrically, since they may be granted ictus in verses like *dreamleas gebad* (*Beowulf* 1720b). The point is corroborated by the treatment of semi-lexical morphemes with respect to the rule of the coda. Certain prefixes reduce morphemes to semi-lexical status (see p. 176, n. 14 above), such as *ond-* in *ondslyht ageaf* (2929b); compare *ondweard undyrne* (*Christ III* 1540a, next to *Ondweard ne mæg* 1528b).[74] Thus, words with light second elements reduced by such prefixes perhaps ought to occupy an ambiguous position with regard to the rule of the coda, since they are closer to having secondary stress

---

[73]Although the verse conforms either way, here *utan* belongs in the off-verse, *ymbeþohte*, where *ymbe-* ought not to be stressed, and undoubtedly stands for *ymb-*, as elsewhere in the *Meters*.

[74]Corroborative evidence for the intermediate position of words with such prefixes may also be derived from Cable's findings about their distribution in verses of types D and D\* (*English Alliterative Tradition*, pp. 147–48).

than words like weak verbs of the second class. The word *ondwlita* does in fact seem to conform to Kaluza's law instead of the rule of the coda, as we might expect if it had greater than tertiary stress. In the onset of the verse there are no examples in the test group, but *ondwlitan swa some* (*Christ III* 1122b) and *andwlitan seon* (*Christ and Satan* 377b; *seon* is not in the manuscript) may be noted.[75] The only example of *ondsaca* in the onset of the verse is in *andsaca ne wæs* (*Daniel* 668b), and the only example of inflected *ondgiet* in the onset (cf. n. 75) is in *ondgete swa some* (*Christ III* 1242b). Words with the prefix *un-* (*unbrice, unfæger, unfremu,* and *unwrecen,* for a total of six verses) should receive the same treatment —to *uncuð gelad* (*Beowulf* 1410b) compare verses like *þe þone unræd ongan* (*Genesis A* 30a) and *þæt unlæd nimeð* (*Maxims I* 119b)—but none of them appears in the onset. These conform to the rule in the coda, with the exception of *æte þa unfreme* (*Genesis A* 893a; but cf. below, 251). The noun *andswaru* perhaps belongs here, too. It appears three times in the onset, in *ondsware cyðan* (*Elene* 318a), *ondsware agef* (*Andreas* 628b), and *andsware findan* (*Meters* 22.43b). The instance in *Andreas* violates the rule, though its evidence is slight, since it is opposed to twenty-one instances of *ageaf andsware* (with minor variations) in Old English verse, nearly half of them in *Andreas* itself. And it is of course itself unique, so that scribal corruption is a possible explanation. The entrenchment of the formula *ageaf andsware* is at any rate demonstrated by the fact that it is consistently used in violation of Kuhn's first law. Excluding this formula, *andswaru* appears twelve times in the test group—that is, in the coda—ambiguously in seven instances, and with ictus on *-swar-* in four.[76] The one exception is *him on ondsware* (*Beowulf* 1840b, with alliteration on *h*). The status of the stem *ondswar-* is particularly ambiguous, since *swar-* is a bound morpheme (and was ever since the phonemicization of umlaut), while *wlit-* and *giet-* are not. It is perhaps for that reason that the poets of *Andreas* and *Christ and Satan* consistently privilege the rules of medial resolution (see the next chapter) over the rule of the coda with respect to this word, while it is never resolved in other poems.[77]

§235. On the evidence of verses like *Hroðgar geseon* (*Beowulf* 396b) and *Higelac ongan* (1983b), the second elements of Germanic personal names ought also to be ambiguous with regard to the rule of the coda. Several name-elements used as the second part of compounds have etymologically short vowels, and so still carried stress at the time of high-vowel syncope: these are *-dene* (including *Suðdene,* etc.), *-here, -waru, -wela,* and

---

[75]There are four violations in the Paris Psalter (e.g. *and me andwlita onfeng* 68.29.2a), but once again the psalter is metrically too deficient to serve as evidence. To this verse may be compared *þæt him yþende mod* (54.22.2a), *Wærun wigbedu þin* (83.3.1a), and similar. Cf. also *þæt us andgytes ma* (73.8.3a).

[76]The four are at *Beowulf* 1493b, *Elene* 375b and 642b, and *Andreas* 315b; the seven are at *Beowulf* 354a, 2860a, *Elene* 567a, 1001a, *Andreas* 319a, 508a, and *Meters* 22.51a.

[77]There is one exception, *yrre andswarode* (*Daniel* 210a; cf. 127b, 134b, and 741b).

*-wine* in *Beowulf*, along with the place-name *Frēswæle* (dat. sg.). These occur fifty times in the poem, but just four times in the first foot:[78]

463b  Suðdena folc
783b  Norðdenum stod
1009b Healfdenes sunu
1329b swylc Æschere wæs

Here only the last does not necessarily violate the rule of the coda, and so these are in contrast to verses like *þreatedon þearle*. In other words, the name-elements almost always bear ictus on the short syllable, regardless of position. On the other hand, these names do not behave like compounds with secondary stress, either, since they do not conform to Kaluza's law in the instance of *heah Healfdene* (57a). Given the fidelity of *Beowulf* to Kaluza's law, secondary stress here is unlikely. Loss of stress is at any rate a prerequisite for sound changes in some name-elements, such as *-ferþ* > *-friþ*. The only evidence in the test group outside of *Beowulf* is found in *Maldon*:

80a   Ælfere and Maccus
192a  Godrine and Godwig
211a  Ælfwine þa cwæð
231a  Hwæt þu, Ælfwine, hafast
244a  Leofsunu gemælde
255a  Dunnere þa cwæð

Here the treatment of the name-elements is inconsistent, but unlike the treatment in *Beowulf*, since these names more frequently conform to the rule of the coda. This difference accords with the evidence that stress on personal names changed between the composition of Æthelwulf's *De abbatibus* and Wulfstan of Winchester's life of St. Swithun, mentioned above (§212). Comparison with the *Maldon* poet's treatment of long second elements is instructive, since *Swa hi Æþelgares bearn* (320a) and *ær him Wigelines bearn* (300a) are peculiar; by comparison, of the sixty-five instances in *Beowulf* of inflected forms like *Hrōþgāres* with a long middle syllable, in just one instance does the word not fill three metrical positions (at 501b: see below). Outside the test group there are twenty-three instances of light second elements, such as *Ælfheres sunu* (*Waldere I* 11b) and *mid ðy ðu Guðhere scealt* (25b).[79] Most instances of the relevant name are in the onset, and the only certain exceptions to the rule of the coda are a small group in *Widsith*: *Wulfhere sohte ic ond Wyrmhere* (119a),

---

[78]There is also one violation in the second foot, *Dead is Æschere* (1323b).
[79]The others are at *Widsith* 26a, 28a, 32a, 33a, 57b, 58b, 62b, 66a, 70b, 74b, 98b, 113b, 117a, 119a, 123a, 123b, *Wulf and Eadwacer* 16a, *Battle of Finnsburh* 18b, *Waldere II* 11a, 18b, and *Death of Alfred* 6a.

*Rædhere sohte ic ond Rondhere* (123a), and *Rumstan ond Gislhere* (123b). Their grouping reinforces the impression that the constraints of meter have been slackened here for the purpose of accommodating a great number of proper names. Indeed, it is surprising how metrically regular *Widsith* is, given its material. Note that in these verses, as in *Beowulf*, light personal name elements like *-wine* and *-here* are generally subject to the rule of the coda. Light tribal name-elements are not attested in the onset outside *Beowulf*, but there the evidence suggests that they bear secondary stress (as Bliss suggests, §32, n. 1), since they achieve ictus and conform to Kaluza's law. The distinction between the two types of names is to be expected, since personal compounds are certainly older than tribal ones—and Klaeber's practice of hyphenating tribal names is thus preferable to Dobbie's practice. *Maldon* (along with *Waldere*) then does appear to be exceptional, apparently reflecting metrical change.

§236. The rule of the coda applies also to verse in other early Germanic languages. So in the elder *Edda* the suffix *-lig-* and the middle syllable of preterites of the second weak class bear ictus in the coda, but usually not in the onset: compare *Árliga verðar* (*Hávamál* 33.1), *heitr þú fljótliga fǫr* (*Grípisspá* 35.7), *kallaði þá Knefrøðr* (*Atlakviða* 2.5); so also *Gunnari til handa* (*Grípisspá* 35.5); but compare *kǫlloðo Karl* (*Rígsþula* 21.3) and *kallaðir frá kvǫlum* (*Sólarljóð* 24.6: this is *ljóðaháttr*, comparable to *líknfastan at lofi* at *Hávamál* 123.6).[80] In the *Heliand* the suffix *-lîc-* is always long and ictus-bearing, while second-class preterites conform to the rule in the onset: compare *uundarlîcas filo* (36b), *munilîca magað* (252a), *bisorgoda sie an is gisîðea* (334a), *uuardoda selƀo* (384b), and *folgodun ferahtlîco* (659a); and compare *Manag fagonoda* (526b), *up sîðogean* (594b) and *Sô gornode* (5021a).[81] But even closed syllables in this position may lack ictus: compare *Afhôƀun thô hêlagna sang* (414a), *alomahtigna god* (416b, vs. *hêlagna Krist* 460a), *uualdande mid iro uuordun*

---

[80]Sievers (*Altgerm. Metrik*, §38.2a) concludes that these short syllables always bear ictus in *fornyrðislag* and *dróttkvætt*, but all his examples are in the coda. He says that ictus may be lost in *málaháttr*, e.g. *ok fagnaði komnom* (*Atlamál* 47.4) and *glumruðu gylfringar* (5.7) in Eyvindr skaldaspillir's *Hákonarmál*; but cf. *brotnuðu skildir* (*Hákonarmál* 5.6) and *tjǫrguðum ǫrum* in Þorbjǫrn hornklofi's *Haraldskvæði* 5.7. He would no doubt regard verses in *fornyrðislag* like *Árliga verðar* as five-position verses (§16.6). Sievers also says that words that become trisyllabic by enclisis are exceptions to his rule, as in *myndiga ek lostig* (*Helgakviða Hjǫrvarðssonar* 42.5) and *kalliga ek Hǫgna* (*Guðrúnarkviða III* 8.2), but that the final syllable in such words may also be a lift, as in *at ek stǫðvigak* (*Hávamál* 150.5). But all the instances with the supposed second lift necessarily occur in the coda, and thus it is perhaps simpler to assume a uniform effect of the rule of the coda than a variable scansion of the final syllable, which is, after all, ad hoc. See further below, p. 222, n. 94. The eddic verses cited in this paragraph are in Neckel's edition; the other Norse verses are in *Den norsk-isländska skaldediktningen*, ed. Ernst A. Kock, 2 vols. (Lund: Gleerup, 1946–49). The verses from the *Heliand* are in Behaghel's edition.

[81]So Campbell's remark (p. 35, n. 3) that OSax. *-od-* virtually never receives half-stress must be qualified, as it is true only of the onset.

(432a), *uualdanda at them uuîha* (462a, vs. *uualdandas craft* 469b, *uualdandes uuord* 575a), and similar; see further Sievers, *Altgerm. Metrik*, §§106.1, 107.3. So, too, syncopated syllables restored by analogy occasionally bear ictus in the coda, as in *bodo drohtines* (702a) and *is engilun* (1087a); compare *Thu scalt ûses drohtines uuesan* (264b).

§237. There seems no linguistic motivation for the rule of the coda, since it is metrically conditioned: the metrical value of short syllables under tertiary stress is determined by position in the verse rather than any phonological property of the syllable. There may have been some facet of early Germanic meter that made it inevitable that such a rule should arise. But more likely it originated by analogy to Kaluza's law. Under Kaluza's law, a long final syllable in the onset of the verse prevents resolution, as in *beaghroden cwen* (*Beowulf* 623b). But such verses are rare—there are just six in *Beowulf*, according to Bliss—and so usually two short syllables are resolved in the onset of the verse. That the rule of the coda should have arisen by analogy to these regularities under secondary stress implies that the law is archaic, and it casts doubt on Alistair Campbell's suggestion that the looseness of Old Saxon meter does not represent a metrical system in decline, but that the relative strictness of Old English meter is an insular refinement of the metrical tradition.[82]

§238. Regardless of the general linguistic significance of the rule of the coda, its significance in the present context is that it eliminates from consideration the vast majority of the apparent violations of the rules of stress as set forth by Campbell (§185 above). Forms with tertiary stress that are not subject to the rule of the coda generally do not lose that stress. This includes all words with long non-high vowels in the position for tertiary stress, as long as they were not shortened by prehistoric loss of stress: the point was illustrated above (§222) with all the relevant examples of *missēre* and the suffix *-dōm-* in the test group. The number of verses conforming to Campbell's rules for tertiary stress thus is enormous, in comparison to which the exceptions seem few. All the remaining exceptions in the test group of poems may be listed:

| Genesis A | Daniel |
|---|---|
| 1055a  Se æresta wæs | 247a  iserne ymb æfæste |
| 1134a  se yldesta wæs | 646a  witegena wordcwyde |
| 1155a  Þære cneorisse wæs | *Beowulf* |
| 2176a  freomanna to frofre | 501b  wæs him Beowulfes sið |
| 2304b  ymb XIII gear | 534a  earfeþo on yþum |

---

[82]"The Old English Epic Style," in *English and Medieval Studies Presented to J. R. R. Tolkien*, ed. Norman Davis and C. L. Wrenn (London: Allen & Unwin, 1962), p. 16, n. 1. Campbell's argument is specifically in regard to Kuhn's first law, but he refers also to "some other refinements." Campbell's suggestion is in opposition to the standard view that Old Saxon and Old High German meters represent a system in decline, as argued for instance by Lehmann, *Verse Form*, p. 89 and passim.

| 932b | þæt ic ænigra me | 3.2b | *þæt sweorcende mod* |
|------|------------------|------|----------------------|
| 949b | Ne bið þe nænigra gad | 17.18b | nænigne *metað* |
| *Exodus* | | 20.18a | Nis nan mihtigra |
| 326a | ðeoda ænigre | *Brunanburh* | |
| *Elene* | | 64a | grædigne guðhafoc |
| 42b | Þa se casere heht | *Judith* | |
| 998b | Hie se casere heht | 10a | ealle ða yldestan ðegnas |
| *Fates of the Apostles* | | | (hypermetric) |
| 91a | friðes ond fultomes | *Maldon* | |
| *Andreas* | | 25b | stiðlice clypode |
| 288a | þeoden leofesta | 28a | ærænde to þam eorle |
| 339a | on eowerne agenne dom | 234b | oþerne bylde |
| 412a | hlaforde æt hilde | 261b | heardlice feohtan |
| 490a | syxtyne siðum | 265b | geornlice fylstan |
| 517a | manna ænigne | 300a | ær him Wigelines bearn |
| 770b | Þær orcnawe wearð | 320a | Swa hi Æþelgares bearn |
| 1037b | þær he nænigne forlet | *Death of Edward* | |
| 1081b | ænigne to lafe | 22b | freolice in geatwum |
| *Metrical Epilogue to the Pastoral Care* | | 28a | soþfæste sawle |
| 27b | ðyrelne kylle | *Durham* | |
| *Meters of Boethius* | | 12a | Osuualdes, Engle leo |
| 1.61b | *þæt se casere eft* | | |

§239. Some omissions should be mentioned. The verse *frecenra siða* (*Genesis A* 1427b) perhaps has nonparasiting: see n. 29 to Chapter 1. In verses like *niðas to nergenne* (*Daniel* 284a) the inflected infinitive stands for an uninflected one. The verse *þara ymbsittendra* (*Beowulf* 9b) can hardly be scanned under the assumption that tertiary stress has been lost, and so Klaeber (after Sievers, "Rhythmik," p. 256) is doubtless right to omit *þara*.[83] Verses like *þæt hie eagena gesihð* (*Andreas* 30b) are not exceptional, since *eagena* is orthographic for *eagna*. Rather, the *e* in gen. pl. *-ena* makes position only after short roots and those ending in resonants, as in *wītgena* and *eldrena*: see Brunner, §276, n. 4a. The verse *wiðerweardes hwæthwugu* (*Meters* 11.52b) appears to be an example of loss of stress until it is recognized that *hwæthwugu* at the other place it appears in the *Meters* is also difficult: compare *wið fyre hwæthwugu* (20.111a). Substitution of the more poetic *hwæt* at both places seems preferable: compare how *ymbe* in the *Meters* generally stands for *ymb*. Also in the *Meters*, in *þe he hine eallunga ær* (25.66a) the last word probably should be put into the off-verse, *underþiodde*: compare *a underþeodan* three lines above it, as well as 14.8b and 16.4b; but also compare simple *underþieded* (17.24b). At 16.7b, *siofunga ana* is unreliable because *ana* is emended from the Cottonian manuscript's reading *and*—an unacceptable alteration. Sievers (*Altgerm. Metrik*, §78.4) points

---

[83]John C. Pope offers a persuasive explanation for the scribal error in "The Irregular Anacrusis in *Beowulf* 9 and 402" (see above, p. 59, n. 99).

to *and feowerðe lyft* (20.61b) as an exception, but in fact the normal form is *feorðe*: *feowerðe* is analogical to *feower*.

§240. Some verses on the list ought probably to be omitted. Luick (§306, n. 2) notes that *yldsta* might in fact be old rather than a late West-Saxon innovation—an idea that derives support from Alois Walde's analysis of the structurally parallel syncope in forms like Li. *gehers ðu* (§320 below)—and so *Genesis A* 1134a and *Judith* 10a are ambiguous, as are perhaps *Genesis A* 1055a and *Andreas* 288a. See also above on *Genesis A* 51a (p. 95, n. 3) and *Daniel* 215a (p. 205, n. 70); and compare page 100, note 8 above for Sievers' position. The treatment of *-st-* as if it were a unit phoneme, and thus providing an environment for syncope, at any rate should not be surprising (as Russom remarks, p. 120), since the syllable onset may begin with *s* rather than *t*. The cluster behaves this way, for instance, in the early Middle English shortening of long vowels in closed syllables (Jordan, §23; Luick, §352). *Genesis A* 2176a might be hypermetric, since lines 2167–74 show inconsistent hypermetricity. The verses with *cāsere* < *\*kaisārjaz* show a regular distribution rather like that prescribed by Kaluza's law: just as with the Germanic masculine *i*-stems (the *ja*-stems are uncertain: see Appendix A), the nominative and accusative singular does not make an extra position, while (as with the *ja*-stems) the other cases do. Compare, for example, *þam casere* (*Elene* 70a) and *caseres mæg* (330b).[84]

§241. At *Beowulf* 534a the emendation of Heyne, Bugge, and Trautmann to *eafeþo* makes the variation in the passage more regular:

> Soð ic talige,
> þæt ic merestrengo    maran ahte,
> eafeþo on yþum,    ðonne ænig oþer man. (532b-34)

The use of the plural is paralleled at line 1717a:

> Ðeah þe hine mihtig god    mægenes wynnum,
> eafeþum stepte. (1716a-17a)

Nearly all other instances of inflected *earfoþ-* in verse bear tertiary stress, for example *earfoða dæl* (*Genesis A* 180a) and *earfeða dreag* (*Juliana* 626b; other examples and discussion below, §§258f.). The reading *earfeþo* provides not variation but mere parallelism, under Arthur Brodeur's definition of the terms,[85] while *eafeþo* provides true variation and parallelism. This is not a decisive argument in favor of the emendation, but it is nonetheless a remarkable coincidence that the form that would solve the metrical problem also happens to make a natural variation with

---

[84]The only exceptions, out of nineteen instances, are *fleah casere* (*Meters* 1.20b) and *heah casere* (*Lord's Prayer II* 60b).

[85]*The Art of Beowulf* (Berkeley: Univ. of California Press, 1959), pp. 39ff.

parallelism, certainly a far commoner rhetorical device in *Beowulf* than mere grammatical parallelism. More telling is the semantic difficulty raised by the manuscript reading. In this passage Beowulf is countering the accusation of Unferth that he lost the swimming contest with Breca. Unferth ends his speech with the words that make its point explicit: if Beowulf failed on that earlier occasion,

> Ðonne wene ic to þe   wyrsan geþingea,
> ðeah þu heaðoræsa   gehwær dohte,
> grimre guðe,   gif þu Grendles dearst
> nihtlongne fyrst   nean bidan. (525–28)

What Unferth has called into question is Beowulf's physical ability to withstand Grendel's assault, and so the most appropriate response for Beowulf is to reaffirm his physical prowess. This is in fact his first reaction (after accusing Unferth of drunkenness), as demonstrated by his reference to his *merestrengo* in the first part of the passage in question. The change of topic to *earfeþo* seems something of a counterproductive non sequitur in this context. But more important, to make sense of the word at all requires that its meaning be construed in an unusual way. Klaeber and Dobbie, in retaining the manuscript reading, must understand the word to have a positive sense in this context: Beowulf is clearly boasting of his prowess, and so his claim that he had more *earfeþo* in the water than any other man can only mean that *earfeþo* are something good —presumably a series of trials such as a hero ought to have in order to prove his worth. But elsewhere in verse the word never has this meaning. Usually the meaning is purely negative, as at *Genesis A* 180a, where *earfoða dæl* refers to what Adam did not suffer when God removed his rib. Even in the passage most susceptible to positive interpretation, at *Christ III* 1423b-27, in which Christ explains how he suffered incarnation for the sake of humankind, the word is intended to evoke pity for his sacrifice rather than confidence in his prowess. Thus the word makes some strained sense in the passage in *Beowulf*, but does not represent either the self-confidence expected of Beowulf in this context or the most natural variation on *merestrengo* (533a). Since the substitution of *eafeþo* resolves all these difficulties, and in view of the fact that Bliss is obliged to classify the verse as type 1A\*1a(ii), though no other of the 604 verses of type 1A\* in the poem has a similar dissyllabic expansion, the emendation seems probable.

§242. The two verses in *Beowulf* with *(n)ænigra* are also dubitable, on syntactic grounds. The contexts are these:

> Þæt wæs ungeara   þæt ic ænigra me
> weana ne wende   to widan feore
> bote gebidan. (932–34a)

>               Ne bið þe nænigra gad
> worolde wilna,     þe ic geweald hæbbe.  (949b-50)

Both instances are like Modern English *to have need of any help*, synonymous with *to have any need of help* (though in the former passage there is a slight difference in meaning between the two interpretations, and the context shows that *ænig* really ought to modify *bōte* rather than *wēana*). The preference in Old English verse seems to be for the latter pattern, as in the following:

> Hie þæt ne wiston,     þa hie gewin drugon,
> heardhicgende     hildemecgas,
> ond on healfa gehwone     heawan þohton,
> sawle secan,     þone synscaðan
> ænig ofer eorþan     irenna cyst,
> guðbilla nan,     gretan nolde.  (*Beowulf* 798–803)

>               ah he þara wundra a
> domagende,     dæl nænigne
> frætre þeode     beforan cyðde.  (*Andreas* 569b-71)

> ne þe ænig nedþearf     næs æfre giet
> ealra þara weorca     þe þu geworht hafast.  (*Meters* 20.20–21)

>               nysses þu wean ænigne dæl.  (*Christ III* 1384b)

The point is underscored by the fact that these two verses in *Beowulf* are the only instances of the genitive plural of *(n)ænig* in poetry, and so of course there are no other verses syntactically like these. Then *ænigra* at 932b perhaps ought to be *ænige*, modifying *bōte* (and then the *i* is to be ignored in scansion, as usual), and *nænigra* at 949b should be *nænig*, agreeing with *gād*. In the former instance a scribe would have had a clear reason to change *ænige* to *ænigra*, since the word is far removed from *bōte*, but close to *wēana*, so that a certain amount of confusion results. The same motive does not apply to the second instance, but it should be pointed out that *nænigra* is the product of two emendations, since the manuscript reads *ænigre*. It can at any rate be concluded that the evidence of *Beowulf* 932b and 949b cannot carry much weight.

§243. This leaves only the first of the six verses, *wæs him Beowulfes sið*, as evidence for the loss of tertiary stress in the second thesis of type B in *Beowulf*. The verse seems sound, and so the only reasonable objection is to its uniqueness—not because it is the only instance in *Beowulf* in which a proper name improperly loses its tertiary stress (as well as the only one in which a medial syllable made long by two consonants, rather than by vowel length, loses its stress), since that is the point to be settled, but because it is the only type B verse of its kind (3B2), once the two verses with *(n)ænigra* (above) are eliminated.[86] The point is worth making because the *Beowulf* poet so clearly and frequently does just the opposite, stressing a syllable that ought to lose its tertiary stress, as in *Higelac ongan* (1983b), and all other verses of type 2E1. And the number of counterexamples for personal names is large: there are forty-three instances in *Beowulf* with stress on an etymologically long syllable in this position, as in *Ecglafes bearn* (499b).[87]

§244. But it matters little whether or not these exceptional verses are genuine, because no convincing chronology could be based on a criterion that requires the attribution of so many exceptions to scribal interference, and because it is nonetheless apparent from this list of exceptions that neither Sarrazin's nor Sievers' claim is true: *Beowulf* does not markedly differ from *Genesis A* in its treatment of tertiary stress in this respect, nor do the *Meters of Boethius* differ strikingly from these two.

§245. Rather, the one remarkable fact about the list is the frequency of exceptional verses in the last three poems. The poetry dated from 991 to the end of the Old English period, though it constitutes less than 3 percent of the verses in the test group, accounts for a quarter of the exceptional instances, even when the total includes the verses from earlier poetry that, it was shown above, probably ought to be eliminated. Some of the same metrical peculiarities observable in these poems also characterize other supposedly late compositions, such as *Judgment Day II* and the Psalms of the Paris Psalter. The treatment of ictus at the tertiary level exemplified in classical verse seems to have been in the process of change by the end of the tenth century. This conclusion of course is of no great value as a dating criterion, since the change occurred so late in the period. It does stand as a counterprobability to some of the more extreme proposals about the dating of Old English verse.

G.   The Domain of the Rule of the Coda and
Bliss's Theory of the Caesura

§246. The pattern dictated by the rule of the coda is paralleled by the facts about Kaluza's law. Examination of the data in the preceding chapter reveals that in *Beowulf* resolution under Kaluza's law is restricted almost entirely to the onset of the verse, and nonresolution to the coda. In Bliss's classificatory system there are just two verse types that permit

---

[86]Dobbie reads *Ic on Hygelac wat* (1830b) where Bliss, following Klaeber, retains MS *Hygelace*. The emendation resolves the lack of congruence with *Geata dryhten* (1831a). Dobbie compares *God wat on mec* (2650b). Klaeber justifies the manuscript reading by comparison to *wæs him Beowulfes sið*.

[87]Another twenty-one instances are ambiguous, almost all of them because they are light verses in the on-verse, the exception being *dohtor Hroðgares* (2020b), on which see above, p. 86, n. 45.

nonresolution in the onset: these are 3E3 and 3E*3, with just six examples in *Beowulf*, as opposed to the thirty-seven verses with resolution. In the coda, resolution is found in types 1A2a(ii), 1A2b(ii), 1A*2a(ii) and 2A2(ii), for a total of seven verses, according to Bliss, as opposed to the forty-three verses without resolution. The rule of the coda is apparently a property of verse independent of Kaluza's law, since verses with tertiary stress conform to the rule of the coda, but not Kaluza's law. For example, in the above list of verses like *þreatedon þearle* with a weak verb of the second class in the first foot (p. 205 n. 70), four of the thirteen examples in *Beowulf* bear consonantal endings, though of course *Beowulf* conforms well to Kaluza's law. Similarly, three of the eleven verses with *-scipe* and *-sum-* in the same position have long endings. (On the reason Kaluza's law does not apply to suffixes like *-scipe* and *-sum-*, see below, §262.)

§247. Yet the similarity between the demands of the rule of the coda and the distribution of verses affected by Kaluza's law makes it tempting to speculate whether the domain of the former might not be expanded to include verses containing secondary as well as tertiary stress.[88] Verses like *Suðdena folc* (*Beowulf* 463b) without resolution in the onset are not strong counterevidence to this speculation, since it was demonstrated above that in the test group, deviations from the rule of the coda in the onset are numerous. More significant are verses like *deorc ofer driht-gumum* (1790a), which Bliss would classify as type 1A2b rather than 1D*3(ii) on the basis of his theory of the caesura (see his §45). According to Bliss, the caesura falls before any proclitics preceding the second stressed element of a verse. Thus, when he finds that in all indisputable instances of verses of type D* the caesura falls immediately before the second stress, as in *cealdum cearsiðum* (2396a), while it may fall immediately after the first stress in type 1A, as in *ecg wæs iren* (1459a), the implication is that verses like *deorc ofer drihtgumum* must belong to type A, and therefore must have resolution of the final two syllables. His evidence for the metrical significance of the caesura is statistical: in verses of type A in the on-verse, when the caesura falls immediately before the second lift, as in *lange þrage* (114a), there is double alliteration in fewer than a third of the instances in *Beowulf*; but when there is a proclitic syllable after the caesura, as in *ecg wæs iren* and *eldum swa unnyt* (3168a), 93 percent of the verses take double alliteration (Bliss, §43). These statistics do undoubtedly prove that the caesura, or some larger syntactic or morphological property governing it, has metrical significance. It does not, however, prove that *deorc ofer drihtgumum* must be classified

[88]I had considered and rejected this idea when Thomas Cable convinced me that the matter was worth reconsidering. I am pleased to acknowledge the indebtedness of the remainder of this chapter to our correspondence, and to the current research on syllable counting at the end of the verse that he has kindly shared with me before publication, just as he has so graciously acknowledged the influence of my findings about Kaluza's law on his current theories.

as type A rather than D. Bliss's own statistics show that double alliteration is not quite compulsory in verses like *ecg wæs iren*; in the same way it could well be that the position of the caesura immediately before the second lift, while certainly the norm, is not quite compulsory in type D. Thus the choice whether to privilege resolution or the caesura as the deciding factor in the classification of verses is a subjective one, and the ramifications of the choice should be explored.

§248. One reason the caesura seems necessary is that it explains a restriction on anacrusis in verses of type A. Bliss finds that in *Beowulf* initial anacrusis is permitted, and indeed is relatively frequent, in verses like *swa guman gefrungon* (666b), but that it is disallowed when the caesura falls immediately before the second lift—that is, there are no verses like *\*gemæne wæron*—even though verses of type 2A1a are far commoner than those of type 1A1a. But to say that anacrusis is disallowed in type 2A1a because of the different placement of the caesura is to explain the unknown by the unknown. Rather, Daniel Donoghue has argued that in verses like *swa guman gefrungon* in the off-verse, the first syllable is not anacrustic: *ge-* instead is extrametrical, and the verse belongs to type C rather than A.[89] If Donoghue is right, there is no anacrusis in the off-verse. It can now be added that this idea may explain why verses like *\*gemæne wæron* do not occur, given that the last syllable of the first word cannot be extrametrical.

§249. The chief reason Bliss offers for maintaining the significance of the caesura is that it explains why verses like *\*wīgendes egesan* are disallowed, while those like *æþeling to yppan* are not (Bliss, §43). But it was demonstrated above (§214) that since tertiary stress is required for other reasons, and will account for this regularity as well, the assumption of caesura is not actually necessary. Granting the rule of the coda precedence over the caesura would actually result in few changes in Bliss's analysis of *Beowulf*, since there are few verses that require resolution in the coda under his system. They may be listed:

Type 1A1a(ii):
  Dead is Æschere  (1323b)
  eard ond eorlscipe  (1727a)
  him on ondsware  (1840b)
  lif ond leodscipe  (2751a)
Type 1A1b(ii):
  word wæron wynsume (612a)
Type 1A2a(ii):
  fleon on fenhopu  (764a)
  bær on bearm scipes  (896a)

win of wunderfatum  (1162a)
lond ond leodbyrig  (2471a)
Type 1A2b(ii):
  deorc ofer dryhtgumum  (1790a)
Type 1A*2a(ii)
  wongas ond wicstede  (2462a)
Type 2A2(ii):
  modges merefaran  (502a)
  fyrdsearu fuslicu  (232a)

---

[89]"On the Classification of B-Verses with Anacrusis in *Beowulf* and *Andreas*," *N&Q* 232, n.s. 34 (1987), 1–5. Cable's theory of clashing stress might account for the inserted syllable; but see his *English Alliterative Tradition*, p. 143.

There are also a few verses like *mearcað morhopu* (450a) that Bliss scans as type 1D*3, though they might be analyzed as type 2A2(ii) under his system: see p. 159, n. 15 above. In addition there are twenty-six verses of type 2A1a(ii), all but one being examples of the formula *Beowulf maþelode, Hroðgar maþelode*, and such. The one exception, and the only verse of the type in the off-verse, is *wæpen hafenade* (1573b). These verses were discussed above in Chapter 1 (n. 45), and in this chapter it was pointed out that every other instance of a weak verb of the second class in the coda in *Beowulf* conforms to the rule of the coda (§230). Bliss's reasons for classifying these verses as type A are two: (1) all other verses of type 1D*1 have double alliteration;[90] and (2) granting *maþelode* or *hafenade* three metrical positions would infringe upon Sievers' observation that a single short syllable may not serve as a half-lift immediately after a resolved lift: rather, resolution is required in such an instance. In regard to the latter point, *maþelode* is not necessarily an exception to Sievers' rule, since *maþel-* is etymologically monosyllabic (cf. Gothic *maþl*), and so may show nonparasiting. We in any case have no assurance that the *Beowulf* poet did not actually use the form *gemælde* in each of these instances: with just three exceptions in verse the verb is *maþelode* (*-ade*) rather than *(ge)mælde* in the formula X *maþelode*; and yet outside of this formula the verb is always *(ge)mælan*.[91] This suggests that *(ge)mælan* may have been the verb of preference, and that it was changed by scribes in a common formula. It might also be true that the root of *hafenade* is etymologically monosyllabic, though there are no Norse or Gothic cognates to compare. At any rate an original monosyllable is likelier, since the root is PIE *kəp-, and while the PIE suffix *-no- is common, as here, in the formation of nouns with reduced grade of the root (cf. Gk. ὕπνος, Lat. *fornus*, OIcel. *þorn*, and similar), the variant *-eno-/-ono- is generally reserved in Germanic for the formation of nonfinite verb forms. If *hafen-* is etymologically monosyllabic, there is no obstacle to classifying it as type 1D1, with nonparasiting in *wæpen*. Moreover, regular as Sievers' rule is, there are still quite a few exceptional verses in the test group: for example, *heofoncyninge(s)* forms a verse unto itself at *Genesis A* 1315b, 2918b, and *Exodus* 410b, as well as in some poems outside the test group (see Chap. 8). Exceptions are relatively frequent in *Genesis A* (cf. *þæs þe on woruld cymð* 2321b, *on woruld sunu* 2344a, 2608b, *on woruld cumen* 2365a, *se ðe sigor seleð* 2809a); and in *Beowulf* itself there are the exceptions *gold glitinian* (2758a) and *hord openian* (3056b). Under exceptional circumstances there may be room for doubt, and this is particularly true in regard to *modges merefaran* (*Beowulf*

---

[90]Bliss examines the apparent exceptions in §64.

[91]Cf. *Christ* 797b, 1337b, 1363a, *Genesis* 524b, 2220b, *Guthlac B* 1202b. The formula with *gemælde* appears (beside the one with *maþelode*) in *Genesis B* and *Maldon*. *Mælan* of course derives from the same root as *maþelian*.

502a), where Bliss's assumption of final resolution would be in violation of Kaluza's law, despite the *Beowulf* poet's otherwise careful observance of the law. It is difficult to say which rule should take precedence, and Sievers himself apparently did not consider his own rule so firm, since he classified all examples of the *maþelode* formula as belonging to type D* ("Rhythmik," p. 303). As for classifying verses like *Beowulf maþelode* as type 2A1a(ii) on the basis of its single alliteration, this is no longer an admissible argument, now that Calvin Kendall has shown that compounds with secondary stress normally alliterate in *Beowulf* (see above, §66). This explains why double alliteration is more or less compulsory in all verses of type D except 1D1, and thus also why the appearance of any verse of type D except 1D1 is not to be expected in the off-verse. Since *maþelode* does not bear secondary stress, double alliteration should not be required in verses like *Beowulf maþelode*. Moreover, as remarked above, in the parallel instance Bliss excuses single alliteration in two verses of type 1A*1 in *Maldon*, *Offa gemælde* (230a) and *Leofsunu gemælde* (244a), on the basis of the observation that "it would be unreasonable to restrict the useful verb *gemælde* to proper nouns beginning with *M-*" (§117; and see n. 45 to Chap. 1 above).

§250. Some of the other verses on the list may be eliminated, or at least classified as ambiguous. The last element of *lond ond leodbyrig* (2471a) is etymologically monosyllabic: compare nom. *burh*. Both *win of wunderfatum* (1162a) and *deorc ofer dryhtgumum* (1790a) violate Kaluza's law if scanned as type A; and so, once again, because the *Beowulf* poet is so faithful to the law, it is dubitable whether the placement of the caesura ought to take precedence. In *bær on bearm scipes* (896a) the verb need not be stressed, as it begins a clause, and Bliss finds that when the verb is the only particle in the clause before the first clearly stressed element it may or may not be stressed (§§15–17), though it usually is. As type A the verse would offend against Kaluza's law. In view of the slight evidence that *Beowulf* is a Mercian composition (see §420 below) it is possible that we should read *wynsum* in *word wæron wynsume* (612a), as in VP, where the final *-u* in *-sumu* is missing in the feminine nominative singular and the neuter nominative and accusative plural. (The form *-sume* is late and/or West-Saxon.) There are no other examples of the feminine nominative singular or neuter nominative or accusative plural inflection with *-sum-* in the test group of poems. These eliminations leave just seven verses that undeniably demand final resolution under Bliss's theory of the caesura, a number small enough that the advantage of privileging the caesura over the rule of the coda may be questioned. Most of these seven offer no other obstacle to scansion as type D. There are three exceptions. Two of them, *fleon on fenhopu* (764a) and *wongas ond wicstede* (2462a), would violate Kaluza's law. These should be weighed against the four violations of Kaluza's law that result if Bliss's scansion of all these lines is allowed. But the latter would also be anomalous because in the rare instances in which there are two syllables in the expansion of type D* in *Beowulf*, they are examples of short syllables under tertiary stress, and so subject to the rule of the coda: the two examples in *Beowulf* are *sellice sædracan* (1426a) and *eahtodan eorlscipe* (3173a). The remaining exception, *fyrdsearu fuslicu* (232a), will not scan at all without final resolution, since secondary stress in the expansion of type D* is unknown. It would be necessary to assume some more drastic scribal interference, such as transposition of the two words.

§251. Outside *Beowulf*, the verses *witegena wordcwyde* (*Daniel* 646a) and *wrætlicu wægfaru* (*Exodus* 298a) would violate Kaluza's law if resolution were forbidden in the coda. There is also a group of words with medial resolution violating the rule, for example *cealdum cylegicelum* (*Andreas* 1260a). These are discussed in the next chapter, where it is demonstrated that they are governed by a rule related to Kaluza's law that overrides the rule of the coda.[92] And there are few verses discussed in this chapter whose classification would be affected by the assumption that resolution is not permitted in the coda. From the list of verbs of the second class (§230) there are just four: *eaforan bytlian* (*Genesis A* 2177b), *folc awæcniað* (2293b), *deade gefeormedon* (*Andreas* 1090a), and *fæder getiohhode* (*Meters* 29.37b). These would be unusual, since type D* is not found in the off-verse in *Beowulf*, and in the on-verse it always has double alliteration; but the first two, at least, are perhaps to be explained otherwise (see p. 205, n. 72). At *Daniel* 554a, *yrre and egeslicu* would offend against Sievers' rule that a short half-lift should not follow immediately upon a resolved lift. It would also put two syllables not subject to the rule of the coda into the expansion of type D* (as remarked in the preceding paragraph in regard to *wongas ond wicstede*); and the same may be said about *æte þa unfreme* (*Genesis A* 893a), where *æte* must be stressed under Kuhn's first law. More telling are the three extraordinary verses from *Widsith* discussed in §235, *Wulfhere sohte ic ond Wyrmhere* (119a), *Rædhere sohte ic ond Rondhere* (123a), and *Rumstan ond Gislhere* (123b). As remarked above, the rules of meter may have been attentuated in these instances in order to accommodate so many personal names; and yet what these lines seem to prove is that at least in some instances Anglo-Saxon poets could resolve two syllables at the end of a verse, since it is implausible that these could be scanned any other way.

§252. In the final assessment, then, the rule of the coda cannot be regarded as exceptionless at the end of the verse, since there are a few verses in Old English in which the scop clearly intended resolution on other than primary stress in the coda. Yet some of the verses that Bliss scans as type A might still be better regarded as belonging to type D—especially verses like *Beowulf maþelode*, for the reasons given above.

---

[92]That is, unless the second vowel in *-gicel-* is analogical, as Terasawa supposes (p. 78, n. 33 above). But cf. also §276 below.

Moreover, Bliss's account also produces some unlikely scansions, for example, of *win of wunderfatum* (*Beowulf* 1162a) and *deorc ofer dryht-gumum* (1790a) as type A, though they would then violate Kaluza's law. Thus, neither analysis produces an exceptionless explanation. Yet while the difference between the theoretical implications of the rule of the coda and Bliss's theory of the caesura is important, the practical difference is clearly very small. The verses that might have resolution in the coda without primary stress are not numerous, and the list of them above is most likely liberal: for instance, Sievers himself apparently allowed just two or three such verses in *Beowulf*.[93] The sheer statistics do not allow certainty in choosing between these analyses: either is possible, and neither is statistically improbable.

§253. Rather, the choice between the two must then be based on considerations other than the sheer statistics of Old English verse. When comparative and general theoretical matters are taken into account, the advantages of preferring the rule of the coda to the caesura are clear. The evidence of verse in other early Germanic languages is unambiguous. The rule of the coda is observed with absolute fidelity at the end of the verse in Old Icelandic, and also very well in Old Saxon, even though the comparative laxness of the rules of ictus in Old Saxon might lead one to expect otherwise.[94] By comparison, the caesura is of no metrical significance in Old Icelandic. So although Bliss finds that the caesura must immediately precede the second lift in type D* in Old English, this is not so in Norse: to *dísir suðrœnar* (*Helgakviða Hundingsbana I* 16.4) compare *Seggr inn suðrœni* (*Sigurðarkviða* 4.1) and *Gefa mundu Guðrúno* (56.1). Nor is the caesura relevant in the *Heliand*: to *manno mêndâdi* (1007a)

---

[93]"Rhythmik," p. 280. As remarked above (§249), he regarded examples of the formula with *maþelode* as belonging to type D*. There is some inconsistency in his position, since in his *Altgermansiche Metrik* he still regarded *fyrdsearu fuslicu* (*Beowulf* 232a) as belonging to type A (§80.3a), though there he also concludes that the final thesis of all verses of types A, C, D, and D* is consistently monosyllabic (§82.6).

[94]To the Norse evidence might be raised the objection that all noninitial syllables in stressed words fill a metrical position in eddic verse, according to Sievers (*Altgerm. Metrik*, §38). Thus, conformity to the rule of the coda, at least in the coda itself, is of no significance as evidence. But it was demonstrated above (§236) that verses like *Árliga verðar* and *heitr þú fliótliga fǫr* suggest that Sievers' conclusion is incorrect. Under secondary stress there are no words in Norse like OE *gicela*, with a short medial syllable, since such syllables were always syncopated after a short syllable: cf. cognate OIcel. nom. sg. *jǫkull*, pl. *jǫklar*. And it is demonstrated in the next chapter that in conservative Old English verse, words like *cyningas*, with a long second syllable, are not resolved under secondary stress. Thus it is not surprising that there is no resolution under secondary stress in Old Icelandic. The morphological gap created by the syncope in forms like *jǫklar* produces the result that the only forms in which Sievers' conclusion can be tested are those under tertiary stress. And so it is not difficult to see how Sievers reached the wrong conclusion, and also why infrequent verses like *Árliga verðar* and *heitr þú fliótliga fǫr* are of the first importance in settling the question. If *-liga* may lack ictus in the onset, then it is metrically significant that it never lacks it in the coda.

compare *engil thes alouualdon* (251a) and *hoƀos endi hîuuiski* (3310a). Thus, although the rule of the coda is corroborated in the verse of other early Germanic languages, the caesura is not.

§254. So also the rule of the coda is to be preferred on theoretical and methodological grounds. It can readily be integrated into a general theory of Germanic meter, such as Sievers' and Cable's theories of four-position verses, since it is predicated on the counting of metrical positions, on which these theories are based. The caesura, on the other hand, may have practical but no theoretical value. It is independent of the positional analysis of Old English meter, as it may fall either at the boundary of a metrical position (as in type 1A1a, e.g. *dæges ond nihtes* at *Beowulf* 2269a) or in the middle of the position (as in type 1A*1a, e.g. *sylfe geweorðan* 1996b). The caesura does not in fact seem to corroborate or be corroborated by any other analytic principle in Old English metrics, or to be related in any way to other discoverable features of verse construction. The choice between caesura and the rule of the coda also depends upon the way ictus is defined at the tertiary level. If it correlates to syllable length, then the caesura is an untenable hypothesis. The nature of ictus is examined, and an answer to the question proposed, in the following paragraphs.

## H.  Ictus as Stress or Length

§255. Since before the time of Sievers the general assumption among metrists has been that the primary phonological correlate of ictus in Old English verse is stress. Syllable length plays a contributory role, inasmuch as short full lifts are exceptional; but otherwise the pattern of lifts, half-lifts, and drops in Sievers' five metrical types is determined solely on the basis of stress.[95] Now it appears that syllable length plays a greater role than previously imagined: in the preceding chapter it was demonstrated that the length of endings is essential to determining resolvability under secondary stress in *Beowulf* (Kaluza's law); in this chapter it was shown that whether or not syllables with tertiary stress must bear ictus depends upon syllable length (e.g., the second syllable of *wealdendes* must bear ictus, regardless of its position in the verse, while the second syllable of *wīsode* need not do so, and usually does not, in the onset of the verse); and in the next chapter it will be demonstrated that the resolvability of internal syllables (as in *sæcyningas*) depends upon the length of the second of the resolvable syllables. The construction of Old English verse, which has never seemed simple, thus begins to appear extraordinarily

[95] A minor exception is the assumption that a short half-lift must not immediately follow a resolved lift, though it was demonstrated above that the assumption is subject to exceptions, such as *heofoncyninge* (*Genesis A* 1315b). Bliss argues that a short lift must follow a long syllable (§31), but the usual formulation is that it must follow half-stress.

complex and cumbersome. It strains credibility to suppose that stress and length both played such pervasive roles; and since length now appears to be of particular importance, the question arises whether the role of stress has been overestimated, and ought to be simplified. For example, it might now be argued that it does not matter whether or not there is any phonological stress on the second syllable of *hlāforde*: in the verse *hlaforde leof* (*Meters* 1.47b) the ictus referred to throughout this chapter as "tertiary stress" is determined solely by length. This would be a welcome simplification, since stress alone will not account for the different metrical treatment of *hlāforde* and *wīsode* in this position, while syllable length might.

§256. The greatest obstacle to this revision of metrical theory is the one discussed above (§214): verses like *\*wīgendes egesan* are disallowed, while *Herebeald ond Hæðcyn* (*Beowulf* 2434a) and *æþeling to yppan* (1815a) are not. These suggest that it cannot be syllable length alone that determines ictus in the second position. Unless Bliss's idea of the caesura is appealed to, the only likely conclusion seems to be that *wīgendes* must have metrically significant stress on the second syllable—stress that is missing from the final syllable of *Herebeald* and *æþeling*. Nor can this stress be identical to secondary stress, since the behavior of derivational and lexical morphemes is different, as demonstrated when they are short syllables, at least in *Beowulf*: *þrēatedon þearle* is a normal verse in *Beowulf*, while *\*wordcwidum wealdan* is not. These examples also demonstrate that short syllables under tertiary stress need not bear ictus in the onset (and usually do not), while short syllables under secondary stress must always do so, or at least participate in ictus, if resolved. So also a short derivational morpheme may appear in the expansion of type D\*, as in *eahtodan eorlscipe* (though the type is rare), but not a short lexical morpheme. A difference in the metrical treatment of long derivational and lexical morphemes is also demonstrable, in type D: the type with tertiary stress is common in the off-verse, while the type with secondary stress is rare or nonexistent. In *Beowulf* Bliss finds 220 examples of the former type, and 2 of the latter. The reason for this, again, is that compounds with secondary stress normally alliterate (see above, §66).

§257. Decisive evidence could be derived from words in which a short medial syllable with tertiary stress normally demands ictus in the onset of the verse. In that event it would have to be concluded that tertiary stress may indeed determine ictus independent of syllable length. *Casere* is normally assumed to be such a word, but its evidence was shown above to be ambiguous (§240; and cf. Sievers, *Altgerm. Metrik*, §77, n. 1): in a manner reminiscent of Kaluza's law, the middle syllable bears ictus in the onset only when the inflection is etymologically long. The second syllable of *missēre* is generally assumed to be long.[96] Inflected forms of *sīðfæt*

---

[96]The word derives from *\*mis-jǣr-*, lit. 'half-year', but since the word is exclusively poetic it may contain the poetic or Anglian equivalent *\*-jēr-*. Thus the *e* in the second

appear only in the coda. The decade-forming suffix *-tig-* was shown above to appear in the onset only in *Genesis A* and the *Death of Edgar* (§231), for a total of three instances, violating the rule of the coda in the former, though the comparative evidence shows the vowel to be etymologically short. Shortness is corroborated by late spellings like *þrittega*. This evidence is too meager because of the uncertainties involved: because the East and North Germanic cognates show the suffix as a separate word (Gothic *twai tigjus*, *þrins tiguns*, OIcel. *þrír tigir*, etc.), possibly the suffix is semi-lexical and carried secondary stress in early verse; the point cannot be determined by the vocalism, since both stressed and unstressed *i* remain before *g* (see below, §261).[97] If this is the case, the difference in metrical treatment between *Genesis A* and the Chronicle poem may be due to the metrical change evidenced in the latter.

§258. But there does appear to be one word that satisfies the requirements: inflected forms of *earfoþ* nearly always fill three metrical positions in the onset of the verse. All the examples in verse may be listed:

> earfoða dæl  (*Genesis A* 180a)
> earfeþu swa some  (*Christ III* 1272b)
> forðon ic þæt earfeþe wonn  (*Christ III* 1427b)
> earfeþa mæst  (*Guthlac A* 207a)
> earfeða dreag  (*Juliana* 626b)
> earfeþa gemyndig  (*Wanderer* 6b)
> sumum earfeþa dæl  (*Fortunes of Men* 67b)
> earfoþa dreag  (*Deor* 2b)
> earfoða dæl  (*Deor* 30b, emended from *earfoda*)
> earfoþa fela  (*Wife's Lament* 39a)
> earfeþo on yþum  (*Beowulf* 534a)
> earfoðes feala  (*Psalms* 70.19.1b)

The alternation between *e* and *o* in the medial syllable could be due to a number of causes, including analogical extension of nom. *-eþ* < *-æþ* into the inflected cases, vowel harmony, and suffix confusion (Campbell, §§356, 386, 648.4). Whichever of these explanations is correct, the medial vowel ought originally to have been *o* < *ā* < *ai* (cf. Gothic *arbaiþs*). The middle syllable bears ictus in all but the three verses from the *Wanderer*, the *Fortunes of Men*, and *Beowulf*. (The verse at *Christ III* 1427b is hypermetric.) The last of these exceptions is dubitable on both stylistic and semantic grounds, as explained above (§241). The remaining verses appear to indicate that a short syllable under tertiary stress may regularly bear ictus, and therefore stress rather than length is the determinant of ictus.

---

syllable may represent either a long or a short vowel. The vocalism of the alternant *missār-* is obscure: Sisam (*Studies*, p. 43n) suggests Latin influence. The metrical treatment of the second syllable is always long (as above, §222).

[97] Another source of uncertainty is that *-tiges* may stand for *-tigra*.

§259. Yet not all of these obstacles are as insuperable as they seem. In regard to verses like *earfoða dæl* there is the possibility that the second syllable was actually long. The grammarians tell us that the shortening of long vowels in medial syllables took place in the prehistoric period (Luick, §350; Campbell, §394). Yet it is also clear that the monophthongization and shortening of WGmc. *ai* took place in at least three stages in Old English. If the diphthong lost stress early it developed to *æ*, whence OE *e*; if later, it developed to *ā*, whence OE *o*. Thus, since tertiary stress was retained longer in middle syllables than final, the result is nom. *earfeþ*, but inflected *earfoþ-* (Campbell, §356). Still later this same *ā* remains unreduced in inflected forms of the suffixes *-hād-* and *-lāc-*, and personal names like *Hrōðgār-*, but is shortened to *a* in uninflected *-had*, *-lac*, and *Hrōðgar*, according to the standard view. Yet this last shortening perhaps had not taken place when *Beowulf* was composed, since the verses *Hroðgar geseon* (396b) and *Higelac ongan* (1983b) are among those like *uppriht astod* (2092b) that receive unexpected ictus on the second syllable (§210 above). The second syllable of inflected *earfoþ-* thus occupies a middle position in the chronology of these changes, between changes attributable to the prehistoric and historical periods. Dating the change precisely is difficult, but *eofot* < *\*eƀ-hait-* takes the form *ebhat-* in Ép. and Erf., suggesting that the shortening was not prehistoric.[98] In that event the vowel may have been long when the earlier poems were composed—as apparently assumed by Sarrazin (see §184 above)—or the scansion of the word might have been preserved as an archaism.[99] But the word is too sparsely attested in verse to serve as a dating criterion.

§260. If in fact the second syllable of inflected *earfoð-* was long at the time these poems were composed, or the scansion antiquated, there is no good evidence that any short syllable under tertiary stress normally bears ictus in the onset of the verse. This suggests that there is something defective about our definition of tertiary stress. According to the assumptions about tertiary stress outlined by Campbell (§185 above), half-stress falls on all medial syllables (except those like the second syllable of *rūmedlīce*). From this it may be concluded that any medial syllable without secondary stress has tertiary stress. But this definition is based ultimately on Sievers' findings about the treatment of medial syllables in verse (*Altgerm. Metrik*, §78), and so the definition must be changed or the reasoning will be circular, now that short syllables in the onset have been shown not to require ictus. At this point it would appear that a new definition should state that any *long* medial syllable without secondary

[98]The later *Corpus Glossary* has *eobot-*. But note that in the later Northumbrian texts the stem *ebals-* appears beside *ebols-* < *\*eƀ-hāls-*. For other examples of medial *ā* < *ai* see Brunner, §43, n. 4.

[99]The latter point of view is advocated by Philip E. Webber, "Preliterate Formulaic Patterns Suggested by Old English *earfoðe*," *Michigan Germanic Studies* 9.2 (1983), 109–12.

stress has tertiary stress. But if the definition is actually predicated on syllable length, stress becomes a secondary and dispensable factor, for which the verse provides no direct evidence.

§261. Rather, it becomes clear now that the most fundamental flaw in the definition of tertiary stress is that it is based on meter rather than phonology. If tertiary stress exists, it cannot be verified in verse, and at any rate ought not to be, since it is circular reasoning to equate ictus with stress on this basis. Instead, to justify the assumption of its existence there must be evidence in the phonology of Old English. But when we turn to the phonology, though it does lend some support to the concept, the distribution it suggests is different from the distribution of metrical ictus at the tertiary level. The phonological evidence does corroborate the necessary change in the definition of tertiary stress mentioned above, since it shows that there was no tertiary stress on short medial syllables. It was pointed out above (§196) that the existence of tertiary stress at the phonological level is undeniable, since otherwise the vocalism of suffixes like -dōm, -fæst, -lēas, and -hād could not be explained: if unstressed, these would have developed to *-dam, *-fest, *-las, and *-hod. But these are all long syllables. When short syllables with tertiary stress are taken into consideration, the vowel qualities also seem to be preserved as if under stress; but in fact wherever those qualities are preserved, their retention is attributable to the influence of adjoining consonants. Thus the flanking palatal consonants prevent the lowering of i in -scipe, -lic-, and (since it receives ictus in late verse, and thus may be considered here) -ig-. That these vowels had actually lost stress, however, is demonstrated by the fact that -lic- and -ig- may appear as -lec- (or -luc-) and -eg- when a back vowel follows.[100] In the present stem of weak verbs of the second class, -i- stands for -ig-, i.e. [ij], and is sometimes so written.[101] Thus the palatal glide prevents the lowering of i. So also -sum does not become *-som because u is preserved before m in unstressed as in stressed syllables, as in fultum, wæstum, māþum, dat. pl. -um (not *fultom, etc.: Campbell, §373). If so many of these short suffixes had not preserved their vowel qualities by this means it would perhaps

---

[100]The lowering does not take place in -scipum because the palatal consonant precedes i, and thus is unaffected by the back vowel. In -licum and -igum, on the other hand, the normally palatal consonants are velarized (Campbell, §§426–43), and thus exert no raising influence on the preceding vowel. The suffix -scipe is perhaps from *-skipi rather than *-skapi (Brunner, §105, n. 1).

[101]Presumably the reason the adjective suffix -ig- is consistently written with g, but the verb suffix only occasionally (in West Saxon), is that in the former, g stands for both a palatal glide and a velar fricative, while in the latter it can only be a glide. The velar fricative is phonemic, while the glide is not: the allophone of /i/ before a vowel in Old English is [ij]. Although allophonic variation need not be regularly recorded in a language (hence the facultative status of -ig- in verbs), the fricative must be written because it is a phoneme; and because Old English orthography tolerates very little paradigm allomorphy, the glide is also regularly recorded in the adjective paradigm.

have been obvious from the beginning that our definition of tertiary stress is inadequate. These short suffixes do not in fact carry any phonological stress, as is apparent in the case of the two separable suffixes that do not contain consonants that affect the quality of the vowel: they are *-(n)oþ* /-(n)aþ*, as in *fisc(n)oþ, hunt(n)oþ*, and such, and the preterite marker *-od-/-ad-* in weak verbs of the second class.[102] The former does not appear in inflected form in the onset anywhere in verse. Both suffixes have clearly undergone shortening, from *\*-nāþ* (cf. OHG *-nand*) and *-ud* /-ōd-*, and so it is equally clear that they lack stress.

§262. In a stress-based prosodic system it is conceivable that a syllable should lack phonological stress and still bear ictus. For example, it would hardly be reasonable to conclude on the basis of the iambic verse *Swa lufede þe Laferrd Godd* (*Ormulum* 16712) that the final syllable of *lufede* normally had phonological stress. But such verses are exceptional because they are jarring, and it is difficult to imagine a stress-based meter that *regularly* assigned ictus to unstressed syllables. That short syllables like *-lic-* and *-od-* are phonologically unstressed, then, and yet bear ictus in the coda of the verse, tells against the supposition that ictus in the coda has anything to do with stress. The rule governing ictus in the coda of the verse, that is, the rule of the coda, in fact makes no reference to stress below the level of primary stress: the rule is simply that every syllable after the last full lift in the verse must bear ictus—regardless of length or stress. And of course since these short syllables normally bear no ictus in the onset—and thus stress plays no role in their treatment in the onset, either—there is neither a phonological basis nor a metrical one for assigning any sort of stress at all to such short syllables, anywhere in the verse. This explains why Kaluza's law does not apply to syllables under tertiary stress: although some long syllables bear tertiary stress, no short one does; and since stress is a prerequisite for resolution (cf. the discussion below of the different definitions of length in stressed and unstressed syllables, n. 104), there are no relevant short syllables.

§263. Since short syllables cannot bear phonological stress at the tertiary level, it would seem to follow that tertiary stress and syllable length in medial position are identical, and that stress is a superfluous feature for which length may be substituted. But in actuality the two are not identical, since *-dōm-, -fæst-*, and the like, are not the only syllables below the level of secondary stress that bear ictus in the onset. There are also several closed syllables that do not bear phonological stress, since they have the vocalism of unstressed syllables. The three commonest in verse are participial *-end-* < *\*-andj-*, the suffix *-ing-* (at least outside proper names: see p. 189, n. 35 above), and superlative *-est-/-ost-* < *-ist-/-ust-*. Only the last of these is definitive, since the development of the vocalism in *-end-* and *-ing-* would be identical in fully stressed syllables.

---

[102]So also participial *-en-* < *-æn-*, *-in-*, since it gains ictus occasionally in late verse.

Less common but with clearly unstressed vocalism are *-erne* (e.g. *sūperne*, as in *superne gar* at *Maldon* 134b: cf. OIcel. *suðrœnn* < \**-rōni*) *-els* < *-isl-* (e.g., to *fǣtels* cf. OS *dōpisli* 'baptism'), and *-ness* < *-nass-*, *-nissi*, *-nussi*. Despite the phonological ambiguity, it is clear that *-end-* and *-ing-* belong with this group rather than with *-dōm-* and *-fǣst-*, since the latter are semi-lexical morphemes: they carry a significant degree of semantic integrity, less than that of the purely lexical morphemes that form the second elements of compounds with secondary stress, but greater than the mainly grammatical and classificatory significance of purely derivational suffixes. Yet these long derivational suffixes consistently bear ictus when medial, even though they lack phonological stress. It follows that the decisive factor in assigning ictus below the level of secondary stress is not phonological stress but syllable length.[103]

§264. And so to return to the counterevidence presented above (§256), there must be some explanation other than stress to account for the fact that *Herebeald ond Hæðcyn* and *æþeling to yppan* are acceptable verses in *Beowulf*, while \**wīgendes egesan* is not. Bliss's theory of caesura will account for the difference, but there is perhaps another explanation. Verses like *æþeling to yppan*, with a long syllable in the position of *-ing*, are actually remarkably rare in *Beowulf*. Aside from a few verses beginning with a personal name, of the type *Herebeald ond Hæðcyn*, the only other example is *æþeling on elne* (2506a).[104] The rarity of the type is

---

[103]Doubtless the pattern of stress that Campbell describes, with half-stress on all long medial syllables, did apply to a particular class of words in Old English. This assumption is required, for instance, in order to account for the preservation of stressed vocalism in, e.g., *Æþelgār*, but not in WS *Cūðferþ*—both show leveling in the paradigm. This situation is paralleled in Old Norse, where the names *Óláfr* and *Þorlákr* take the datives *Óleife* and *Þorleike*: see Adolf Noreen, *Altnordische Grammatik I: Altisländische und altnorwegische Grammatik*, 5th ed., unrev. (Tübingen: Niemeyer, 1970), §54.3b. But names and semi-lexical morphemes like *-dōm-* certainly retained a degree of semantic integrity, and thus stress, longer than mere suffixes like *-end-* and *-els-*: the former still contain long vowels in the *Ormulum*, while there is no evidence for stress on the latter sort of suffix in Old English, and a great deal of evidence for lack of stress.

[104]It is an anomaly of most metrical analyses of Old English that syllable length is defined differently in stressed and unstressed syllables. For example, both Sievers and Bliss regard the second syllable of *Hreðel cyning* (*Beowulf* 2430b) as short (see above, §207), while under primary stress the word *scip* is a long syllable regardless of its position in the verse, and regardless of what follows it. But the discrepancy is not phonologically improbable. Comparison with Modern Icelandic is instructive. There vowels are long in open and short in closed syllables, so that the vowel in, for example, the adjective stem *fljót-* 'rapid' is long in most forms (masc. nom. *fljótur*, fem. *fljót*), and short when an inflection beginning with a consonant follows (neut. *fljótt*). But it is not shortened when a word beginning with a consonant follows (e.g. *fljót þyrla* 'a fast helicopter'), nor even when mere juncture above the inflectional level intervenes (e.g. *fljótlega* 'quickly'). So, too, the treatment of vowel length is not identical in stressed and unstressed syllables. Within the sentence, vowels in unstressed syllables are shortened, and may even be elided when another vowel follows. Long consonants, on the other hand, as in the ending *-inn*, tend to retain their length. In Old English it is not

remarkable, considering that there are 547 verses of type 1A\*1a in *Beowulf*, according to Bliss—nearly 10 percent of the verses in the poem —and considering how many words there are in *Beowulf* like *æþeling*, with a long, unstressed final syllable, such as *hlāford*, *brenting*, adjectives in *-isc* like *eotonisc*, superlatives like *ǣrest* and *mǣrost*, and agentives like *wīgend* and *Waldend*. This evidence is not conclusive, but it does tend to support the overall point.[105] If a long syllable is disfavored in this position, it is not surprising that most of the exceptions are personal names, given that the *Widsith* poet seems also to have allowed unusual verse types for the sake of fitting personal names into his verse (§235 above), and the *Beowulf* poet himself, along with other Old English poets, allows verses like *Beowulf maþelode* in the off-verse (§249 above). That such rare verses as *æþeling on elne* are found at all should also be judged in light of the fact that secondary stress finds its way into the same position on an exceptional basis, as in *gealorand to guþe* (*Beowulf* 438a), *gamolfeax ond guðrof* (608a), and *wreoþenhilt ond wyrmfah* (1698a). For examples in other poems see Sievers, *Altgerm. Metrik*, §85.2 and n. 1.

§265. Further evidence for the primacy of syllable length in the determination of ictus at the tertiary level may be derived from Cable's observation that verses like *hlyn swynsode* (611b), ending in a verb of the second weak class, are confined to the off-verse in *Beowulf* (*English Alliterative Tradition*, p. 145). By comparison, verses like *leod Scyldinga* (1653a) may occur in either half of the line. The reason for the restriction

surprising, then, that in unstressed syllables, where the articulation is similarly less distinct, it should also require two syllable-final consonants to establish length, but not in stressed syllables.

[105]There is still room for some doubt on this score. If length rather than stress is the primary correlate of ictus at the tertiary level, one might expect heavy syllables to be avoided in a position in which secondary stress is also avoided. So, for example, heavy syllables are indeed infrequent in the second thesis of verses of type B and the drop of type E. In Bliss's type 3B1b in *Beowulf*, the most frequent exceptions involve personal names, e.g. in *Þonan Biowulf com* (2359b; cf. Sievers, *Altgerm. Metrik*, §81). Perhaps verses like *se ðær lengest hwearf* (2238b) ought also to be excluded, given, once again, the ambiguous nature of the *st* cluster. This leaves just six exceptions in 358 verses. Yet long syllables also seem to be infrequent in some positions in which secondary stress is not avoided. For example, heavy syllables are perhaps commoner in the first thesis of Bliss's type 2A1a in *Beowulf*, but they are still remarkably infrequent. This evidence is then inconclusive, though avoidance of heavy syllables in the second thesis of type B in classical verse still seems probable, given the frequency with which this general pattern is violated in some late and metrically inferior verse: see below, §307. Verses like *hêleand the gôdo* (*Heliand* 4032a) and *uualdand fan themu uuîhe* (4271a) are commoner in Old Saxon, but so also are those like *godspell that guoda* (25a) and *craftigaro kunnio* (4217a). Another source of doubt is the observation (§210 above) that the second metrical position in verses like *dreamleas gebad* (*Beowulf* 1720b) is generally occupied by a lexical morpheme. Yet there are exceptions, e.g. *Hengest þa gyt* (1127b) and *Nægling forbærst* (2680b); and derivational morphemes in this position are particularly frequent in Norse and Old Saxon (see the examples in §210 above).

is not obvious, though the situation is perhaps comparable to that in Middle English alliterative verse, where, as Cable points out (p. 86), the off-verse is consistently lighter than the on-verse. Whatever the reason, in this instance syllable length at the tertiary level clearly affects the distribution of verse types.

§266. In sum, it must be concluded that the ictus associated with tertiary stress is not stress-related at all, but is predicated on syllable length. This is not to say that stress is irrelevant to the construction of Old English verse. Clearly, primary stress is of the first importance in determining the position of lifts, and secondary stress is also still relevant, since short syllables with secondary stress bear (or participate in) ictus in the onset, while short syllables with "tertiary stress" normally do not. Secondary stress is also significant because verses like *flod fæðmian* (1D1) appear 220 times in the off-verse in *Beowulf*, while there are just 2 examples with secondary stress in the off-verse, *feond mancynnes* (164b) and *hroden ealowæge* (495b). So, also, Kaluza's law applies under secondary but not tertiary stress. This conclusion does not reduce the number of levels of phonological stress required in Old English, since tertiary stress is still required on suffixes like *-dōm* and *-lēas*, and this stress must still be distinguished from secondary stress, which is not lost finally. But at the metrical level it appears to be possible to simplify the description and reduce the number of levels of stress required, perhaps even to two—that is, stress and no stress—since ictus at the tertiary level apparently amounts to syllable length, and secondary stress can be distinguished from primary on a purely positional basis: it is any full stress that immediately follows another full stress.[106] Therefore it need not be phonologically any different from primary stress. Reducing the requisite number of levels of stress to two is perhaps preferable, since Thomas Cable has pointed out that acoustic experiments designed by Philip Lieberman demonstrate that subjects are able to make only binary distinctions between levels of stress.[107] This is not to say that prosodic

---

[106]This definition will seem an oversimplification in view of the Sieversian analysis of, for example, *gomen gleobeames* (*Beowulf* 2263a) as containing two full lifts and one half-lift. Rather, under Cable's interpretation of Sievers' five types we should understand the verse to contain four metrical positions of descending prominence, with three stresses. Though phonologically the stress on *glēo-* might be equal to that on *gomen*, metrically its ictus is inferior. The point is demonstrated in the next chapter, where it is shown that verses like *fyll cyninges* (*Beowulf* 2912b) are metrically correct, since resolution is forbidden in this position. Thus, although the first syllable of *cyninges* receives stress that we call primary, its metrical treatment is what we should call secondary, since short syllables in Sievers' analysis may serve as lifts under secondary stress, but not primary. The terms *primary* and *secondary* as applied to stress are convenient, but the distinction seems to have little to do with metrical realities.

[107]*Meter and Melody*, pp. 96–99; Lieberman (as above, p. 189, n. 36), pp. 144–47. More recently Cable has depreciated the significance of Lieberman's findings: see his "Old and Middle English Prosody: Transformations of the Model," in *Hermeneutics and*

systems in natural languages do not recognize more than two levels of stress. Intuition tells otherwise: to take an example familiar to metrical phonologists, few would deny that there must be at least three levels of stress (including nonstress) in the phrase "law degree requirement changes." Regardless of the physiological facts, at least psychologically *law* has greater prominence than the second syllable of *degree*; but then the second syllable of *degree* must have greater prominence than the first, as one syllable preserves vowel quality and the other (at least in rapid speech) does not. Or, to take another familiar example, *gymnast* and *modest* both bear stress on the first syllable, yet the second syllables of the words do not receive the same degree of stress.[108] Current phonological theory accounts for the seemingly multivalued hierarchy of stress in many prosodic systems with the construction of metrical trees, which are predicated on the assumption that stress is constituted as a binary distinction between strong and weak nodes, but that each node dominates one or more subdistinctions, which are also binary. Thus, three or four levels of psychological prominence in Old English may be derived from two levels of physiological stress, and the binary nature of stress recognition may be preserved.[109] But such distinctions can only have been extraordinarily fine, and this is the primary consideration that has prompted Cable recently to abandon the concept of metrical contours.[110]

---

*Medieval Culture*, ed. Patrick J. Gallacher and Helen Damico (Albany: State Univ. of New York Press, 1989), pp. 201–11, at 203. And indeed, metrical phonologists feel unconstrained by Lieberman's findings, as demonstrated by the studies cited in the following notes. But since Cable remarks there that a metrical system with intermediate ictus would be unique not just in Germanic, but in Western verse forms, Lieberman's experiments explain the absence of a parallel.

[108]Conversely, Christopher McCully argues that four peaks of stress in an utterance must have different degrees of intensity, and yet may be perceived as accentually identical: see "On Old English Verse Rhythm: A Reply," *ES* 65 (1984), 385–91. The first example derives from M. Liberman and A. Prince, "On Stress and Linguistic Rhythm," *Linguistic Inquiry* 8 (1977), 249–336, a study influencing much subsequent work in metrical phonology. For the second see Richard Hogg and C. B. McCully, *Metrical Phonology: A Coursebook* (Cambridge: Cambridge Univ. Press, 1987), chap. 3.

[109]The current alternative to tree structures is metrical grids: for references, and a demonstration that the differences between trees and grids are not as profound as they seem, see B. Elan Dresher's review of M. Halle and J.-R. Vergnaud, *An Essay on Stress*, in *Phonology* 7 (1989), 171–88. Tree structures with binary nodes are the basis for Russom's approach to Old English meter; and see also B. Elan Dresher and Aditi Lahiri, "The Germanic Foot: Metrical Coherence in Old English," *Linguistic Inquiry* 22 (1991), 251–86. On the status of stress on suffixes like -*dōm* and -*lēas* in a binary system, see above, p. 189, n. 36.

[110]Professor Cable confirmed this reason for departing from his earlier position, in the discussion following his paper "Why Rhythm is More Basic than Melody in Old English Meter," at the 1991 Congress on Medieval Studies in Kalamazoo. This paper will be published under the title "Type D Verses as Evidence for the Rhythmic Basis of Old English Meter." See also his *English Alliterative Tradition*, pp. 37–40.

Still, because these metrical contours are so useful, and provide a convenient means of conceptualizing verses like *fyll cyninges* (see below, §275), the correlation of ictus and syllable length at the tertiary level might be invoked to resolve the difficulty.

§267. It should also be apparent now why the structure of early Germanic verse has always seemed so arcane to students of the literature that frequently nonlinguists have doubted even the most basic of Sievers' conclusions about what constitutes an acceptable metrical pattern. Modern English stress patterns do not seem different enough from Old English ones that a stress-based metrical system should be so difficult for the uninitiated to grasp. If early Germanic meter is predicated primarily on syllable length, however, it ought to seem unfamiliar to speakers of modern Germanic languages, since all Germanic languages have undergone standardization of vowel quantities since the early medieval period —that is, long vowels have been shortened in closed syllables, and short vowels lengthened in open syllables. Modern English makes a particularly bad comparison to Old English on this basis, because after the standardization of quantities, vowel length was eventually lost altogether, and then was reintroduced as an allophonic property governed by the voiced or voiceless quality of postvocalic consonants. The closest parallel among the modern Germanic languages to the situation in Old English is Danish, in which vowel quantities have been in part re-phonemicized by the simplification of medial geminates. But that simplification itself reduced the extent of syllable length oppositions in unstressed syllables, and in general a word may contain no more than one long vowel, so that the parallel with Old English holds true only for syllables bearing primary stress. Even there the analogy is only partial, since Danish has no long vowels in closed syllables.

§268. To summarize: The standard view on half-stress in Old English, as represented by Campbell (see §185 above), cannot be correct, in view of the regularity that the short medial syllable in a word such as *weardode* receives different metrical treatment in the onset and the coda of the verse, as dictated by the rule of the coda. The rule is predicated on syllable length rather than stress, since long syllables with tertiary stress, as in *winnende*, do not conform to the rule. It appears, then, to be possible to say that ictus at the tertiary level has nothing to do with stress, but with syllable length only. The small amount of counterevidence to this conclusion, in the form of verses such as *earfoða dreag* and *æþeling to yppan*, perhaps can be explained otherwise. This conclusion is clearly supported by the evidence of phonology, which shows that the second syllable of *weardode* (and *gyrdelse*) must be unstressed regardless of where it appears in the verse; and the standard analysis of half-stress must be wrong, since it is based on the evidence of metrical ictus rather than phonology, thereby employing circular reasoning. The role of stress then looks severely diminished, because although it is required to form a lift, it does not define ictus at every level, while length does, being required at the primary level to form a lift, at the secondary level to determine resolvability, and at the tertiary level as a prerequisite to ictus. Accordingly, Old English prosody looks closer to classical and Indo-European models than was formerly suspected.

## I.  Summary of Chronological Findings

§269. To summarize the evidence of this chapter in regard to the dating of verse: (1) The adjective suffix -ig-, when an inflection is added, forms a syllable almost exclusively in verse attributed to Alfred's reign and later (§§215ff.). The distribution of this feature is perhaps partially dialectal, but it is certainly also only a late development. (2) The adjective suffix -lic- can be either long or short in verse presumably composed before the ninth century, but from that time on it is always long (§§221ff.). The reason is that in the course of the Old English period, variation between the long and short forms was eliminated, the long form being extended analogically into all positions. The development of -lic- to -lec- or -luc-, which must antedate the analogical replacement by -līc-, also appears to be a sign that a poem has been transmitted in a manuscript tradition dating at least to the Alfredian period (§225). (3) In the *Death of Edward* and *Maldon* the adverb suffix -līce almost certainly still has a long vowel, but in these poems it sometimes loses ictus (§227). Apparently, then, the rules governing the assignment of ictus were undergoing change in the last quarter of the tenth century, and this assumption is corroborated by the occasional loss of ictus from the long second elements of inflected personal names in *Maldon* and *Durham*, as well as by the multitude of verses like *operne bylde* in the last poems of the test group (§245). The adjective suffixes -ig- and -lic- are unlike other short medial syllables, such as the preterite suffix -od- in weak verbs of the second class, and they suggest chronological development while those others do not, because they reflect the effects of analogical developments: -ig- replaced nonsyllabic medial -g- in the course of the Old English period, and short -lic- was replaced by -līc-, by analogy to forms in which the suffix remained stressed and long, such as *bismerlīcum*. Changes in the treatment of these syllables in verse thus record the progress of analogical, not phonological, developments. Syllables like -od- suffered no analogical process after the prehistoric period, and show no clear pattern of development in their metrical treatment. They generally conform to the rule of the coda, but there are exceptions in verse throughout the period. All syllables subject to the rule of the coda are the result of either analogical processes or reduction of stress in the historical period, since short unstressed vowels in the relevant position should all have been syncopated before the beginning of the Old English period.

§270. The combination of these three criteria suggests a broad chronology: (1) an early group comprising *Genesis A, Daniel, Beowulf,* and *Exodus* (with insufficient evidence in the three short Northumbrian poems), characterized by both long and short treatment of the adjective suffix *-lic-*; (2) a second group comprising Cynewulf's signed poems and *Andreas,* which, though not demonstrably like the first group in regard to treatment of *-lic-,* is also without metrical restoration of the adjective suffix *-g-* to *-ig-,* with just one possible exception (though dialect origins might also play a role here); (3) a third group including Alfred's verse and *Judith,* with frequently syllabic *-ig-* and consistently ictus-bearing *-lic-*; and (4) a final group comprising all the externally datable verse from the last quarter of the tenth century and later, characterized by various signs of change in the rules for the assignment of ictus at the tertiary level.

# VIII

# ICTUS AND RESOLUTION
# IN NONFINAL POSITION

§271. The preceding two chapters confined their scope to word-final position. But resolution and the assignment of ictus are not haphazard in other positions, at least in presumably early verse. First a distinction must be drawn between two types of structures, those in which the second of the resolvable syllables is short (e.g. the third syllable of *wīgheafolan*) and those in which it is long (e.g. the third syllable of *sǣcyningas*). In regard to the former type, as in Chapter 6, forms with parasite vowels must be distinguished from those with etymological vowels: for example, *-gicel* is of the latter type, being cognate with OIcel. *jǫkull*, while *feðer, leðer,* and *fugol* have parasite vowels, as demonstrated by comparison with OIcel. *fjǫðr, leðr,* and *fugl.* Thus, words like *feðer* are irrelevant to resolution, and must always be scanned as monosyllables.

§272. In the *wīgheafolan* type, resolution always applies in the test group of poems, and this is true in both light and normal verses. Examples are *sǣfaroða sand* (*Daniel* 322a), *cealdum cylegicelum* (*Andreas* 1260a), and *under heahrodore* (*Genesis A* 151a). Among the seventy-five examples in the test group there is just one exceptional verse, *weoruld-welena* (*Meters of Boethius* 19.26a).[1] The exception is significant, though many of the verses that conform to the rule are not, as they perhaps ought to be scanned as if with syncope, for example *cealdum cylegiclum*

---

[1] The relevant verses are as follows: *Genesis A* 151a, 1311a, 1620b, 1948b, 2117a, 2411b, 2493a; *Daniel* 321b, 322a; *Beowulf* 468b, 744a, 911a, 1260a, 1308b, 1389a, 2583b, 2650a, 2661b, 2708a, 2780b, 2908b, 2917b, 2921b; *Exodus* 121b, 128b, 134a, 167b, 195b, 251b, 329b, 357a, 361b, 425b, 447b, 478b; *Elene* 64b, 113b, 170a, 251a, 461a, 564a, 878a, 981b; *Fates of the Apostles* 100a; *Juliana* 322a, 437a, 514b, 544b; *Christ II* 731a, 833b; *Andreas* 197a, 289a, 351a, 375b, 435b, 586b, 728b, 791a, 799b, 875a, 1260a, 1298a, 1650b; *Meters of Boethius* 7.36a, 7.47a, 13.17a, 16.6a, 17.15a, 17.21a, 19.21b, 19.26a, 25.23a; *Judith* 39a, 180b, 315b. This list is not very exclusive, including some dubitable and emended forms. It includes forms with the prefix *un-*, since the example of *uncuð gelad* in *Beowulf* (see above, §§210, 234) suggests that elements after *un-* might take secondary rather than tertiary stress on occasion. Also included are forms like *-mægen-*, which might show parasiting, and *-egsa*, since the syncope here may be simply orthographic: see Campbell, §§388–89. On the other hand, in a verse like *þæt hio leod-bealewa* (*Beowulf* 1946a) the last *e* is clearly excrescent; and many verses, such as *cealdum cylegicelum*, might also contain excrescent vowels: see below, §276. Such dubitable cases are included because the uncertainties are such that it is impossible to construct a reliable list of relevant examples, and because the point is to demonstrate that there are practically no exceptions to the rule.

(see n. 1). On the other hand, resolution in the *sǣcyningas* type ought always to be significant, since syncope does not occur in such words until the end of the Old English period (see below, §276). These are unlike the *wīgheafolan* type, as they usually, though not consistently, remain metrically unresolved. The following are the unambiguous instances in the test group of poems:[2]

*Genesis A*
124a  heahcininges hæs
1060a  sweordberende
1100a  soðcyninges
1145a  sædberendes
1315b  heofoncyninge
1955a  feorhberendra
1965a  þeodcyningas
1974b  folccyningas
2041a  æscberendra
2074b  folccyningas
2337a  woruldcyningas
2754a  folccyninge
2884a  gastcyninge
2918b  heofoncyninges
*Daniel*
305a  eorðcyninga
*Beowulf*
2a      þeodcyninga
372b, 535b  cnihtwesende
1039b  heahcyninges
1155b  eorðcyninges
1187a  umborwesendum ær

1684b  woroldcyninga
2382b  sæcyninga
2503b  Frescyninge
2694b  þeodcyninges
3180b  wyruldcyninga
*Exodus*
231a  garberendra

373a  mismicelra
392b  eorðcyninga
410b  heofoncyninge
*Elene*
170b  þæt hit heofoncyninges
219a  æðelcyninges rod
367a  hu ge heofoncyninge
624b  radorcyninges
747b  heofoncininges lof
886b  rodorcyninges beam
1173b  eorðcyninga
1282a  reordberendra
*Fates of the Apostles*
18b  ðeodcyninges
*Juliana*
360b  þæt þu heofoncyninge
447a  rodorcyninges giefe
*Christ II*
727a  rodorcyninges ræs
*Andreas*
92b      heofoncyninges stefn
723b, 998b  heofoncyninges þrym
821b  heofoncyninge neh
1381b  heofoncyninges word
1679a  æþelcyninges ar
*Meters of Boethius*
9.47a  *hu he eorðcyningas*
22.32b  *oforgiotolnesse*
*Death of Edward*
34b      þæs þeodkyninges

§273. Here there is almost no resolution in the supposedly early group of poems, up to and including *Exodus*: the only exceptions are at

---

[2]There are ambiguous instances at *Genesis A* 111b, 1384b; *Elene* 291b, 962a, 1321a; *Juliana* 248b; *Andreas* 418a, 801a (hypermetric?), 1430a, and 1447b. On *herige hæðencyninga* (*Daniel* 54a) see above, p. 89, n. 53. Verses like *sawlberendra* (*Beowulf* 1004b) and *aldorduguðe* (*Genesis A* 2081b) are almost certainly of type 241, as *sawl-* and *aldor-* are etymologically dissyllabic. Verses like *forðsnoterne* (*Elene* 1052b; cf. *forðsnotterne* 1160b) must be excluded: see p. 73, n. 21. An example with *un-* (on which see the preceding note) is *Unstaðolfæste* (*Meters* 28.70a). On the participle *-buend-* see §§108f.

*Genesis A* 124a and *Beowulf* 1187a, and the latter, at least, might be due to scribal corruption, since *ǽr* is inessential to the sense of the passage. Hans Kuhn suggests that *ǽr* is ultimately due to a dittography with *arna*, the next word, in the off-verse.[3] Cynewulf uses both the resolved and unresolved types, though the former predominates. Then in the list from *Andreas* onward only the resolved type is found. Variation in medial resolution thus correlates well to the presumed chronology in much the way final resolution does. Kaluza's law then appears to have wider application than has yet been realized. Although only the *Beowulf* poet convincingly observes Kaluza's law in final position, the poets of *Genesis A*, *Beowulf*, and *Exodus*, and perhaps also *Daniel*, were clearly aware of the restriction against resolution of a long syllable with a preceding syllable in medial position, while later poets were not. That uncertainty about final position should have arisen before changes in internal position is to be expected, because the regularity would at first have continued undisturbed in medial position: for etymological reasons there were no circumflected long vowels internally in the relevant forms, and thus no length distinctions after the shortening of noncircumflected vowels, as in final position. Thus the law could be retained in medial position relatively easily, since the distinction depended simply on whether or not the internal syllable was closed by a consonant. Presumably the law was eventually lost in medial position simply because the distinction was no longer important enough once it was no longer observed in final position; and the example set by final position could in fact be just the opposite of the situation in medial position. For example, while medial *-faroð-* was always resolved, final *-faroð* was not. That the poets of *Genesis A*, *Exodus*, and perhaps *Daniel*, but not later poets, should have observed the law in medial position accords with the evidence of Chapter 6 (see §180) that poets continued to avoid resolving long final syllables, now limited to consonantal endings and *-a*, after the shortening of other long vowels.

§274. As for the rule of the coda, it will be noted that all the verses in the supposedly early group, including the two verses with resolution, conform to the rule, inasmuch as they have resolution before the last full lift, but not after it. Cynewulf, on the other hand, violates the rule in three out of twelve instances, and the rule is consistently violated in the four verses from the Boethian *Meters* and the *Death of Edward*. While the instances in *Andreas* consistently violate Kaluza's law, they all conform to

---

[3]"Westgermanisches," p. 193 (*Kleine Schriften* 1:496). Kuhn anticipates some of these observations, finding that words like *cyningas* without resolution are common in *Beowulf*, and grow progressively scarcer in the works of Cynewulf, the *Heliand*, and the Alfredian *Meters*. But variation within the Old English corpus he attributes in part to the extent of Continental influence on Old English verse, rather than to date of composition. This is in accordance with the thesis of the article, that the heroic poems of the *Edda* are translations from West Germanic—an untenable position, though the extensive discussion of resolution in Old Norse is valuable.

the rule of the coda, and so possibly with the disruption of Kaluza's law in final position by the shortening of circumflected vowels, the *Andreas* poet simply privileged the rule of the coda in its place. But he does not consistently observe the rule of the coda, as there are several exceptions in the *wīgheafolan* type, such as *on merefaroðe* (289a). Another way of summarizing the treatment of the *sæcyningas* type is to observe that there are three verse types involved, 1D1 (e.g. *þēodcyninga*), 3E2 (e.g. *hēah-cininges hǣs*), and d2 (e.g. *þæt hit heofoncyninges*). In the group of purportedly early poems only the first two types are permitted, though the latter is so infrequent that the instances might be due to scribal corruption. In *Andreas* only the second type is permitted, while all three types are permitted in the rest of the poetry. The unique treatment of these verses in *Andreas* is consonant with the fact that *Andreas* is also intermediate in the metrical treatment of the verb *andswarian* (§278 below).

§275. Resolution under primary stress (in the Sieversian analysis) appears to be compulsory, as in *mid sunum sinum* (*Genesis A* 1599a), *ham staðelian* (1556b), and *to sæs faruðe* (*Andreas* 236b). There are six apparently exceptional verses:[4]

> *Daniel*:
> | 129b | swefen cyninge |
> | 148b | swefn cyninge |
> | 163b | dom micelne |
> | 165b | swefen cyninge |
>
> *Beowulf*:
> | 1210b | feorh cyninges |
> | 2912b | fyll cyninges |

It is important to note that in each instance the second of the resolvable syllables is long. By contrast, when that syllable is short, resolution always

---

[4]Under Sievers' and Bliss's analyses, verses like *wælreow wiga* (*Beowulf* 629a) and *ondslyht giofan* (2972b) would also appear to be exceptions. However, Sievers' stipulation that the short second lift must follow a long stressed syllable (*Altgerm. Metrik*, §§9.2, 16.1b; cf. Bliss, §31) raises the likelihood that such verses are to be analyzed as having a continuously descending metrical contour—perhaps based on syllable length rather than stress. Kaluza believed that such verses conform to his law; see also the dissertation of B. R. Hutcheson (as above, p. 66 n. 2), pp. 360–63. But verses like *flodblac here* (*Exodus* 536b), *hyðweard geara* (*Beowulf* 1914b), and *uhthlem þone* (*Beowulf* 2007b; and similar verses ending in *þone*, 2334b, 2588b, 2969b, and 3018b), are difficult, since they have short vocalic endings: see Appendix C. Yet *þone*, at least, perhaps does not bear secondary stress, and so is not subject to Kaluza's law. In verses like *wælreow wiga* it may well be that the second word bears secondary rather than primary stress, given the analysis of secondary stress below (n. 6). This assumption would preserve the regularity that resolution is compulsory under primary stress. The permissibility of the short second lift, at any rate, is clearly dictated by position in the same way that the definition of secondary stress is.

applies, with just one exception in the 117 relevant verses.[5] To understand why uncompounded *cyninge* and *micelne* may be unresolved in these verses, which are all of type D, but in no other type (e.g., *\*cyninges hǽs* is impossible), it is only necessary to observe that in type D, *cyninge* immediately follows a lift with primary stress, while this is not true in any other type: there are no verses like *\*ond sēo hǽs cyninges*, though of course the compounded type *hū hē eorðcyningas* may appear in later verse. This then appears to be confirmation of Thomas Cable's assertion that the second of two adjacent stresses is necessarily subordinated (*Meter and Melody*, chap. 5). This is to say that in type D, Kaluza's law, which normally applies only under secondary stress, may apply to *cyninge* because its stress is subordinated to that of the preceding word, in accordance with Cable's description of type D as containing four metrical positions of continually decreasing prominence. After all, Cable's theory obliges us to regard the metrical contours of types 1D (e.g. *wig Hengeste* at *Beowulf* 1083a) and 1D1 (e.g. *niwtyrwydne* 295a) as identical, and so if Kaluza's law applies to the latter type, as it certainly does, then it ought to apply to the former, regardless of the distinction usually drawn, assigning primary stress in the former where the latter has secondary stress.[6] Verses like *feorh cyninges* are infrequent, but that is to be

[5]This then is an additional reason to doubt Krapp's reading *þe ic wægþrea on / liðe* [MS *hliðe*] *nerede* at *Genesis A* 1490b–91a. In addition, *-þrea* as the second element of a compound never receives this metrical treatment elsewhere in the poem: cf. *oðþæt brohþrea* (1813b), *mid cwealmþrea* (2509b), and *Grap heahþrea* (2547b). The exceptional verse is *rodor swipode* (*Exodus* 464b). The relevant instances occur only in types C and D, for reasons made clear in the following paragraph. They are at *Genesis A* 1556b, 1688b, 2529b; *Daniel* 306a, 533b, 717b; *Beowulf* 28b, 164a, 813b, 914a, 922b, 1158b, 1530b, 1603b, 1703a, 1870b, 1897a, 2025b, 2062a, 2096b, 2161a, 2206b, 2386b, 2424a, 2758a, 2769a, 2796b, 2958b, 3056b, 3128b; *Exodus* 408b; *Elene* 14b, 50b, 108a, 427b, 461a (*bis*), 474b, 488a, 493a, 564a (*bis*), 623b, 624a, 646a, 686b, 796b, 1093b, 1099b, 1308a, 1318b; *Fates of the Apostles* 115b; *Juliana* 222a, 270b, 271b, 364b, 437b, 484a, 641a; *Christ II* 478b, 488b, 493a, 521b, 554a, 570b, 643a, 864b; *Andreas* 82b, 99b, 164a, 236b, 619a, 622b, 639b, 681b, 707a, 714a, 760a, 815b, 866a, 868b, 870a, 881b, 912a, 942a (emended), 945b, 955b, 996a, 1005a, 1077a, 1217b, 1218b, 1260b, 1280a, 1398b, 1409b, 1410b, 1536a, 1556b, 1557a, 1658a; *Meters of Boethius* 1.47a, 7.25a, 9.60a, 10.37a, 11.4b, 13.29b, 26.81b, 26.89b, 26.91b; *Judith* 37b, 157b, 272a; *Coronation of Edgar* 9a; *Maldon* 42b, 66a, 228b, 256b, 309b. The list again is unselective, and probably not exhaustive. This type violates the rule of the coda (see Chap. 7), and so it must be assumed that the rules governing resolution take precedence in such instances.

[6]It should be pointed out that this is not an ad hoc rejection of the usual means of distinguishing primary from secondary stress, since anyone who accepts Cable's theory has implicitly conceded the inadequacy of these terms as used by Sievers and Bliss. Rather, the facts of Kaluza's law provide needed confirmation of Cable's predictions that the second lift in type D is subordinate to the first, and that the metrical contours of types 1D and 1D1 are identical. Russom's observation that the probability of resolution correlates to metrical strength (p. 115) supports this analysis (though Russom would insist on the significance of the distinction between primary and secondary stress that such verses seem to abrogate: see above, §266). Further support for Cable's position may be derived from the rarity in classical meters of verses of the type *He on weg*

expected, since under this analysis they are metrically identical to *þeodcyninga*, a type that is regular only in presumably early verse. That verses like *feorh cyninges* are found only early in the chronology supports the chronological conclusion about the other type.

§276. Accordingly, it is now possible to explain the following three apparently anomalous verses in *Beowulf*, *secg betsta* (947a, 1759a) and *ðegn betstan* (1871b). Various proposed emendations were discussed above (§205). But the verses are not anomalous once it is recognized that *betsta(n)* stands for *betosta(n)*, as suggested by John Pope (p. 320): compare *Nu is ofost betost* (3007b), where *o* in *betost* is also required by the meter. Geoffrey Russom (p. 120) points out an obstacle to Pope's solution in Sievers' earlier assertion ("Rhythmik," pp. 462–63) that there were only syncopated forms of the word in the poet's dialect. But Sievers' evidence is unpersuasive because it is based on circular reasoning. His intention is to demonstrate that there is no resolution in the second position of a three-position foot—for example, *þeodcyninga* cannot have resolution, and must fill four positions—and his method of proving this is to show that in all apparent counterexamples syncope rather than resolution may be assumed: e.g., *blōdegesa* may stand for *blōdegsa*.[7] The circularity of this reasoning should be apparent from the preceding demonstration that in verses like *þeodcyninga*, resolution is precluded by the weight of the third syllable. This is why the only indisputable counterexample in *Beowulf* to Sievers' assertion is *wīgheafolan bær* (2661b)—the evidence of which is weightier than Sievers supposes, since *heafola* is one of the few words with a syllable structure like *egesa* that is not subject to orthographic syncope. At any rate, the fact that *betost* must be dissyllabic at 3007b seems sufficient justification for Pope's emendation. The metrical pattern of *ðegn bet[o]stan* is paralleled in Old Icelandic, where verses like *lítt megandi* (*Vǫluspá* 17.6) and *margs vitandi* (20.2) are found. It should be pointed out, incidentally, that although syncope in words with a structure like *woruld* is attested only late in the Old English period, early syncope is possible with the superlative suffix, as discussed above (§240). As mentioned there (and, Russom points out, as a solution to the conflict between Sievers' findings and Pope's proposal), *st* might have been treated as a unit phoneme. Otherwise it is difficult to explain why syncope is early and frequent in *æf(e)st*, *of(o)st*,

---

*losade* (*Beowulf* 2096b) and *þe ic her on starie* (2796b), with a resolved lift after an unresolved one in type C, in favor of the type *wið wrað werod* (319a). The positive avoidance of the resolved type and the frequency of the unresolved type, given that resolution is otherwise demanded under primary stress, implies that the second arsis in type C bears not primary but secondary stress. To explain the anomaly by concluding simply that a primary stress that immediately follows another is an exception to the usual metrical treatment of primary stress is to concede the point that the behavior of what we call primary stress is as much defined by position as by phonological stress.

[7]This is also the position of Terasawa: see above, p. 78, n. 33.

and *ef(e)stan*, but generally late and infrequent in *cyn(in)g*, *wor(u)ld*, and *ber(er)n* (Campbell, §391). The co-occurrence of *ofst* and *ofost*, and the like, is due to paradigm regularization, since this syncope was restricted to the inflected cases (Campbell, §343).

§277. By contrast, the only certain violations of Kaluza's law in initial position appear in presumably ninth-century verse: compare *fram fruman worulde* (*Elene* 1141b), *from fruman worulde* (*Juliana* 509a), and *and eac dysegran* (*Meters of Boethius* 19.41b).[8] But this evidence is less persuasive, since ambiguous instances in supposedly early verse seem more likely violations than nonviolations.[9]

§278. It was remarked above (§229) that in present participles like *gnorniende* the *i* never bears ictus. The evidence at the tertiary level, parallel to the facts about Kaluza's law in nonfinal position at the secondary level, otherwise seems to be restricted to the verb *andswarian*—if in fact this bears tertiary stress (see above, §234). There are twenty-four instances with ictus, mostly in early verse, for example the verse *andswarede* (*Genesis A* 872b).[10] To these are opposed nine instances without, all but one of these in *Andreas*, for instance *Him ða ondswarude* (*Andreas* 202a).[11] This peculiarity of *Andreas* is reminiscent of the way that that one poem stands out in regard to internal resolution in type 3E2 (e.g. *heofoncyninges stefn* 92b, §273 above). The possibility thus arises that the treatment of *andswarian* also correlates to chronology: in the earliest verse the word conforms to the rule of the coda (except at *Daniel* 210a); in *Andreas* it violates the rule (except at 857b); the word is generally avoided by Cynewulf (appearing only at *Elene* 396b); and it is dropped altogether in verse after Cynewulf's. Avoidance of *andswarian* may be due to uncertainty about its metrical treatment, since it is clear that by the time of *Andreas,* treatment with and without ictus on the relevant syllable were both possible. This assumption is corroborated by the facts about the formula *agēaf andsware* (and similar). This appears twenty times in the test group of poems, but never earlier than Cynewulf, and almost always in violation of Kuhn's law. Presumably, then, the formula came into use because of uncertainty about the metrical value of *andswarian*.

---

[8]The first two must belong to type C, since anacrusis in type D demands double alliteration. Probable instances are forms of the formula *in woruld weorulda* (*Elene* 452a; so also *Christ II* 778a and *Andreas* 1686a), though anacrusis is possible here.

[9]*Wæs se fruma egeslic* (*Beowulf* 2309b) is ambiguous because *eges-* may stand for *egs-* (see Campbell, §389); but if *Beowulf* is as early as other metrical criteria suggest, *egs-* seems unlikely. Perhaps *Niht somod and dæg* (*Daniel* 374b) should be included here.

[10]The others are at *Genesis A* 882b, 896b, 1005b, 1022b, 2136b, 2173b, 2187b, 2256b, 2273b, 2280b, 2354b, 2436b, 2477b, 2513b, 2527b, 2691b; *Daniel* 127b, 134b, 741b; *Beowulf* 258b, 340b; *Elene* 396b; and *Andreas* 857b.

[11]The others are at *Daniel* 210a and *Andreas* 260a, 277a, 290a, 343a, 510a, 623a, 925a. Interestingly, all these are in the on-verse, while all instances without resolution (see the preceding note) are in the off-verse.

# IX

# MISCELLANEOUS PROPOSED
# CHRONOLOGICAL VARIABLES

§279. Eric Stanley points to the forms *Dena* and *-wina* in *Beowulf*, for earlier *Deni(ge)a* and *-winia*, as evidence that the poem is not early:

In *Beowulf* the metre requires the *-i-* of *Denia* (variously spelled) and *winia* (variously spelled). Thus *Denia leode* (line 2125b) and *winia bealdor* (2567a) would be short without the *-i-*. The poem elsewhere also has the form *Dena* and forms like *Ingwina*, so that genitival *-i-* of *i*-stems is no longer compulsory. The forms with *-i-* would require careful pronunciation; if we were to substitute carelessly in our reading a form without *-i-* we should be opening the door to short half-lines. Such half-lines exist—for example *kyning mænan* (3171b) where we must not add *ond* if we are to avoid breach of Kuhn's Law, as well as two (or conceivably three) other lines, as well as some bad lines with *fæder*. These lines could be of a kind to which a man who no longer says *Denia* but normally says *Dena* grows accustomed metrically. He is, however, at least old enough to know about the old forms, though young enough to feel perhaps that the old forms mispronounced licence the short half-line which he occasionally allows himself to use.[1]

The point of this argument apparently is to illustrate the conclusion that the metrical evidence for language variation is unreliable because meter is unreliable—that is, odd metrical types may be permissible because language change itself licensed them.[2] The general principle of licensing new metrical types that result from language change is valid: compare the discussion of verses like *morgenlongne dæg* above (§95). But it is not required in order to explain the metrical treatment of the genitive plural of short-stemmed *i*-stems. The form without *-i-* appears in *Beowulf* in the following instances:

---

[1]"The Date of *Beowulf*: Some Doubts and No Conclusions," in the Chase volume, pp. 197–211, at 209.

[2]This is what the context implies. The preceding portion of the paragraph reads, "Philological evidence is cumulative. As we have the rule that the strength of a chain is that of its weakest link, so the strength of cumulative evidence is that of its strongest constituent part. I sense in everything that *Beowulf* is relatively early. But when I look for the details of why I feel that the poem is early the hoped-for solid facts melt in my hands like battle-icicles" (pp. 208–9). As should be apparent from the discussion in the Introduction above, the analogy of the chain is appropriate to deductive reasoning (as in a mathematical proof), but not to inductive reasoning, which is not sequential but, as Stanley says, cumulative.

| 1a | Hwæt! We Gardena | 657a | ðryþærn Dena |
|---|---|---|---|
| 242a | þe on land Dena | 668a | ymb aldor Dena |
| 253b | on land Dena | 1044a | eodor Ingwina |
| 392a | aldor Eastdena | 1069a | hæleð Healfdena |
| 427a | brego Beorhtdena | 1319a | frean Ingwina |
| 463b | Suðdena folc | 1769a | Swa ic Hringdena |
| 498b | Dena ond Wedera | 1904b | Dena land ofgeaf |
| 609a | brego Beorhtdena | 2035a | dryhtbearn Dena |
| 616a | ærest Eastdena | | |

In each instance except 1904b, the alternate form with -*i*- would scan as well.[3] By contrast, all verses with the extra -*i*- in the manuscript would be spoilt metrically by the substitution of a form without it:[4]

| 155b | mægenes Deniga | 1323a | Denigea leodum |
|---|---|---|---|
| 271a | Deniga frean | 1582a | folces Denigea |
| 350b | Ic þæs wine Deniga | 1670a | deaðcwealm Denigea |
| 359a | Deniga frean | 1680b | Denigea frean |
| 389a | Deniga leodum | 1712b | Deniga leodum |
| 465b | folce Deniga [MS *de ninga*] | 2125b | Denia leode |
| 599a | leode Deniga | 2567a | winia bealdor |
| 696a | Denigea leode | | |

A complementary distribution of such regularity cannot be accidental. Rather, this distribution is the one to be expected if a late copyist wrote the only form familiar to him wherever the meter did not require the unfamiliar form. There is abundant evidence that scribes did operate in this manner, substituting late West-Saxon forms for archaic and Anglian ones wherever the meter permitted: see §369 below and the discussion of the metrical Psalms of the Paris Psalter in Appendix A.

§280. Thus, the distribution of *Dena* and *Deniga* cannot be interpreted as supporting the idea that the *Beowulf* poet permitted verses like *kyning mǽnan*, with a short initial lift, by analogy to verses like *\*Dena lēodum*. The latter type does not occur in *Beowulf* or any other poem, and ought not to be expected, since the complementary distribution of *Dena* and *Deniga* demonstrates that the variation between them (with the possible exception of verse 1904b)[5] is almost certainly scribal rather than author-ial. If verses like *kyning mǽnan* are to be admitted, it must not be on the

---

[3]With -*i*- added, verses like *frean Ingwinia* would take resolution under the principles discussed in Chap. 8, as in *Ic þæs wine Deniga* (350b) and *He on weg losade* (2096b).

[4]Verse 1670a is a quasi-exception, since *deaðcwealm Dena* would make an accept-able verse, though the resolved second lift is certainly preferable. The form with -*i*- is required in 350b, since the verse *Ic þæs wine Dena* would offend against Sievers' rule that a short lift may not immediately follow a resolved lift: see §249 above.

[5]If this verse requires explanation it may be supposed that the original reading was *Deneland*, altered to *Dena land* because the word seemed peculiar in the later period, when *Denemearc* was the standard form: cf. the comparably archaic *Scedelandum* (19b).

basis of verses with *Dena*. But in fact the objection to the reading *ond kyning mænan* (as Klaeber, Dobbie, and others have it) is inapposite, as *ond* does not produce an unmetrical verse—compare *ond on bæl don* (1116b), *ond to fæder fæþmum freoðo wilnian* (188), and *ond þe þa ondsware ædre gecyðan* (354). Rather, for the purposes of Kuhn's laws, a distinction must be observed between adverbial conjunctions, which are sentence particles, and copulative conjunctions, which are not.[6] The three metrically parallel verses that Stanley cites (1889a, 1980b, 2299a) are unlikely evidence.[7] They are at any rate too few to justify the assumption that a short initial lift in verses of type A is acceptable in *Beowulf*, given the rate of scribal error in Old English manuscripts (§31 above). On problematic verses containing *fæder*, such as *fæder minum* (*Elene* 438b, etc.), see above, §199. The fact that they all contain *fæder* of course indicates that these are not to be admitted as verses with a short initial lift, but that there is something peculiar about this word.

§281. That the use of the genitive plural in *-i-* is a sign of a poem's antiquity cannot be proved, though it seems probable. Certainly it is an archaism, as it is not used in Old English prose texts. And since a late copyist found it advisable to delete the vowel wherever he could without spoiling the meter, apparently the genitive in *-i-* is not a feature of the poetic koine. The only orthographic instance in verse other than those listed above is in *gewiten, winiga hleo* (*Guthlac B* 1365a, for MS *wiinga* or *wunga*), perhaps preserved only through scribal error. The evidence, such as it is, suggests that the poet of *Guthlac B* was roughly contemporary with Cynewulf: see Appendix A. Perhaps the only additional secure instance in which the short form is required by the meter is in *and Dena weoldon* (*Death of Edward* 19a).[8] This evidence is compatible with the assumption that the longer form should be restricted to relatively early verse, as Stanley implies; but the instances are too few to afford certainty.

§282. The genitive plural of *dæg* is a weak form *dagana/dagena* in some late texts in both Anglian and Southern dialects, for example Li.,

---

[6]*Adverbial* and *copulative* are the terms used by Calvin B. Kendall, *The Metrical Grammar of "Beowulf"* (Cambridge: Cambridge Univ. Press, 1991), esp. chaps. 2 and 8.

[7]The first, *hægstealdra heap* (*heap* not in the MS) is not actually a parallel, since it does not have a short first lift; and in any case three-position verses were shown above to be improbable (§§205ff.). The latter two verses seem to involve some sort of scribal corruption. If *hwearf* is put into 1981a, that verse is still metrically anomalous, having just one thesis after the initial lift, and no secondary or tertiary stress. In any case *hwearf* ought not to belong to 1981a, where it would alliterate in preference to the following *reced*, contravening Sievers' rule of precedence (p. 182 n. 23 above). Conversely, at 2298b, *gefeh* may belong to the next verse, since 2298b is certainly corrupt, lacking alliteration.

[8]In *wina uncuðra* (*Genesis A* 2699a), stress may fall on the fourth syllable. Feminine *i*-stems must be excluded, as they are confused early with *ō*-stems, and in late West Saxon the latter take gen. pl. *-ena*. Thus, although *fremena* (*Genesis B* 437b) is perhaps a late Southernism, it might be argued that it stands for earlier *\*fremiga*.

Rit., Ru.[1], and many of the Mercian-based psalter glosses. In late West Saxon it appears in Ælfric and in Byrhtferth's *Manual* (one instance each), but in early West Saxon only in the originally Mercian translation of Bede's *History*. These instances in Bede (in the Tanner MS) are perhaps the earliest recorded—there are no examples, for instance, in the earlier gloss on VP, which has only *dæga/dega*. In verse there are instances in *Elene* (193a), *Christ II* (467b), *Christ III* (1586b), *Guthlac B* (949a), the metrical Psalms of the Paris Psalter (77.32.1a, 88.39.1a, 101.21.5b, 118.84.1b), and the *Menologium* (64a, 169b), most of which are confirmed by the meter. *Daga* appears in some of the same poems, but this is not surprising, as clearly both forms were acceptable in all dialects in the later period, and were interchangeable in a variety of texts, though the weak form is much commoner north of the Humber than south of it. Such evidence as there is suggests that of the poetic texts with *dagena*, only *Christ III* might be older than the age of Cynewulf (see Appendix A). *Genesis A* and *Daniel* have only *daga*; the genitive plural of this word is unattested in *Exodus* and *Beowulf*. Another weak genitive plural, to *lim*, appears at *Solomon and Saturn I* 102a; compare the strong form at *Guthlac A* 221b, *Guthlac B* 1046a, and *Riming Poem* 8b. So also *godena* appears twice in the metrical division of the Paris Psalter (135.2.2a, 135.28.1a); compare *goda* at 85.7.1a, as well as *Andreas* 1319a and *Juliana* 146a and 619b; and see Sievers, "Rhythmik," pp. 484, 485.

§283. The accusative singular *i*-stem ending was syncopated after long stems, leaving an inflectionless form, but eventually the feminines came to be inflected like the otherwise identical *ō*-stems. It has been argued that this variation reflects a poem's date of composition.[9] Frederick Tupper ("Philological Legend," p. 273) overstates the case when he objects that there are just "one or two" examples of inflected forms in verse, but his overall point is valid, since the instances are certainly too few to support the construction of a chronology. Nor do there appear to be any significant statistical differences among the longer poems. In *Genesis A* there are two inflected forms that can be confirmed by the meter (*bryde* 2661a, *-þryðe* 2240b), and only a few more that are simply orthographic (1340a, 2639a, 2710a), though the number of feminine *i*-stems attested in the accusative singular in this poem is large.[10] The difficulty of compiling statistics is compounded by uncertainty about the number and case of specific forms. Thus, Klaeber (p. lxxxv) eliminates all examples in *Beowulf* but *dæde* at 889a. Examples in the Cynewulf canon,

---

[9]See Philipp Frucht, *Metrisches und Sprachliches zu Cynewulfs Elene, Juliana und Crist* (Greifswald diss.; Greifswald: J. Abel, 1887), pp. 83–84; Trautmann, *Kynewulf*, pp. 80–81; and Sarrazin, "Chronologie," pp. 150–51, 158–59, 190. Sarrazin implies that the change occurred earlier in the Anglian dialects than in the Southern ones, but the inflected form is common in both VP and early West-Saxon texts.

[10]Cf. *ætwist, brȳd, -byrd, cyst, (-)dryht, ēst, fyrd, miht, neod, -sceaft, (-)spēd, tīd, (-)wist, wyrd*.

*Andreas*, and the *Meters of Boethius* do not seem significantly more numerous than in *Genesis A*.[11]

§284. George William Small examines comparative constructions in Old English, and finds historical decline in the use of the dative of comparison (e.g. *stane heardran* at *Elene* 565b), in favor of the construction with *þon* or *þonne* (e.g. *se wæs betera þonne ic* at *Beowulf* 469b).[12] Several limiting factors must be taken into account, such as the possibility of the influence of Latin constructions in translations, and the necessity of excluding *þonne* constructions to which there is no dative equivalent (e.g. *He eow neon gesceod / ða he aferede of fæstenne / manncynnes ma þonne gemet wære* at *Andreas* 1176b-78). The prevailing pattern in the history of the Indo-European languages is for a particle construction to replace comparison by case, and this is what Small finds in Old English, as well. In prose of the Alfredian period, the case construction is already moribund, with an incidence of 11 percent, and it has died out entirely by the start of the eleventh century (p. 80). In verse the overall incidence is much higher, at 45 percent (p. 55). It is the conservative nature of poetic diction that accounts for the difference in incidence between prose and verse: compare Alfred's translation of Boethius, in which the prose has an overall incidence of 4 percent, to the verse, with an incidence of 45 percent (p. 58). But as an indicator of chronology in verse, comparative constructions have no practical value. It is clear that even late verse such as the *Meters of Boethius* has a high incidence of the conservative construction. More important, the overall incidence of relevant examples in verse is remarkably low (p. 52), so that the figures for any given poem are of little statistical significance. For example, Small finds that *Genesis A* contains just one example relevant to dating, a *þonne* construction in which the dative might have been used instead (p. 52). Bruce Mitchell (§§1359–64) approves Small's findings.

§285. Charles R. Sleeth (pp. 31–34) argues that the proportion of verses of type A with alliteration only on the second lift to all other verses of type A may have some bearing on the chronology of verse. He examines a variety of poems and finds that, for the most part, the incidence of the type with single alliteration is low in poems thought to be relatively early, and high in later poems—for example, the proportion amounts to a percentage of 8.77 in *Genesis A*, 9.77 in *Beowulf*, 10.92 in the Cynewulf canon, 18.84 in the *Meters of Boethius*, and 20.82 in the *Battle of Maldon*. He might be right that the type was used with increasing frequency over the course of the Old English period, but there is no initial

[11]For the data on Cynewulf and *Andreas* see Johann Josef von der Warth, *Metrisch-Sprachliches und Textkritisches zu Cynewulfs Werken* (Bonn diss.; Halle: E. Karras, 1908), pp. 7–11. In the *Meters* there are probable examples at 4.49b, 9.15b, 9.30b, 11.14b, 26.4b, 26.12a, 26.43a, and perhaps a few other places.

[12]*The Germanic Case of Comparison, with a Special Study of English* (Philadelphia: Linguistic Society of America, 1929).

probability of this, since there is no apparent linguistic reason for such an increase in incidence. Rather, if there was such a change, it must have been stylistic in nature, and so evidence such as this is on considerably less firm ground than forms of metrical change dependent upon language change. In addition, the design of the experiment relies upon the fairly uncertain assumption that "type A with alliteration on the second lift only" is somehow related to all other verses of type A. Grouping the two types together is perhaps more a classificational convenience within Sievers' and Pope's systems than a strong claim about the nature of Old English meter. Bliss, for example, classifies the former as belonging to the light type a, so that comparison with type A needs to be justified on independent grounds.

§286. Lehmann (*Verse Form*, pp. 99–100) argues that *Judith* is a later composition than *Beowulf* because in the former there is an instance of unstressed *ān*, an early occurrence of the unstressed indefinite article (*anes monðes fyrst* 324b). But compare *an gara laf* (*Genesis A* 2019a) and *anne manlican* (*Daniel* 174a). See also Mitchell, §§232–35.

§287. It has often been suggested that the earliest Germanic verse was end-stopped, and that enjambment is a later development.[13] This is not properly a metrical feature, but a stylistic one; and, as has already been observed, it is more difficult to prove the chronological relevance of stylistic features, since it usually cannot be shown that they changed in a particular direction over time, and thus might correlate to detectable change in verse, while this can be demonstrated about linguistic features like parasiting and contraction.

§288. Meter does not provide the only evidence for a chronology of verse, though its evidence is perhaps the strongest of all linguistic factors, as it is least subject to scribal alteration. The possibility of scribal alteration, for example, is Amos' chief objection to a variety of non-metrical means of dating texts, especially syntactic ones. Yet, at the conclusion of a judicious survey of lexical arguments, in which she rightly rejects a great deal of spurious evidence, Amos is nonetheless inclined to regard the evidence of vocabulary as fairly significant (chap. 3; see esp. p. 156)—leading her to the conclusion, for instance, that *Genesis A* is likely to be a relatively early composition (p. 147). It is of course true that

---

[13]For references see Daniel G. Calder, "The Study of Style in Old English Poetry: A Historical Introduction," in *Old English Poetry: Essays on Style* (Berkeley: Univ. of California Press, 1979), pp. 1–65, at 37–39. See also T. Gregory Foster, *Judith: Studies in Metre, Language and Style*, Quellen und Forschungen 71 (Strassburg: Karl Trübner, 1892), 40–44; and E. G. Stanley, "The Ruthwell Cross Inscription: Some Linguistic and Literary Implications of Paul Meyvaert's Paper 'An Apocalypse Panel on the Ruthwell Cross'," in his *Collection of Papers with Emphasis on Old English Literature* (Toronto: Pontifical Institute of Mediaeval Studies, 1987), pp. 281–97, at 288–91. Alfred B. Lord correlates enjambment to literacy and general sophistication of composition in *The Singer of Tales* (Cambridge: Harvard Univ. Press, 1960), pp. 54ff. See below, §§314ff., for a discussion of the decline of enjambment in the transition to Middle English.

vocabulary could be altered over time—see, for example, J. J. Campbell's study of the shifting vocabulary in the manuscripts of the Old English Bede. But there are counterexamples, such as the Anglian vocabulary studied below in Chapter 11; and in any case, alteration of the vocabulary seems less probable in verse, because of the constraints of meter, and also because poetic language naturally licenses such obscure vocabulary as is not found in prose, or meanings not found in prose usage.[14] Already the evidence of the lexicon has been employed to good effect, for example in Girvan's and Whitelock's arguments in regard to words such as *forscrīfan*, *gīgant*, *nōn*, and *Scedenig* (cf. the Alfredian borrowing *Scōneg*) in *Beowulf*.[15] Lexical and semantic evidence is bound to grow in importance as tools for the study of the Old English lexicon improve, but already some valuable work has been done.[16]

§289. There is also a variety of nonmetrical evidence in the form of copyists' errors. For example, Girvan offers the manuscript spelling *hrærg-* (for Anglian *herg*, WS *hearg*) at *Beowulf* 175b as evidence of an early date of composition: "The anticipation of *r* is a common type of textual error, but that need not concern us further. Once miswritten, it was copied mechanically and preserved because no longer understood. If the scribe

---

[14]This point is relevant to the argument of Kevin S. Kiernan, in *Beowulf and the Beowulf Manuscript* (New Brunswick: Rutgers Univ. Press, 1981), pp. 21–22, that the word *here*, used in a positive sense when applied to the Danes at *Beowulf* 1248a, demonstrates that the poem must have been composed in the eleventh century, because in the Chronicle before the reign of Cnut the word is applied exclusively to the hated army of the Viking Danes. And had *Beowulf* been composed before the Viking invasions, the word surely could not have survived unaltered in manuscript transmission through the Viking Age. He has reiterated this argument in "The Legacy of Wiglaf" (as above, p. 205, n. 70). Phillip Pulsiano and Joseph McGowan attempt to demonstrate that the word could be used in a nonpejorative sense before the eleventh century: see "*Fyrd, here*, and the Dating of *Beowulf*," *Studia Linguistica Posnaniensia* 23 (1990), 3–13. But it is perhaps more significant that the word does not seem to have exclusively negative connotations in verse. For example, in other poems it is applied to the Israelites on their journey from Egypt (*Exodus* 551b), to the host of the saved in the Harrowing of Hell (*Christ II* 574b), to the ranks of angels (*Christ III* 1277a), and to the army of Constantine the Great (*Elene* 101a), as well as to bands of demons, and so forth. Regardless of whether these poems were composed as early as is generally thought, at least the Cynewulfian instances forbid Kiernan's conclusion, since both manuscripts are from the tenth century.

[15]See Girvan, pp. 24–25, and Whitelock, *Audience*, pp. 5–6, 10–11, and 26. Roberta Frank objects to the evidence of the last of these in the Chase volume, p. 125, n. 8; but cf. *PQ* 61 (1982), 343.

[16]See Amos' discussion, pp. 141–56. One promising lexical study that has appeared in the meantime is that of Alan Crozier, who argues that the meanings of *drēogan* and the use of *ādrēogan* vary in such a way as to support the division of verse into Cædmonian, Cynewulfian, and later periods: see "Old English *drēogan*," *ES* 68 (1989), 297–304. It is difficult to say to what extent his findings might be due to dialect variation: e.g., he finds that *Genesis A* and the riddles of the Exeter Book are more archaic than *Beowulf* in this respect, but the findings of the next chapter and Appendix A suggest that of the longer poems, these two are the likeliest to be of Northumbrian origin.

had understood the word he would have made it *herg* or *hearg* as it appears elsewhere, but by an accident we can restore an older and more original spelling" (p. 14). The argument is based on the observation that smoothed *æ* before *r* remains as such only in the early glossaries; by the time of the gloss on the Vespasian Psalter it is consistently represented as *e*, as it is also in the tenth-century Northumbrian glosses. This same *æ* is also found in *stærced-* in *Elene* and *Andreas*, which is shown below (§342) to preserve its *æ* because the word was unfamiliar to the scribes. The Anglian texts testifying to the change of *æ* to *e* in this position of course are few, but they are consistent, and so the sound change may be considered reasonably certain (see Campbell, §§222f.). On the other hand, this is not a very finely tuned dating criterion, since it clearly does not distinguish the dates of *Beowulf*, *Elene*, and *Andreas*. It does, however, set these apart from *Judith*, which has *sterced-* twice, thus suggesting the validity of Girvan's point. Another piece of evidence of this sort is the form *secan* (1602b), which the editions emend to *setan* (i.e. *sǣton*) or the like. The preservation of Anglian *ē* in such verbs is rare, and so the scribe's error suggests an Anglian original. Such evidence is not directly relevant to metrical history, though it supports metrical conclusions. Some other copyists' errors are studied in Appendix A.

# X

# LATE DEVELOPMENTS

§290. Most of the metrical change examined up to this point has been in the treatment of individual words and morphological structures, as with parasiting, contraction, and so forth. But the metrical system itself also changed, again for linguistic reasons that can be independently confirmed outside the realm of pure metrics. One change of this sort is the loss of Kaluza's law, treated above in Chapters 6 and 8. With a few minor exceptions, such as the appearance of verses like *Neorxnawong stod* (208b) and *dreorigmod tu* (2805b) in *Genesis A*, the remainder of these changes belong to the end of the Anglo-Saxon period: with the exception of the loss of Kaluza's law, the rules of Old English meter, as opposed to the scansion of individual items, are remarkably stable until the later tenth century, if the presumed chronology is correct.

§291. At the end of the Old English period there was apparently a slow process of change in the metrical rules, though how early the evolution away from classical norms began is difficult to determine. Certainly the composition of the *Meters of Boethius* strays markedly from earlier norms. A line of verse such as *Gif þæt nære, þonne hio wære* (20.103) shows extraordinary treatment of particles: if the on-verse consists entirely of particles, it is unusual for any but the last to be stressed, especially if only the last is a finite verb; and Bliss would regard it as a violation of Kuhn's first law to stress *þonne* but not *hio*.[1] And Cynewulf, for example, wrote nothing like the following verses:

> Þonne hio ymb hire scyppend    mid gescead smeað,
> hio bið up ahæfen    ofer hi selfe,
> ac hio bið eallunga    an hire selfre,
> þonne hio ymb hi selfe    secende smeað. (20.218–21)

But this is not necessarily evidence of metrical change. Alfred is generally acknowledged not to have been a good poet (see §39 above), and he faced the additional difficulty that the philosophical reasoning of the *Consolation* does not consistently provide appropriate matter for good Old English verse. The peculiarities of this passage are more stylistic than

---

[1]Alfred's faults as a poet should not be exaggerated. One of the metrically more peculiar passages in the *Meters* has been rendered less anomalous by Denise Cavanaugh's observation that *hit* at 29.70a corresponds to *gehyt* (to the verb *hȳdan*) in the prose: see "A Note on *Meter* 29 of the Old English *Meters of Boethius*," *N&Q*, n.s. 31 (1984), 293–96.

metrical: it would certainly be wrong to suppose, for instance, that the aberrant and fluctuating metrical treatment of pronouns, or the faulty alliteration in the last line, reflects a linguistic change in progress. Actual language change is infrequently attested in the *Meters*: it is evident in Alfred's treatment of the adjective suffix *-ig-* (see above, §§216ff.), while the most striking metrical innovation of the *Meters*, the appearance of syncope in verb forms like *wyrð* and *begð*, more likely represents Saxonization of the poetic tradition than the beginnings of a sound change (see Chap. 11 below). In just one instance, however, do the *Meters of Boethius* seem to mark the start of a small change in the metrical rules themselves. In classical verse Bliss's type a2 (e.g. *Me þone wælræs* at *Beowulf* 2101a) must have a single word filling the two final syllables of the verse (as remarked by Russom, p. 54). There are no certain exceptions in the presumed chronology before the *Meters*, and although the verse type is not one of the commonest, it is still frequent enough to afford certainty: Bliss finds twenty-six examples in *Beowulf*, for example. In the Alfredian *Meters* appear verses like *Ne synt þa word soð* (2.18b), along with three other certain examples and several probable ones.[2] Other late verse in the presumed chronology shows a few examples: see *Maldon* 239a and 270a, *Death of Edward* 34a, and *Durham* 9a. The type is clearly modeled on type a2: note that all these but one are on-verses. There are also examples in the presumably Alfredian *Genesis B*: see Doane, *Saxon Genesis*, p. 86.

§292. By the late tenth century, scribes regularly confuse all unstressed vowels, indicating the sort of vowel centralization that accompanies the general lowering of levels of stress. This centralization affects not only final syllables, but also many medial ones: for instance, by the late tenth century the preterite ending *-ode/-ade* of weak verbs of the second class could also be written *-ede*.[3] Certain types of shortening also occurred in medial syllables before the end of the Old English period. For example, Middle English forms such as *briȝthede, kinrade(n)*, and *knowlache(n)* (beside *-reden* and *-lechen*) require late Old English shortening of *ā* and *ǣ* (Luick, §443 and n. 2; Jordan, §137 and n.). Reduction of stress in a compound with original secondary stress is

---

[2]See 20.28a, 22.37a, 28.80a, and probably 20.37a. The words *ān* and *riht* are perhaps actually prefixes at 21.10a, 21.13a, 22.53a, and 25.1a: cf. *ðæt an god is* (17.8a), which is aberrant, and will not scan at all if *god* is a separate word.

[3]Luick (§440) dates this change to the tenth century in Northumbria and the eleventh in the South, but Kemp Malone has shown that all four of the tenth-century poetic codices show the same confusion of unstressed vowels: see "When Did Middle English Begin?" in the *Curme Volume of Linguistic Studies*, ed. James Taft Hatfield et al., Language Monographs Published by the Linguistic Society of America 7 (Baltimore: Waverly Press, 1930), 110–17. On conjugational endings in particular see Albert H. Marckwardt, "Verb Inflections in Late Old English," *Philologica: The Malone Anniversary Studies*, ed. T. A. Kirby and H. B. Woolf (Baltimore: Johns Hopkins Univ. Press, 1949), pp. 79–88. In medial syllables the change is not to be confused with the eighth-century one affecting two successive back vowels, e.g. in *-odon* > *-edon* (Luick, §347).

suggested by the rhyme of *headeor* and *fæder* in the Peterborough Chronicle under the year 1086. Such developments are difficult to date, owing to the extraordinary conservatism of the West-Saxon literary standards of orthography in late Old English. The weakening of unstressed vowels is apparent, however, in texts not dominated by the West-Saxon standard, as in the spellings *hlaferd, hiorades,* and *moneð* in Rit. and Li.[4] In these texts also, there is a tendency for some unstressed medial syllables to disappear altogether, as in *geembehta, geondswærde,* and *world.* But even in West-Saxon texts, with their conservative orthography, there is much evidence of change in unstressed medial syllables, e.g. in the loss of such syllables, as in *æftra* and *fulhtere* (Campbell, §§392f.), and in the development of parasite connecting vowels like those that are so common in early Middle English texts (see Campbell, §367). But the weakening of unstressed syllables is apparent in West-Saxon texts already in the *Meters,* since geminates after unstressed vowels are frequently simplified, as in *ōpera* and *æmetig* for *ōperra* and *æmettig* (Campbell, §457). After the breakdown of Old English spelling standards, such changes are evidenced across dialects—for example, *-erd* in the reflex of OE *hlāford* (where *-er* represents syllabic *r*) is found in the *Ormulum,* in Laȝamon's *Brut,* and in the *South English Legendary,* among others.

§293. There are numerous counterexamples to the assumption of loss of stress on semi-lexical elements of compounds, for example *swikedome* in Laȝamon's *Brut, manifolde* and *Guldeforde* in the *Owl and the Nightingale* (but cf. *bisemar, cartare, munekes,* and others, the last already in the Peterborough Chronicle, as well), and *kinedom* in the *Ormulum* (with a long vowel; so also *-dom* rhymes with *com* in the *South English Legendary;* but *-dōm* elsewhere: Jordan, §137). Yet in most of these instances the vowel does fall in a stressed syllable (cf. the remarks on *rūmedlīce* above, §203); and otherwise they are subject to analogical replacement on the basis of such forms, such as *maȝȝphad* beside *maȝȝdennhad* in the *Ormulum.* Compare, in the same text, *saccless* (but also *endeless*) beside *gilltelæs, reckelæs,* and such (but also *skilllæs, wittlæs*). It is perhaps significant that the long ending *-dom* in Orm nearly always appears after an unstressed syllable (*allderrdom, haliȝdom,* etc.), and that in *horedom* and *swikedom* an anaptyctic vowel is required (OE *hōrdom, swicdom;* but cf. Orm's *þeowwdom, wissdom*). Possibly, the same occurred in personal names, for example *Wolston* and *Oswold* on the basis of comparison to *Apelston* and *Erkenwold.*

§294. So, too, it is possible that in the latter part of the period there was a decline in the levels of secondary stress. Such a decline cannot be proved on a phonological basis: if vowel quantities and qualities were

---

[4]On the confusion of unstressed vowels in Li. see H. C. A. Carpenter, *Die Deklination in der nordhumrischen Evangelienübersetzung der Lindisfarner Handschrift,* Bonner Studien zur Englischen Philologie 2 (Bonn: P. Hanstein, 1910), pp. 38ff.

restored analogically in semi-lexical morphemes under tertiary stress, certainly no orthographic changes should be expected at the secondary level. The change is suggested instead by the dramatic decline in the incidence of poetic compounds of the Old English sort in early Middle English poetic vocabulary. This perhaps is not surprising in Eastern texts like the *Owl and the Nightingale* and *Floris and Blauncheflour*, which have abandoned Old English meters for the iambic rhythms to which compounds with secondary stress do not on the whole lend themselves well. So, too, these poems tend to follow the Modern English pattern of borrowing Romance vocabulary to express complex ideas, rather than the Old English method of compounding. But these conditions are not found in Western texts like the *South English Legendary*, Laȝamon's *Brut*, and Robert of Gloucester's *Chronicle of England*. The vocabulary of both prose and verse in the West remained remarkably impervious to French influence until a fairly late date, and the verse rhythms are much freer. Yet these texts seem no richer in compounds, poetic or otherwise. The disappearance of compounds is better explained by the assumption that declining stress at the secondary level threatened to collapse the difference between poetic compounds and everyday compounds with second elements of obscured meaning.[5] The distinction is essential to the construction of verse, since innovative compounding is the chief poetic effect of early Germanic verse. It is also metrically significant: because of the demands of alliteration, compounds with secondary and tertiary stress are distributed differently in verse. For example, type D with tertiary stress in the coda is most frequently found in the off-verse, while the type with secondary stress is almost never found there. Thus, any disruption of the process of compounding was bound to have a significant effect on meter.

§295. If the decline of compounding evident in early Middle English verse did begin in the later Old English period, it ought to be evident in the meter, since those metrical types most dependent on the formation of compounds ought to show the effects. Thus Oakden (p. 133) attributes the decline in the incidence of verse types D and E in late Old English to diminished use of poetic compounds. The evidence of the *Battle of Maldon* supports this view. It might be objected that other clearly late verse, such as the *Menologium*, naturally has few compounds because the subjects treated are less suited to poetic diction. But in fact the *Menologium* has a higher incidence of compounds with secondary stress than *Maldon*: there are twenty-three in the last hundred lines of the

---

[5]This is not to underrate the effect of the loss of poetic tradition: see below, §§316f. Nor is this to say that OE *swanrād* had greater secondary stress than MnE *swan-road*. Rather, the assumption here is that compounds retained from Old English tended to become lexicalized, their second elements growing obscure and bearing reduced stress, and that many fewer new compounds were formed than had been used in Old English. Thus, the change posited here is an increased proportion of words with reduced stress, not a reduction in the levels of stress of which the phonological system was capable.

former (not counting constructions like *ymb seofon niht þæs* 137a: see above, §199), and in the last hundred of the latter there are twenty-two.[6] By comparison, in the first hundred lines of *Genesis A* there are forty; of *Beowulf*, fifty; and of *Elene*, forty-eight. This is an unscientific sample, but it is nonetheless representative of differences in general between late and presumably early verse.

§296. Thomas Cable ("Metrical Style," p. 80) quantifies the drop in the incidence of types C, D, and E at the end of the Anglo-Saxon period. He finds that they comprise just 14.3 percent of the verses in *Durham*, while even as late as 1066, the *Death of Edward* shows 24.9 percent, and *Maldon* (991) 24.5 percent. Of course the sample in the former two poems is very small, but if it is reliable, it represents a significant decrease from the 34.5 percent found in the *Meters of Boethius* (897), a percentage also representative of the Cynewulf canon and *Andreas*.[7] Cable's computed percentages of types C, D, and E extend also to presumably early verse. His purpose is to date *Beowulf*, and his conclusion is that in this one regard *Beowulf* and *Exodus* are more similar to *Andreas* and the signed poems of Cynewulf than to *Genesis A* and *Daniel*. The figures are these:

| | |
|---|---|
| *Genesis A (I)* | 29.0 |
| *Genesis A (II)* | 32.4 |
| *Daniel* | 33.6 |
| *Beowulf* | 38.3 |
| *Exodus* | 40.8 |
| *Elene* | 35.8 |
| *Fates of the Apostles* | 34.0 |
| *Juliana* | 34.5 |
| *Andreas* | 36.8 |

Thus, the percentages are lowest in the first group (*Genesis A* and *Daniel*), highest in the second (*Beowulf* and *Exodus*), and intermediate in the third (the remainder). Statistically, then, the second group is closer to the third, and on this basis he concludes that a ninth-century *Beowulf* is not unlikely. Since this conclusion conflicts with the evidence of the preceding chapters of this book, however, it ought to be remarked that the statistical variation among the poems is small. This is demonstrated by the observation that the statistical variation within any given poem is high. For example, in the first hundred lines of *Beowulf*, of types C, D,

---

[6] The last hundred lines are selected because Scragg (p. 32) notes that nominal compounds in the poem are commoner in the battle description than elsewhere. There is in fact just one compound with secondary stress in the first twenty lines.

[7] Note, incidentally, that Cable's figures include all verses of types C, D, and E, not just those with secondary stress under the standard definition. Type C ought to be included under the revised definition (§275 above).

and E there are sixty-nine verses (giving an incidence of 34.5), while in the second hundred there are eighty-two (at 41).[8] These samples are too small to be conclusive, but they suggest that the margin of error is sufficient to allow for all the statistical variation, at least up to and including the works of Cynewulf. Larger samples would be more accurate, and might lower the margin of error, but still the statistical differences do not seem large enough to justify chronological conclusions. The incidence of types C, D, and E is certainly related to the incidence of compounds, and the figures above in regard to the varying incidence of compounds in the first hundred lines of *Genesis A*, *Beowulf*, and *Elene* suggest that this alone might be sufficient to account for the varying incidence of metrical types. And at least before the later tenth century, variation in the incidence of compounds seems to be a matter of style, dictated in part by the poet's skill.[9]

§297. Whether such verses as *stiðlice clypode* (25b) and *Swa hi Æþelgares bearn* (320a) in late poems like *Maldon* arose because of purely linguistic change, or whether there was also change in some of the finer metrical principles toward the end of the Anglo-Saxon period, is difficult to say. Metrical change seems to be required to explain the frequent aberrant anacrusis in *Maldon*, and the lapses in alliteration, along with much repetition and some unusual treatment of poetic compounds.[10] Yet there is also orthographic evidence of a declining ability to distinguish the quantities of unstressed syllables already at the end of the ninth century, with the concomitant simplification of geminates between unstressed vowels. (Given the conclusions of Chap. 7 above, declining stress levels in fact are probably significant in large part because they led to a decreased ability to distinguish the quantities of noninitial syllables.) There is also the point to be made that despite the peculiarities of his versification, the *Maldon* poet was by no means ignorant of classical norms, as evidenced for example by his use of *wæpen* as a monosyllable in 130b, and by his general conformity to the four-position structure of the verse. It is difficult to believe, then, that he could have intended *Æþelgāres* to fill just two metrical positions if it actually had a long

---

[8]This count is based on Pope's findings, since Cable, in compiling his statistics, did not employ Bliss's concept of the light verse.

[9]Of course it is possible that the low incidence of compounds in *Maldon* is also a matter of style. But the statistical difference is great enough to suggest otherwise, and the drift away from compounds as the language evolved into Middle English, a development with which the trend in late Old English verse concurs, is difficult to account for simply as a matter of style.

[10]See below, §303. It is sometimes difficult not to portray late aberrations from classical norms as representing decline rather than simple change. This is admittedly a jaundiced view, analogous to calling Shakespeare's English degenerate by comparison to Chaucer's. But because we tend to regard apparently earlier verse as representing a metrical standard, it has not always been possible in this chapter to characterize metrical change impartially.

penultimate syllable. And if the *Maldon* poet's unusual practices are due to incompetence rather than language change, it is remarkable that so much clearly late verse shows similar features, as discussed in the following paragraphs. It is therefore of some importance that Douglas Moffatt finds that inflected compounds with tertiary stress are treated more or less as dissyllables in the early Middle English *Soul's Address to the Body* (e.g. *pineþ þene licame* and *on holie wisdome*), while inflected compounds bearing secondary stress generally make three metrical positions (e.g. *et þen fontstone* and *þu hauest kinemerke*), with few exceptions.[11] Similarly, Jakob Schipper remarks the rarity of rhyme on syllables with secondary or tertiary stress in Laȝamon's *Brut*.[12] Reduction in tertiary stress thus perhaps did play a role in the evolution of metrical standards away from classical models. It is one very likely explanation for the decreased incidence of types C, D, and E: when words like *wisdome* could no longer fill three metrical positions, the considerable majority of verses requiring three-position feet were disallowed.

§298. Early Middle English alliterative poetry generally has two stresses per verse, with unstressed syllables distributed around these in a largely unrestricted manner: see below, §314. This pattern follows naturally from the loss of compounding, and hence of verses of types C, D, and E, leaving only types A and B. The loss of the Old English rules severely limiting the environments for anacrusis perhaps also follows from the loss of the compounded verse types: as types D and E do not take anacrusis, their loss considerably reduced the internal evidence for the restrictions on anacrusis. Thus, poets learning their metrics from the reduced inventory of types would have seen little reason to avoid types like *ouer alle blissen* (*Proverbs of Alfred*),[13] which had been disallowed in classical verse. The increased incidence of irregular anacrusis in *Maldon* is thus very likely related to its sometimes odd treatment of tertiary stress.

§299. A peculiarity of the later Anglo-Saxon period discussed in Chapter 7 (§§238ff.) is a rise in the incidence of verses of types A and B with an unusual stressed syllable in one thesis—again very likely a result of the late Old English decay of stress, allowing many formerly stressed syllables to be treated as unstressed. These verses are so unusual in classical Old English poetry that the known instances are probably due to scribal corruption. For example, when tertiary stress is properly defined there remain just four examples of such verses in *Beowulf*, three of which can be explained otherwise (see §§241f. above). By contrast, there are seven instances in *Maldon*, such as *Hwæt þu, Ælfwine, hafast* (231a).

---

[11] *"The Soul's Address to the Body": The Worcester Fragments* (East Lansing: Colleagues Press, 1987), p. 30.

[12] *A History of English Versification* (Oxford: Clarendon, 1910), pp. 73–74.

[13] Edited by O. Arngart, *"The Proverbs of Alfred": An Emended Text*, Studier utgivna av Kungl. Humanistiska Vetenskapssamfundet i Lund, Scripta Minora, 1979–80.

§300. The metrics of the Chronicle poems included in the test group are remarkably regular. It has been pointed out (§39) that *Brunanburh* includes just one metrically anomalous verse (64a). But even the *Death of Edward* (1065) is surprisingly regular, with just three verses of types clearly disallowed in an earlier age: *befæste ðæt rice* (29b) is a type not found in *Beowulf*, where anacrusis is not encountered in type A*1 in the off-verse. Verse 34a was mentioned above (§291); and its companion *ðæs ðeodkyninges* demands resolution in a position not found in classical verse. Another anomalous verse, *freolice in geatwum* (22b), can be regularized by the adoption of the reading *freolic* from the Worcester text.[14] The verse *soðfæste sawle* (28a) is of the type mentioned above, with anomalous tertiary stress in the first thesis. The metrical regularity of these poems is paralleled by the paucity of prosaic vocabulary (Stanley, p. 389).

§301. Earle and Plummer print as verse several late passages from the Worcester (D) and Peterborough (E) Chronicles that are not included in the ASPR edition: for a list see ASPR 6:xxxiii, n. 1. None of these is relevant here, since they either do not alliterate (and so might not have been intended as verse) or do rhyme, in which case they are unreliable witnesses to metrical developments, since even Cynewulf sacrifices metrical niceties for the sake of rhyme (see, e.g., *Christ II*, lines 591–96). A good example is the line *sume hi man wið feo sealde, sume hreowlice acwealde* (*Death of Alfred* 8). An exception occurs in the D Chronicle under the year 1067, in the middle of an account of King Malcolm of Scotland's wooing of Margaret, sister of Edgar Ætheling:

> *and* cwæð *þæt* heo hine ne nanne habban wolde.
> gyf hire seo uplice arfæstnys geunnan wolde.
> þæt heo on mægðhade mihtigan drihtne.
> mid lichoman(licre) heortan. on þisan life sceortan.
> on clænre forhæf(e)dnysse cwéman mihte.  (1:201)

Here the alliteration is flawless, and the significance of the pointing is unambiguous. Four verses scan properly (*habban wolde*; *þæt heo on mægð-hade*; *mihtigan drihtne*; *cwéman mihte*), though three of the four are of the same type. Otherwise, syllables with tertiary or no stress are freely disregarded. That something other than strict verse is intended might be concluded from the fact that two years earlier, the chronicle incorporates a poem with very few departures from classical norms, the *Death of Edward*. It of course is not necessary to assume that one chronicler is responsible for both this passage and the *Death of Edward*.

§302. As is well known, palatal and velar *g* no longer alliterate in the latest verse. In the Chronicle poems the only very probable exceptions are in *Brunanburh*: *garum ageted* (18a) and *giungne æt guðe* (44a). Bliss

---

[14]Another possibility is to read *getawum*: cf. *Beowulf* 395b, and see Pope, p. 322.

(§115) remarks that these exceptions must be genuine, since they are both of type 1A*1a, and therefore require double alliteration. In *Beowulf* the proportion of verses of this type with single alliteration to those with double (15:270) is high enough to support this conclusion: one example of single alliteration might be possible in *Brunanburh*, but two instances are improbable, and so it must be assumed that velar and palatal *g* alliterate here. All the other instances in the Chronicle poems distinguish the two: see *Brunanburh* (937) 15, 50, 64, *Coronation of Edgar* (973) 10, *Death of Edgar* (975) 8, 19, 26, and *Death of Edward* (1065) 3. The *Maldon* poet also distinguishes the two types of *g*, with instances at lines 13, 32, 35, 46, 61, 67, 84, 94, 100, and elsewhere. There are no instances in *Durham*, and *Judith* does not keep the two sounds separate, for example in *þæs ðe Iudith hyne, gleaw on geðonce* (13). On the other hand, the velar and affricate pronunciations of *c* are not indisputably distinguished in any poem. A line such as *swa ymbclyppað cealde brymmas* (*Death of Edward* 12) might be explained as derived from an original with poetic *calde*, but in this and other poems that distinguish the two types of *g* this sort of explanation is not always possible, as in *to cynerice, cild unweaxen* (*Death of Edgar* 11). Ælfric, in his alliterative prose, also generally keeps velar and palatal *g* separate. This does not help to date the later verse, since it is not necessary to assume that Ælfric felt his prose constrained by the same rules of alliteration that bound verse in the classical tradition.

§303. *Maldon* is considerably less regular than any of these Chronicle poems, and this is the subjective impression with which it leaves most readers. Surprisingly, then, Bliss finds little to criticize in the poem's metrics (§§117–21). And so to set matters straight D. G. Scragg (pp. 28–35) lists the features that contribute to the overall impression of altered standards. Those dealing with poetic form may be summarized and supplemented here: (1) There are frequent defects of alliteration, including alliteration on the second lift in the off-verse, or on a word of insufficient sentence stress, as well as a lack of any alliteration at all in one verse (183). In addition, as Bliss points out, occasionally there is alliteration only on the second lift of the on-verse (§120); and alliteration on *l* in *he let him þa of handon* (7a) violates Sievers' rule of precedence (p. 182, n. 23 above), though Bliss would emend to *landon* (§121). Alliteration of *st* with *s* in *æfre embe stunde he sealde sume wunde* (271) is perhaps a liberty dictated by the rhyme. (2) There is freer treatment of unstressed syllables. This is particularly true with regard to anacrusis, which is extraordinarily frequent and often anomalous, as in verses like *mid gafole forgyldon* (32b) and *To lang hit him þuhte* (66b).[15] But as Scragg remarks, there is also in general less economy with regard to unstressed syllables

[15]Bliss's remark that "there are no instances of irregular anacrusis" (§118) is misleading, since regular types of anacrusis are often found in the off-verse, where they are not found in *Beowulf*: see John Pope's remark, cited above, p. 89, n. 49.

than in other verse: he compares, for example, *flugon on þæt fæsten and hyra feore burgon* (194) to *flugon on fæsten and feore burgon* (*Elene* 134).[16] (3) The verb phrase frequently spans the verse boundary, weakening its effect, as in *þæt se eorl nolde yrhðo geþolian* (line 6). It may be added that the effect of the verse boundary is also weakened when a noun and a modifier in attributive position are in opposite halves of the line, and this situation is less frequent in other verse: compare *þon we swa hearde hilde dælon* (33).[17] (4) As remarked above, the incidence of verses of types D and E is smaller than in presumably earlier verse, comprising less than 10 percent of the total. Also there is less variety in the subtypes of type A represented. (5) The poem shows much repetition, as several verses, or even lines, and syntactic frames appear more than once, such as *wordum mælde* at 26b, 43b, and 210b.

§304. In *Durham* about a quarter of the verses are defective. Some defects are no doubt due to faulty transmission, but since the proportion is so high, not all these verses can be explained this way. The alliteration is unobjectionable, aside from the *locus desperatus* in 16b, *on gecheðe*[18] —even the limitation on the alliteration of *st* is observed in line 2—and there is no rhyme or secondary alliteration. In line 19 the alliteration shows that the stress is on the third syllable of *unarimeda*, but this occurs occasionally with *un-* in other verse: for instance, there are two certain examples in *Beowulf* (Klaeber, n. to 1756a), and many in the metrical Psalms of the Paris Psalter. Extraordinary anacrusis might account for four anomalous verses: *on floda gemonge* (5b), *and Aidan biscop* (12b), *and Boisil abbot* (15b), and *ðe clene Cudberte* (16a). Other defective verses cannot be explained this way:

| | | | |
|---|---|---|---|
| 4a | ea yðum stronge | 15a | and breoma bocera Beda |
| 7b | wilda deor monige | 16b | on gecheðe |
| 8b | deora ungerim | 17b | and he his lara wel genom |
| 9a | Is in ðere byri eac | 20a | ðær monia wundrum gewurðað |
| 12a | Osuualdes, Engle leo | | |

The second of these can be righted by the substitution of *wilddeor* (cf. the parallel in *Daniel* discussed above, p. 89, n. 50), and the third by the substitution of *unrim*, which is common in verse, while *ungerim* is unique. The fourth is perhaps an example of verses like *Ne synt þa word soð*

---

[16]Cf. Mitchell, who points out, "The early poetry tends to do without dependent *se* more often than the prose and later poetry" (§336). Lehmann (*Verse Form*, chap. 3, esp. p. 97) regards a paucity of unstressed syllables as characterizing the most conservative verse in the Germanic languages. Old Saxon and Old High German show the most innovation in this regard.

[17]Also 51, 109, 132, 151, etc. As do others, Scragg remarks that a large proportion of the lines in *Maldon* are end-stopped. On this as a sign of lateness see §287 above.

[18]Holthausen's emendation to *on cildhade* seems likely.

(*Meters of Boethius* 2.18b) that appear only in relatively late verse (see §291 above). The fifth verse shows the same anomalous treatment of personal names as in *Maldon*, and perhaps should be classified as belonging to type D, but the sixth will not scan even if tertiary stress is ignored. In the poem there is one example of a long syllable in the thesis of type E (cf. the discussion of similar verses of type B below, §307), in *wudafæstern micel* (6b).

§305. Aside from the Chronicle poems, along with *Maldon* and *Durham*, there are no poems in Old English indisputably datable on the basis of nonmetrical evidence to the tenth century or later, though there seems to be a consensus about the later origins of several short poetic works.[19] One poem, the *Menologium*, is very probably to be dated sometime after ca. 965. The reference to the Benedictine Rule in lines 42b–44a suggests a date after the Benedictine reform gained momentum in England. The relative lateness of the poem is further suggested by the fact that lines 60–62 are adapted from Psalm 117.22 in the Paris Psalter, a text also assumed to be late, only because of its faulty metrics. (But other evidence for the lateness of this text will be found below in Appendix A.) And so a comparison of the metrics of the *Menologium* with those of the datably late poems ought to be worthwhile.

§306. Like *Maldon*, the *Menologium* does not mix palatal and velar *g* for the purpose of alliteration: *his gast ageaf* (217a) may be assumed to have single alliteration, and compare 10, 39, 100, 101, 109, 113, 117, 132 and 171. Palatal and velar *c* alliterate once, at 31. There is no alliteration in the off-verse of 117, and so there may be scribal error here, especially as the syntax is unusual;[20] and *s* is proved not to alliterate with *sc* by the verses *And þæs symle scrip* (136b) and *on þas sidan gesceaft* (227b). There are no very convincing examples of rhyme, and alliteration of the type *abab* is limited to three verses (9, 81, 145), a number small enough to suggest accident.

§307. The treatment of unstressed syllables is not so free as in *Maldon*. Anacrusis is rare, occurring only in *on neorxnawange* (151a) and *besenctun on sægrund* (212a), though the former is a type that does not occur in *Beowulf*. But tertiary stress is clearly on the wane, since it is disregarded in two verses, *eadigne upweg* (193a) and *haligra tiida* (229a); *prowedon on Rome* (123b) shows conformity to the rule of the coda. More

---

[19]For example, Eric Stanley (in the Chase volume, p. 199, n. 18) lists the following as surely or probably belonging to the tenth century or later: *Maldon*, the Chronicle poems, *Durham*, *Solomon and Saturn*, the *Menologium*, poems in CCCC MS 201 and MS Junius 121, the Kentish poems in Cotton MS Vespasian D.vi, *Gloria II, Thureth*, the *Seasons for Fasting, Instructions for Christians, Epilogue to MS CCCC 41*, and some of the charms.

[20]Donoghue (p. 10) notes that monosyllabic stressed auxiliaries are usually verse-final: to *wearð acenned* (*Menologium* 117b) cf. *acenned wearð* (*Elene* 5a, 178a, 775a, etc.). And so see the proposed emendations discussed by Dobbie, ASPR 6:172.

remarkable is the frequency with which a long second thesis occurs in verses of type B. Adopting Campbell's model of half-stress, and limiting the examples to instances of final syllables bearing half-stress, or those that would acquire it by the addition of an ending—for example *habbað foreweard gear* (6b; cf. *wiðerweard gesceaft* at *Meters* 11.41b, 11.49a)—there are seventeen such verses in a poem of 231 lines.[21] By contrast, there are no examples in the first 231 lines of *Beowulf*.[22] In addition, under similar circumstances ictus is lost in *Ne hyrde ic guman a fyrn* (101b), reminiscent of verses like *Se flod ut gewat* (72a) in *Maldon*, which Bliss despairs of scanning (§121). In *forþan heo Crist on þam dæge* (21b), *þam* is unstressed: compare *Christ III* 1096b, 1371b, *Beowulf* 197a, 790a, 806a, and so forth. The verse *cyninge lof secgað* (93b) is a type that ought not to appear in the off-verse, and requires double alliteration. Verse types D and E are not rare in the *Menologium*: there are perhaps as many as 52 instances, comprising more than 8 percent of the verses. But this is still a small proportion by classical standards: Bliss finds 1001 examples in *Beowulf*, or better than 15 percent. As in *Maldon* there is considerable repetition, especially with respect to the word *middangeard* (36a, 53a, 92a) and the cheville *tō tūne, on tūn* (8b, 28a, 34b, 78a, 89b, 108b, 183a, 219b).

§308. Although several other short poems are thought to be late compositions, there is no evidence for this aside from their faulty meter. And defective meter alone is not proof of lateness, since there is again the possibility that the poets were simply incompetent. Yet we have already seen (above, §291) that King Alfred's inferior command of verse technique generally results in metrical peculiarities of a different order from those that characterize genuinely late poems like *Maldon*, the latest Chronicle poems, and *Durham*. Similarly, it is widely acknowledged that the poet of *Genesis A* was not very skilled in verse technique; but when Dietrich Hofmann appeals to the poet's faults as evidence of late composition, Edward B. Irving, Jr., rightly replies that his shortcomings are unlike those of verifiably late poets.[23] Almost certainly, then, a distinction must be drawn between deficiencies in the poet's skill and metrical change that is most likely dictated by language change. If the metrical faults of externally undatable but presumably late poems are the same as those of *Maldon* and other verifiably late compositions, this would constitute evidence against mere incompetence.

§309. *Judgment Day II* may be taken as an example. There are several instances of rhyme or near rhyme in the poem (3, 6, 28, 82, 147, 266), in

---

[21]See 6b, 7a, 11b, 24b, 41a, 46a, 55b, 76a, 137a, 140b, 144a, 151b, 153b, 154a, 173b, 174a, 222b. For another comparison with *Beowulf* see above, p. 230, n. 105.

[22]At 6b *ærest* is an adverb, and thus not to be inflected.

[23]Hofmann, "Untersuchungen zu den altenglischen Gedichten Genesis und Exodus," *Anglia* 75 (1957), 1–34, at 7–11; and Irving, "On the Dating of the Old English Poems *Genesis* and *Exodus*," *Anglia* 77 (1959), 1–11, at 2–3.

each instance interfering with the alliteration.[24] The final lift in line 222 alliterates, where perhaps *wihte* is for *auhte*. And there is no alliteration in 42, 152 (MS *blawað* for *floweð*?), 169 (inversion?), 190, 202 (*nāwiht* for *nē wiht*?), 251, and 255. As in *Maldon*, velar and palatal *g* do not alliterate with each other. Three times the poet alliterates *sw* with *sw* (49, 105, 199), and once *sl* with *sl* (241), but *sw* also frequently alliterates with *s* (12, 29, 67, 108, etc.). The clusters *sp, st*, and *sc* are treated as in classical verse, and *s* is proved not to alliterate with *sp* by the verse *sib mid spede* (268b). Alliteration on the pattern *abab* is infrequent (88, 102, 247, 279), and so probably accidental.

§310. The treatment of unstressed syllables is similar to that in *Maldon*. Anacrusis is frequent: because of the treatment of tertiary stress it is sometimes difficult to determine whether anacrusis is intended, but it occurs possibly in thirty-nine verses, or more than 12 percent. For comparison, Bliss finds fifty-five examples in *Beowulf*, or less than 1 percent. The anacrusis is often peculiar, as well, appearing in a type that does not take it in *Beowulf* (e.g. *and dædbote do* 85a and *awyrgedon gastum* 184a), or in the off-verse (e.g. *for synnum on eorðan* 87b and *hu micel is that wite* 92b), though 1A1a(i) is the only type that takes anacrusis in the off-verse in *Beowulf*. As with *Maldon*, there is occasionally a proliferation of unstressed syllables, as in *Ic bidde, man, þæt þu gemune* (123a). And as in other late verse, normally unstressed words often receive stress: for instance, King Alfred could well have composed a verse like *and þonne mot* (252b). This peculiarity arises in large part because particles are frequently postponed, and do not appear in the first drop of the verse clause. The result is a variety of violations of Kuhn's first law, including *swyþe nele brysan* (49b; cf. 155b), *genipu mæge flecgan* (110b) and several others. Kuhn's first law is violated in other ways, as well, for example by the stressing of the preposition before a noun in *gemang þam werode* (303b; cf. 282a) and *butan ende forð* (306b).

§311. Tertiary stress is frequently ignored, as in *nu þu forgifnesse hæfst* (68a), *ænigre wihte* (203b), and several others. Conversely, *-leas* takes unusual stress in *heortleas and earh* (125b; cf. 126b), as in *Beowulf* and the *Meters*. The incidence of verses of types D and E is small, 26 verses at most out of 306 lines, or a little more than 4 percent. As with *Maldon* and the *Menologium*, verses of type B not infrequently have in the second thesis a long syllable that would gain tertiary stress by the addition of an inflection, for example in *wið scyppend god* (73a) and *eal arleas heap* (175a). In type a2 the last two syllables may be separate words (see §291 above), in *Ðis is an hæl* (43a), *Hwæt miht þu on þa tid* (177a; cf. *Judith* 306a), and perhaps *Ufenan eall þis* (145a, 213a, 272a), if the preposition is not stressed here. This last example also illustrates the use of chevilles.

---

[24]Rhyme is probably also intended at line 4, where the alliteration is faulty, and *secge* may stand for *sæge* or *sege*, though the subjunctive would be unusual in this context.

The rule of the coda is consistently observed with respect to the adjective suffix -lic-, but the adverb suffix -līce is treated the same way (160b, 273b), as in *Maldon*. Even after peculiar anacrusis and failure to observe tertiary stress are taken into account, several verses remain unclassifiable, such as *earme geþanc* (65b, Bliss's type 2E1 having been eliminated) and *ungerydre sæ* (102b, with vocalic alliteration).

§312. Thus the metrical faults of *Judgment Day II* are not random, but follow the same patterns found in demonstrably late verse. Particularly telling is the avoidance of alliteration between the velar and palatal varieties of *g*, as this cannot be considered merely a stylistic fault. Since this and most of the other features discussed characterize verse of the late tenth century or later, but not verse that is merely stylistically inept, such as the *Meters of Boethius*, they constitute fairly firm evidence against the view that metrical anomalies such as these may as well be attributed to stylistic causes as to actual linguistic change. Accordingly, *Judgment Day II* should be dated no earlier than the second half of the tenth century, as is widely assumed. Poems displaying similar metrical faults, then, are also most likely rather late: these include the *Exhortation to Christian Living* (along with *A Summons to Prayer*),[25] the *Lord's Prayer II*, the metrical Psalms of the Paris Psalter, and the *Judgment of the Damned*.[26]

§313. Transitional and early Middle English alliterative verse show a more advanced state of the same tendencies. There is little verse in this category, since rhyme takes the place of alliteration quickly after the Conquest, and most of the alliterative poems themselves have a noteworthy admixture of rhyme. The meter of the *Grave* is measurably different from that of *Durham*: the verses are longer, containing more unstressed words, there are just two compounds in twenty-five lines (*helewaȝes, sidwaȝes*), neither poetic, there are no verses of type C, D, or E, the alliteration is inferior, and the language is decidedly prosaic.[27] Yet this is recognizably verse and not prose.[28] The same characteristics are

---

[25]Fred C. Robinson has offered weighty reasons to regard these two poems as one: see "'The Rewards of Piety': Two Old English Poems in Their Manuscript Context," in *Hermeneutics and Medieval Culture*, ed. Patrick J. Gallacher and Helen Damico (Albany: State Univ. of New York Press, 1989), pp. 193–200.

[26]On the last of these see E. G. Stanley, "*The Judgement of the Damned* (from Cambridge, Corpus Christi College 201 and Other Manuscripts), and the Definition of Old English Verse," in *Learning and Literature*, pp. 363–91. The metrical faults of *Genesis B* are of a different order: such metrical faults as there are resemble the verse patterns of the Old Saxon original. See the studies cited above, n. 24 to Chap. 1.

[27]Edited by Arnold Schröer, *Anglia* 5 (1882), 289–90. Some verses may have been added later. The excess of unstressed words can be related to Cable's observation (*English Alliterative Tradition*, p. 57) that although verses of type A are common in the poem, there are none with just four syllables—even though this is the commonest pattern in type A in classical verse—and very few in other Middle English alliterative verse.

[28]On the difficulty of distinguishing some late Old English verse from prose see the article by Stanley mentioned above, n. 26.

observable in the Worcester fragments of the *Soul's Address to the Body*, the *Proverbs of Alfred*, the Chronicle entry for 1036, the *Bestiary*, and Laȝamon's *Brut*.

§314. Norman Blake points out that enjambment is rare in Laȝamon's *Brut*, each verse or line forming a syntactic unit, and Carolynn Van Dyke Friedlander extends this observation to all the verse in this category.[29] It is certainly true of the *Grave*, though not of *Durham*. Aside from the syntactic integrity of verse and line, Friedlander concludes that the only norm of early Middle English alliterative poetry is that verses generally contain two stresses, though their contours are not always similar to Old English verses of types A and B. Rather, there seem to be no restrictions, other than the necessary syntactic ones, on the distribution of unstressed syllables around the two stresses. It is not a far route to travel from *Maldon* to this state of affairs, once verses of types C, D, and E are eliminated, given the irregularities of anacrusis in *Maldon*.

§315. Changes in the metrical system cannot readily be isolated from the non-metrical characteristics of verse. It was remarked above (§§295ff.) that the decline of compounding led directly to decreased incidence of types C, D, and E, and increased incidence of irregular anacrusis. But the loss of compounds was bound to have more wide-ranging consequences, since poetic vocabulary, and particularly poetic compounding, is the primary aesthetic feature of Old English verse, serving much the same function as metaphor in Greek and Latin verse. Variation is a product of the importance of poetic vocabulary, since it is the means by which such a large variety of vocabulary is introduced into verse. Variation, in turn, is related to enjambment, since the impulse to expand and prolong the syntax of the poetic clause through variation labors against the natural impulse to contain the syntax within the long line. Thus, the loss of compounds contributed to the suppression of variation, and the latter, in turn, to the decline of enjambment. Lehmann (*Verse Form*, chap. 3) convincingly demonstrates that in comparison to more conservative Old English, the loss of poetic vocabulary in Old Saxon and Old High German verse can be correlated to an increase in the incidence of unstressed syllables. The loss of compounding may perhaps even be related to the rise of rhyme, since the loss of the chief aesthetic principle of verse can hardly have gone uncompensated, and since rhyme has so thoroughly supplanted compounding in most early Middle English verse. In a similar vein, M. S. Griffith points out that the poet of the Paris Psalter avoids heroic poetic vocabulary, that this has the effect of limiting the formulism of the poet's diction, and that it is precisely the dearth of

---

[29]Blake, "Rhythmical Alliteration," *MP* 67 (1969), 118–24; Friedlander, "Early Middle English Accentual Verse," *MP* 76 (1979), 219–30. On lack of enjambment as a feature of early Middle English verse see Valerie Krishna, "Parataxis, Formulaic Density, and Thrift in the *Alliterative Morte Arthure*," *Speculum* 57 (1982), 63–83, esp. 68–71.

poetic formulas that is most responsible for the prosaic impression that the Psalms present.[30]

§316. The thoroughness and swiftness with which rhyme replaced alliteration was certainly not motivated simply by the formal appeal of rhyme. After all, although there is rhymed verse in Old English, the amount is small, and even in the later period, though its meters were altered, native tradition seemed in no danger of being swept away until the sudden onset of the changes that followed the Conquest. Most would probably agree that it seems a poor trade, substituting the purely formal features of rhyme and homomorphic feet for the entire tradition of Old English poetic diction. To explain the change, it will be useful to elaborate on some remarks presented elsewhere on the general characteristics of Old English verse, and the transition to Middle English.[31] It should be remembered above all that Old English verse is a highly artificial medium, both in diction and sentiment. The language of verse was far removed from everyday speech, not only in its vocabulary, but even in its spelling system. This poetry is aristocratic, at least in the sense that subjects appropriate to the elevated diction of verse were severely limited —there is nothing in Old English comparable to the playfulness, or frivolousness, of the *Owl and the Nightingale*. And subjects appropriate to verse tend to be filtered through a medium of epic attitudes, so that Christ's saints, the phoenix, and even objects in the *Riddles* are described in the same martial terms as heroes of Germanic legend. The traditions of Old English verse are extraordinarily conservative: were it not for its metrical aberrations and its externally datable setting, the *Battle of Maldon* could have been composed in the seventh century. The world it describes does not seem far removed from that described by Tacitus, though social conditions in England at the close of the tenth century were nothing like the world described by Tacitus.[32] That poems such as *Beowulf* and *Widsith* continued to be copied late in the Anglo-Saxon period is sufficient evidence of the antiquarian bent of verse traditions. The changes in both the form and content of verse after the Norman Conquest are not plausibly to be attributed to any sudden, fundamental changes in English interests and character. Rather, the changes are so thorough only because the traditions were so artificial. The development of the language itself

---

[30]"Poetic Language and the Paris Psalter: The Decay of the Old English Tradition," *ASE* 20 (1991), 167–86. For references to other studies arguing a relationship between formulae and meter see Pat Belanoff, "The Fall(?) of the Old English Female Poetic Image," *PMLA* 104 (1989), 822–31, at 830 n. 4.

[31]See "The Old English Period" in the *Norton Anthology of English Literature*, 6th ed., gen. ed. M. H. Abrams, vol. 1 (New York: Norton, forthcoming).

[32]See Rosemary Woolf, "The Ideal of Men Dying with Their Lord in the *Germania* and in *The Battle of Maldon*," *ASE* 5 (1976), 63–81; and Helmut Gneuss, *Die Battle of Maldon als historisches und literarisches Zeugnis* (Munich: Bayerische Akademie der Wissenschaften, 1976).

provides a parallel. It was once widely taught that the differences between Old and early Middle English are somehow attributable to the deleterious effects of the Norman Conquest on native speech. Rather, Old English as written in the tenth and eleventh centuries was an artificial language.[33] With the Norman decimation of the Anglo-Saxon lay and ecclesiastical intelligentsia, the social system required to maintain linguistic standards and the training of scribes in native traditions was swept away, along with the orthographic conventions that concealed language change and dialectal diversity.

§317. In the same way, all the artificial and aristocratic conventions of Old English verse were lost when their conservators were dismissed from the positions in which they had maintained the standards of tradition. The verse that emerges, like the language itself, is no doubt considerably closer to the forms in popular use. Possibly, as suggested by Angus McIntosh, rhymed verse was far more popular in the Old English period than the surviving records suggest—though this is not necessarily the case, since rhyme was originally a learned affectation borrowed from Latin literature, and the homomorphic feet that usually accompany Middle English rhymed verse are not found in the Old English period at all.[34] Possibly, also, Blake and McIntosh are substantially right that early Middle English alliterative verse owes as much to Old English alliterative prose like Ælfric's as to verse of the classical sort, since, as E. G. Stanley has demonstrated, the line between the two cannot always be drawn with assurance. The primary difference between Ælfric's most verselike prose, such as his *Life of St. Edmund*,[35] and classical verse is not so much the distribution of stressed and unstressed syllables as the absence of purely poetic vocabulary. The result is that in this text there are no unambiguous verses of type D or E (as remarked by Cable, *English Alliterative Tradition*, p. 45). But also, as John Pope observes, syllable length is irrelevant to Ælfric's rhythmical prose, and half-stress is ignored.[36] Whether or not such prose actually served as an example, it was certainly produced under conditions similar to the milieu of transitional verse, retaining only as much of the form of strict verse as the language requires once it is freed from the constraints of poetic diction.[37] Unstressed

---

[33]The re-emergence of linguistic diversity as the product of the decline of artificial orthographic norms is now the standard view, as expressed, for example, by Campbell, §329, and by H. R. Loyn, "The Norman Conquest of the English Language," *History Today* 30 (April, 1980), 35–39. On the artificiality late Old English spelling standards see Chap. 11 below, esp. p. 286, n. 43.

[34]McIntosh, "Early Middle English Alliterative Verse," in *Middle English Alliterative Poetry*, ed. David Lawton (Bury St. Edmunds: D. S. Brewer, 1982), pp. 20–33, at 26–27.

[35]In *Lives of Three Saints*, ed. G. I. Needham, (London: Methuen, 1966).

[36]*Homilies of Ælfric: A Supplementary Collection*, I, EETS, o.s. 259 (1967), 117–18.

[37]That is, given the requirement of two stresses per half-line. After all, Thomas Cable has ably demonstrated the difference between Ælfric's nonrhythmical prose and

syllables were weakened toward the end of the Old English period, and this may well be in part the cause of the decline of classical meters even in a poem as conservative in style as *Maldon*. So, too, early Middle English alliterative verse may owe much to Old English rhythmical prose, though it was demonstrated above that with the decline in compounding, early Middle English verse types are not so very difficult to derive from those found already in late Old English, with their unusual anacrusis and peculiar treatment of tertiary stress. But it was the loss of Anglo-Saxon poetic traditions, especially poetic compounded vocabulary, under the suppression of the Anglo-Saxon intelligentsia at the time of the Conquest, that was most responsible for the changes in English verse in the transitional period.

---

his rhythmical compositions: see *The English Alliterative Tradition*, pp. 46–47. In this chapter he offers the most detailed argument to date for the derivation of this verse from the tradition of rhythmical prose.

# XI

# SYNCOPATED ENDINGS OF LONG-STEMMED VERBS AND OTHER PRESUMED INDICATORS OF DIALECT ORIGINS

§318. A few variables usually associated with dialect origins may have some bearing on the dating of verse. Two of these, negative contraction and analogical restoration of the adjective suffix -*ig*-, were discussed above (Chap. 3 and §§216ff.). A similar case is syncope in verb endings. It was Eduard Sievers who first argued that there is evidence of a poem's dialect of composition in its metrical treatment of the second and third person singular indicative endings of long-stemmed weak verbs of the first class and strong verbs, and of the preterite participial ending of long-stemmed weak verbs of the first class with stems ending in an oral dental stop.[1] Up to the end of the Old English period these inflections remain unsyncopated in Anglian prose texts, though they are usually syncopated in West Saxon and Kentish.[2] For example, *lǣtst*, *lǣtt*, and *gelǣd(d)* may appear in Southern texts, corresponding to Anglian *lǣdes(t)*, *lǣdeþ*, and *gelǣded*.[3] Sievers points out that the meter requires the syncopated forms in several poems, most of which we have some reason to believe were composed in the South. He concludes that as a dialect indicator this criterion is absolute: if a poem displays metrically confirmable syncopated forms it is of Southern provenance; otherwise it was originally composed in an Anglian dialect.

§319. Several scholars have suggested that Sievers' reasoning is flawed, and though it seems only Kenneth Sisam's response is remembered now, this is not entirely unjust, since his objections are the most detailed.[4] He remarks, "Evidence is wanting that the short forms were characteristic of West Saxon in earlier times, say in the eighth century" (*Studies*, p. 123), and while observing that the evidence is scant, he points

---

[1]"Miscellen," p. 273; "Zum Codex Junius XI," *PBB* 10 (1885), 195–99, at 196; "Rhythmik," pp. 464–75.

[2]See n. 12 below. For the Middle English evidence see Oakden, p. 35.

[3]In the past participle, syncope affects open syllables in all dialects (e.g. in *ahyrde* at *Psalms* 119.4.2b in the Paris Psalter, from *\*ā-hard-id-ǣ*), but closed ones only in Southern texts, for example in Southern acc. sg. masc. *sendne*, but Anglian *sendedne*.

[4]*Studies*, pp. 119–39. Cf. ten Brink, p. 213; Trautmann, *Kynewulf*, p. 71n; and Tupper, "Philological Legend," pp. 255–61, and "Notes on Old English Poems," *JEGP* 11 (1912), 84–85.

to Saxon and Kentish charters antedating Alfred's reign that have only uncontracted forms.[5] Under the older interpretation of this syncope, which was standard in Sievers' day, and according to which the change applied in all dialects but was later removed analogically in Anglian, Sisam's objection is linguistically insupportable. Although it is true that Sievers' syncope cannot be dated on the basis of attestation in the existing Southern records, still almost certainly this sound change took place at the beginning of the seventh century or earlier. This is the likeliest date for the loss of unstressed *i* in other positions (Luick, §309). Luick expresses some doubt about whether this syncope in verbs occurred at the same time as the loss of final *-i*.[6] But in the same place he reiterates the standard view that the Anglian unsyncopated forms are the result of analogy. If this is so, then in any case this syncope antedates the earliest Anglian glossaries, since they show only unsyncopated forms. And since the earliest glossary manuscript is now possibly to be dated to the seventh century (see below, §400), if this syncope did not occur at the same time as the loss of final *-i*, it cannot have occurred much later. Demonstrably, at any rate, the change was initiated before the loss of intervocalic *h*, since otherwise it would not be possible to explain forms like WS *siehþ* and *onlīhþ*; and the loss of *h* can be dated to ca. 700, according to Luick (§249), yet is probably even earlier (see below, §§395ff.). Dating Sievers' syncope to the beginning of the seventh century also accords with the observation that the Anglian unsyncopated forms, restored by analogy, are already in use in verse, with its conservative language, in the early Northumbrian poems, including the inscription on the Franks Casket (*drigiþ*, right side, 2a), usually dated ca. 700, and *Bede's Death Song* (*uuiurthit*, 1b), A.D. 735. (In the latter instance the earliest manuscript is from the ninth century, but in both instances the unsyncopated form is required by the meter.) And so syncope would appear to have occurred so early that it should perhaps be evidenced in verse composed in Wessex before Alfred's reign.

§320. But while Sisam's objections are untenable under the older interpretation of syncope in verbs, this is not so under Alois Walde's hypothesis that this syncope originally occurred only when a pronoun followed, as in *bin(t)st þū*, contrasted with *þū bindes*.[7] Presumably, then, the Anglian and Southern dialects have leveled the variants in opposite directions. There is no very strong direct evidence for this view in the

[5]Tupper surveys the charter evidence in "Philological Legend," p. 257. The following discussion of the origin of syncopated forms applies only to present-tense verbs. Syncope in preterite participles like *gelǽd(d)* apparently arose in inflected forms, whence it was extended to uninflected ones. Thus in the Anglian dialects *gesended* (usually WS *gesend*) is normal beside inflected *gesende*.

[6]"Es ist nicht deutlich, ob dieser Schwund mit dem von auslautendem *i* in Zusammenhang steht; wahrscheinlich ist es nicht" (§304, n. 1).

[7]*Die germanischen Auslautgesetze* (Halle: Niemeyer, 1900), p. 125, n. 1.

Old English records, and yet it seems the most probable explanation. If the process is the same as early seventh-century *i*-syncope, the development is anomalous, since *i*-syncope does not in other grammatical categories apply to a final syllable if it is closed by a consonant. Walde's idea obviates this difficulty, assuming close juncture between the verb and the following pronoun, since the pronoun is stressed if the verb is (cf., e.g., *for hwon secest þu, Genesis A* 873b; also 2200b, 2248a, 2271a, etc.), and this creates an environment in which syncope is known elsewhere to apply, as in compounds such as *giesthūs* and *hȳþgyld*. The parallel is particularly close because *i*-syncope is much more regular after long syllables in such compounds (e.g. *giesthūs* beside *seledrēam*), just as Sievers' syncope is much more regular in long-stemmed verbs (e.g. West-Saxon *bin(t)st* beside *fremest*). The low stress before enclitic pronouns perhaps also explains the reduction of various plural endings to *-e* in expressions like ind., sj., and imp. pres. *binde wē*, and pret. *bunde wē*: see Brunner, §360, n. 5, for details. Verb forms with orthographically enclitic *-þū* of course occur occasionally, especially in Northumbrian texts, for example Li. *gesiistu, cuoeðestu*, and *hæfdestu*. Such enclisis is a widespread phenomenon in early Germanic, as in OIcel. *skaltú < skalt-þú* and *gekktú*, and OHG *forsahhistu, gilaubistu* (Tatian) and *lisistu, suachistu, thenkistu* (Otfrid). Enclisis is the source of *-t* in the Old English ending *-st* (frequently still *-sð* in the Hatton manuscript of the *Cura Pastoralis*), which derives from PGmc. *\*-is(i)*: the same change occurred in Old High German, where the earliest texts have *-is*, later beside *-ist*; and the reverse development is apparent in Icelandic, where 2. pers. pl. pron. *þér* arose from *ér* in enclitic forms like *skuluðér* 'you shall'. Thus, that West Saxon adopts the *-t* is not surprising, and supports Walde's analysis, since this dialect generalizes the syncopated, enclitic forms in which *-t* arose, while Anglian, which retained the unsyncopated, nonenclitic forms, usually has the original ending without *-t*. It may be mentioned as well that in those few instances in which there is syncope in the second person singular in Anglian texts, there is always a pronoun following: compare VP *acers ðu* and Li. *gehers ðu*.

§321. The objection has been raised to Walde's explanation that syncope does not normally apply in closed syllables, and so it should not be expected in *bindistū*. But there are parallels in compounds, such as *nȳdgripe*, and in the structurally parallel superlatives, such as West-Saxon *hīehsta*, and *nīehsta*. It was remarked above (§240) that the *-st-* cluster in these superlatives may have been regarded as a unit phoneme, as it was when early Middle English long vowels were shortened in closed syllables, since both consonants may be analyzed as belonging to the following rather than the preceding syllable. So also there is no serious obstacle to assuming (with Luick: see n. 8 below) that constructions like *\*bindiþ hē* were pronounced *\*bindiþē*. The objection to Walde's explanation also seems weak in view of the linguistic difficulties that the hypothesis resolves. It was pointed out above that there is no trace of syncope in the earliest Northumbrian poems, or in the early glossaries. And yet this is peculiar if the unsyncopated forms are an Anglian innovation: by comparison, parasiting leaves traces of variation in verse late into the Old English period. So also the absence of unsyncopated forms in the early glossaries is surprising in view of the fact that *i*-mutation is still in the process of being leveled out in these texts: compare Ép. *caelith* (561), *milciþ* (628), and *scripit* (906), beside *suggit* (455). But mutation should have been leveled out at the same time that the unsyncopated endings were restored. Walde's hypothesis also obviates the necessity of assuming a phonologically unnatural syncope rule. Syncope does not apply to final syllables when they are closed by a consonant, except in this instance. To limit the application of syncope on a morphological basis in this way is a linguistic improbability, since phonological change, except when it is analogical, always begins with purely phonetic conditioning, and is only later morphologized. Accordingly, it is not surprising that Luick retracted his earlier view and embraced Walde's hypothesis, as did several other Germanic philologists.[8]

§322. Walde's hypothesis removes the objection of §319 above to Sisam's suggestion that unsyncopated forms may have been characteristic of West Saxon before Alfred's reign, since it demands the assumption that syncopated forms were originally restricted to a particular environment, and were only later generalized; and this analogical change may have occurred at any time between the loss of unstressed vowels and Alfred's reign. The sudden appearance of syncopated forms in Southern verse during Alfred's reign does seem a contradiction of Sisam's charter evidence, given that the language of verse is more conservative than that of prose. But the charters in all likelihood ought to be disregarded, anyway, because in the ninth century, West-Saxon and Kentish orthography were still "fighting against the strong traditions of Mercian spelling" (Campbell, §§16, 207). For example, in *se alda suínhaga utsciote∂* (West-Saxon charter of Æthelwulf, Sweet's no. 20, A.D. 847) the verb is indeed unsyncopated, but *alda* is a Mercian form. Moreover, Sisam's remarks might give the incorrect impression that syncopated forms are not found in the earliest Southern charters, and so attention should be drawn to the form *limp∂* in the Kentish endorsement on a charter of Æthelberht (Sweet's no. 28, A.D. 858) along with *geli∂* in a Surrey charter (Sweet's no. 45, A.D. 871–89), one of the four charters that Sisam calls "perhaps the best witnesses for the South before Alfred's reign," and which he mistakenly says has only uncontracted forms (p. 124).

---

[8]Luick, review of Horn, *Sprachkörper und Sprachfunktion*, in *Englische Studien* 56 (1922), 185–203, at 196–97. Campbell (§347) seems unaware of Walde's theory, while Brunner (§358.2) mentions it without comment. For a history of responses to Walde's view see M. T. Löfvenberg, *On the Syncope of the Old English Present Endings*, Essays and Studies on English Language and Literature 1 (Uppsala: Lundequist, 1949), 17–23.

§323. Yet there remains the possibility that "the long forms may have been a feature of the old poetic diction, and the appearance of the short forms in some late pieces may be part of the breakdown in the traditional verse technique of which there is other evidence" (Sisam, p. 124). Sisam's suggestion derives some benefit from the fact that most verse showing Sievers' syncope is rather bad, at least formally, exemplifying the poetic tradition in decline.

§324. Initially Sisam's objections to Sievers' dialect criterion should have made little difference, since the uncertainty they add could easily be rectified by reference to other dialect indicators accepted in Sievers' day, which point overwhelmingly to Anglian origins for most verse. But Sisam in fact casts doubt on the validity of those other criteria. He contends that it is necessary to set aside as unreliable all dialect indicators that cannot be confirmed metrically (pp. 121–23): for example, a scribe might alter *wealdend* to *waldend* without leaving any evidence of meddling, but a change of *sendest* to *sen(t)st* would affect the meter in many instances, and is therefore "structural," to use his term. Nonstructural criteria are particularly unreliable because it may be that there existed a poetic koine, a common poetic language for all the Anglo-Saxon kingdoms, containing archaic and dialectal forms like *waldend*. Few of Sisam's objections had not been raised before, but the act of collecting, synthesizing, and rendering them accessible to an audience of nonlinguists lent them a degree of influence they had long deserved but never achieved. Hardly an edition of Old English verse has appeared since 1953 in which the prefatory discussion of dialect features does not begin with a disclaimer about the reliability of dialect indicators and a reference to Sisam's essay. But as happens so frequently when complex linguistic issues are taken for settled, the genuine worth of his argument has been obscured by popular misunderstandings: for instance, frequently he is credited with having invented the idea of an Anglo-Saxon poetic koine,[9] and he is sometimes said to have proved the unreliability of all dialect, or even dating, criteria.[10] The consequence of this latter misunderstanding is that Sisam, the proponent of philological (though not textual) conservatism, is made to champion some philologically extreme claims about date and dialect, for instance that *Beowulf* is an eleventh-century West-Saxon poem, or that all poems except the lyrics actually attested in Northumbrian versions are

---

[9]See, for example, R. T. Farrell, ed., *Daniel and Azarias* (London: Methuen, 1974), pp. 11–12 and 17–18; to which cf. Klaeber, p. lxxxviii, with references at n. 3. (The Collitz article that Klaeber mentions actually posits a koine for Old Saxon rather than Old English.) Add also Cecilia A. Hotchner, *Wessex and Old English Poetry, with Special Consideration of "The Ruin,"* (New York Univ. diss.; Lancaster, Pa.: Lancaster Press, 1939), pp. 86ff.

[10]See, e.g., Howell D. Chickering, Jr., *Beowulf: A Dual-Language Edition* (Garden City, N.Y.: Anchor, 1977), p. 248; Busse, p. 43; and Doane, *Genesis A*, p. 25.

tenth-century West-Saxon compositions.[11] Such assertions in fact run counter to Sisam's thesis, which is that presumably early verse (cf. his title "Dialect Origins of the Earlier Old English Verse") is as likely to derive from Wessex as from anywhere else. His point about Sievers' criterion of syncope in verbs is that it proves only that the bulk of Old English verse is *not* late West-Saxon in origin. Accordingly, his view is that most Old English verse is still to be considered either early or Anglian—or both.

§325. Certainly, Sievers' logic is not conclusive. Undoubtedly he is right that a poem with structurally confirmed syncopated forms is a Southern composition: the incidence of unsyncopated forms in Anglian prose texts is negligible,[12] and since the language of verse is conservative, it is improbable that a text with such forms should have been composed by an Anglian rather than a Southerner. But the corollary, that texts without syncopated forms are either Anglian or early, is objectionable. There are of course texts that offer no metrically confirmable evidence— for example, *Maldon*, which is certainly not early, and is most likely from Essex.[13] On the other hand, given a poem rich in unsyncopated forms and devoid of syncopated ones, such as *Genesis A*, it may be debated whether the poem could not be a late West-Saxon composition. In another context Dorothy Whitelock, followed by others, has argued that apparent archaisms may simply have a stylistic basis (see §35 above). Given this assumption it might be argued that a late West-Saxon scop well versed in the older poetic practices might avoid syncopated forms as a stylistic choice. As before, the likelihood of these suggestions cannot be gauged in a linguistic vacuum. Sievers' criterion of syncope must be viewed in the context of other dialect indicators, for the greater the number of linguistic differences between, for example, *Genesis A* and late Southern compositions like the Boethian *Meters*, the less likely it is that *Genesis A* could have been composed in Wessex at any date. The matter can be put beyond reasonable doubt if it can be shown that late Southern poems as a group share a significant number of linguistic characteristics that are not shared by poems like *Genesis A*, and that as a group they lack a significant array of features characteristic of poems like *Genesis A*, and

[11]The former is the argument of Kevin S. Kiernan, *Beowulf and the Beowulf Manuscript* (as above, p. 249, n. 14); this book, along with some other scholarship arguing for a date for *Beowulf* after the age of Bede, is examined in "Dating *Beowulf* to the Viking Age," *PQ* 61 (1982), 341–59. The latter argument is that of Busse.

[12]Johannes Hedberg provides an exhaustive survey of such forms in prose, and finds that the proportion of syncopated to unsyncopated forms is 5:1283 in Northumbrian texts and 39:883 in Mercian. See *The Syncope of the Old English Present Endings: A Dialect Criterion*, Lund Studies in English 12 (Lund: Gleerup, 1945), 285.

[13]See below. *To heanlic me þinceð* (55b) is inconclusive because anacrusis exceeds its normal limits in this poem: see above, §303.2. There is orthographic syncope in *Gehyrst* (45a) and *stynt* (51a). On *segeð* (45b, in a defective line) see below, §353.

shared by prose written in non-West-Saxon dialects. Such evidence would discount not only the possibility that the avoidance of late Southern forms in most verse is merely stylistic, but also the more likely objection raised by Sisam that the appearance of syncopated forms in some verse is merely indicative of the late degeneration of the poetic tradition.

§326. Another result of examining the characteristics of late Southern compositions as a group will be to shed light on the question of the value of spelling alone as an indicator of dialect. A frequent misconception about Sisam's work is the supposition that he has disproved the value of nonstructural dialect criteria. It must be conceded from the start, it is certainly true that some supposedly Anglian habits of spelling are common to all verse. For example, the "Anglian" spelling *waldend*, for West-Saxon *wealdend*, is frequent not only in such undeniably Anglian poems as those of Cynewulf, but also in the clearly Southern *Meters of Boethius* and *Battle of Maldon*.[14] Moreover, dialect determinations of Old English verse that rely uncritically on spelling tend to reach the embarrassing conclusion that most poems have passed through Anglian, Kentish, and early West-Saxon recensions before reaching their final, late West-Saxon state, owing to the mixture of dialect forms they evince. To a certain extent, then, skepticism about the value of spelling is salutary. Nonetheless, in some instances spelling is a reliable indicator. Several such indicators are discussed below (§§340ff.), but one example may suffice here. Sievers observes that the West-Saxon forms of the second and third person singular present indicative of the verb *habban* appear only in poems known or presumed to be of Southern provenance ("Rhythmik," p. 471): the West-Saxon forms *hæfst* and *hæfþ* (also *næfst* and *næfþ*; cf. Anglian *hafas(t)* and *hafaþ*) appear in nine poems, thirty-three instances in all; and all but two of these instances appear in poems that evince structural syncopation, and must therefore be Southern.[15] This regularity is the more remarkable because *hafast* and *hafaþ* usually are metrically indistinguishable from their contracted counterparts, and in any of these thirty-three instances substitution might have taken place, if indeed the scribes had considered *hæfst* and *hæfþ* foreign to the poetic koine. Two

---

[14]E. G. Stanley offers a detailed study of the distribution of this spelling in "Spellings of the *Waldend* Group," in *Studies in Language, Literature and Culture of the Middle Ages and Later*, ed. E. Bagby Atwood and Archibald A. Hill (Austin: Univ. of Texas Press, 1969), pp. 38–69. See also Angelika Lutz, "Spellings of the *Waldend* Group— Again," *ASE* 13 (1984), 51–64.

[15]The exceptions are at *Maldon* 237b and *Psalms* 71.12.3b, though the former of course is considered Southern on other grounds. Included are some instances that Sievers does not mention: *Genesis B* 360b, 361a, 392b, 395b, 504b, 507a, 569a, 570b, 617b, 791a, 818b; *Meters* 10.67b, 11.22a, 11.31a, 11.55a, 11.64a, 20.36a, 20.143a, 20.190a, 20.191a, 24.37b, 28.26b; *Rune Poem* 23b, 41a; *Menologium* 146b; *Judgment Day II* 68a, 109a, 164a; *A Prayer* 25; *Seasons for Fasting* 172a, 196b. As remarked below (§331), the last of these has just one example of a metrically syncopated form, and so whether it is Southern is not as certain.

conclusions follow: (1) at least some purely orthographic, nonstructural features are not random, but display the same distribution as structural ones, and thus seem to be reliable indicators of date or dialect (whichever features like Sievers' syncope turn out to be), and (2) for the majority of Old English poems, and particularly lengthy ones such as *Genesis A* and *Beowulf*, there is initially a certain amount of improbability attached to the notion that they could have been composed in the South, given the regularity with which *hafaþ* and *hafast* are used in them. That degree of improbability increases with the number of features that distinguish poems like *Genesis A* and *Beowulf* from those with Sievers' syncope. On the possibility that such differences are merely stylistic, see further below (§333).

§327. To determine the value of nonstructural features, then, the known corpus of late Southern verse should be examined to see what nonstandard features it shares and does not share with presumably Anglian verse. It will thus be possible to distinguish genuine dialect features from aspects of the poetic koine. As explained above (§325), it will be safe to regard as Southern any poem for which we can be reasonably certain that the poet used syncopated forms of long-stemmed strong and first-class weak verbs. This syncope also applies to short-stemmed verbs (though see Campbell, §753 end, on Anglian preterite participles); but usually the syncopated and unsyncopated forms of these are not metrically distinguishable. Examples of exceptions are *on last cymeð* (*Genesis A* 1099b) and *eall þing birest* (*Meters of Boethius* 20.276a). Short-stemmed weak verbs of the first class are like these examples because they have no gemination in the relevant forms, for instance *frem(e)þ* < *\*framiþ*, beside inf. *fremman* < *\*frammjan*, and *cēð* < *\*kau(w)iþ*, beside inf. *cīegan* < *\*kau(w)jan*.[16] Proto-Germanic geminates must be distinguished from West Germanic: *fyllan* is a long-stemmed verb (cf. Gothic *fulljan*), for example. Verbs with *h* in the second and third person singular must be discounted: for instance, *anfehst siþðan* (*Psalm 50* 135b) is of no significance, since *-fēhst* could stand for Anglian *-fæst*, with contraction after loss of *h*.

§328. Sievers finds that syncopated forms, beside unsyncopated ones, are required by the meter in eleven poems, all of which are known or presumed to be of Southern provenance: these are the *Metrical Preface* and *Epilogue to the Pastoral Care*, the *Meters of Boethius*, the *Menologium*, *Genesis B*, *Soul and Body I* and *II*, *A Prayer*, the *Lord's Prayer II*, the *Creed*, and the *Rune Poem*. Most of these are generally regarded as Southern compositions.[17] The first three are of course known or presumed to be by

---

[16]But analogical forms of *cīegan* are found in Anglian as well West Saxon (Campbell, §237.1, n. 1), and so cf. *cleopað and cigeð* (*Genesis A* 1013a) beside *ond him dryhten gecygð* (*Phoenix* 454b), and see §§118 and 120 above.

[17]See, e.g., J. J. Campbell, p. 353, n. 17.

King Alfred (§72 above). The *Menologium* is usually thought to be late, since lines 60–63 are adapted with little change from verse 22 of Psalm 117 in the Paris Psalter, which is itself very probably late.[18] Moreover, Rudolf Imelmann argues that the reference to *rincas regolfæste* (44a) who honor St. Benedict indicates the year 963 or later as the likeliest time of composition, given the progress of the Benedictine reform.[19] There is room for doubt: Imelmann regarded the poem as Anglian in origin, and Jordan thought this possible, on the basis of the frequent appearance of *in* in the poem (treated below, §362; *Eigentümlichkeiten*, p. 67, n. 2). But Kenneth Sisam expresses current consensus when he calls the case unconvincing, and pronounces the *Menologium* a late Southern text (*Studies*, p. 125, n. 3 and p. 129). The *Creed* is associated with the Benedictine Office (Dobbie, ASPR 6:lxxv–lxxviii), and so is also likely to be no earlier than the latter part of the tenth century. Lateness proves nothing decisive about dialect, but it surely increases the probability of Southern composition. Sievers offers the alliteration of *g* with a vowel in *georne togenes and sædon ealles þanc* (238) as evidence for late Kentish composition of *Genesis B*.[20] This seems probable, though such a development is also known in late West Saxon.[21] And there is other evidence for Kentish influence on *Genesis*: see below, §§335.8, 335.18, and 362. Dobbie dates the *Rune Poem* "fairly early, say in the eighth or early ninth century" because "the regularity of the meter, together with the poet's general adherence to the style and diction of the older poetry, places a pre-Alfredian date of composition almost beyond question" (ASPR 6:l). The poem's most recent editor rightly responds that conservative meter and diction also characterize the *Battle of Brunanburh*, composed A.D. 937 or later, and so there is no reason to reject the possibility of composition in the tenth century.[22] As for the claim that the meter of the poem is regular, this is not strictly true, since *langsum geþuht* (63b) is unusual, *-sum* normally being unstressed.[23] Several other verses, such as *(Tir) biþ tacna sum* (48a) and *(beorc) byþ bleda leas* (51a; see also 10a, 32a, 74a, 84a), seem to have peculiar placement of the

---

[18]Dobbie associates these psalms with the monastic revival of the later tenth century, and with the Worcester school (ASPR 6:lxxviii); cf. Krapp: "latter ninth or early tenth century" (ASPR 5:xvii).

[19]*Das altenglische Menologium* (Berlin diss.; Berlin: E. Ebering, 1902), pp. 52–53.

[20]"Zum Codex Junius XI," *PBB* 10 (1885), 195–98.

[21]As remarked by Gradon, p. 10. See Brunner, §§125a, 212, n. 2; and Campbell, §303. It might be argued that *georne* here stands for *eorne*, to which cf. *Elene maðelode þurh eorne hyge* (*Elene* 685). But double alliteration in the on-verse seems likelier—in this metrical type it occurs in 270 out of 295 instances in the on-verse in *Beowulf*.

[22]Maureen Halsall, *The Rune Poem* (Toronto: Univ. of Toronto Press, 1981), p. 32.

[23]Cf. *Þæt is wynsum wong* (*Phoenix* 13a), *cymeð wynsum stenc* (*Whale* 54b), and *and his weorc wynsum* (*Psalms* 106.21.2a). This *-sum* is a suffix, not a compound element, and since it has no obvious connection with any separate word, it perhaps ought not to be included in the class of "semi-lexical" morphemes discussed above in §§210ff.

caesura.[24] Because of its diction, Eric Stanley ("Prosaic Vocabulary," p. 391) doubts an early date of composition.

§329. The remaining poems in which Sievers finds metrically confirmed syncopated forms are too short to afford evidence of date or dialect of composition, though the survey of features of spelling (§§335ff. below) does not suggest Anglian origins. One example that Sievers finds of a syncopated form confirmed by the meter in a presumably early poem is *forlæt* at *Genesis A* 2440b. The poem's most recent editor regards this as a preterite form—that is, standing for *forlēt*—and compares *lēt* at 2111b, definitely a preterite (Doane, pp. 301, 310, and 350). But this seems unlikely, given the context:

> Wit be þisse stræte    stille þencað
> sæles bidan,    siððan sunnan eft
> forð to morgen    metod up forlæt. (2438–40)

But it must be conceded that it would not be impossible for *forlæt* to be a preterite standing for a future perfect if Bruce Mitchell is right that under similar circumstances *gewitan* (for *gewiton*) in a subordinate temporal clause at *Ruin* 9a is a future perfect:[25]

> Eorðgrap hafað
> waldend wyrhtan    forweorone, geleorene,
> heardgripe hrusan,    oþ hund cnea
> werþeoda gewitan. (6b-9a)

Syncopated forms are also relatively frequent in two poems Sievers does not consider:

*Judgment Day II*
66b    þæt þu ðe læce ne cyþst
87a    and þe sylfum demst
108a    and seo sunne forswyrcð
166b    ræscet fyre
172a    ac ealle þurhyrnð

290b    hwyrfð mædenheap
292a    þe ealle læt
*An Exhortation to Christian Living*
26b    gif heo inne wyrð
34b    þe on god gelyfð
39    gif he him god ne ondræt

It is worth noting incidentally that *Judgment Day II*, *An Exhortation to Christian Living*, and the *Lord's Prayer II* also have in common that they are all uniquely preserved in MS 201, Corpus Christi College, Cambridge. *A Summons to Prayer*, also uniquely preserved there, has no syncopated forms, but it is just thirty-one lines long.[26]

---

[24]This assumption about placement of the caesura is what makes it necessary to assume that *Beowulf* 1790a is an exception to Kaluza's law (§172).

[25]"Some Problems of Mood and Tense in Old English," *Neophil.* 49 (1965), 44–46.

[26]Because of Fred Robinson's argument that *An Exhortation to Christian Living* and *A Summons to Prayer* are one poem (see above, p. 264, n. 25), the latter perhaps should

§330. Syncopated forms are to be found in *Instructions for Christians*:

| | | | |
|---|---|---|---|
| 51b | oððe his wita onleoht | 151b | swa him Crist onlænð |
| 96a | Se þe ear gifð | 168a | and fulfæstlice þencð |
| 129b | to swiðe ahefð | 173b | and maran forlæt |

The second is merely orthographic, as the meter requires *gifeð*. The third is not secure, as the metrical pattern of *mid feondes larum* (143b) is found several times in the poem. The remainder are probable examples, though the meter of the poem is rough. In addition, there are several clear Southeastern features in the orthography, and the spelling of the twelfth-century manuscript is relatively capricious. As regards phonological features, then, the poem is not a good comparison to classical verse—for example, it shows non-Saxon back mutation in *weolan* (136b), *weogas* (257a), and elsewhere, not because of the poetic koine, but because it was composed and/or copied by a Southeasterner, as demonstrated by such spellings as *diæðes* (32a), *unþiaw* (45a), and *diað* (219a), and by vocalic alliteration on *geornlice* (247b). Thus, it should not be included in this group of poems. It may be said that the only specifically Anglian features to be noted are in *oferseagon* (128b; see Campbell, §207) and *sealo* (223a); and the latter is perhaps due to the general confusion of *æ*, *a*, and *ea* in the poem (see Rosier, p. 9).

§331. Less significant are a few isolated instances of syncope:

> ne her draca ne fleogeð  (*Finnsburh* 3b)
> Wealdest eall on riht  (*Gloria I* 7b)
> ac he on hinder scriþ  (*Seasons for Fasting* 173a)

It would perhaps be rash to label a poem late West-Saxon on the basis of a single contracted form, especially a poem with as many uncontracted forms as the *Seasons for Fasting*. It seems significant also that in two of these three instances an uncontracted spelling is used, while generally contraction is both orthographic and metrical, as in the examples from *Judgment Day II* and *An Exhortation to Christian Living*, above, and as discussed below in regard to Sievers' findings (§§353ff.) Three examples in *An Exhortation to Christian Living*, especially when spelt contracted, seem sufficient grounds to consider that poem Southern, but given the vagaries of manuscript transmission, one example in *Finnsburh* is insufficient: might not the second *ne* in 3b be scribal, for example? Multiple negatives are much less common in verse than in prose, as Mitchell points out, noting that *næfre* "stands without *ne* before the verb in seven of the eight clauses in which it appears in *Beowulf*" (§1609).

---

be included in the Southern group of poems. But its inclusion would make little difference, since the only relevant forms in the poem are *Þænne* (1a), *onsended* (15a), *bodade* (17a), and *æcum* (26a), only the last of which is of much significance.

Indeed, *ne* appears before the verb just five times in *Beowulf*. Moreover, the scribal addition and deletion of negation are common in verse: for example, in *Beowulf* there are four instances in which the editor of the ASPR edition has been obliged to add or delete *ne* (648b, 1130a, 1805a, 2006a). Therefore, although these might be late Southern compositions, it is best not to draw any conclusions as to the original dialect of a poem with a single syncopated form. On the basis of this conclusion it is also necessary to exclude the *Creed* and *Soul and Body*, though in these instances the syncope is also orthographic.[27]

§332. Another probable instance of mere metrical irregularity is *Maxims I*, with four examples of metrical but not orthographic syncope:

> 30b    þe heonan of cyþþe gewiteþ
> 143b   to fela gestryneð
> 147b   Ful oft hine se gefera sliteð
> 149b   nales þæt heafe bewindeð

These are all perhaps hypermetric, as is most of the poem; and the last three in fact begin and conclude a hypermetric passage. The nonhypermetric verses of the poem, at any rate, are somewhat irregular: for instance, there are no metrical parallels in *Beowulf* to five verses in the first section of the poem alone (9a, 11a, 13a, 17b, 33b). So also a line of the *Riming Poem* is inconclusive: *Ær þæt eadig geþenceð, he hine þe oftor swenceð* (80). To this must be compared *se ær in dæge wæs dyre. Scriþeð nu deop in feore* (45). The fact is that in rhyming verse the meter may be wrenched, and this is apparent, for example, in the rhyming passage at *Christ II* 591–96.

§333. There is then a group of ten poems that may on the basis of Sievers' syncope criterion be regarded as late Southern. The nonstandard features that these share with, for example, *Beowulf*, may be taken to represent aspects derived from the poetic koine, and features *Beowulf* does not share with them may be regarded in all probability as genuine dialect indicators. But it will be useful to add some poems to this group. Supposing it is true that the use of nonstandard forms is a matter of stylistic choice, it may be charged that there is circular reasoning in defining the late Southern group by a feature, syncope, that is characteristic of unconservative style. It has been argued, for example, that the linguistic differences between the *Meters of Boethius* and other verse may not be taken for sound chronological or dialectal evidence, since the

---

[27]*Soul and Body* seems particularly dubitable, since against the rhyme at *II* 114 (*I* 119) stand eleven unsyncopated forms in *II*, seven of them confirmed by the meter (3b, 6a, 21b, 37b, 43b, 53b, 112b; also 16a, 94a, 99a, 116a). Nonetheless, the syncopated form *þurhsmyhð* must be correct: the rhyme with *totyhð* need not be intentional, but the Anglian form *þurhsmūgeð* would vitiate the meter (while Anglian *totīþ* would not—assuming vowel contraction after loss of *h* in smoothed *totīhiþ*).

*Meters* follow the prose translation of the *Consolation* closely, and thus may display features that would not normally be found in West-Saxon verse.[28] It should not be assumed that the *Meters* are merely prose set to meter, since they contain some purely poetic features, as demonstrated by the frequent substitution of Anglian forms for verbs that are syncopated in the prose version.[29] And as with Whitelock's observations on style considered above (§35), this objection can be shown to be unreasonable if there is a large number of features that the *Meters* share with other poems of the Southern group, but not with supposedly Anglian verse, since it is unlikely that poems as diverse in style and subject as, for example, the *Meters* and *Genesis B* should share so many features, due to the prosaic nature of the former—and this is an especially apt comparison, since the latter is widely regarded as a translation of the Alfredian period.[30] Although *Beowulf* and *Genesis B* are both written in epic style, the nonstandard dialect features of the latter are like those of the *Meters* rather than of *Beowulf*. And eleven poems of diverse subject, from the heroic to versified catalogues, could not reasonably be claimed to evince the same style by mere coincidence. But it is preferable to be as cautious as possible in this instance, and so to help ensure against stylistic interference it will be useful to add to the group some late Southern verse that is defined as Southern by some means other than the syncope criterion—and that is preferably of conservative style. *Maldon* and the

[28]See Kiernan (as above, p. 249, n. 14), pp. 45–46; and Hiroshi Ogawa, *Old English Modal Verbs: A Syntactical Study*, Anglistica 26 (Copenhagen: Rosenkilde & Bagger, 1989), p. 50; and cf. the review of the latter in *JEGP* 90 (1991), 546–49.

[29]A few of the features of the poetic koine studied below in §335 are frequent in the *Meters* but not the corresponding prose translation. But in general it is true that the nonstandard features of the *Meters* also characterize the prose, and so must be regarded as due to Anglian and Kentish influence on early West-Saxon spelling rather than to poetic usage (Campbell, §§17, 258).

[30]This dating of the poem is probably correct: see the review of Doane's *Saxon Genesis* forthcoming in *PQ*. Kiernan also objects to the use of *Genesis B* as a testing ground for Southernisms, because it is a translation from Old Saxon. His objection is sound to the extent that the poem's origins have been employed to excuse the application of a double standard: frequently its Southernisms have been taken for reliable dialect evidence, and its possibly Anglian features explained as due to Old Saxon influence. Its Southern features, too, Kiernan objects, might derive from Old Saxon. But clearly the objection does not justify ignoring *Genesis B* altogether. The matter can only be judged on a case-by-case basis, by a comparison of dialectal features with Old Saxon equivalents in instances in which conclusions depend heavily on the evidence of *Genesis B*. Sievers' syncope, for example, is a feature that is clearly not due to Old Saxon influence, and so it would be wrong to disallow evidence such as this. Thus, certain features of the poem may still be disregarded as evidence on the basis of the assumption that they are due to Old Saxon influence, as long as those features are not found in other poems of the Southern group. The influence of the Old Saxon *Genesis* is undeniably very strong in *Genesis B*, and the point is perhaps best demonstrated by the large number of foreign words in the poem: see Timmer's edition, pp. 27–39.

four tenth-century Chronicle poems (Parker MS) should suffice.[31] They lack structural syncope only for reasons of content, and the possibility that they are not Southern is remote enough that most scholars consider it negligible.[32] In the case of *Maldon* there is also a small amount of linguistic evidence: the form *gofol* (61b) is a Southeastern spelling not found elsewhere in verse, though *gafol-* and *gaful-* are found several times; also, *stynt* is a Southeastern form. Other spelling criteria are less decisive.[33] These poems are also considered conservative in their style.[34] It will in fact be demonstrated below that there is no significant variation in dialect features across this body of late Southern verse: for example, though the style of *Brunanburh* is conservative, and that of the *Meters of Boethius* unconservative, the nonstandard dialect features encountered in the two are roughly the same. This is a conclusion of the first importance, for it provides counterevidence to the hypothesis that the incidence of nonstandard dialect forms is dictated by poetic style. Thus in one of the few instances in which it is possible to test Whitelock's objection that the incidence of dating and dialect indicators may also be a correlate of style, the suggestion proves to be unfounded.

[31]Since some scholars seem not to be aware of the fact, it ought to be pointed out that the dialect of Essex was Saxon, not Anglian, and thus had Sievers' syncope, as confirmed by the Middle English evidence. For example, B. J. Timmer mistakenly attributes the view to E. V. Gordon that *Maldon* was originally written down in an Anglian dialect: see his *Judith*, p. 5. The dialect origin of the *Death of Edward* (1065) is less certain. The poem is contained in just two of the Chronicle manuscripts, C (BL MS Cotton Tiberius B.i, probably written at Abingdon) and D (BL MS Cotton Tiberius B.iv, from the West Midlands, probably Worcester). In the C version cf. *weolan* (7b, D *weolm*), *Walum* (9b), *Sexum* (11a, D *sæxum*), and the like. For much of the eleventh century, the entries in C and D are closely related, indicating a common source, and the section containing these affinites encompasses both the *Death of Edward* and the *Death of Alfred* (1036). The latter poem contains the rhymes *cōmon : nāmon* (12; Anglian *nōmon*), and *gȳt : hēt* (16; *gēt* is rare in West Saxon: see §360, with n. 132). In line 15, the rhyme *scylde : acwealde* seems to demand *cylde*, to *cyllan* (see the *OED* s.v. *kill*).

[32]E.g., Campbell remarks, "The two poems on the victories of Æthelstan and Eadmund in 937 and 942 can hardly be regarded as non-West-Saxon in origin" (§18). See also Jordan, *Eigentümlichkeiten*, p. 64; and J. J. Campbell, p. 353, n. 17. These poems are historical narratives, and so offer few verbs in the present tense. The only relevant form in the *Chronicle* poems is metrically confirmed *gebeded* (*Brunanburh* 33b); on instances in *Maldon* see above, p. 274, n. 13.

[33]See Scragg's edition, pp. 24–25 and 28. The errors in the burnt manuscript might suggest that it was at some remove from the autograph or fair copy, and so spelling is an especially untrustworthy indicator in this instance. But it is debatable whether all the errors are not Casley's; and in any case it would be something of a coincidence if the poem was not composed in Essex, and happened to acquire East Saxon features in the course of transmission. As always, such evidence is only probabilistic, but the probability that it suggests is not negligible.

[34]E.g., Dobbie remarks, "In style and diction the *Battle of Brunanburh* follows the older poetry rather closely" (ASPR 6:xl), and "In style and vocabulary the *Battle of Maldon*, despite its late date, clearly belongs to the traditional heroic poetry" (p. xxxi).

§334. The Southern group thus comprises the three poems by Alfred, *Genesis B*, *Judgment Day II*, *An Exhortation to Christian Living*, the *Rune Poem*, the *Menologium*, the *Lord's Prayer II*, *A Prayer*, *Maldon*, and the tenth-century Chronicle poems. The *Kentish Hymn* and *Psalm 50* will not be included in the Southern group because the point of this survey of features is to determine whether the common deviations from West-Saxon standards of orthography encountered in verse are genuine dialect indicators or aspects of the koine. These two poems, on the other hand, are so thoroughly imbued with a variety of unmistakably Kentish features that they are linguistically unique in verse, and do not represent the koine well.[35] But they may be employed for comparative purposes with regard to Southeastern dialect features in the Southern group. The only syncopated form in these poems is *anfehst* (*Psalm 50* 135b), but even orthographically unsyncopated forms are few: compare *sitest* (*Kentish Hymn* 30a), *standeð* (*Psalm 50* 44b), and *geeadmeded* (128a).

§335. It should be established at the outset that many of the orthographic peculiarities that have been suggested as possible non-West-Saxon indicators of dialect can be found in this Southern group of poems. Except for Kentish features that are not paralleled in supposedly Anglian verse, these peculiarities must therefore be regarded in general as aspects of the poetic koine. The phonological/graphic dialect indicators most commonly cited may be listed as follows.

(1) Anglian retraction of *æ* (WS *ea*) to *a* before covered *l* (Luick, §§138, 146; Campbell, §143; Brunner, §85): spellings such as *ald*, *cald*, *haldeð*, *waldend*, and *waldeð* are to be found in most of the Southern poems. The Kentish *Psalm 50* has *aldor* (40a, 69b, 103a) and *waldend* (92b, 116a, 150a). Middle English place-name evidence confirms the testimony of Old English texts that this feature was confined to the Anglian areas, and *ea* was general throughout the South.[36] And so the common spellings in early West Saxon with *a* (examples are provided by Tupper, "Philological Legend," pp. 248–49) are to be regarded as due to Mercian influence on Alfredian spelling: see below, §337.

(2) Anglian (mainly Northumbrian) retraction of *æ* (WS *ea*) to *a* before covered *r* (Luick, §147; Campbell, §144; Brunner, §84, n. 1): the only instance is *gegarwod* (*Genesis B* 431b). But especially since the Anglian form of the verb is usually *gearwian*, the form in *Genesis B* is

---

[35]It should be said that the cause of the Kentish influence on these poems is disputed. Dobbie (ASPR 6:lxxxii–lxxxiii) suggests that they are West-Saxon in origin, and were simply copied at St. Augustine's in Canterbury. This seems to be Kenneth Sisam's view, as well: see "Canterbury, Lichfield, and the Vespasian Psalter," *RES*, n.s. 7 (1956), 1–10, 113–31, at 125, n. 2. But counterarguments are offered below (§335.5)

[36]See Eilert Ekwall, *Contributions to the History of Old English Dialects*, Lunds universitets årsskrift, n.s. pt. I, vol. 12, no. 6 (Lund: Gleerup), 1–39. For ordinary prose evidence in the Middle English etyma of words like *bold*, *hold*, *told*, and *fold*, see the *Linguistic Atlas of Late Mediaeval English*, dot map 930.

perhaps likelier to be due to the influence of the Old Saxon original (cf. OSax. *garuuuian*), which is the cause of many of the peculiarities of the language of *Genesis B*.[37] There are no sure examples of this feature in the test group of poems. Klaeber (p. lxxiv) suggests that Anglian *\*barn* underlies the form *brand* in the manuscript at *Beowulf* 1020b.

(3) Anglian (mainly Northumbrian) *æ* as the *i*-mutation of *a* derived from *æ* before covered *r* (Luick, §188.1; Campbell, §193a; Brunner, §96.4; cf. (2) above and (6) below): *hwærfð* (*Meters* 20.217b), *hwærfeð* (20.211b). Compare *hwerfeð* (28.15b), and *hwerfð* three times in the prose text. Outside the Southern group are *gegærwan* (*Genesis A* 2856b, to be compared with *gegarwod* under (2) above), *wærc-* (*Guthlac B* 1028a and twice in the metrical charms), and *wærgð-* (*Christ I* 57a, 98a, *Christ III* 1271b, *Christ and Satan* 89b), in the last instance perhaps due to hypercorrection, as discussed under (5) below. See also Tupper, "Philological Legend," p. 249.

(4) Anglian *æ* as *i*-mutation of *a* before covered *l* (Luick, §188.1; Campbell, §200.1; Brunner, §96.4): *befælled* (*Genesis B* 361a). To this may be compared *ældran* and *ælde* in the Kentish *Psalm 50* (65a, 142a): this looks like an Anglian form (Campbell, §290), but it is perhaps due to hypercorrection (see (5) below). This feature is not uncommon in the test group of poems in forms of *bæld-* (*Andreas* 1186a, and perhaps *Beowulf* 2018a: see Klaeber's note), *-wælm-* (*Genesis A* 980b [MS *hyge wælmos*], *Beowulf* 2066a, 2135a, 2546b, *Andreas* 452a, 1542a, *Christ II* 831a), *æld-* (*Cædmon's Hymn* 5b, *Juliana* 727b, *Christ II* 582a, 620b, 780b), and *bælc* (*Judith* 267a). Compare (7) below. Ekwall (see (1) above) studied the distribution of reflexes of OE (WS) *-wiella* (Angl. *-wælla*, Kent. *-wella*) in Middle English place-names, and found that reflexes of OE *ie* are found in the West and South Saxon areas; of *æ* throughout most of the West Midlands; and of *e* everywhere else, including the entire East Saxon area (Essex, Middlesex, and part of Hertfordshire).[38]

(5) Mercian and Kentish raising of *æ* to *e* (Luick, §180; Campbell, §§164–69, 288; Brunner, §52): compare *beþ* (*Rune Poem* 46b)[39] and

[37]For a survey of such influence see Erwin Hönncher, "Zur Interpolation der ags. Genesis Vers 235–851," *Anglia* 7 (1884), 469–96.

[38]Pp. 40–65. See also A. H. Smith, *English Place-Name Elements*, English Place-Name Society 25–26 (Cambridge: Cambridge Univ. Press, 1956), s.vv. *wella* (2:250–53), *welm* (2:253), *belg* (1:27), and *elf* (1:149). Gillis Kristensson confirms Ekwall's conclusions, finding that the *wæll(e)* forms predominate in the dioceses of Lichfield and Hereford, and argues further that the same geographical distribution should be assumed for the second fronting: see "A Middle English Dialect Boundary," in the Fisiak Festschrift, 1:443–57. See also his *Survey of Middle English Dialects 1290–1350: The West Midland Counties*, Skrifter utgivna av Vetenskapssocieteten i Lund 78 (Lund: Lund Univ. Press, 1987), 42.

[39]Possibly *e* here is Hickes's error for *ę*. But there are other forms in this poem suggesting Southeastern influence: cf. *(wen)ne* (22a, the name supplied from the margin), *semannum* (45a), and possibly *breneð* (43a) and *iar* (corrected to *ior*, 87a). The

*westrn* (*Death of Edgar* 37b); and in *Maldon, (ea)steðe* (63a), *leg* (276b), and *wrec* (279a).[40] A result of the merger of the two sounds is that West Mercian and Kentish scribes will frequently employ hypercorrections, as in *Psalm 50, brega* (2a), *gefræmmað* (14b), and so forth. The confusion of the sounds is also especially frequent in *Christ and Satan*: see Appendix A. In the Southern group the only examples of this confusion are two instances of *stæfne* in the *Lord's Prayer II* (11b, 50b), which is also found in the Worcester (D) Chronicle version of *Brunanburh* (34a); but this spelling of the word is found in other texts in the same manuscript,[41] such as *Apollonius of Tyre* and the *Regularis concordia*, and so it may be a scribal addition.[42] The form *þægne* at *Genesis B* 409a is a late West-Saxon spelling, perhaps indicating vocalization of *g* (Brunner, §55 n.).

---

form *wintergeteles* (*Coronation of Edgar* 14a) is not an example of this raising, since *-tēl-* can be shown to have a long vowel on grounds independent of the meter: see Arthur S. Napier, "Aeng. *getæl, getel* 'Zahl'," *PBB* 24 (1899), 246–48.

[40]That this feature is genuine in *Maldon* is confirmed by some examples of hypercorrection, *stæde(fæst)* at 127a, and *(wæl)ræste* at 113b. There are also unstressed examples in *hælæð* (249b) and *æræende* (28a). The *Linguistic Atlas of Late Mediaeval English* indicates that 'had' is spelt with *e* in the Southwest Midlands (including the lower Severn), Kent, and in scattered instances in Essex and southern Suffolk (dot map 12). Similarly, a modern survey finds [ɛ] in *apple* in parts of Kent, Surrey, and Sussex, with an isolated instance at Little Baddow in central Essex. Essex more clearly shares with Kent the post-Old English raising in *man* and *carrots*: see Harold Orton et al., *The Linguistic Atlas of England* (London: Croom Helm, 1978), phonological maps 1, 2, and 5. In Essex place-names *e* for *æ* is rare: see P. H. Reaney, *The Place-Names of Essex*, English Place-Name Society 12 (Cambridge: Cambridge Univ. Press, 1935), p. xxxvi.

[41]Cambridge, Corpus Christi College, MS 201. This manuscript also shows frequent examples of *æ* for WS *e* as the *i*-mutation of *a* before nasal consonants, and on this score Helmut Gneuss uses it to illustrate the dangers of relying heavily on Middle English dialect evidence to localize Old English texts: the manuscript need not come from Essex or Middlesex, he says, because some other Old English manuscripts which "display this very same phonological or orthographic feature, quite definitely come from other parts of England—Kent, for example" ("Origin," p. 72). For references to manuscripts containing this feature see Gneuss, *Hymnar und Hymnen im englischen Mittelalter* (Tübingen: Niemeyer, 1968), pp. 160–61. But Karl-Gustav Ek has shown that this must also have been a dialect feature of (in addition to Essex and Middlesex) Hertfordshire, Surrey, and East Sussex, with just a few instances in Kent: see *The Development of OE æ (i-mutated ă) before Nasals and OE æ in South-Eastern Middle English* (Lund: Gleerup, 1975).

[42]*Stæfn* is frequent in some other West-Saxon texts, as well (as Campbell notes, §328). The change perhaps arose by analogy to the alternation between *hræfn* and *hremn*, which Bülbring (§170 n.) and Luick (§186) explain as due to raising of *æ* before *m*. Campbell (p. 74, n. 4) rejects this explanation, suggesting that the words were originally *i*-stems; but the comparative evidence is rather negative: cf. OIcel. *stafn, hrafn*. Bülbring and Luick's explanation better accounts for the difference in vocalism between *stefn* and *hræfn*, given that the former seems to have etymological *m*, and the latter *ƀ*, as remarked by H. M. Flasdieck, "OE *nefne*, a Revaluation," *Anglia* 69 (1950), 135–71 (at 142–43), and 70 (1951), 46. It does not appear possible to localize *stæfn* very well on the basis of Middle English evidence.

Confusion of *æ* and *e* is frequent in the test group of poems: for example, Klaeber lists eighteen examples in *Beowulf* (pp. lxxiv–lxxv, §§7.1, 8.1). It is also found in the *Kentish Hymn* (*sigefest* 16a, *heleða* 34b, *fegere* 43a) and *Psalm 50* (*efter* 35a, *elmehtig* 77a, etc.). Instances of *e* for WS *æ* in texts without hypercorrective *æ* thus do for the most part seem likely to be due to non-West-Saxon origins. Hypercorrective *æ* is due to the attempts of non-West-Saxon scribes to write the standard language, and so for an originally West-Saxon poem to show hypercorrective *æ*, it would first have to have been "translated" into another dialect, in order to require re-Saxonization. It is more likely, then, in the absence of counterevidence, that texts with hypercorrective *æ* are not West-Saxon compositions. For this reason Dobbie's and Sisam's suggestion (see above, p. 283, n. 35) that the *Kentish Hymn* and *Psalm 50* are West-Saxon compositions that acquired Kentish features by copying at Canterbury seems unlikely: if the poems were originally West-Saxon, the Kentish scribe must have been singularly inept at writing his own dialect to have substituted Kentish forms for West-Saxon ones on such an irregular basis. And if his intent was rather to write standard West Saxon, it is not very credible that he should have done such a singularly poor job of copying a West-Saxon exemplar. More probably the poems are Kentish in origin, and the Kentish scribe of MS Vespasian D.vi, who wrote good Kentish in the prose portion of his work, was merely attempting to write the standard poetic language in the poetic portion: it must be remembered that although the koine as attested in the existing manuscripts exhibits many non-West-Saxon features, it is still primarily West-Saxon in nature, and thus more difficult for non-West-Saxon scribes than for West-Saxon ones. (The point is demonstrated by the scribes of *Christ and Satan*: see Appendix A.) It is difficult to explain the presence of hypercorrective *æ* under any assumption other than that the scribe was a Kentishman attempting to write West-Saxon. In the parallel instance of prose, there is abundant evidence that West Saxon, as the standard dialect of the later period, was written at monasteries all over England, with varying degrees of success.[43] The geographical distribution of this feature has been

---

[43]See Campbell, §8, with the Mercian and Northumbrian charters cited there; and see C. R. Hart, *The Early Charters of Northern England and the North Midlands* (Leicester: Leicester Univ. Press, 1975). For Kentish, Richard Taxweiler traces the gradual subordination of Mercian and Kentish features in the charters to the West-Saxon standard, in his Berlin doctoral dissertation, *Angelsächsische Urkundenbücher von kentischem Lokalcharakter* (Berlin: Mayer & Müller, 1906), esp. p. 58. Further examples are provided by Willy Schlemilch, *Beiträge zur Sprache und Orthographie spätaltengl. Sprachdenkmäler der Übergangszeit*, Studien zur englischen Philologie 34 (Halle: Niemeyer, 1914), pp. 69–71. Helmut Gneuss (*Hymnar*, pp. 188–89: see n. 41 above) offers a similar explanation for the mixture of Kentish and West-Saxon forms in the Latin hymns in Durham, Cathedral Library MS B.iii, on which see also von Schaubert, pp. 135–37. The standard West Saxon that was the literary dialect in prose of the later period could be strange and difficult even for West-Saxon scribes, for whom it was also

studied in both Middle and Modern English dialect surveys: see above, p. 41, n. 70.

(6) Non-WS *e* (eWS *ie*) as the *i*-mutation of *æ* broken to *ea* before covered *r* (Luick, §194; Campbell, §200.2; Brunner, §96.4): in the *Meters of Boethius* are *amerred* (8.44a), *oncerran* (10.39b), *behwerfed* (13.77b), *hwerfeð* (28.15b), and so forth. (On *werð* < *wiorþiþ* at *Metrical Epilogue* 21b see Brunner, §107, n. 1). But in the Southern group this feature appears only in the *Meters*, and so the counterevidence is inconclusive, since the Cotton manuscript shows considerable imitation of non-West-Saxon spelling (Campbell, §17, and see below, p. 294, n. 59). Thus for instance *amerred, oncerran*, and *behwerfed* also appear in the prose of the *Consolation*. Yet it may be doubted whether this feature is of any significance, since the same development before *h* is found in *bilgeslehtes* (45b) and *hlehhan* (47b) of the Parker MS version of the *Battle of Brunanburh* (see below, n. 53; and cf. *-meht-* in the Kentish poems). This feature is frequent in the test group of poems: in *Andreas*, for example, *awerged* (1299a), *ermðu* (1162a), *gerwan* (1634a; cf. (3) above), *herd* (1213a), and *werig-* 'accursed' (86a, 615a). It is also found in *Psalm 50* (*ferdrinc* 22a, *gecerre* 64b, *derne* 70b, etc.).

(7) Kentish *e* (eWS *ie*) as the *i*-mutation of *æ* broken to *ea* before covered *l* (Luick, §194.2; Campbell, §200.1): for example *felð* (*Meters* 5.15b), *widgel* (10.10b), *æwelm* (20.259a), *wel-* (*Metrical Epilogue* 7b, 24b), *eld-* (*Rune Poem* 77b, 81b), *heaðowelm* (*Genesis B* 324a). But this feature is also found in supposedly Anglian verse in the stem *eld-* (five times in *Beowulf*; also *Elene* 476a, *Andreas* 1057a, and elsewhere); and in *-welm-* (*Elene* 579a, 1257a, *Andreas* 495b, *Christ and Satan* 27a). This *e* is also found in Anglian prose texts, beside *æ*, as in *belg, eldra, cwelman*, and others in the Rushworth Gospels (see Brunner, §96, n. 6). These Anglian attestations are not surprising in view of Ekwall's findings (see (4) above), according to which this feature should also be expected in the East Saxon and Kentish areas; yet it is not found in the *Kentish Hymn* and *Psalm 50*, where *æ* appears instead.

(8) Southeastern confusion of *e* and *y* (Luick, §183; Campbell, §§288ff., 298; Brunner, §31, n. 1): *merge* (*Meters* 13.45a), *rene* (29.10a), *(wen)ne* (*Rune Poem* 22a, but the name is supplied from the margin), *untryowða* (*Genesis B* 581a; cf. *fyore* at *Genesis A* 1184b, and *wryon* at 1572b), and possibly *styde* (*Genesis B* 356a, but see Brunner, §263.1 and n. 5).

---

artificial, due to various sound changes, especially the merger of unstressed vowels to a central sound. The point has been demonstrated particularly well by René Derolez, "Norm and Practice in Late Old English," *Proceedings of the Eighth International Congress of Linguists*, ed. Eva Sivertsen (Oslo: Oslo Univ. Press, 1958), pp. 415–17. For this reason it can be said that the dramatic changes in the English language reflected in some early Middle English texts represent less likely an acceleration of language change after the Conquest than a breakdown of the Anglo-Saxon institutions that maintained orthographic standards (see above §§316f.).

Probable examples in less than fully stressed syllables are *unnet* (*Meters* 10.17b, 21a, etc.), *stynt* (*Maldon* 51a), and *ættrynne* (47a). If *trym* at *Maldon* 247a is not an example, then *trem* at *Beowulf* 2525a is; but it seems likelier that *trem* is the form of the standard dialect.[44] The etymology of *hildepremman* (*Juliana* 64a) is unknown. The only other example in the test group of poems is MS *syndon* at *Daniel* 412b; but see Campbell, §326. The spellings with *yo* for *eo*, at least, are peculiar enough that they seem to demand the assumption of genuine Kentish influence; and the Junius MS has in fact usually been thought to come from Canterbury.[45] The texts that it contains very possibly underwent a thorough revision at the time *Genesis B* was inserted into *Genesis A* (see below, §362). In *Psalm 50* compare *sceldig* (20b), *sennum* (38a), *geltas* (39b), and so forth. On the basis of Middle English evidence, Karl-Gustav Ek identifies Kent, Essex, and Suffolk as the central area of the region in which this development took place, though *e* is also predominant in East Sussex, eastern Surrey, Middlesex (including London), Hertfordshire, and Cambridgeshire; the original area probably included Norfolk, as well.[46] This conclusion agrees in general with the findings of the *Linguistic Atlas of Late Mediaeval English* (dot map 1057) that instances of *-e-* in late Middle English forms of *pride, hide,* and *bride* are restricted to the area that Ek demarcates, with a few isolated exceptions in the South and West.

(9) *æ* for *ē*, *i*-mutation of *ō*, perhaps due to scribal misinterpretation of Northumbrian and archaic *œ*, such as apparently underlies similar instances in the Old English translation of Bede's *History*.[47] But this could also be simply a late orthographic feature.[48] The only example is *sæl* (*Meters* 15.10a), and this feature is also found in the prose of the

---

[44]Either way, the word must show *i*-mutation, and so it is a *ja*-stem, with final *-m* standing for *-mm*. The *ja*-stems in Proto-Indo-European were mainly denominative adjectives that could be substantivized: see Karl Brugmann, *Grundriss der vergleichenden Grammatik der indogermanischen Sprachen*, 2nd ed., vol. 2.1 (Strassburg: Trübner, 1906), §109. And so cf. Gk. δρόμος 'race, race-course', with full grade of the root; and also Skt. *dandramyatē* 'runs about'.

[45]M. R. James first identified the Junius MS as the "Genesis anglice depicta" listed in the catalogue of Christ Church, Canterbury, from the early fourteenth century. Peter J. Lucas has adduced arguments for attributing the work to Malmesbury: see his edition of *Exodus*, pp. 2–5. But the evidence for a Canterbury provenance seems more reliable: see the responses by David Jost in his review of Lucas' book, *Speculum* 54 (1979), 829–31; Thomas Shippey's review, *MLR* 75 (1980), 616–18; and Rodney Thomson, "Identifiable Books from the Pre-Conquest Library of Malmesbury Abbey," *ASE* 10 (1981), 1–19, at 16–18.

[46]*The Development of OE ӯ and ēo in South-Eastern Middle English*, Lund Studies in English 42 (Lund: Gleerup, 1972), p. 122.

[47]See Max Deutschbein, "Dialektisches in der ags. Uebersetzung von Bedas Kirchengeschichte," *PBB* 26 (1901), 169–244, at 200, n. 3.

[48]See Schlemilch, p. 21 (as above, n. 43); and Campbell, §198.

*Consolation*,[49] but in no non-Alfredian verse of the Southern group. The *Kentish Hymn* has *blætsiað* (8a): compare Northumbrian *gebloedsiga*.

(10) Non-WS *ē* for Gmc. *ǣ* (Luick, §§117–18; Campbell, §128; Brunner, §§62–63): *mece* (*Meters* 9.29b, *Maldon* 167b, etc.), *geþwerað* (*Meters* 29.46b), *receð* (*Meters* 29.61a), *femnena* (*A Prayer* 46a), *beron* (*Maldon* 67b), *wegon* (98b), *gefrege* (*Coronation of Edgar* 9b, *Death of Edgar* 34b), and probably *ofet* (*Genesis B* 638b et passim; cf. *ofætes* 461b and passim). Yet all of these spellings are more or less conventional in verse, while *Psalm 50* has some unusual ones: forms of *ded* appear four times (19a, 44a, 84a, 147b), and nowhere else in verse, though the spelling *dæd* in simplices and compounds is very common in verse. Similarly, at *Beowulf* 1135b, acc. pl. *sele* (to *sæl*) is found, the only instance of such a spelling of this root in verse, though the word and its derivates are fairly common. The verse in which it appears is slightly obscure, suggesting perhaps that *e* was left unchanged because of uncertainty about the meaning.[50] So also, *e* for *ǣ* is found in *(-)red* only at *Beowulf* 3006a and *Ruin* 19a. There are also several probable examples in the preterite of strong verbs of the fourth and fifth classes, e.g. *bere* at *Daniel* 747b. These observations suggest that the spelling *e* for Gmc. *ǣ* is a reliable dialect indicator in some of the less conventional items of vocabulary: compare *hǣlend* under (11) below. Clearly, for some words the poetic koine normally had *ē* (e.g. *mēce*), and for others *ǣ* (e.g. *lǣce*, *mǣre*, *mǣg*). And so although Sisam (pp. 126–28) is right to object to the way in which *mēce* has been used as a dialect indicator, it is an overgeneralization to conclude that the spelling *e* for Gmc. *ǣ* has no bearing on dialect origins. The geographical distribution of this feature has been studied repeatedly. Perhaps the most important and reliable study is that of Alois Brandl, who finds on the basis of alternation between *strat-* and *stret-* (shortened from OE *strǣt-* and *strēt-*) in Middle English place-names that the isogloss runs more or less along the northern border of ancient Wessex (but including parts of Gloucestershire, Worcestershire, and Warwickshire), east to the middle of Essex, and then north to the middle of Norfolk.[51] This line is

---

[49]Cf. *gefægð* at p. 54, line 17 of Sedgefield's edition. On the other hand, *gedræfð* (*Meters* 18.3a, 25.42a) and *gedræfnesse* (22.61a) are probably not examples of *ǣ* for *ē* but of confusion of *drǣfan* 'drive' (cf. Gothic *draibjan*) and *drēfan* 'trouble' (Gothic *drobjan*), which is understandable given the similarity of meanings. Although confusion of *ǣ* and *ē* does occur infrequently in West-Saxon prose, instances of *ge-, tōdrǣf(ed)ness* are too frequent to be explained this way.

[50]"oþðæt oþer com / gear in geardas, swa nu gyt deð, / þa ðe syngales sele bewitiað, / wuldortorhtan weder" (1133b–36a).

[51]*Zur Geographie der altenglischen Dialekte*, Abhandlungen der kgl. Preußischen Akademie der Wissenschaften, Phil.-hist. Klasse, 1915, no. 4 (Berlin: Reimer, 1915). Other studies of the problem include those of Alois Pogatscher, "Die englische *ǣ/ē* Grenze," *Anglia* 23 (1901), 302–9; Otto Ritter, "Zur englischen *ǣ/ē* Grenze," *Anglia* 37 (1913), 269–75; James Hulbert, "The 'West Midland' of the Romances," *Modern Philology* 19 (1921), 1–16 at 7; R. M. Wilson, "*ǣ*[1] and *ǣ*[2] in Middle English,"

generally confirmed by the findings of J. P. Oakden (pp. 23–24) with regard to Middle English rhymes of tense and lax varieties of *ē*. Other types of evidence in regard to geographical distribution are for the most part inconclusive. Recently Richard Hogg and Eric Stanley have presented good evidence suggesting that the development of *ǣ* to *ē* in Kentish is a relatively late development, observable in the historical records.[52] Tupper ("Philological Legend," p. 247) argues that there is a tendency for *ǣ* to be represented as *ē* after palatal consonants in some Southern texts.

(11) Kentish and (before dental consonants) Anglian *ē* (WS *ǣ*) as *i*-mutation of *ā* from Gmc. *ai* (Luick, §187; Campbell, §§288, 292; Brunner, §97, n. 1): *semannum* (*Rune Poem* 45a), *gebeded* (*Brunanburh* 33b), *let* (from *lǣdan*: *Judgment Day II* 296a). The last of course is not an Anglian form. The first two again possibly show *e* for *ę*: see note 39 above, and compare MS *nęgled* at *Brunanburh* 53b. The latter is the reading of the Parker manuscript; the others have *gebǣded*.[53] This feature is infrequent elsewhere in the test group of poems: compare *gesne* (*Judith* 112a), and perhaps *stenan* (MS: *Elene* 151b), *elðes* (Gradon's correction of MS *eðles* at *Elene* 1294a), and *snedeþ* (Klaeber's correction of MS *sendeþ* at *Beowulf* 600a). *Psalm 50* has *helo* (113a) beside *hǣlo* (100a). This feature is perhaps a reliable indicator of dialect, especially when it is found in unconventional circumstances. For example, there are seventy-two forms of *hǣlend* in verse with the spelling *æ*, but just three with *e* (*Psalm 50* 50a, *Christ and Satan* 54a, 86a, the latter a poem with pronounced West Mercian features: see Appendix A). Oakden (p. 24) finds that this feature before dental consonants is evidenced by the rhymes of Middle English verse north of a line from mid-Shropshire to the Wash. The Middle English evidence for the Midlands is eastern; but

---

*Proceedings of the Leeds Philological and Literary Society*, Lit. and Hist. Sec. 3 (1935), 342–46; and Lee Lamar Snyder, "The Old English Dialect Boundaries: Some Place-Name Evidence" (Univ. of Pennsylvania diss., 1969), pp. 40–42. On the reason that a West-Saxon feature should be found also in the southwest Midlands in the Middle English period, see above, §52.

[52]Hogg, "On the Impossibility of Old English Dialectology," in *Luick Revisited*, pp. 183–204, at 193ff.; and Stanley, "Karl Luick's 'Man schrieb wie man sprach' and English Historical Philology," also in *Luick Revisited*, pp. 311–34, at 318.

[53]*Brunanburh* in the Parker Chronicle evinces an interesting array of orthographic features not paralleled in the other versions, esp. *e* for *ȳ/ī(e)* in *herefleman* (*Brunanburh* 23a), *geflemed* (32b), *Gelpan* (44b), *bilgeslehtes* (45b), and *hlehhan* (47b). It also has some conservative West-Saxon forms in comparison to poetic ones in the other manuscripts, e.g. *afaran* (7a, 52b, but also *aforan* in C) and *mæca* (40a; MS *mæcan*). So, too, it shares some typically early West-Saxon features with the work of the earlier hands in the manuscript, e.g. *o* for *a* in *condel* (15b), *ondlongne* (21a), and so forth. The prose written by this hand (annals for 925–955) is too meager to afford certainty, but spellings like *geflemed* are not characteristic of the preceding hands, and so may not be due to general Mercian influence on early West-Saxon orthography.

in Old English there are also many examples in VP.[54] Tupper ("Philological Legend," p. 251) rejects the significance of this feature, but confuses the Kentish and Anglian changes.

(12) Non-WS $\bar{e}$ (WS $\bar{\imath}e$) as $i$-mutation of $\bar{e}a$ (Luick, §194; Campbell, §200.5–7; Brunner, §106). Spellings such as *becnan, cepan, geman, hehst, henðo, heran* and *ned* are to be found in nearly all the poems of the Southern group. Compare *ales* (*Kentish Hymn* 33a) and *herdon* (*Psalm 50* 56b). The peculiar forms *sceone* and *sceonost* (*Genesis B* 549a, 704b) are difficult to explain; Timmer suggests that they are influenced by OSax. *skōni*, and Doane agrees.[55] This is no doubt correct, *e* being a glide (Campbell, §179). See also Tupper, "Philological Legend," p. 250.

(13) Southeastern confusion of $\bar{e}$ and $\bar{y}$ (Luick, §183; Campbell, §§288–91; Brunner, §31, n. 1): *getede* (*Meters* 13.44a). The form *niðhedige* (*Beowulf* 3165a) seems to be the only example elsewhere in the test group of poems. The *Kentish Hymn* has *gerena* (11b), and *Psalm 50* has *-cyne* (10b), *ontende* (28b), and *leðre* (41b). Compare (8) above.

(14) Kentish *eo* for *io* (eWS *ie*) as $i$-mutation of *io* before covered *r* (Campbell, §§201, 297): *beorhto* (*Meters* 21.39b; cf. VP *birhtu*), *weorð* (*Genesis B* 405b, 519b). This feature is largely confined to Kentish because in the Anglian dialects, *i* in the position for $i$-mutation before *r* usually failed to be affected by breaking (Luick, §139.2; Campbell, §154.3 and nn. 3–4; Brunner, §83 n.), and of course in West Saxon *io* was mutated to *ie*. Compare *feorran* (*Beowulf* 156a), as opposed to Li., Ru.[1] *afirr-*; but also *aferre* (*Psalm 50* 97a). Yet *eorre* and *eormen-* may also be Anglian: see Campbell, §154.3 and n. 3. Since *beorhto* in the *Meters* lacks smoothing, and *weorð* in *Genesis B* may be a hybrid (cf. poetic and Anglian *weorðeþ*), there is not actually any firm evidence in the Southern group for Anglian *eo* corresponding to eWS *ie* as the $i$-mutation of *io*, and so this possibly is a reliable indicator of non-West-Saxon origins. Forms of *eorre* appear in the clearly Kentish *Psalm 50*, and in *Beowulf, Elene, Andreas, Christ and Satan*, and *Solomon and Saturn*, beside forms of *yrre*, which is widely distributed in verse. *Eormen-* appears in *Beowulf, Solomon and Saturn II*, and the *Fortunes of Men*, beside *yrmen-* in *Beowulf, Juliana, Christ II*, and the *Menologium*. *Psalm 50* has *eorre* (24b), but also *hiorde* (101b, 107b). Compare (17) below.

---

[54]See Jordan, §48, n. 2. But in *Sir Gawain and the Green Knight* there is one instance of *clene* (line 146; OE *clǣne* < *klain(i)jaz*; cf. *clene* in Ru.[1] and Rit.) rhyming with *sene* (OE *-sēne*) and *grene* (OE *grēne*), as pointed out by Joyce Bazire, "ME $\bar{e}$ and $\bar{\text{e}}$ in the Rhymes of *Sir Gawain and the Green Knight*," *JEGP* 51 (1952), 234–35. For the examples in VP see Campbell, §292. In addition to the studies mentioned by Jordan see Luick, §§187, 361, n. 2; Joyce Bazire, "An Examination of Rhymes Containing Middle English $\bar{e}$," *Studia Neophilologica* 29 (1957), 111–22; and Gillis Kristensson, *A Survey of Middle English Dialects 1290–1350: The Six Northern Counties and Lincolnshire*, Lund Studies in English 35 (Lund: Gleerup, 1967), 49–53.

[55]Timmer, *The Later Genesis*, p. 24; Doane, *Saxon Genesis*, pp. 49–50.

(15) Kentish *io* for *eo* by breaking (Luick, §260; Campbell, §297; Brunner, §84, n. 5): *gewiorðan* (*Meters* 11.39b), *fior* (20.222a). Compare *biorg* (three times in *Beowulf*, once in *Guthlac A*), and *biorn* (twice in *Beowulf*). These spellings with *io* in *Beowulf* are all in the work of the second scribe, who does not change *eo* to *io* in *Judith*—suggesting that his *Beowulf* exemplar had *io*. In the Vercelli Book, *io* for *eo* of diverse origins is frequent. *Psalm 50* has forms of *hiort* three times (34b, 88b, 127b).

(16) Kentish *io* for *eo* under West-Saxon conditions for back mutation (Luick, §260; Campbell, §297; Brunner, §111): *siofian* (*Meters* 2.2b, 26.82b), *siofunga* (16.7b), *hiofones* (21.39a). But these forms also occur in the prose of the *Consolation*; and this feature is found in *Beowulf* (see Klaeber, p. lxxix, §14.2) and the Vercelli Book (as with (15) above). Forms of *hiofen* are frequent in the two Kentish poems. Compare examples of non-West-Saxon conditions for back mutation below, §343.

(17) Mercian *ēo* (eWS *īe*) as the *i*-mutation of *īo* (Luick, §261.1; Campbell, §§293–95; Brunner, §§38, 107): *steoran* (*Meters* 4.49b), *deore* (*Rune Poem* 74b, *Genesis B* 261a). But these may be West-Saxon (Campbell, §202; Brunner, §107): both are found in the prose of the *Consolation*, and the former spelling, at least, is also found in as good a witness of late West Saxon as Chrodegang's *Rule for Canons*. So also *geortreowe* (*Meters* 5.35a) is paralleled by *geortreowan* and several forms of *getrīewe* 'faithful' with *eo* in the prose. The form *oðeowde* (*Meters* 28.75a) probably does not belong here, as other forms of the verb in the *Consolation* belong to the stem with the short root vowel (a semi-analogical creation: see Campbell, §763 and p. 328, n. 2): compare inf. *eowian*, sg. *geewð* beside pl. *eowað*.[56] Compare (14) above. Forms like *þeostru* are common in late West-Saxon prose, but *deogol-* is confined to verse and the originally Mercian translations of Gregory's *Dialogues* and Bede's *Ecclesiastical History*. Other examples are *(-)heor-* (*Beowulf* 987a, 1372b, *Andreas* 34b), and the verb stem *treow-* (*Daniel* 268b, *Beowulf* 1166b, *Juliana* 435b). This feature is not found in the two Kentish poems.

(18) Southeastern *īo* for WS *ēo* (Luick, §260; Campbell, §297; Brunner, §38): this spelling is very frequent in the *Meters* and the *Metrical Epilogue* in words such as *bioð, glio-, hio, hrioh, lioð, siowian, gestrion,* and *þios,* in both verse and prose. Outside the Alfredian works in the Southern group it appears only in *Genesis B: niotan* (235a, 401b, 486b), *niobedd* (343a), *Hio* (684a), *sniomor* (830a) and *niod* (835b). These could be due to the influence of Old Saxon spelling (cf. OS *niotan, sniumo,* and *niud*), but *untryowða* at 581a (see (8) above) is difficult to account for except as the result of genuine Kentish influence. Yet orthographic *io* for

---

[56]Brunner (§§126, n. 2, 408, n. 14) offers the explanation of development of *ēw* to *ēow* for some later examples; but this change is not attested until the eleventh century, and at any rate this leaves unexplained the evidence of short vocalism in the *Consolation*.

*ēo* is also found in the second scribe's work in *Beowulf* (see Klaeber, p. lxxx, §17.1), and in the Vercelli Book; and so this criterion is unreliable. This feature is very frequent in the two Kentish poems, in *hlioðor-* (2a), *liof-* (3a), *þioda* (9b), and so forth, in the *Kentish Hymn*. Campbell regards this as simply a Kentish development, but Ek (see (8) above) concludes on the basis of Middle English place-name evidence that this *īo* had the same distribution as the change of *ȳ* to *ē̆*.

(19) Non-WS *io* (eWS *īe*) as the *i*-mutation of *īo* (Luick, §191; Campbell, §201.3–4; Brunner, §107): this is a feature of the *Consolation*, both verse and prose, in forms of *diore, stioran* and *ðiostre, ðiostro*. Elsewhere it does not occur in the Southern group. Only the last of these cannot be West-Saxon (see (17) above), and it may be Kentish (cf. MS *ðriostre* for *ðiostre* at *Kentish Hymn* 28b), given the other Kentish forms in the *Consolation* considered under (6), (8), and possibly (13)–(16), (18), and (20). Such spellings are not uncommon in the supposedly Anglian poems of the test group, as in *liodgeard* (*Genesis A* 229a; see Campbell, §202), and *-siona* (*Beowulf* 995b). *Psalm 50* has *ansione* twice (85a, 95a). In the Southeast, Ek finds that this feature has the same distribution as (18) above.

(20) Non-WS failure of diphthongization by initial palatal consonants (Luick, §172; Campbell, §185; Brunner, §§90ff.): in the *Meters* appear *sceldas* (1.2b; also in the Orosius), *ged* (2.5b), *gelp* (10.2a, 13b, 17b), *sceppend* (4.30a, 11.1a, etc.), *geta* (7.3b, 8.33b, 24.46a), and so forth. This is also a feature of the prose *Consolation*, and outside the *Meters* in the Southern group it appears only in *get* (*Coronation of Edgar* 13b). The rarity of this feature outside the *Meters* is noteworthy, since it is common in supposedly Anglian verse.[57] Examples in *Psalm 50* are common, for instance *sceppen(d)* (8b, 39a, 45b, 63b), *forgefenesse* (37a), and *begeton* (57b).

(21) Anglian retention of *-þl-* (WS *-tl-*) after a short vowel (with later voicing and metathesis: Luick, §§638.1, 673, 693.2b; Campbell, §§419–20; Brunner, §201.3): *bolde* (*Rune Poem* 73a), though this is emended from MS *blode*. *Bold-* does appear in the *Rule of Chrodegang*, a reliable witness of late West Saxon. As a place-name element the word is not found in East Anglia or the South, except for dubitable examples in Devon, Somerset, Hampshire, and Wight; and the form *bold* is restricted almost entirely to Mercia.[58]

---

[57]For examples in *Beowulf* see Klaeber, pp. lxxv–lxxvii (§§7.4, 8.4, 10.3–4). Robert Farrell, in his edition of *Daniel* and *Azarias* (London: Methuen, 1974), explains *agæf* at *Daniel* 452a as possibly due to the monophthongization of *ea* that begins to be attested in the eleventh century (Campbell, §329.2). This is not unlikely, given the other apparent instances of the change in this manuscript.

[58]See Smith (as above, p. 284, n. 38), 1:44 and map 8 in the back pocket of vol. 2; also Eilert Ekwall, "Ae. *botl, bold, boðl* in englischen Ortsnamen," *Anglia Beiblatt* 28 (1917), 82–91; and Bertil Sundby, *Studies in the Middle English Dialect Materials of Worcestershire Records* (Bergen: Norwegian Universities Press, 1963), p. 214.

§336. Some of these criteria cannot be considered disproved, since the counterevidence is weak. Among the possibly reliable dialect indicators are second fronting (5), Southeastern confusion of $\breve{y}$ and $\breve{e}$ (8 and 13), Mercian $\breve{e}o$ (eWS $\bar{\imath}e$) as the $i$-mutation of $io$ and $\bar{\imath}o$ (14 and 17), non-WS $\bar{\imath}o$ (eWS $\bar{\imath}e$) as the $i$-mutation of $\bar{\imath}o$ (19), and non-WS failure of diphthongization by initial palatal consonants (20). Some others may be reliable when applied only to unconventional spellings, especially non-WS $\bar{e}$ for Gmc. $\bar{æ}$ (10) and Kentish and (before dental consonants) Anglian $\bar{e}$ as $i$-mutation of $\bar{a}$ (11).

§337. In the Southern group some of these features are instanced only in Alfredian verse, yet are also attested in the prose of the *Consolation*. It is dubitable whether any of the more significant non-West-Saxon phonological features of the *Meters* are not also to be found in the prose work. The value of the evidence of the *Meters* may thus be questioned, since these features may simply result from the influence of non-West-Saxon spelling on Alfredian texts. Some Alfredian translations are clearly the work of Mercians: Bishop Wærferth of Worcester translated Gregory's *Dialogues* at Alfred's behest, and the vocabulary of the translation of Bede's *Ecclesiastical History* points unmistakably to a Mercian translator.[59] Yet even the best witnesses of "pure" early West Saxon—the first hand (at least) in the Parker manuscript of the Chronicle, the Hatton and Cotton manuscripts of Alfred's translation of Gregory's *Cura Pastoralis*, the Tollemache Orosius, and Sweet's charters 3 and 20—display an admixture of apparently Mercian features.[60] For example, *a*

---

[59]On the vocabulary of the Bede translation see J. J. Campbell. On the other hand, there is the possibility that the strongly Kentish color of some Alfredian texts derives from the originals. The matter cannot be settled conclusively with regard to the *Consolation*, but there is some circumstantial counterevidence. Prose and verse are preserved in B (BL MS Cotton Otho A.vi), a manuscript from the middle of the tenth century—the prose version in MS Bodley 180 in the Bodleian Library, from the beginning of the twelfth century, is too late to have any bearing on the question—but the lower half of a folio from another manuscript, N (formerly used as an end-leaf to Bodleian MS Junius 86—not Bodley 86, as Krapp has it), was edited by A. Napier before it was misplaced: see "Bruchstück einer altenglischen Boetiushandschrift," *ZfdA* 31, n.s. 19 (1887), 52–54. The fragment has not been found since. Napier dated the hand to the first half of the tenth century, and so this antedates B. The two parallel passages are brief, corresponding to pp. 32.18–33.10 and 34.15–35.7 in Sedgefield's edition, but the few definite Kentishisms in B are not paralleled in N: *þiof-* (B, p. 33.10 in Sedgefield) = *þeof-* (N); *get* (B, pp. 34.25, 35.6) = *git* (N); *leg* (B, p. 34.27) = *lig* (N). The evidence in the case of Alfred's translation of Augustine's *Soliloquies* is more conclusive. The *Dialogue of Solomon and Saturn*, in the same manuscript and the same scribal hand, also has marked Kentish features. Moreover, the early West-Saxon features of the text are so few that it is not plausible that original Kentish features should have been preserved any better than these; and thus the Kentishisms must be the result of later Kentish influence.

[60]Charter 3 (a grant of land by Cynewulf, king of Wessex) is a copy, but is nonetheless early: Bruckner dates it to the end of the eighth or the beginning of the ninth century (3:53), or simply to the eighth century (4:xiii).

is frequently unbroken before *l* in these texts, as in *onwald, saldon*, and *allum*; *o* for *a* before nasal consonants is widespread, as in *monig, monn, ond*, and *long*; and especially in the *Pastoral Care*, verbs are frequently immune to Sievers' syncope, as in *lædeð* and *drifeð*.[61] It is implausible that such spellings should reflect the actual state of affairs in early West-Saxon: *a* is not an earlier stage in the development of *ea* before checked *l*, but an Anglian innovation, and an early one, since breaking is an archaic development; before nasal consonants *a* is unlikely to have been rounded and subsequently unrounded in Wessex, and the evidence of the *Linguistic Atlas of Late Mediaeval English* shows this to have been a stable characteristic only of the West Midlands and parts of the North as far back as its geographical distribution can be traced; and although Walde's hypothesis does not rule out the possibility that unsyncopated verbs were common in Wessex before Alfred's reign, the particularly heavy incidence of unsyncopated forms in the *Cura Pastoralis* in comparison to other early West-Saxon texts seems better explicable as orthographic convention than as morphophonological reality—especially since other works that also purport to be by Alfred himself are not as rich in such forms.[62]

§338. Thus, the supposition that early West-Saxon orthography was influenced by Mercian standards of spelling seems likelier than the alternative explanations that have been proposed for the Anglianisms in early West-Saxon prose.[63] This, for example, is the opinion of Campbell (§§17, 185), Flasdieck,[64] Sisam (*Studies*, p. 294), Vleeskruyer (pp. 41–62), and Gneuss ("Origin," p. 82). The assumption derives support from the probability that early West-Saxon scripts are based on Mercian models:

---

[61]For a listing of unsyncopated forms in early West-Saxon texts see Hedberg (as above, p. 274, n. 12), pp. 111–12, 159, 201–2, 253–54, and 270. C. L. Wrenn discusses such features of early West Saxon in "'Standard' Old English," *Transactions of the Philological Society*, 1933, pp. 65–88. Vleeskruyer (p. 42, n. 4, and p. 43, n. 3) lists a variety of West Mercian features found in Alfredian prose and Æthelwulf's charter of 847, respectively; and Toon (chap. 3) traces in detail the rise and decline of Mercian *o* for *a* before nasal consonants over the course of the eighth and ninth centuries.

[62]This is then additional counterevidence to the view of Richard Hogg that alternations such as these are not merely orthographic, and are class-based: see above, p. 41, n. 71.

[63]Hedberg (again, as above, p. 274, n. 12) lists some other possibilities: "With regard to the Alfredian translations it has been surmised that the divergencies might be due to the difficulty of creating a water-tight standard which was previously non-existent. They have been explained as occasioned by non-West-Saxon scribes, by the lingering tradition from Mercian scriptioriums, and by the cropping-up of non-standardized West Saxon speech, called *patois* by Bülbring" (p. 6). The supposition that Mercian scribes are involved does not conflict with the conclusions presented here, but it does not seem likely: though possibly Alfred brought Mercian scribes to West-Saxon monasteries to carry out his literary and educational plans, this leaves the Anglianisms in the charters of Cynewulf and Æthelwulf unexplained.

[64]"Zur Charakteristik der sprachlichen Verhältnisse in altengl. Zeit," *PBB* 48, pt. 2 (1924), 376–413, at 388.

see Vleeskruyer's comparison (p. 44) of letter-forms in the Hatton manuscript of the *Pastoral Care* to those in the charters of Cenwulf (king of Mercia 796–821). Support also comes from the parallel instance of early Kentish orthography, which is perhaps universally acknowledged to bear the impress of Mercian conventions.[65] Early Kentish, best attested in Sweet's charters 34 and 37–42, and the endorsements to 28, 30, and 44, shows some of the same Mercian features as Alfredian texts, including the three features mentioned above. These features grow scarcer over the course of the ninth century, and are almost entirely missing from the tenth-century *Kentish Glosses*. Mercian influence on Kentish orthography is so widely acknowledged because Mercian domination of the Kentish church and state in the eighth century and the early ninth is well documented. But although the sources of information for Wessex in this period are sparser, it seems the West Saxons were no less subject to Mercian control.[66] Æthelbald of Mercia was able to style himself *rex Britanniae* in his charters after the death of Wihtred of Kent, in 725, and the abdication of Ine of Wessex, in 726, and as Bede tells us, all the kingdoms south of the Humber were subject to him. He dominated the South for nearly thirty years after. Following Æthelbald's murder in 757 the West Saxons were to reestablish a degree of independence for a few years; but after the mutually fatal struggle between Cynewulf and Cyneheard, in 789 Offa of Mercia was able to install his man Beorhtric on the West-Saxon throne, marrying his daughter to him and helping to drive his opponent, Alfred's grandfather Ecgberht, out of England. Mercian domination of Wessex thus prevailed until the battle of Ellendun in 825, when Ecgberht established the power of the West-Saxon kings once for all. Because relations between Wessex and Mercia were little different from those between Kent and Mercia, the political and cultural reasons advanced for Mercian influence on Kentish orthography apply no less to early West-Saxon scribal practice. And we have the additional evidence that when Alfred gathered ecclesiastics to help him in his

[65]The idea dates at least to H. M. Chadwick, "Studies in Old English," *Transactions of the Cambridge Philological Society* 4 (1899), 85–265, at 91, 183. William F. Bryan collects the evidence and details the political and religious history of Mercian domination in Kent, in *Studies in the Dialects of the Kentish Charters of the Old English Period* (Menasha, Wisc.: George Banta, 1915). See also Flasdieck (as in the preceding note), pp. 385–7, and *Forschungen zur Frühzeit der neuenglischen Schriftsprache*, Studien zur Englischen Philologie 25–26 (Halle: Niemeyer, 1922), 2:30, n. 2, with the references there; also Hedberg, p. 6; Campbell, §§207, 247, 258, 290; Brunner, §2, n. 3, etc. There is some evidence that despite spelling conventions, æ had already become e in Kent as early as ca. 710: see Blackburn, pp. 151–53.

[66]Toon chronicles the historical and cultural evidence for the Mercian domination of the South in the period of Mercian ascendency, pp. 16–43; see also his article "The Socio-Politics of Literacy in Early England: What We Learned at Our *Hlaford*'s Knee," *Folia Linguistica Historica* 6 (1985), 87–106.

program of reviving scholarship, he looked first to the Mercian church.[67] Chambers and Sisam have argued that there was little vernacular prose literature in England before Alfred's day.[68] As Chambers points out, this is what Alfred himself tells us in his preface to the translation of the *Pastoral Care*:

Ða ic þa ðis eall gemunde, þa wundrode ic swiðe swiðe þara godena witena þe giu wæron geond Angelcynn, & þa bec befullan ealla geleornod hæfdon, þæt hi hiora þa nanne dæl noldon on hiora ægen geðiode wendan.

Alfred's account of the decline of Anglo-Saxon scholarship is perhaps exaggerated.[69] But it cannot be so very far from the truth, since his contemporary ecclesiastical audience for this preface would certainly have known it if this were a severe distortion of the facts. It is at any rate clear now that the written homiletic tradition in Old English is late and Southern.[70] If this particular claim of Chambers' is in the main correct, the adoption of Mercian standards of spelling in the South should not be viewed as a supersedure of earlier traditions, but as an important factor in the initial formation of vernacular standards.[71]

§339. If there was strong Mercian influence on early West-Saxon prose, the Anglianisms in the three Alfredian poems perhaps ought not to be considered very strong evidence that the Anglianisms in poems like *Genesis A* are due to a poetic koine rather than to Anglian origins. But

---

[67]In Asser's account (chaps. 77–79), Alfred called upon the Mercians Wærferth, bishop of Worcester; Plegmund, whom he made archbishop of Canterbury in 890; and the priests Wærwulf and Æthelstan, who were his chaplains. Asser himself came from St. David's in Wales, and the other two assistants of Alfred mentioned by Asser (John and Grimbald) came from the Continent.

[68]R. W. Chambers, "The Lost Literature of Medieval England," *The Library*, 4th ser., vol. 5 (1925), 293–321, at 311, rpt. in *Essential Articles for the Study of Old English Literature*, ed. Jess B. Bessinger and Stanley J. Kahrl (Hamden, Conn.: Archon, 1968), pp. 3–26; and Sisam, *Studies*, p. 133 and n. 3. On the other hand, Vleeskruyer (pp. 18–22) argues that the *Life of St. Chad* must derive from a vital West Mercian prose tradition before Alfred's day. But the contradiction he remarks in Chambers' advocacy of a body of lost Mercian prose is mistaken, since Chambers regarded this homily as post-Alfredian.

[69]See especially Jennifer Morrish, "King Alfred's Letter as a Source on Learning in England in the Ninth Century," in *Studies in Earlier Old English Prose*, ed. Paul E. Szarmach (Albany: State Univ. of New York Press, 1986), pp. 87–107; and Allen J. Frantzen, *King Alfred*, Twayne's English Authors Series 425 (Boston: Twayne, 1986), pp. 5–6 and 110–11, with the references there. But cf. also David Knowles, *The Monastic Order in England*, 2nd ed. (Cambridge: Cambridge Univ. Press, 1949), chaps. 2–3.

[70]D. G. Scragg, "The Corpus of Vernacular Homilies and Prose Saints' Lives before Ælfric," *ASE* 8 (1979), 223–77, finds that the homiletic tradition antedating Ælfric is a late and narrow one, with Canterbury as its center.

[71]In reference to the alternative view that there was a Mercian standard literary dialect in use over a wide area of England in the eighth and ninth centuries, see the discussion and references given by Crowley, pp. 201–6.

then the same might be said of *Genesis B*, since this is widely regarded as an early West-Saxon translation.[72] The only very strong evidence in the Southern group for use of a poetic koine ought then to be the poems that are almost certainly post-Alfredian Southern compositions, such as the *Menologium*. Yet such material is sparse enough that the absence of certain Anglian features in it should not be surprising. There are other ways to prove the existence and detect the features of the poetic koine. As Sisam points out, unsyncopated verb forms are considerably more frequent in the *metra* of the *Consolation* than in the prose, and so Alfred must have regarded this as a feature of poetic language. The Southern group of poems also contains some vocabulary that is found in Anglian but not West-Saxon prose, and this vocabulary was thus most likely regarded by West-Saxons as poetic (see below, §367). Moreover, it should be observed that the evidence of Alfredian verse cannot be discounted altogether, since some Anglian features are common in early West-Saxon prose and others are not. Although *a* is rounded to *o* before nasal consonants with great frequency before the tenth century throughout the South, and this feature predictably has no reliable dialectal significance in verse, Anglian smoothing and back mutation in certain environments are not common features of Mercian-influenced Southern prose, and so features such as these could be taken as aspects of the poetic koine if found in the Southern group of poems.

§340. Anglian smoothing is almost unknown in the Southern group. It is of course impossible to predict which Anglian or archaic features will become part of the poetic koine and which will not, but perhaps a contributing factor here is the lateness of smoothing: it is one of the last of the "prehistoric" changes of Old English, later than the development of *æ* to non-WS *ē*, retraction of *æ* to *a* in *ald-* and such, mutation of *ea* to *e*, and other Anglian features found in the Southern group. It is in fact usually assumed not to have been completed at the time of the earliest texts (Luick, §240; Campbell, §222), though this is questionable (§398 below). If the main features of the poetic koine were established before this sound change was completed, it should not be surprising if the feature was of restricted occurrence in Southern verse, while other Anglian features were more general. Smoothing in the word *ferhð* must be disregarded in this context, since this is purely an item of poetic vocabulary, apparently otherwise unknown to the West Saxons.[73] Otherwise the only undeniable examples of smoothing in the Southern group are *sperca* (*Judgment Day II* 219b) and *berhtre* (*Meters* 22.22a); *tyhhað* (*Lord's Prayer II* 97a), whatever its significance, is not an Anglian spelling. As for *swiran* (*Meters* 10.19a; cf. *swyran* at 9.56a), with a long root vowel required by the meter, leaving aside the etymological difficulty (Campbell,

---

[72]See the editions of Timmer (p. 43), Doane (pp. 47–54), and Krapp (ASPR 1:xxvi.)
[73]See "Unferth and His Name," *MP* 85 (1987), 114, n. 8.

§241.2, n. 5), this must be discounted, anyway, since it also appears in the corrresponding prose of Alfred's translation (p. 46, l. 8 in Sedgefield's edition).

§341. The incidence of smoothing in the Southern group (3,700 lines) may be compared to that in *Beowulf* (3,182 lines), the Cynewulf canon (2,601), and *Genesis A* (2,319). Cynewulf's works of course are known to be Anglian by the rhymes in *Elene* (on which see below, §§389ff.). Comparison with *Beowulf* and *Genesis A* is appropriate, as these are the only presumably Anglian poems of a length approaching that of the Southern group, and they should help to ensure that the statistical differences between the Southern and Cynewulfian groups are not accidental. Information on the remaining longer poems of the test group is given in a more summary fashion, as they are not comparable in length.

(1) *Beowulf* displays a wide variety of smoothed diphthongs: (a) *æ* appears for WS *ea* in *hærgtrafum* (175b, MS *hrærg trafum*), *geæhtlan* (369a) and *geæhted* (1885a); (b) *æ* appears for WS *eo* in *wiðerræhtes* (3039b)—compare *cnæht, gefæht, -sæh* (imperative) beside *cneht, -feht, -seh* in Anglian texts (Brunner, §119, n. 5d); (c) *e* appears for WS *ea* in *hergum* (3072a); (d) *e* appears for WS *eo* in *ferhwearde* (305b) and *ferh* (2706b);[74] (e) *æ* appears for WS *ēa* in *ægwearde* (241b); (f) *ē* appears for WS *ēo* in *fela* (1032a: see Campbell, §229); (g) *ī* appears for WS *ēo* in *wigweorþunga* (176a, where *-ig- = -ī-*: see Campbell, §230) and five instances of *Wihstanes* (2752b, 2907b, 3076b, 3110b, 3120b; cf. *Weoxstanes* 2602b, *Weohstan* 2613b, *Weohstanes* 2862b).[75] Forms like *gefeh* (827b), *beg* (3163b), and *þeh* (fourteen times in verse, once in the Southern group) must be disregarded, as they may be due to the late West-Saxon smoothing of *ĕa* before *c, g,* and *h* (Campbell, §312). This includes most of the forms listed by Klaeber, §§8.3b, 10.5 (pp. lxxvi, lxxviii).

(2) Smoothing is less frequent in the signed poems of Cynewulf, but it is nonetheless well attested: (a) *æ* appears for WS *ea* in *stærcedfyrhðe* (*Elene* 38a)[76] and *æht* 'counsel' (473b); (b) *e* appears for WS *eo* in *wideferh* (*Christ II* 583a, *Juliana* 223a) and *wideferg* (*Juliana* 467b); (c) *e* appears for WS *ea* in *hergas* (*Christ II* 485b).

---

[74]In addition, instances of *wideferhð* (702a, 937b, 1222a) must be scribal alterations of *-ferh*: *wideferhð* is semantic nonsense, and *-ð* must have been added because *-ferh*, without breaking, looked odd. Cf. *wideferh* at *Christ II* 784a. The word appears once in prose, in the form *widefeorlic* (see the *Microfiche Concordance*), with normal WS *eo*.

[75]The verb *līxan*, mainly poetic, and unattested in early West Saxon, shows the later West-Saxon monophthongization of *īe* before palatal consonants (Campbell, §301). The stem *līex-* occurs just once in the Old English records, at *Azarias* 106a.

[76]Pamela Gradon, in her edition of *Elene* (p. 12, n. 1) assumes that *æ* here represents the *i*-mutation of *æ* retracted to *a* before *r*; but as *\*stiercan* is not attested as a verb, the suffix is perhaps that found in forms like *æppled* (OSax. *-ōdi*). Cf. *stearcferþe* (*Juliana* 636b), and see below, §342. For a parallel to the addition of *\*-ōdi* to an adjective stem cf. OHG *armōti* 'needy'.

(3) In *Genesis A* smoothing is found under similar circumstances: (a) *e* appears for WS *ea* in *wexað* (196a), and perhaps in MS *werg* (906b, emended to *werig*);[77] (b) *ī* appears for WS *ēo* in *wibed* (1791a, 1806a, 1882b; cf. *weobedd* 2842a) and in *twih* (2255b); and again, *wideferhð* (906a) is best understood as a scribal corruption of *wideferh*.

(4) Elsewhere in the test group of poems Anglian smoothing is found in forms of *æht* 'counsel' (*Andreas* 410b, 608b), *-berge* (*Exodus* 175a), *berhtm-* (*Daniel* 380a; cf. *Breahtmum* at *Azarias* 161b), *betwīnum* (*Andreas* 1103a), *herg* (*Daniel* 181a, 714a, *Exodus* 46a, *Andreas* 1124a, 1687b), *wīh-* (*Daniel* 182a, 201a, 207b), *stærced-* (see below), and possibly *werig-* (*Andreas* 1169b).[78]

§342. Most of these are words that a West-Saxon scribe might not have known or recognized in their Anglian form, and so left unaltered. Indeed, it is difficult to imagine how *wideferhð* could have arisen except from an Anglian exemplar; and that some scribes found it advisable to alter the word is evidence that it is not simply an aspect of the poetic koine. But the point can also be demonstrated with particular clarity, and an objection answered at the same time, by reference to the form *stærced-fyrhðe* in *Elene*. The word appears at *Judith* 227b in the form *stercedferhð*, and in his edition (p. 5) Timmer remarks that the unbroken vowel need not be regarded as an Anglianism, since *æ* appears for *ea* twice in *Genesis B* (*hwærf* 240a, *folcgestælna* 271a, though of course these are not examples of smoothing), a poem that never existed in an Anglian recension. Presumably he means that the first *e* in *stercedferhð* is confused with *æ*, the latter of which need not be smoothed, but may represent such haphazard orthographic failure of breaking[79] as is found in the two words in *Genesis B*. But this explanation is unlikely. First it should be said that failure of breaking is not a characteristic of the orthography of *Judith*. And then the word actually appears twice in the poem: compare *stercedferhðe* (55b). It seems unlikely that the vowel should be *e* here, too, simply as the result of a haphazard orthographic peculiarity. This is particularly true because Timmer's explanation actually requires two separate accidents, failure of breaking and confusion of *æ* with *e*. And so it does not seem plausible

---

[77]Doane (p. 123) edits lines 906–7 to read *þu scealt wideferhð, werg, þinum breostum / bearme* [MS *bearm*], *tredan brade eorðan*. Regardless, Krapp's *werig* is odd, as a weak form would be normal here if the word were an adjective: cf. *Soul and Body II* 22a. On the problems associated with the adjective see Klaeber's *Beowulf*, note to line 133 (p. 133). But only the noun is relevant here, as the adjective has *i*-mutation. Cf. *wergas* at *Dream of the Rood* 31b, and *wearh* at *Beowulf* 1267a, *Elene* 926a, and *Maxims II* 55b.

[78]Brooks, in his note to this line, identifies *weriges* as a noun (see the preceding note), i.e. a corruption of *werges*. But in the parallel instance at *Daniel* 267a, *werigra* is used as a substantive, though the ending is clearly adjectival—for which reason Farrell's identification of the word as a noun (p. 130) is puzzling.

[79]Actually, it is probably late monophthongization: see Luick, §356; Campbell, §329.2. See also Celia and Kenneth Sisam, *The Salisbury Psalter*, EETS, o.s. 242 (1959), §§45, 61.

that the vocalism here could simply be accidental. More evidence derives from the fact that the vowel is also smoothed or unbroken in *Elene*, and in the one other place the word occurs (*stærcedferþne*, at *Andreas* 1233b, emended from MS *stærced ferþe*). It is unlikely to be an accident that the word never appears with a diphthong, and yet this consistency is itself remarkable, since smoothing is not generally found with such regularity in verse. Perhaps the only very likely explanation is that West-Saxon scribes did not recognize the word, and so left it unaltered in its smoothed, Anglian form. This is probable because neither *stærced(-)* nor any other spelling occurs outside of verse. Corroboration can be derived from the form *stearcferþe* (*Juliana* 636b; cf. the only other forms of the compounded morpheme in verse, *stearcheort*, at *Beowulf* 2288b, 2552a, and *stearcheard*, at *Judgment Day II* 201b). Here the word lacks the unusual suffix -*ed*-, and so is readily converted into good West Saxon. Finally, it was pointed out above that Timmer's explanation requires two separate accidents, failure of breaking and confusion of *æ* with *e*. The parallels he adduces from *Maldon* are not apposite, because in these *e* stands for *æ*, not *ea*. On the other hand, the assumption of smoothing disposes of the problem, since smoothed *æ* was later raised to *e* before *r* (Campbell, §222). In sum, it seems unlikely that *stærcedfyrhðe* in *Elene* can be explained convincingly as anything but a smoothed form. A more significant question is whether the form is a relic of an Anglian recension or simply a poetic convention. The dearth of smoothed forms in the Southern group argues against the latter proposition, and supports the evidence above that *stærcedfyrhðe* remains smoothed because it was unfamiliar, not because it was a common poeticism. On the dating value of these observations see above, §289.

§343. Non-West-Saxon back mutation is markedly limited in the Southern group. Again this is usually thought to be a late prehistoric sound change, coeval with smoothing (Luick, §240; but cf. below, p. 347, n. 170). With a few exceptions (e.g. *neoðan*), back mutation is considered non-West-Saxon when it applies across consonants other than labials and liquids; but some other forms may also perhaps be Anglian or Kentish if they have alternate, supposedly West-Saxon forms, such as *eafora* beside *afora*, and *dearoð* beside *daroð*. In a few instances these supposed West-Saxon forms can be checked against forms in prose (though this leads to some caprices of classification: e.g., although forms like *beofian, seofian*, and *seomian* ought to be normal in West Saxon, *bifian, sifian/sefian*, and *semian* do sometimes occur, and the mutated forms must therefore be classed with *eafora* and *dearoð*). In most instances, however, it cannot be proved that the forms without mutation are West-Saxon—most such words are strictly poetic vocabulary—even though a West-Saxon origin is undoubtedly the likeliest explanation for their existence. Less well founded is the assumption that *eafora* and *dearoð* must *not* be West-Saxon. Nonetheless, with or without the conventional assumptions it is still clear that back mutation in the Southern group is limited. The difference is both quantitative and qualitative:

(1) Back mutation is most diverse in the *Meters of Boethius*, but even here it is not encountered nearly as often as in presumably Anglian poems. But the reason back mutation appears as frequently as it does in the *Meters* is that it is also a feature of the prose, as in *gefrioðode* (133.11–12), forms of *headorian* (49.6, 57.5, 128.21), *neoðeran* (11.25), and *niodor* (80.30, 147.10; cited by page and line from Sedgefield's edition). The *Meters* thus are not trustworthy on this account, as this is another instance of Anglian influence on Alfredian spelling. Nonetheless, the sixteen instances in the *Meters* may be listed: (a) *ea* for WS *a* appears in *beadurincum* (1.18b), *eafora* (26.35a), *geador* (13.49b, actually the usual West-Saxon form), *headorian* (11.31a, 13.6a), *headorinca* (9.45a), *wearoð* (1.14b; also *wearod* 8.30b); (b) *ea* appears for WS *e* in *eaforas* (26.81a); (c) *eo* appears for WS *e* in *feola* (13.16b); (d) *eo* appears for WS *i* in *sincgeofa* (1.50a), *neoðemest* (20.85b); (e) *io* appears for WS *i* (or *e*) in *siofian* (2.2b, 26.82b), *siofunga* (16.7b), *ðiossum* (Proem 4a).

(2) In the remainder of the Southern group there are nineteen instances, nearly all of them in exclusively poetic vocabulary: (a) *ea* appears for WS *a* in *beadu-* (*Maldon* 111a, 185a, *Brunanburh* 48a), *eafora* (*Coronation of Edgar* 17b, *Genesis B* 399a, 550a, 623a), *heaðo-* (*Menologium* 14a, *Brunanburh* 6a, *Genesis B* 324a); (b) *eo* appears for WS *e* in *meodo* (*Maldon* 212b), *meotod* (*Menologium* 51b, 82b, 86b, 129b, *A Prayer* 27b); (c) *eo* appears for WS *i* in *geofian* (*Genesis B* 546a); (d) *io* appears for WS *i* in *lioðobendum* (*Genesis B* 382a) and *siodo* (*Genesis B* 618b).

(3) There are 149 instances of non-West-Saxon back mutation in *Beowulf*. They are listed by Klaeber (§§12.1, 12.2, 13.1a, 13.1b, 13.2a, 14.1, pp. lxxviii–lxxix).[80]

(4) The signed works of Cynewulf contain ninety-one instances of non-West Saxon back mutation: (a) *ea* appears for WS *a* in *Elene* in forms of *beadu-* (31b, 34a, 45a, 152a, 1003a, 1184b), *deareð-* (37a), *eafora* (353b, 439b), *eatol* (901a), *-fearoð-* (226b, 251a), *geador* (26b, 888b), *heaðo-* (130a, 579a, 1305a), *geheaðrod* (1275b), and *-treafum* (926a); in the *Fates of the Apostles* in *bealo-* (44a, 78a); in *Christ II* in *heafelan* (505b); in *Juliana* in *beaduwe* (385a), *eaferum* (504b), *eafoða* (601b), *geador* (163b, 714b); (b) *ea* appears for WS *e* in *feala* (*Elene* 362b, 636a, the latter emended), *teala* (*Christ II* 792a); (c) *eo* appears for WS *e* in *eodera* (*Juliana* 113a), *leopo-* (*Elene* 522b, 1250a, *Juliana* 592a), *meotod* (*Elene* 366a, 461a, 474b, 564a, 686b, 985a, 1042a, *Christ II* 452b, 589a, 629b, 716a, *Juliana* 182a, 306a, 436a, 667a, 721b); (d) *eo* appears for WS *i(e)* in *Elene* in *beofaþ* (758a),

---

[80]Although Klaeber includes *heonan* (twice in *Beowulf*), this is the normal West-Saxon form of the word, e.g. Ælfric's form. Included is *(on)geador* (491b, 835b, 1595b): see Brunner, §109, n. 3. Note that back mutation is normal in West Saxon in most of the forms that Klaeber lists in §14.2 (but cf. *semian*, *giefan*).

*beweotigaþ* (744b), *cleopigan* (696b, 1099b, 1319a), *freoðode* (1146b), *fyrnweota* (343a), *geofenes* (227a, 1200a), *Leomu* (882b), *nedcleofa* (711b, 1275a), *reodode* (1238b), *seonoð-* (552b), *stangreopum* (823b), *stanhleoðum* (653a), *þreodude* (1238a), *uðweotan* (473a), *wuldorgeofa* (681a); in the *Fates of the Apostles* in *cleopigan* (115b), *þreodode* (18a); in *Christ II* in *beofiað* (827a), *cleopedon* (508b), *gefreopade* (588a), *freoþa* (773b), *geofum* (686b), *heahhleoþu* (745a), *leomu(m)* (628a, 777a); in *Juliana* in *beofað* (708b), *cleopian* (271b, 618a), *gefreoðade* (565a), *sweopum* (188a); (e) *io* appears for WS *i* (or *e*) in *Elene* in *fyrnwiota* (438a), *siomode* (694a), *sionoðe* (154a), *sioððan* (1146b); in the *Fates of the Apostles* in *seomaþ* (121b); in *Juliana* in *seofian* (537a), *seomað* (709a).

(5) There are sixty-four instances in *Genesis A*: (a) *ea* appears for WS *a* in *ceara* (2281a, 2733b), *cearum* (2795a), *eafora* (forty-one forms; twice *afora*), *geador* (2559b; MS *eador*: see Campbell, §303); (b) *ea* appears for WS *e* in *teala* (1232b); (c) *eo* appears for WS *e* in *meotodes* (189a), *seomodon* (72a); (d) *eo* appears for WS *i* in *aleoðode* (177a), *beorhhleoþum* (2160a), *cleopað* (1013a), *freoðo(-)* (79a, 1045a, 1198a, 1347b, 1760a, 1838b, 2303a, 2499a), *geofonhusa* (1321a), *hleoðo, -u* (1459b, 1803a); (e) *eo* appears for WS *a* in *deoreðsceaftum* (1984a); (f) *io* appears for WS *i* in *hlioðo* (1439a).

(6) In the remaining longer poems of the test group there are examples of *beadu-*, *breogo(-)* *breomo* (*Andreas* 242b), *cear-* (cf. phonologically correct *carleasan* at *Exodus* 166a), *cleofu*, (*Andreas* 310a), *cleopian*, *eafera*, *freoðo*, *geof-* (*Andreas* 62a, 551b, 1282a), *heaðo-*, *-hleoðu* (*Exodus* 70a, beside *-hliðu* at 449a), *hneotan* (*Andreas* 4b), *-leoda* (*Exodus* 374a, *Andreas* 500a), *meotod*, *gemeotu* (*Andreas* 454a), *ondsweorodon* (857b), *sceoran* (1181b), *seoðþan* (534a), *-smeoðas* (1220a), *Geweotan* (801b).

§344. But conclusions about the incidence of back mutation as a dialect indicator must not be based solely on statistics of sheer quantity. Although *Beowulf* and the Cynewulf canon show a wide variety of mutated forms, the figures for *Genesis A* are distorted by forty-one instances of *eafora*, a greater number than the instances of non-West-Saxon back mutation in the Southern group altogether. When *eafora* is set aside, the incidence of back mutation in *Genesis A* is unremarkable, at least in terms of sheer numbers. Of course it cannot be concluded that *Genesis A* is not an Anglian poem: it may simply be that the poem has undergone a particularly thorough Saxonization (see below, §362). The argument cannot be reversed, however, and applied to the Southern group, since that group comprises a wide variety of texts and manuscripts. Thus the very low incidence of back mutation confirms expectations, given the dialect origins of the Cynewulfian and Southern groups, and argues for a non-West Saxon origin for *Beowulf*.

§345. Setting aside the quantitative evidence of the data, the qualitative evidence points more persuasively to the same conclusion. There is a wide variety of mutated types represented in the data above, on a scale from the conventional to the unusual. Most of the morphemes represented occur only in verse, and of those, several never appear without mutation, for example *beadu-* and *heaðo-*, even though these are very frequent, and *geador* and *leoðo-*, which are less frequent. Such words are useless as evidence for dialect origins, and clearly derive their spelling from poetic convention rather than Anglian originals.[81] Some other spellings are only slightly less prescribed by convention: for instance, *afora* and other forms of the word without mutation appear seven times in the poetic records, while forms with mutation are found in sixty-seven places. Also more or less prescribed seem to be *geofian* and *(ge)heaðorian*, for although they also appear in prose, they are rarely or never without mutation. Leaving aside the Alfredian *Meters*, then, there are just three morphemes in the Southern group with mutation that do not fall into these prescribed categories. And even those three can hardly be thought of as showing unconventional mutation, since they are mutated roughly half the time in the poetic records: for *meotod, meodo,* and *siodo* the proportion of mutated to unmutated forms in verse is 145:120, 20:22 and 1:1, respectively. As for the *Meters* themselves, they display just two forms that can be considered unconventional: *wearoð* has mutation twice in verse (twelve times without) and *ðiossum* thrice (forty-four times without). These of course may once again be due to Anglian influence on Alfredian spelling: compare *þiosum, þioson, þiossum* nine times in the Hatton manuscript of the *Pastoral Care.*

§346. By contrast, back mutation in the presumably Anglian poems is frequently unconventional. Especially noteworthy are those few instances in *Beowulf* in which ordinary prosaic words, particularly in paradigmatic alternation, show an instance of mutation unique, or nearly so, in poetry. Such are *riodan* (3169a) and *scionon* (303b), as well as *wreoþen-* (1698a), though it is less common a verb. The forms *hneotan* (4b) and *Geweotan* (801b) in *Andreas* should be included here. These are perhaps the only instances of mutation in strong verbs of the first class in verse. Given that the conditions for mutation are limited only to the preterite plural and participle in paradigms of the first class, it is difficult to believe that these are not instances of genuine phonological conditioning rather than of convention. Similar are *sceoran* at *Andreas* 1181b (a strong verb of the fourth class) and gen. pl. *weora* (*Beowulf* 2947a), the latter of which also occurs in the Kentish *Psalm 50*; compare in poetry ninety instances of *wera*, sixty of *weras*, and thirty-three of *werum*, including compounds. At *Andreas* 857b, the vocalism of *ondsweorodon* is distinctly Mercian, and is found just a few times in prose—in VP, in the originally Mercian translation of Bede's *Ecclesiastical History*, and in Ru.[1]. The normal

---

[81]The same sort of restriction of certain types of spellings to particular items of vocabulary is well known in prose—e.g., Toon finds that in the Corpus Glossary, several words have exclusively *o* for *a* before nasal consonants, while other words have exclusively *a* (p. 105).

spelling with -*a*- in the root of the preterite stem is found thirty-five times in verse. Also in *Andreas*, -*smeoðas* (1220a) is unique in verse (as opposed to fourteen mutatable instances with -*i*-), as are *breomo* (242b) and *gemeotu* (454a), matched by seven and three undiphthongized instances, respectively. At 209a and 305a, *breogo(-)* may be Kentish—it in fact occurs in *Psalm 50*, as well—but it may also be Mercian (Campbell, §210.2).

§347. More numerous are words that show mutation only infrequently in verse, and these are especially common in *Beowulf*, *Andreas*, and Cynewulf's poems. Forms of *eatol-*, *eatul-* occur five times in verse (twice in *Beowulf*, once each in *Elene*, the *Riming Poem*, and *Widsith*), while *atol-* and *atul-* appear forty-seven times (once in *Judgment Day II*). There are sixteen instances of *seoððan, sioððan* in verse (seven times in *Christ and Satan*, three times in *Beowulf* and *Psalm 50*, once each in *Elene*, *Andreas*, and *Solomon and Saturn II*), and 279 of *siððan*, with instances in most of the Southern poems. The verb *(be)weotian* (including *(un)wiotod*, etc.) has mutation ten times (three times in *Beowulf* and *Andreas*, once in *Elene*, *Christ and Satan*, *Solomon and Saturn II*, and *Maxims I*), and is without it twenty-four times (including examples in *Genesis B* and the *Meters of Boethius*).[82] There are seven instances of forms of (-)*weota/wiota* with mutation (three times in *Elene*, twice in *Andreas*, once in *Beowulf* and *Solomon and Saturn II*), and forty-one without (thirteen times in the Southern group); and -*cleofu(m)* occurs four times (once each in *Beowulf*, *Andreas*, *Christ III*, and *Riddle 3*), but -*clifu(m)* eight times. Likewise -*fearoð*- appears twice (in *Elene*), but -*faroð*- and such seventeen times; and *deareð-*, *deoreð-* once each in *Elene* and *Genesis A*, respectively, but *daroþ*- and the like elsewhere eleven times.

§348. Again in this respect *Genesis A* does not seem as different from the Southern group as *Beowulf* and Cynewulf's poems do, but there is perhaps some evidence that the reason is scribal normalization of spelling. There is a tendency in these presumably Anglian poems for back mutation to appear more frequently in compounds than in simplices. In *Genesis A*, *freoðo*- is always mutated as an element of a compound (six times), but just three out of six times as a simplex. In *Beowulf* also, *medu* is the simplex (twice), but *meodu-/meodo-* is the compounded form in five of sixteen instances; and although *hafela* is the normal uncompounded form (eleven of thirteen instances), the one compound of the word is *wigheafolan* (2661b). The principle is more pronounced in Cynewulf, where, for example, we find that the simplex *wita* has no mutation (twice: *Elene* 544b, *Juliana* 98a), while the compounded form has it in three of five instances (*Elene* 343a, 438a, 473a, but 455a, 1153a). Incidentally, six

---

[82]Spellings like *weotan* under conditions for combinative back mutation do occur in West Saxon (see Campbell, §218); but they are restricted to Alfredian texts, and so are less likely to be forms later exterminated than examples of Mercian influence on Alfredian spelling.

of the sixteen instances of compounded *-wita* are in the Southern group (*Meters* 10.50a, 20.184a, 22.54a, *Menologium* 166a, *Judgment Day II* 300a, *Brunanburh* 69a). It is difficult to understand why scribes should have written *eo/io* for *e* in compounds while avoiding doing so in simplices; but the reverse (i.e., changing the exemplar's *eo* in simplices in only a desultory fashion) makes good sense, since compounds were naturally less familiar, and at any rate were more clearly poetic. The same principle no doubt explains, for instance, why Anglian *īo* for West-Saxon *ī* by smoothing is found in *Beowulf* only in the compound *wigweorþunga* and the personal name *Wīhstan* (§341): ordinary words were more readily Saxonized.

§349. Conversely, in a few words there is a particularly high incidence of nonmutated forms in the Southern group. This is most apparent in words that do not frequently show nonmutated forms in verse. The clearest example is *cleopian*, with forms in verse showing mutation forty-three times, and lacking it just thirteen times. Eight of those thirteen instances, however, are in the Southern group: *Lord's Prayer II* 2b, 12a, 24a, 45b, *Menologium* 214b, *Judgment Day II* 138b, *Maldon* 25b, 256b. So also *heofon* should show back mutation in all dialects, but perhaps for analogical reasons *hefon* could appear in West Saxon (Campbell, §210.1; Brunner, §110.1). Ten of the twelve instances in verse are in the Southern group, at *Meters* 4.2a, 4.4a, 6.4a, 9.18a, 11.31b, *Metrical Epilogue to the Pastoral Care* 8a, and *Genesis B* 633b, 642a, 659a, 808b. This is too high a proportion to be regarded as accidental, and although of course it does not prove that poems outside the Southern group are not West-Saxon in origin, it raises a significant probability of that.

§350. Back mutation exceeding West-Saxon limits is found in all the non-West-Saxon dialects. However, back mutation of *a* to *ea* is limited to a part of the West Midlands, because only in this area was the *a* that had been restored before back vowels fronted again, rendering it subject to diphthongization. There are no unconventional instances of *ea* corresponding to WS *a* in *Genesis A*, where *cear-* is the only form that does not also appear in the Southern group. Among the unconventional instances listed above, *Beowulf* has only *eatol*, while Cynewulf has also *-fearoð-*, *deareð-*, and *-treafum*. Cynewulf is in fact widely believed to have been a Mercian, and this belief is supported elsewhere (§§16, 361, 391).

§351. Another non-West-Saxon dialect feature frequently cited is the orthographic confusion of *eo* and *ea*, primarily a Northumbrian phenomenon, though it appears to a lesser extent in Mercian and Kentish texts, more frequently in the earliest ones (Campbell, §§275–81; Brunner, §35, n. 1). There is one instance of such confusion in the Southern group, *ymbhwearfest* at *Meters* 4.4a, for Anglian *ymbhweorfes(t)*, WS *ymbhwierfst*; but this is perhaps a scribal change, as the prose version has *ymbhweorfest*. There are several examples in *Beowulf*: *fea* (156b), *Geotena*

(443b), *beorn* (1880a), *abreot* (2930a).[83] Additionally, the manuscript reading *þeod* (1278b, emended to *deað*) implies an earlier *\*deoð* (cf. *deoth-* in *Bede's Death Song* 5a).[84] There are a few examples in *Genesis A*: *deoreð-* (1984a), *feallan* (2038b), *-treawa* (2369a), *beheowan* (2645a, MS *-heopan*). But Doane (p. 31) correctly points out that *beheowan* could be a late West-Saxon form, with assimilation of *ēa* to the following *w* (Campbell, §274). Less likely is his suggestion that *feallan* is a present subjunctive (p. 298). In Cynewulf's verse the only example is *beorn* (*Christ II* 540a). In the remaining longer poems of the test group compare *feala* (eleven times in *Andreas*, but also frequent in the works of Ælfric), *feoh* (MS *fea*, *Daniel* 66a), *hwearf on* (MS *hweorfon*, *Daniel* 266a), and *teala* (*Andreas* 1612b).[85]

§352. N. F. Blake, followed by others, objects to the confusion of *eo* and *ea* as a dialect indicator, on the basis of Willy Schlemilch's observation that such confusion is also encountered in some West-Saxon texts of the period 1000–1150.[86] It would seem possible to shed light on the dispute in regard to *Beowulf*, at least, by examining the other texts in the manuscript to see whether the confusion of *eo* and *ea* is merely a scribal habit or a feature of the language of *Beowulf* itself. But the problem is complicated by the fact that the prose texts preceding *Beowulf* in the

[83]The form *neon* (3104b; also at *Andreas* 1176b) does not show confusion of *ēa* and *ēo*, but is Anglian and Kentish, where the root originally had *ē* corresponding to WGmc. and WS *ǣ*.

[84]George Brown argues that the manuscript reading makes sense, and should be retained: see "*Beowulf* 1278b: 'sunu þeod wrecan'," *MP* 72 (1974), 172–74. But *wrecan* 'avenge' takes just two types of accusative object, a person killed or a wrong committed: see the examples in Bosworth and Toller's dictionary. Moreover, Brown's hypothesis faces the difficulty that the accusative form ought to be *þēode* rather than *þēod*—demanding the assumption either that the poem is a late Anglian composition or that it has at some point been copied by a late Anglian scribe, since it is in these dialects that *ō*-stems with long stems may take endingless accusatives (Brunner, §252, n. 2). Thus, paleographically, *þēod* demands about as much conjecture as *dēað*; and since the construction would be syntactically unparalleled if *þeod* were retained, the emendation of the major editions to *dēað* or *dēoð* is to be preferred.

[85]Lucas suggests several examples in *Exodus*. He analyzes *reodan* (413b) as an adjective, but the syntax makes a verb seem more natural, and as a verb 'redden' in the sense 'kill' it has the support of *Meters* 8.34b. At 61a, *mearchofu morheald* is admittedly unconvincing, but as a verb, *heald* seems semantically awkward, and metrically anomalous: in *Beowulf* a finite verb never appears as the final syllable of a verse of type A. His emendation of MS *beo hata* (253a, divided at the end of a MS line) to *beodohata* seems likelier than any other, but is still too speculative to be regarded as evidence. The same may be said of his emendation of MS *geneop* to *gehneop* (476b).

[86]Blake, ed., *The Phoenix* (Manchester: Manchester Univ. Press, 1964), p. 6; Schlemilch (as above, p. 286, n. 43), pp. 26, 32, 36. Tupper ("Philological Legend," pp. 246–47) provides evidence for the interchange of *feala* and *feola*, *dēagol* and *dēogol*, in West-Saxon texts. But the former pair appears to represent a special case (see Brunner, §110, n. 5), and both alternants of the latter pair are perhaps correct: on *dēogol* see Brunner, §141, n. 2, in reference to the process that Campbell describes in §202.

manuscript are not all purely West-Saxon. The first item, the *Letter of Alexander the Great to Aristotle*, is certainly based ultimately on an Anglian original, as it shows several unmistakable signs of Anglian usage that do not normally appear in West-Saxon prose. An indisputable sign is the form *foeran* at line 6 on fol. 118ᵛ, as in Stanley Rypins' edition.[87] Another clear sign is the relatively frequent appearance of non-West-Saxon back mutation in a nonpoetic text, as in *heahcleofan* (fol. 109ᵛ, line 15), *wolbeorendan* (fol. 125ʳ, line 8; 110ʳ, lines 16–17), *siogorum* (fol. 128ʳ, line 20) and *sioððan, seoððan* (passim).[88] The second prose text, the *Wonders of the East*, has also been thought by some to derive from an Anglian original.[89] But if this is so it is considerably further removed from that original than is the preceding piece of prose, as the supposedly Anglian features are rather few. In the third item, the *Life of St. Christopher*, Anglian features are weak and inconclusive, and it is regarded by most as entirely West-Saxon in character.[90] In the light of these observations there is perhaps some significance in the distribution of *eo* and *ea* in this manuscript, since they are confused only in *Beowulf* and the Anglian *Letter*. In the latter are found *reode* (fol. 124ʳ, line 17; and cf. *read-* five times in the *Wonders*, once in *Judith*, at 338a) and *breastum* (114ʳ, line 6). The confusion of the two diphthongs in the manuscript appears not to be merely scribal, since the confusion is found in the work of both *Beowulf* scribes but not in the other texts each copied, excluding the *Letter*. Possibly, *Beowulf* was copied faithfully from a very recent exemplar affected by this supposed West-Saxon confusion. Yet this proposition seems improbable. It requires the construction of an ad hoc history of the text to account solely for this confusion—a construction that is unnecessary, given that other linguistic features demand an Anglian original, anyway. In addition, as Schlemilch points out, many of his examples are questionable; they are, in any case, inadmissible in this context, as they derive from texts showing other signs of Anglian influence, such as Gregory's *Dialogues*.[91]

§353. In addition to the absence of Anglian smoothing, unconventional non-West-Saxon back mutation and, perhaps, confusion of *eo* and *ea*, there are other orthographic properties of the Southern group that set it apart from presumably Anglian verse. While editions of Old English

[87]*Three Old English Prose Texts*, EETS, o.s. 161 (1924, for 1921).

[88]For some morphological and lexical evidence see Rypins' edition, pp. xxxviii–xxxix, and more particularly his article "The Old English *Epistola Alexandri ad Aristotelem*," *MLN* 38 (1928), 216–20.

[89]Thus Rypins; see also J. J. Campbell, p. 353.

[90]Vleeskruyer, pp. 55–56, argues for an Anglian original, but cf. Campbell's review of Vleeskruyer's book, in *Medium Ævum* 24 (1955), 52–56, at 56.

[91]J. J. Campbell (pp. 353–54) offers a convenient summary of conventional views on the dialectal affiliations of prose texts.

poems often devote detailed attention to phonology, many of these other features are rarely, if ever, remarked:

(1) Mentioned above (§326) was Sievers' observation that syncopated forms of the verb *habban* (*hæfst, hæfþ, hæfst, næfþ*), which are foreign to Anglian prose texts, in thirty-three of thirty-four instances in the poetic records appear in presumably Southern poems. But he also finds that the poetic manuscripts are remarkably correct as regards syncope in other verbs, since the poetic meter almost never contradicts the manuscript forms, even in the Southern group, where contracted and uncontracted forms alternate. In the Southern group the only long-stemmed exceptions he finds that can still be considered exceptions, given Bliss's assumptions about metrics, are in the *Meters of Boethius*: compare *blate forbærnð* (8.54a) and *Gif ðu weorðest* (24.44a, MS *wyrft* or *wyrst*). These are to be set against more than 160 instances of unexceptionable usage. With one possible exception discussed above (§329), the few syncopated forms found outside the Southern group are short-stemmed, so that they usually do not affect the meter. Sievers lists just five instances in which syncope in a short-stemmed verb does make a metrical difference:[92]

> þæs þe on woruld cymð (*Genesis A* 2321b)[93]
> nu þu ymb þa burh sprycest (MS *spryst*, *Genesis A* 2528b)
> Swa þin blæd lið (*Daniel* 562a)
> oðþæt þu eft cymst (*Daniel* 584b)
> Eftwyrd cymð (*Exodus* 540b)

Doubtless the frequency of orthographic syncope in short-stemmed verbs is a scribal convention, though perhaps the practice arose because in most instances syncope makes no metrical difference in these verbs.[94] The fact that, for instance, *cymst/cymð* violates the meter in four of the fifteen places it appears in verse demonstrates that the infrequency of orthographic syncope in long-stemmed verbs, where metrically it is more easily detected, is more likely to be due to scribal convention than to the scribes' awareness of the meter, though admittedly the tendency to write syncopated forms of the short-stemmed verbs may have its origin in scribes' knowledge of poetic meter. Scribal conservatism in regard to syncope is at any rate amply demonstrated by the distribution of *hæfst, hæfþ*. Syncope in the other verbs of the third weak class is less regular in West Saxon (Campbell, §762; Brunner, §417, nn. 3a, 4a), and so forms like *hygeð* (*Meters* 19.1b), *sægeð* (*Genesis B* 682b), and *segeð* (*Maldon* 45b)

---

[92]Though Sievers does not list them, a few such exceptions also occur in the Southern group, e.g. at *Meters* 6.11b and *Genesis B* 806a.

[93]But note that the verse would still be metrically peculiar with dissyllabic *cymeð*, since this requires a short lift after a resolved one.

[94]Note, however, that *cweþan* takes the form *cwið* in VP: see (12) below.

in the Southern group are not surprising. Yet these forms of *secgan* are still significant, as the usual forms in verse are 2. sg. *sagast*, 3. *sagað*, and imp. *saga*, found in *Genesis A, Andreas, Elene, Christ I* and *III, Guthlac B, Juliana*, the *Riddles, Solomon and Saturn II*, and the metrical preface to Wærferth's translation of Gregory's *Dialogues*. Compare also *sægst* (*Genesis B* 570a) and imp. *sege* (*Maldon* 50a) and *sæge* (*Genesis B* 617a, but also *Solomon and Saturn II* 210b, 339b; cf. *saga* at 237b, 332b; and *gesegð* at *Christ III* 1309b). The forms with *a* in the root occur in Mercian and Mercian-influenced texts, but they are extremely rare in pure West Saxon (Brunner, §417, n. 3): the only exceptions are two examples in the *Rule of Chrodegang* and one in the laws of Alfred. So also from *hycgan* there is *hogaþ* at *Riming Poem* 81b, but *hygeþ* (as above) at *Solomon and Saturn II* 239b.

(2) Forms of the verb *libban* with the stem *libb-* are foreign to non-West-Saxon texts, which have *lifi(g)-* or *lifg-* instead (Campbell, §762; Brunner, §417, n. 2b). In verse the stem *libb-* occurs only in the Southern group: see *Meters* 10.64b, 13.33b, 20.107b, *Metrical Epilogue to the Pastoral Care* 4b, *Genesis B* 482b, 787a, 805a, 851b. Although the form with *b* is confined to West Saxon, the form with *f* is also common in West Saxon; thus, compare *lif(i)g-* at *Meters* 20.278b and *Lord's Prayer II* 25b, 101b. In the findings of the *Linguistic Atlas of Late Mediaeval English*, forms with *b* are confined to the Saxon and southwest Mercian areas, with the exception of a single source from northern Cambridgeshire (Oxford, University College 45, *Piers Plowman*, hand A—see dot map 468—but of course Langland's own dialect must have been that of the Worcester area), and two from Canterbury (to which compare only forms with *f* in *Psalm 50*, at 101a, 112a, 126a, 139b). The heavy concentration of late Middle English forms with *b* in the Southwest Midlands is surprising in view of the absence of such forms in VP, but as, for example, the *Katherine* Group and the *Ancrene Wisse* demonstrate, the language of this area came to be heavily influenced by the standard dialect before the end of the Old English period, at least in its orthography, if not in its actual phonology and morphology.[95]

(3) Less decisive, but nonetheless remarkable, is the distribution of 1. sg. pres. ind. *hafo, hafu*, to *habban*. This is the Northumbrian form, to be distinguished from the subjunctive *hæbbe*; compare WS ind. *hæbbe* and Kentish *hebbe* (Campbell, §762; Brunner, §417, n. 1f). The first person singular indicative is unattested in VP and Ru.[1], but *lifgu, secgu, sæcge*, and such, in these texts (cf. Northumbrian *li(o)fo, sægo*) suggest that

---

[95]See, for example, the maps provided by Peter M. Anderson, *A Structural Atlas of the English Dialects* (London: Croom Helm, 1987); and also the article by Martyn Wakelin mentioned above, p. 43, n. 74. Sisam, for instance, remarks that "contemporary Worcester charters leave no doubt that West Saxon had become the official language at Worcester by the end of the tenth century" (*Studies*, p. 121).

*hæbbe* may have been current at least in parts of Mercia. This is also what the Middle English evidence suggests, as 1. sg. *habbe*, 2. *hauest*, 3. *haueð* are found in the *Katherine* Group. In the sources of the *Linguistic Atlas of Late Mediaeval English* the paradigm has been regularized to the extent that all forms of the verb with *b* are restricted to the Saxon, Kentish, and Southwest Mercian areas, with rare scattered exceptions in East Anglian sources, and in the *Pearl* manuscript. Thus, 1. sg. ind. *hæbbe* (so also *lifge, secge*) seems to be a Southern or West Mercian character-istic in verse—though because these are clearly the original forms, and Northumbrian *li(o)fo, sægo* analogical, it cannot be said with assurance that structural instances could not reflect early Northumbrian or East Mercian usage. In fact, although the Mercian records are ambiguous, and too many areas of Anglo-Saxon England are unrepresented in the sur-viving texts to afford any firm conclusions, still it seems unlikely that *hæbbe* and *secge* should delimit the same area, since the distribution of the two types is not the same in verse: the latter is found everywhere in verse, even beside *hafo, hafu*, in *Beowulf* and the signed poems of Cyne-wulf. *Hafo* and *hafu* appear seven times in Old English verse, always in poems known or suspected to be Anglian (*Beowulf, Elene, Guthlac B, Riddles*). *Hæbbe* is also found in these four texts, but is required by the meter instead of *hafo* only in *heafod hæbbe* (*Riddle 81* 2a). *Hæbbe* is also required by the meter at *Christ I* 169b, *Resignation* 78b, *Solomon and Saturn I* 1b, and *Psalms* 118.50.1b, 118.111.1b, 143.3.2b. First person sg. ind. *secge* is structural in a variety of poems, including *Genesis A* and *B, Daniel, Beowulf, Juliana, Andreas*, the *Meters of Boethius, Judgment Day II*, and others.

(4) Although there are prominent exceptions, the preterite of *cuman* in Anglian prose texts is normally *cwōm(on)*, and in West-Saxon texts *cōm(on)* (Brunner, §390, n. 3; Campbell, §742). All preterites of *(be-, for-, ofer-)cuman* in the Southern group lack the *w*: compare *Meters* 1.66a, 1.77b, 13.70b, 17.3b, 20.30b, 20.240a, 26.59b, 28.73b, *Brunanburh* 37b, 70b, 72b, *Maldon* 58b, 65a, *Genesis B* 255b, 598b, 602b, 627b, 679b, 683b, 723b. Both forms are very common in other verse, and they appear with about equal frequency. For example, in *Beowulf* there are twenty-six instances with *w* and twenty-four without it. It is a point of interest that only forms without *w* are found in *Genesis A* and *B*, while the other poems in the hand of the scribe of Liber I in the Junius manuscript show a mixture of forms. For a possible explanation see §362; see also Sisam, *Studies*, p. 103. The works of Cynewulf, on the other hand, though found in two manu-scripts, have almost exclusively the forms with *w*, the one exception being at *Elene* 150b. Yet this is not so very significant in regard to the Exeter Book, which almost consistently has forms with *w*.

(5) A clearer indicator is the preterite plural of *sēon*, which is *sēgon* in Anglian prose texts (whence the scribal hybrid *sǣgon* by Saxonization), but *sāwon* in West-Saxon. So also the Anglian preterite participle is

*gesegen*, but WS *gesewen* (Campbell, §743). The Southern group has only forms with *w*: compare *Meters* 8.13a, 8.36a, 10.5a, 13.37b, *Maldon* 84b, *Genesis B* 783b, 830a *Death of Edgar* 22a. By contrast, more than half the instances with *g* are in *Beowulf* and in Cynewulf's signed poems, and the rest in verse known or suspected to be Anglian: compare *Exodus* 178b [MS *onsigon*], *Beowulf* 1422b, 3038a, 3128a, *Elene* 68b, 71a, 75a, 389b, 1104b, *Christ II* 495b, 498a, 506a, 536b, 554b, *Juliana* 291b, *Andreas* 455a, 581b, 711b, 881a, *Christ III* 1127b, 1153a, *Riming Poem* 5a, *Christ and Satan* 527a, *Guthlac A* 266a, 630b, *Psalms* 90.8.2a, *Instructions for Christians* 128b.

(6) Beside the normal verb *(æt-, oð-, ge-)īewan*, belonging to the first weak class, there is a nonmutated Anglian form *ēawan* (Brunner, §408, n. 14; Campbell, §764). The form appears also to be Kentish.[96] The two stems must originally spring from a weak verb of the third class with 1. sg. *īewe*, 2. sg. *ēawast*, and so forth. This interpretation is supported by the co-occurrence of, for instance, Mercian *ēawde* and *ēawade*. (On related forms belonging to the paradigm of *eowian* see above, §335.17.) The Anglian form does not appear in the Southern group: compare *Beowulf* 276a, 1194a, *Guthlac A* 86a, *Phoenix* 322b, 334b, *Psalms* 149.7.2b, *Christ I* 55b, *Christ III* 955b, 1604a, *Soul and Body II* 70b. The connection of the last poem with the South is dubitable: see above, §331. By contrast, *īewan* (or *eowian*) is more common, and is not infrequent in the Southern group: compare forms in the *Meters* (13.60a, 28.75a, 29.33a, 29.71a), *Genesis B* (540a, 653a, 714a, 774a), the *Menologium* (142b, 180a), and the *Death of Edgar* (29a).

(7) In West Saxon, *e* is not broken before *lf* in *self* as it is in other dialects (Brunner, §85; Campbell, §146). In verse, *seolf-* occurs 35 times, always in presumably Anglian poems (*Genesis A, Daniel, Christ and Satan, Andreas, Elene, Beowulf*). *Self-, silf-,* and *sylf-* are very frequent in verse, appearing 490 times, 82 times in the Southern group.

(8) In Anglian prose texts, the equivalent of lWS 1. sg. pres. ind. *bēo* is *bēom* or *bīom*.[97] The spelling *beom* is found in verse at *Juliana* 438a, along with one example at *Christ III* 1490b, and four in the *Riddles* (3.74b, 7.8b, 16.4a, 23.4b). Other forms of the verb 'to be' may also be relevant. Campbell (§768) remarks that the infinitive is *bēon* (*bīon, bīan*) in West Saxon and Mercian, and *wosa* in Northumbrian, though *wesa* is found once in Ru.[1], and *bian* once in Li. In verse, *wesan* is found in a wide variety of texts, including the *Meters* and *Judgment Day II*. Since *wesan* is not found in early West-Saxon prose (Brunner, §427, n. 9), Alfred must have regarded it as a poeticism. The distribution of *beon/bion* is more

---

[96]There is one instance of *ateauð* 'aparuit' in the *Kentish Glosses* (1117 in Sweet and Hoad's edition). The *u* is added above the line: see Zupitza, *ZfdA* 22 (1878), 225.

[97]Unfortunately, the word is not attested in early West Saxon. But *\*bēom* seems less likely than *\*bēo*, since reflexes of the PIE *-mi* ending are otherwise unknown in West Saxon: see above, §126.

restricted: it is found in the *Meters, Genesis B, Maldon*, and *Judgment Day II*, while the only other example in the test group of poems is at *Daniel* 557b. The subjunctive *bīo/bēo(n)* (cf. *sīen*) appears in verse only at *Meters* 10.65, and in the Paris Psalter at 118.78.1a and 148.12.1a.[98] In Anglian texts, *sīe(n)* is the usual subjunctive, though forms like *bēo* appear twice in Li., and ten times in the Mercian portion of the Rushworth Gospels.[99] The subjunctive *bēo* is also attested in early West Saxon, and is the prevailing form in the later language. Indicative *wesað* and subj. *wese* seem to be late Southernisms,[100] but they are perhaps also Mercian, as there is an example of the former in one of the *Blickling Homilies*, and the latter is very frequent in the metrical Psalms of the Paris Psalter.[101] Unmistakably Anglian *earon, earun* appears twice in the same text (101.21.7a, 104.7.2a). The back mutation in these forms is typical of the second fronting dialect of the Southwest Midlands, and in Old English such forms are restricted to West Mercian and Kentish texts.[102] *Aren* occurs occasionally in the *Katherine* Group.[103]

(9) In prose, West Saxon and Mercian generally use the stem 2. pers. pl. *ūr(e)* for the possessive adjective (but cf. *userne* once in Ru.[1]), while Northumbrian texts use *ūser* (Campbell, §§705–6; Brunner, §335 n.). In verse the two are fairly well mixed, yet the former clearly predominates

---

[98]Inf. *beon* (118.46.4a) is dependent on *mote* (cf. Grein's *Sprachschatz*, p. 44).

[99]The figure is Matti Kilpiö's, *Passive Constructions in Old English Translations from Latin*, Mémoires de la Société Néophilologique de Helsinki 49 (Helsinki: Société Néophilologique, 1989). He finds fifty-one examples of *sīe(n)* and such in the text.

[100]They are found, e.g., in the Canterbury Psalter and the Lambeth Psalter, the latter associated with Winchester (see Gneuss, "Origin," pp. 77–79), and others.

[101]On the Mercianisms in the *Blickling Homilies* see, among others, R. J. Menner, "The Anglian Vocabulary of the *Blickling Homilies*," in *Philologica: The Malone Anniversary Studies*, ed. Thomas A. Kirby and Henry Bosley Woolf (Baltimore: Johns Hopkins Univ. Press, 1949), pp. 56–64; Vleeskruyer, pp. 56–57; and Hans Schabram, *Superbia: Studien zum altenglischen Wortschatz, I: Die dialektale und zeitliche Verbreitung des Wortguts* (Munich: W. Fink, 1965), pp. 73–77.

[102]They are found in VP, the *Life of St. Chad* (probably from Worcester), and a Worcester charter dated 880 for 887, Sawyer's no. 217. The Kentish instances of *earan* are in Sweet's Kentish charters 34 and 58, and in the Kentish-colored translation of the *Visio Sancti Pauli*. In addition to the linguistic evidence for a Kentish provenance of the *Visio*, Antonette diPaolo Healey presents some external evidence for locating the manuscript at St. Augustine's, Canterbury, in the later Middle Ages: see *The Old English Vision of St. Paul*, Speculum Anniversary Monographs 2 (Cambridge, Mass.: Medieval Academy of America, 1978), 16–18.

[103]In Middle English the heaviest concentrations of the 'are' type are in the North, East Mercia, and East Anglia, with sparser examples in the West Midlands and the London area. See the *Linguistic Atlas of Late Mediaeval English*, dot maps 118–22, and cf. the distribution of the reflexes of *bēoð*, which are more or less restricted to the South and the West Midlands (dot maps 128–30). This confirms the evidence of Old English, since, excluding the instances of *earon* mentioned in n. 102, the 'are' type is restricted to Northumbrian texts, with one exception in Ru.[1]: the facts are collected by Gerhard Heidemann, "Die Flexion des Verb. subst. im Ags.," *Archiv* 147 (1924), 30–46.

in the Southern group. *Ūre* is the exclusive stem in *Maldon* (56a, 58a, 232b, 240b, 313b, 314a) and *Lord's Prayer II* (1a, 14a, 68b, 77b, 83a, 84a, 85a, 100a, 102a, 106a, 107a). It is almost exclusive in *Genesis B* (261a, 360a, 411b), which also has an instance of *ūser* (536a). Only the *Meters* show a thorough mixture of forms, with six instances of the stem *ūre* (20.33b, 20.252b, 20.258a, 20.261b, 21.14b, 22.54b), and seven of *ūser* (8.40b, 20.249b, 20.265b, 20.267b, 21.12a, 21.35a, 23.11b). There is perhaps some dating significance to this distribution, as *ūre* is used in a great many poems thought to be late compositions (*Judith*, the Psalms of the Paris Psalter, the *Lord's Prayer III*, the fragments of Psalms in Bodleian MS. Junius 121, the *Seasons for Fasting*, and *Instructions for Christians*, along with several poems thought to be earlier). The use of *ūser* must be either a poeticism or a sign of relatively early composition, as the dialect evidence as a whole suggests that very few Old English poems might be Northumbrian in origin. *Ūser* predominates in most of the longer poems of the test group, but only the pattern in *Genesis* is remarkable. In the first part of *Genesis A*, to line 234, and all of *Genesis B*, only *ūre* is used (ten times), with the exception of one instance of *ūser*, mentioned above. After the end of *Genesis B* the stem is consistently *ūsser* (sixteen times), always with geminate *s*, with the exception of one instance of *ūre* at 2827b, which is also the last instance of the word in the poem. The genitive of *wē* is distributed in prose much the same way as the possessive adjective—*ūser* is Northumbrian (but also *ūsra* in Rit.), and *ūre* is Mercian and West-Saxon. Both are employed in verse, and instances are too few to suggest the avoidance of the latter in any poem.

(10) The conjunction *ac* is commonly spelt *ah* in Mercian and Northumbrian texts (VP, Ru., Li., Rit.) and texts of Mercian origin (the translation of Bede's history, the *Life of St. Chad*, the *Blickling Homilies*). This spelling appears just twice in pure early West-Saxon texts, and in no pure late ones.[104] The spelling is always *ac*, for example, in the Chronicle, in Ælfric, in the genuine homilies of Wulfstan, the West-Saxon gospels, MS A of the *Benedictine Rule*, the Junius Psalter, *Lǣceboc*, and the *Rule of Chrodegang*. In verse *ah* is frequent in *Christ and Satan*, a poem that has exceptionally marked West Mercian characteristics above

---

[104]Cf. Brunner (§210.3) and Campbell (§452). The two Alfredian instances are in the *Pastoral Care* (Hatton MS, p. 305, line 1 in Sweet's edition) and the Orosius (p. 69, line 6 in Bately's edition). By comparison, there are thirty examples in the Old English Bede. The only other instances are in texts of a mixed dialectal nature or of uncertain origins: these are the Lenten homily edited by Belfour (one instance); some of the spurious "Wulfstan" homilies edited by Napier; the martyrology edited by Herzfeld, with the fragments printed by Sweet (*Oldest English Texts*) and C. Sisam; the so-called *Iudicia Dei IV* and *V* printed by Libermann (both with very strong Anglian characteristics); the full interlinear gloss on the Rule of St. Benedict (not the West-Saxon translation); some of the Psalter glosses of type D (see below, p. 330, n. 135); and the Aldhelm fragments at Yale University. For more specific references see the *Microfiche Concordance*.

and beyond the usual Anglianisms found in verse: see §335.5 and .11
above, and Appendix A below. Elsewhere in verse it appears only in the
*Fates of the Apostles* (115a), and in *Andreas*, eight times (23b, 232a, 281a,
569b, 1083a, 1209b, 1670b, 1703b), along with one instance of *ach*
(1592a). It clearly is not a feature of the poetic koine, and so it is
probable evidence of the Anglian origins of *Andreas* and the *Fates of the
Apostles*, or at least of an earlier Anglian recension. In late Northumbrian
texts final *c* is spirantized in a variety of words, but only *ac* is affected in
Mercian texts. The restriction of the change to the word *ac* in verse thus
suggests a greater probability of Mercian origins than Northumbrian for
these poems, though of course this evidence cannot be called firm.

(11) After long or resolved syllables, the connecting vowel *-i-* in the
present participle and inflected infinitive of weak verbs of the second
class is regularly lost in Anglian prose texts, with the exception of VP,
though the loss is occasionally represented there, as well. In Northumbrian texts the loss is also frequent after short syllables. For example,
Ru.[1] *lōkende* corresponds to WS *lōciende*: see Campbell, §757; Brunner,
§412, n. 10; and also p. 204, n. 69 above. Spellings without *-i-* are frequent in supposedly Anglian verse, for example at *Elene* 1257b, *Beowulf*
2761b, and *Solomon and Saturn* 77b. They do not occur in the Southern
group, which has only spellings with the connecting vowel, at *Judgment
Day II* 25a, 44a, 112a, 215a, 286a, and *Genesis B* 347b, 841a, and perhaps
243a (see the note just mentioned). The significance of this evidence is
limited, as there are no examples of any sort after long syllables in the
works of Alfred.

(12) In some Mercian prose texts, the third person singular present
indicative form of the verb *cweðan* is syncopated (Campbell, §733a;
Brunner, §358, n. 7). Thus, *cwið* is found in VP and Ru.[1], and syncope in
verbs ending in a dental consonant is frequent in the *Katherine* Group.
The appearance of *cwið*, then, and perhaps other syncopated forms with
roots ending in a dental consonant, in a poetic text that otherwise does
not show Sievers' syncope, is probabilistic evidence of Mercian origins. It
does not seem likely that a West-Saxon poet, regularly decontracting his
own contracted verb forms for the sake of conforming to the koine, would
have known that *cwið* should not be decontracted, considering the
demonstrable variety of fairly elementary blunders that scribes make in
copying the poetic koine. Rather, this is fairly convincing evidence of
Mercian composition. The form *cwið* is found in *Christ II* and *III*, *Guthlac
A*, and *Beowulf*; cf. *cwepeð* once in the metrical Psalms of the Paris Psalter
(57.10.1a).

(13) The use of *in-* as a verb prefix roughly equivalent to Modern
English *en-* is effectively limited to Anglian and Anglian-influenced texts:
for example, to Southern *onlīhtan* corresponds *inlīhtan* in VP, Ru., Li.,
Rit., the Old English Bede, Wærferth's translation of Gregory's *Dialogues*,
and other texts. This is true only when *in-* denotes inception, as in

*inbryrdan* 'inspire' and *inhǣtan* 'inflame'; forms in which *in-* means 'in', like *ingān*, are as likely to be Southern as Anglian, and *on-* as an indicator of the reversal of an action, as in *onbindan* 'unbind' and *onlūcan* 'open', is also common to all dialects. *In-* in forms like *ingān*, however, is stressed, while inceptive *in-* is not. In verse, inceptive *in-* is never found in the Southern group, though it is infrequent in the test group of poems, as well. Examples are at *Elene* 812a, 841a, 1045a, and *Juliana* 535a. It is also found in *Christ I*, *Guthlac A*, and *Maxims I*. Cf. Campbell, §76.

(14) Vleeskruyer (p. 27) points out that West-Saxon scribes tend to change Anglian *fore* to Southern *for*. The former is the form used in VP, Ru., Li., and Rit. It is also found in the *Life of St. Chad*, Wærferth's translation of Gregory's *Dialogues*, the translation of Bede's *History*, and some other texts of Mercian origin. In pure West-Saxon texts, *fore* appears only when stressed—that is, as an adverb or a postposed preposition. In verse, unstressed *fore* is very common, but it never appears in the Southern group of poems. It is found in the Northumbrian texts of *Bede's Death Song*, *Beowulf*, all the signed works of Cynewulf, *Andreas*, *Christ III*, the *Guthlac* poems, *Azarias*, the *Phoenix*, the metrical portion of the Paris Psalter, one of the psalm fragments in Bodleian MS Junius 121, and a variety of lyrics in the Exeter Book. Remarkably, there is not a single instance in the Cædmon MS, and this is especially peculiar given the variety of evidence that the scribes of *Christ and Satan* were Mercians (see Appendix A). This should probably be regarded as further evidence for the thorough revision of this manuscript (see §362 below).

(15) In the Saxon dialects *g* was lost before dental consonants other than liquids (Luick, §251; Campbell, §§243–45; Brunner, §214.3). The Saxon distribution of the change is confirmed by Middle English evidence. Forms like *gefrunon* and *þenað* (for *gefrugnon* and *þegnað*) occur throughout the corpus, and need not indicate Saxon origins. So also forms that retain *g* sometimes appear even in Saxon texts, for example *legdun* at *Brunanburh* 22a, and *þegnunga* at *Meters of Boethius* 11.46b, 25.24b, 25.32b. Yet the distribution of forms is sometimes suggestive. For example, although forms of *(a-, ge-, on)sæd-* do occur in the presumably Anglian texts *Genesis A* (238b), *Daniel* (4 examples), *Christ and Satan* (5 examples), *Andreas* (1022b), and *Beowulf* (1696a, 1945b), forms with *g* in these texts are overall much more frequent, e.g. with more than 20 examples in *Genesis A*. By comparison, the incidence of forms without *g* is disproportionately high in the Southern group: cf. *Meters* 9.61b, 20.182a, 25.54a, 25.60b, 26.74a, and *Maldon* 120b, 147b, 198b. Nor are there any examples of *sægd-* in the Saxon poems of the Southern group, if *Genesis B* is regarded as most likely a Kentish translation. Similarly, of the 23 instances of *-ren-* for *-regn-* in verse, seven are found in the *Meters*, one in *Maldon* (161b); and forms of *mægden* twice have *g* (*Christ III* 1419b, *Juliana* 608a), and twice do not (*Judgment Day II* 290b, 295b).

(16) It was shown above (§225) that the adjective suffix *-lic-* was

frequently spelt -lec- in the Alfredian period, but not later. Similarly, the word *heofon* was often spelt *hefon, hefen* in early West-Saxon, or perhaps throughout the South during the Alfredian period (Brunner, §110.1). Only the diphthongal spelling is found in such late West-Saxon texts as the works of Ælfric and Wulfstan. In verse the monophthongal spelling is found in the *Meters of Boethius, Genesis B*, and *Solomon and Saturn*; it is also found once each in the metrical epilogue to the *Pastoral Care, Daniel, Andreas*, and *Beowulf*. The lone instances may not signify anything, since lone instances occur in a variety of prose texts, including Li. But when there are several instance in a single text, this seems an estimable sign of a stage of transmission that is Southern and dates to the Alfredian period.

(17) It was pointed out above (§348) that non-West-Saxon back mutation is especially frequent in compounds, no doubt because they are less familiar than simplices. The same principle applies to personal names, and thus the preservation of some non-West-Saxon spellings in personal names seems especially good evidence of dialect origins. It is difficult to believe, for instance, that a scribe would have altered five of eight instances of *Wēohstan* to *Wīhstan* in *Beowulf* (especially as the same smoothing is found in *wigweorþunga*), while the opposite alteration is both credible and probable (§341). Similarly, the co-occurrence of *Hrǣdles, Hrǣdlan* with *Hrēðel, Hrēþles* < *\*Hrōþil-* in *Beowulf* seems incomprehensible without the assumption that *ǣ* is a scribal misinterpretation of archaic and/or Northumbrian *œ*.[105] That this is the case is implied also by the interchange of *d* and *þ*, which is not readily understandable unless it is due to the archaic use of *d* to represent the sound [ð] (Campbell, §55).[106] Unfortunately, few Old English poems contain Germanic proper names, though it may be pointed out that *Widsith* contains some apparent dialect forms (e.g. *Meaca* 23a, *Breoca* 25a, *Alewih* 35b, *Freoþeric* 124a, and others), while *Maldon* does not. The Germanic proper names in the *Meters* are of a different order. *Aleric* (1.7a, 1.19b) is not a dialect form: it is not even an Old English form, but is taken from a Latin source. *Eallerica* in the prose version (p. 7, line 2 of Sedgefield's edition) is perhaps a mere guess at the Anglo-Saxon equivalent, which actually should be *Ælric*.[107]

---

[105]It was shown above (§335.9) that *ǣ* is occasionally found for *ē* in early West-Saxon prose, and once in the Boethian *Meters*. However, that this happens more than once in the name *Hrēþel*, co-occurring with the substitution of *d* for *þ*, demonstrates that the phenomenon in this instance is of a different order.

[106]Original paradigmatic alternations under Verner's law are out of the question in *a*-stems, since the Proto-Indo-European accent did not alternate in these. And the co-occurrence of *Hrēþles* and *Hrǣdles* tells against the supposition of an original accentual difference between strong and weak paradigms.

[107]The name occurs several times in the Anglo-Saxon records. The earliest instance of *Ælric* is in an East Saxon charter dated 704, but which is probably a copy made late in the eighth century: see Bruckner, item 188 (Sawyer's no. 65). The attestation is early enough that it must be authentic rather than a corruption of *Ælfric*. Yet *Alric* may be a corruption of Anglian *Ald-*. *Ealle-* is not an authentic Old English name-element.

Yet it could be an inheritance corrupted over time, since, for example, the names in *Beowulf* are frequently close to their Scandinavian equivalents, but inexact (see Klaeber, p. xxxii, with n. 5). Similarly, at the same place in the *Consolation*, *Rædgota* (in the verse *metra* cf. *Rædgod* 1.7a, *Rædgot* 1.19b) seems to be a guess at the equivalent of Latin *Radagaisus*, which should actually be *Rædgar* (attested as *Rædgær*, *Ratgær*, *Re(h)dger*). The use of *-gota* is undoubtedly based on the fact that the man was a Goth: *-got* is not an Old English personal name-element, and *-god*, because it is a genuine name-element, is thus the *lectio facilior*.

§354. Purely orthographic evidence such as this must be treated with especial caution, and it is truer of this than of other types of evidence that no single criterion is very persuasive in its own right. For example, even though some orthographic features do seem to correlate to the division between the Southern group and the rest of the test group of poems, it is conceivable that a poem should have acquired some of these features by copying in an Anglian area at some time after the poem was first committed to parchment. Some assumption of this kind seems necessary in order to account for the presence of Anglian back mutation in the longer poems, if any of them are to be dated before the early glossaries, in which back mutation is orthographically incipient (see p. 347, n. 170 and §398 below). Thus Sisam is right that only "structural" evidence can afford certainty; and yet although the evidence of individual orthographic dialectal features means little on its own, as support for structural features it is certainly significant.

§355. Several types of structural evidence may be considered here:

(1) With negligible exceptions, the preposition *mid* is found only with the dative and instrumental cases in Southern prose texts, while it may take the accusative in Anglian ones.[108] With just one apparent exception, *mid* never takes the accusative in the Southern group, though the word appears 198 times.[109] In *Beowulf* there are 6 instances with the accusative (out of 72 occurrences of the word); in Cynewulf there are ten instances (out of 62); in *Genesis A* there are eight (out of 93).[110]

---

[108]Mitchell, §1195. He remarks, "Only sporadic examples of *mid* + accusative are found outside *Bede* and the poetry," but Thomas Miller finds that about a third of the instances in Li. and Ru. take the accusative. In VP the incidence is much lower, at 25 accusatives out of 192 instances: see *The Old English Version of Bede's Ecclesiastical History of the English People*, I, i, EETS, o.s. 95 (1890), xlv–xlvi. See also A. S. Napier, "Ein altenglisches Leben des heiligen Chad," *Anglia* 10 (1888), 131–56, at 138–39.

[109]The one exception is nonstructural, *mid gescead smeað* (*Meters* 20.218b). *Smeað* is monosyllabic at *Meters* 20.214b and 20.221b, but probably dissyllabic at 20.215a. In *mid bitere care* (*Judgment Day II* 214a), *bitere* may stand for either *biterre* or *bitre* (Campbell, §§457, 643.4).

[110]These instances with the accusative are at *Beowulf* 357b, 633b, 662b, 879b, 1672b, 2652a, *Elene* 275b, 297b (Campbell, §574.2 n. 2), 736b, 997a, *Fates of the Apostles* 74a, *Christ II* 461a, 515b, 519b, *Juliana* 668b, 681a, *Genesis A* 20a, 1210b, 1733–34, 2210a, 2255b, 2723a, 2786a, 2869a.

(2) *Sæ* is almost always masculine in Anglian prose texts.[111] In West-Saxon it is usually feminine: for instance, it is almost exclusively feminine in Ælfric. Whether there is a chronological element to the distribution of genders may be doubted, as the masculine form is hardly commoner in early West-Saxon texts than in later ones, with the exception only of the Old English Orosius.[112] The distribution in verse matches these facts fairly well. The word is masculine at *Genesis A* 958b, 1375b, 1452b, 2453a, *Exodus* 134b, 467a, 473a, *Beowulf* 507a, *Elene* 728a, *Christ II* 677a, 852a, *Andreas* 236b, 1658a, and in several poems outside the test group; it is feminine at *Meters of Boethius* 5.7a, 6.13b, 11.3b, 27.3b, 28.33b, and *Judgment Day II* 102b. There are three exceptions, at *Beowulf* 2394a, *Meters* 19.16a, and the *Metrical Preface to the Pastoral Care* 2a. The exceptions can perhaps be explained otherwise, but whether or not this is so seems unimportant, given the general conformity of the data, and the slight variability in prose.[113]

(3) Sievers ("Rhythmik," pp. 498–99) points out that the meter indicates two forms of *fæger* in verse, with a long and short root-vowel.[114] He offers this as a dialect criterion, and this is presumably correct, as the

---

[111]There are just three feminine instances in pure Anglian texts, one each in the headings to readings in Li. and the Canticles and Psalms of VP.

[112]Already in early West-Saxon texts the masculine form is infrequent. For example, Sedgefield in his edition of the *Consolation* counts eighteen feminine instances and two masculine (presumably he means in the prose), and Helen Bartlett (to whom all the following figures are due) reports the proportion of masculine to feminine forms as 1:4 in the Hatton MS of the *Pastoral Care* and 0:3 in the Parker Chronicle. The exception is the Old English Orosius, with a proportion of 39:11 (with seven of the latter in the passage about Ohtere and Wulfstan). Masculine forms are commoner in two West-Saxon texts of Anglian origin, the translation of Bede's *History* (14:13) and the Peterborough Chronicle (3:1). Bartlett finds just one masculine instance in the later West-Saxon texts she surveyed, in Thorpe's edition of the homilies of Ælfric (33:1); cf. consistently feminine forms in the Heptateuch, the West-Saxon Gospels, and the prose portion of the Paris Psalter.

[113]Because the masculine form is frequent in Alfredian prose, the two instances in Alfredian verse are not especially surprising, particularly as they are both instances of a formula, *on sealtne sæ* (cf. *Christ II* 677a). The exception in *Beowulf* (*ofer sæ side*) is suspicious in view of the formula *on/ofer/geond sidne sæ* (*Beowulf* 507a, *Christ II* 852a, *Phoenix* 103a, *Psalms* 134.6.3a, 145.5.2a) and the related formula with *sealtne*. Arguably, *side* is a mistake for *siðe*: cf. *æfter sæsiðe* (1149a).

[114]A. S. C. Ross offers an etymological explanation for the difference in "Notes on Some Old English Words," *Englische Studien* 67 (1932–33), 343–49, at 346–47. He proposes two ablaut grades of the root, with PIE *o* and *ē*; but under the laryngeal hypothesis such an alternation seems unlikely, and the comparative Germanic evidence is all negative. Alfred Bammesberger suggests that in verse the first syllable could be scanned long simply by analogy to the long, monosyllabic stem in the oblique cases (PGmc. *\*fagra-*); but this leaves unexplained the spelling with *e*. See his *Beiträge* (as above, p. 142, n. 2), pp. 46–47. Spellings like *fægger* and *fæiger* are exceedingly rare in Old English, though in Middle English the geminate is common early on: for example, already in the *Ormulum*, where consonants are not geminated after short vowels in open syllables, the word is consistently *faȝȝerr*.

word is consistently spelt *feger(-)* (i.e. *fēger*, corresponding to WS *\*fǣger*) in Li. and Rit. This is also the spelling in VP, but there *e* may stand for WS *ǣ*; and the spelling *fæger* is found in Ru.[2] (Jn. 18:1). Joseph Wright reports the pronunciation "*fiə(r)*" in widely scattered Anglian areas, including southeast Lancashire, northeast Shropshire, northern Cumberland, and the Isle of Man, as well as "*viə(r)*" in Dorset.[115] Most examples in verse are ambiguous, but the unambiguous ones conform largely to general assumptions about dialect in verse. Long forms are required at *Beowulf* 773a, *Elene* 242b, 910b, *Precepts* 12a, *Christ and Satan* 79b, 387b, *Homiletic Fragment I* 17b, *Dream of the Rood* 73a, *Azarias* 119a, *Phoenix* 85b, 182b, 232b, 307b, *Riddle 31* 17b, *Psalms* 54.23.2b, 77.61.2a, 112.7.2b, 115.5.1a, *Guthlac A* 748b and *Panther* 29a. There are no unambiguously long examples in the Southern group, and there are three short forms in one poem of the group: cf. *Rune Poem* 31b, 85b, 88b. Exceptions are few: *þæt fægerro lyt* (*Genesis A* 1852b, emended), *on fægerne sweg* (*Exodus* 567a), and *fæger halignes* (*Psalms* 95.6.2a); and perhaps *fah wyrm þurh fægir word* (*Genesis A* 899a), though there is no parallel to the metrical type in *Beowulf*. But since both *fæger* and *feger* appear in Anglian texts, the occurrence of short forms in supposedly Anglian verse does not constitute counterevidence: only the occurrence of long forms is significant. This evidence is hardly conclusive, but it is suggestive.

(4) At the same place Sievers points out that the meter frequently requires *dǣdon* for *dydon* in verse, and that *dǣdon* is actually attested a few places in verse—compare *dēdon*, found mainly in Li. He provides examples from *Genesis A* (142a, 2894a), *Daniel* (196b), *Beowulf* (1828b), and the Psalms of the Paris Psalter (61.3.2b, 77.32.1b). To these may be added *Daniel* 262b and *Wulf and Eadwacer* 14a. There is a prominent exception, *þæt hie to mete dædon* (*Genesis B* 722b), which Sievers explains as due to the influence of OSax. *dādun*. The first and third person singular preterite indicative should not have the long vowel, but the optative perhaps should (as at *Genesis A* 2894a). In that event, the second person singular preterite perhaps also should agree with the plural in root vocalism, as with the Old Saxon and Old High German cognates. If so there are also examples at *Psalms* 84.3.1b, 87.8.1a, 118.65.1b, 137.3.3b, and 141.5.1b. But the long form is metrically inadmissible at *Psalms* 118.98.1a, 118.132.2b, 144.12.1a, *Fragments of Psalms* 24.5.2a, 50.1.1b, and *Christ and Satan* 623b. In regard to the plural, the appearance of the short form in supposedly Anglian verse is of no significance, since *dydon* and *dydun* are common in VP, Li., and Ru. For this reason clear examples with a short root vowel in the Southern group (of which there are none) would not render this criterion considerably more effective. Its value is limited, but it lends support to other dialect indicators.

---

[115]See *The English Dialect Grammar* (Oxford: Clarendon, 1905). *Fair* became *fār* in the North during the Middle English period.

(5) Sievers ("Miscellen," p. 252; "Rhythmik," p. 483) remarks that nom. and acc. pl. *fēondas* and *frēondas* (for WS *fīend* and *frīend*) are probably not attested in prose outside Northumbrian texts. Metrically confirmable instances appear in *Daniel, Azarias, Guthlac A, Solomon and Saturn* and the Paris Psalter. Nonstructural examples occur also in the *Dream of the Rood*. But while it is true that these are the normal forms in the late Northumbrian glosses, it should also be pointed out that there are a few instances in Mercian texts, in Farman's gloss to Matthew (5:44, 10:36, 22:44), in a Mercian charter of the last part of the ninth century, granting rights at Worcester (Sawyer's no. 223), and in the originally Mercian Alfredian translations of Gregory's *Dialogues* and Bede's *Historia*. There are no other instances outside Northumbrian, though in Northumbrian texts there seem to be no examples without the *-as* inflection. As for the shorter forms in verse, the following are the structural instances:[116]

> Fynd gold strudon  (*Genesis A* 2006b)
> fynd bysmriað  (*Psalms* 79.6.3b)
> wið ealle fynd  (*Psalms* 88.9.3b)
> þæt heora fynd ehton  (*Psalms* 105.33.1b)
> unholde fynd  (*Psalms* 108.11.1b)
> þe þine frynd wærun  (*Psalms* 138.15.4a)
> wið ða fynd weredon  (*Maldon* 82b)

The remaining examples of the Southern forms—that is, the nonstructural ones—appear in three poems of the Southern group, i.e. *Genesis B, Judith*, and *Maldon*, as well as in *Genesis A, Elene, Maxims I,* the *Wife's Lament*, and the Paris Psalter. The presence of the Southern forms does not prove that a poem is not Anglian in origin—for example, it is not known when the analogical forms with *-as* replaced the originals in the Midlands and the North—though the presence of the Northern forms is certainly good evidence of Anglian composition, and the complete absence of such forms from the Southern group is good probabilistic evidence.

(6) Sievers ("Rhythmik," pp. 463–64) argues that Hygelac's name must have been *Hyglac* in the *Beowulf* poet's dialect, since the name several times begins the second foot of a verse of type D, a position in which resolution is unusual. If the name lacked the *e*, then the poet's dialect should have been Northumbrian, since this name-element (and, like it, *Sige-*) regularly lacks the *e* in the North, but not in the Midlands or the South. But this argument is unpersuasive. Although resolution is admittedly rare in the relevant position, it does occur in several verses in

---

[116]Sievers offers *feogað frynd hiera* (*Elene* 360a) as a structural example, but with the substitution of *frēondas* this could belong to type 1D\*5. *Fynd gold strudon* (*Genesis A* 2006b) must be a structural example under the rule of the coda, forbidding resolution in *strudon* (see Chap. 7); and as pointed out above (p. 307, n. 85), a finite verb would be unusual in final position in a verse of type A.

the poem.[117] And ten Brink argues (pp. 213–16), with some reason, that the rarity of the metrical type is dictated by the structure of the language, rather than by purely metrical concerns. More important, it is clear that Anglo-Saxon poets were willing to construct metrically unusual verses for the sake of accommodating personal names (see, e.g., §§235, 264 above). The spelling *Hylaces* does occur once in the poem (1530b), but this is not itself a Northumbrian spelling, and forms of *Sige-* and *Hyge-* without *e* do occur a few times in non-Northumbrian texts (Sievers lists four instances on p. 464).

(7) A distinction in form between accusative and dative personal pronouns may be regarded as semi-structural, since the difference between forms like *ūsic* and *ūs* can be detected in the meter, while the difference between *mec* and *mē* cannot.[118] The forms *mec, þec, incit, uncit, ūsic,* and *ēowic* are characteristic of Anglian and Anglian-influenced prose texts, but not of pure Southern prose texts: they are absent, for instance, from the genuine works of Alfred, and from Ælfric, the West-Saxon Gospels, the Chronicle, the genuine homilies of Wulfstan, and the *Benedictine Rule*, as well as from some less certainly pure texts, such as the laws. In verse these forms are found in a wide variety of poems, including the *Leiden Riddle, Genesis A, Daniel, Exodus, Beowulf, Andreas,* and the Cynewulf canon. They are not found in any poem of the Southern group. Thus, these pronouns may be regarded as good evidence for dialect origins. Most of these presumably Anglian poems also have instances of *mē* for *mec, þē* for *þec,* and the like, and it is only by means of the meter, and then only in regard to the dissyllabic forms, that it can be determined whether this is scribal substitution or inherent variability. The former appears to be the case: for instance, the Vercelli scribe writes *eow* for both dative (ten times) and accusative (six times) throughout *Elene*. But at the only place where the accusative pronoun is stressed and structural, *ēowic* is required by the meter: Krapp and others emend to *for eowic forð* (318b). In *Genesis A* the dative *ūs* (thirteen times) is correctly distinguished from the accusative *ūsic* (four times) in all but one instance, where *ūs* is not structural: compare *ac us hearde sceod* (997b). The clearest evidence for Saxonization of such Anglian pronouns in the course of scribal transmission comes from the Exeter Book, in which *usic* and *þec* are common; and yet in one poem, the *Descent into Hell*, they have regularly been altered to *us* and *þe* by erasure. Usually these

---

[117]See 487a, 495b, 1897a, 2161a, 2206b, 2424a, 2613a, and 2708a. That the type is rare is not surprising under the rule of the coda, in conjunction with the assumption that the initial lift of the second foot of type D is subordinated to that of the first foot (see §275 above).

[118]On the use of *mec* in two short inscriptions see E. G. Stanley in the Chase volume, pp. 210–11. Stanley is right not to draw any firm conclusions, since the provenance of such objects is even more difficult to determine than that of most manuscripts.

pronouns are unstressed, and even when they are stressed they are not always structural, or unambiguously so; but the structural instances tend to confirm the dialectal distribution. Out of more than sixty structural instances of *ūs*, just a few suggest *ūsic* is required instead, and these are in presumably Anglian poems. These verses from the Paris Psalter are relevant:

> gebeltsige us    bliðe drihten  (66.6.2)
> and alys us,     lifigende god  (78.9.2)
> and þine bletsunge    bring ofer us  (113.21.2)

Since the metrics of the Psalms are so aberrant it is not safe to base any firm conclusions on them, but the facts are worth examining. The second of these requires an accusative pronoun, and *ūsic* would mend the meter. The third ought to have an accusative after the verb of motion—and compare *swyþe ofer usic* (64.3.1b) and *heah ofer usic* (89.19.3b)—and this would mend the meter here, as well. The first example offends against Kuhn's second law if the first syllable is not anacrustic, and the accusative case is required after the verb. Anacrusis is not found in this type in *Beowulf*, and so the example is uncertain. But since *ūsic* is required in the other two instances, and the word actually appears three times in the Paris Psalter, perhaps it is to be preferred here. In the *Fragments of Psalms* the meter seems to require *ūsic* in *wel ofer us* (32.18.2a), though the sense seems to demand a dative form. But the metrics of these fragments are like those of the Paris Psalter, and *ūsic* in dative use seems unlikely. In *God wæs mid us* (*Christ I* 124b) stress on *mid* before a pronoun is possible (see p. 35, n. 65 above), though possibly instead *ūsic* should be substituted under the assumption that this is an instance of an Anglian accusative with *mid* (as under (1) above). An accusative is required in *Ic bidde eow* (*Judgment Day II* 33a), and *ēowic* would be unmetrical; but this is not proof of accusative *ēow* in the poet's dialect, since the unmetrical type is paralleled in the poem, as in *gelice alyfed* (144a) and *awyrgedum gastum* (184a). Accusative *ēow* is required in *þæt ge recene eow* (*Judith* 188b), however, where *ēowic* is ruled out by the meter. This appears to be the only very good metrical evidence of a Southern origin for *Judith*.[119]

(8) The use of *ac* as an interrogative particle equivalent to *numquid* is found in VP, Ru., and Li. It is not found in any text of a predominantly West-Saxon nature, where *numquid* is generally translated *cwyðst þu*, or

---

[119]Most earlier scholars regarded *Judith* as an Anglian composition. Those arguing for West-Saxon origins have done so not so much on the basis of the claim that the poem contains Southern features, but that it contains no definitive Anglian ones: see Tupper (as above, p. 4, n. 6); Dobbie, ASPR 6:lxiv–lxv; and Timmer's edition, pp. 2–6. See also below, p. 335, n. 147, on the poem's vocabulary.

*is þæs wen*, as in the Canterbury Psalter.[120] In verse, the only certain examples of the use of *ac* in this sense are the following:

> Hu lomp eow on lade,   leofa Biowulf,
> þa ðu færinga   feorr gehogodest
> sæcce secean   ofer sealt wæter,
> hilde to Hiorote?   Ac ðu Hroðgare
> widcuðne wean   wihte gebettest,
> mærum ðeodne?  (*Beowulf* 1987–92a)

> Æþelinge weox
> word ond wisdom;   ah he þara wundra a,
> domagende,   dæl ænigne
> frætre þeode   beforan cyðde?  (*Andreas* 568b–71)[121]

*Ac* perhaps translates *numquid* once in the metrical Psalms of the Paris Psalter:

> Ac we þæs ne wenað,   þæt us witig god
> mæge bringan to   beod gegearwod
> on þisum westene   widum and sidum.  (77.20.5–7)

This passage translates "numquid poterit deus parare mensam in deserto," and here once again Krapp, following earlier editors, has inserted an unncessary *ne* (see n. 121). But *we þæs wenað* is also a translation of *numquid*, of the *is þæs wen* type. Possibly the poet was working from more than one prose translation: compare 87.12.1a, where *numquid* is translated *cwist þu*.[122] *Ac* also introduces several questions in *Solomon and Saturn II*, such as *Ac forhwon fealleð se snaw* (302a); but in these instances it may consistently be translated "but" or "and." It is very unlikely that the use of *ac* as an interrogative particle was an actual feature of Anglian speech. Rather, more likely it arose in Anglian translations from Latin as a device for dealing with an untranslatable Latin word. Yet even if this is the case, the recording (and very likely the composition) of *Andreas* and *Beowulf* in a monastic scriptorium[123] is sufficient explanation for the

---

[120]See Napier (as above, p. 318, n. 108), p. 138; Klaeber, p. xcv; and Vleeskruyer, pp. 25–26, with the references there.

[121]This passage is quoted from Brooks's edition, as Krapp emends *ænigne* to *nænigne*—an unnecessary change, once it is recognized that *ac* is an interrogative particle. That it is interrogative is demonstrated by the Latin and Greek texts: see Brooks's note, p. 81.

[122]That the metrical portion of the Paris Psalter is versified from interlinear psalter glosses has been demonstrated by Sarah Larratt Keefer, *The Old English Metrical Psalter: An Annotated Set of Collation Lists with the Psalter Glosses* (New York: Garland, 1979).

[123]See Fred C. Robinson, "Old English Poetry: The Question of Authorship," *ANQ*, n.s. 3 (1990), 59–64.

intrusion of such learned jargon—compare, for example, the use of *nōn* at *Beowulf* 1600a.

(9) The use of the weak form 1. and 3. sg. pret. ind. *funde* (*a-*, *ge-*, *onfunde*, etc.) to *findan* is generally regarded as West-Saxon, corresponding to Anglian *fand, fond*: see Campbell, §741; Brunner, §386, n. 2. The relevant forms in the Southern group are *fond* (*Meters* 2.9b) and *funde* (*Meters* 8.58b, *Menologium* 99b); compare also *anfunde* at *Psalm 50* 25b. *Funde* is probably also indicative at *Genesis B* 455b, since the subjunctive is not usual in *ōððæt* clauses (Mitchell, §2743); but the same reasoning applies to *Beowulf* 1415b and *Elene* 830b. There are also indicative instances at *Juliana* 490b and *Judith* 2b and 278a. In actuality, neither *fond* nor *funde* is in evidence in any of the pure Mercian Old English texts, and so it cannot be said with assurance that this is only a Southern feature. The evidence of the Old English Bede and Wærferth's translation of Gregory's *Dialogues*, in which *funde* is frequent, of course is suggestive rather than probative. Certainly *fond* was in use in parts of Mercia, given the Middle English evidence. But there is also a small amount of evidence for the use of *funde* there, including two examples in the Worcester Chronicle (one of them also in the Peterborough manuscript), and in *Havelok the Dane* and *Dame Sirith*.

(10) The Anglian preterite finite and participial suffix is *-ad-* (more commonly WS *-od-*) in weak verbs of the second class (Campbell, §757; Brunner, §§413–14; and see above, §228). In the *Meters* the instances are *geswiðrad* (5.45b), *earnade* (9.20a), *geweorðad* (10.28a), *geheaðorad* (13.6a), *gesamnade* (17.13a), *gestaðoladest* (20.161a), *gesomnade* (20.246a), *bereafad* (28.43b), and *staðolade* (29.84b); there are also 28 instances of *-od-*, and 4 certain examples of *-ed-* in these verbs. All three variants are frequent in the prose of the *Consolation*, along with occasional *-ud-*. Elsewhere in the Southern group, *-ad-* is found only in *prowade* (*Menologium* 25b), *geweorðad* (154b), and *geearnade* (*Judgment Day II* 32a). By comparison, there are 28 instances of *-ad-* in *Beowulf*, as compared to 132 of *-od-* and 22 of *-ed-*; *-ad-* is frequent in the Exeter Book: see Appendix A below. There are perhaps 26 instances of *-ad-* in *Andreas*, 61 of *-od-*, 9 of *-ed-*, and 2 of *-ud-*.[124] The evidence indicates that, in general, statistics of incidence alone will not mark this as a dialect indicator in verse.

(11) Anglian (?) inflection of the noun *bend* as an *ō*-stem (Brunner, §266, n. 1) is seen in *irenbenda* (*Genesis B* 371b, nom. pl.; *-s* added by a later hand). Few other syntactic features have been suggested as dialect indicators.[125]

---

[124]These are the figures of H. Bauer (p. 90: see the reference under the *Phoenix* in Appendix A, p. 402 below), whose findings are not consistently reliable.

[125]See von Schaubert, *passim*; Vleeskruyer, pp. 15–16, 48, 140; Kilpiö (as above, p. 313, n. 99), pp. 98–101; and Ogawa (as above, p. 281, n. 28), *passim*, esp. pp. 45–46 and 50—but cf. the review in *JEGP* 90 (1991), 546–49. Only the last of these is primarily concerned with verse.

§356. Many differences in pure dialect vocabulary have been suggested—that is, differences in terms of choice of lexical items rather than of phonologically or metrically differentiated variants of the same word. These are important as corroboration of the preceding evidence, being of a different order. But since these lead somewhat afield of the topic of metrics, it will be sufficient merely to mention a few of the more convincing examples. It seems advisable to do this here because of the impression Sisam creates that the evidence of vocabulary is negligible, concluding, as he does, that in "the present state of the investigation, vocabulary remains unsatisfactory or inconclusive as evidence of the original dialect of poems presumed to be early; and too many favourable hypotheses are used to reproduce the result that all the earlier poetry is Anglian" (*Studies*, p. 131). As always, Sisam's remarks are worthy of the most careful consideration, and his counterexamples must be rebutted if dialect vocabulary is to merit any credence.

§357. The value of vocabulary as a means of identifying the original dialect, or even the author, of works in prose, has been sufficiently demonstrated, for example by Janet Bately's splendid studies of the vocabulary of the Alfredian canon.[126] In verse, matters are not so straightforward. The general difficulties involved in using vocabulary as an indicator of dialect for verse have been summarized well by Robert J. Menner in a study of the vocabulary in *Judgment Day I* and *II*.[127] The

---

[126]See "King Alfred and the Old English Translation of Orosius," *Anglia* 88 (1970), 433–60; "The Compilation of the Anglo-Saxon Chronicle, 60 B.C. to A.D. 890: Vocabulary as Evidence," *Proceedings of the British Academy* 64 (1980 for 1978), 93–129; and "Lexical Evidence for the Authorship of the Prose Psalms in the Paris Psalter," *ASE* 10 (1982), 69–95. Some other studies that employ vocabulary as a key to authorship are by Karl Jost, "Unechte Ælfrictexte," *Anglia* 51 (1927), 81–103 and 177–219, along with his *Wulfstanstudien* (Bern: Francke, 1950); John C. Pope, *Homilies of Ælfric: A Supplementary Collection*, EETS, o.s. 259–60 (1967–68), 1:94–105; E. Liggins, "The Authorship of the Old English *Orosius*," *Anglia* 88 (1970), 289–322; Dorothy Whitelock, "The Authorship of the Account of King Edgar's Establishment of Monasteries," in *Philological Essays in Honour of Herbert Dean Meritt*, ed. James Rosier (The Hague: Mouton, 1970), pp. 125–36; Peter Clemoes in *The Old English Illustrated Hexateuch*, ed. C. R. Dodwell and P. Clemoes, Early English Manuscripts in Facsimile 18 (Copenhagen: Rosenkilde & Bagger, 1974), 42–53; and Peter S. Baker, "The Old English Canon of Byrhtferth of Ramsey," *Speculum* 55 (1980), 22–37. The last of these discusses some of the genuine dangers in applying this method without considerable care; and Malcolm Godden points out another interfering factor, changes in an author's vocabulary over the course of his lifetime, in "Ælfric's Changing Vocabulary," *ES* 61 (1980), 206–23.

[127]"The Vocabulary of the Old English Poems on the Judgment Day," *PMLA* 62 (1947), 583–97. For some other studies dealing with dialect vocabulary see Menner's "Date and Dialect of *Genesis A* 852–2936 (Part III)," *Anglia* 70 (1951/52), 285–94; Elmar Seebold, "Die ae. Entsprechungen von Lat. *sapiens* und *prudens*," *Anglia* 92 (1974), 291–333; Franz Wenisch, "*Judith*—eine westsächsische Dichtung?" *Anglia* 100 (1982), 273–300; Jane Roberts, "The Old English Prose Translation of Felix's *Vita sancti Guthlaci*," in *Studies in Earlier Old English Prose*, ed. Paul E. Szarmach (Albany: State Univ. of New York Press, 1986), pp. 363–79, with the references in n. 17; and the

chief difficulties are that the number of distinctive lexical items is small, since poets avoid prosaic words, and yet only words found also in prose can be verified as belonging to a particular dialect; that there is a great deal of dialectal impurity in some prose texts that might be used for corroboration, such as the Alfredian translations of Gregory's *Dialogues* and Bede's *History*; and that many "dialect" words are actually part of the poetic koine, and so may appear in Southern texts despite their Anglian form: for instance, *mēce* is the Anglian form of WS *mǣce* (recorded only in the Parker Chronicle version of the *Battle of Brunanburh*), and yet *mēce* is found in the *Meters of Boethius*, *Maldon*, and even Laȝamon's *Brut*. Yet these are not insuperable difficulties, because after attention to these problems has eliminated a great deal of spurious evidence, there still remains a core of words that are distributed along presumed dialect boundaries in verse.

§358. Another point Sisam raises is that vocabulary can be misleading if it is not structural, that is, if it is not bound by meter and alliteration (*Studies*, pp. 130–31). For instance, any scribe could methodically change *on* to *in* throughout his text—and indeed, it must be assumed that this is precisely what has happened in the text of the *Menologium* if *in* is to be assumed to have any validity as a dialect word (see below). That scribes did perform such changes, at least in prose, has been amply demonstrated, for example by J. J. Campbell. And yet this objection is not convincing in regard to verse texts of any length, since these all contain a variety of dialect vocabulary. In addition to displaying Anglian phonological and morphological features not found in the Southern

---

studies mentioned in the following notes. Caution must be urged in the use of two studies that have been widely cited: G. Scherer, *Zur Geographie und Chronologie des ags. Wortschatzes* (Berlin diss.; Leipzig: Mayer & Müller, 1928); and Hildegard Rauh, *Der Wortschatz der altenglischen Übersetzungen des Matthäus-Evangeliums* (Berlin diss.; Berlin: Paul Funk, 1936). P. N. U. Harting, "The Text of the Old English Translation of Gregory's 'Dialogues'," *Neophilologus* 22 (1937), 281–302 at 283–86, has shown that Scherer's work is based not on an original exmination of the vocabulary of the *Dialogues*, but on secondary sources, and thus reaches faulty conclusions based on incomplete data; see also Amos, pp. 152–53. David Yerkes provides a thorough listing of the relevant material in *The Two Versions of Wærferth's Translation of Gregory's Dialogues: An Old English Thesaurus* (Toronto: Univ. of Toronto Press, 1979). The problems of Scherer's work to a certain extent also affect Rauh's, which relies on Scherer's. For a critique of these and other studies of dialect vocabulary see Otto Funke, "Altenglische Wortgeographie (Eine bibliographische Überschau)," *Anglistische Studien: Festschrift zum 70. Geburtstag von Professor Friedrich Wild*, ed. K. Brunner et al., Wiener Beiträge zur englischen Philologie 66 (Vienna: W. Braumüller, 1958), 39–51. There are also considerable difficulties with the conclusions of P. Meissner, "Studien zum Wortschatz Ælfrics," *Archiv* 165 (1934), 11–19, and 166 (1935), 30–39, 205–15; cf. Hans Schabram, "Kritische Bemerkungen zu Angaben über die Verbreitung altenglischer Wörter," *Festschrift für Edgar Mertner*, ed. B. Fabian and U. Suerbaum (Munich: Fink, 1969), 89–102. For some Middle English evidence see Rolf Kaiser, *Zur Geographie des mittelenglischen Wortschatzes*, Palaestra 205 (Leipzig: Mayer & Müller, 1937).

group, poems like *Genesis A*, *Beowulf*, and the signed works of Cynewulf show a high incidence of a variety of very common Anglian words such as *nymþe* and *gēn(a)*, which are not found in the Southern group. The coincidence is not credible, nor is the assumption that the scribes, who were not effective at altering the dialect of prose texts without leaving traces, could have produced such seamless regularity in verse texts, which by their very nature are more resistant to alteration.

§359. But Sisam points out a further difficulty, that there are no pre-Alfredian West-Saxon prose texts for comparison with the Anglian ones, and therefore it cannot be proved that any supposedly Anglian word was not in use in West-Saxon verse before Alfred's reign. Thus, presumably early verse could still be West-Saxon.[128] Menner ("Judgment Day," p. 586) replies:

> This contingency seems highly unlikely in itself. But, if it were true, we should then certainly expect that some words which became restricted to West Saxon prose (as opposed to Anglian) would be found in the poem [*Solomon and Saturn II*], just as we have, in admittedly Anglian poems, words which became restricted to Anglian prose (as opposed to West Saxon). Such words, with one doubtful exception, *clūd*, 'rock,' 185, we do not find.

Sisam's rejoinder (*Studies*, p. 130) is in the form of a set of counter-examples:

> Since he used "West Saxon" in the strict sense, excluding texts that are not pure, "Anglian prose" should be similarly defined. Then several words in *Salomon and Saturn II* that are (I believe) lacking in Anglian prose are found in Alfred's West Saxon prose, e.g. *gielpen* 'boastful', *leoftæl* 'well-liked', *getigan* 'to tie', *weorðgeorn* 'desiring honour'.

As he makes clear, Sisam does not mean to argue that *Solomon and Saturn II* is a West-Saxon composition, but that Menner's method of identifying Anglian vocabulary can be shown to produce clearly erroneous results in a parallel instance. Yet his objection to Menner's using "West-Saxon" in the strict sense of the word is not convincing, since pure West-Saxon texts are so much more extensive than pure Anglian ones, with the result that apparently West-Saxon lexical items are likelier to be missing from Anglian texts by chance than apparently Anglian lexical items from West-Saxon texts. More important, his counterexamples fail to convince because they are so rare in prose. Only *getīgan* has any frequency—there are twenty-four instances in prose, according to the *Microfiche Concordance*—while the other three words appear just thrice each.[129] To be

---

[128]Sisam, review of Menner's *Poetical Dialogues of Solomon and Saturn*, in *MÆ* 13 (1944), 28–36, at 32.

[129]Sisam counts two extra instances of *gielpen* in the *Pastoral Care*, but he seems to have counted the same readings twice, in different manuscripts.

sure, some words attested as few as twenty-four times have been offered as evidence of dialect origins—for example, Menner's identification of *(eormen)strȳnd* in *Solomon and Saturn II* as Anglian—but this is not true of all vocabulary regarded as Anglian, or even of all of Menner's own evidence. When very common words like *in, gēn(a)*, and *nympe* show an exclusively Anglian distribution in prose, with a corroborating distribution in verse, Menner's position remains valid to the extent that in the verse Sisam would like to call early West-Saxon rather than Anglian there are no similar words restricted to West-Saxon use in prose—that is, words common enough in prose that their nonattestation in Anglian prose texts cannot be mere chance.[130] And so while Sisam's objection might be valid in regard to relatively rare lexical items, it is not so in regard to common ones. Yet even relatively rare words can be shown to be non-West-Saxon if it can be demonstrated that West-Saxon scribes regularly altered or avoided them. This is true, for example, of Menner's *strȳnd*, which in prose is found in Rit., Li., Ru., and one of the *Blickling Homilies*. It is also found in the most conservative manuscripts of the (originally Mercian) translation of Bede's *History*, but in the less conservative, more Saxonizing ones (especially Cambridge, Corpus Christi College 41) it may be changed to *cynn* or *gestrēon* or *gebyrd*.[131]

§360. Nonetheless, the most convincing evidence remains the vocabulary that is very well attested, and just a few of these words need be mentioned here. The most thorough studies of the problem are by Richard Jordan and Franz Wenisch, and their findings about some individual items of vocabulary may be summarized. One fairly clear example is the use of *gēn(a)* beside *gīet(a)*. Both are found in Anglian prose, but only the latter in pure West-Saxon texts. As for verse, there are nineteen instances of *gēt(a)* or *gīet(a)* in the poems of the Southern group; for comparison, Jordan finds seventeen in *Genesis A*, eighteen in *Beowulf*, and two in the signed works of Cynewulf.[132] On the other hand, Wenisch finds seven instances of *gēn(a)* or *gīen(a)* in *Genesis A*, thirteen

---

[130]Joseph Tuso argues that *Beowulf* contains some West-Saxon dialect vocabulary: see "*Beowulf*'s Dialect Vocabulary and the Kiernan Theory," *South Central Review* 2 (1985), 1–9. But since his items of West-Saxon vocabulary are *āhsian, ansȳn, būtan, cȳðan, faran*, and so forth, the methodology used is not that of excluding all words except those used in one dialect or set of dialects.

[131]See Wenisch, pp. 228–29. For other examples see J. J. Campbell; C. and K. Sisam, (as above, p. 300, n. 79), §77; and Raymond Grant, *The B Text of the Old English Bede: A Linguistic Commentary*, Costerus, n.s. 73 (Amsterdam/Atlanta: Rodopi, 1989).

[132]Jordan neglected a few instances in the Southern group, and so the number nineteen is based on the entries in the ASPR concordance. Jordan's study is important, but with better reference works available, his figures can now frequently be corrected. Thus, in instances in which Wenisch offers data, his are preferred here. The form *gēna* has Anglian or Kentish vocalism, and is rare in good West-Saxon prose. Yet it is frequent in the *Consolation*, prose and verse, perhaps as another Southeasternism.

in *Beowulf* and twenty in Cynewulf, but just one in the Southern group, at *Genesis B* 413b.[133]

§361. Another Anglian word is conj. *nympe* or *nemne/nefne* 'nisi', which may be used exclusively in Anglian prose texts, or beside *butan*, *bute*.[134] In Northumbrian, *nympe* and *butan* are used to the exclusion of *nemne*, which then is only Mercian. On the other hand, Jordan finds that only *butan* is used in the major West-Saxon prose texts, that is, in Alfred, Ælfric, the West-Saxon gospels, Wulfstan, the Chronicle, the laws, and the translation of the *Benedictine Rule*.[135] In verse there are 9 examples of conj. *butan* in the Southern group, in addition to one in *Genesis A*, five in *Beowulf*, and four in Cynewulf. *Nympe* and *nemne* do not appear at all in the Southern group, while there are, according to Jordan, six instances of *nympe* in *Genesis A*, ten of *nemne* and two of *nympe* in *Beowulf*, and one of each in the longer poems of Cynewulf (to which may be added

[133]Jordan excludes this example because he follows the view that the metrically most irregular section in the middle of the poem is a separate composition.

[134]The Anglian nature of the word was independently recognized first by Frank J. Mather, "Anglo-Saxon *nemne* (*nymðe*) and the Northumbrian Theory," *MLN* 9 (1894), 152–56 (with support from A. S. Napier, "Old English *nemne* (*nymðe*)," in the same volume, p. 318); and Bartlett, pp. 18–19. Hermann Flasdieck argues that the spelling *nefne* cannot be dated later than ca. 725: see "OE *nefne*: A Revaluation" (as above, p. 285, n. 42), with a detailed list of all instances in Old English, pp. 137–40. But this argument rests on some conjecture, e.g. that the reason for the alternation between -*fn*- and -*mn*- in similar words is that the change was originally restricted to inflected forms (as Luick has it, §681). It also demands that *Blickling Homily XVIII* be dated to the beginning of the eighth century (p. 168), which seems improbable, though Vleeskruyer (pp. 56–57) would also like to date the *Blickling Homilies* before 900. See Vleeskruyer, p. 32, for further references on *nemne*.

[135]Anglian *nympe* is found in some Psalter glosses of the D type, a family including the Royal, Canterbury, Stowe, Vitellius, Arundel, Salisbury, Blickling, and Bosworth Psalters, and at least partially the Lambeth Psalter. The language of these is mainly West-Saxon, but they also contain some marked Anglianisms: see C. and K. Sisam (as above, p. 300, n. 79), §108; and the discussion, with references, in von Schaubert's study, p. 134. For more recent references see Phillip Pulsiano, "Defining the A-Type (*Vespasian*) and D-Type (*Regius*) Psalter-Gloss Traditions," *ES* 72 (1991), 308–27. As Wenisch correctly points out (pp. 99–100), the Sisams' doubts about the connection between the D and A gloss types (§111) does not affect the evidence of Anglian origins. Tupper ("Philological Legend," p. 260) objects that *nymne* is found once in a Kentish charter of the year 805 (Sweet's no. 34), and *nymðe* appears three times in a grant of Æthelberht, dated 864, to the church of Sherborne, Dorset—Birch's no. 510, edited by Agnes Robertson, *Anglo-Saxon Charters* (Cambridge: Cambridge Univ. Press, 1939), no. 11 (pp. 16–21). Tupper remarks in a note that the charter contains only West-Saxon and Kentish forms. Certainly there are some apparent Southeastern features, including *sye*, *genæmned*, *siondon*, *syondon*, *Eongolcynne*, and *bynyopan*. But there are also Anglian habits of spelling, including retraction of *æ* in *walдеð* and *alra*, consistently unsyncopated finite verb forms, and possibly an attempt at smoothing in *Westsaxna*. Some other features may be either Kentish or Anglian, including those seen in *forgyfo* and *lifi(g)ende*. Just possibly, then, *nympe* is Kentish as well as Anglian, but more likely these examples demonstrate the particularly strong Mercian influence in ninth-century Kentish documents.

*nemþe* at *Fates of the Apostles* 114a). Other poems containing examples of *nymþe* are *Exodus, Daniel, Christ and Satan, Christ I,* the *Riddles,* the *Wanderer, Judgment Day I, Judith,* the Psalms of the Paris Psalter, the fragment of Psalm 58 in Bodleian MS Junius 121, and the homiletic verse fragment in the Vercelli Book. That *nymðe* was perceived as an Anglian word even in verse in Anglo-Saxon times is demonstrated in the Cædmon MS, where the corrector who substituted West-Saxon for Anglian spellings throughout *Christ and Satan* has written *buton* over *nymðe* at 18b (see Appendix A below). As *nemne* appears to be an exclusively Mercian lexical item, it is worth noting that it appears in *Andreas, Guthlac A,* the *Phoenix, Juliana,* the *Seafarer, Maxims I,* the *Riming Poem,* the *Wife's Lament,* and *Beowulf.*

§362. It has often been remarked that the use of *in* as a preposition (better, unstressed *in*) is an Anglian feature, since there is a clear preference for *on* in purely West-Saxon texts.[136] In general, unstressed *in* is rare in the Southern group and common in other verse. Excluding the *Menologium* there are just three instances in the Southern group, one each in the Alfredian *Meters* (20.238a), the *Death of Edgar* (6a), and *Judgment Day II* (190a). The only unusual text in the Southern group is the *Menologium,* with eleven instances (15a, 39b, 40a, 43a, 75b, 97a, 117a, 134b, 155b, 173a, 201a). *Maxims II* in the same manuscript has one instance (41b). In other verse *in* is frequent, appearing, for example, in unstressed position forty-five times in *Beowulf,* eighty times in *Elene,* four times in the *Fates of the Apostles,* thirty-six times in *Christ II,* forty-three times in *Juliana,* sixty-four times in *Andreas,* and ten times in *Judith. In* is in fact very frequent generally in poetry outside the Southern group, with two surprising exceptions: there are just five instances in the originally Anglian Psalms of the Paris Psalter (59.8.3a, 77.31.1a, 77.43.3a, 78.2.2a [emended], 82.6.1b; on these see Appendix A), and three in *Genesis A* (1707a, 2540a, 2835a). Except for *Genesis B,* which has no instances, the other poems in the hand of the first scribe of the Junius MS have a sufficient number of examples, with seventeen in *Exodus* and fifty-five in *Daniel.* Thus the outlines are somewhat blurred, and the sort of scribal tampering of which Sisam warns must be assumed to have interfered. But still the general conformity of the data to the dialectal distribution of *in* forbids attribution to chance: given all the other evidence for a dialect difference between the Southern group and the rest of Old English verse, it is difficult to believe that dialect is not responsible for the low incidence of *in* in the Southern group. It is perhaps possible that the

---

[136]See, e.g., the *OED,* s.v. *in* preposition; and A. Napier, "Ein altenglisches Leben des heiligen Chad," *Anglia* 10 (1888), 131–56. Summaries of the distribution in prose are given by Miller (as above, p. 318, n. 108), pp. xxxiii–xliv, and Mitchell, §§1191–93. "Unstressed *in*" is preferable to "preposition *in*" because it excludes not only the adverb but also the postposed preposition, e.g. in *winburgum in (Juliana* 83a) and *sæstreamum in (Meters* 1.15b).

exceptional distribution in the *Menologium*, the metrical Psalms of the Paris Psalter, and *Genesis A* is due not to scribal alteration but to a more complex isogloss than the distinction between Anglian and Southern dialects, a possibility suggested by Miller's conclusion that in Anglian, *in* predominates in the North and in West Mercia (p. xlii; see also the *OED* entry); because the evidence for East Anglia is scant, however (p. xxxviii), his assumption that this distribution is the result of West-Saxon influence, beginning with Alfred's reign, is debatable. Nonetheless, the possibility of scribal alteration should not be discarded lightly. After all, there is considerable evidence for scribal tampering with *in*/*on*: for example, not a single one of the ten instances of *in* in the portion of *Azarias* that closely parallels *Daniel* (i.e. lines 1–72 and 279–361, respectively) corresponds to an *in* in *Daniel*. In six of these instances *Daniel* in fact has *on*.[137] Likewise the one instance of *in* in the tenth-century Chronicle poems (*Death of Edgar* 6a, Parker MS) is paralleled by *on* in the other two manuscripts that contain the poem. And for evidence of scribal removal of *in* in the Paris Psalter see Appendix A. It may well be then that most instances of *in* were excised from *Genesis A*, especially if Doane (*Genesis A*, p. 36) is right that *Genesis A* was revised at the time *Genesis B* was inserted into it, and more particularly if the reviser was the translator of *Genesis B*, who never uses *in*. The latter assumption seems virtually assured by the evidence of Barbara Raw and Thomas H. Ohlgren that the illustrations in the Junius MS are based on an Old Saxon original.[138] Such thorough revision of the text would also explain the low incidence of back mutation in *Genesis A* in comparison to other poems with Siever's syncope in verbs (see above, §§343ff.).

§363. In prose the verb *sceððan* is found only in Anglian and Anglian-influenced texts.[139] In verse the verb appears in *Genesis A, Exodus, Daniel, Beowulf,* the signed poems of Cynewulf, *Andreas, Christ and Satan,* the *Dream of the Rood, Guthlac A* and *B,* the *Riddles,* the Psalms of the Paris Psalter, and others. It appears in no poem of the Southern group. The Southern equivalent is *derian,* which appears in no pure Anglian prose text. In verse it appears in the *Meters, Genesis B, Maldon, Judgment Day II, Instructions for Christians, An Exhortation to Christian Living,* the fragments of Psalms in Bodleian MS Junius 121, the third metrical charm,

---

[137]The six are at *Azarias* 10b, 17a, 27a, 53b, 61a, 65a; and *Daniel* 289b, 296a, 306a, 337b, 345a, 350a, respectively.

[138]Raw, "The Probable Derivation of Most of the Illustrations in Junius 11 from an Illustrated Old Saxon *Genesis*," *ASE* 5 (1976), 133–48; Ohlgren, "Some New Light on the Old English *Cædmonian Genesis*," *Studies in Iconography* 1 (1975), 38–75; and for the significance of this see Doane's discussion, *Genesis A*, pp. 16–24, and *Saxon Genesis*, pp. 41–2, 49, 54.

[139]See K. Wildhagen, *Der Psalter des Eadwine von Canterbury,* Studien zur englischen Philologie 13 (Halle: Niemeyer, 1905), 185; and Wenisch, pp. 211–15.

and in one metrical crux in *Daniel* (*Him þær on ofne owiht ne derede* 273, *on ofne* not in the MS), where it is in nonalliterating position.

§364. Conversely, some lexical items appear to be restricted to Southern texts in both prose works and poetry. Franz Wenisch points out that *gehende* 'iuxta, prope, vicinus' is such a word, appearing in verse only at the *Death of Alfred* 24b, *Judgment Day II* 59b and 171b, and *Maldon* 294b. Similarly, *ætforan* appears in verse only at *Maldon* 16a.[140] Robert J. Menner finds a variety of exclusively Saxon (or perhaps Southern) vocabulary in *Judgment Day II*: in addition to *gehende* there are *ymtrymmað* (128b), *gemang* as a preposition (284b, 303b; cf. Anglian *inmong*), and *murcnigende* (25a); and to these should probably be added *afeormad* (157b).[141] In the *Meters of Boethius* he finds *āxung* (22.41a), *tūcian* (24.60b), *ymbhoga* (7.28a, 7.36a, 16.6a, 22.10a), *ealneg* (7.40b, 7.53a, 10.21b, 21.15b, 22.15b, 28.58b, 28.70b), *ēaðmētto* (7.33a, 38a), *ofermētto* (7.8a, 25.44a), *rēcelīest* (25.53a), and *tōhopa* (25.50a; but cf. n. 147 below).

§365. A good example of the impreciseness of lexical evidence of this sort can be derived from Hans Schabram's findings about the dialectal distribution of words denoting pride.[142] He demonstrates that *ofermōd* and its derivates are restricted in prose to Southern texts, corresponding to Anglian *oferhygd/oferhycgan*, and that the distribution in verse generally conforms to this pattern, given widespread assumptions about the dialect origins of Old English verse. But there are some exceptions to this pattern, as words of the Southern type are found four times in supposedly Anglian verse, in *Daniel* (656b), *Vainglory* (75a), *Solomon and Saturn II* (452b), and the metrical Psalms of the Paris Psalter (118.51.1a). So, too, *oferhygd* is found once in *Genesis B* (328a). Schabram explains the latter exception as due to the influence of *oðarhugd* in the Old Saxon original (though this portion is not actually preserved), and the former exceptions

---

[140]Wenisch, "Sächsische Dialektwörter in *The Battle of Maldon*," IF 81 (1976), 181–203. The Saxon nature of *gehende* had earlier been recognized by Rauh.

[141]"Vocabulary," pp. 592–7 (as above, p. 326, n. 127). He chooses his dialect words from Rauh's unreliable study, but checks them against the Old English corpus. His findings are confirmed now by an examination of the *Microfiche Concordance*. He rightly expresses doubt about the dialectal nature of many verbs distinguished only by their prefixes—*feormian*, for example, is common to all the Old English dialects, while *āfeormian* is not found in Anglian texts—and suggests that nonattestation of *āfeormian* in the Anglian dialects is due to chance. Yet he does admit *ymbtrymman*, and it is now possible to say that this word is not as frequently encountered as *āfeormian*: in the *Microfiche Concordance* there are fewer that fifty forms of *emb-, ym-, ymb(e)trymman, -tremman* in prose (plus seven of *ymbtrymming* and one of *ymbtrymnys*), and more than a hundred of *āfeormian* (plus four of *āfeormung*). On the other hand, he is right to reject the evidence of the rare word *ofergēotan*.

[142]Schabram (as above, p. 313, n. 101), esp. pp. 123–31. His findings are supplemented in "Das altenglische *superbia*-Wortgut: Eine Nachlese," in *Festschrift Prof. Dr. Herbert Koziol zum Siebzigsten Geburtstag*, ed. G. Bauer et al., Wiener Beiträge zur englischen Philologie 75 (Vienna and Stuttgart: H. Braumüller, 1973), 272–79. On Kevin Kiernan's objections to Schabram's findings see above, p. 281, n. 30.

as due to later scribal change (since none of the instances is structural). The exceptional uses of *ofermōd* are in fact countervailed by six examples of *oferhygd* in *Daniel*, four in *Vainglory*, and sixteen in the metrical Psalms, so that scribal change in the exceptional cases is not improbable. But since the exceptions must be explained this way, the point cannot be proved, and it is surely too absolute to insist that one or the other form could not have been used outside its normal dialect range. This conclusion does not deny the general value of these words as dialect criteria: despite the exceptions, no one can fail to be struck by the distribution of the two words and their derivatives, the Anglian type appearing fifty-two times in verse (excluding the exception above, in *Genesis A*, *Daniel*, *Exodus*, *Christ and Satan*, *Andreas*, *Guthlac A*, *Azarias*, *Juliana*, *Vainglory*, *Resignation*, *Beowulf*, and the metrical portion of the Paris Psalter), and the Southern type twenty-one times (excluding the exceptions above, in *Genesis B*, the *Meters of Boethius*, *Maldon*, and *Instructions for Christians*). Rather than insist on the absoluteness of this criterion and assume scribal tampering, it is sufficient to note that the distribution is regular enough that it cannot be explained as mere coincidence. Therefore this evidence supports in a general way the usual assumptions about dialect origins, and when several dialect indicators of this caliber are discovered to agree, their evidence approaches a certainty that no single criterion could afford.

§366. Another sort of lexical evidence is furnished by the word *weorc*. In pure West-Saxon prose texts it has the meaning 'labor', while in texts of Anglian coloring, such as the *Blickling Homilies*, it may also mean 'pain'. It also has both meanings in verse. The mixture of meanings in poetic and Anglian-colored texts is due to the unfamiliarity of West-Saxon scribes with the exclusively Anglian word *wærc* 'pain' (see Jordan, *Eigentümlichkeiten*, pp. 51–53), which they altered to *weorc*. The point is illustrated in the West-Saxon translation of Bede's *History*, where the scribe of B (MS CCCC 41, the most thoroughly Saxonized of the manuscripts) has altered *wærces* to *weorces*.[143] The word *weorc* in the sense 'pain' does appear in *Genesis B* (296a, 786a); but this is to be expected, as *wærc* is an *i*-stem, and thus the Old Saxon cognates of *wærc* and *weorc* fell together in *werk*: compare, for example, *That uuirðid thi uuerk mikil, / thrim te githolonna* (*Heliand* 501b-502a). And so a West Saxon translating the Old Saxon *Genesis* into the koine would have faced the same problem with this word as when he translated an Anglian text. Otherwise, *weorc* is not found in this sense in the Southern group, though it is frequent elsewhere in verse, appearing in *Genesis A*, *Daniel*, *Beowulf*, the signed works of Cynewulf, *Andreas*, *Guthlac B*, the *Riddles*, and the *Dream of the Rood*. The adjective construction with dative of person, for example *Me*

---

[143]See Fr. Klaeber, "Zur altenglischen Bedaübersetzung," *Anglia* 25 (1902), 257–315, and 28 (1904), 399–435, at 418.

*þa fraceðu sind . . . mæste weorce* (*Juliana* 71–72) also appears at *Genesis A* 2792a, *Beowulf* 1418b, and *Juliana* 135a. In the present century, *wark* and *warch* (verbs) are confined to the North of England.[144] Since this word represents a misunderstanding on the part of West-Saxon scribes, it is less likely than other items of vocabulary to be simply part of the conventional poetic language, especially in such an idiomatic construction as the adjective one.

§367. Although Sisam's objections to Menner's conclusions about the usefulness of dialect vocabulary cannot stand unqualified, nonetheless caution is necessary in regard to the use of the lexicon as a determinant of dialect origins, since it is clear that some words, obsolete in the South but still in use in the Midlands and the North, were regarded by Southerners as appropriate to verse. For example, Wenisch finds that *snyttru*, which is common in verse and in Anglian prose, is almost entirely unattested in pure West-Saxon texts, where *wīsdom* is used instead.[145] Yet the word is also found in Alfred's metrical preface to the *Pastoral Care* (7a) and in the Kentish *Psalm 50* (71a). Similarly, *nǣnig* is exceedingly rare in genuine West-Saxon prose texts, yet is frequent in the *Meters of Boethius* (but never in the prose of the *Consolation*), and appears twice in *Judgment Day II* (pp. 189–205). And as has often been pointed out, the clearly Anglian verb *lēoran* appears at *Menologium* 208b. Conversely, at least one item of Southern vocabulary is known to appear in apparently Anglian verse: although Wenisch demonstrates convincingly that *fægnian* is a Southernism in prose, it also appears in the *Riming Poem, Beowulf* (1333a, emended), and the Psalms of the Paris Psalter.[146] Yet some words thought to be Southern might more correctly be regarded as late: *hopian* at *Judith* 117b is very likely a word of this sort.[147] Major class

---

[144]See Clive Upton et al., *Word Maps: A Dialect Atlas of England* (London: Croom Helm, 1987), map 1.

[145]*Wortgut*, pp. 218–21. Menner, "Judgment Day" (as above, p. 326, n. 127), also offers the examples of Anglian *mægwlite* (31.5a) and *worn* (9.7b, 26.33b) in the *Meters*.

[146]Wenisch, "*(ge)fægnian*: Zur dialektalen Verbreitung eines altenglischen Wortes," in *Problems of Old English Lexicography*, ed. Alfred Bammesberger, Eichstätter Beiträge 15 (Regensburg: Friedrich Pustet, 1985), 393–426.

[147]The view that *Judith* is a late West-Saxon composition, first promoted by Tupper, rests on its vocabulary, and primarily on this word. Wenisch, in his article on the poem (see above, p. 326, n. 127) adequately accounts for the other supposedly Southern vocabulary, and demonstrates the high incidence of Anglian lexical items, including *nymðe* and *in*. He regards *hopian* as a late substitution for Anglian *hyhtan*, but this seems conjectural. Rather, the nonattestation of *hopian* (and related forms, e.g. *hopa*) in Anglian texts seems at least as much a matter of date as of dialect. The word is rare in early West Saxon—there are just three examples of unprefixed *hopa* and *hopian* in Alfredian prose, but about two hundred in later texts—and thus it seems to have been added to the vocabulary of Old English relatively late. In early Middle English it appears already in Anglian texts as dialectally diverse as the *Katherine* Group and the *Ormulum* (both ca. 1200). It also appears in the Northern dialect, although this is not well attested until much later. As the gloss on VP dates to the middle of the ninth century or earlier,

words like *sceððan* that are well attested in supposedly Anglian verse but missing entirely from the Southern group are few in number, and in view of the distribution of words like *snyttru, nænig,* and *lēoran* it does not seem implausible that even a well-attested major class word should be missing from Southern verse merely by chance. And so certainly the most secure lexical evidence of Anglian origins is function words like *in, nymþe,* and *gēna.* Such words have unambiguous West-Saxon equivalents that were clearly acceptable in Southern verse, and were frequently altered by scribes to their West-Saxon equivalents—see, e.g., the evidence of the Paris Psalter in Appendix A. There seems to have been less of a tendency to alter major class words, and this is not surprising, since words contributing to the essential meaning of a text, rather than simply to its grammatical structure, are likelier to have been regarded by West-Saxon scribes as poetic vocabulary, and thus left unaltered.[148] And so given the scribal tendency to alter them, the appearance of Anglian function words in verse is especially likely to be a sign of non-West-Saxon origins. To this evidence may be added that of Southern vocabulary like *gehende* and *ealneg,* which adequately proves the Southern origins of poems with verbs showing Sievers' syncope. The absence of such words from other verse cannot be said to prove conclusively its Anglian origins, because there remains the possibility that the Southern group displays Southern features merely because it manifests the poetic tradition in decline, as Sisam suggests. Yet the greater the number of vocabulary items involved, the less likely this objection seems, since the poetic tradition is likelier to have suffered slow decline than such a sudden abandonment of standards as Sisam must assume in order to explain the large array of absolute differences between the Southern group and other verse. Moreover, the parallel evidence of dialect vocabulary in prose suggests the improbability

---

*hopian* may well have been as common in the South Mercian of the tenth and eleventh centuries as it is in West Saxon. That, at any rate, is what the Middle English evidence of the AB dialect suggests. That the word is a late addition to Old English vocabulary was suggested very early by Franz Dietrich, "Hycgan und Hopian," *ZfdA* 9 (1853), 214–22; see also T. Gregory Foster, *Judith: Studies in Metre, Language and Style,* Quellen und Forschungen 71 (Strassburg: Trübner, 1892), 88–89; Amos, p. 149; and cf. the *OED,* which refers to *hopa* as late Old English (*hope* sb.¹). For a study of this sort of vocabulary and its relevance to the philology of verse, see Stanley, "Prosaic Vocabulary." He points to the prepositions and adverbs *beæftan, binnan, of dune,* and *on ufan* (p. 390) as evidence for the Southern origin of *Judith,* but Wenisch (pp. 283–84) lists the not infrequent examples of the first three in Anglian prose. As for *on ufa(n),* it is found in Ru.² (Lk. 24:49) and Rit. (twice). And so these expressions are prosaic rather than Southern, and Stanley now regards them as indicators of date rather than dialect (see the Chase volume, p. 198). For an example of the danger inherent in basing chronological conclusions on prosaic vocabulary, see Levin Schücking, "Die Beowulf-datierung: Eine Replik," *PBB* 47 (1923), 293–311, at 303–11.

[148]Comparison with verse in the modern European languages is instructive, as it contains much poetic vocabulary, but very little of it in the form of function words.

of Sisam's objection. Work such as Wenisch's *Wortgut* and Jackson J. Campbell's article on the manuscripts of Bede's history demonstrates not only that there are unmistakable vocabulary differences among the Old English dialects—differences recognized by the Old English scribes who altered unfamiliar vocabulary—but also that a great deal of West-Saxon prose, perhaps the majority of it, either has been "translated" from non-West-Saxon originals, or was written in non-West-Saxon areas by scribes attempting to use the West-Saxon literary standard. The evidence for the translation of a great deal of prose into West Saxon from other dialects should not be surprising, since it is hardly to be supposed that after the reign of Alfred, Wessex was the only kingdom that produced any considerable literary activity. And given the evidence that so much prose preserved in late manuscripts was not actually composed in West Saxon, it cannot be thought likely that that one Southwestern kingdom was actually responsible for the composition of the majority of surviving Old English verse. Thus the proposition that vocabulary such as *in, nymþe,* and *gēna* is simply archaic rather than dialectal, and that vocabulary such as *gehende* and *ealneg* is simply degenerate, cannot be ruled out; but given these probabilities, it cannot be called the most reasonable or likely assessment of the facts.

§368. But any remaining doubts about the significance of dialect vocabulary in verse must be satisfied when this evidence is compounded with all the other evidence for the dialect origins of Old English verse examined in this chapter. These are of unequal value: the phonological evidence is largely indeterminate, though certain examples of unconventional Anglian smoothing and back mutation are difficult to account for in any other way; and the morphological, syntactic, and lexical evidence is on the whole more convincing. But collectively the various types of evidence confirm the testimony of Sievers' syncope that there are regular linguistic differences between the Southern group and poems generally regarded as Anglian. Many of these differences can only be dialect differences, and not simply differences in date of composition. In a few instances there is ambiguity: *hæfst* and *hæfþ* cannot be separated from Sievers' syncope; *cwōm(on)* may exclusively have been the very early form of the word in West Saxon, with later loss of *w; in* was surely commoner in prehistoric West Saxon than it was later, and the same reasoning applies to pronominal forms like *mec* and *ūsic,*[149] along with *ūser* and *dǣdon;* and all individual items of Anglian vocabulary conceivably might have been found in West Saxon before the reign of Alfred, and subsequently lost. But it is unlikely that pre-Alfredian West Saxon should have had *lifg-* for *libb-:* cf. OSax. *libbian* and Old Frisian *libba.* And nearly

---

[149]*Mec* and *þec* reflect Proto-Germanic forms, as demonstrated by the cognates Goth. OIcel. OSax. *mik,* etc. Forms like *ūsic* are analogical to the etyma of *mec* and *þec,* but probably arose no later than the Proto-West-Germanic period: cf. OHG *unsih, iuwih.*

all the other criteria are the result of Anglian innovations: there was never smoothing of *wīoh-* to *wīh-* in West Saxon at any time, and West-Saxon forms are conservative with regard to back mutation, confusion of *ĕo* and *ĕa*, Anglian *hafo, sēgon, ēawan, seolf, ah, fēger, fēondas* and *frēondas*. Sisam's explanation that unsyncopated forms may have been the rule in West-Saxon prose and verse before Alfred's reign will not account for such Anglianisms. And his alternative explanation, that syncope characterizes only degenerate Southern verse, and not earlier, more conservative compositions, faces the two difficulties already mentioned: (1) the Southern group comprises a variety of styles, from the conservative, epic style of *Maldon* and *Genesis B* to the prosiac *Meters*, and (2) it is not plausible that such a wide array of features should be distributed according to an absolute difference between conservative and degenerate compositions. Rather, if the linguistic variables studied here were related to the decline of the poetic tradition, that decline ought not to have been so sudden. Nor can the idiosyncrasies of the Southern group represent simple abandonment of the koine, since these poems still display many Anglian features of the koine. To be sure, all this Southern verse fares poorly in comparison to classical verse in terms of style and metrical competence. But it is not uniformly bad: the *Menologium* and *A Prayer*, for example, are for the most part metrically presentable, and E. G. Stanley (pp. 390, 391) finds few examples of prosaic vocabulary in them.

§369. There remains the problem of scribal tampering, since a Southern composition could have acquired some Anglian features through copying in an Anglian area, or by an Anglian scribe.[150] The problem is perhaps most apparent in the language of the Exeter Book, which, it has frequently been pointed out, is remarkably uniform in character. For example, *cwōm*, preterite of *cuman*, is nearly universal, and the proportion of instances of *-ad-* in the preterite and past participle of weak verbs of the second class to those of *-od-* and *-ed-* is fairly constant.[151] It seems entirely probable that a number of such orthographic

---

[150]Sisam raises the latter possibility when he remarks that the literate class of Anglo-Saxon England was relatively mobile: see his article on the Vespasian Psalter (as above, p. 283, n. 35), p. 123. Gneuss thinks that at least during the Benedictine reform, the inhabitants of monasteries were mostly from the neighboring area ("Origin," p. 72). But certainly, movement among monastic houses must be allowed. For example, Flasdieck observes that in the later period many monks from Worcester studied at Canterbury: see his article on linguistic relations (as above, p. 295, n. 64), p. 410. For discussion and further references see Crowley's dissertation, pp. 194–97; and Michelle P. Brown, *Anglo-Saxon Manuscripts* (Toronto: Univ. of Toronto Press, 1991), p. 21.

[151]For precise figures on these other features, see Appendix A, and cf. Sisam, *Studies*, pp. 100ff. N. F. Blake, assuming that the scribe of Bodleian MS Bodley 319 is the same scribe who wrote out the Exeter Book (on the basis of Ker's observation that the two hands are very similar, p. 316), points out that the spelling practices in the two manuscripts are very different, that the spelling in the Exeter Book is less likely to be the scribe's own than that in the Bodleian manuscript, and, therefore, that the

features have been regularized throughout the collection, and therefore that their testimony in regard to the poems of the Exeter Book is questionable. But structural features cannot be changed so easily, and their congruence with orthographic features in terms of distribution in the poems studied in this chapter renders the evidence of the latter probable under most conditions. As explained in the Introduction, the most credible hypothesis is the one that relies the least on attribution to chance, and also explains the widest variety of facts under a single explanation. The assumption of Anglian origins for all the longer poems of the test group best satisfies these conditions. Moreover, most of the evidence for scribal normalization is of the opposite sort: that is, in many texts, one or more scribes have clearly normalized the language to conform to West-Saxon standards, eliminating Anglianisms. A particularly clear example is the metrical portion of the Paris Psalter, in which a variety of features attests to such normalization: for example, the Anglian form *fēondas*, which is frequent, usually appears only where it is required metrically, while *fēond* and *fȳnd*, which are also frequent, may almost always stand metrically for *fēondas*. Similarly, aside from forms of *cweðan*, which are syncopated in VP, the few genuine instances of Sievers' syncope are limited almost entirely to contract verbs in which the substitution of the syncopated form does not affect the meter. These and a variety of other features discussed in Appendix A are best explained by the assumption that a revisor altered Anglian forms in the psalter wherever the Southern equivalents did not disrupt the meter. Similarly, Saxonization is evidenced by instances in which scribal error has led to the preservation of Anglian forms. For example, at two places in the riddles, Anglian *swē* is preserved in the Exeter Book because of mistranscription of the surrounding letters, rendering the passage unintelligible to the scribe: see the discussion in Appendix A, and see above, §279. Thus, even in the Exeter Book, which shows the clearest tendency to regularization of language, there is good evidence for the Saxonization of originally Anglian texts.

§370. In regard to the possibility that Southern verse generally lacks the Anglian characteristics discussed in this chapter simply because it is all fairly inept, and thus incapable of conforming to the koine, it should be pointed out that not all metrically inept verse lacks these Anglian characteristics. The discussion of the metrical Psalms of the *Paris Psalter* in Appendix B demonstrates that at least one poet who was not skilled

---

uniformity of spelling in the Exeter Book probably derives from the exemplar. See "The Scribe of the Exeter Book," *Neophilologus* 46 (1962), 316–19. But the findings of this chapter and Appendix A demonstrate that scribes did tend to follow different conventions of spelling in prose and verse. Thus, because the English in the Bodleian manuscript is simply an interlinear gloss, the spelling in the Exeter Book could still be that of this same scribe.

in the metrical patterns of classical verse used as wide a variety of Anglian features as Cynewulf or the *Beowulf* poet. But it should be possible to disprove the objection more conclusively if it can be shown that Southern verse conforming to classical standards does not display these Anglian characteristics. In that event, certainly these features must not be contingent merely upon the poet's skill at producing the poetic koine. The *Meters of Boethius*, though somewhat inept, metrically are mostly regular. The only other certainly Southern verse that conforms generally to classical standards of meter (i.e., among other things, excluding Sievers' syncope) is the set of tenth-century Chronicle poems. These display many of the Anglian phonological features that can safely be regarded as conventional, such as Mercian back mutation in *beadu-* (*Brunanburh* 48a), with *ea* in all manuscripts. Anglian retraction of *æ* before covered *l* is found in *waldend-* (*Death of Edgar* 17b, 22b, 34a, all MSS), *aldor* (12a, in B and C), and *gewalc* (25b, in B and C). Anglian smoothing is frequent in B and C, as in *(Wes)sex-* (*Brunanburh* 20b, 59a, 70a), *-fex* (45a), and *unwexen* (*Death of Edgar* 11b). In the Parker Chronicle (A), *e* for eWS *ie* of various origins is frequent, as in *gelpan* (*Brunanburh* 44b), *bilgeslehtes* (45b), *hlehhan* (47b), and others. Alistair Campbell provides a more complete list of such features in the various manuscripts of *Brunanburh*, and concludes that they are authorial, and introduced as mere adornment.[152] Yet the phonology still shows Southern characteristics that are unusual in verse. The form *mæca* (*Brunanburh* 40a, MS *mæcan*; cf. 24a) in A only, beside *mec(e)a* in B and C, is the only example of this word in verse with WS *æ* instead of Anglian *ē*—and forms with *ē* appear nearly twenty-five times in verse. Similarly, although spellings of *eafora* with intial *ea-* and *a-* are both found in the poems, it is remarkable how frequent the latter is. In the four instances of the word in these poems, the B version has only *ea-*, while A and C have *a-* three times. This seems significant, as the Southern spelling with *a-* occurs just three other places in verse, one of which is in a presumably Southern composition (*Genesis A* 967b, 2054a, *Menologium* 136a).

§371. The Anglian morphological, syntactic, and lexical features studied in this chapter are missing from these poems, however. *Mid* does not take the accusative case, though it does take the dative three times (*Brunanburh* 26a, 37b, 47a). The preterite of *cuman* lacks *w* in all manuscripts, at *Brunanburh* 37b and 72b. There are two instances of the Southern equivalent of Anglian *gēn(a)* in all manuscripts (*Brunanburh* 66b, *Coronation of Edgar* 13b). The past participle of *sēon* takes the Southern form at *Death of Edgar* 22a (*-sewen* in A, *-sawen* in B and C). There is one instance of unstressed *in*, at *Death of Edgar* 6a, in A only; but *in* is found occasionally in other poems of the Southern group, and in fact there are several examples of prepositional *in* in the prose of the

---

[152]*The Battle of Brunanburh* (London: Heinemann, 1938), pp. 8–15.

Parker MS where the other manuscripts all have *on* (*s.a.* 626, 635, 666, and 709 *bis*). The verb *ætȳwan* at *Death of Edgar* 29a has only its Southern form in all manuscripts. There are no relevant accusative pronouns, Anglian or otherwise. On the other hand, there is positive internal evidence for a Southern provenance, as *welhwær* (*Death of Edgar* 17a) appears to be a West-Saxonism. In prose it appears only in the Chronicle (*s.a.* 897) and in two sets of glosses.[153] Elsewhere in verse it appears only in the *Meters of Boethius* (12.4b and 28.83b) and the *Menologium* (138b, for MS *wel hwæt*). The significance of this dearth of Anglian features, along with the positive internal evidence of Southern origins (*mæca, afaran, welhwær*), should be apparent from comparison with the data on any of the poems examined in Appendix A. To be sure, the sample that comprises the Chronicle poems, at 143 lines, is shorter than any of the poems examined in the appendix; but it is still long enough that the absence of such Anglian features is remarkable. The point can be corroborated by comparison with an unquestionably Anglian poem roughly comparable in length, the *Fates of the Apostles* (122 lines). Aside from the usual phonological features, *mid* appears with the accusative case once (74a), and unstressed *in* occurs in *hames in hehðo* (118a), along with five instances before Mediterranean place-names. Unstressed *fore* is encountered four times (11a, 18a, 36a, 71a). To Southern *ūre* corresponds *usse* (116a). Unmistakably Anglian are *nempe* (114a) and *ah* (115a). The closest parallel to *utu* (115a) is *wutu*, found only in Ru.¹ (three times). *Habban* has 3. sg. *Hafað* (73b). Taking another manuscript, comparison may also be made to the first 143 lines of *Exodus*. There *mid* takes the accusative case once (9b), and unstressed *in* appears four times, though in the same manuscript there are no indisputable examples in *Genesis A* and *B*, the only unstressed examples appearing before biblical place-names, and thus very likely influenced by the Latin. The Anglian verb stem *lifig-* appears once (6a), and the preterite *cuman* is spelt twice with *w* (91b, 135b), and twice without it (21a, 46b). The preterite of *sēon* twice takes the Southern form (103b, 126a), but *sæ* is masculine at 134b. Unmistakably Anglian is *nymðe* (124a). To be sure, there is variability in the number of Anglian features encountered in each text. But even *Beowulf*, which has perhaps the fewest Anglian features in its first 143 lines of any presumably Anglian poem, has Anglian *gen* (83b) and seven instances of unstressed *in*. It also of course lacks positive Southern features like *mæca, afaran*, and *welhwær* in the Chronicle poems. And even an unmistakably Anglian poem as brief as *Durham* contains a variety

---

[153]The word appears twice each in BL MS Cotton Cleopatra A. iii, ed. Thomas Wright and Richard Paul Wülcker, *Anglo-Saxon and Old English Vocabularies*, vol. 1, 2nd ed. (London: Trübner, 1884), 467 and 495; and in CCCC MS 173, in glosses on Sedulius' *Carmen paschale*, ed. Herbert Dean Meritt, *Old English Glosses* (London: Oxford Univ. Press, 1945), pp. 35, 38. The latter is possibly a Winchester manuscript: see Ker, item 40.

of Northumbrian features.[154] Thus, the Chronicle poems are identifiable as Southern on the basis of the dialect criteria discussed in this chapter, and since the poems conform well to classical norms of meter, it may be concluded that the Anglian features discussed in this chapter cannot all simply be aspects of the poetic koine.

§372. Nor is it after all an improbable development that most surviving verse should have been first composed in an Anglian dialect. Sisam argues at length that early Wessex and Kent had the cultural richness to produce memorable verse, and the scholarly tendency to ascribe verse to the Anglian realms has much to do with the fact that we know so much more about the North than about the South before Alfred's reign, owing to Bede's history. But Bede is not the only witness. The oldest English manuscripts are from the North, and it is perhaps no accident that few Saxon charters survive from the early period. More important, there are several short vernacular literary texts from the North that can be dated to the eighth or ninth century, or perhaps earlier: the two Northumbrian versions of *Cædmon's Hymn*, *Bede's Death Song*, the inscription on the Franks Casket, the *Leiden Riddle*, and the inscription on the Ruthwell Cross.[155] There is nothing comparable from the South, where linguistic

---

[154]See Toon, p. 92, for an analysis.

[155]Eric Stanley, building on the argument of Paul Meyvaert that the runic inscription on the Ruthwell Cross might be considerably later than the construction of the cross itself (though he was not the first to suggest this: in addition to the article by R. I. Page below, which Stanley cites, see Sisam, *Studies*, p. 34), reviews the linguistic evidence and concludes that the runic poem could have been inscribed as late as the first half of the tenth century: see "The Ruthwell Cross Inscription" (as above, p. 248, n. 13). Sir Christopher Ball remarks that the difference in layout between the upper and lower stones suggests that the main runic inscriptions are a later addition: see "Inconsistencies in the Main Runic Inscriptions on the Ruthwell Cross," in Bammesberger, *Runes*, pp. 107–23, at 108–9. Although it is scant, the linguistic evidence tells against Stanley's argument. Raymond Page had earlier pointed out that the etymological accuracy of the inscription in respect to unstressed vowels is so high that a date in the tenth century is unlikely: see "Language and Dating in OE Inscriptions," *Anglia* 77 (1959), 385–406. The evidence of the Conclusion below suggests that unstressed *æ* and *i* had fallen together by the middle of the ninth century in Northumbria—thus, following Page's line of argument, rendering a date very long after that for the Ruthwell inscription fairly improbable. Ball believes that the hypercorrective spellings *rodi* and *bismærædu* (for *rodæ* and *bismæridu*) prove that the runes were carved after the coalescence of unstressed *æ* and *i* in Northumbrian; but he also points out that *hrofe* at *Cædmon's Hymn* 6a (Moore version), *deothdaege* at *Bede's Death Song* 5a, *giuæde* at *Leiden Riddle* 12b, and *twœgen* on the Franks Casket show that early Northumbrian texts "without exception show the same pattern of *e*-spellings encroaching upon the older tradition of *-i* or *-æ*" (p. 121). The Moore version of *Cædmon's Hymn*, at least, must belong to the eighth century: see Appendix D below. The distinction that the Ruthwell inscription shows between *k* and *c* suggests a relatively early date. Elsewhere Ball argues that the latter is an affricate in *kyniŋc*: see "Problems in Early Northumbrian Phonology," in *Luick Revisited*, pp. 109–17. But as he points out there, the *ŋ*-rune would be surprising before an alveopalatal affricate. And since in the same place he argues that *k* and *k̄* are merely spelling variants of the same sound, and the latter therefore does not represent a palatal stop, it seems

records of any sort are extremely sparse before the reign of Alfred. This is a peculiar situation if there was any appreciable production of vernacular literature in the South before the middle of the ninth century, considering that after the beginning of the Viking onslaught, Southern manuscripts had a considerably greater chance of survival than Northern ones. Moreover, it would be an extreme coincidence if it were mere accident that four of these five poems exist in West-Saxon "translations." Rather, a great deal of Anglian verse must have been so converted, and that assumption is corroborated by the two instances in which rhymes may be used to determine a poem's original dialect, in *Elene* and the *Riming Poem*. To this may be added the evidence that early West-Saxon and Kentish vernacular texts display considerable Mercian influence, as discussed above (§§337ff.). Had there been any very considerable writing in the vernacular before Alfred's time, we should expect otherwise. Aside from the story that Bede tells concerning Cædmon, we know practically nothing about the conditions under which vernacular poetry was committed to writing. As most of the verse thought to be Anglian in origin is religious narrative adapted from Latin sources, presumably it was for the use of those members of religious houses who could not read Latin—though in the later period translation could also be undertaken for the use of laymen, as demonstrated by Ælfric's preface to the Hexateuch.[156]

---

likelier that *c* represents a palatal stop not yet affricated, even in *riicnæ, ic*, and *licæs*—especially since the first of these, etymologically, should not have been affricated (see Campbell, §435). This would date the inscription most likely before the early ninth century: see Luick, §687. Clearly the date of the inscription is very uncertain, and I incline to the view that it is later than has usually been thought, though not so late as Stanley suggests. Stanley also argues that the Ruthwell inscription is an abridgement of a longer text, more accurately reflected in the *Dream of the Rood*. He suggests that *[..]geredæ hinæ ḡod almeʒttig* in the inscription has been shortened from *Ongyrede hine þa geong hæleð (þæt wæs god ælmihtig)* in the Vercelli version (39). There are metrical difficulties here. *Ongyrede hine þa geong hæleð* is not a known verse type (see Bliss, p. 163). In the next line, *strang ond stiðmod. Gestah he on gealgan heanne* (40), the on-verse is not hypermetric, and the off-verse violates the condition that a finite verb ought not to alliterate in preference to a following noun (see above, p. 182, n. 23). This is suspicious, as the Vercelli poem is not on the whole metrically deficient. The corresponding Ruthwell verse *þa he walde on ḡalḡu gistiḡa* (the off-verse to the verse above) is metrically unexceptionable, and it is perhaps too much of a coincidence that the Ruthwell poet should have found in his exemplar precisely the words he needed in order to reduce four verses, three of them metrically aberrant, to two regular verses. Ball's idea ("Ruthwell Cross," p. 113) that *[..]geredæ hinæ* and *ḡod almeʒttig* are intended to be two separate verses of the normal sort seems unlikely. The former, reconstructed +*Ondgeredæ hinæ*, offends against Kuhn's second law; this reconstruction pairs a normal verse with a hypermetric one in the second line; and nearly every other finite verb at the beginning of a verse clause in the inscription is in a hypermetric verse. The Vercelli version is made unambiguous by the insertion of *þa*, which could not remain unstressed if *hine* were stressed.

[156]Whether such laymen were literate is not known. Brown (as above, p. 338, n. 150) suggests they may have required the aid of a priest to read their books (p. 25).

Such translations may have been undertaken in a haphazard fashion, or they may have resulted largely from the educational program of a particular monastery or at the behest of a particular royal house, as with Alfred's program of prose translation.[157] And so there is no great improbability attached to the assumption of Anglian origins, and several reasons to think it probable.

§373. But there are other types of evidence, as well. The history of the Anglo-Saxon coinage suggests the backwardness of Wessex until the middle of the ninth century. Finds of the so-called sceattas, issued mostly in Kent and East Anglia from the late seventh century to the middle of the eighth, are abundant and widely distributed in Northumbria, Mercia and east Kent, but are considerably less frequent in Wessex, especially through the first quarter of the eighth century.[158] Moreover, most of the Wessex finds are in south Hampshire, an area that was Jutish rather than West-Saxon at least until Cædwalla's reign. West-Saxon sceat types are also exceedingly few in comparison to types from other parts of the country.[159] Coins appear not to have been minted in the royal town of Winchester before the reign of Alfred.[160] The Northumbrian coinage remains on the sceat standard, and becomes debased, but remains vital and prolific right up to the Viking conquest. Offa perhaps was not after all responsible for the reformed coinage based on Frankish *deniers*, introduced in 755 on the Continent, but his coins dominate the finds of the latter part of the eighth century.[161] By contrast, in the Saxon South the new coinage is only scantily represented before the reign of Ecgberht of Wessex, and then only in the latter part of his reign, after 825, when all of the South came under his control. It must be remembered, too, that Wessex was still a frontier kingdom at least until the close of the seventh

[157]Vleeskruyer (pp. 56–62) advances a similar argument regarding the West Mercian homiletic tradition from which the *Life of St. Chad* springs.

[158]See the maps and discussion in David Hill's *Atlas of Anglo-Saxon England* (Toronto: Univ. of Toronto, 1981), pp. 121–23. D. M. Metcalf isolates the finds of the earlier part of the period in the maps accompanying his "Monetary Expansion and Recession: Interpreting the Distribution-Patterns of Seventh and Eighth-Century Coins," in *Coins and the Archaeologist*, 2nd ed., ed. John Casey and Richard Reece (London: Seaby, 1988), pp. 230–53, at 235 and 238. See also S. E. Rigold and D. M. Metcalf, "A Check-List of English Finds of Sceattas," *British Numismatic Journal* 47 (1977), 31–52, and Blackburn's table of single-finds for the runic Crowned Bust/Standard types, p. 151.

[159]For a list of types see *Coins of England and the United Kingdom*, 23rd ed. (London: Seaby, 1987, for 1988), items 751–872. S. E. Rigold identifies the West-Saxon coinage (Series H) in "The Principal Series of English Sceattas," *British Numismatic Journal* 47 (1977), 21–30.

[160]See Martin Biddle, "*Felix Urbs Withonia*: Winchester in the Age of Monastic Reform," in *Tenth-Century Studies*, ed. David Parsons (London: Phillimore, 1975), pp. 123–40, at 131.

[161]Possibly the Kentish kings Ecgberht and Heahberht were the first to introduce the type: see Lyon, pp. 178–79, and Metcalf (as above, n. 158), pp. 239ff. But certainly most of the new coins were struck with Offa's name.

century. There are no pagan Saxon burial grounds in Dorset; the invasion of east Somerset did not begin until 658; the western half of Wessex was not organized as a diocese until 705; and the kingdom of the Dumnonii remained in existence until at least 710.[162] It is demonstrated in the Conclusion that some of the longer poems of the test group cannot have been composed much later than this, unless they are Northumbrian in origin. Similarly, the South Saxons were not converted until 685. D. R. Kirby points out that in Wessex the "influence of Christianity was at first very limited," and he illustrates from the history of the conversion of the West-Saxon monarchs: "Centwine, a king of the western Saxons in the late 670s and 80s was not a convert until shortly before his abdication c. 685, and Caedwalla who established himself as king in 686, was not baptized until he went as a pilgrim to Rome following his abdication in 688."[163] Wessex was not a very influential kingdom until the latter part of the reign of Ecgberht (i.e. after 825), who wrested Essex, Middlesex, and Kent from Mercian control, and eventually conquered Mercia itself. All of this is not to say that verse could not have been recorded in Wessex at an early date, but that if no such verse survives, this should not be surprising, as the kingdom is not to be compared with the Anglian realms before the latter part of Ecgberht's reign. Then the half century preceding Alfred, while a more reasonable time to expect the preservation of verse, will not accord well with Sisam's view, since it would be rather coincidental if the wide variety of linguistic changes characterizing West Saxon, as demanded by his hypothesis, should all have taken place in this period, and *after* the composition of the verse he would like to call West-Saxon. And while it might be true that the Anglian kingdoms have been favored simply because we know more about them in the early period, so, too, the tendency to attribute much importance to Wessex simply because of its later prominence must be avoided.

§374. More important than the political history of Wessex is ecclesiastical history, since it is dubitable whether documents of any sort were produced by anyone but churchmen before the eleventh century. Even if there was a central royal chancery earlier than this—a disputed issue—it cannot have been in existence before the tenth century, and in any case was certainly not involved in the production of books of verse.[164] At any

---

[162]See Sir Frank Stenton, *Anglo-Saxon England*, 3rd ed. (Oxford: Clarendon, 1971), pp. 63–73.

[163]*The Earliest English Kings* (London: Unwin Hyman, 1991), p. 49.

[164]Pierre Chaplais argues against the existence of a central royal chancery before the eleventh century in "The Origin and Authenticity of the Royal Anglo-Saxon Diploma," *Journal of the Society of Archivists* 3, no. 2 (1965), 48–61, and "The Anglo-Saxon Chancery: From the Diploma to the Writ," ibid. 3, no. 4 (1966), 160–76. See also Nicholas Brooks, "Anglo-Saxon Charters: The Work of the Last Twenty Years," *ASE* 5 (1974), 211–31, at 217–20. Simon Keynes argues that some of the charters of Æthelred II are the product of such a royal writing office, in *The Diplomas of King Æthelred 'The Unready' 978–1016* (Cambridge: Cambridge University Press, 1980), p. 80. But

rate, Helmut Gneuss finds that for the extant manuscripts of the period written in England, "the known places of origin or provenance in Anglo-Saxon England are almost exclusively cathedrals, cathedral priories and Benedictine abbeys and nunneries."[165] And Mary P. Richards points out that the surviving copies of texts even as secular as the law codes were produced at ecclesiastical centers, and that some were even composed by churchmen, such as Wulfstan.[166] Undoubtedly, any Anglo-Saxon kingdom had the cultural richness to produce verse, but it was only at ecclesiastical centers that it could be recorded. It is significant, then, that the only properly West-Saxon monastery Bede mentions in his *Ecclesiastical History* is Aldhelm's establishment at Malmesbury.[167] Yet it is debatable whether even Malmesbury may properly be regarded as Saxon in the early period, as the English settlements of the lower Severn were annexed to Mercia long before the end of the seventh century. According to the earliest charters of the abbey at Malmesbury, Aldhelm received lands in Gloucester and north Wiltshire from Æthelred of Mercia in 681, and others in Gloucestershire four years later from Æthelred's nephew Berhtwald, in a gift confirmed by Æthelred himself.[168] And at least some dialect criteria place the settlements of the lower Severn in the Anglian group, for example retraction of *æ* before covered *l*, and second fronting.[169] This observation renders more plausible the suggestion that

---

reviewers of the book seem unconvinced: see the references provided by Brigitte Bedos Rezak, "The King Enthroned, a New Theme in Anglo-Saxon Royal Econography: The Seal of Edward the Confessor and Its Political Implications," *Acta* 11 (1986, for 1984), 53–88, at 71, n. 27, and Chaplais, "The Royal Anglo-Saxon 'Chancery' of the Tenth Century Revisited," in *Studies in Medieval History Presented to R. H. C. Davis*, ed. Henry Mayr-Harting and R. I. Moore (London: Hambledon, 1985), pp. 41–51. For references to earlier views on the existence of a central chancery, see p. 19, n. 8 of the article by Richards mentioned below, n. 166. The controversy continues. Fred C. Robinson discusses the evolution of critical opinion on the composition of Old English verse, from earlier belief in its secular origins to current trust in its ecclesiastical provenance, on pp. 59–60 of the article mentiontioned above, p. 324, n. 123.

[165]"A Preliminary List of Manuscripts Written or Owned in England up to 1100," *ASE* 9 (1981), 1–60, at 4.

[166]"Elements of a Written Standard in the Old English Laws," in *Standardizing English: Essays in the History of Language Change*, ed. Joseph B. Trahern, Jr. (Knoxville: Univ. of Tennessee Press, 1989), pp. 1–22, at 4–5.

[167]He refers to Redbridge, but this is in the Jutish area opposite the Isle of Wight, mentioned above. West of London, the only other monasteries in the South that Bede mentions are at Chertsey, Surrey, in the kingdom of the East Saxons, and Bosham and Selsey, in west Sussex. Sussex was, however, in the see of Winchester until the end of the seventh century. Bede also mentions churches at Dorchester and Winchester. The meagerness of Bede's information about the Saxon South seems more likely due to the meagerness of monastic activity than to lack of sources. Bede did, for example, correspond with Daniel, bishop of Winchester.

[168]Stenton (as above, n. 162), p. 69.

[169]See, respectively, Ekwall's findings (as above, §335.1), and p. 285, n. 40, above.

Ép. and Erf. spring ultimately from Aldhelm's establishment, though their dialect is primarily Mercian.[170] Though Bede mentions only Malmesbury, there were surely ample monasteries in Wessex in the eighth century; and yet the evidence indicates that they were small and fairly primitive.[171] This is especially clear when the manuscript production of Wessex in the early period is compared to that of Mercia and Northumbria, for which there is clearly evidence of an old and refined tradition in the production of books. Given, once again, the fact that the Viking depredations render the survival of early manuscripts in the South more likely than in the North, the dearth of surviving manuscripts from Wessex, both Latin and English, before the tenth century is remarkable.[172] None of this is to say that verse could not have been recorded in Wessex before the reign of Alfred, but rather that conditions were much more favorable elsewhere, and it should therefore not be surprising if most of the longer poems of the test group show evidence of Anglian origins.

§375. The question posed at the beginning of this chapter was whether Sievers' syncope should be regarded as an indicator of dialect or date. The matter can only be determined by an examination of a wide variety of apparent dialect features. Consideration of the question has sometimes strayed from the subject of meter, since structural features are too few to settle the matter, and must have the support of purely orthographic features. But given the wide variety of apparent dialect features distributed in the same way as syncope, Sievers' syncope seems unlikely to be an indicator of date.

[170]Henry Bradley first suggested this connection, on the basis of the observation that the glosses drawn from the works of Aldhelm in Ép. are generally correct, unlike some of the later, blundered glosses: see "Remarks on the Corpus Glossary," *Classical Quarterly* 13 (1919), 89–108, at 101–2. Pheifer (p. lvii) supports Bradley's view with the observation that Aldhelm apparently borrowed from this family of glossaries. On the basis of the rarity of back mutation in the glossaries, Gustav Neckel would place their origins in Wessex or a neighboring area: see "Die Verwandtschaften der germanischen Sprachen untereinander," *PBB* 51 (1927), 1–17, at 15. But this assumption is unnecessary, as Sir Christopher Ball and Patrick Stiles have shown that apparent instances of back mutation in the early glossaries may be explained otherwise, and back mutation may not have begun until after the time of these manuscripts: see "The Derivation of Old English *geolu* 'Yellow', and the Relative Chronology of Smoothing and Back-Mutation," *Anglia* 101 (1983), 5–28. Sherman Kuhn had earlier attempted to redate back mutation, in "The Dialect of the Corpus Glossary," *PMLA* 54 (1939), 1–19, and "*e* and *æ* in Farman's Mercian Glosses," ibid. 60 (1945), 631–69; but apparently insuperable obstacles to Kuhn's line of reasoning are mentioned by Campbell (§239 n. 1) and Christopher Ball, "Mercian 'Second Fronting'," *Archivum Linguisticum* 14 (1962), 130–45, at 134–35. Second fronting of *æ*, also characterizing the dialect of the lower Severn, is a feature of the language of Ép., Erf., and Cp. about a third of the time, and of *a* somewhat more often: see Campbell, "The Glosses," p. 87. And although Neckel's argument on the basis of back mutation is not tenable, still there is some clear Saxon influence on a few forms in the early glossaries: see Pheifer, §90.

[171]See Knowles (as above, p. 53, n. 88), p. 22.

[172]See Gneuss's list of manuscripts (as above, p. 346, n. 165).

# CONCLUSION:
## RELATIVE AND ABSOLUTE DATING

### A. Summary of the Evidence for a Chronology

§376. The evidence of the preceding chapters indicates that there was measurable historical and regional variation in Old English meter over the course of the Anglo-Saxon period. The broad chronology and dialect distribution suggested by metrical variation are remarkably similar to those based on the impressions of earlier philologists:

(1) The distribution of parasited and nonparasited forms in verse (Chap. 1) suggests that *Beowulf*, *Genesis A*, and *Daniel* are the most conservative of the longer poems; and *Exodus*, if it belongs with this group, is the last of the four, as is commonly supposed. *Andreas* and the signed works of Cynewulf would appear to be measurably later, and the *Meters of Boethius* and *Judith* are last, with no instances of nonparasiting. Interpreted very strictly, the noteworthy departures from Cable's chronology are just two: the figures put *Beowulf* earliest, earlier than *Genesis A*; and *Andreas* comes before Cynewulf rather than being contemporary with him. But it would be unreasonable to press the statistics so far. Perhaps the most that should be concluded is that the poems studied fall into three recognizable groups: a group of mainly "Cædmonian" poems (but including *Beowulf*) that appear to be earliest, showing relatively few instances of parasiting, and a lexically varied collection of forms without parasiting; a middle group of "Cynewulfian" poems (including *Andreas*), containing few instances of nonparasiting; and the group of Alfredian and later poems, that is, the *Meters of Boethius*, *Judith* and the datably late short lyrics.

(2) The evidence of contraction following the loss of intervocalic *h* (Chap. 2) also suggests that *Genesis A*, *Daniel*, and *Beowulf* are earliest, with a relatively high incidence of uncontracted forms. *Exodus*, the Cynewulf canon, *Andreas*, and Alfred's *Meters* form another statistically fairly homogeneous group in which noncontraction is infrequent. *Judith* and the late historical poems come last in the statistics, showing no instances of non-contraction.

(3) Contraction in both negated verbs and indefinite pronouns also supports the chronology. Undoubtedly there was a dialectal difference in regard to the distribution of contracted and uncontracted verb forms in Old English, but as demonstrated in Chapter 3, dialect differences alone

will not account for the data. This is especially true of *Genesis A* and *Beowulf*, which show no instances of contraction at all—a pattern not to be expected in any dialect, but which may be accounted for as an archaism. Again the presumed chronology is supported: *Genesis A* and *Beowulf* appear to be earliest, *Daniel* has a few contracted forms, Cynewulf proportionately more, and the *Meters* and *Maldon* quite a few. *Andreas*, as in the case of parasiting, falls statistically between the earliest poems and Cynewulf.

(4) With regard to the analogical shortening of vowels lengthened by the loss of postconsonantal *h* (Chap. 4), only the instances in *Beowulf* and *Andreas* are numerous enough to be significant, though the criterion does indicate the anteriority of *Beowulf*. And although none of the other poems has many instances, the combined figures for the scriptural narratives are compatible with the assumption that these are earlier than the rest of the poems of the test group, except for *Beowulf*.

(5) The analogical lengthening of root vocalism in inflected forms of diphthongal stems is considered in Chapter 5. The results again are meager, but they confirm the general outline of the presumed chronology, since only the *Meters of Boethius* and *Judith* show such lengthening, and thus presumably are last in chronological order.

(6) From the discussion in Chapter 6 of Kaluza's law in final position it emerges that *Beowulf* is the only poem in the test group that undeniably conforms to the law in its most conservative form. *Genesis A* perhaps also conforms, though the instances are too few to afford certainty. The dearth of relevant forms is itself suspicious, suggesting that perhaps the *Genesis A* poet practiced a pattern of avoidance because of uncertainty about the metrical value of vowels in final position under secondary stress. Such a pattern of avoidance is what should be expected at an intermediate stage in the development of the change. All the remaining longer poems show sufficient exceptions to leave no doubt. In regard to the number of discoverable exceptions, *Daniel* and *Exodus* fall statistically between *Beowulf* and Cynewulf/*Andreas*, though this is probably of no significance: one expects that a poet was either aware of the metrical value of final vowels or not, with no middle ground, especially since the shortening of final long vowels took place relatively early (see below).

(7) Chapter 7 examines a number of metrical variables usually associated with tertiary stress. Only in *Beowulf* and the Cædmonian narratives may the adjective suffix *-lic-* be either long or short. Thereafter it is always long, though the dearth of examples in Cynewulf's verse is significant, suggesting a pattern of avoidance like that remarked in the preceding paragraph. This distribution of long and short *-lic-* is due to analogy rather than changes in stress. Analogy and stress seem to have worked together to produce the result that the adjective suffix *-ig-* forms a metrical syllable almost exclusively in verse from the last part of the chronology—from the *Meters* onward—with just two minor exceptions.

This distribution might be governed in part by dialect, but if so, dialect is not the only determining factor. The combination of these two factors, the metrical treatment of -*lic*- and -*ig*-, serves to divide the poems examined into the three aforementioned groups, corresponding to Cædmonian, Cynewulfian, and later verse. The last group may be further subdivided, since poems assigned to the last quarter of the tenth century and later display a variety of signs of change in the way ictus is assigned at the tertiary level.

(8) As in final position under Kaluza's law, resolution is governed by syllable weight in internal position (Chap. 8), at least in presumably early verse. In *Beowulf* and the Cædmonian poems, normally resolution is required in the middle syllables of words like *wīgheafolan*, where the third syllable of the word is open, but forbidden in the type *þēodcyninga*, where it is closed. In Cynewulf, words like *sǣcyningas* may or may not be resolved, while in the rest of the test group from *Andreas* onward there is always resolution in internal syllables, regardless of the weight of the second of the resolving syllables. Apparently Kaluza's law originally governed resolution in medial as well as final syllables. It is natural that it should have lingered longer in medial syllables: in final syllables the law was lost when long vowels were shortened, but in medial syllables there were were no vowels with broken intonation, and thus the law depended solely on whether the syllable was open or closed.

(9) Since Sisam argued that it might be a dating rather than a dialect criterion, unsyncopated verb forms like *cēosest*, *cēoseð*, and *sended* (WS *cīest*, *cīest*, and *send*) are examined in Chapter 11. To test Sisam's claim, poems exhibiting this syncope are compared with the rest of the test group in order to see whether other dialect criteria are distributed in the same way along this dividing line between undeniably Southern and supposedly Anglian verse. The criteria examined include Anglian smoothing, non-West-Saxon back mutation, orthographic confusion of *eo* and *ea*, forms of the verb *libban*, use of Anglian *hafo, hafu, cwōm(on)*, *sēgon, ēawan, seolf*, forms of the copula, *ūser, ah* 'but', inceptive *in*-, *fore*, *mid* with the accusative, masculine *sǣ, fēger, dǣdon*, agentive-stem plurals in -*as*, Anglian personal pronouns, and a few others, among them some purely Anglian vocabulary. The distribution of these features is indeed parallel to that of the syncopated verb forms. This would be a remarkable coincidence if any poems outside the Southern group were actually early West-Saxon in origin. In any case, some of the features examined are Anglian innovations, and so could not be found in early West-Saxon poems unless they came to be part of the poet koine; yet identifiably Southern poems do employ other, mainly phonological aspects of the koine while they do not employ these morphological, syntactic, and lexical features—which then cannot readily be called features of the koine. And since Cynewulf can be proved by his rhymes to have been an Anglian, the similarity of poems like *Beowulf*, the biblical paraphrases, and *Andreas* to

Cynewulf in this respect is telling. Thus, syncope in verbs must be contingent upon dialect rather than a date, and the common view that most Old English verse is Anglian in origin must be correct. This conclusion in turn tells against the assumption that Old English verse should be uniformly late. It would be peculiar if most of the preserved verse should have been composed in Anglian areas at precisely the time that Wessex was culturally ascendant. Under these circumstances we should expect a much greater quantity of distinctly West-Saxon verse.

§377. As remarked in the Introduction, no single piece of evidence for metrical history could be very convincing by itself. But when several combine to produce the same results, the probability derived from that combination may approximate certainty. That is the case here: although some of these metrical variations provide evidence only for portions of the test group, their combined effect points unambiguously to at least four rough periods in the development of Old English meter. This conclusion is supported by the evidence of Appendix A: although the evidence found there is small by comparison, poems outside the test group displaying extensive parasiting tend also to display extensive contraction, and so forth. Cable's precise ordering must not be insisted upon, since, all in all, the chronological and dialectal distinctions suggested by these criteria are not very fine. For example, on this basis it cannot be determined with assurance whether *Genesis A* or *Beowulf* is older. On the other hand, the general outline of the chronology is clear: several criteria affirm that both of those poems are older than Cynewulf's verse and *Andreas*, which in turn are older than Alfred's *Meters*.

§378. The purpose of this concluding chapter is to examine the possibility of correlating the given chronology to absolute dates in time. The Alfredian *Meters* provide a valuable reference point, demonstrating that *Beowulf*, the biblical poems, the Cynewulf canon, and *Andreas* cannot belong to the tenth century, and probably not to the second half of the ninth, either. But how much earlier might they be? Some of the sound changes underlying the metrical developments examined in the previous chapters, along with some other phonological developments, place *termini ad quem* and *a quo* on the composition of some of these poems. But before examining these developments it will be useful to review the evidence of date and dialect furnished by Cynewulf's methods of individualizing his verse.

## B. Dating and Localizing Cynewulf by His Rhymes and Runic Signatures

§379. Ralph W. V. Elliott fairly represented the majority opinion on Cynewulf when he recently wrote,

We still do not know who he was, when he lived, or where he wrote, although the consensus seems to see him as a Mercian ecclesiastic, probably a monk, whose life-span bridges the latter half of the 8th century and the first half of the 9th. That he may have been associated with Lichfield is a possibility but remains unproven.[1]

A *terminus ad quem* cannot be set to Cynewulf's works before the date of the manuscripts themselves, both of which are generally assigned to the second half of the tenth century. It ought, however, to be possible to set a date before which he cannot have written, on the basis of the spelling of his name in his runic signatures. In *Elene* and *Juliana* the runes spell out CYNEWULF, while in *Christ II* and the *Fates of the Apostles* the name is CYNWULF, without the E. Sievers, in an article that has become the basis for all subsequent discussion, surveyed the evidence of the charters in Sweet's *Oldest English Texts*, along with some of the early Northumbrian evidence, and concluded that the change of unstressed *i* to *e* began about 740 and was completed about 750; and Cynewulf then must not have composed these poems before about 750.[2] The form CYNWULF, on the other hand, is no guide to dating, since *Cyn-* appears beside *Cyni-* in even the earliest texts (e.g. *Cynuise* in Bede's *Historia*, beside frequent forms in *Cyni-* and never *Cyne-* in the earliest manuscripts), but also beside *Cyne-* in later texts (e.g. *Cynred* beside *Cyneðryþ*, *Cyneferð*, and *Cyneberht* in Sweet's authentic Mercian charter no. 47, A.D. 836).[3]

§380. Sievers' account is widely adopted in the handbooks (see, e.g., Luick, §325 and n.). And aside from a particularly vexed rebuttal by Frederick Tupper, Jr. (see n. 8 below), Sievers' conclusions remained unchallenged until Kenneth Sisam reexamined the linguistic evidence in 1933 (*Studies*, pp. 2–7) and raised some important objections. His formulation of the charter evidence is that "forms with *e* are not recorded in Southern documents before 740, or in South Midlands documents before 770" (p. 3), the distinction being meaningless for dating Cynewulf unless his argument is that the change was later in the Midlands than in the South. But in fact the latter date cannot be maintained, since Hermann Flasdieck points out that earlier unstressed *i* is *e* in the name *tilhere* in an authentic Mercian charter of 759 (Sweet's no. 10);[4] and, it should be added now, also in the only other relevant instance in the charter, in the

---

[1]"Coming Back to Cynewulf," in Bammesberger, *Runes*, pp. 231–47, at 231.

[2]"Zu Cynewulf," *Anglia* 13 (1891), 1–25, at 13–15.

[3]The reason for this alternation is not known for certain. See the explanation offered below (n. 8), and the discussion by Hilmer Ström in *Old English Personal Names in Bede's History*, Lund Studies in English 8 (Lund: Gleerup, 1939), 120. Other *i*-stem name-elements show the same alternation already in the earliest texts, e.g. *hyg-*, never *hygi-* in the early Northumbrian documents, and *her-* in *herred* beside *here-* and *-heri* in the *Liber Vitae*.

[4]"Zur Datierung des Wandels *īo* > *ēo* im westlichen Mittelland," *Anglia Beiblatt* 41 (1930), 37–39, at 39.

place-name *meosgelegeo*.[5] There are no clearly authentic Mercian charters between 736 and 759, and so there is no reason to suppose that the change proceeded at a different rate in the South and the Midlands. However, Sievers' conclusion that the change was completed by 750 must not be taken to mean that forms with *i* are not to be found after that date in the South and Midlands. Flasdieck, reviewing this evidence, nonetheless dates the change in the Midlands a decade later than Sievers had put it: "Man wird also im Mittelland die Vokalverschiebung auf ca. 750 datieren dürfen; doch war sie kaum vor ca. 775 durchgeführt" (p. 39; as above, n. 4).

§381. Another objection that Sisam raises undermines support for the position that the change was later in the Midlands than in the South, since he argues that the two charters containing the earliest evidence for the change in the South, dated 740 and 742 by Sweet (nos. 7 and 17), are actually somewhat later.[6] The one exception Sievers found to his evidence that the change is first attested in the middle of the eighth century (two instances of *e* for *i* beside several instances of *i* in Sweet's no. 1, from the period 685 × 694, probably 690 × 693) is also accounted for, since it is now known that the portion of the document in which these two instances of *e* appear is a late eighth-century addition.[7] Thus

---

[5]Location unknown. E. Ekwall identifies *Onnan ford*, mentioned in the same set of boundaries, as Andoversford, near Cheltenham: see *The Concise Oxford Dictionary of English Place-Names*, 4th ed. (Oxford: Oxford Univ. Press, 1960), s.v. *Andover* (but cf. Bruckner, pt. 3, item 179, n. 5: "? Onford, co. Worcester"). H. P. R. Finberg corroborates Ekwall's view, identifying *uuisleag* in the same document as Wistley Hill, about three miles from Andoversford by the A436 to Gloucester: see *Roman and Saxon Withington: A Study in Continuity*, Dept. of English Local History Occasional Papers 8 (University College, Leicester, 1955), 7. G. Storms cautions that the evidence of the prefix *ge-* is questionable because of Gothic *ga-*: see "The Weakening of O.E. Unstressed *i* to *e* and the Date of Cynewulf," *ES* 37 (1956), 104–10, at 110. However, the earliest Old English texts always have *gi-*, never *ga-*, and there is no indisputable evidence that *ga-* survived at all into prehistoric Old English.

[6]P. 3, n. 1. In regard to no. 7 his objection is that the indiction number is wrong. On the significance of the indiction see Kenneth Harrison, "The Beginning of the Year in England, ca. 500–900," *ASE* 2 (1973), 51–70. Bruckner (item 192) agrees that this charter is a copy, but places it probably in the late eighth century. In regard to no. 17, elsewhere Sisam explains that there is no example of *wynn* in other such early pieces of work: see "Anglo-Saxon Royal Genealogies," *Proceedings of the British Academy* 39 (1953), 287–348, at 310, n. 5. And elsewhere again he remarks that in no. 17, *g, t*, and *ð* have forms not generally encountered in so early a charter, as they are characteristic rather of Mercian royal charters of the early ninth century. And so the charter is probably a copy made "two or three generations" later: see "Canterbury, Lichfield, and the Vespasian Psalter (Concluded)," *RES*, n.s. 7 (1956), 113–31, at 117, n. 1. Bruckner apparently agrees, as the charter is not included in his collection.

[7]See Chaplais's findings (below, §415). But even before Chaplais's discoveries this charter came to be generally regarded as an eighth-century copy. In addition to n. 9 below, see the references provided by Dorothy Whitelock, *English Historical Documents, I: c. 500–1042*, 2nd ed. (London: Eyre Methuen, 1979), p. 486; and also F. M. Stenton, *The Latin Charters of the Anglo-Saxon Period* (Oxford: Clarendon, 1955), p. 10.

Tupper's objections to the charter evidence are satisfied.[8] The result is that there are now no indisputable instances of *e* for unstressed *i* in a charter of any dialect before 759, though also there are no authentic, original charters between 736 and that date, and so the change may have started as early as the late 730s.[9] Moreover, rather than lagging behind

---

[8]Tupper, "Philological Legend," p. 240. The one other point of real significance to the charters that he raises is the claim that "unstressed *e* [for *i*] appears once in a Charter of 700–15," by which he presumably means Sweet's no. 5. Here appears the form *bereueg*, probably 'barley-way', where *bere-* would indeed seem to stand for earlier *\*beri-*: on the etymology of this word see "An Eddic Analogue to the Scyld Scefing Story," *RES*, n.s. 40 (1989), 313–22. But it is also possible that the *e* is a parasite vowel (Campbell, §367). This explanation might also account for the co-occurrence of *Cyn-* and *Cyne-*, *Hyg-* and *Hyge-*, etc.; at any rate, since *Cyn-* and *Cyne-* co-occur throughout the Old English period, it must not be supposed that the alternation in Cynewulf's spelling of his own name represents a diachronic development. Tupper's views, it should be remarked, are not consistently reasonable: he remarks, for instance, that Cynewulf might himself have spelt his name *Cyni-*, but used CYNE- in his runic signatures because "to introduce I (*īs* 'ice') into his acrostics would have taxed his ingenuity too far" (p. 242).

[9]Although "Sweet's work was soundly done" (Campbell, §8), some alterations to his conclusions are inevitable. Bruckner's findings with regard to Sweet's charters in the British Museum from the seventh and eighth centuries (*Chartae*, pt. 3) may be summarized as follows. Nos. 1, 2, 3, and 7 are later copies, but 1 and 7 were still probably made in the eighth century, and 2 and 3 possibly. (Actually, no. 1 is authentic up to the beginning of the bounds: see §415 below.) Campbell (§§8, 14 n. 1) would have no. 4 a later copy, though no later than 750. But Bruckner regards it as "contemporaneous, probably original" (pt. 3, item 182), and Pierre Chaplais finds that it is original, though the list of witnesses is in a different but contemporary hand—perhaps satisfying Campbell's unspecified scruple: see "Some Early Anglo-Saxon Diplomas on Single Sheets: Originals or Copies?" *Journal of the Society of Archivists* 3 (1965–69), 315–36. To Sweet's eighth-century charters may be added Bruckner's no. 195 (Sawyer's 35, Birch's 227, Kemble's 132; Kentish, dated 778); no. 196 (Sawyer's 1861, Birch's 364, Kemble's 1028; Mercian, 796 × 821); and no. 222 (Sawyer's 123, Birch's 247; Mercian-Kentish, dated 785). He also dates Sweet's no. 34 to 799. In addition, his no. 188 (Sawyer's 65, Birch's 111, Kemble's 52; from Essex), a copy of a charter dated 704, was probably made in the late eighth century; and no. 193 (Sawyer's 96, Birch's 181, Kemble's 100; Mercian) is a copy made ca. 800 of a charter assigned to 757. Unaccountably, he also includes no. 223 (Sawyer's 155, Birch's 293, Kemble's 1020) among the charters that are "certainly" from the "eighth century, but cannot be classed as strictly contemporary" (4:xiii), even though he remarks elsewhere that both sides of the charter are in one hand, on the verso to be assigned to 844/845 (pt. 3, item 197). As for charters outside the British Museum (pt. 4), he regards Sweet's nos. 13 and 18 as "contemporaneous, very probably original," but he does not discuss nos. 15 and 17, the implication being that they are copies later than the eighth century. The former is nearly identical to no. 16, which is probably original. The latter was discussed above. To the eighth-century charters Campbell (§8) would add Birch's no. 1334 (Chichester, Diocesan Record Office, Cap. I/17), and Bruckner agrees that both sides are "contemporaneous, probably original" (pt. 4, item 236). This is a Sussex charter dated 780 on the recto, with a confirmation by Offa on the verso, assigned to the period 787/789 × 796: see also Chaplais, "Diplomas," pp. 333–35; and H. L. Rogers, "The Oldest West-Saxon Text?" *RES*, n.s. 32 (1981), 257–66. T. A. M. Bishop regards at least the verso as original: see Sawyer, item 1184. A. Campbell regards several eighth-century Rochester charters, not

the Southern dialects, Mercian now leads the way, since there are no contemporary charters for comparison in the other dialects until somewhat later: ca. 767 in Kent (Sweet's no. 8), and not until the ninth century for the Saxon areas if Sweet's no. 3, dated 778, is a copy, as is now widely believed (see n. 9, and Campbell, §8). But if the bounds and witness list of Sweet's no. 1 are an addition of the later eighth century, they give evidence for at least mixed *e* in eighth-century Essex.

§382. Unfortunately, the evidence of coins does little to supplement the charter evidence, and numismatic evidence must be approached with caution.[10] There are no relevant names on Kentish coins until the reign of the usurper Eadberht Præn (796–798), when the name of the moneyer EÞELMOD appears.[11] Æthelheard, archbishop of Canterbury (791–805), however, on coins struck during the reign of Cœnwulf (796–807), spells his name AEDILHEARD—at least a quarter of a century after *aethelnothes* appears in Sweet's Kentish charter no. 8. This seems evidence for Sievers' claim ("Zu Cynewulf," p. 14; as above, p. 352, n. 2) that the name-element *Æðil-* is subject to the influence of spelling conventions (as discussed below). Further evidence for this assertion comes from the striking example of an East Anglian coin of the reign of Æthelstan I (ca. 825) that has AEDELSTAN REX on the obverse and EDILHELM MON[ETA] on the reverse.[12] Before this the evidence for East Anglia is scant and contradictory: EFE appears on a coin of Beonna (ca. 758); and there is a coin of Æthelberht (d. 794), spelling the name with I.[13] For Wessex there are no examples of older *i* at all, the first instances of *e* appearing in the reign of Ecgberht (802–39), with moneyers TILVVINE and

included in Sweet's edition, as genuine: see *Charters of Rochester*, Anglo-Saxon Charters 1 (London: Oxford Univ. Press, 1973), pp. xxii–xxiii. These are Sawyer's nos. 27, 30, 32–34, 36–37, 105, 129–31; and probably in part Sawyer's no. 35 (see p. xiv). But of these only the last is preserved on a separate sheet, the rest being copies written into the *Textus Roffensis*. Thus they do not have the linguistic value of originals.

[10]Crowley (p. 164) describes the sources of uncertainty in regard to the linguistic evidence of coins, including the possibility that die-makers were not local citizens at the mint site, and that the spelling on coins might be that of the issuing authority rather than of the die-maker. But he overstates the case when he concludes that numismatic evidence thus normally cannot be admitted. Similar uncertainties beset assumptions about manuscript production; and at any rate when there is a large number of coins involved, with frequent spellings of a particular type, from a variety of moneyers, their evidence can hardly be doubted.

[11]Georg Galster, *Royal Collection of Coins and Medals, National Museum, Copenhagen, Part I: Ancient British and Anglo-Saxon Coins before Æthelred II*, Sylloge of Coins of the British Isles 4 (London: Oxford Univ. Press, 1964), item 642.

[12]J. D. A. Thompson, *Ashmolean Museum, Oxford: Anglo-Saxon Pennies*, Sylloge of Coins of the British Isles 9 (London: Oxford Univ. Press, 1967), item 59.

[13]The coin of Beonna is item 57 in ibid. *Efe* is a genuine name: e.g., cf. the place-name *Evesham*. For the coin of Æthelberht see C. H. V. Sutherland, *English Coinage 600–1900* (London: Batsford, 1973), plate 3, no. 29.

TIDEMAN.[14] On the other hand, the evidence for Mercia is good. The evidence begins with the introduction of the new Carolingian-inspired penny standard during the reign of Offa (757–796).[15] From the beginning these show both *i*- and *e*-types, though the former is rare (e.g. Mack [see n. 14], items 561 and 562). After Offa only the *e*-type is found. Accordingly, at least for Mercia the evidence of the coinage does not conflict with the charter evidence, and the change may be assumed to have begun before 759. How much before this the change began is difficult to say, but it is not impossible that it began at least two decades before—a possibility suggested by the appearance of several forms like *gegeruuednae* in Ép., a manuscript, probably made in England, that recent scholarship suggests is rather old, perhaps even to be dated as early as the end of the seventh century.[16] But there is firmer evidence in the development of the corresponding unstressed back vowel, *u*, to *o*. The two vowels should have changed at the same rate, because if structuralism has demonstrated anything it is that phonemic systems tend to change in symmetrical fashion. The evidence for the change of *u* to *o* is much scanter, but the earliest instance is in a Mercian charter dated 736 (Sweet's no. 9), which appears to be reliable: Bruckner, for example, considers it contemporaneous, and very probably original (pt. 3, item 183). The name *Bercol* appears in the charter; compare *Bercul* in Sweet's no. 17, a ninth-century copy of a charter dated 742.

§383. Whether the change of *i* to *e* actually took place later in the South than in the Midlands is irrelevant to the dating of Cynewulf's verse, since the rhymes at *Elene* 1236–49 prove that the poet composed in an Anglian dialect (see below, §§391ff.). The general consensus, however, is that it cannot be determined from the rhymes whether Cynewulf was a Mercian or a Northumbrian; and the chronology of the change in Northumbria is a considerably more difficult problem, not least of all because there are no early Northumbrian charters. On this score Sisam

[14]R. P. Mack, *R. P. Mack Collection: Ancient British, Anglo-Saxon and Norman Coins*, Sylloge of Coins of the British Isles 20 (London: Oxford Univ. Press, 1973), items 699 and 702.

[15]It was once believed that silver "sceattas" with the name ÆÞILIRÆD in runes were Mercian, from the reign of Æthelred (675–704), but now the name is more usually thought to be a moneyer's: see George C. Brook, *English Coins from the Seventh Century to the Present Day* (London: Methuen, 1932), p. 7. Seaby's catalogue (as above, p. 344, n. 159) suggests a date "c. 750–775" (p. 40); but cf. below, §404. If these coins are not Æthelred's, there is no identifying their provenance on archeological and numismatic grounds more narrowly than "England": see Sutherland (above, n. 9), p. 6. But the linguistic evidence points to a Saxon area: see below, §403.

[16]See below, §400. For other examples of *e* for unstressed *i* in this glossary see the article by Storms mentioned above, n. 5; and for numerical summaries see Dahl, p. 190, and Pheifer, §63. Dahl, adopting Sweet's dating of the early glossaries, and unaware that the bounds clause and witness list of Sweet's charter no. 1 are later additions, concluded that the change began toward the end of the seventh century (p. 191).

raises another series of objections to Sievers' dating. The Northumbrian *Liber Vitae Dunelmensis* (early ninth century, perhaps as late as 840) has *cyni-* in more than a hundred instances, and never *cyne-* (pp. 3–4). Sievers ("Zu Cynewulf," p. 14; as above, n. 2) ascribes this peculiarity to faithful copying of earlier spellings, especially since *e* predominates for unstressed *i* in the "Northumbrian Genealogies" (edited by Sweet, pp. 167–71), the first hand of which can be dated to the period 811–14 by means of identification of the names recorded. But as Sisam points out, the continuation of the lists of the bishops of Lichfield and, later, Leicester indicates that the genealogies were almost certainly written out in the former see, even if they are based on records in other dialects. Spellings in *e* rather than *i* may then be due to Mercian scribal practice. Therefore the evidence of the *Liber Vitae* must take precedence, and there is no reason to suppose that *Cyni-* had become *Cyne-* in Northumbria by ca. 830 or 840 (pp. 4–6).

§384. It should be said that Sievers' assumption of the interference of spelling conventions was not motivated simply by a desire to reconcile the evidence of the "Northumbrian Genealogies" and the *Liber Vitae*. He points out that in certain cases conservative *i* is retained, especially in the name-element *Æðil-*, in charters at the end of the eighth century, and even occasionally into the ninth (p. 14). Credibility is now lent his position by those instances of earlier charters considered to have been copied later, such as Sweet's nos. 2 and 7, in which *i* is found preserved. Storms provides a detailed defense of the assumption of conservative Northumbrian scribal practice in a reply to Sisam's objections, and scribal conservatism of this sort is in fact a widely held assumption.[17] Bede was fifty-nine when he finished the *Historia* in 731, and his spelling, says Storms, is unlikely to have changed significantly over the course of his lifetime. Likewise the names in the *Liber Vitae* derive mostly from older records. And so Storms surveys the spellings of unstressed *i* in English names in all six of the eighth-century manuscripts of Bede's *Historia*.[18] He finds that although *i* clearly predominates, several instances of *e* are to be found. But a few adjustments to his data are necessary. Most of the instances of *e* are to be found in C (BL MS Cotton Tiberius C.ii); but this manuscript must be excluded, since it was almost certainly copied in

[17]Storms (as above, n. 5), pp. 104–10. Campbell (§369, n. 2) assumes rather that the change was later in Northumbria, but he nonetheless agrees with the principle of scribal convention to explain apparent phonological conservatism, since he invokes it himself to account for the apparent lateness of changes in the Kentish front vowels (§290).

[18]This excludes the insignificant fragment in the Pierpont Morgan Library (Lowe, XI, 1662). Storms also includes Ép. and Cp. because his purpose is not to consider just the Northumbrian evidence, but to counter also what he perceived as Sisam's rejection of all the charter evidence. In actuality Sisam had rejected just three charters, Sweet's nos. 1, 7, and 17.

the South.[19] Then aside from some instances of -*uine* in B and N,[20] and of -*stede* and *sebbe* once each in K,[21] the only relevant forms are examples of *here* as a name-element. These appear in all manuscripts, including the very earliest, the famous Moore (M) and St. Petersburg (P) manuscripts.[22] But there is a limited distribution to these: in M, P, and K, *here-* is not uncommon as a first element, but as a second element -*here* is found just twice in P and K, and never in M. Raymond Page suggests that the pattern here reflects a change of *i* to *e* "when medial and after *e* in the preceding syllable."[23] By comparison, the name-elements *æðil-*, *cyni-*, and -*uini* always have *i* in these manuscripts. These are the only remaining relevant forms, except possibly for *bosel* (twice; cf. *boisil*) in all manuscripts.[24] This pattern is corroborated later in the *Liber Vitae* (edited by Sweet, pp. 153–66). Here once again there are some lone instances of *e* for *i*, such as *embe* (line 440), *hiodde* (328; cf. 100, 253, etc.), *boesel* (51), and others.[25] But *eðil-* and *cyni-*, with more than a hundred instances of each, always have *i*, while normally *dene(-)* and *here-* have *e* as simplices or as the first elements of compounds. Yet -*heri* is more frequent than -*here* finally, as in P.

§385. The same pattern again is found in the names of kings, archbishops and moneyers on the Northumbrian coinage.[26] Campbell believed

---

[19]Lowe remarks, "Written in England, probably in the South, as script and ornamentation suggest. The textual connexion with Durham may be due to its Northumbrian exemplar" (2:191).

[20]B (for "burnt") is BL MS Cotton Tiberius A.xiv, which Lowe dates to the middle of the eighth century, and which he finds must have been written in Northumbria: see item 1703 in his Supplement. Likewise D. H. Wright dates it not long after 746, and places it at Wearmouth-Jarrow: see his review of Peter Hunter Blair, *The Moore Bede*, in *Anglia* 82 (1964), 110–17, at 115–16. N is the manuscript in Namur, Bibliothèque de la Ville 11, and is probably actually from the ninth century. That apparently was Lowe's opinion, since he did not describe it.

[21]K is Kassel Landesbibliothek MS Theol. Qu. 2, thought to be a Northumbrian manuscript from the latter half of the eighth century: see Lowe, VIII, item 1140, and the discussion of the evidence in T. J. M. van Els's *Kassel Manuscript of Bede's "Historia Ecclesiastica Gentis Anglorum" and Its Old English Material* (Assen: Van Gorcum, 1972), pp. 23–37.

[22]On the dating of the Moore and St. Petersburg manuscripts see Appendix C.

[23]"Language and Dating in OE Inscriptions," *Anglia* 77 (1959), 385–406, at 395.

[24]Sweet, p. 144, ll. 307–8. Sweet does not collate P, for which see Arngart (Anderson), p. 108; and on the absence of umlaut see p. 106. For K see van Els (above, n. 21), pp. 115–77. Van Els remarks that the *e* in *Bosel* is perhaps attributable to the fact that the man was bishop of the Hwicce, his see being located at Worcester (p. 205). The name may be Celtic: see M. Redin, *Studies on Uncompounded Personal Names in Old English* (Uppsala: E. Berling, 1919), p. 141.

[25]See Rudulf Müller, *Untersuchungen über die Namen des nordhumbrischen Liber Vitae*, Palaestra 9 (Berlin: Mayer & Müller, 1901).

[26]There is a good introduction to the linguistic use of numismatics by Fran Colman, "Anglo-Saxon Pennies and Old English Phonology," *Folia Linguistica Historica* 5 (1984), 91–143. But Colman deals exclusively with pennies of Edward the Confessor, and the

that the "sceattas" and "stycas" of the eighth and ninth centuries prove that the change of *i* to *e* was later in Northumbria than farther south, since "*Eaduine* occurs on one coin of Eanred (*c.* 807–*c.* 840), but otherwise *e* spellings are not found before the reign of Æthelred II (*c.* 840–*c.* 849), when they become frequent" (§369, n. 2; see also Dahl, p. 188). But closer examination reveals some complexities. It is true that it is not until the reigns of the Northumbrian Æthelred II (840/841–844 and 844–848/ 849)[27] that unstressed *i* is replaced by *e* with any frequency: for example, his name is still usually spelt EDIL-, but also quite often EÐEL-, and the name of the moneyer Cynemund has both the forms CVNI- and CVNE-.[28] Similarly, among the coins of the archbishops of York the change is first found with any frequency on the coins of Wigmund (831–54). On the other hand, when the name-element -HERE first appears on the Northumbrian coinage (also in the reigns of Æthelred II), it is always spelt thus, never -HERI (i.e. never with the fluctuation found in *æðil-* and *cyni-*). It thus appears that the change of *i* to *e* in this name-element had been established before Æthelred's reign, as the manuscript evidence suggests. Moreover, it must be pointed out that the only numismatic evidence for the retention of *i* before the coinages of King Æthelred II and Archbishop Wigmund is the spelling of names in *Æðil-*, and this name-element is attested very infrequently: it appears with I (AEDIL-, EDIL-) on coins of Æthelred I (774–779 and 789/90–796?) and Archbishop Eanbald II (796–?).[29] To say that the change of unstressed *i* to *e* in Northumbria

---

main sources of linguistic uncertainty that attend these coins are not relevant to Northumbrian "sceattas" and "stycas."

[27]The dates given are those provided in Symeon of Durham's *Historia regum* and the anonymous earlier portions of the *Flores historiarum*, compiled by Roger of Wendover in the thirteenth century, which two sources are not always in agreement. Their conflicting versions are separated by a virgule. "Æthelred I," however, is known only by his coins. Hugh E. Pagan, in "Northumbrian Numismatic Chronology in the Ninth Century," *British Numismatic Journal* 38 (1969), 1–15, offers some ingenious arguments for dating several of the ninth-century Northumbrian kings and archbishops of York about fifteen years later than this. According to Pagan's view the monarchs known by their coinage should be dated as follows (all dates approximate): Æthelred I (date uncertain), Eanred 825–854; Æthelred II 854–858 and 858–862; Redwulf 858; and Osberht 862–867. For an additional piece of evidence for Pagan's view see Lyon, p. 191.

[28]See, e.g., Galster (above, n. 11), item 272; Mack (above, n. 14), item 20; and Jeremiah D. Brady, *American Collections: Ancient British, Anglo-Saxon, and Norman Coins*, Sylloge of Coins of the British Isles 30 (London: Oxford Univ. Press, 1982), item 120.

[29]Names in *-wini* are not relevant here, since in at least some parts of Northumbria unstressed *i* is not regularly lowered after *i* in the preceding syllable, even in tenth-century texts (Luick, §325 n.; Campbell, §369), and with the one exception noted by Campbell, there is no variation of this spelling with *-i* on any of the sceattas or stycas. The moneyer Odilo does not precede Æthelred II and Archbishop Wigmund, since his name is also on a coin of Redwulf (between the reigns of Æthelred) and on a coin that "can be shown to date from the middle of the ninth century" (Galster [above, n. 11], opposite Plate 8, item 192). In any case, his name is almost certainly not English.

comes in the middle of the ninth century is thus to say simply that EDEL-never appears earlier than this. But the issue raised by Sievers and Storms is precisely whether *Æðil-* (and so also *Cyni-*) represents a conventional spelling or actual pronunciation.

§386. Is there a linguistically plausible explanation other than orthographic conservatism? If the difference is not due to spelling convention, then the change of unstressed *i* to *e* in Northumbria must have been accomplished in two stages. (1) By a kind of vowel harmony, *i* was assimilated to *e* in the preceding syllable (*Here-*, *Dene-*). This change began before the time of the earliest manuscripts, since it is found in the Moore Bede. But it was at first restricted morphologically, since it is found much more frequently when *here-* is the first element than when it is the second element of a name. This morphological restriction is improbable, as new phonological rules are phonologically rather than morphologically conditioned—morphologization is a later development. Spelling convention is thus a more plausible explanation for the *here-/-heri* contrast. (2) In the middle of the ninth century, lowering affected *i* in all other unstressed positions. However, *i* must have remained unchanged longer in certain environments, given the evidence of tenth-century texts: in Li. and Rit. it frequently remained unchanged longer after high front vowels, *g*, and dental consonants; and in Rit. and Ru.[2] it also is usually found in the prefixes *bi-* and *gi-* (Campbell, §369). As a phonological development this is implausible, as the rule is not natural—for example, even without the peculiar, specific stipulations necessary for Li. and Rit., and other allowances for subdialectal differences, the process could not be formulated for any subdialect as a single rule in generative notation, since all "except-for" stipulations violate naturalness. Moreover, those exceptions are inconsistent, since the condition that *i* should remain after high front vowels is violated already in the ninth century: even though *-uini* always has *i* (after the one early exception noted by Campbell), the moneyer Cynemund, as remarked above, sometimes spells his name with E.[30] And the one instance of *cyne-* 'royal' in tenth-century Northumbrian texts has *e* rather than *i*.[31] Some of the irregularity of the change might be accounted for by appealing to the principle of lexical diffusion; but it now appears that lexically irregular sound changes ought to be restricted to high-level changes of the semi-morphological (e.g. metathetic and dissimilatory) and analogical types, rather than affecting low-level phonetic processes like weakening and assimilation.[32] Subdialectal differences do

---

[30]See n. 28 above, and see also C. E. Blunt, F. Elmore-Jones, and R. P. Mack, *Mrs. Emery May Norweb Collection: Ancient British, Anglo-Saxon and English Coins to 1180*, Sylloge of Coins of the British Isles 16 (London: Oxford Univ. Press, 1971), item 76.

[31]See T. J. Brown, ed., *The Durham Ritual*, Early English Manuscripts in Facsimile 16 (Copenhagen: Rosenkilde & Bagger, 1969), fol. 12ᵛ6.

[32]There is an informative discussion in Hans Henrich Hock's *Principles of Historical Linguistics* (Berlin: Mouton de Gruyter, 1986), pp. 649–59.

remain a possibility to be reckoned with: the preservation of *i* after high front vowels is found in Aldred's "Northern Northumbrian" glosses to Li. and Rit., and not in the "Southern Northumbrian" of Ru.[2]. But the proposed distinction between "Northern" and "Southern" Northumbrian, the latter less conservative in its unstressed vocalism, is not supported by the evidence of prefixes.[33] And at any rate, subdialectal differences will not account adequately for all of the irregularities: for example, it would be too much of a coincidence to suppose that King Osberht's moneyer WINIBERHT should have been the only moneyer to write exclusively an *i*-preserving subdialect when -*wini* also happens to be the only name-element other than *Cyni*- that meets the conditions for preservation of unstressed *i* in Rit.[34] Accordingly, spelling convention is again a more plausible explanation than a purely phonological change.

§387. Still, there are some seemingly insurmountable obstacles to Sievers' position. The absolute consistency with which *Æðil*- and *Cyni*- are spelt with *i* until the middle of the ninth century tells against the assumption that the sound had actually been lowered. Even if the possibility is granted in regard to scribal practice, it is hardly credible in regard to the coinage, as the blunders on these suggest that many of the moneyers were barely literate. They can hardly, then, be credited with consistently inscribing I (few as the instances admittedly are) if the sound had actually changed a century earlier. But even if Sievers' point were conceded, this would not dispose of the problem that Cynewulf himself wrote his name with *e*. If he was a Northumbrian, and if the scribes of Northumbrian monasteries consistently wrote *i* in his lifetime, it is not a very plausible assumption that he would have done any differently, himself. Therefore Storms's response to Sisam that the evidence of all examples of unstressed *i* ought to be considered, not just *i* in *Cyni*-, is untenable, since clearly not all names with unstressed *i* were treated alike, regardless of whether the reason is phonological or orthographic. If Cynewulf was a Northumbrian, it is thoroughly unlikely that he wrote before the middle of the ninth century, when *Cyni*- begins to appear as *Cyne*-.

§388. This conclusion renders it improbable that Cynewulf was a Northumbrian, since it was shown in the preceding chapters that in terms

---

[33] The epigraphic evidence is better localized, though less secure as to date. The Dewsbury Cross fragment (Yorkshire West Riding, prob. second half of ninth cent.) has GI-, while the Thornhill Cross fragments (Yorkshire West Riding, same date) have *ge*- (as well as the name-element *epel*- twice), and the Falstone Hogback (Northumberland, ninth cent.) also has GE- (as well as hypercorrective AEFTAER three times): see Sweet and Hoad, p. 104; and on the dates see Dahl, Chap. 1. Dahl's evidence from and datings for the Urswick and Ripon crosses (p. 187) are less reliable. None of this of course is sound counterevidence, but neither does it support the Northern/Southern distinction. That Aldred writes generally *gi*- in Rit. but *ge*- in Li. is ample demonstration of the intractability of all the evidence.

[34] It should be added that at any rate the subdialectal boundary could not be as simple as the distinction between Southern and Northern varieties of Northumbrian.

of relative chronology the works of Cynewulf across the board are metrically more conservative than the *Meters of Boethius*. Since a Northumbrian Cynewulf could not have composed much before the composition of the *Meters*, he is more likely to have been a Mercian. Granted that there might have been consistent differences in metrical practice between Northumbria and Wessex, still the variety of criteria distinguishing Cynewulf's work as earlier than the *Meters* is sufficient to rule out simple dialect differences as the reason for the metrical disparities. This conclusion accords with Sisam's own contention (a widely shared view) that Cynewulf is more likely to have been a Mercian because of close linguistic and stylistic affinities between his verse and the *Guthlac* poems (*Studies*, p. 134).[35]

§389. As mentioned above, Cynewulf's dialect is known to have been Anglian because of his rhymes. Sievers pointed out in 1884, in a footnote about the *Riming Poem*, that the rhyming passages in that poem as well as *Elene* and *Christ II*, which are irregular in their late West-Saxon recensions, can be made regular by the substitution of Anglian forms.[36] For example, *riht* and *geþeaht*, *miht* and *þeaht* obviously do not rhyme in West Saxon, though their Anglian counterparts might rhyme, having either *æ* or *e* in the root. Cynewulf's two rhyming passages are these:

> Þus ic frod ond fus      þurh þæt fæcne hus
> wordcræftum wæf      ond wundrum læs,
> þragum þreodude      ond geþanc reodode
> nihtes nearwe.   Nysse ic gearwe
> be ðære rode riht      ær me rumran geþeaht
> þurh ða mæran miht      on modes þeaht
> wisdom onwreah.   Ic wæs weorcum fah,
> synnum asæled,      sorgum gewæled,
> bitrum gebunden,      bisgum beþrungen,
> ær me lare onlag      þurh leohtne had
> gamelum to geoce,      gife unscynde
> mægencyning amæt      ond on gemynd begeat,
> torht ontynde,      tidum gerymde,
> bancofan onband,      breostlocan onwand,
> leoðucræft onleac.   Þæs ic lustum breac,
> willum in worlde.      (*Elene* 1236–51)

> Hwæt, we nu gehyrdan      hu þæt hælubearn
> þurh his hydercyme      hals eft forgeaf,
> gefreode ond gefreoþade      folc under wolcnum,
> mære meotudes sunu,      þæt nu monna gehwylc
> cwic þendan her wunað,      geceosan mot

---

[35]The poems' most recent editor finds that *Guthlac B* has close affinities to the Cynewulf canon, but *Guthlac A* does not: see Roberts' edition, p. 61.

[36]"Miscellen," p. 235, n. 1. See also the discussion in Pamela Gradon's edition, pp. 13–14; and Sisam, *Studies*, p. 2.

swa helle hienþu     swa heofones mærþu,
swa þæt leohte leoht     swa ða laþan niht,
swa þrymmes þræce     swa þystra wræce,
swa mid dryhten dream     swa mid deoflum hream,
swa wite mid wraþum     swa wuldor mid arum,
swa lif swa deað,     swa him leofre bið
to gefremmanne,     þenden flæsc ond gæst
wuniað in worulde.     (*Christ II* 586–98)

The rhyme is usually exact, but occasionally it is simply assonance, that is, vowel-rhyme, as with *wæf : læs, onlāg : hād, ontȳnde : gerȳmde,* and *gebunden : geþrungen.* That the examples of rhyme with imperfect assonance could be due to some cause other than Anglian provenance is not a notion that has been widely entertained; but since H. L. Rogers urges this view, the matter should be considered here.[37] The methodological implications of his argument were explored in the Introduction (§13), and so here it is necessary only to consider the plausibility of his explanation as an alternative to Sievers'. His argument is that the passage from *Elene* displays not rhyme but a variety of formal foregrounding devices—full rhyme, internal rhyme, assonance and consonance—in such a way that any one of them will suffice, and emendation to produce full rhyme is unnecessary. Thus for instance the sequence *-yn-* (or *-ȳn-* or *-ȳm-*) is repeated in rhymed and unrhymed words in lines 1246–48; and in 1249 the first three sounds in *bāncofan* almost participate in the rhyme, while there is assonance between *-cofan* and *-locan.* For comparison he presents an analogue in Latin verse by an Anglo-Saxon:

In this respect Cynewulf's Epilogue containing his runic "signature," bears some resemblance to the verses at the end of Boniface's letter to Nithard, which contain the name NITHARDVS in the initial letters. The Latin verses have end-rhyme, but not consistently (*florentibus : viribus; domino : solio; cuneo : aethereo; apostolicis : laudibus* etc.); there are also comparable additional decorative features:

apostol*orum* edit*us*     et prophet*arum* fili*us*. (p. 51)

He also quotes some verses at the end of a short poem by Alcuin "in which rhyme, assonance, and consonance variously appear":

Sed egi, vidi, feci, cum fecero favi,
Et sedi, iuvi, fodi, cum fodero cavi,
Hoc emi, sevi sivi, cum sivero cevi,
Hod odi, fovi, lavi, cum lavero iunxi.[38]

---

[37]"Rhymes in the Epilogue to *Elene*: A Reconsideration," *Leeds Studies in English,* n.s. 5 (1971), 47–52.

[38]"Versus Albini magistri de laude metricae artis feliciter amen," *Poetae Latini Aevi Carolini*, vol. 1, ed. Ernest Dümmler, Monumenta Germaniae Historica (Berlin: Weidmann, 1881), p. 347. The last line corrects the mistranscription in Rogers' article.

But neither of these analogues is apposite. Boniface's verses in fact have full rhyme in all but one line, since clearly rhyme is required only on the last syllable, the more important requirement being that stress fall on the antepenultimate syllable of the verse:

| | |
|---|---|
| Vale frater, florentibus | iuventutis cum viribus, |
| ut floreas cum domino | in sempiterno solio— |
| qua martyres in cuneo | regem canunt aethereo, |
| prophetae apostolicis | consonabunt et laudibus, |
| qua rex regum perpetuo | cives ditat in saeculo— |
| iconisma sic cherubin | ut et gestes cum seraphin, |
| apostolorum editus | et prophetarum filius. |
| Nitharde, nunc nigerrima | imi cosmi contagia |
| temne fauste—Tartarea | haec contrahunt supplicia— |
| altaque super aethera | rimari petens agmina, |
| deum quae semper canticis | verum comunt angelicis, |
| summa sede ut gaudeas | unaque simul fulgeas, |
| excelsi regni praemia | lucidus captes aurea |
| inque throno aethereo | Christum laudes praeconio.[39] |

Thus, in both Latin poems there is an unmistakable pattern: rhyme in Boniface's, and in Alcuin's a phonological, syntactic, and metrical frame X VB-*i*, VB-*i*, VB-*i, cum* VB-*ero* VB-*i*, where the third and fourth verb roots are identical. What Rogers proposes for Cynewulf is something different, since it removes all regularity of repetition. But form consists only in the repetition of one or more linguistic elements—that is, in the much-quoted dictum of Roman Jakobson, "The poetic function projects the principle of equivalence from the axis of selection into the axis of combination."[40] And so to remove the element of regularity from Cynewulf's rhymes is to argue for their relative formlessness. Even if this did not contradict what I believe is every reader's sense of these passages— that Cynewulf is here attempting to impose a different sort of form from that of normal Old English verse—it would be belied by the fact that most of the verses do in fact rhyme (i.e. have vowel-rhyme or perfect rhyme). In other words, there is sufficient form that if Cynewulf's intention was not to impose regularity, it is peculiar that there is so much of it. It would also be peculiar that the substitution of Anglian equivalents in each instance furnishes rhyme, if this were mere coincidence.

§390. The Latin examples then are not convincing, since they do not provide a parallel on the crucial point, which is whether Cynewulf might purposely have written irregular lines. And turning to Latin analogues is not a convincing method when Old English material may be appealed to, instead. There is in fact no convincing parallel in Old English verse to

[39]Ibid., p. 18.

[40]"Linguistics and Poetics," in *Style in Language*, ed. Thomas Sebeok (Cambridge, Mass.: MIT Press, 1960), p. 358.

the sort of sustained and irregular use of a variety of formal parallelisms that Rogers proposes. There is, on the other hand, a parallel to the use of rhyme, in the form of the *Riming Poem*.[41] And here, too, Anglian forms must be substituted in order to restore the rhyme. But most important—and perhaps it is the most telling objection to Rogers' argument—although there are several instances in the *Riming Poem* and in Cynewulf's rhyming passages in which the substitution of Anglian forms mends the rhyme, there are no instances in which the substitution of one or another Anglian form for a West-Saxon one would spoil the rhyme.[42] This would be a remarkable accident, since it is true of three separate poems, and considering how frequently Anglian forms do produce regularity. And finally, arguing against the Anglian forms when they regularize the rhymes so well seems especially vain in the light of all the other evidence that Cynewulf wrote in an Anglian dialect. This evidence was summarized in the Introduction (§16): the evidence of present-tense strong verb endings (§§318ff.), of Anglian spellings other than poetically conventional ones (§§340ff.), of nonconventional Anglian vocabulary

---

[41]Tupper ("Philological Legend," p. 258), argues that Old English poets did not require precise rhymes, and points to several imprecise ones—though his references are incorrect, and are repeated, errors and all, in *JEGP* 11 (1912), 86. All but one of these are isolated instances, however, so that it is not certain that rhymes are actually intended. His overall point is not clear, as he apparently did not intend this objection seriously, referring to himself as "the devil's advocate," and ultimately concluding that Cynewulf's rhymes do show him to have been an Anglian (p. 259).

[42]O. D. Macrae-Gibson argues that the rhymes *beofode* : *hlīfade* (30), *nimeþ* : *becymeð* (73), and *getēoh* : *onwrāh* (2) indicate late West-Saxon provenance for the *Riming Poem*: see *The Old English Riming Poem*, corrected reprint (Woodbridge, Suffolk: D. S. Brewer, 1987), p. 4. Yet the form *bifade* required by the rhyme may as well be Anglian as West-Saxon, as the unmutated vowel is very frequently restored by analogy in all dialects (Campbell, §212). And the unrounding of *y* required for full rhyme in *becymeð* can probably be identified as a relatively late West Mercian feature, since the AB dialect of early Middle English, which otherwise spells the reflex of OE *y* as *u*, has *kimest, kimeth*. J. A. W. Bennett and G. V. Smithers explain this anomaly as "probably due to rhyme-association with *nimeð* through the preterites (*nom, nomen*: *com, comen*)": see *Early Middle English Verse and Prose*, 2nd ed. (Oxford: Clarendon, 1968), p. 399. VP has *cymes, cymeð*. As for the supposition that *gewrāh* (2b) should be emended to *gewrēah*, a late West-Saxon analogical form, this depends on the assumption that the rhyming word is a verb (it is usually taken for a noun), that the MS reading *geteoh* is an error for *geteah*, and that the poet departed from his usual practice in the first twenty-six lines of the poem, here rhyming two rather than four verses. The same reasons must answer Anne L. Klinck's proposal that the two words are not meant to rhyme: see "The Riming Poem: Design and Interpretation," *NM* 89 (1988), 266–79. By comparison, the evidence of Anglian rhymes is firm, e.g. *frætwum* : *geatwum* (38), *gewæf* : *forgeaf* (70), *biscyrede* : *generede* (84), and so forth. Macrae-Gibson's argument that the Anglian rhymes in the poem are merely due to the West-Saxon poet's familiarity with "different dialectal possibilities" (p. 2) is difficult to credit. Presumably such a poet would use Anglian rhymes because they were part of the poetic koine; and yet the scribes behind the manuscript tradition of this poem, also writing the koine, clearly regarded many of the poet's forms as foreign to the koine, altering them at will.

(§§356ff.), and of the widespread impression that his poems are stylistically and linguistically affiliated at least with *Guthlac B* (§388). Again, none of these sorts of evidence is alone decisive, but all are shown in the sections cited to carry greater force than any alternative explanation proposed, and the probability derived from their combined force is a high one.

§391. As mentioned above, it is generally believed that it is not possible to determine from the rhymes which Anglian dialect Cynewulf spoke. A closer examination suggests otherwise. Sievers' statement of the matter indicates that he believed the rhymes at *Elene* 1241–42 should be emended to *reht : gepæht* and *mæht : pæht*, and at *Christ II* 592 to *leht : neht*. These are (supposedly) Northumbrian forms. No doubt these emendations were influenced by two considerations: first, in 1891 Mercia was not considered a likely place for the composition of lasting verse, and the natural inclination was to assign all early verse to Northumbria;[43] and second, at that time the differences among Anglian dialects had not been studied as carefully as they were to be later. As a result, Sievers' emendations present two problems:

(1) The Northumbrian pair *reht : gepæht* is not a rhyme, nor is it assonance, but consonance, which was shown above not to be permitted in Cynewulf's other rhymes, nor in the *Riming Poem*. Yet *ræht* is a very unlikely emendation—as Sievers clearly recognized, since he avoided it. The stem *ræht-* appears just once in the Northumbrian records, at Matthew 3:3 in Li., as against more than fifty instances of *reht-*. Nor is there any known phonological reason for *\*reoht-* ever to have been smoothed to *ræht* rather than *reht* in any dialect, and so this appears to be simply a lone orthographic aberration. Likelier therefore is the rhyme *reht : gepeht*, since the stem *gepeht-* is attested in VP and Ru.¹ (three times all told).[44] It is true that *gepæht-* is commoner in these texts, but *gepeht-* perhaps is also phonologically valid, at least in Ru.¹ (see below). Campbell (§223) regards *gepeht-* as an umlaut variant in VP, like *neht* and *meht* beside *næht* and *mæht*. This is dubitable, since the word is not mutated in other dialects (cf. WS *gepeaht*); but this is not decisive counterevidence, since, for instance, *næht* is used to the complete exclusion of *neht* in Northumbrian, and thus it is remotely possible that the mutated form was leveled out in other dialects. But regardless of

[43]In his edition of *Christ* A. S. Cook chronicles the emergence of a consensus placing Cynewulf in Northumbria: see *The Christ of Cynewulf* (Boston: Ginn, 1900), p. lxxi.

[44]At Psalm 105:13, Hymn 7.56–57, and Mt. 12:14. The two former are cited by verse or line from Sweet, the latter from Walter W. Skeat's *Gospel according to Saint Matthew* (Cambridge: Cambridge Univ. Press, 1887). Pamela Gradon also seems to favor *reht : gepeht* in the discussion in her edition, pp. 13–14. Rogers, it should be noted in passing, argues that this rhyme could be Kentish as well as Mercian (p. 49). But *leoht* and *niht* cannot be made to rhyme in Kentish, and at any rate Rogers says that he does not mean to argue that Cynewulf was from Kent. The objection thus does not seem relevant.

whether or not there ever was a mutated form, *geþehtung* at least must be valid in Ru.[1], since Campbell notes that there are many similar spellings there with *e* before *h* that cannot be explained as analogical, for example *wexan*, *exlan*, *ehtu* and *wexeþ*.

(2) At *Christ II* 592 the emended *neht* conflicts with Sievers' *geþæht*, *mæht*, and *þæht* in *Elene*, since this is not actually a Northumbrian form. The word is well attested, and appears only as *næht* in the tenth-century Northumbrian texts. As the rhyming word cannot be *\*læht* under any circumstances, it is again necessary to assume Mercian forms. The dialect of VP is a possible analogue, since it has *neht(-)* twice, beside consistent *leht*; but *næht*, without *i*-umlaut, is the usual form in the psalter. And so a better match is again the dialect of Farman's gloss on the Rushworth Gospels, since he writes *niht* and *liht* almost consistently, with palatal umlaut.[45] Among the early glossaries 'light' appears just once, in Cp. *lehtfaet* (Sweet, line 1194), which also has *neht-* and *naect-* once each (52 and 1746). In the other glossaries (Ép., Erf., Ld., Royal) *neht-* is common, beside *næht-*. Unfortunately, Cp. cannot be localized with any assurance, and if Farman worked in West Yorkshire, as is widely believed, his dialect must not be regarded as a local one. In that event, the most that can be said about it is that he was not from the second fronting area of the West Midlands.[46]

---

[45]See Campbell, §§308–10. He regards *līht* as retaining its quantity even after palatal umlaut. This is possible, but it is irrelevant to the rhyme: the same quantitative disparity between 'night' and 'light' applies to all Old English dialects; and at any rate even the *Riming Poem*, which has stricter rhyme than Cynewulf, permits long and short vowels to rhyme, as in line 30, and perhaps 67. Line 26, with the rhyme *wǣr* (Angl. *wēr*) : *bescǣr* is probably not an example: the latter ought to have *ē* leveled from the plural, as frequently in Northumbrian texts. The same substitution perhaps is to be found in Farman's Rushworth gloss, as suggested by R. J. Menner, "Farman Vindicatus," *Anglia* 58 (1934), 16.

[46]Yet even this conclusion might be contested, since Sherman M. Kuhn argues in "*e* and *æ* in Farman's Mercian Glosses," *PMLA* 60 (1945), 631–69, that Farman's dialect does show second fronting. The *Harawudu* at which Owun locates Farman is usually taken to be Harewood, near Leeds, though Max Förster argues for a spot near Ross-on-Wye in Herefordshire: see *Der Flussname Themse und seine Sippe* (Munich: Beck, 1941), p. 474. But the dialect of a Herefordshire Farman ought to show clearer evidence of second fronting, or at least be less differentiated from the dialect of the Vespasian glossator. Paul Bibire and Alan S. C. Ross offer a list of other possible sites in "The Differences between Lindisfarne and Rushworth Two," *N&Q* 226 (1981), 98–116, at 98. There is no reason to suspect that there was a monastery at any of these places, but then Owun's reference to Farman as *sē prēost æt Harawuda* suggests we need not expect one. The location north of Leeds better explains why a Mercian and a Northumbrian collaborated, and why Farman must have been in Chester-le-Street or Durham during a good portion of his work (as Bibire and Ross demonstrate, pp. 115–16; and Ross, in the same volume, pp. 6–11). The location near Leeds was certainly not in Mercian territory, and, of course, wherever *Harawudu* was, it need not have been Farman's native ground. Therefore Luick (§24) might be right to place Farman's dialect in the eastern part of the country. Alistair Campbell is right that Luick makes a poor case for this location: see his comments in "The Glosses," p. 89, n. 4. Perhaps a better case could

§392. Conclusions can only be regarded as probable at best, since it must not be assumed that the few preserved Northumbrian records adequately represent speech across the entire North, or for the entire historical period. But since the Anglo-Saxons based their political boundaries primarily on population rather than geography, absolute differences between Northumbrian and Mercian are not unlikely. As for the difficulty that conclusions about *næht* in Northumbria are based exclusively on tenth-century texts, it should be observed that this is actually the more conservative form, and so *neht* is very improbable for any earlier period in the North. Thus, the degree of probability that can be achieved in this instance is relatively high for such a small body of evidence. This conclusion derives support from a variety of dialect indicators studied in the previous chapter: for example, the use of Mercian *nemne* at *Juliana* 109b, *ah* and *utu* at *Fates* 115a, the absence of such distinctively Northumbrian features as characterize the riddles of the Exeter Book (see Appendix A), and the general similarity of Cynewulf's language to that of the *Guthlac B* poet.

§393. In sum, Cynewulf must have been an Anglian, and almost certainly not a Northumbrian. Because spellings like *Cyne-* are not found in Mercian charters before the middle of the eighth century, he must have composed sometime after ca. 750. He is not likely to have composed after ca. 850, since his metrical practices are clearly differentiated from Alfred's. This terminus of 850 is another reason to doubt a Northumbrian provenance, as the spelling *Cyni-* is consistent in eighth-century Northumbrian documents, and *Cyne-* first appears on the Northumbrian coinage in the middle of the ninth century. These conclusions about Cynewulf are of benefit to dating the rest of the verse in the test group.


C.  Establishing a *Terminus a Quo* for the
Longer Poems: Dating the Sound Changes

§394. A few of the early poems of course may be dated by external means: *Bede's Death Song* dates to A.D. 735; *Cædmon's Hymn* to the period 657–680, when Hild was abbess at Whitby; and the inscription on

---

be made. For example, normal patterns of dialect geography suggest proximity to a Saxon dialect, given Farman's frequent use of *æ* for Anglian *ē*, the usual failure of Anglian smoothing to affect *ĕo* (Luick, §§237, n. 2, and 238, n. 2; Campbell, §227, nn. 2–3; and see below, §399), failure of the general Anglian change of *īo, ēo* to *īa, ēa* before non-high vowels under contraction (Luick, §248), and individual forms of a generally Southern character that crop up in his work. A useful comparison is between Farman's language and the English bounds in a probably good copy of a charter from Thorney Abbey, Sawyer's no. 556: see C. R. Hart, *The Early Charters of Eastern England* (Leicester: Leicester Univ. Press, 1966), p. 156. But the apparent Southernisms could be due to the influence of the standard literary dialect, and the language of the gloss shares so many more features with Northumbrian than do the Vespasian Psalter and the *Royal Glosses* that a more northerly location does seem more likely.

the Franks Casket to the first half of the eighth century at the latest. But the evidence of these poems is of limited value, since they are not substantial enough to exhibit the sort of metrical information by which the longer poems may be ordered chronologically. Nonetheless, *Genesis A*, *Daniel*, and *Exodus* are most likely to be dated after *Cædmon's Hymn*, since Bede apparently regarded this as the initial effort of the first religious poet in English. *Beowulf* of course could be earlier, but relative chronological criteria suggest that it is roughly coeval with *Genesis A*.

§395. More substantial evidence for the actual dates of the longer poems can be derived from information about the dates of various sound changes. For example, no longer poem can be older than contraction after the loss of intervocalic *h*, since all contain some examples of contraction. Luick dates contraction in words like *sēon* < *\*seohan* to the beginning of the eighth century, for two reasons:

> Die Kontraktionen, welche durch den Ausfall des *h* veranlaßt wurden, sind sicher zu datieren, da dieser sich erst kurz vor unseren ältesten Aufzeichnungen (die noch *h*-Schreibungen aufweisen) vollzogen hat: sie sind in derselben Periode, vermutlich bald nach jenem Ausfall, erfolgt. Dazu stimmt aufs Beste, daß sie deutlich jünger sind als die Ebnung. (§249; see also §291)

The former argument is based on a number of forms, in the early glossaries only, that seem to preserve intervocalic *h*. It would appear, then, that loss of *h* was not yet complete when these glossaries were compiled. This is in fact the standard view: see, for instance, Campbell, §461. Amos compiles a list of such forms (p. 42, cited by line from Pheifer's edition, or from Sweet):

> Ép. Erf. 171 *crocha*, Cp. 461 *croha*
> Ép. Erf. 579 *scocha*
> Ép. 785 *faehit*, Erf. 785 *faethit*, Cp. 1582 *faehit*
> Ép. Erf. 799 *nihol*, Cp. 1659 *nihold*
> Ép. 840 *aehrian*, Erf. 840 *aegrihan*, cf. Cp. 1696 *aegnan* (< *\*æhurjō(n)* with
>    metathesis)
> Ép. Erf. 1066 *uuolohum*, cf. Cp. 2122 *uuloum*
> Ép. Erf. 1080 *ryhae*, cf. Cp. 2126 *rye*, Ld. 42.2 *rihum*
> Ép. Erf. 1081 *ryhae*, cf. Cp. 2128 *ryee*
> Ép. 3 *thohae*, Erf. 3 *thoæ*, Cp. 207 *thoae*
> Ép. 654 *scyhend*, cf. Cp. 1286 *scyend*, Ld. 47.35 *scyhend*
> Ép. 1062 *suehoras*, cf. Erf. 1062 *sueoras*, Cp. 2121 *sueoras*
> Erf. 1020 *hyrhae*, cf. Ép. 1020 *ryae*, Cp. 1977 *rye*

Examples could be added from Cp.: see Campbell, §461. But intervocalic *h* here cannot stand for a consonant sound, because in at least one word, *nihol* (WS *neowol*) it is inorganic. There never was an *h* in *neowol*, which must derive from West Germanic *\*niwal*: compare Gk. νειόθεν < *\*νειφόθεν* 'from the bottom', νέατος, νείατος 'lowest', and Old Church Slavonic *ńiva* 'field', indicating organic *w* but no Proto-Indo-European velar consonant.[47] In another instance intervocalic *h* is not a consonant in *geholu* (Erf. 1064; *geolu* Ép. 1064, Cp. 2095), a form that shows back mutation. Therefore it appears that at least in some instances intervocalic *h* in these glossaries is either meaningless or is used as an orthographic representation of hiatus, the way it is commonly used in Old Saxon and Old High German manuscripts.[48] Initial *h* was of course silent in Latin words—for example, names like *Helias* and *Heliseus* take vocalic alliteration in Old English verse—and it is also used as a marker of hiatus internally, as in names like *Emmanuhel* (132a) and *Gabrihel* (201b) in *Christ I*, and *Danihel* in Sawyer's charter no. 88. And so there are analogues to its use as a silent orthographic device in the early glossaries. This conclusion follows as well from Pheifer's observation about forms like *sceptloum* (106) and *(h)ry(h)ae* (1020) in Ép. and Erf.: "The apparent preference for uncontracted forms with Prim. OE. *ō* and *ȳ* suggests that hiatus persisted longer where the first vowel was rounded" (p. lxxiii). Persistence of hiatus after rounded vowels makes phonological sense, given their tendency to produce a glide in hiatus; persistence of *h* under the same conditions has no straightforward phonological explanation. Nor is it very likely that *h* and hiatus should both have been preserved late under these conditions, and so the preservation of *h* seems unlikely.

§396. A few forms remain to be explained. Clearly, *ch* cannot be simply a hiatus-filler in *crocha* and *scocha*; but neither is it simply *h*. For example, although the former is spelt *croha* at Cp. 461, it is *crohha* at 1254. These should never have been regarded as examples of intervocalic *h*, since West-Saxon forms reveal that they contain geminate consonants, and perhaps even stops (see Brunner, §220 and n. 2; Campbell, §464). Similarly, geminates may be assumed before resonants in *thuachl* (Erf. 326; cf. Li. *ðuahles*, Jn. 12:3, otherwise not to be accounted for: see Campbell, §242) and *aehrian* (cf. Northumbrian *æhher*).[49] To judge by the spelling, *bituicn* (Ép. 546; Erf. *bituichn*) may be another example of a geminate, though possibly also it is simply influenced analogically by *bitwīh*. Analogy, Campbell agrees (§227), is also responsible for the *h* in *sceolhegi* (Ép. 981, vs. *sceolegi* Erf. 981, *scelege* Cp. 1939); and the same reasoning may apply to *furhum* (nom. *furh*) in the glossaries, and to the

---

[47]For other possible cognates see Julius Pokorny, *Indogermanisches etymologisches Wörterbuch*, vol. 1 (Bern: Francke, 1959), p. 313; and Holthausen's dictionary, s.v. *niowol*. The hiatus probably originated in the ablaut variant *\*niwil*: see Brunner, §88, n. 2; and Campbell, §406.

[48]See, for example, Ferdinand Holthausen, *Altsächsisches Elementarbuch* (Heidelberg: Winter, 1900), §218, n. 1; and Braune and Eggers, §152b.

[49]Alfred Bammesberger points out that single *h* in forms of this word must stand for a geminate: see "Zur Vorgeschichte der altenglischer Wörter für Ähre und Träne," in *The History and the Dialects of English: Festschrift for Eduard Kolb*, ed. Andreas Fischer (Heidelberg: Winter, 1989), pp. 47–52, at 47–48.

name *Uelhisci* in Sweet's charter no. 4.[50] This leaves only *ebhatis* (Ép. Erf. 854; *eobotum* Cp. 1705, from *\*eƀ-hait-*), which does after all seem to preserve *h*. Yet there is a reason for the late preservation of *h* in this word. In the second syllable *\*ai* develops to *a* ( > *o*), as in other compounds that lost stress on their second elements relatively late. In words that loss stress on their second elements early, on the other hand, *\*ai* develops to *æ* > *e* (Campbell, §§336, 356). Since *eofot* therefore retained stress on the second element relatively late, this explains the preservation of *h*: compare how *h* is preserved at the beginning of second elements in *holthana* (Ép. 41, but *holtana* Erf. 41), *alerholt* (Erf. 46), *uuorhana* (Ép. 424), and the like, though it is sometimes also lost (examples given by Pheifer, §72). The point is corroborated by the fact that *eofot* (with back mutation) lacks compensatory lengthening, though the parallel construction WS *īfig* (from *\*iƀ-hīej-*: cf. *ifeg* Erf. 392; *ifegn* Cp. 718; *ibaei* Ld. 44; OHG *ebahewi, -houwi*) does have lengthening. Luick (§250.1) remarks that the reason for the failure of lengthening in *eofot* is unknown. Clearly, loss of *h* in *eofot* took place at a later date than in *īfig*—it in fact constitutes a different sound change altogether, since it did not produce compensatory lengthening in *eofot* any more than in *uuodae(h)uistlae* (Ép. 248). The distinction is an important one, since it means that while loss of *h* at the beginning of the second elements of compounds may indeed have developed relatively late, the process we usually have in mind when we mean loss of internal *h*—that is, in simplices with no interference from secondary or tertiary stress—was in fact completed at the time the Mercian glossaries were written or compiled. The glossaries do, on the other hand, record the preservation of the hiatus left by that loss of *h*, though there are no certain examples in any other reliable text.[51]

§397. One further piece of evidence is derivable from the early glossaries. Luick (§250, n. 3) points out that compensatory lengthening

---

[50]Morsbach (pp. 262–63) points out that *uuestanae* in the same charter has lost interior *h*; and the same may be said of *liminaee* in Sweet's no. 5 (A.D. 697 in the Stowe version). Whitelock (*Audience*, pp. 27–28) calls attention to the name of an abbot *Heaha* in an apparently genuine list of witnesses to a Berkshire will (Birch, no. 74; Sawyer, no. 252) that she dates 705–709, and she concludes that intervocalic *h* may have survived into the eighth century. But Amos correctly points out that this may be a hypocorism (p. 41, n. 6). A charter in the twelfth-century *Textus Roffensis* that Campbell regards as a faithful copy of one dated 738 (Sawyer's no. 27; see above, p. 354, n. 9) contains the place-name *Andscohesham* (cf. *Hondsciōh* in *Beowulf*) and the personal name *Dimheahac*. The latter is probably a Celtic name, but the former seems unobjectionable. Yet since the charter is a copy, its evidence is dubitable, especially in view of the loss of *h* in earlier and contemporary charters, in *aethiliaeardi* (Sweet's no. 6) and *moreb* (beside *moerheb*, no. 9).

[51]Girvan (p. 20) believes that *Treenta* (beside *Treanta*) in the Moore MS of Bede's *Historia* is uncontracted, and this also appears to be the opinion of Arngart (Anderson, p. 83). But this spelling for an uncontracted diphthong seems fairly uncertain in view of the fact that the contracting vowel is *a* (the form is from Brythonic *\*trihanton*), and there are examples of geminates for long vowels in the manuscript, e.g. *thuuf* and *hooh*.

from loss of *h* has already taken place in these texts. This is observable from the fact that *onettae* (Ép. 712, *onete* Erf. 712, from \**an-hæt-*) is spelt with initial *o*. Short *a* before a nasal consonant is never spelt *o* in Ép., and so lengthening must already have taken place here. So also the spelling indicates lengthened vowels in *steeli* (Ép. 49, from \**stæhlij-*) and *ungiseem* (Erf. 333, for *-seeni*—cf. *ungesene* Cp. 682—if from Gmc. \**-sæhnij-*): see Campbell, §241, and Pheifer, §§50.3, 60. Compensatory lengthening cannot be any later than the loss of *h* itself, and so this is further evidence for the status of *h* in the early glossaries.

§398. The conclusion that *h* was lost before the compilation of the early glossaries conflicts with another common assumption about them, that they reflect a state of the language in which Anglian smoothing is not yet completed. This, for instance, is the view of Luick (§240) and Campbell (§§225, 227). Since *h* is one of the consonants that produce smoothing, the vowel change should be thought of as completed before the loss of *h*, and so ought to be in a finished state in the glossaries. The matter is complicated, however, by the fact that in some instances, loss of *h* seems to have preceded smoothing, and for this reason Luick (§240) concludes that the two sound changes must have taken place at roughly the same time. The evidence for this limited loss of *h* before smoothing is of two sorts:

(1) Campbell (§231) remarks that smoothing is normal before *lh* and *rh* before a front vowel, but not before a back vowel, and he concludes that *h* was lost earlier in the latter instance (so also Brunner, §120, n. 1). The evidence is to be found in later as well as earlier texts, for example *elch* (Ép. Erf. 1001) beside *eola* (Erf. 346a, Cp. 627b), and VP *ætfealan*, beside pres. subj. *fele*. Campbell naturally assumes lengthened vocalism in all of these except *elch*. But if internal *h* was lost before the early glossaries were compiled, it could have been lost quite early indeed (see below, §401). It could in fact have been lost early enough that analogical replacement with the short vowel (e.g. smoothed \**elha* > \**ēla* > \**ela*, as in verse forms like *feore*, Chap. 4 above) should be assumed already in the earliest records. In that event all of these words should have short root vocalism, their diphthongs being due to back mutation.[52] Luick (§239)

---

[52]This explanation is rendered possible by Ball and Stiles's demonstration that smoothing must precede back mutation (see above, p. 347, n. 170). They find that none of the very earliest texts evinces back mutation without smoothing, while several show smoothing without back mutation, including *Cædmon's Hymn*, the inscription on the Franks Casket, Sweet's Mercian charters 9 and 12, and the early Anglian glosses in Bodleian MS Add. C. 144 printed by Arthur S. Napier, *Old English Glosses, Chiefly Unpublished* (Oxford: Clarendon, 1900), no. 53. They offer alternative explanations for the few forms in Ép. that appear to have back mutation; but the point is not essential to their argument, since the occurrence of a few unsmoothed forms in the glossary does not prove that smoothing was not yet complete when the glossary was written. Compare the Bodleian glosses just mentioned, in which internal *h* is already consistently lost, as in *thuæle*, *ibig-*, and *fiil*, though orthographically the diphthongs are mostly unsmoothed,

in fact acknowledges that this is the standard interpretation, but he rejects it because smoothing followed by the loss of *h* followed by back mutation would require a greater span of time than related sound changes seem to permit. But this conclusion is based on the assumption that loss of *h* is still not completed in the early glossaries. That was shown above not to be an obstacle, and it might well be that both smoothing and the loss of *h* took place more than a century earlier than Luick assumes. This solution seems preferable to Luick's, since it simplifies the grammar of Old English, attributing the diphthongs to a change already known to have occurred, rather than requiring the formulation of an ad hoc rule like Campbell's.

(2) Campbell's remarks in §230 may be summarized as follows: Normally *h* is lost before voiced consonants, as in *wībedd*, *bitwīnum*, and *fīl*. Sometimes, however, *h* must have been lost before smoothing, given the evidence of a wide range of Anglian texts, from the earliest to the latest, such as Cp. *hēalēcas* and *ēorod-*; VP *hēanis*, *nēosian*, *nēowist*, *nēolǣcan*; personal names in *Hēa-* in the *Liber Vitae*, the "Northumbrian" *Genealogies*, and in the Mercian charters; the name-element *Plēo-* in the *Liber Vitae*; and some other forms in the tenth-century Northumbrian glosses. This analysis is no doubt correct, but it is not evidence for dating smoothing to about the same time as loss of *h*, as Luick concludes that it is (§§239–40). It will be noticed that all the forms with early loss of *h* are compounds with reduced stress on the second element. By contrast, *wībedd* has secondary rather than tertiary stress on the second element, and in *fīl* and *betwīn* (to which *bitwīnum* is analogical) the loss occurs in fully stressed syllables, under the same conditions as in contract verbs. Whatever the precise phonological reason for the different treatment of *h* in compounds with secondary and tertiary stress, the regularity of the difference is assured by the analogous developments at the beginning of

---

as in *ymbeactę*, *-leac*, *-heacan*, and perhaps *heagotho*; and, what is more striking, compare the preservation of unsmoothed forms in a text as late as the early ninth-century *Liber Vitae Dunelmensis* (see Campbell, §225). Under analogous circumstances, breaking is frequently unexpressed in early texts, including Bede's *History* and the inscription on the Franks Casket. It may also be noted that in the *Glossae in Psalmos* in Vatican MS. Pal. Lat. 68 (Napier, no. 54; from the eighth century, according to Ker), the form *selas* contradicts Campbell's explanation of Erf. *eola*, though the form is to be expected if smoothing preceded back mutation. The attribution of the diphthong in *eola* to back mutation does not contradict their argument about the early glossaries, as they note that the language of Erf. is somewhat later than that of Ép., and they would admit back mutation in *-foedur* (Erf. 1039; Ép. *-fedor*, Cp. *-feoðor*), and perhaps *beoso* (Erf. 409; Ép. *baeso*, Cp. *beosu*). Since it was concluded in the preceding chapter that back mutation may be a genuine Anglian feature of *Beowulf* and the Cynewulf canon, this might suggest that these poems postdate the later development of the normal orthographic expression of back mutation. Since we know nothing about the scribal histories of these poems, however, it is not possible to rule out the possibility that they attest back mutation because they continued to be copied in Anglian areas. This, for example, is Girvan's position (p. 11).

second elements of compounds: *h* is usually preserved under secondary stress, as in *fenhop, felahrōr,* and *fyrdhrægl,* but lost under tertiary stress in compounds that lost their stress early, as in *īfig* < \**ib-hīej-*, and *ōrettan* < \**or-haitjan*; less regularly in compunds that lost their stress later, as in *wælrēow* beside *wælhrēow*, and *Waldere* beside *Wealdhere* (see Campbell, §468).[53] And so because the early loss of *h* in forms like *nēolǣcan* is predictable on a regular basis, it is not then a random occurrence—that is, it is not evidence that the regular loss of internal *h* started before smoothing, and was running its course as smoothing began. Rather, it represents a sound change that may have been separated by a consider-able amount of time from the regular loss of internal *h*, that is, the sort found in contract verbs. Smoothing may have occurred at any time between the two developments, and there is no reason to assume that smoothing and the regular loss of *h* were coeval.

§399. And so because smoothing did in all probability precede the loss of *h*, it is intrinsically unlikely that the early glossaries should provide evidence that smoothing was still in progress when they were compiled. This is a difficult matter either to prove or to disprove, and there is wide divergence of opinion. Although smoothing is usual in the glossaries, undeniably there are quite a few examples of unsmoothed diphthongs, es-pecially in Ép. Pheifer (§57) lists the relevant examples in Ép. and Erf., and his results may be tabulated as follows:

|  | SMOOTHED | UNSMOOTHED |
|---|---|---|
| *ēa* | Ép. 8, Erf. 15 | Ép. 9, Erf. 4 |
| *ea* | Ép. 10, Erf. 13 | Ép. 5 |
| *ēo* |  | Ép. 1, Erf. 2 |
| *eo* | Ép. 10, Erf. 11 | Ép. 2, Erf. 2 |
| *īo* | Ép. 2, Erf. 3 |  |
| *io* | Ép. 2, Erf. 2 |  |

All the examples of unsmoothed *eo* except *algiuueorc* (Ép. 556, cf. *algiuerc* Erf. 556) should be eliminated: *eola* (Erf. 346a) and *(e)oritmon* (Erf. 320) were treated above (§398.1, 2), and *sceol(h)egi* (981) may be subject to the same early loss of *h* (see Campbell, §232). But three forms may be added from Cp.: compare *-beorg* (1771), *-biorg* (1672), and *leactrogas* (540, as in

---

[53]Perhaps the reason for the early loss is that *h*, already an acoustically weak consonant, was entirely obscured when followed immediately by a consonant of consid-erable articulatory force, i.e. at the beginning of a syllable bearing half stress in close juncture. Compounds like *wībedd* remained unaffected because their juncture was open, and equivalent to a word boundary—indeed, such compounds are still frequently written as separate words in the manuscripts. Late retention of *h* in such forms can at any rate be attributed to the analogical influence of the corresponding simplices (see, e.g., Campbell, §232), an analogical influence not available to compounds with obscured second elements.

the other glossaries). Brunner (§119, n. 2) assumes that these unsmoothed forms are the result of either early scribal uncertainties or mixture of Anglian and other scribal practices. Campbell assumes that they are mostly genuine, but he also resorts to the acknowledged dialectal mixture in the origin of the glossaries in order to account for the unsmoothed diphthong of *buturfliogae, -o* (Ép. Erf. 817; Campbell, §227; see also "The Glosses," p. 87 and passim). While acknowledging the dialectally mixed origins of the early glossaries (§90), Pheifer (§58) regards the dialectal explanation as less likely, since "the fact that the numerous unsmoothed forms in Épinal are mostly ones containing Prim. OE. *ǣo* and Prim. OE. *ǣo* and *ĕu* by breaking before *r* plus a back consonant suggests that the pattern is chronological rather than dialectal, i.e. that Anglian smoothing first affected short diphthongs immediately before *h*, which is inherently reasonable and borne out by the evidence, as far as it goes, of other early texts (cf. Campbell, §§223ff.)." The observation that the unsmoothed short diphthongs are almost all before *r* is a valuable one, but the explanation offered is untenable, since Campbell's discussion does not in fact include any evidence that could be construed as indicating that smoothing occurred earlier before *h* than before *r*, aside from the examples in the early glossaries themselves. On the contrary, aside from the forms treated above, the only examples of unsmoothed diphthongs in relatively early texts that he offers are immediately before velar consonants: he cites *eac* on the Bewcastle Column, *Beag-* in the *Liber Vitae*, *Uueoht-* in Sweet's Mercian charter no. 47, and *Alouuioh* in the Lichfield *Genealogies*. To these may be added *-leag* and *leah* in Sweet's Mercian charters 10 and 14 (beside four instances of *-berht* in each), and some names on Anglian coins, such as EALMUND beside ALHMUND, and BEAG- beside BAH- on coins of Offa.[54] As for later Anglian texts, the only example before *r* in Farman's work is *weorc* (beside *werc* and *wærc*). And this must be weighed against Farman's forms cited by Campbell, *feoh, beseoh* (imper.), *-sēoc, lēoht, wēox, flēoh* and *atēoh* (the last two imperatives), as well as *þēah* and *ēage* (the former also in Rit.), most of these also beside smoothed forms. Thus it appears to be unlikely that the examples of unsmoothed diphthongs before *r* in the early glossaries reflect a chronological cause rather than a dialectal one. The point should be particularly clear in view of the large number of unsmoothed forms just cited from Farman's tenth-century glosses: it cannot be argued very reasonably that these reflect a state of the language in which smoothing was not yet complete, and so it is generally agreed that they represent a dialect mixture of some sort. Such an explanation is not intrinsically any less probable for the early glosses, especially as they are agreed to reflect dialect mixture in other ways. The appearance of a few unsmoothed

---

[54]For references see Veronica Smart, *Cumulative Index of Volumes 1–20*, Sylloge of Coins of the British Isles 28 (London: Oxford Univ. Press, 1981), pp. 16, 32.

forms in the early glossaries is then no stranger than the appearance of a few forms without parasiting (e.g. -*beacn*, Ép. 992), which Luick and Campbell agree does not reflect a change still in progress, but the effects of either analogy or scribal practice: after all, Luick dates parasiting to the seventh century. Rather, unsmoothed forms are perhaps to be expected if these glossaries spring ultimately from Aldhelm's Malmesbury (see above, p. 347, n. 170).

§400. Regardless of whether or not the early glossaries evidence an uncompleted stage of smoothing, the limit they place on the date of smoothing and the loss of *h* is not very severe. The orthography of Ép. and Erf. is extraordinarily conservative, generally preserving, for instance, the distinction between Germanic *b* (spelt *b*) and *f*.[55] This means either that the Épinal manuscript is quite old, or that the orthographic practices evident in the glossary are considerably older than the manuscript, since the regular use of *b* for *f* among the charters is restricted almost exclusively to seventh-century documents.[56] Earlier scholarship generally dated the manuscript to the eighth or early ninth century.[57] But recent paleographical scholarship suggests that it belongs more properly to the turn, or even the last part of the seventh century.[58] The linguistic probability of such a dating is difficult to gauge. The glossary has several instances of *e* for unstressed *i*, but possibly these do not have any phonological significance, and are like the occasional examples of *e* for *i* in the early Bede manuscripts (cf. §§384ff. and 415). Comparatively they are so few (Pheifer, p. lxxv, finds that the proportion of *i* to *e* is 134:11 in medial

[55]See Sievers, "Altangelsächsisch *f* und *b*," *PBB* 11 (1886), 542–45.

[56]The use of *b* for *f* in the charters is surveyed by Sievers, "Zu Cynewulf" (as above, p. 352, n. 2), p. 15. The Erfurt scribe of course is also conservative, but he was not an Englishman.

[57]Among those who would place it in the first half of the eighth century are Sweet, p. 3; W. M. Lindsay, *Notae latinae* (Cambridge: Cambridge Univ. Press, 1915), p. 456; E. A. Lowe (6:760); Brunner, §2, n. 3; and Pheifer, §88 (though subsequently Pheifer has adopted Parkes' view, below). Ker (item 114) also calls it an eighth-century manuscript. Earlier scholarship tended to date it later, to the beginning of the ninth century. This was the opinion of Sir Edward Maunde Thompson, as reported by H. Sweet, *The Épinal Glossary, Latin and Old English, of the Eighth Century*, EETS, o.s. 79b (1883); and Wolfgang Keller, *Angelsächsische Palaeographie I*, *Palaestra* 43 (1906), 17; further references are given by Pheifer, §5, n. 6. Thompson's and Keller's opinion is based on comparison with the script of Sweet's charter no. 37 (Kentish, A.D. 805 × 810). However, Pheifer remarks, "This opinion has been widely accepted, but the resemblance on which it is based is not really very close, and the consistently archaic character of the Old English favors the earlier date" (§5).

[58]See T. J. Brown, "The Irish Element in the Insular System of Scripts to circa A.D. 850," in *Die Iren und Europa im früheren Mittelalter*, ed. H. Löwe, vol. 1 (Stuttgart: Klett-Cotta, 1982), 101–19, at 109 and n. 12; and Malcolm Parkes (with Bernhard Bischoff), "Palaeographical Commentary," in *The Épinal, Erfurt, Werden, and Corpus Glossaries*, ed. Bernhard Bischoff et al., Early English Manuscripts in Facsimile 22 (Copenhagen: Rosenkilde & Bagger, 1988), 13–25, at 16.

syllables and finally before consonants, and 82:8 in absolute finality) that if the glossary is coeval with Sweet's reliable late seventh-century charters, nos. 1 (A.D. 685 × 694, prob. 690 × 693; see above, p. 354, n. 9), 4 (A.D. 679), and 5 (A.D. 697 in the Stowe version), whatever the reason for the appearance of *e* in the glossary, its absence in these charters might be explained as due to the paucity of relevant forms. The evidence of the change of *æ* to *e* is compatible with a date in the late seventh century. Pheifer finds that in the glossary, the proportion of *æ* and *ae* to *e* is 30:16 in medial syllables and before final consonants, and 192:8 in absolute finality. The change is thus considerably more common non-finally. It is unattested in the earliest charter (no. 4; the only instance is in final position, in *uuestanae*), but it is found consistently in the other two in non-final position (see §415 below). In this respect, then, the glossary is actually more conservative than the earliest charters. But the statistical difference is small, and the significance of the orthographic evidence is disputable (see §415 below). Perhaps the linguistic evidence does not forbid a date in the seventh century for the Épinal manuscript; but in order for this to be possible, the evidence that the glossary provides in respect to the development of unstressed *i* and *æ* must be regarded as negligible. In regard to the Erfurt Glossary it may be noted that the foreign scribe's divergences from his exemplar can only be errors, not modernizations of the spelling, since he clearly did not understand English. The version of the glossary preserved in the Épinal manuscript in any case probably cannot be earlier than A.D. 685, as the glossary apparently incorporates glosses on Aldhelm's riddles, which cannot have been composed earlier than this.[59] Nonetheless, the material in the Épinal-Erfurt exemplar is of diverse origins, and the ultimate source of at least some of its material was interlinear glosses in books.[60] Accordingly, the language of some of the material in the glossaries may be even older than Aldhelm's riddles. And so even if one accepts Luick's and Campbell's analysis of the language of the early glossaries, it is not necessary to assume that smoothing, loss of *h*, and contraction were not completed before the end of the seventh century.

§401. But since it was shown above that it is in fact likely that parasiting, smoothing and loss of *h* were completed before the early

---

[59]See Michael Lapidge and James L. Rosier, *Aldhelm: The Poetic Works* (Cambridge: D. S. Brewer, 1985), pp. 11–12; and see Pheifer, p. lvi, n. 3, and his notes on glosses 218, 569, and so forth. Pheifer himself allows slightly more latitude in the date, using as his touchstone the composition of Aldhelm's prose *De viginitate*, with a date between 675 and 690 for the *terminus a quo*: see "Early Anglo-Saxon Glossaries and the School of Canterbury," *ASE* 16 (1987), 17–44, at 18 and n. 6. Lapidge has offered cogent reasons to believe that the *glossae collectae* on which Ép.-Erf. draws were compiled at Canterbury under Archbishop Theodore (669–690) and Abbot Hadrian (671–709 or 710): see "The School of Theodore and Hadrian," *ASE* 15 (1986), 45–72.

[60]Chadwick (p. 68) was perhaps the first to point this out, drawing attention to glosses of more than one word, e.g. *þorh byrgeras* glossing *per uispellones* (Ép. 760).

Mercian glossaries were compiled, there is no compelling reason they could not have occurred soon after *i*-mutation. And since Luick dates *i*-mutation to the sixth century, and probably the first half, these changes may be very early—too early to establish a useful *terminus a quo*.

§402. The apocope of *-i* and *-u* seems to set a dating limit, since none of the longer poems contains verses that will not scan correctly without the final vowel, though all contain examples of verses that would be spoilt metrically by the addition of the vowel.[61] But this evidence cannot be considered fully secure, since it is not unlikely that the loss of *-i* and *-u* was attended by alterations in the acceptability of certain verse types: for instance, the rules governing Germanic meter were certainly different ca. 400 when a certain Holsteiner inscribed *ek hlewagastiR . holtijaR . horna . tawiðo* in runes on the gold horn found at Gallehus.[62] This point is all the more significant because apparently unstressed high vowels were lost medially at the same time as finally, so that countless verses like *ond his heafdes segl* (*Andreas* 50b, with *hēafdes* < *hēafudæs*) would have been affected by the change, as well. Moreover, dating the loss of these vowels is a controversial problem. Morsbach (pp. 253–62) collects the early evidence for the loss or preservation of final *-i* and *-u*, and ultimately finds just one example of preserved *-u*, the form *flōdu* on the Franks Casket, really convincing. Amos (pp. 18–29) reviews the evidence, sharing Morsbach's own doubts, but also rejecting even the word on the casket, on the grounds that "no interpretation of 'flodu' has established itself as preeminent."[63] Yet the alternatives to Morsbach's explanation all seem improbable. Chadwick's proposal (p. 69, n. 4) that *fisc flodu* is an error for *fiscflod up* (endorsed by Campbell, §346, n. 2, and Brunner, §273, n. 4)

---

[61]Sarrazin ("Chronologie," pp. 178–79) offers examples of verses in *Genesis A* that he says require *-u*, and this provokes a controversy: see Richter, p. 23; Sarrazin, *Kädmon*, pp. 25–27; and Amos, pp. 26–27. Amos' discussion contains some errors, but her conclusion is reliable that the poem contains no examples of verses requiring pre-apocopic forms, and several requiring post-apocopic ones, e.g. *siððan folca bearn* (1087b) and *Flod ealle wreah* (1386b). Morsbach (pp. 269–73) applies the same test to *Cædmon's Hymn*, *Bede's Death Song*, the *Leiden Riddle*, and *Beowulf*, finding that all contain verses requiring post-apocopic forms except for the first, which offers no unambiguous examples.

[62]On early inscriptions in verse see Lehmann, *Verse Form*, pp. 28–29, 77–80.

[63]P. 24. Alfred Bammesberger is rightly skeptical in regard to the view that the inscription SKANOMODU on an early gold *solidus* shows a nominative *u*-stem ending: see "SKANOMODU: Linguistic Issues," in *Britain 400–600: Language and History*, ed. Alfred Bammesbergeer and Alfred Wollmann (Heidelberg: Winter, 1990), pp. 457–64, at 461. New runic evidence has been discovered since Amos reached her conclusions, among the most important of which is the Undley bracteate: for a survey of inscriptions relevant to dating apocope see John Hines, "The Runic Inscriptions of Early Anglo-Saxon England," pp. 437–55 in the same volume. Hans F. Nielsen remarks the surprising number of early runic *u*-inflections in what appear to be *a*-stems, and concludes that *u*- is simply a representation of the reflex of Gmc. *-a*: see "Unaccented Vowels in Runic Frisian and Ingvaeonic," in Bammesberger, *Runes*, pp. 299–303.

would spoil the meter.[64] Page's suggestion (pp. 176–7) that *flōdu* is analogical to plural forms like *wintru* (see n. 71 below), *applu*, and some dissyllabic neuters plural in Cp., faces the difficulty that the word is masculine. Sir Christopher Ball regards both of these explanations as desperate, and suggests the morphologically most plausible solution proposed to date: *fiscflodu* is a compound with an ending of the *n*-stems (cf. OE *brū* beside *oferbrūwa*, and *pād* beside *hoppāda*), in the accusative case (cf. *galgu* on the Ruthwell Cross and *foldu* in *Cædmon's Hymn*).[65] Yet even this ingenious explanation is not entirely satisfying: in context it seems unlikely that *flōdu* could be anything but nominative singular, as the verses almost certainly describe the stranding of a whale.[66] The name *ægili* in a panel on the lid also suggests that final high vowels had not yet been apocopated when the casket was made, although its evidence is less firm (cf. Dahl, p. 56, and Girvan, p. 21, neither explanation very likely). Nonetheless, there are real obstacles to the evidence of *flōdu*. Two other forms in the inscription have lost a final high vowel, *end* (Brunner, §79, n. 4) and *wylif*. More important, smoothing has already applied to *fegtaþ*, *fergenberig*, *-bergæ*, *drigiþ*, and *unneg*; and yet smoothing is later than the apocope of high vowels, since it follows parasiting (e.g. Anglian *bēcun* rather than *\*bēcen*: Luick, §320), which in turn follows apocope (e.g. *\*frōfru* > *\*frōfr* > *frōfor*).[67] It is also remarkable that the spelling on the casket is more modern than the spelling in the early glossaries—Arthur Napier points out that *f* instead of *b* in *wylif* and *sefa* (to which *afitatores* may be added), and loss of *-n* in *sefa*, point to a date in the eighth century at the earliest[68]—and yet there are no masculine forms comparable to *flōdu* in the early glossaries (on *aetgaeru* see above, p. 174, n. 11), and final *-n* is preserved in *uullan* in the *Leiden Riddle*. It is thus not credible that *flōdu*, whatever its significance, could represent a genuine survival of unapocopated *-u*, especially because the verses containing *flōdu* appear to describe the stranding of the whale from whose bone the casket was made, and thus should have been composed at that time.

---

[64]By the reading *fiscflod u[p]ahof* Chadwick seems to have intended *up-* as an unstressed prefix. But *up* is never an unstressed prefix in verse. Nor is the word ever unstressed as an adverb. Cf. *flod up ahof* (*Genesis A* 1419b).

[65]"Problems in Early Northumbrian Phonology," in *Luick Revisited*, pp. 109–17, at 110–11.

[66]This is also the view of Alfred Becker, *Franks Casket: Zu den Bildern und Inschriften des Runenkästchens von Auzon*, Regensburger Arbeiten zur Anglistik und Amerikanistik 5 (Regensburg: Hans Carl, 1973), p. 19: "Daß *flodu* hier Nominative Sing. ist, läßt sich der Satzaussage zwar nicht mit Sicherheit entnehmen, es ist aber nach dieser Texterörterung recht wahrscheinlich."

[67]See also Ball, "Problems" (n. 65), pp. 110–11, and cf. above, §398.1.

[68]"Contributions to Old English Literature, 2: The Franks Casket," in *An English Miscellany Presented to Dr. Furnivall* (Oxford: Clarendon, 1901), pp. 362–81, at 380.

§403. Ritchie Girvan offers another piece of evidence for late apocope: "Now we have coins of Æthelred of Mercia with runic inscriptions in the two forms *Æþiliræd* and *Æþilræd*. As we can hardly imagine the name as built with two different elements we must conclude that one is an earlier, the other a later, spelling. His regnal years are 675–704" (p. 22). Actually, the one example of this coin known to me without the second *i* has instead ÆÞIL.RÆD. On most of the other coins the I is smaller than the rest of the runes, made to fit under the upper part of the runic L. The point after the L thus is not insignificant, since it corresponds to I on the other coins. Possibly, then, this coin is a blundered copy, with the smaller I mistaken for ornamentation at the end of the first line of runes. It should be remembered that many Anglo-Saxon coins are merely copies of successful issues, not authorized by the original issuers, but made to resemble original issues because of the authority thereby lent them. Raymond Page in fact offers a reason to believe that some of the coins reading ÆÞILIRÆD are copies of this sort.[69] And so this coin does not offer clear evidence of a change in progress.

§404. Nor is its evidence of an unapocopated high vowel reliable. It is now known that the coins were not issued by Æthelred of Mercia—indeed, this should always have seemed improbable, given the spelling -RÆD, indicating a Saxon provenance even if the coins were issued in the seventh century—and the name on the coins must be that of the moneyer. The coins should in fact be dated to the eighth century, probably the second decade.[70] This is clearly much too late for apocope not to have applied—in a genuine Kentish charter dated 679 (Sweet's no. 4) apocope has already applied, even to this same name-element in *aedilmaeri*. And so whatever the significance of the name on these coins, it cannot be regarded as evidence for the date of apocope.

§405. The one linguistic fact that does show some promise of setting a *terminus a quo* for the composition of the longer poems is the occurrence of noncontraction in the early glossaries. Admittedly, the evidence is somewhat ambiguous. Certainly forms with intervocalic *h* are uncontracted, yet contraction does seem to have set in in other instances.

---

[69]He points out that three specimens have an unusual form of the D-rune, missing the final upright. "These were probably copied from imperfect coins of this issue, which were poorly centred on the flan so that the second stem of the last letter missed it" (p. 127). Page supplies line-drawings of some of the coins; for photographs see Mack (as above, p. 356, n. 14), item 312; Seaby's catalogue, item 837 (as above, p. 344, n. 159); Sutherland, pl. 2, item 21 (as above, p. 355, n. 13); and J. J. North, *English Hammered Coinage, I: Early Anglo-Saxon to Henry III, ca. 600–1272* (London: Spink & Son, 1980), pl. 1, item 60. Since the time of Page's study, ten more examples of the coin have been located, for a total of nineteen so far: see Blackburn, pp. 157–8, with the references there.

[70]See Blackburn's discussion of the dating, p. 157, though he would attribute the coins to Kent.

For example, *æ* and *i* remain uncontracted in 3. sg. pres. *faehit* (Ép. 785), but not in the preterite *faedun* (Ép. 797; see Pheifer, §59, for other examples). Such variation may be due either to scribal alteration or to variability in the original language of the glosses. All that can be concluded is that contraction was certainly not completed at the time the glosses used to compile these glossaries were written, again perhaps even earlier than A.D. 685. Noncontraction is clear frequently enough in the early glossaries that a measurable difference can be observed between the glossaries and the verse of Cynewulf in this regard. In earlier verse the distinction is less pronounced. Thus, *Beowulf* and the Cædmonian narratives are unlikely to have been composed much before ca. 685, though they may be considerably later than that.

## D. Dating *Beowulf* by Kaluza's Law

§406. The most important criterion of the preceding chapters with respect to absolute dating is Kaluza's law. Bliss recognized the value of the criterion in this regard, and attempted to demonstrate that the distinction the *Beowulf* poet observes between long and short vocalic endings need not have been lost when the phonological difference was lost, but could have been morphologized at that time, and have remained active at least to the end of the Old English period (see Appendix B to his book, pp. 118–21). He never actually formulates the morphological rule, but states the general rationale in the form of a proportion: "nominative plural *scipu* and *hus* and genitive plural *scipa* and *husa* are equivalent both in grammar and in metre" (p. 120). In other words, under Kaluza's law nom. pl. *scipu* and *hūs*, though they differ in syllable count, receive identical metrical treatment, a rule learnable by association with the grammatical rule that the ending *-u* is used with short-stemmed nouns like *scip* and not long-stemmed ones like *hūs*; and gen. pl. *scipa* and *hūsa*, with identical syllable count, also receive identical metrical treatment, a rule learnable by association with the grammatical rule that the two stem types take the same genitive plural ending. The effect of presenting this proportion is to advance the claim that the metrical value of short vocalic endings is predictable on the basis of whether or not their appearance in grammar is regulated by the length of the root syllable to which they are attached—that is, endings that disappear after long syllables are metrically short, and all others are long. Once the rule is thus actually formulated it becomes apparent that the proportion is untenable. One difficulty is that the analogy does not hold true in all instances. For example, in the feminine *ō*-stems the acc. sg. *ceare* is not metrically equivalent to *lāre*, which in turn is metrically equivalent to dat. sg. *ceare*, which is not metrically equivalent to acc. pl. *ceare*, which is metrically equivalent to gen. sg. *ceare*, even though the appearance of none of these phonologically identical endings varies according to the weight of the root syllable. The accusative and genitive are attested in *Beowulf*; and thus Bliss is obliged to explain the two instances in *Beowulf* of acc. sg. *-ceare* (*modceare micle* 1778a, *modceare mændon* 3149a) with the assumption that *mōdceare* in both instances is a scribal substitution (p. 119).

§407. Similarly, at least in *Beowulf*, although nom. *i*-stem *gripe* is metrically equivalent to nom. *stān*, and gen. pl. *gripa* to *stāna*, still dat. sg. *gripe* is not equivalent to *stāne*: this is instanced in *mundgripe mægenes* (*Beowulf* 1534a). Bliss discards this evidence on the basis of the observation,

The Old English dative combines the functions, and presumably the endings, of two cases, the dative and the instrumental; of these, the first should be retained after a long stem-syllable and the second should perhaps be lost. Since it is impossible to be certain that the single example in *Beowulf* of the masculine *i*-stem, dative singular, does not represent a survival of the old instrumental, this instance must be considered doubtful. (p. 119)

But both the old dative and instrumental endings should almost certainly be short. Bliss himself implicitly concedes the point when he classifies the nom. pl. masc. *i*-stem ending as short, even though it derives from PGmc. *-îz*: the reason, as demonstrated above in §§187ff., is that the shortening of high vowels took place before the shortening of other vowels (see the discussion of the nom. pl. masc. *i*-stem ending in Appendix B), again as Bliss himself claims. And so the confusion of long and short *-e* in the dative singular of *i*-stems is due rather to the analogical substitution of the *a*-stem ending, as demonstrated in some early texts, for example in forms like Ép. *faengae* and *suicae*. But even if Bliss were right about the source of short *-e*, his objection would be irrelevant, since the question is not actually how dat. sg. masc. *i*-stem *-e* got to be short in *Beowulf*, but whether the analogical proportion he proposes could have been used by the *Beowulf* poet. In this instance the answer is surely no, regardless of the poet's reason for using a short ending: this ending is just as certainly an exception to Bliss's proposal, whatever its origin, and so represents another obstacle to the learnability (and therefore the naturalness and credibility) of the supposed morphological rule.

§408. Bliss rejects one other exceptional ending: "The normal ending of the masculine *u*-stem, accusative plural, is *-a* in Old English, and it is retained after a long stem-syllable; but the single instance in *Beowulf* (*bordwudu beorhtan* 1243a) retains the older ending *-u*, which is lost after a long stem-syllable" (p. 119). Essentially the same criticism must be raised here, that the explanation is beside the point: granted that etymologically this ending ought to be short, it is still an instance that a scop using Bliss's morphologized rule would need to have learned as an exception. The reason is that while it is technically true that the ending *-u* "is lost after a long stem-syllable," it is only true in the diachronic sense, since long-stemmed masculine *u*-stem nouns like *feld* are never *\*feld* in the accusative plural, but *felda*, occasionally *feldas*, and thus do not provide the requisite analogical proportion.[71] Considering the absence of the acc. pl. *\*feld* type from the Anglo-Saxon records, the regular alternation between acc. pl. *-u* after short syllables and nil after long must have broken down, at the latest, at about the same time that the metrical alternation would need to have become morphologized, and therefore there never was a time when a scop could have determined (or would have needed to determine) the metrical value of *-wudu* on the basis of comparison to *\*feld*.

§409. This reasoning also applies to Bliss's remark, "The ending of the masculine *i*-stem, nominative plural, preserved mainly in tribal names such as *Engle, Mierce*, etc., is retained after a long stem, but this retention appears to be analogical" (p. 119). This is in explanation of a verse without a proper name, *laðbite lices* (*Beowulf* 1122a). The objection might be valid if the long-stemmed nouns were normally inflectionless in the nominative plural, but this is not the case: there are no such forms attested, and in the earliest texts there are a few examples of the type with the original ending (e.g. Cp. *daele*) beside the forms with analogical *-as* (e.g. Cp. *hegas*, and *uyrmas* in the *Leiden Riddle*). The analogical addition (or retention) of *-i/-e* thus cannot be dated, but it must have been fairly early. And so there is no evidence for a time when Bliss's analogical proportion would have applied to these nouns. More important, for the most part, long-stemmed masculine *i*-stems were inflectionally indistinguishable from *a*-stems (though the former had *i*-mutation in the root-syllable), and so there could not have been any analogical proportion in this stem class.

§410. A further complication is that what Bliss actually means in calling *scipa* and *hūsa* metrically equivalent is that they receive the same metrical treatment under secondary stress.[72] It is certainly not true under primary stress, where, for instance, *scipa* and *hūsa* are never metrically equivalent, the former always requiring resolution. This stipulation, in conjunction with all the preceding exceptions, characterizes a rule too complex to be learned as a simple analogical proportion to a morphological alternation. After all, as Bliss himself remarks, whatever

---

[71]It is true that the accusative plural of *winter* is sometimes *winter*, but it is also *wintru*; and Brunner (§273, n. 3) might be right that acc. pl. *winter* was regarded as neuter: cf. *ðurh tyn winter full* in Bede's *History*, bk. 1, chap. 6. Forms like *flōdu* on the Franks Casket and *aetgaeru* in the Erfurt Glossary are too disputed to serve as counterevidence to Bliss's view. Alfred Bammesberger derives the newer ending *-a* from an Indo-European dual in "Die Endung für Nom. Akk. Pl. bei altenglischen *u*-Stämmen," *Anglia* 103 (1985), 365–70.

[72]Technically, even this is not quite accurate, as the type *\*ond seofon scipa* is avoided, under Sievers' principle that a short lift should not follow a resolved lift.

the basis of the distinction, "it must have been easily accessible to the poets, whom we must not credit with too much philological acumen" (p. 118). And since *Beowulf* violates the analogical proportion in every one of the five instances in which it provides relevant examples for testing the hypothesis (i.e. short endings that do not disappear after long syllables), especially when the poet is meticulous about observing Kaluza's law in other respects, it follows that Bliss's morphological explanation is implausible.

§411. The alternative that Bliss proposes to his morphological proportion is a distinction that he considers purely phonological (p. 120), that is, the fact that for the most part the short vocalic endings derive etymologically from high vowels, and the long endings from non-high ones. But this is more properly regarded as another morphological distinction, since any rule stating that low vowels resist resolution after secondary stress clearly is not motivated by any natural phonological conditioning, there being no innate phonological connection between vowel height and resolvability. Rather, if such a rule existed it must have been a morphologization of an earlier rule based on a quantitative distinction; and such a rule may indeed have been purely phonological, since there is a clear connection between resolvability and vowel length, for instance in the fact that acc. sg. *lāre* may never be resolved. Of course, regardless of whether or not Kaluza's law was ever regulated on a morphological basis, this earlier, purely phonological rule must be assumed, since morphophonemic rules do not arise *ex nihilo*: they must be either morphologizations of phonological rules or the result of analogical pressures, the latter possibility being irrelevant in this instance. Bliss's alternative rule then ought to be assumed to have arisen out of the accident that Proto-Germanic vowels with the broken accent nearly always produce Old English non-high vowels: when the length distinction between long vowels with and without the broken accent was eliminated, the rule of resolvability that depended on that distinction was (perhaps) morphologized by transferral to the nearly identical distinction in vowel height.

§412. Bliss's alternative formulation, this second morphological rule, is not as incredible as the first, but it still depends on some implausible assumptions. The fit again is not exact, since the feminine *ō*-stem accusative singular ending, though metrically short, does not derive from a high vowel, and there are two examples in *Beowulf* (given above) to confirm that the ending is indeed short. There are some short endings from other non-high vowels—the feminine *ō*-stem accusative plural, the *n*-stem nominative and accusative singular neuter, the *n*-stem nominative singular feminine, and a few others—though unfortunately none of these endings is attested in the relevant position in *Beowulf*. In any case, the regularity with which the *Beowulf* poet observes Kaluza's law lends significant weight to the two feminine accusative singular counterexamples. So also there are exceptions to the grammatical rule that Bliss's scop would have had to learn, for instance the ending -*u* preserved after a long syllable in the nominative and accusative plural of long-stemmed neuter *ja*-stems. Moreover, the general idea of a morphologized rule of resolution is not convincing. This is not to say that it is impossible, but that it is difficult to imagine a close prosodic parallel. Older metrical values may be preserved artificially, for example in the Renaissance scansion of English *heaven, never,* and the like; but this is on a lexical rather than a morphological basis—for example, Shakespeare frequently has dissyllabic *heaven* (cf. "Sometime too hot the eye of heaven shines," *Sonnet 18*) whereas Marlowe consistently has a monosyllable (cf. "Sweet Faustus, think of heaven and heavenly things," *Doctor Faustus* II.i.21). And when such artificial metrical values are employed, they are readily learnable and easily passed on to the next generation of poets because they are implanted in the matrix of living prosodic rules, and so are recognized by all listeners: the rhythm of the line from Marlowe above would be seriously disrupted if *heaven* were read as a dissyllable. This is not the case in the situation Bliss envisages, because after the loss of the distinction between long and short unstressed vowels the prosodic system could no longer depend upon such a distinction—though exceptions like *heaven* can be taken into account, the actual, regular rules of a prosodic system cannot be based on regularities no longer existent in the phonological system. The fact that, under secondary stress, *scipa* never resolves, while *scipu* does, would not have been foregrounded by the prosodic system, the way the scansion of *heaven* is foregrounded by the overlay of iambic pentameter. This means that unless a new generation of scops were actually told in so many words that low vowels are not resolved after secondary stress (and of course living metrical systems are not learned this way, and Old English almost certainly lacked the terminology to express such a rule),[73] then it is unlikely that such a regularity would have been noticed.

§413. Even if Bliss's second explanation were believable, loss of the distinction underlying Kaluza's law would still have to be dated relatively early. This is because the distinction between unstressed *æ* and *i* was eliminated about the middle of the eighth century south of the Humber, and the middle of the ninth north of it. As demonstrated above in the discussion of Cynewulf's runic signatures, that is the period when unstressed *i* begins to be written as *e* with some regularity; and as demonstrated below, unstressed *æ* perhaps changed to *e* even earlier. Bliss recognized that his second explanation demands a relatively early date. A peculiar mistake in his presentation of this point perhaps explains why he devotes an appendix to defending these two morphological explanations, when they both must have seemed improbable to as acute an observer as he. He says that the distinction between etymologically high and low unstressed vowels persisted "as late as the early seventh century"

---

[73]See above, p. 167, n. 19.

(p. 120). The error in dating implies much. The early seventh century has always seemed too early a date for *Beowulf*—Girvan, for example, who favors a fairly early dating of ca. 680–700, rules out any date earlier than the second half of the seventh century (p. 20). No one claims it was composed so early, and it was shown above that *Beowulf* and the early scriptural narratives cannot be dated much earlier than ca. 685. Bliss's "purely phonological" solution must have seemed improbable to him on that account, inducing him therefore to argue at greater length the virtue of his first morphological solution—even though he frankly admits that the second explanation otherwise makes better sense.[74]

§414. Of course if both of the morphological solutions that Bliss proposes are implausible, then the only remaining explanation is that Kaluza's law was governed by genuine differences in vowel length. But Bliss rejects this possibility from the start, because "it is at least clear that no distinction of quantity can have survived into historic Old English, since the early coalescence of final -*æ* and -*i* clearly implies that the original long vowels had been shortened" (p. 118). Again he must be assuming too early a date for this shortening: he later implies that the

---

[74]P. 121. B. R. Hutcheson has offered another explanation for the preservation of Kaluza's law in *Beowulf*. In sec. V.D. of his dissertation (see p. 66, n. 2 above) he argues that it is due to the poet's use of formulaic language. (This is in response to the 1989 MLA paper mentioned in the Preface above.) The relevance of formulaic language to the partial preservation of the law in verse other than *Beowulf* was in fact suggested above (§179). But the regularity of the *Beowulf* poet's adherence to the law raises difficulties. This explanation might be plausible in regard to verses like *nydwracu niþgrim* (193a), but it is difficult to credit in the instance of verses like *mundgripe mægenes* (1534a) and *modceare mændon* (3149a), in which the compound may have a varying metrical value in the paradigm of the word, depending upon what case-inflection -*e* represents. Another difficulty is that Kaluza's law appears not to apply to verses of type C (see above, §§174f.). Hutcheson argues that his explanation accounts for this anomaly, since it may be supposed that the poet innovated in verses of type C, but conformed to traditional diction in the other relevant verse types. But the anomalous type C seems to tell against the hypothesis rather than for it. It is not plausible that a poet should have retained formulaic diction in all but 2 of 108 instances in other types, but not in type C—this is explaining the unknown by the unknown. Methodologically the purely metrical explanation—i.e., that the law simply does not apply in type C—is preferable, since the formulaic explanation incorporates it. That is, the formulaic explanation, while labeling the difference formulaic, still relies at its core on a distinction between verses of type C and other types—which is precisely the metrical distinction. And so formulism seems a distraction from the real issue, which is the metrical one. Hutcheson's idea that the other verse types are more conservative than C because they arose earlier in the development of Germanic meter faces some difficulties: the comparative evidence demonstrates that type C is common to all the early Germanic languages, and so must have arisen long before the Old English period; and Hutcheson agrees (private communication) that whatever the conditioning for the law at the time *Beowulf* was composed, the conditioning must originally have been phonological. Yet such phonological conditioning cannot have been lost as early as the supposed origin of the metrical pattern of type C, since final quantities were certainly preserved past the Ingvaeonic period, as the comparative evidence indicates.

coalescence of final -æ and -i took place in the early part of the seventh century (p. 120). It was demonstrated by Sievers, and confirmed above (§§379ff.), that there is no secure evidence for the regular change of -i to -e south of the Humber before the middle of the eighth century, and at least in the name-elements *Cyni*- and *Æðil*- until about a century later in the North. On this score, then, there is no evidence for dating the shortening of -ī before the first half of the eighth century in the Midlands and the South, and possibly even later in the North.

§415. Since so few instances of OE -e actually derive from *-ī (only the nom.-acc. plural of *i*-stems is relevant to Kaluza's law), more important ought to be the evidence for the centralization of -æ to -e, setting a terminus to the shortening of *-ǣ. This change is sometimes thought to have occurred earlier than the lowering of -i (as Girvan remarks, p. 23), though the evidence is less abundant than for -i. The earliest reliable charter to furnish any evidence is Sweet's no. 1, an Essex document that is original in the main, though the bounds and witnesses (starting with *termini sunt autem isti*) are an addition of about a century later.[75] The preceding portion thus dates to the period 685 × 694, and it contains examples of e for unstressed æ, in *angenlabeshaam* and *uuidmundesfelt*.[76] Next is no. 5, a Kentish document to be dated to 697 in the Stowe version (edited by Sweet and Hoad, p. 201). Here æ is twice reduced to e in the genitive ending of *wieghelmes* and *meguines*, though finally æ is preserved in *limingae* (*aedilburgae* has a Latin dative ending). Probable instances of *ae* for æ are *liminaee* (no. 6, Kentish, A.D. 732; cf. *balth-haeardi*, *aeanberhti* in the same document) and *liminaea*, *liminiaeae*, *liminiaee* in no. 7 (Kentish, A.D. 741, for 750?), that is, *limingæ-ea*. Next there is *husmerae* in no. 9 (Mercian, 736), but *ibe* and *pede* in the same charter are probable instances of centralization. In no. 8 (Kentish, ca. 767) there are three genitives in -es and none in -æs. These appear alongside two genitives in -is (!), demonstrating that the change is phonological, not merely orthographic, and not new in 767. Even in the very conservative no. 11 (Mercian, 767), which has unstressed i in *middil-saexum*, *bituih*, and *ciltinne*, æ has become e in *liddinge* and *ciltinne*, but remains in *hergae*. This evidence might be interpreted to mean that the change had begun by the end of the seventh century at the latest in the South, and that it could be that old in the Midlands, as well. Yet the parallel instance of occasional e for i and æ in the early Bede manuscripts (see below) suggests the possibility of a small inherent variability in the spelling of unstressed vowels even before these sound changes occurred. This seems likelier than the assumption that the sound change spanned as many as sixty years or more. It would be best then to date the change not to the first instances of e for æ, but to a time shortly before e begins

---

[75]See Chaplais, "Anglo-Saxon Diplomas" (as above, p. 381, n. 9).
[76]The form *hedilburge* has a Latin dative ending.

to replace *æ* with some regularity. At any rate, the change is no younger than the middle of the eighth century in Mercia. Dahl (pp. 194–96) reaches a similar conclusion.

§416. The Northumbrian evidence again suggests a later change. Dahl (p. 187) finds that *-e* is commoner than *-æ* in both the Moore and Namur manuscripts of Bede's *Historia*; but Arngart (Anderson, pp. 110–13) demonstrates that these are almost all instances of datives, and so may represent Latin or Latinized endings. Still, the proportion of *-es* to *-æs* is 6:12 in the Moore MS (but 2:14 in the Leningrad and Namur MSS). And even in *Cædmon's Hymn* we find *heben*, *hrofe*, and *haleg*.[77] On the other hand, in the *Liber Vitae* the proportion of *-e* to *-æ* is 2:7, which cannot be reconciled with the supposition that the change had made much progress by the beginning of the ninth century: rather, it implies that earlier instances of *e* for *æ* are merely orthographic. Unfortunately, the "stycas" furnish almost no evidence, and what little there is is unreliable, since E is frequently written for Æ on these coins, as in EDILRED. But the change had certainly taken place by the latter part of the ninth century, as demonstrated by forms in inscriptions, for example *sete*, *arærde*, *berhtsuiþe*, and *saule* on the Thornhill Cross fragments. Likewise, *saule* appears on the Falstone Hogback, along with a few instances of the hyperurbanism *æftær* (for *æfter*) in both runic and roman characters. It is safest to suppose that in Northumbria, unstressed *æ* changed to *e* at the time that *i* underwent the same change, that is, in the middle of the ninth century.

§417. How long before the change of unstressed *æ* to *e* the shortening of *ǣ* occurred (meaning, of course, the vowel with abnormal intonation) it is not possible to say for certain. At a minimum, a generation ought to be allowed between the start of one sound change and the next. This follows, for instance, from William Labov's findings in regard to the centralization of /aw/ on Martha's Vineyard.[78] The oldest informants showing any significant amount of centralization were about thirty years older than the oldest informants whose distribution of centralized and non-centralized varieties was regulated by the environmental conditioning characteristic of all the younger informants. Between these two, variation was haphazard with regard to environment, a characteristic of a sound change still in progress. The same span of time and intermediate haphazardness are findings of L. Gauchat's and Eduard Hermann's studies of sound change in Charmey, a French-speaking mountain village in Switzerland.[79] Shortening of final long vowels and lowering of high vowels are

[77]Some other early forms that look like hypercorrections are *ofaer* in the *Leiden Riddle*, *bismæradu* on the Ruthwell Cross, and *gibroþær* on the Franks Casket; and probably also *rodi* on the Ruthwell Cross and *-cæstri* on the Franks Casket.

[78]See "The Social Motivation of a Sound Change," *Word* 19 (1963), 273–309; rpt. in his *Sociolinguistic Patterns* (Philadelphia: Univ. of Pennsylvania Press, 1972), pp. 1–42.

[79]Gauchat, "L'unité phonétique dans le patois d'une commune," *Aus romanischen Sprachen und Literaturen: Festschrift Heinrich Morf* (Halle: Niemeyer, 1905),

sequential sound changes—that is, one is a prerequisite to the other—and so they cannot be assumed to have overlapped in time. At least a generation should then be assumed between the first appearance of shortening of *ǣ* in Old English (after which time Kaluza's law could no longer be applied as accurately as the *Beowulf* poet applies it) and the beginning of the change of shortened *æ* to *e*.

§418. Another method of dating the shortening of non-high circumflected vowels is suggested by the change of *ô* to *a*, as in the nominative singular of masculine *n*-stems and the genitive plural of all declensions. One might assume on structural principles that shortening preceded this change, and that the shortening occurred at the same time as the shortening of *ǣ*. But the relevant endings are spelt *-a*, not *\*-o*, even in the earliest records, while *-ǣ* is still frequently spelt *-æ* in the same places. This might be interpreted to mean that *-ô* was shortened before *-ǣ*. But the evidence of Kaluza's law suggests otherwise. Ép. always has *-a* rather than *\*-o*, though the glossary seems at least as conservative as *Beowulf*, if not more conservative, with regard to contraction after the loss of intervocalic *h*, especially considering that the glossary's preservation of uncontracted forms is not attributable to poetic convention. Rather, it seems necessary to assume that *ō* changed to *ā* before shortening. In support of this assumption it may be remarked that this *ō* appears as *a* in Old Frisian, as well, suggesting perhaps an Anglo-Frisian development considerably anterior to the period under study here. The view, at any rate, that the vowel was still *o* when it caused back mutation (see, e.g., Campbell, p. 85, n. 2) is untenable in the light of Ball and Stiles's demonstration that back mutation must postdate the language of Ép. (see above, p. 347, n. 170).

§419. And so the *Beowulf* poet's observance of Kaluza's law establishes a *terminus ad quem* for the composition of the poem because it depends on the preservation of original quantities in final vowels with Indo-European and Germanic broken intonation: after these vowels were shortened, it was no longer possible to observe Kaluza's law in many words. The shortening of these vowels cannot be dated precisely, but it certainly took place at least a generation before the centralization of *-æ* to *-e* began. Thus, if *Beowulf* was composed by a Southerner or a Midlander it might have been made as late as the first quarter of the eighth century—that is, a generation before the regular changes of unstressed vowels in Southumbrian documents begin. A *terminus ad quem* of about a century later is possible for a Northumbrian composition. The latter limitation is corroborated by the limiting observation that the relative dating criteria place *Beowulf* before Cynewulf, who cannot have written

---

pp. 175–232; and Hermann, "Lautveränderungen in der Individuelsprache einer Mundart," *Nachrichten der Gesellschaft der Wissenschaften zu Göttingen*, phil.-hist. Klasse 9 (1929), 195–214.

after about 850; and the metrical differences between the two are sufficient that probably at least a generation should be assumed to have elapsed between them. These of course are the very latest dates afforded by the evidence, and the poem might be earlier. As for a *terminus a quo*, it was demonstrated above (§400) that the linguistic evidence does not rule out a date even before ca. 685, though such an early date is considerably less probable.

§420. In brief, *Beowulf* almost certainly was not composed after ca. 725 if Mercian in origin, or after ca. 825 if Northumbrian. These findings confirm and support the relative chronological evidence that it is one of the earliest poems in English. Whether *Beowulf* is Northumbrian or Mercian in origin cannot be determined with assurance, but what evidence there is suggests that it is Mercian. The most direct evidence is the poet's use of *nemne* 'nisi' (see §361 above). But unlike conclusions for which there is the evidence of a variety of dialect features, a conclusion based on a small number of criteria faces many uncertainties.[80] This is not to say that the evidence of *nemne* is worthless—it does indeed create a higher probability for a Mercian origin than for any other. And the distribution of the word in verse lends further support to the evidence of prose: it occurs only in *Andreas, Guthlac A*, the *Phoenix, Juliana*, the *Seafarer, Maxims I*, the *Riming Poem*, the *Wife's Lament*, and *Beowulf*. Because of their subject, the *Guthlac* poems are almost certainly Mercian (see Sisam, *Studies*, p. 134), and Cynewulf was shown above almost certainly to have been a Mercian, by his rhymes and by the affinities between the language of his verse and *Guthlac B*. The evidence of spirantization in *ah/ach* for *ac* (§353.10 above) suggests a greater probability of a Mercian than a Northumbrian origin for *Andreas*—and this evidence is of a different sort from that of *nemne*, as *ah* clearly is not a poeticism. The Mercian distribution of *nemne* in verse is also supported by the parallel distribution of unconventional Mercian back-mutation of *æ* to *ea*. It was pointed out above (§350) that this development is found in Cynewulf and *Beowulf*, but not in *Genesis A* or the Southern group.[81] Neither does it occur in *Daniel* or *Exodus*: the former has no examples, and the latter only the conventional *beado-* and *heaðo-*.[82] It does,

---

[80]Jordan (*Eigentümlichkeiten*, p. 65), for example, in discussing the evidence of *nemne*, points out that isolated dialect words in verse may be inheritances from archaic times when they were common to all dialects; or, if not structural, they may be attributable to scribal interference.

[81]Again, with regard to *Genesis A* this evidence is merely suggestive, as the back mutation of *æ* is found only in a portion of the West Midlands.

[82]Farrell (p. 15; as noted above, p. 293, n. 57) remarks that *Agæf* (*Daniel* 452a), if not a late development, seems to be a Mercian or Kentish form, and he cites Campbell, §187, in support. Actually *gæf* is found beside *geaf* in Northumbrian (Campbell, §186). Also, Lucas (p. 37) says that *dægsceldes* (79b) is probably Mercian, and cites Campbell, §183; but this section of Campbell's grammar actually refers to developments between

however, occur in both *Guthlac* poems: compare *þeara* (398b; see Campbell, §708, n. 5) and *heafelan* (1270a). These regularities are mirrored in the fact that *nemne* is not found in the biblical narratives of MS Junius 11. Another Mercian feature may be observed in the evidence for Sievers' syncope. In *Beowulf*, this syncope is limited to contract verbs (*gesyhð* 2041b, 2455a, *lyhþ* 1048b) and forms of *cweðan* (*cwið* 2041a, *acwyð* 2046b). Syncopated contract verbs are not uncommon in the orthography of all Old English verse, and they may represent a scribal convention of the koine stemming from the recognition of the distinction between Anglian forms like *weorðeþ*, which clearly were readily comprehensible to Southerners, and forms like *gesi(i)þ* (WS *gesyhþ*), which probably were not so clear. Possibly, however, the practice began because of the appearance of a few familiar, syncopated contract forms in some Anglian verse: for example, *gesihð* is found beside *gesið* in Farman's work in the Rushworth Gospels—such forms perhaps arose in enclisis, as the second person singular forms with *h* occur only when enclitic *-tu* or *þu* follows, and so they may be genuine and old—and therefore such forms might have occurred in some Anglian verse. But the use of *cwið* in *Beowulf* cannot be explained this way. Sievers' syncope is rare in pure Anglian texts (Brunner lists the instances, §358, n. 7), but the syncopated forms are the only ones used to the verb *cweoðan* in VP (six instances of *cwið* and one of *cyð*), and probably in Ru.¹ (*cwiðst* and *cwið* once each).[83] It would be a remarkable coincidence if a scribe Saxonizing an Anglian text, in addition perhaps to a few contract verbs, happened to insert syncopated forms only of the sole verb that is regularly syncopated in the Mercian dialect of the Vespasian Psalter. More likely the Mercian forms were in his exemplar. Again, if *Beowulf* was not composed in a Mercian dialect, any of these features might have been added by copying in a Mercian scriptorium in the course of its manuscript transmission, particularly before the rise of the poetic koine based on West-Saxon standards. But since this is an unwarranted complication of the poem's scribal history, Mercian composition does seem likelier. Thus, although the evidence for a Mercian origin for *Beowulf* is not incontestable, neither is it inconsiderable.

§421. As for *Daniel* and *Exodus*, these should probably be dated after the shortening of final *-æ*, as they do not conform to Kaluza's law. This change again cannot be dated—although an upper limit of ca. 850 can be set for Northumbria, the shortening could have taken place at any time before that, and so no useful *terminus a quo* can be established. Like *Beowulf*, these poems are metrically more conservative than Cynewulf's,

---

*sc* and back vowels. Rather, *sceld* is the proper Northumbrian form, attested twice in the *Durham Ritual*.

[83]For *ait, inquit*, and *dicit, cweþ, cwæþ*, and *cwęþ* are used interchangeably, and they are probably all preterites. Excluded are instances in which enclitic *-tu* or *þu* follows the verb, as these are treated differently in the Anglian dialects: see above, §126.

and so a probable *terminus ad quem* of ca. 825 should also be placed on them. The same reasoning applies to *Genesis A*, as it also probably does not conform to Kaluza's law. But since the relative criteria make it and *Daniel* roughly contemporary with *Beowulf*, these probably cannot be much later than ca. 725 if *Beowulf* is Mercian, and of course they may be earlier than that. This conclusion accords with the observation that *Genesis A* seems to have been composed too early for the poet to have used *nænig* (see above, §148), though the word appears already in *Bede's Death Song*, A.D. 735. Corroborative evidence in this regard may be derived from the facts about contraction upon loss of *h*. It was demonstrated above (§§123ff.) that noncontraction in the Cædmonian group must be an archaism rather than an Anglian innovation: particularly telling is the verse *hæfde wordbeot* (*Genesis A* 2762b), since *-bēot* contains no juncture, and thus cannot have acquired its dissyllabicity by the analogical process that produced forms like *doað* in Anglian prose of the ninth century and later. The effect of this analogical development no doubt was to reverse the previous situation, making contracted forms seem archaic (and thus more poetic), and uncontracted ones innovative, at least in the Anglian dialects. Hence the low incidence of uncontracted forms in Cynewulfian verse. Although the Anglian analogical development cannot be dated with assurance, it seems to have been in progress in the early ninth century, since VP has some analogically decontracted forms, but not consistently. Cædmonian verse therefore seems unlikely to have been composed later than the first half of the ninth century, when VP was glossed, and it may be earlier.

# APPENDIX A:

# CHRONOLOGY AND DIALECT IN THE REMAINING LONGER POEMS

As explained in §71, the test group of poems includes most Old English works of sufficient length to provide creditable evidence for tracing metrical history. This appendix compiles the evidence for all the remaining works greater than four hundred lines in length. These are *Christ and Satan, Christ I* and *III, Guthlac A* and *B*, and the *Phoenix*. The evidence is also presented for *Riddles 1–59* and *61–95* in the Exeter Book, not under the assurance that they are all the work of a single author, but as a test of that hypothesis. They are examined as two groups because that is how they are presented in the manuscript, and thus each group has a better chance of being a single composition than all the riddles combined. Similarly, it is possible that the two parts of the *Phoenix*, the translation and the exegesis, are not by the same poet, and so these data may be used to pursue the question. *Solomon and Saturn* is not included in this appendix, as the two parts are clearly different compositions, and neither approaches four hundred lines in length. Even some of the poems that meet this minimal standard are still too short to yield sufficient chronological data. The metrical Psalms of the Paris Psalter again are metrically too irregular to furnish reliable evidence about metrical variation in Old English, but their dialect features are examined below.

All the texts treated but the first and the last are contained in the Exeter Book, which, it has frequently been pointed out, has some exceptionally regular orthographic features, suggesting scribal normalization in the exemplar, in which most or all of these poems were surely collected already. Sisam (*Studies*, pp. 100–108) lists some of these features. For example, although it is not quite true, as Sisam remarks, that preterite forms of *cuman* contain -*w*- without exception, the counterinstances are very few. Similarly, in preterites and past participles of the second class of weak verbs, the proportion of instances formed with -*ad*- to those with -*od*- and -*ed*- is fairly constant throughout the manuscript. And so it is not to be supposed that all the orthographic features listed below are genuine indicators of dialect in this manuscript: some of these data are offered only for comparative purposes, as supplementary tests of the limits to the reliability of purely orthographic variables. This is particularly true of features like the use of the verb stem *lifg*-. The precise incidence of such features in any given poem is of no significance per se, since such forms are also found in the Southern group of poems. There might be some significance to the frequency with which such forms are encountered, given that the stem *libb*- is never found outside the Southern group; but especially as the scribe is regular in writing *lifg*-, never *lifi*- or *lifig*-, the listing of such forms here is intended merely to chronicle the absence of the Southern equivalent.

The data given on chronological variables such as parasiting and contraction differ widely from those offered by Amos. The reasons may be found in Chapters 1–4. Dialect indicators are examined first, then chronological variables.

### *Christ and Satan*

This poem was copied into the Junius MS by perhaps three scribes, the first writing pp. 213–15 (ll. 1–125), the second pp. 216–28 (ll. 125–709), and the third p. 229 (ll. 710–30)—if the third is not identical to the first, as argued by Barbara Raw, "The Construction of Oxford, Bodleian Library, Junius 11," *ASE* 13 (1984), 187–207, at 189, n. 7. It stands apart from the rest of the longer works, as it shows a particularly heavy incidence of Anglian features, along with such a multitude of hyperurbanisms that the only poems like it in this respect are the *Kentish Hymn* and *Psalm 50* (see §§334 and 335.5). It is also exceptional in that the poem as a whole, and particularly the work of the first scribe, has been very frequently corrected in a contemporary hand, and the purpose of the corrections is clearly to eliminate dialectal features and bring the spelling into conformity with the poetic koine, mainly by changing Anglianisms to Saxonisms. For example, among other changes, in the first hundred lines the corrector has changed *e* in second fronting environments to WS *æ* four times, in *heleð* (47a), *Segdest* (63a), *ðes* (77a), and *nessas* (90a); he has changed Anglian *ē* to *ǣ* three times, in *weron* (23a), *gredige* (32a), and *forleton* (69b); he has changed Anglian *ē* (the front mutation of *ā*) before coronal consonants to *ǣ* five times, in *clene* (18a), *helend-* (54a, 86a), *bedelde* (68a), and *geledde* (88b); he has substituted broken diphthongs for Anglian retracted *a* four times, in *alda* (34a), *swarte* (52a), *gewald* (86b), and *alle* (92a); he has removed the effects of Anglian smoothing twice, in *henne* (17a) and *liht* (68b); he has changed Anglian *ea* to *eo* in *scealdon* (54b); he has changed Anglian *seolfe* to *sylfe* (23a); and he has glossed Anglian *nymðe* (18b), writing *buton* above it.

These examples illustrate not only the variety of Anglian features in the poem, but also their frequency, since those listed are only the ones changed by the corrector in the first hundred lines. More significant than the sheer incidence is the unusual nature of many examples. For instance, although *wald-* and its derivates are considerably more common than *weald-* in verse, and thus clearly represent a conventional spelling of the koine, *eal(l)-*, except in some compounds such as *alwihta* and *alwalda*, is used to the nearly complete exclusion of *al(l)-*. In *Christ and Satan*, however, *al(l)-* appears as a simplex ten times; elsewhere it appears only in *Elene* (645a, 815b), the metrical preface to Wærferth's translation of Gregory's *Dialogues* (13b), and *Instructions for Christians* (198b). Similarly, the poem contains roughly a third of the instances of smoothed forms of *hēh* in verse, as well as one of the two instances of smoothed *þæh*, all three instances of *līht* (n.), and the only instance of *werc*. Back mutation is also very common, and much of it is clearly unconventional, e.g. *spreocan* (78b, as in VP: see Campbell, §210.2), *Neoman* (197a), *beoran* (205a), and *geseotu* (601b). There is also one nonconventional example of the back mutation of *æ* (*eaples* 409b), restricted to the second fronting dialect in prose.

There is evidence of hypercorrection of *ē* to *ǣ* in *hær* (101b), and of *e* to *æ* in *bættran* (49b), the latter possible only in the second fronting dialect. Hypercorrection is also possible in *rægnas* (11b), *-ðægn* (66a), and forms of *ængel* (81b, 94a, 122a); but all of these, though infrequent, are also found in Anglian prose texts (Campbell, §§193d, 328; Sleeth, p. 35). Note that all of these are in the work of the first scribe. The only other dialect feature influenced by the change of scribes is the preterite and participial suffix of weak verbs of the second and third classes: *-ed-* appears occasionally throughout the poem, but otherwise the first scribe has only *-ad-* (eight times: 3a, 29b, 51a, 66b, 75a, 78a, 84b, 102a), and the second almost exclusively *-od-*. Some of the first scribe's examples of *-ad-* are unconventional, e.g. *andsweradan* (51a), which is the only example of the verb in verse with *-ad-*, beside thirty-seven instances in verse with *-od-* or *-ed-*; and *hogade* (84b), the one example of the verb in verse with *-ad-*, beside twenty-five with *-od-*, *-ed-*, or *-d-*. For a more complete list of Anglian phonological features evident in the orthography of the poem (some of which, however, must be disregarded), see Sleeth, pp. 34–48.

Anglian morphological, lexical, and syntactic features are numerous. Occasional West-Saxon forms like *sylfa* appear, but usually the spelling is *seolf-*. Anglian *nymðe* appears six times (18b, 330b, 334b, 349b, 491b, 675), and forms of Anglian *oferhygd* and *oferhycgan* appear eight times (50a, 69a, 113a, 196a, 226a, 250a, 304a, 369a). There is enclisis of *-tu*, a common feature in Anglian prose texts, in *earttu* (57b) and *hafustu* (64b). Anglian pronouns are *ðec* (60b, 537a) and *usic* (254a). Adjective *fæger* has a metrically long first syllable at 79b, 212a, and 387b; it is ambiguous at 307a, 328a, 455a, and 545a. Conjunctive *ac* is spelt *ah* nine times, not counting some instances altered to *ac*, and the verb stem *lifig-* is always spelt thus (284b, 298b, 573a, 677a), never *libb-*. The preterite plural of *sēon* is once *gesegon* (527a), beside four instances of *gesawon*; and there is one instance of *becwom* (178b), beside several of *(be)com*. The Anglian copula *eam* (WS *eom*: see Campbell, §768) appears once (167a); and the subjunctive *seo* (as in Ru.[1], and in Sweet's Surrey charter no. 45, beside other forms) appears five times (212b, 264b, 687b, 703a, 706b). The Anglian form *-end-* of the present participial ending of long-stemmed verbs of the second weak class is found in *(be)gnornende* (52b, 133a) and *reordende* (624; corrected). Unstressed *in* appears more than sixty-five times, though it is rare in *Genesis A* in the same manuscript. The use of the accusative after *mid* is found in verses 60b, 359b, 375a, 611a, and 614b; and substitution of an accusative form would mend the meter at 203b. But a short vowel in *dydon* is required by the meter in *swa oðre dydon* (623b). The plural of *fēond* is spelt *feond* (twice), but in *hu þa blacan feond* (195b), where *blacan* can hardly have a long vowel, the substitution of *feondas* would correct the meter; in the other instance (*Feond seondon reðe* 103b), *Feondas* would also be metrically permissible. The ending of adv. *feolo* (419a) is also an Anglian feature (Campbell, §666). There are no examples of Sievers' syncope required by the meter. The one orthographic example is in a short-stemmed verb, in *þær he sylfa sit* (217a), and this may be Mercian (see §353.12 above). Anglian forms of *habban*, such as *Hafað* (586b), are consistent.

This evidence points to a Mercian dialect. Second fronting of both *æ* and *a* are found in the text, and the spellings *eam* and *seo* of the copula are Mercian (though the latter is also found in the Surrey charter mentioned above). Although the language of the poem in many respects resembles that of VP, there are also some divergences, of a (probably) more northerly character. Loss of final *-n* in *Uta* (216b, 250a), along with MS *wea* (319b) and *werga* (710a), is mainly a Northumbrian feature, but it is also found in Ru.[1]. Retraction of *æ* to *a* before checked *r* is also a Northumbrian feature that is found occasionally in Mercian texts (see Campbell, p. 56, n. 1).

There are three structural examples of parasiting in the poem (6a, 183b, 320a), and three of nonparasiting. But the latter three are dubitable: *mid wuldorcyninge* (223b) and *þær heo mid wuldorcyninge* (311a) perhaps should have acc. *-cyning* after *mid*; and in regard to *and eorðan tudor* (657b) it should be kept in mind that unusual anacrusis appears several times in the poem—cf., just a few verses before this, *and eadige sawla* (651b).

There is no unambiguous evidence relevant to contraction upon loss of intervocalic *h*. The only unambiguous verse relevant to contraction in negated verbs is *þæt awriten nære* (674b).

In regard to Kaluza's law cf. *wloncra winsele* (93a) and *wide geond windsele* (384a). Medially the law is observed in verses 1b (cf. 683b) and 51a, but disregarded in 182a, 316a, 435b, and 683b. At 223b and 311a, again, accusatives after *mid* might be substituted. The rule of the coda is observed in the onset in *Is ðæs walica ham* (99a) and *gearwian us togenes* (286a); it is violated in *reordian and cweðan* (728), which, however, is corrupt, having no off-verse.

Clearly the metrical practice of the poem is not as archaic as that of *Beowulf*, but the evidence is too meager to suggest where it ought to be placed in the chronology.

## *Christ I*

Because of the normalization of the orthography in the Exeter Book, there are few phonological criteria in *Christ I* that are sufficiently unusual to merit remark. Examples of smoothing are fairly conventional, perhaps even in *wideferh* (163a), which is found several times in the Exeter Book. The form *gereht* (133b) is paralleled at *Instructions for Christians* 107b, and in Ælfric; and 1. sg. sj. *slæce* in *Apollonius of Tyre* suggests that *geslæhte* (149a) may be a normal Southern analogical form: see Campbell, §753.9b(1). So also *eld-* (311a) and *ermþ-* (271b) are paralleled in the *Meters of Boethius*, and *æld-* (406a) in *Psalm 50*. For a discussion of other non-Saxon phonological features see Jackson J. Campbell, *The Advent Lyrics of the Exeter Book* (Princeton: Princeton Univ. Press, 1959), pp. 36–42.

Morphological, syntactic, and lexical criteria indicating Anglian origins are numerous. Certain examples of *mid* with the accusative are at 122a, 217b, 237b, 347b, 349a, and 355b. Unstressed *in* is found nearly forty times. Anglian forms of the present participle are *sorgende* (26a) and *geomrende* (90a), beside Southern *efeneardigende* (237a). In the preterite of this class of verbs, *-ed-* appears once, *-od-* five times, and *-ad-* fourteen times. The preterite of *cuman* consistently has *w* (46b, 74b, 148a, 290b, 413b, 420a, 436b), and there is one instance of Anglian *eawed* (55b). There are several examples of *ȳwan* (245a, 257b, 335a), but that at least one is a scribal substitution is suggested by the verse *arfæst ywe* (245a): as Sievers remarks ("Rhythmik," p. 485), an imperative *ȳwe* is improbable, and so the authorial form was probably *ēowa* or *ēawa*. There are ten instances of Anglian pronouns (*ūsic, þec*), and the 1. pl. poss. adjective is never *ūre*, but *ūser* (28a, 261a, 370b, 398b; *ure* 362b is a genitive pronoun). The copula has the 1. sg. form *eam* (167b, 206b), and the 2. sg. pres. and weak pret. inflection of verbs takes the form *-es* (108b, 161b, 240b, 259a, 289b, 290a, beside *-est*, e.g. at 176b, 288a, 408a), which is the normal form in Anglian prose texts. (It is also found in early West-Saxon texts, including the *Meters*, apparently under Mercian influence.)  The verb stem *lifg-* (194b, 231b, 273b, 437a) is used to the exclusion of *libb-*. *In-* is inceptive in forms of *inlīhtan* (43b, 108b, 115a; cf. *Meters* 11.62a, 20.267a, etc.) and *inhebban* (313b, MS *in hebba*). Anglian *nymðe* appears once (324b), beside one instance of conj. *butan* (272a). There are two instances of *gen* (192b, 198b), and two of *giet* (318b, 351a). But the preterite participle of *sēon* is Southern *gesewen* (125a). There are two instances of 1. sg. ind. *hæbbe* (*worde hæbbe* 169b; *Ic to fela hæbbe* 181b), both structural, beside one structural instance of *hafað* in *þe gemynd hafað* (431b; cf. also 256a). So also there is a structural instance of 1. sg. ind. *secge* (197a), beside imp. *saga* (209b). Sievers' syncope never applies. The use of *sunu* (91a) as nominative (vocative) plural is mainly Anglian—see Brunner's examples, §271, n. 2. The considerable variety of Anglian features suggests a Mercian or Northumbrian origin; and *eam* is an exclusively Mercian form. On the other hand, the extension of the ending *-e* to long-stemmed weak imperatives like *gesece* (254a, structurally probable) is known in Northumbrian and West-Saxon, but not Mercian texts (Brunner, §410.3).

Nonparasiting is found in *Næfre wommes tacn* (54b) and *wundurclommum bewriþen* (310a). There is parasiting in *secg searoþoncol* (220a) and *wuldorweorudes* (285a), and two kinship terms in *-r* have syllabic finals (191b, 425b). There are no unambiguous forms relevant to contraction upon loss of *h*. The rule of the coda is generally observed in the onset (see 8a, 83a, 372a, 394a), and disregarded once verse-finally (396a). There are no examples of negative contraction in a verb that are required by the meter, though there is one example with a pronoun, at 189b. Indefinite pronouns are contracted at 189b and 238a, but not at 248b and 343b (the last three are structural). In *feore, eo* is short at 230b and 277b. Kaluza's law is observed internally at 350a, 381b, and 404a, and disregarded finally at 382a. Such as it is, the evidence does not suggest a very late date of composition, nor a very early one, though it is too meager to afford any firm conclusions. Nonlinguistic evidence speaks for the probability of a date between the late eighth century and the middle of the tenth: see Susan Rankin, "The Liturgical Background of the Old English Advent Lyrics: A Reappraisal," in *Learning and Literature*, pp. 317–40, at 333–34.

## Christ III

As with *Christ I*, non-West-Saxon phonological features are mostly conventional, though a few spellings might be due to Anglian origins. Anglian *ē* corresponding to WS *æ* is perhaps not simply a poeticism in *fere* (867a; cf. *afærde* 892a), as this spelling is unusual in verse: Grein lists more than thirty examples of the noun stem *fær-*, and just two others of *fēr-* (*Juliana* 649b, *Exodus* 119a). This interpretation is supported by the blunder at 952a, where the manuscript reads *feore*, though apparently 'fear' is meant: the Anglian spellings of WS *feore* and *fære* would both be *fere*. So also *gefon* (1353b) is perhaps preserved because of confusion with *gefōn*. As the reflex of Gmc. *\*skaldj-* in the Exeter Book is usually *scild-* (cf. *scild-* at *Christ II* 675a, 761a, 775a, 781b, *Guthlac A* 457b, etc.; occasionally *scyld-*), the form *sceldun* (979b) is unusual. It may be Kentish, but it is also paralleled in the phonology of Ru.[1] (see Campbell, §193a). Smoothing is unusual in *brehtme* (881a), which otherwise appears only in *Andreas* (but cf. *berhtm-* at *Daniel* 380a): the spelling is usually *breahtm-* or *bearhtm-*, as in *Genesis A*, *Exodus*, *Beowulf*, *Elene*, *Judith*, *Guthlac A* and *B*, *Riddles*, *Azarias*, the *Phoenix*, the *Wanderer*, *Vainglory*, *Precepts*, and elsewhere in *Christ III* (950b,

1144a). Smoothing is also unusual in *sinnehte* (1542a, 1631a; also a few leaves later in the manuscript at *Guthlac A* 678a; and cf. *sinneahtes* at *Christ I* 117a), which is perhaps best explained under the principle that conservative spelling features are better preserved in compounds than in simplices (see above, §348).

Anglian morphological, syntactic, and lexical features are again more numerous. *Mid* is used with the accusative at 941b, 1489a, and 1664b, and unstressed *in* is used nearly twenty times. Unstressed *fore* appears thirty times. (There are no examples in *Christ I*, and three in *Christ II*.) In the second class of weak verbs, the present participle has -*end*- four times (889b, 992a, 1016b, 1266a), but cf. *sceawianne* (914a)—which, however, may also stand for the uninflected infinitive. In the preterite of these verbs, there are three instances of -*ed*-, six of -*od*-, and twenty-four of -*ad*-. The preterite of *cuman* consistently has *w* (1105b, 1113a, 1160b), and there are two instances of Anglian *ēawan* (955b, 1604a; cf. 894a, 904b, etc.). Anglian accusative pronouns (*mec, þec, ūsic*) are found nine times, and the 1. pers. pl. poss. adjective is *ūser* (1084a, 1313a, 1328a). The copula has the 1. sg. pres. form *beom* (1490b), and the weak pret. 2. sg. desinence is consistently -*es*, more than ten times. The verb stem *lifg*- is frequent (1156a, 1211a, 1326b, 1381b, 1453b), never *libb*-. The first syllable of *fæger* may or may not be long in *on gefean fæger* (912a). Anglian *gēn* appears once (1457b), and the verb *sēon* has the Anglian preterite with -*g*- twice (1127b, 1153a). Except for nonstructural *gesegð* at 1309b, there is no evidence of Sievers' syncope, though there is one instance of Mercian *cwið* (1518a: see above, §353.12). The verb *habban* has 2. and 3. sg. *hafast, hafað* (eight times), and is never syncopated. Forms of *sæ* are consistently masculine (966b, 1144b, 1163b). Thus again there is a considerable body of evidence for Anglian origins, though Northumbrian and Mercian features for the most part cannot be differentiated. Only *cwið* suggests that Mercian is likelier than Northumbrian composition.

Nonparasiting is frequent, and is found in a variety of items of vocabulary, *wuldor*- (1010a, 1079a), *wundor*- (1139a), *tuddor* (1416a), *broþor* (1499b: acc. pl., and so etymologically correct), *facen*- (1565a), *morþor*- (1611b, 1624a), and *ealdor*- (1615a). Parasiting is restricted to *wundor*- (905a) and *tungol*- (1150b); at 1419a, dissyllabic *modor* is etymologically correct. There is perhaps an example of unetymological nonparasiting in *mines eþelrices* (1461a); but the preceding verse will not scan.

Noncontraction with intervocalic *h* is also frequent, in forms of *þrēan* (1023a, 1563a), *onfōn* (1031a), *hēah* (1064b), *fāh* (1082a), *sēon* (1244a, 1270a, 1300b, 1416b, 1580a, 1611b), *þwēan* (1320a), and perhaps also in *wynsum gefea* (1252b), where either the verse has a short second lift or -*sum* is accorded unusual ictus. Contraction occurs in forms of *fāh* (1538a, 1614b, 1632a) and *þrēan* (1320b).

There is structural contraction of the particle *ne* in *næron* (1130b), *nyle* (1199b, as required by the alliteration), and *nysses* (1498b), but not in *þonc ne wisses* (1473b), or in hypermetric *þu þæs þonc ne wisses* (1385b). Nonstructural examples are contracted (e.g. 1015a, 1384b, 1568b, 1573b, 1599b, 1660b). In the indefinite pronouns, there is structural noncontraction in *ac þær æghwæþer* (1576b). Nonstructural examples of noncontraction are at 922b and 1474b.

Compensatory lengthening upon loss of postconsonantal *h* is preserved in *feores frætwe* (1073a), *fira feorum* (1592a), and probably *se þe nu his feore nyle* (1573b). The short vowel is restored in *ond þæs to widan feore* (1343a), *to widan feore* (1543a), and probably *Feores unwyrðe* (1562b). Thus, in general, shortening is found in formulae.

Word-finally in the onset of the verse, Kaluza's law is observed at 1001a, 1011b, 1275b, 1536a, and 1615a. It is violated in *proht peodbealu* (1267a). Internally it is usually observed (886b, 916a, 961a, 1024b, 1055a, 1086a, 1206a, 1368a, 1516a, 1654a), but it is violated four times (906a, 942a, 1513a, 1524b). The rule of the coda is also violated in *singað ond swinsiap* (884a).

These criteria suggest a relatively early date, perhaps in the same period as the "Cædmonian" poems. The archaisms *bifen* (1157b), structurally contracted, beside structurally uncontracted *-fongen* 1183a and *gefengen* 1512a), *forden* (1206a) and *gedenra* (1265b) corroborate the general signs of antiquity.

## Guthlac A

Once again, the Anglian phonological features of *Guthlac A* are few and largely conventional. Anglian back mutation is perhaps not merely poetic in *meodumre* (384a), *breodwiað* (287b), and *wiperbreocum* (294b), though it is analogical in the last instance if it is not Kentish (see Campbell, §210.2). Particularly convincing is *peara* (398b), which is Mercian, not Kentish (Campbell, §708 and n. 5), and which is unique in verse. But if Campbell is right that the form shows shortening of *pāra* in unstressed position, followed by second fronting and back mutation, in this poem this spelling must be considered the result of copying by a Mercian scribe, rather than authorial, as the meter requires *pāra*, with a long vowel. Forms of *giefu* with *eo* in the root (as at 530a) are found throughout the Exeter Book, and appear to be a scribal habit; and at any rate, *geofu* is found in late West Saxon (Campbell, §220). Smoothing might be significant in *sinnehte* (678a: see above, under *Christ III*), *geræhte* (768b), and *(-)ferh* (603a, 671a, 817b). *Beorgsepel* (102a) represents the only instance of Anglian *sepel* in verse, as opposed to numerous instances of *setl*—more than thirty instances of the uncompounded form alone. Jane Roberts provides a thorough discussion of the phonology of the poem in her edition, pp. 63ff.

The morphology, syntax, and vocabulary of the poem conform to a variety of Anglian standards. *Mid* takes the accusative case at 14a, 90b, 303a, 318b, 439b, and 530a, and unstressed *in* appears more than a hundred times. There are sixteen examples of unstressed *fore*. The present participle in the second class of weak verbs has *-end-* twice (232a, 679b). In the preterite of these verbs, there are eight instances of *-ed-*, seven of *-od-*, and thirty-one unambiguous instances of *-ad-*. There is consistently a *w* in the preterite of *cuman* (eleven instances), and there is one instance of Anglian *ēawan* (86a; cf. 143a, 502b). Anglian accusative pronouns (*mec*, *pec*, *ūsic*) appear twenty-nine times, and the 1. pers. pl. poss. adjective is *ūser* rather than *ūre* (401b, 750b, 753b). The copula has the 1. sg. pres. form *eam* once (246a), beside six instances of WS *eom*; and the weak pret. 2. sg. desinence is twice *-es*. The verb stem *libb-* is not found, while *lifg-* appears three times (273a, 460b, 818a). Use of inceptive *in-* is found in *inbryrded* (654a; cf. *onbryrded* at 335a) and *inæled* (668a; cf. *onæled* in B, at 955a). The first syllable of *fæger* is unequivocally long in *Hwylc wæs fægerra* (748b), as well as in *pær he fægran* (382b), where *fēgerran* is required by the meter. Anglian *gēn(a)* is found six times (155a, 233a, 446a, 515b, 521a, 538b), and the verb *sēon* has the Anglian preterite with *-g-* twice (266a, 630b; cf. *gesawe* 468a). There is no structural evidence of Sievers' syncope, though there is one instance of Mercian *cwið* (4a: see above, §353.12). The verb *habban* has 3. sg. *hafað* (three times), and is never syncopated. Anglian *oferhygd* is used three times (269a, 634a, 661a), and Mercian *nemne* once (367b). The nom.-acc. plural of *fēond* is consistently spelt *feondas* (218a, 421a, 748a).

Most of these features may be either Mercian or Northumbrian, but a few are specifically Mercian: *eam* and *nemne* are important in this respect; so is *þeara*, though it is probably not authorial. Of course *cwið* may be Southern as well as Mercian, but since it is the only form subject to Sievers' syncope, it would be a remarkable coincidence if it were not Mercian.

Uncontracted forms with loss of intervocalic *h* are not infrequent (16b, 63a, 252b, 412b, 504b, and probably 301a and 574a), but there are also some clearly contracted ones (73b, 74a, 649a; perhaps 754b). Nonparasiting is found at 86b and 735a; parasited forms are at 304a and 817a; and *broþorsibbe* (804b) has syllabic *-or-*. Unetymological nonparasiting is found in *eþelriehte feor* (216b). The verse *ealdfeonda* (475a), if authentic, is the only example in verse of non-contraction in *fēond, frēond*. For a suggested emendation see Jane Roberts, "A Metrical Examination of the Poems *Guthlac A* and *Guthlac B*," *Proceedings of the Royal Irish Academy*, sec. C, 71 (1971), 91–137, at 96, n. 24.

*Ne* is uncontracted with a following verb at 196b, 246a, 326b, and 355b. Only the first of these is structural. The only relevant indefinite pronoun is uncon-tracted *owiht* (319b). The original long form of the diphthong is required in inflected forms of *feorh* (130b, 291b; probably 13a, 548a) and *mearh* (286a), but not in *feores orwene* (627b), which again is the most formulaic instance of the word among these examples: cf. *Andreas* 1107b and *Fortunes of Men* 40b. The verb *þeowian* has short root vocalism at 69a, 80a, and perhaps 502a, but long at 91b, where the word must belong to the third class of weak verbs. Substitution of forms from the second or third class in the other instances is possible.

Kaluza's law is observed finally in *modcearu mǣgum* (195a), but not in *gyldan gyrnwrǣce* (434a). Internally it is observed in *heofoncyninges* (617b), and perhaps *hyge staþeliað* (66b), but not in *heofoncyninges bibod* (807b). In the onset of the verse, the rule of the coda is always observed, as at 795a and 800a; it is violated in the coda at 156a.

The chronological evidence is not extensive enough for very firm conclu-sions, but what evidence there is largely supports Jane Roberts' view that the poem belongs with *Genesis A, Beowulf, Exodus*, and *Daniel* rather than with the works of Cynewulf: see her edition, p. 70, and also her "Metrical Examination," p. 116. Uncontracted forms predominate, and nonparasiting is found, though the instances of parasited and unparasited forms are too few to afford certainty. But unetymological nonparasiting in *eþelriehte* is a probable sign of relative earliness. The remaining chronological evidence is compatible with this conclusion.

## Guthlac B

Anglian phonological features in the poem are generally inconclusive. Second fronting in *meþel-* (1007a, 1015b, 1219a) is paralleled in a variety of poems, and probably represents a general poeticism. The spelling *-weg* (985a, 991a) for Anglian *wēg*, WS *wǣg*, is perhaps due not to poetic usage, but to confusion with *weg* 'way', as it certainly is elsewhere, e.g. at *Andreas* 1532a. Aside from two instances in the metrical charms, *wærc* (1028a) is the only example of this word in verse that has not been changed to *weorc*. (The form *wærcfæc* in the ASPR concordance is a typographical error.) The spelling *Teagor* (1340b) is unique, and difficult to explain as anything but a genuine dialect form: if *g* were merely orthographic, as in *Heagum* (*Genesis A* 8b), this would leave the back mutation of the root vowel unexplained.

*Mid* is followed by the accusative case at 999b, 1215b, and 1372a, and *in* is unstressed more than forty times. Unstressed *fore* is used five times. There is thus notable variability in the distribution of *in* in the Exeter Book, as *Guthlac A* is half again as long as *Guthlac B*, but has two and a half times the incidence of unstressed *in*; and *Christ III*, which is only a few lines shorter than *Guthlac A*, has one fifth the incidence of unstressed *in*. The present participial ending after long stems in the second class of weak verbs is *-end-* four times (1048b, 1061a, 1209b, 1379b). In the preterite of these verbs there are four instances of *-ed-*, five of *-od-*, and twenty-one unambiguous instances of *-ad-*. The preterite of *cuman* has *-w-* seven times, but cf. *Com* (1141b). There are no instances of Anglian *ēawan*. Anglian accusative pronouns (*mec, þec*) appear just three times. The form *usse* appears at 973b; and *ussera* is required in *sume in urra* (876b). For the verb stem *libb-* appears only *lifg-* (831b, 1099a, 1234a). Anglian *gēna* occurs once (1270b), beside *giet* (1221b). The verb *sēon* has only Southern forms in the preterite (1128a, 1313a). Sievers' syncope is unattested. The verb *habban* has 1. sg. *hafu* (1067b), but also *hæbbe* (1207b; the former is structural and the latter probably so); and *secgan* has 1. sg. *gesecge* (1179a) and imp. *saga* (1192b). These Anglian features are fewer than in *Guthlac A*, and could be either Mercian or Northumbrian in origin. There is no evidence on this score to distinguish the dialect from that of *Guthlac A*, though other considerations, especially sentence structure, suggest stylistic affinities, on the one hand, between *Guthlac A* and the early group including *Beowulf* and the early biblical paraphrases, and on the other between *Guthlac B* and Cynewulfian verse: see A. Rynell, *Parataxis and Hypotaxis as a Criterion of Syntax and Style, Especially in Old English Poetry*, Lunds universitets årsskrift 48 (Lund: Gleerup, 1952), 36. See also Sisam, *Studies*, p. 134.

There is no evidence of etymological nonparasiting in the poem, and considerable evidence of parasiting, in forms of *ādl* (978b, 1064b; but cf. 1008a), *leahtor* (1072a, 1087a), *tācen* (1293a), *bēacen* (1309b), *hlēoþor* (1323a), *bealdor* (1358a), and probably *ēastor-* (1102b). At 1358b, *broþor* is nominative singular, and so is correctly dissyllabic; but *sweostor* (1179b) is dative singular, and so ought etymologically to be monosyllabic. Of all these, the forms of *ādl* are particularly significant, as these are the only examples in verse of parasiting with *l* after a dental consonant, and so these seem particularly late forms. On the other hand, there is unetymological nonparasiting in *from æfenglome* (1291a), a phenomenon found elsewhere only in apparently early verse.

With loss of intervocalic *h*, only contracted forms are found, though they are few (1024a, 1155a, 1168b). The substitution of *frīgea* is possibly required in *ær þu me, frea min* (1222a), but the poem shows verses of the type *Hwæt, þu me, wine min* (1227a), characteristic of late poetry (see §291 above).

*Ne* is uncontracted with a following verb at 1200b and 1221b, where the uncontracted forms are required by the meter; and orthographically at 987b and 1229b. The contracted form is required by the alliteration in *Huru, ic nolde sylf* (1234b). There is a short *eo* in the formulaic *to widan feore* (840a) and in *þeowan* (922a, MS *þeowon*, dat. sg.).

In final position, Kaluza's law is observed at 1219a and 1331b; it is violated internally in *deaðberende gyfl* (850b). The rule of the coda is never violated in the onset; in the coda it is violated at 1172a, 1284a, and 1331a.

The evidence of parasiting suggests a rather late date of composition, especially the parasiting in *ādl*. The evidence of contraction is meager, but it supports this conclusion, as does the appearance of verses like *Hwæt, þu me, wine min* (1227a). The only sign of earliness is the unetymological nonparasiting in *from æfenglome* (1291a). This conclusion is corroborated by Roberts' finding ("Metrical Examination") of considerable differences between the metrics of *Guthlac A* and *B*, and it is compatible with the widespread assumption that the poem is no older than the age of Cynewulf. These findings in fact suggest perhaps a somewhat later date. The internal evidence of the poems, though somewhat vague and debatable, tends to support the distinction in dating between the two *Guthlac* poems, as the former characterizes Guthlac's struggles with the devils as having taken place in recent memory ("Eall þas geeodon in ussera / tida timan" 753–54a), and the latter, clearly based on Felix of Crowland's *Vita sancti Guthlaci*, appeals only to the authority of books ("Us secgað bec / hu Guthlac wearð . . ." 878b–79a). Guthlac died in A.D. 714, from which it may be concluded that the first half of the eighth century is not an unreasonable time for verse with the metrical characteristics of the "Cædmonian" poems to have been composed. Felix's *Vita* is from the middle of the eighth century, as it is dedicated to Ælfwald, king of East Anglia, who died in 749. And so *Guthlac B* is not likely to have been composed before the second half of the eighth century, and may be considerably later.

## The Phoenix

The only very remarkable Anglian feature of the phonology is the unconventional back mutation in *gefreogum* (29b). Perhaps noteworthy also is *gebreadad* (372b, apparently for *gebreodad*), beside *gebredade* (592a), though these are the only attested uses of the verb, and there are no convincing Germanic cognates. N. F. Blake, in his edition, would give these long root vocalism, but in both instances this would produce metrically unacceptable patterns: see *The Phoenix* (Manchester: Manchester Univ. Press, 1964). Blake declines to discuss the Anglian phonological features of the text: see instead Hermann Bauer, *Ueber die Sprache und Mundart der altenglischen Dichtungen Andreas, Gûðlâc, Phönix, hl. Kreuz und Höllenfahrt Christi* (Marburg diss.; Marburg: R. Friedrich, 1890), which, though it is the most complete treatment, contains errors and is not thorough.

    *Mid* takes the accusative case at 483b and 560a, and unstressed *in* appears nearly sixty times. There are two examples of unstressed *fore* (514a, 600a). The present participle of *drūsian* is *drusende* (368a). In the preterite of weak verbs of the second class, there is one certain instance each of *-ed-* and *-od-*, and twenty-seven of *-ad-*. The Anglian verb *ēawan* is attested twice (322b, 334b). The only Anglian accusative pronoun is *ūsic* (630a), but the absence of *mec* and *þec* is not surprising in view of the subject: *mē* and *þē* appear three times all told. The 1. pers. pl. poss. adjective is *ūser* rather than *ūre* (414a, 438a). The verb stem *libb-* is not found, while *lifg-* appears twice (596a, 672a). The first syllable of *fæger* is unequivocally long in four instances (85b, 182b, 232b, 307b), is probably so in one other (125a), and may be so in the remainder. There is one instance of *gin* (236b), probably for *gien*, a hybrid with Saxonization of the root vowel. There is no structural evidence of Sievers' syncope: the form *gecygð* (454b) may as well stand for contracted Anglian *gecēð* (see above, §118). The verb *habban* has 1. sg. *hæbbe* at 1a and 569b, the latter instance being structural; and 3. sg. *hafað* (175a, 667a) is never syncopated. 3. sg. *weseð* (373b) is unique in prose and verse, and so perhaps represents a poetic creation rather than a Southernism (see §353.8 above). Mercian *nemne* appears once (260b). An apparently Mercian feature is the plural *fotas* (311a), in verse paralleled only in the metrical Psalms of the Paris Psalter (121.2.1b, 137.7.3a, 139.5.5a), and in prose only in the Mercian-influenced martyrology fragment edited by Sweet (178.23). Similarly, the plural *toþas* (407b) is paralleled in verse in *Soul and Body II* (114b), in the metrical portion of the Paris Psalter (57.5.1a), and in *Solomon and Saturn I* (114b). In prose it appears only in the Vespasian and Arundel psalters. On *fōtas* and *tōþas* see Sievers, "Rhythmik," pp. 483–84. A remarkable feature of this poem is that inflected forms of *glæd* require a long first syllable: cf. 92a, 289a, 303a, and 593a. Sievers ("Rhythmik," p. 501) points out the rhyme of *glæd* and *blæd* at *Fortunes of Men* 68a. Otherwise, in all other verse where the quantity may be determined, the syllable is short, with instances in *Genesis A*, *Daniel*, *Beowulf*, *Christ III*, *Riddle 24*, and the metrical Psalms of the Paris Psalter. There is no Old English evidence linking this feature to any particular dialect. There is later evidence for a form with a long vowel in parts of the North: e.g., there is the spelling *glaid* in Barbour's *Bruce*, and in the *Cursor Mundi* (beside *glæd* and *gladd*), and Joseph Wright reports the pronunciation "*glēd*" in northeast Scotland: see *The English Dialect Grammar* (Oxford: Clarendon, 1905). Possibly the spelling *glead* in the AB dialect of early Middle English indicates a long vowel, as in *neauere, sea* < OE *næfre, sæ*, etc.; but *ea* here may also represent West Mercian back mutation leveled into the nominative, as in *beað, steaf*, etc., in the same texts. Although Laȝamon rhymes forms of *glæd* with the reflexes of OE *ræd, gelædde*, and *dēad*, his rhymes frequently disregard quantities—e.g., he also rhymes the reflexes of OE *fēt* and *bet, geseah* and *nēah, west* and *ēast, on* and *dōn*, and *bicōm* and *mon*.

Again the evidence suggests a Mercian rather than a Northumbrian provenance. The firmest evidence is *nemne*, though perhaps structural *hæbbe* also tells against Northumbria. The evidence of *fōtas* and *tōþas* is not strong, but also suggests Mercia.

Parasiting is frequent, occurring in forms of *winter* (18b), *tācen* (51b, 254b, 510b, 574a), *wundor* (127b, 359b), and perhaps *hādor* (212b) and *swongor* (315a). Nonparasiting is limited to *fodorþege gefean* (248a). Contraction is also frequent, but limited to forms of *fōn* and its derivatives (143a, 192a, 276a, 433b, 533b). Noncontraction also occurs, in *hea hlifiað* (32a) and *Ðæt is se hea beam* (447a).

In one instance *ne* is uncontracted with a following verb, in *þæt ne wat ænig* (357b), with alliteration on *w*. The diphthong is short in *treowum* (76a) and *cleowenne* (226a).

Kaluza's law is observed finally in *sunbearo lixeð* (33b) and *willsele stymeð* (213b). Internally it is observed in *caldum cylegicelum* (59a), and perhaps *woruld staþelode* (130b), but not in *ond heofoncyninges* (616b). There are no violations of the rule of the coda, but *wrætlice wrixled* (294a; cf. 297a, etc.) shows the same treatment of adverbial *-līce* as in *Maldon* and other late verse.

The most abundant of the chronological indicators is parasiting, which suggests a date no earlier than the time of Cynewulf. The evidence is limited, but the other criteria do not conflict with this conclusion. It may also be remarked that there are no striking differences of distribution with respect to these features between the two parts of the poem, the translation and the exegesis.

Some features in fact may be taken as evidence for unity of authorship, e.g. the frequency of parasiting and the distribution of both *hæbbe* and *hafað* in the two parts, and especially the length of the root syllable in inflected forms of *glæd* throughout the poem.

## The Riddles

There is considerable scholarly disagreement about whether the Old English *Riddles* are the work of a single poet. Unity of authorship of course is difficult to prove, and so it is not surprising that the evidence is not compelling: see the arguments discussed in the edition of Frederick Tupper, Jr., *The Riddles of the Exeter Book* (Boston: Ginn, 1910), pp. lxiii–lxxix. More telling is the counter-evidence. If there is unity of authorship, it is unlikely to encompass all the riddles of the Exeter Book, as *Riddle 30* on fol. 108$^r$ is repeated almost verbatim twelve folios later. The compiler of the Exeter Book or its exemplar, then, seems to have added riddles to the collection as they became available (as Sisam argues, *Studies*, p. 97)—an assumption that derives support from the insertion of several lyrics after *Riddle 59*. Thus, although the thirty-five riddles at the end could be the work of the poet who composed the first fifty-nine (if they are themselves the work of a single poet), the circumstance that the compiler probably did not find them in the same source suggests otherwise.

Certain differences of tone and subject within the collection also suggest diverse origins. For example, it has often been remarked that the "storm" riddles (the first three) are marked by an elevated style and heroic diction that set them apart from the others, even to the extent that the pretext of the genre, the riddle game itself, seems subordinated to a larger rhetorical purpose: see Tupper, p. lxvi, and see the edition of Craig Williamson, *The Old English Riddles of the Exeter Book* (Chapel Hill: Univ. of North Carolina Press, 1977), who regards the first three as a single riddle. Similarly, the lofty tone, the series of paradoxes, and the very length of *Riddle 40*, translated from Aldhelm's "creatura" riddle, set it apart from the more mundane verses surrounding it—elements inherent perhaps in the Latin, but suggesting that the position of this riddle is better explicable as the choice of a compiler than of a poet making and shaping a collection. Katherine O'Brien O'Keeffe has argued that this translation was made from the copy of Aldhelm's "creatura" riddle in a manuscript in the Bodleian Library, and that the translation depends upon certain corrections in the Bodleian manuscript that were made in the early tenth century: see "The Text of Aldhelm's *Enigma* No. C in Oxford, Bodleian Library, Rawlinson C. 697 and Exeter Riddle 40," *ASE* 14 (1985), 61–73. Regardless of whether or not this is correct, there is certainly a degree of probability that *Riddle 40* is not an early composition, since it translates a version of the "creatura" riddle in which lines 61–67 of the Latin text have been moved, appearing between lines 43 and 44—a displacement known only in a family of continental manuscripts, none of which is earlier than the ninth century. This probability tells against unity of authorship, as the original of *Riddle 35* is probably older than the ninth century. In the main it represents the same text as the *Leiden Riddle*, the language of which, however late the continental manuscript itself might be, represents an historical stage of the Northumbrian dialect anterior to that of the early ninth-century *Liber Vitae Dunelmensis*. For example, the *Leiden Riddle* has both *a* and *o* before nasal consonants (*ouana* 8a, *uong* 1a), preservation of

WGmc. *iu* (*fliusum* 3b, *niudlicae* 14b), and possibly *æ* as the mutation of *a* before nasal consonants (*cæn[.]æ* 2b; but cf. Malcolm Parkes in *ASE* 1 [1972], 208–10), while the *Liber Vitae* has almost exclusively *o*, *eo*, and *e*, respectively. In comparison to the early texts of *Cædmon's Hymn*, the *Leiden Riddle* is in some respects more conservative in regard to unstressed vocalism, e.g. with preservation of final *-æ* in *cæn[.]æ* (2b), *innaðae* (2a), *biuorthæ* (3a), *ueflæ* (5a), and *hafæ* (5b), beside *hrofe* (6a) in the Moore version of *Cædmon's Hymn*. In other respects the riddle is less conservative, e.g. in regard to *aerest* (2b) beside *-ist* in both the Moore and Leningrad versions of the hymn, and perhaps *hrutendu* (7a), if Parkes's reading with *-o* is correct. Perhaps most important, the riddle contains an example of *b* for later final *f* (*ob* 14b), a feature that Sievers has shown to have disappeared in final position well before the end of the eighth century, and to occur rarely in medial position for a short time after that (see §400 above). These considerations suggest that the language of the *Leiden Riddle* should not be dated later than the eighth century: see A. H. Smith, *Three Northumbrian Poems* (London: Methuen, 1933), p. 37. This is probably too early for *Riddle 40* to have been composed at the same time. *Riddle 23* very likely also is to be dated no later than the eighth century, as the solution offered in the first line (*Agof is min noma eft onhwyrfed*) demands the assumption that *agof* stands for earlier *agob*, i.e. *boga*: see Sievers, ibid., p. 15. Tupper (p. lvii) mistakes Sievers' point, and Williamson, oddly, first rejects it (pp. 5–6), then concedes it: "Still it does seem likely that the mistake arose because some scribe at some point was copying an exemplar containing riddles or poems in which the spelling *b* for voiced *f* was common and had to be changed to accord with the scribe's own usage" (p. 205). Similarly, the final *-æ* of the runic solution HIGORÆ to *Riddle 24*, unless it is a Northumbrianism, suggests a date earlier than the ninth century. None of this evidence is conclusive, but if some of the riddles are not early, it is an extraordinary accident that so many of the structural features suggest that they are.

The internal linguistic evidence to a small degree also suggests diverse origins. There are some Northumbrian dialect features, one of which is *ehtuwe* (36.4a: see Brunner, §235); but the Mercian and Kentish forms are unattested. Possibly the *Leiden Riddle* is translated from another Old English dialect, but more likely *Riddle 35* should be regarded as Northumbrian in origin. In any case there is one piece of evidence that *Riddle 35* is based on a Northumbrian or archaic original, as the spelling of the adverb *ærist* (2b) is unique in verse, beside more than a hundred instances of *ærest*. *Riddle 35* also has 1. sg. *hafu* (also at 40.98a), though *hæbbe* is common in the collection (see below). Conjunctive *nymþe* is found six times (five of the six in *Riddles 1–59*), and never Mercian *nemne*. So also Mercian *eam* is missing, though there are four instances of *bēom* (all in *1–59*, beside *beo* 23.7b). Runic HIGORÆ, as above, if it is not simply archaic, must also be a Northumbrianism; and *wræce* (1.2b, 20.18a; Brunner, §391, n. 5), apparently a present subjunctive, along with *geonge* (21.2b: Campbell, §173; cf. Klaeber, p. lxxix, §13.5) appear to be. On the other hand, 1. sg. ind. *(on)hæbbe* appears eight times, and this form is not Northumbrian, unless such a form was in use in the North in the early period, for which there is no evidence. Just possibly the one structural instance (*heafod hæbbe* 81.2a) is of the rare metrical type represented by *Hreðel cyning* (*Beowulf* 2430b); but as *hafu* appears to be an acceptable form in the koine, there is not much motivation for it to have been changed to *hæbbe* here. So also runic COFOAH, i.e.

*haofoc*, is perhaps best understood as showing an archaic attempt to represent the West Mercian back mutation of *æ*: cf. the earliest representations of the reflex of Gmc. *au* as *aeo* (Campbell, §275); but cf. also Sievers, ibid., pp. 18–19. Eric Stanley's idea that *aeo* represents scribal experiment rather than actual pronunciation, even if it is correct, does not alter the probability that *aeo* is an early attempt to represent the diphthong *ea*: see "Problems in Early Northumbrian Phonology," in *Luick Revisited*, pp. 311–34, at 316–17. The forms *swa þeana* (58.13b) and *seþeana* (88.7b) are paralleled only in the almost certainly East Anglian *Guthlac A* (110b, 409b). The spelling *heasewe* (40.61b), if not simply a poeticism, is Mercian. MS *wær* (46.1a), *wægas* (51.6b), and *wæg* (53.8b), if original, are probably Mercian rather than Northumbrian (Campbell, §328; cf. one instance of *wæg* in Li.), though they might also render Northumbrian *wær* and *wæg*. Certainly all the most secure evidence is for a Northumbrian provenance for the riddles, but these possibly Mercian features contribute to the uncertainty about the unity of origins.

Even if the riddles are of diverse origins, undoubtedly small groups of them stem from a single source. The best evidence for this is the use of formulae in series. For example, the formula *ic eom wunderlicu wiht* initiates nos. 18, 20, 24, and 25; and this is varied with *ic eom wrætlic wiht* at 23.2a, and *Da cwom wundorlicu wiht* at 29.7a. It appears in no other riddle. This small group, then, is very likely by a single poet. For lists of other formulae see Tupper, p. lxv. The unified origin of the first three riddles is suggested by the evidence of Kaluza's law. As in most Old English verse, the evidence for Kaluza's law is sparse in the riddles—except in the first three, where there are four verses that conform (1.5b, 2.5a, 3.8b, 3.71a), and two violations (3.26a, 3.37a). The verses that conform are all of the type *folcsalo bærne*, and the violations are both of the type *stealc stanhleoþu*, reminiscent of *steap stanhliðo* (*Beowulf* 1409a). In the remainder of the riddles there are just two unambiguous verses relevant to Kaluza's law in final position (23.9a, 40.2a; to which cf. 38.2a; 23.14a is emended). The Beowulfian proportions of the incidence in the first three riddles corroborate the stylistic impression, mentioned above, that these form a unified group, separate from the remainder.

On the other hand, the remaining dialectal evidence suggests that all the riddles are Anglian in origin. And the chronological evidence tends to the conclusion that most or all are relatively conservative in their metrical features, in a fairly uniform manner. The evidence may be summarized as follows.

### RIDDLES 1–59

The riddles are no exception to the rule of normalized orthography in the Exeter Book. One Anglian spelling is perhaps preserved in two places because obscured by scribal error: for MS *sweon leorum*, nearly all editors read *swe on hleorum* (15.4a); and for MS *snearlice*, all editors read *sue, swe*, or *swa arlice* (9.6a). There is Anglian back mutation in a compound in -*hleoþ*- (27.2b, 57.2a), and an unusual instance in a simplex is *heasewe* (40.61b). Unusual examples of smoothing are *bæg* (4.8a), *eh* (22.11a), and *ehtuwe* (36.4). The last form is fairly convincing, as it is a form that was perhaps unfamiliar to West-Saxon scribes, and yet one that was required by the meter, which would have been spoilt by the substition of WS *eahta*. 1. sg. opt. *sy* 'see' (40.65a) is probably to be explained as replacing *sīe*, the Anglian form (see Brunner, §374, nn. 2–6), as opposed to WS *sēo*. The context is such that the verb might be mistaken for 'be', as in fact Holthausen would have it: see his review of W. S. Mackie, *The Exeter Book, Part II*, in *Anglia Beiblatt* 46 (1935), 5–10, at 9. Just possibly runic AGEW (19.6a) for *wiga* is a relic example of *a*-mutation, a process that must at one time have been more widespread, and that was reversed in order to reduce paradigm allomorphy: for other possible examples see Otto Ritter, *Vermischte Beiträge zur englischen Sprachgeschichte* (Halle: Niemeyer, 1922), pp. 173–76. But such a form cannot be associated with any particular dialect. For other phonological features of interest in the *Riddles*, see Moritz Trautmann, "Sprache und Versbau der altenglischen Rätsel," *Anglia* 38, n.s. 26 (1914), 355–64, at 355–57, and August Madert, *Die Sprache der altenglischen Rätsel des Exeterbuchs und die Cynewulffrage* (Marburg diss.; Marburg: Heinrich Bauer, 1900), pp. 126ff. Few of Trautmann's and Madert's dialect indicators are reliable.

Several morphological, syntactic, and lexical features may be added to those mentioned above. There are no unequivocal instances of the use of the accusative case with *mid*, and no examples of unstressed *fore*. Unstressed *in* appears twenty-five times. There are two probable instances of *-end-* in the present participle of the second class of weak verbs (3.47a, 8.9b). In the preterite of these verbs, there are six unambiguous instances of *-ed-*, six of *-od-*, and fourteen of *-ad-*. The preterite of *cuman* is consistently spelt with *w*, in five instances all told. Possessive *ūser* is found once, in the formula *waldend user* (40.89b). The verb stem *libb-* does not occur, while *lifg-* appears six times (10.9a, 12.14a, 28.9a, 39.22a, 40.64b, 41.6b). The first syllable of *fæger* is unequivocally long in *fæger hleopor* (31.17b). Anglian *gēn* (also *gena, geno, gien*) is found five times (9.2b, 20.25b, 20.29a, 40.58b, 49.8b). There is no evidence of Sievers' syncope (the alliteration shows 40.5b to be corrupt), except in contract verbs: cf. *tyhð* (34.4b), and see the discussion of syncope in contract verbs below, in the discussion of the metrical portion of the Paris Psalter. The verb *habban* has 3. sg. *hafað* (eleven instances), and there are also eleven instances of imperative *saga*. Beside the usual 1. sg. pres. ending *-e* there is one instance of Anglian *-o* in a verb other than *habban* (15.28a), and one of *-a* (MS, 3.8a). The latter does occur rarely in Anglian texts, but it is perhaps better understandable as due to the copyist's confusion of *u* and open *a* in an exemplar written in Anglian or archaic pointed minuscule. To *willan* there is the preterite *walde* (29.5a), a spelling that is standard in most Anglian texts, and almost unknown in pure West-Saxon ones. The form *eðþa* (43.16a) is not confined to Northumbrian (cf. *aeththa* at *Bede's Death Song* 4b), as it occurs twice in Ru.[1] (Mt. 5:17, 5:18). But it probably at least represents a more northerly dialect than that of VP, and it is certainly unique in verse, tending to support some of the more unusual dialectal features of these riddles.

Both parasited and nonparasited forms are common: there are seven unambiguous examples of the former, in forms of *þoncol* (2.12b), *wundor* (29.1b, 31.5b, 40.85b), *hlēopor* (31.17b), *hungor* (43.3a), and *tācen* (59.10a). Nonparasiting is more varied and frequent, with eleven examples, in forms of *wæpn* (3.58b), *wolcn* (3.71a), *winter* (4.7a; but the following verse is corrupt), *wunder* (18.1a, 20.1a, 25.1a, 29.7a, all examples of a formula), *hlēopor* (24.5a), *sundor* (39.3b, 39.5b), and *tācen* (55.5a). The kinship terms in *-r* are frequent, and sometimes the etymologically monosyllabic forms are dissyllabic, as at 31.22b, 40.45b, and 43.14a. There appears to be unetymological nonparasiting in *þurh dune þyrel* (15.21b); but as the manuscript reads *dum* rather than *dune*, other emendations are possible, e.g. *duruþyrel* and *dunþyrel* (see Williamson, p. 177). On *þyrel* cf. the discussion of *Riddles 61–95* below.

There is one example of contraction upon loss of intervocalic *h* (*geþeon þrymme* 40.91a)—perhaps significantly, in the riddle that O'Keeffe argues must be late. Noncontraction, on the other hand, is very common, in forms of *hēah* (1.10b, 3.24a, 7.4b, 22.7b, 22.19a), *nēah* (3.64b), *sēon* (5.3b), *þēon* 'press, urge' (12.8b, 21.5b), *tēon* (34.4b), *bifōn* (40.52a), *þēoh* (44.1b), and *wrēon* (50.5a). The verse *farende flan* (3.57a) should also be remarked.

There is one structural example of noncontraction of *ne* with a following verb, in *Stælgiest ne wæs* (47.5b). But nonstructural examples are frequent, at 9.2b, 13.5b, 35.3a, 36.9b, 39.10a, 39.16a, 39.18a, 39.27a, 43.10b, and 49.9a; also 40.98a, on which see Williamson, p. 274. There are no structural examples of contraction in this type, and even nonstructural examples are relatively infrequent (3.6b, 15.16b, 27.14b, 32.5a, 40.68a, 40.86a). In the indefinite pronouns there is noncontraction in *nowiht* (11.5b) and *æghwæðres* (46.5b), and the contraction in *ægþer twega* (39.11b) may be merely orthographic, under the rule of the coda.

The diphthong in *feore* is long at 23.14b and 40.65b, and probably in *on bonan feore* (20.18b) and *ofer mere feolan* (22.5b), as the verse type with a short second full lift after a resolved lift (see above, §249) is exceedingly rare, with just two examples in *Beowulf* (2096b, 2796b; on 2803b see Pope, p. 357). The diphthong is short in *þeowige* (12.15b).

On Kaluza's law in final position, see above. Internally it is observed at 8.11a, 13.10a, 39.6a, and 40.20b. A possible violation is *neahbuendum nyt* (25.2a), if *-bu-* is short, and if this does not stand for *-būndum* (see Campbell, §236.1, and cf. *Beowulf* 117b). There are some striking exceptions to the rule of the coda, of the sort *wrætlice twa* (42.1b; cf. 33.1b) and *wrætlicu wyrd* (47.2a). This is another feature linking the riddles with the earliest narrative verse (see §§221ff. above). Another such feature perhaps is the relative frequency of verses with the unusual metrical pattern of *lagoflod on lyfte* (58.12a; cf. Bliss's types 1A*3 and 1A*4); cf. also the metrically peculiar *eam ond nefa* (46.6a), parallel to *eam his nefan* (*Beowulf* 881a; see §210 above). The riddles resemble *Beowulf* and the older verse in MS Junius 11 in that they, too, contain examples of *frēa* where the meter demands *frīgea* (3.66b, and probably 6.5a). The metrical treatment in *ne eagena* (39.11a) is also peculiar; perhaps it is analogical to *ful cyrtenu* (25.6a), a type discussed above (§192). Finally, *Riddle 40* is exceptional in its treatment of the adverb suffix *-līce*: cf. *þæt mec bealdlice mæg* (40.16b) and *þæt swa fromlice mæg* (40.69a; but cf. 40.85a).

Given the reasons offered above to doubt the unity of the collection, it is remarkable how uniform these features are in their indication of a particular date and dialect. The riddles seem close in date to *Beowulf* and the early biblical narratives, by the frequency of nonparasiting and noncontraction, the incidence of noncontraction of *ne* with *is, willan*, etc. (though this again may be a Northumbrian dialect feature), the treatment of adj. *-lic-*, and the other, minor features listed in the preceding paragraph. It is remarkable, too, that *Riddle 40*, the one riddle that can be shown probably to be a relatively late composition, stands out from the collection in a variety of linguistic as well as stylistic ways. It is mentioned exceptionally frequently in the data above on innovative forms, containing one of the seven examples of parasiting, the only example of contraction, one third of the orthographic instances of negative contraction, and peculiar treatment of the adverb suffix *-līce*. It also contains the only exception to Kaluza's law in the onset of the verse (40.2a), and the only spelling *deagol* (40.39a) in the Exeter Book, or anywhere in verse: elsewhere the manuscript has only *deg-* (six times, twice in the other riddles) and *dyg-* (five times). The circumstance that the poem retains some of Aldhelm's classical allusions (*Ulcanus* 40.56a, *zefferus* 40.68a; cf. also *pernex* 40.66b) perhaps also suggests a relatively late date of composition: an audience that required a translation of Aldhelm's riddle, but still understood such allusions, is less likely to have been an early one. Cf. how classical allusions tend to be reduced in Old English verse translations, e.g. in *Juliana* and the *Phoenix*. These idiosyncratic features tend to support O'Keeffe's argument for the relatively late composition of *Riddle 40*, though the dialect evidence still indicates Anglian origins. Perhaps it is a Mercian composition (cf. *heasewe* 40.61b).

## RIDDLES 61–95

There is unusual smoothing in *pæh* (72.9b), if this is a transfer to the second class. Front mutation is found in *tridep* (84.30b) and *wifeð* (84.33a), forms that are perhaps best explained as Mercian, since in that dialect this mutation is thus limited to verbs with *e* in the root (Campbell, §733a); but cf. *Meters* 20.276a.

Again, there are no unequivocal instances of the use of the accusative case with *mid*, and no examples of unstressed *fore*. Unstressed *in* appears four times. In the preterite of weak verbs of the second class, there are no unambiguous instances of *-ed-*, three of *-od-*, and nineteen of *-ad-*. The preterite of *cuman* is spelt twice with *w* (65.2a, 86.1a), once without (93.18b). The verb stem *libb-* does not occur, while *lifg-* appears twice (67.11b, 85.6b). The Anglian spelling *eawunga* (73.25a) appears once, and the noun *sæ* is masculine (66.3b). Anglian *mec* occurs twenty-five times. There is no evidence of Sievers' syncope, except in contract verbs: cf. *tyhð* (62.6b). The verb *habban* has 3. sg. *hafað* (four instances), and there are six instances of imperative *saga*. See also the features listed above under the general heading.

There is no parasiting. Nonparasiting occurs in forms of *wolcn* (73.2a), *wuldor* (84.25b), *wundor* (87.1a, 88.19a), and *wæpn* (92.5a); and there is unetymological nonparasiting in *his ellen cyðde* (88.27b). In *on þyrelwombne* (81.11a), *on* is not in the manuscript; but the emendation seems possible, as there appears to be unetymological nonparasiting in *þurh þyrel þearle* (72.9a). *Þyrel* scans correctly at 91.5b, and in the first part of the collection at 44.2b.

There is perhaps one example of contraction upon loss of intervocalic *h*, in *hwilum ut tyhð* (62.6b, with alliteration on *h*). But cf. the following off-verse, *hwilum eft fareð*, with vocalic alliteration: if *hwilum* may be stressed in one instance and not the other, presumably the adverb may be, as well. Noncontraction is metrically confirmed in *se mec on þyð* (62.5a), *fægre onþeon* (63.2a), and at 63.6b, where we should doubtless read *fingrum þyð*.

*Ne* is contracted with a following verb at 85.1a and 88.20b, but not at 88.23a, where the alliteration confirms the noncontraction. At 88.27a, contracted *awþer* is not structural. The diphthong is probably long in *on wigan feore* (93.22a).

Kaluza's law is observed internally in *peodcyninges* (67.1b). Violations of the rule like those in the first fifty-nine riddles are encountered in *wrætlice wiht* (67.2a) and *eardian sceal* (88.24b). Also as in the first group of riddles, there are heavy verses of the sort *clængeorn bið ond cystig* (84.27a; see also 87.3a).

Although there are perhaps no distinctive features of sufficient weight to guide opinion on the original dialect and date of composition for this group, the last two features mentioned suggest unity of origins with the first fifty-nine riddles, as does the prevalence of early chronological features (small as the evidence is), especially nonparasiting and noncontraction. Once again, in view of the variety of reasons offered to suppose that this collection was gathered from diverse sources, it is remarkable how uniform the metrical and dialectal features are.

### The Metrical Psalms of the Paris Psalter

The Psalms display a variety of metrical faults. Many verses contain too few syllables to fill four metrical positions, or too many stressed syllables, or unstressed syllables distributed in unusual ways. Many lack alliteration; others show stress on normally unstressed words. These metrical peculiarities are studied in detail by Benno Tschischwitz, *Die Metrik der angelsächsichen Psalmen-übersetzung* (Greifswald diss.; Breslau: H. Fleischmann, 1908); see also Bartlett, pp. 41–49, and Patricia Bethel, "Anacrusis in the Psalms of the Paris Psalter," *NM* 89 (1988), 33–43. Tschischwitz attempts to isolate the commonest sorts of metrical divergences, and to rely on only the surest metrical types, when identifying features like contraction and parasiting. Doubtless, certain examples of these features are very probable (especially in the off-verse, where three-position verses are rare), e.g. in the verses *wuldor stande* (61.12.2b), *drihten, tacen* (85.16.1b), and *ure winter* (89.10.1b). But it is easier to prove the existence of parasited forms by this means than the more archaic forms, and so especially for this reason, a precise count is of little practical value. It can instead be said simply that when the standards of classical verse are applied, innovative forms considerably outnumber archaic ones. Under classical standards, nonparasiting should be expected in *syndon wundorlice* (65.2.2a), *Wærun wuldurlice wið þe* (86.2.1a; but this is hardly a classical pattern), *his fægere wundor* (95.3.2b), and a few others. By contrast, there are dozens of examples of parasiting, if classical standards are applied. Similarly, we should expect noncontraction in *se hehsta* (65.3.5a; also 90.1.2a, 91.1.3a, etc.), *weorðeþ on heagum* (72.9.2b), *heahesta bist* (91.7.2a), and a few others. But examples of contraction under classical standards again number in the dozens, and since noncontraction seems to be limited to forms of *hēah*, the uncontracted forms perhaps represent such a late development as Pope describes (§106 above). All in all, the impression that an examination of metrical chronological features creates is that the Psalms are a very late composition, as one probably should expect from their degenerate metrics. The one possible exception is in the treatment of indefinite pronouns, which are almost always orthographically uncontracted. But this regularity is created largely by a single word, *(n)āwiht/ōwiht*, which has an enormous incidence. Additional metrical evidence of lateness may be derived from the frequency of verses like *Forðam me on sah* (54.3.1a) and *forðon þu me god eart* (58.9.2a), which are very common: see §291 above.

References to verses with parasiting, contraction, and such may be found in Tschischwitz' dissertation, pp. 98ff. Since precise statistics for chronological comparison with other poems are not obtainable, only dialect features will be listed here. This survey should be of value, as there is disagreement about the original dialect of these Psalms, some regarding them as Anglian, others as

Alfredian West-Saxon. The survey will be limited mainly to the first half of the work (to 102.17.2b), as this will be sufficient to demonstrate the generally Anglian, probably Mercian nature of the composition. Since certain Anglian features are rare, or missing altogether, it may be asked whether the remaining instances were added by a poet with limited skill at the poetic koine, or whether they are the remnants left by a revisor who Saxonized an Anglian original. The Psalms provide fairly secure evidence of the latter development, and so they are of some importance in establishing the Anglian, rather than conventional, nature of these dialect criteria in other poems. As mentioned above (§369), the plural of *feond* provides some evidence. *Feond/fynd* and *feondas* occur frequently, and in about equal numbers—there are nearly thirty examples in the first half alone. Yet in most instances in which it appears, the spelling *feondas* is required by the meter (e.g. *feondas mine* 55.2.1b), while in most instances in which *feond* or *fynd* appears, either spelling would be metrically acceptable (e.g. *fynd onfeohtað* 55.1.3a). Tschischwitz lists the exceptions (pp. 102–3), e.g. *hwær fynd mine* (91.10.2a), though they are not so numerous that they could not be explained as due to faulty metrics—cf., in the same psalm, *þe hiom yldo gebidan* (91.13.2a), and many others like it. This distribution is most readily explicable under the assumption that a revisor, who Saxonized the spelling throughout, was aware of the meter, and left metrically requisite Anglian forms unaltered. A more telling example of the same sort of evidence is the treatment of Sievers' syncope. Verbs are rarely syncopated, and the few exceptions generally conform to a pattern. In two instances, substitution of an unsyncopated form would improve the meter, by classical standards: cf. *oððe swa weorð man* (77.65.3a, with alliteration on *w*) and *eall þæt on wege færð* (79.12.2b). In regard to the former instance, however, it should also be observed that the late metrical type is found frequently in these Psalms, and the syncopated verb is paralleled by *gewyrð* in Farman's work in the Rushworth Gospels. At another place, *me anum gehyrst* (80.9.1b), the alliteration demands unstressed *me*, and this is an offense against Kuhn's first law. Rather, *me* should be put into the on-verse, *Gif þu, Israhel*: cf. all the remaining instances of uninflected *Israhel*, in *gif þu, Israhel, a wylt* (80.8.1a), *ne me Israhel behealdan* (80.11.3a), *þær Israhel becwom* (104.19.1a), and *sibb ofer Israhel* (127.7.2b). The revisor apparently made the same error as Krapp, and thus believed that the meter demanded a syncopated form for the unsyncopated one in his exemplar. In one other instance, in *þe on worulde næfð* (71.12.3b) an unsyncopated form would do as well. But the majority of the orthographically unsyncopated verbs in the text are contract verbs, as in *and his handa ðwehð* (57.9.3a; cf. also 58.4.3a, 63.4.4b, 74.7.3b, 79.5.3a). As contraction upon loss of intervocalic *h* is the rule in this text (with the exception of forms of *hēah*), the substitution of Southern forms makes no metrical difference in these instances, though it would make a difference in other sorts of verbs. But cf. the discussion of syncopated forms in *Beowulf*, §420 above. The only remaining exceptions are two forms of *cweðan*, which is syncopated in VP and Ru.[1] (also discussed in §420). The pattern of syncopations thus corroborates the assumption that a revisor who paid attention to the meter Saxonized this text, changing Anglian forms only when the meter was not thereby disrupted. Support for this conclusion may also be derived from some of the other dialect criteria listed below. It may be noted that the Saxonizer was not the scribe of the Paris Psalter, since this text and the nearly identical version of Psalms 90.16–95.2 in Eadwine's Canterbury Psalter derive from a common source: see Peter J. Baker,

"A Little-Known Variant Text of the Old English Metrical Psalms," *Speculum* 59 (1984), 263–81, at 270–71. Cf. also the fragments of the same text in Bodelian MS Junius 121 (ASPR 6:80–86).

The peculiar orthographic features are primarily late rather than specifically Anglian, but a few unusual forms appear that are best explained as Anglianisms. The most important is the unconventional back mutation in *geniomað* (67.16.2b) and *-neomend* (118.63.1a) and, perhaps less significantly, in *wealan* (61.11.1a), for *weolan*. Particularly telling is the Mercian back mutation in *-wearas* (71.9.1a), the form used also in VP. There appears to be second fronting in *þet* (83.1.3b, the only instance in verse), though scribal error cannot be ruled out. For other phonological features see Bartlett, pp. 10–14.

In the first half of the work, a non-Anglian feature is the use of *mid*, which is very frequent, but which never takes the accusative case. Although this is a structural feature, the absence of the accusative after *mid* does not prove that the poet never used the construction, as it is possible that all the accusatives have been changed to datives, especially given the metrical uncertainties of the work. But this seems unlikely, as the number of verses involved is large. Unstressed *in* is relatively rare, appearing only at 59.8.3a, 77.31.1a, 77.43.3a, and 82.6.1b. In all but one of these instances, *in* precedes a foreign, biblical place-name: probably the whole phrase, e.g. *in Idumea*, is taken ultimately from the Latin. In another place, evidence that *on* replaces *in* may be derived from the verse *þeah þe ic on me ingcan* (72.11.2a, though *me* is not in the manuscript), which Sisam (*Studies*, p. 36, n. 1) explains as due to the scribe's normalizing *in* to *on* in *þeah þe ic in ingcan*, the last two words resulting from the obliteration of *t* between them, i.e. *intingcan*, translating *causa* in *sine causa justificavi cor meum*. Similarly, Krapp is no doubt right that MS *hi* is a corruption of *in* at 78.2.2a. There are six examples of unstressed *fore* as a preposition (51.6.1a, 68.22.1a, 79.2.2a, 87.1.3a, 87.13.4a, 100.3.1a). The present participle of *gnornian* is *gnornendra* at 78.11.3b. In the preterite and past participle of weak verbs of the second class, there are nine unambiguous instances of *-ed-*, eleven of *-od-*, five of *-ud-*, and fifty-five of *-ad-*. In the first half there are no instances of the Anglian verb *ēawan*; but cf. 149.7.2b. Though there are hundreds of instances of the pronouns *mē* and *þē*, there are none of *mec* and *þec*; but *ūsic* is found three times (63.4.4b, 64.3.1b, 89.19.3b). In all three instances the dissyllabic form is required by the meter, under classical standards; and so, since *mē* and *þē* are metrically indistinguishable from *mec* and *þec*, this distribution is again compatible with the assumption that a revisor was at work who retained certain Anglian forms only when they were metrically necessary. As in other presumably late verse (see §353.9 above), the possessive adjective *ūre* is commoner than *ūser*, which appears mostly in formulae, e.g. *drihten user* (59.1.1b, 64.1.1b, etc.). In the one instance in which there is a decisive metrical difference between the two, the Anglian form is required. This is in *usserne god* (98.5.2a). In another instance, *Hebbað urne god* (98.10.1a, with alliteration on *h*) is not a metrical type found in classical verse, where type 1D*5 takes double alliteration (twenty-three instances in *Beowulf*). But more likely *urne* is unstressed: cf. *cleopige to þe* (60.1.4a), *God, min gebed* (53.2.1a), and dozens of others listed by Tschischwitz, pp. 58–60. In *helpe usser* (67.20.2b) the word is clearly the genitive pronoun.

The verb stem *libb-* is not found, while *lifi(g)-* (once *lifg-*) appears more than a dozen times. The quantity of the first syllable of *fæger* can only be determined from the faulty meter, but a long syllable seems probable, e.g. in *ne fæger lif*

(54.23.2b), though *ne* emends MS *he*. There is a similar, unencumbered example in the second half of the work, *on fæger lif* (112.7.2b). There is one instance of *gena*, beside four instances of *gyt*, but none of *gyta*. Apparently *gyta* was not in the revisor's vocabulary (it does not occur in West-Saxon prose, except in Mercian-based texts like the translation of Bede's history, and Wærferth's translation of Gregory's *Dialogues*), and so because of the meter he saw no alternative to retaining the Anglian form in *Hwylc þonne gena* (93.13.1a, with alliteration on *h*). In all the instances of *gyt*, on the other hand (77.23.2a, 77.30.1a, 88.5.3b, 91.13.1a), *gēna* would be equally acceptable metrically. This is not true in the second half of the work, but of course the original may also have had *gēn*.

*Sǣ* is usually masculine (68.2.1a, 76.16.1b, 77.27.2a, 88.8.1a, 94.5.1a), though of the first three instances in the Psalms, the first is ambiguous (64.6.3a), and the next two feminine (65.5.2a, 67.22.2a). In these instances, masculine forms would make no metrical difference. The revisor seems to have decided after a short time to allow the masculine forms to stand.

Southern forms like *gesāwon* are frequent, but there is also one instance of an Anglian form, *gesege* (90.8.2a). (Grein's *Sprachschatz* assigns *besegan* 52.4.2a to *besēon*, but it is more likely a corrupted preterite to *(be)sīgan*, as it translates *declinaverunt*. The anomalous metrical type is frequently paralleled in the Psalms: see, again, Tschischwitz, pp. 58–60.) The preterite *dǣdun* occurs twice, at 61.3.2b and 77.32.1b, the latter for MS *dǣdum*. Under classical standards, the form with the long vowel is more probable in *swa hi on wudu dydan* (73.4.3b), and, in the second half, the long vowel seems required in *fleam gedydan* (141.5.1b). In the only other instance, *fyrn geara dydan* (94.9.1b), even if *fyrn* were ever unstressed in verse (it is not: cf. the other fifteen examples in the ASPR concordance), under Kuhn's first law the alliteration on *g* would demand that *fyrn* be put into the on-verse, *Swa on grimnesse*—cf. *Hwæt, me soðfæstnes min* (90.5.1a), *ne on ecnesse ðe* (102.9.2a), and many others listed by Tschischwitz (pp. 42–45). He suggests some places where the long vowel of *dǣdun* ought to be extended analogically to the singular (pp. 106–7), but the examples are inconclusive.

Anglian *nymþe* is frequent in both halves of the work, as is *oferhygd*, with its derivates. Plural *fōtas* (see the discussion of the *Phoenix* above) appears three times in the second half (121.2.1b, 131.7.3a, 139.5.5a), but under classical standards, *fēt* seems to be required metrically at 113.15.3a, 114.8.4a, and 134.18.3a. There is also one example of *tōðas* (57.5.1a). 1. sg. *eam* appears three times in the first half (68.29.1a, 87.8.3a, 101.5.3a), and once in the second (141.1.3a), beside many instances of *eom*. The Psalms contain the only examples of Mercian pl. *earon, earun* in verse (101.21.7a; 104.7.2a), though *næron* (*Seafarer* 82a) probably stands for *nearon* or *naron*. (So also John C. Pope has argued persuasively that another instance in verse is disguised by scribal error: see "*Daniel* 206, *hearan*: The Case of a Misplaced *h*," *N&Q* n.s. 30 [1983], 386–87.) The weak 2. sg. pret. ending is *-es* in *wiðferedes* (76.12.2b), beside many instances of *-est*. On the other hand, sj. *wese(n)*, which may be a late Southernism (see §353.8 above) is very frequent, and is bound by the alliteration at 71.20.2b, 88.46.2b, and in one instance in the second half (105.37.4a). Imperative plural *wesað* also occurs (67.5.1a, 113.23.1a), along with one instance of ind. pl. *wesað* in the second half (119.4.2a).

The (probably Mercian, if authentic) instance of *ac* 'numquid' at 77.20.5a was discussed above (§355.8). Vleeskruyer (pp. 48, 140) characterizes as

Mercian the practice of combining a possessive pronoun with a demonstrative, e.g. *ðas mine gesaldnisse* in Sweet's charter no. 48. This practice probably arose in the glossing of Latin texts, as a method of rendering the Latin inflections precisely, and it is largely limited to Mercian and Mercian-influenced texts, though it is also found in the Alfredian translation of Orosius' history. There are at least two examples in the first half of the Psalms, in *for his þæt gleawe folc* (67.8.1b) and *and his þæt hearde* (73.13.2a).

The verb *habban* has always 1. sg. ind. *hæbbe*, which is structural at a few places in the second half, e.g. *fæste hæbbe* (118.50.1b). 2. and 3. sg. *hafast, hafað* are frequent, with just one instance of *næfð* (see above). To *secgan* are the forms 1. sg. ind. *secge* (structural at 101.21.4b, etc.) and the alternate Southern form 3. sg. *sægeð* (70.14.1a, 3a), which also appears in *Genesis B* (682b).

The evidence on the whole suggests an Anglian original that has been Saxonized. If the work is Anglian, several criteria point to a Mercian rather than a Northumbrian provenance: primarily *eam, earon*, but also *Sigelwearas, cwist/cwyst, þet*, the use of a possessive adjective with a demonstrative, and perhaps *fōtas, tōþas* and *ac* 'numquid'. The only possibly Southern features that are structural are sj. *wese(n)* and, probably, the use of *mid* with the dative only. Given that the translation is most likely late, the former may be due to the influence of the standard language: cf. *weseð* at *Phoenix* 373b (see above), which suggests that these might have been used in poetic language in all dialects in the later period. The use of *mid* exclusively with the dative, however, is better explicable under the assumption that the language of the original text represents a border dialect, or that the isogloss for this feature did not follow the Mercian-Saxon border. The poet's grasp of classical meters is poor enough to cast doubt on the supposition that his command of Anglianisms is poetic rather than native.

The Psalms are probably rather late compositions. They share some metrical faults with the *Meters of Boethius* that are undoubtedly stylistic (particularly the placement of stress on normally unstressed words), but most of its metrical faults are like those of *Maldon* and other presumably late verse. Alois Brandl points out that the alliteration of *s* with *sc* also suggests a late date: see "Geschichte der englischen Literatur," *Pauls Grundriss der germanischen Philologie*, vol. 2, 2nd ed. (Strassburg: Trübner, 1901–9), pp. 941–1134, at 1094. Ælfric links the two sounds in his alliterative prose. How late the translation might be, it is impossible to determine. The Paris Psalter itself dates to the middle of the eleventh century. Baker (pp. 266–67; as above, pp. 411-12) argues that broken spellings like *meæhtig* and *neæhtes* in the metrical and not the prose portion of Eadwine's Psalter suggest that the original text antedates the middle of the tenth century. But the chief obstacle to this argument is that broken spellings are poetic—cf. *meahtig* in the *Kentish Hymn* and *Psalm 50*—and so may have been used in verse at any time, and may be attributable to the scribe of this portion of Eadwine's Psalter, assuming that he was attempting to write the poetic koine here. This seems a better explanation of Baker's observation that the scribe started to write *mihte* at 91.3.2b, but then changed the *i* to *e* and wrote *meæhte*. At any rate, since the metrical portion of the Paris Psalter seems to be based on interlinear glosses (see §355.8 above), broken spellings may also derive from the source.

# APPENDIX B:

# THE DATE OF THE *BATTLE OF MALDON*

Several scholars have suggested in recent years that *Maldon* may have been composed many years after the battle. The linguistic evidence may be considered here. It has long been known that the word *eorl* in late Old English replaces earlier *ealdorman*: see, e.g., Bosworth and Toller's dictionary. John McKinnell studies the word in detail in "The Date of *The Battle of Maldon*," *MÆ* 44 (1975), 121–36, arguing that the change in official documents is to be associated with Cnut's reorganization of the government in 1017. With only very dubitable exceptions, before that date, in charters, laws, and Chronicle entries the word is applied only to Scandinavians, and the English equivalent is always *ealdorman*. After that date, *ealdorman* is generally used of Englishmen given the title during the reign of Æthelred, while *eorl* is used of both Englishmen and Scandinavians titled by Cnut. The result is that *ealdorman* dies out quickly, the only instance in the Chronicle after A.D. 1020 being a lone reference *s.a.* 1036 in the Peterborough Chronicle to the Northumbrian Ælfhelm, who had died thirty years previously. In verse the word *eorl* is frequent in its more general English sense, and it is only in *Maldon* that it is used as the equivalent of *ealdorman*, always referring to Byrhtnoth. John Scattergood argues that *eorl* in the poem is not to be differentiated from the word as it is used in other Old English verse: see *"The Battle of Maldon* and History," in *Literature and Learning in Medieval and Renaissance England*, ed. John Scattergood (Blackrock, Co. Dublin: Irish Academic Press, 1984), pp. 11–24, at 15–16; and cf. Amos, pp. 144–45. But if it did not have this more specific sense it could not be used to distinguish Byrhtnoth from every other Englishman mentioned, as in the following verses (cf. also 132b, 146b, 203a, 233a):

> Þa þæt Offan mæg    ærest onfunde,
> þæt se eorl nolde    yrhðo geþolian . . . (5–6)

> þæt her stynt unforcuð    eorl mid his werode (51)

> Ða se eorl ongan    for his ofermode . . . (89)

In the last instance, Byrhtnoth has not been referred to in more than twenty-five lines. McKinnell concludes that the poem is unlikely to have have been composed before ca. 1020.

The date of the adoption of *eorl* to replace *ealdorman* in official West-Saxon records is not as relevant as it may at first seem. It should be said first that the date "ca. 1020" is not a tenable terminus, since *eorl* is used in the sense 'ealdorman' in Wulfstan's *Institutes of Polity*, a text that McKinnell does not consider, which is to be dated to the first decade of the eleventh century. And as Dorothy Whitelock observes, *eorl* is Wulfstan's own word, since he uses *ealdorman* only when he is quoting earlier legislation: see her edition of *Sermo Lupi ad Anglos*, 3rd ed. (London: Methuen, 1963), p. 45. But even supposing the limit of ca. 1020 were reliable, if it should be imagined that the poet called Byrhtnoth *eorl* because he was too young to know the man's actual title, it is difficult to explain why he uses the word *ealdorman* (219a) in reference to Ealhelm, *ealdorman* of Mercia ca. 940–950 (see Earle and Plummer, 2:170). The poet was not ignorant of the word, but for some reason regarded it as appropriate to Ealhelm, and not to Byrhtnoth. The distinction clearly has no historical basis, since Byrhtnoth was Æthelred's *ealdorman*; nor can the word be merely a poetic variation on *eorl*, since the poet apparently avoided applying it to Byrhtnoth. Unless the distinction is based on essentially imponderable factors (see, e.g., the literary solution proposed by D. G. Scragg in his edition of the poem, p. 27), perhaps the only very likely explanation is dialectal. Though the official West-Saxon records carefully distinguish *ealdorman* and *eorl*, none of these records is from Essex, a kingdom conquered by the Danes in the ninth century and ceded to Guthrum by Alfred. McKinnell depreciates the significance of Danish influence in Essex, noting that the county was recovered early in the tenth century, and that the evidence of place-names suggests only sparse Scandinavian settlement. Yet these arguments can hardly be admitted in regard to a poem that displays Scandinavian influence on its vocabulary and idiom, the clearest instances of which are *grið* (35b) and *drenga* (149a)—though, to be sure, the significance of the former is debatable, as it appears in the Viking messenger's speech. Moreover, though McKinnell objects that none of the Englishmen in the poem bears a Scandinavian name, this is not the case. As Cecily Clark points out, *Þurstan* (298a) certainly is Scandinavian, and his son's name *Wistan* (297b) may be an Anglicization of *Vésteinn*; and *Gadd* (287a) also appears to be Norse: see "On Dating *The Battle of Maldon*: Certain Evidence Reviewed," *Nottingham Mediaeval Studies* 27 (1983), 1–22, at 16–17. Norman Blake agrees, and argues very sensibly that *Maccus* (80a) is not likely to be the Celtic name that it has often been taken for, but an Anglicization of *Magnús*: see "The Genesis of *The Battle of Maldon*," *ASE* 7 (1978), 119–29, at 126. This is certainly what the onomastic evidence suggests: e.g., Symeon of Durham refers to one Maccus, who was the son of Anlaf, and the killer of Eiríkr Blóðøx; and the place called *Macusige* (Maxey, Northnts.), mentioned several times in the list of sureties for Peterborough estates, is said there to be inhabited by one Þur(w)old: see Agnes Robertson, *Anglo-Saxon Charters* (Cambridge: Cambridge Univ. Press, 1939), item 40; and Clark, pp. 16–17. No doubt at least the Scandinavian followers of Byrhtnoth referred to him as *eorl*, and given the evidence of Scandinavian influence on the poet's vocabulary, it should not be surprising that he also refers to him this way.

There are no reliable records from Essex in this period to give evidence one way or the other—possibly the version of the West-Saxon Gospels in BL MS Royal 1 A.xiv (along with Oxford, Bodleian MS Hatton 38, which seems to be a copy of it) is from Essex (see Jordan, §5, "Essex and Middlesex"), but naturally, as it is descended from a West-Saxon original, it should not be expected to contain East Saxon vocabulary—and so only probabilistic conclusions can be drawn. But in a remarkable piece of scholarship mentioned above, Cecily Clark chronicles the evidence for the integration of Scandinavians into the English population throughout the region where Byrhtnoth held estates, an area with tenth-century Essex at its core (an area larger than present-day Essex), but extending into Cambridgeshire, Hertfordshire, East Anglia, and the Midlands—

i.e., the Southern Danelaw. Despite the thin evidence of Scandinavian place-names throughout this area, well over a quarter of the masculine names in the late-tenth-century portion of the *Liber Eliensis* are Scandinavian in origin, and are almost always Anglicized—and it should be remembered that Ely was the foundation that derived the most direct benefit from Byrhtnoth's munificence in his furtherance of the Benedictine Reform, that he is buried there, and that two centuries after his death, his bones were honored by the Ely monks and his last battle recounted in detail in the same *Liber Eliensis*. (Incidentally, Archbishop Wulfstan, who applies *eorl* to Englishmen more than a decade before this usage crops up in the documents studied by McKinnell, had connections with Ely, and is buried there.) Less telling, but still significant, is the extraordinary number of Scandinavian names in the list of sureties for Peterborough estates, mentioned above, and dated 963 × 992; and the smaller variety of Scandinavian moneyers whose names are known from the coinage of the region. Reason dictates that the Southern Danelaw is the likeliest place for such a poem to have been composed, and the linguistic evidence, though it is neither extensive nor conclusive, does point to Essex: see §333 above. Cf. Eric Stanley's list of Scandinavianisms in Aldred's gloss to the Lindisfarne Gospels, which is small, Stanley argues, because Aldred's language is a *Schriftsprache* rather than a record of genuine late Northumbrian speech: see "Karl Luick's 'Man schrieb wie man sprach' and English Historical Philology," in *Luick Revisited*, pp. 311–34, at 321–24.

Even had the poet not referred to Ealhelm as *ealdorman*, a date after ca. 1020 would be difficult to understand, because the poet speaks with assurance about a considerable number of the English participants in the battle. His knowledge of the names and family relations of so many of the men is not likely to be that of someone distantly removed in time from the date of the battle. Norman Blake acknowleges the force of this observation when he opposes it the only way it can be opposed, by doing away with it altogether: the names, he argues, are all fabricated by the poet. Certainly he is right to warn against reading the poem too literally: e.g., it is not to be supposed that the retainers' speeches are substantially genuine, as Laborde claimed (see the article by Scattergood mentioned above), though the difficulty of how the poet should have witnessed all this and yet lived to report it has been relieved by O. D. Macrae-Gibson's observation that battle cannot have been joined before late afternoon, and may have been interrupted by nightfall: see "How Historical Is *The Battle of Maldon?*" *MÆ* 39 (1970), 89–107, at 104. These speeches are reminiscent of those fabricated centuries after the event by the writers of the Icelandic sagas. Yet since the poet uses the word *ealdorman*, a date after the reign of Cnut is unlikely, meaning that many of the children of those who fell in the battle were no doubt alive when the poem was composed, making such a brazen forgery difficult to credit. M. A. L. Locherbie-Cameron has more effectively responded to the various details of Blake's hypothesis, raising a number of telling objections, perhaps the most general of which is that the poet carefully differentiates the two Wulfmærs in the poem, referring to the son of Wulfstan as *se geonga* (155b) in order to distinguish him from the nephew of Byrhtnoth: see "Byrhtnoth, His Noble Companion, and His Sister's Son," *MÆ* 57 (1988), 159–71. The poet is also at pains to keep the faithful Godric separate from the faithless one. It appears, then, that the poet distinguished his characters with the care reserved for actual people. Locherbie-Cameron also gives a detailed examination of the personal names in the poem, and surveys figures named in contemporary documents with whom the poem's characters might be identified: see "The Men Named in the Poem," in *The Battle of Maldon, A.D. 991,* ed. Donald Scragg (Oxford: Blackwell, 1991), pp. 238–49; and see an earlier study of hers, "Ælfwine's Kinsmen and *The Battle of Maldon,*" *N&Q* 25 (1978), 486–87.

It of course cannot be proved when the poem was composed, but that is true of nearly all Old English poems. In sum, the linguistic reasons for supposing a date much later than that of the battle are unpersuasive, and the poet's detailed knowledge of the participants and their family connections, along with his apparent intention to eulogize all of them, grows more difficult to explain the later the poem is assumed to have been composed. For these reasons, Cable's assignment of the poem to the year 991 is likelier than any other for the purpose of constructing a presumed chronology to be tested by the available metrical criteria. This seems to be the general view held in the essays in the anthology last mentioned.

# APPENDIX C:

# LONG AND SHORT INFLECTIONAL SYLLABLES

In conjunction with the discussion of Kaluza's law in Chapter 6, the following remarks are provided as a guide to long and short inflectional endings. An inflection is long if (1) it ends in a consonant in Old English, or (2) the form reconstructed for Proto-Indo-European or Proto-Germanic is written with a circumflex accent, in actuality probably representing dissyllabic pronunciation in Proto-Germanic, since the Proto-Indo-European origin of this type of vocalism appears to be vowel contraction, e.g. in the thematic dative singular endings masc. *-ôy (from thematic -o- plus athematic dative ending -ey-) and fem. *-ây (<*-o-Hey). Likewise the nominative plural i-stem ending, which is not apocopated in Old Saxon and Old High German (as discussed below) arose by contraction in Germanic itself (if it is not analogical: see p. 153, nn. 2f.). It would appear that circumflexion has no bearing on the development of diphthongs (see, e.g., Campbell, §355.2 n. 3, and Krause, §73.3), in which event they should all be regarded as long: e.g., the adjective desinence nom. pl. masc. -e < *-oy, without circumflexion, is clearly long in scapan scirhame (Beowulf 1895a) and elsewhere in Beowulf. Yet this is difficult to prove, as nearly all final diphthongs that can be tested metrically were originally circumflected, and the etymologies of the remainder are debatable: in this instance, Brunner supposes that the ending was in fact circumflected in Proto-Germanic (see below). Admittedly, positing a developmental difference between the two types of diphthongs obviates one difficulty, that unstressed ai and au apparently were monophthongized in final syllables already in Northwest Germanic (an assumption that Campbell shares, §331.7); and so while circumflexion could still distinguish them from original monophthongs, after that point, diphthongal articulation could not. Yet the diphthongs and monophthongs do develop differently, e.g. in ō-stem gen. sg. *-ôz > -e (OSax. -a) and short-stemmed u-stem gen. sg. *-auz > -a (OSax. -o). Another phonological advantage of this alternative analysis is that it provides a motive for the analogical leveling that made early Old English forms like dat. sg. -wini obsolete (Campbell, §601), since the i-stem endings, if uncircumflected and thus shortened, would have been lost after a long syllable, as apparently happened in Old Saxon, where the endings after long syllables are analogical. Yet because the point cannot be settled conclusively, the standard view will be adopted here. Suffice it to say that since most of the relevant final diphthongs were circumflected, they may be regarded as metrically long; and that if diphthongs without circumflexion should be metrically short, Brunner's view will explain the only otherwise very difficult exception, the nominative plural masculine adjective desinence.

In the paradigms below, only early Old English endings are provided, and it must be kept in mind that later, analogical forms like *i*-stem nom. pl. *-cwidas* might represent scribal alteration of earlier forms, in this instance *-cwide*; cf. the equivalence of *hleoðorcwyde* and *hleoþorcwidas* in the corresponding passages in *Daniel* (315b) and *Azarias* (32b). The reconstructions in these paradigms are Proto-Germanic, except that long diphthongs remain unshortened, the better to illustrate the original distribution of long and circumflected vocoids.

NOUNS

1. *a*-stems (masc.)

|  | sg. | pl. |
|---|---|---|
| nom. | *-az > Ø | *-ôs > -as (long) |
| acc. | *-am > Ø | *-ôs (anal.) > -as (long) |
| gen. | *-as(a) > -es (long) | *-ôm > -a (long) |
| dat. | *-ôi > -e (long) | *-omiz > -um (long) |

The neuter *a*-stems are like the masculines, except that *-am in the nom.-acc. singular is apocopated, and *-ō in the nom.-acc. plural gives -u (short) after short stems and is lost after long ones. The masculine *ja*-stems (e.g., with an originally short root, gen. pl. *secga* < *sagjôm*, and long-stemmed nom. sg. *ende* < *andijaz*, with suffixal alternation under Sievers' law) are like the *a*-stems except that *-(i)jaz in the nominative singular and *-(i)jam in the accusative singular give -e. This ending should be short, though in neither case can this be confirmed metrically, as the ending can appear only after a long syllable in Old English, or after *r* (as in *here*; nom.-acc. sg. *sege* and such were replaced analogically by the oblique stem with the geminate final: see Campbell, §576). There are no metrically unambiguous examples after *r* in verse, unless *flodblac here* (*Exodus* 498b) is assumed to conform to Kaluza's law. Yet this -e might appear after a syllable shortened under low stress, as with the agentive suffix *-ere*, and this appears to explain the metrical treatment of *cāsere* (§240), which has the agentive suffix by analogy (Campbell, §518). On the other hand, the masculine *wa*-stems have nom. sg. *-waz and acc. *-wam, both giving -u (short), an ending preserved only after short stems. The long-stemmed *wa*-stems became indistinguishable from *a*-stems. The neuter *ja*-stems are like the masculines. Similarly, the neuter *wa*-stems have nom.-acc. sg. *-wam > -u (short), and only short stems remain in this declension.

2. *ō*-stems (all feminine)

|  | sg. | pl. |
|---|---|---|
| nom. | *-ō > -u/Ø (short) | *-ôz > -a (long) |
| acc. | *-ōm > -e (short) | *-ōnz > -e (short) |
| gen. | *-ôz > -e (long) | *-ôm > -a (long) |
| dat. | *-ôi > -e (long) | *-ōmiz > -um (long) |

Nom. pl. -e in Anglian texts is analogical, as is WS acc. pl. -a: see Frederick Kortlandt, "The Origin of the Old English Dialects," in the Fisiak Festschrift, I, 437–42, at 437–8. The *jō*-stems are like the *ō*-stems except that none survives with -u in the nominative singular (but see Campbell, §591, n. 2 for a possible exception). The *wō*-stems are entirely like the *ō*-stems.

3. *i*-stems (masc.)

|  | sg. | pl. |
|---|---|---|
| nom. | *-iz* > -e/Ø (short) | -e (short: see below) |
| acc. | *-im* > -e/Ø (short) | *-ins* > -e (short) |
| gen. | -es (anal., long) | *-ijôm* > -(ig)a (long) |
| dat. | -e (short: see below) | -um (anal., long) |

The feminine *i*-stems with short roots adopted *ō*-stem inflections early. In the masculine nominative plural, *-e* from *-i* is sometimes found after short stems in early texts, e.g. Cp. *stridi* (cf. *daele*) and VP *gehusscipe*. This archaic ending is also preserved in the forms *byre* and *wine* in verse. But more usually analogical *-as* has been added, as nearly always after long stems. Bliss regards this *-e* in the nominative plural as short, and this must be correct. The usual view is that this ending must reflect PGmc. *-îz* < PIE *-eyes*, and this explains the preservation of the ending in Old Saxon and Old High German, where, if short, it would have been lost after a long stem. Yet the Old High German ending *-i* was certainly short: it is never spelt *-ii*, and in Notker it already shows development to *-e*, as in *géste* (Braune and Eggers, §215, n. 4). Possibly the ending in both Old High German and Old Saxon is analogical to the short-stemmed *i*-stems, and this would explain the preservation of *-i* < *-ins* in the accusative plural, a development that at any rate requires some analogical explanation (see p. 154, n. 3); but then it must be assumed that *-îz* gives a short reflex. If the ending is not analogical, *-îz* must still give a short reflex, though it should then be assumed that the shortening occurred after the syncope of final short *-i*. In either event, it must be concluded once again that the development of high and non-high long vowels is different in West Germanic: as Bliss argues (see §§187ff. above), long high vowels were shortened before long non-high vowels, and this must now include circumflected vowels. This is also the conclusion that the metrical evidence leads to, since the *Beowulf* poet, who is exceptionally faithful to Kaluza's law, treats the Old English ending as metrically short in *laðbite lices* (1122a). The ending also occurs in *burgstede berstað* (*Christ II* 811a), and possibly in *wælgryre weroda* (*Exodus* 137a), though this form could also be singular.

Campbell remarks that the PIE *i*-stem "gen. and dat. sg. were not developed in Gmc., where the endings are from the *a*-stems" (§600). This is the conclusion to which the North and East Germanic evidence points, but it must be modified in view of the evidence of West Germanic. The endings of OE gen. *wines* and dat. *wine* are the same as those of the *a*-stems, but dat. *-e* could as well have developed from *-i*, which happens to be the short-stemmed ending in Old Saxon (cf. long-stemmed *-e*). In Old High German the ending is normally *-e*, but Sievers identifies dat. sg. *meri* as a neuter *i*-stem, a lost category in Old High German: see "Zur Accent- and Lautlehre der german. Sprachen," *PBB* 4 (1877), 522–39, and 5 (1878), 63–163, at 107. In that event, the short-stemmed ending *-i* found beside *-e* in the earliest OHG glossaries is perhaps original rather than analogical to the nominative and accusative (cf. Braune and Eggers, §217, n. 4).

But regardless of whether OE *wine* reflects *wini* or analogical *winæ*, certainly WGmc. *-i* was preserved into early Old English, as it is found in early texts, beside *-æ* (Campbell, §601). This *-æ* may be by analogy to the *a*-stems, as in Gothic. The source of *-i* is more difficult to determine. It may reflect the PIE locative ending of the close-inflected type, *-ēy*, as in the Gothic feminine *i*-stems: see, e.g., Bammesberger, *Morphologie*, §5.2.3.3, and Krause, §§131–3. Yet it is difficult to see how PIE *-ēy* could give *-ai* in Gothic and *-i* in West Germanic, especially if, as Bammesberger points out, the parallel development of *-ēy-* in the third class of weak verbs was to Gmc. *-ai-*. Accordingly, Krahe and Meid (vol. 2, §12) suggest that the *-i* ending derives from a PIE close-inflected instrumental desinence, *-ī*, as in Vedic *ácittī*. Yet this will not account for the long-stemmed feminine ending, since plain *-ī*, without circumflexion, ought to have been lost after long syllables in Old English: cf. *jō*-stems like *bend* < *\*bandī* (Gothic *bandi*).

But the reasoning offered above in regard to the nominative plural desinence provides a solution. It is, after all, simplest to derive the dative ending from a PIE dative, rather than from a locative or instrumental. The PIE close-inflected dative ending was *\*-eyey*, which should have developed in early Germanic to *\*-ijī*, and thence to *\*-î*, just as in the nominative plural. And just as with the nominative plural, in Old High German the reflex *-i* is certainly short (Braune and Eggers, §218, n. 2), even though it is not apocopated after a long syllable. If *\*-î* represents dissyllabic *-ii*, it may be supposed that apocope of short *-i* deleted the second vowel, leaving a short *-i*, as required in Old High German.

Regardless of which of these solutions is correct, the dative singular ending ought to be metrically short, and that is what the evidence of *Beowulf* indicates: cf. *mundgripe mægenes* (1534a). There is also an example of this ending in *ealhstede eorla* (*Daniel* 673a). The genitive singular of short-stemmed *i*-stems is not attested in early Old English records, and so it is impossible to say whether *-es* stands for earlier *-i*, as in the Old Saxon and Old High German feminine *i*-stems. Nor are there any examples in a metrically unambiguous position in the test group of poems.

4. *u*-stems (masc. and fem.)

|      | sg.                       | pl.                               |
|------|---------------------------|-----------------------------------|
| nom. | *\*-uz* > *-u/Ø* (short)  | ?*\*-awiz* > *\*-auz* > *-a* (long) |
| acc. | *\*-um* > *-u/Ø* (short)  | *-a* (anal., long)                |
| gen. | ?*\*-auz* > *-a* (long)   | *-a* (anal., long)                |
| dat. | *-a* (uncertain)          | *\*-umiz* > *-um* (long)          |

There are no neuter *u*-stems preserved as such in Old English. The reconstruction of the dative singular is uncertain. Gothic has *-au*, generally assumed to reflect a PIE locative *\*-ēw*, parallel to *\*-ēy* in the *i*-stems. Cf. Runic *Kunimu[n]diu*, and the ending *-iu* used in the earliest Old High German records, later *-i* > *-e*. But once again this is a poor match with the Ingvaeonic endings: cf. OSax. *-o*. Perhaps this reflects the PIE ablaut alternant *\*-ōw*, as suggested by Krahe and Meid (vol. 2, §17). But again the parallel with the nominative plural suggests that the PIE dative *\*-owey* is a possible source. The genitive singular is reconstructed as *\*-auz* by comparison to Gothic *-aus*, parallel to feminine *i*-stem *-ais*. *Beowulf* contains no metrically unambiguous examples of these endings. In *bordwudu beorhtan* (1243a), *-u* is perhaps an older accusative plural ending, as Klaeber and Bliss have it, from *\*-uns*, and therefore short. Less likely it is accusative singular, in apposition to a plural noun.

5. *n*-stems. Clearly, almost all the inflections in this category are long, since they end in a consonant. As in the other stem classes, the second syllable of gen.

pl. *-ena* derives from *\*-ôm*, and so is long. The nom. sg. masc. ending *-a* is also long, from *\*-ô*, while nom.-acc. sg. neut. and nom. sg. fem. *-e* derive from *\*-ōn*, and so are short.

6. Other athematic stems. There are few ambiguous forms in this category. Among the root nouns, only the feminines *hnutu*, *hnitu*, and *studu* are relevant, and these do not occur in verse. The *nomina agentis* in *-end* (all masculine), like *wealdend*, are irrelevant, never showing a short monosyllabic stem. There are no short-stemmed *s*-stems that have not adopted other declensions. The original nominatives singular to dissyllabic stems in *-þ-* (*hæle*, *ealu*, stems *hæleþ-*, *ealoþ-*) are short.

## PRONOUNS

The first and second person personal pronouns are unambiguous. Among the other pronouns, only a few forms are relevant. PGmc. acc. sg. masc. *\*-n-ōm* gives a short ending in OE *þone*, *hwone*, and gen. sg. fem. *\*-zy-ōz* gives a short one in *hire*, while dat. sg. *\*-zy-ōi* gives a long ending in the homograph *hire*. Gen. pl. *-ra* is long, as always. Note that *gehwǣre* is a late West-Saxonism that generally spoils the meter where it appears, demonstrating that it replaces *gehwæs* or *gehwǣm* (Campbell, §716, n. 4).

## ADJECTIVES

Weak adjectives have the same endings as *n*-stem nouns, except that the genitive plural has *-ra*, long as always. The inflections of the *a*- and *ō*-stems (including most strong adjectives) are an amalgam of pronominal endings and those found in the thematic nouns:

|       | masc. sg.                        | masc. pl.                     |
|-------|----------------------------------|-------------------------------|
| nom.  | *\*-az* > Ø                      | *\*-ai* > *-e* (long)         |
| acc.  | *\*-anōm* > *-ne* (short)        | *-e* (anal., long)            |
| gen.  | *\*-as(a)* > *-es* (long)        | *\*-aizôm* > *-ra* (long)     |
| dat.  | *\*-ozmō(i)* > *-um* (long)      | *\*-omiz* > *-um* (long)      |
| instr.| *-e* (long?)                     |                               |

|       | neut. sg.                        | neut. pl.                     |
|-------|----------------------------------|-------------------------------|
| nom.  | *\*-am* > Ø                      | *\*-ō* > *-u*/Ø (short)       |
| acc.  | *\*-am* > Ø                      | *\*-ō* > *-u*/Ø (short)       |
| gen.  | *\*-as(a)* > *-es* (long)        | *\*-aizôm* > *-ra* (long)     |
| dat.  | *\*-ozmō* > *-um* (long)         | *\*-omiz* > *-um* (long)      |
| instr.| *-e* (short?)                    |                               |

|       | fem. sg.                         | fem. pl.                      |
|-------|----------------------------------|-------------------------------|
| nom.  | *\*-ō* > *-u*/Ø (short)          | *\*-ôz* > *-a* (long)         |
| acc.  | *\*-ōm* > *-e* (short)           | *\*-ōnz* > *-a* (short)       |
| gen.  | *\*-ōizōz* > *-re* (short)       | *\*-ōizôm* > *-ra* (long)     |
| dat.  | *\*-ōizōi* > *-re* (long)        | *-um* (anal., long)           |

Brunner (§150.1) reconstructs a circumflected diphthong in the masculine nominative plural, by addition of PIE pronominal *\*-oy* to the theme vowel; but this is not how the other cases are formed. The masculine and neuter instrumental singular is a puzzle. It is sometimes thought to derive from the PIE athematic locative *-oy, but this leaves OSax. OHG -u unexplained. On the other hand, while PIE thematic instr. *-ō will account for these, it will not explain OE -e. In early texts this appears as -i, and so perhaps ought to be identified with occasional a-stem instrumentals in -i (Campbell, §571), from PGmc. *-ī < PIE *-eyH. If that is so, its retention after long stems is analogical. Presumably it is this retention that prompts Brunner (§150.1, and cf. §44) to reconstruct instr. *-î, which is surely wrong.

There are no ja- or jō-stem adjectives with short stems in Old English. The adjectives in wa- and wō- are like those in a- and ō-, except that they have -u (always short) in the nominative singular of all genders, as well as the accusative singular and nominative and accusative plural neuter.

The i-stem adjectives are declined the same way as the corresponding nouns in Proto-Germanic, but in Old English they are like the short-stemmed a- and ō-stem adjectives, except that they have -e (short) in the nominative singular masculine (from *-iz) and nominative and accusative singular neuter (from *-i). Similarly, the u-stem adjectives occasionally have -u (short) in the nominative singular of all genders.

## ADVERBS

The commonest ending -e, as in hraðe and hrædlīce, derives from the PIE thematic ablative ending *-êd, and so is long. The long ablaut variant *-ôd perhaps is reflected in tela, as it certainly is in adverbs in -inga, -unga. Perhaps also fela has an instrumental ending—cf. Anglian feolu, fealo, which is nominative and accusative singular neuter of the u-stem, as in the other Germanic languages —though whether this reflects *-ôd or the proper PIE instrumental u-stem ending *-ouH, it is impossible to say.

## VERBS

In strong verbs, Anglian 1. sg. pres. ind. -u (short) derives from *-ō. The West-Saxon equivalent -e is of disputed origin: see Warren Cowgill, "The Old English Present Indicative Ending -e," Symbolae linguisticae in honorem Georgii Kuryłowicz (Wrocław: Polska Akademia Nauk, 1965), pp. 44–50, with the references there. The origin of the 2. sg. pret. ind. ending -e is also disputed; but whatever its source, it almost certainly should be short: see Alfred Bammesberger, Der Aufbau des germanischen Verbalsystems, Untersuchungen zur vergleichenden Grammatik der germanischen Sprachen 1 (Heidelberg: Winter, 1986), §5.3. The evidence of Gothic suggests that the present subjunctive of all Germanic strong verbs is based on the PIE thematic optative, i.e. theme vowel plus *-yH- plus athematic secondary ending (*-m, *-s, etc.). Thus the present subjunctive endings all contain PGmc. *-ai- < PIE *-oyH-, and so are long. On the other hand, the preterite subjunctive ending -e, also found in the present subjunctive of preterite-present verbs, reflects the weak-grade form *-ī-, and so is short. Brunner (§150.1) would reconstruct a circumflected vowel here, presumably again to explain preservation of the vowel after long stems; but as -ī derives from PIE *-iHs, *-iHt, there is no call for this. These optative endings are all uncertain, since Bammesberger has shown that analogical changes must have set in relatively early: see "Der Optativ bei athematischen Verbalstämmen im Altenglischen," *Anglia* 100 (1982), 413–18.

Few forms among the weak verbs are ambiguous with regard to final quantities. In the first class, the imperative singular has the short ending *-e*. Luick (§299, n. 1, in reliance on Streitberg, §223) derives this from *-î* < PIE *-eye*, and this seems the best explanation. It accounts for Gothic *nasei* (instead of *nasi*), as well as the preservation of the ending after long stems in Old Saxon and Old High German, though it is lost in this environment in Old English. This is the usual behavior of circumflected vowels in West Germanic (Campbell, p. 242, n. 1; Brunner, §44, n. 1), and it parallels the situation in the nominative plural of *i*-stems (discussed above, where it was concluded that even circumflected high vowels are metrically short). All these developments must otherwise be explained as analogical—as for instance Krahe and Meid have it (vol. 2, §93). They in fact reconstruct PIE *nos-ye*, though in the present paradigm they reconstruct a connecting vowel, e.g. 1. sg. *nos-ey-ō* (§85).

Preterites of the first class like *fremede* are irrelevant to Kaluza's law, as they do not bear secondary stress. In the second class, the imperative ending *-a* is long, to be derived from PGmc. *-ô*. The development of the third weak class is disputed: see "PIE *ə* in Germanic Unstressed Syllables," in *Die Laryngaltheorie und die Rekonstruktion des indogermanischen Laut- und Formensystems*, ed. Alfred Bammesberger (Heidelberg: Winter, 1988), pp. 153–77, at 168–70. And so it is not possible to speak with assurance about resolution in forms like Anglian 1. sg. pres. ind. *hafo* and imp. sg. *hafa*, though they are probably short and long, respectively.

Among the anomalous verbs, the cognates of *dyde* suggest a reduplicated form, but it was argued above (§§112ff.) that the ending is analogical to that of the first weak class. Yet the origin of these desinences is one of the most disputed issues in Germanic philology. The endings of the first and third person singular seem to derive from *-ō(m)* and *-ē(þ)*, in which event they are short. 3. sg. pres. ind. *wile* bears a preterite optative ending, as demonstrated by the Gothic cognate, and so the desinence is short.

# APPENDIX D:

# DATING THE EARLY BEDE MANUSCRIPTS

According to the standard view, the Moore MS (M; Cambridge Univ. Library Kk. v. 16) almost certainly was written in the year 737, and the St. Petersburg (P) no later than 746, though the *Historia* itself could have been copied before the chronological entries at the end that point to this date: see the discussion in A. H. Smith's *Three Northumbrian Poems* (London: Methuen, 1933), pp. 19–23. But O. S. Arngart has pointed out that the chronological calculations in B (BL MS Cotton Tiberius A.xiv) point to the year 746, just as in P. The two calculations contain identical errors that cannot be regarded as independent developments; and B cannot be a copy of P, as Lowe suggests, since it corrects P too frequently. The implication is that the two (or, rather, the memoranda on Northumbrian history in the two, as they are in the hand of a corrector in P, rather than in the hand of one of the main scribes) are copied from a single source, and the chronological calculations may be mere mechanical reproductions, with significance for dating the exemplar, but not the two copies. See Arngart, "On the Dating of Early Bede Manuscripts," *Studia Neophilologica* 45 (1973), 47–52. It makes little difference whether Arngart is right that P and B are independent of each other, or whether B is copied from P, as Malcolm Parkes asserts: see "The Contribution of Insular Scribes of the Seventh and Eighth Centuries to the 'Grammar of Legibility'," in *Grafia e interpunzione del latino nel medievo*, ed. Alfonso Maierù (Roma: Ateneo, 1987), 15–30, at 26–27. Even if B is copied from P, that in itself is evidence that the chronological calculations could be copied without alteration or understanding of their significance, and therefore those in P may also have been copied from an earlier text.

Accordingly, the date of M may also be doubted: although the chronological calculations in the manuscript point to the year 737, they are collected at the end, rather than given in the margins of the summary of major events at the appropriate places. *Cædmon's Hymn* and a few glosses to words from the first three books also appear here at the end. Doubtless the reason is that the margins in M are too narrow, and the Moore scribe wrote out the summary in a single column. And so it is likely that these calculations, too, were copied from the margins of an earlier manuscript, and may also not reflect the actual year that the scribe of M wrote them out: see M. B. Parkes, "The Scriptorium of Wearmouth-Jarrow," Jarrow Lecture (1982), pp. 26–7. It may in any case be said that P and M must be dated to the eighth century on paleographical grounds; and it is also now known that M was in Aachen, in the library of Charlemagne's Palace School, ca. 800, perhaps taken there by, or at the behest of, Alcuin: see Bernhard Bischoff, "Die Hofbibliothek Karls des Grossen," *Karl der Grosse, II: Das Geistige Leben*, ed. Bernhard Bischoff (Düsseldorf: Schwann, 1965), p. 56; and Peter Godman, *Alcuin: The Bishops, Kings, and Saints of York* (Oxford: Clarendon, 1982), p. 131n. In order to explain why not all the memoranda point to the same year, Kevin Kiernan has recently argued that the chronological memoranda in M do not indicate the date of this manuscript or its exemplar; rather, they are intended to trace a manuscript tradition. See "Old English Manuscripts: The Scribal Deconstruction of 'Early' Northumbrian," *ANQ*, n.s. 3 (1990), 48–55. The argument suggests a valuable reservation, since the number of mathematical blunders required under the standard interpretation is surprising; and if the chronological memoranda in M are copied from the margins of another, lost manuscript, as seems likely, the "blunders" may be explained by the assumption that not all the marginal calculations in the exemplar were made in the same year, or even by the same person. But Kiernan carries his healthy skepticism too far, building a hypothesis more extreme than the one he rejects, since he makes the assumption that each calculated date represents the addition of another manuscript to the tradition behind M. The same reasoning applied to other Bede manuscripts would lead to the conclusion that P and B were copied sometime after 861, since both contain a calculation pointing to that date. And of course that is paleographically inadmissible. Thus, at least some of the blundered calculations must be genuine blunders. At any rate, Kiernan's argument does not raise any greater uncertainty than that resulting from Arngart's findings. And Kiernan's argument that M may have been written as late as the early ninth century is implausible, as the language and orthography of M are too different from those of the early ninth-century *Liber Vitae Dunelmensis*. It should also be noted that the accuracy of the work itself in P speaks for an early date. Katherine O'Brien O'Keeffe has recently reminded us that there appear to be just six errors in the text, so that the work must be very close to the author's autograph copy: see *Visible Song: Transitional Literacy in Old English Verse* (Cambridge: Cambridge Univ. Press, 1990), p. 33. This does not prove that it was copied early, but it does render an early date likelier.

Kiernan, reviving an old view, also suggests that *Cædmon's Hymn* is not the original hymn, but a translation of Bede's Latin translation of the hymn: see "Reading Cædmon's 'Hymn' with Someone Else's Glosses," *Representations* 32 (Fall, 1990), 157–74. His chief evidence is that Bede's *debemus* corresponds to Cædmon's *scylun* (1a), without an accompanying pronoun *wē*. From this he concludes that the direction of translation is more likely from Latin to English. But it would be peculiar to suppose that the imagined Old English translator either did not know that *scylun wē* would be a more explicit translation (cf., e.g., Li., where pronouns are usually included in the word-for-word gloss when there is no nominal subject), or that for some unfathomable reason he or she felt obliged to translate each Latin word with one English word. Rather, the reason for the absence of *wē* is more likely poetic, since it is a stylistic feature of the best Old English verse to employ the utmost economy with pronouns and other unstressed words (see Chap. 10 above). And the hortative first person plural subjunctive without a pronoun does in fact appear to be a poetic construction: see Mitchell's examples, §885. More important, since Bede's Latin version corresponds so closely to the Old English, excluding only some poetic variations and one adverb, all ornamental, it would be a remarkable coincidence if Kiernan's conjectured forger should have found that a word-for-word translation provided precisely the words required to form metrically regular and alliterating verses, if these verses were any different from Cædmon's own. After all, the form of the Old English poem is restrictive, while that of the Latin prose is not. Kiernan also argues that the hymn in P is not in the same hand as the main text

(p. 172, n. 16), but his analysis is unconvincing: when the glossator's writing is compared to the first three hands in the manuscript, the difference is so pronounced that, by contrast, the identity of the glossator's hand and the fourth hand seems secure.

# INDEX OF WORDS

Words in the appendices are not indexed. For the purpose of alphabetization, OE *ge-* is disregarded in all parts of speech. The numbers refer to pages.

# INDEX OF VERSES

In general, this index includes verses and lines that are quoted in part or in full, or are singled out for comment, or are listed in tables. Verses in the appendices are not indexed, nor are most untabulated lists of verse numbers, especially in footnotes. Verse and line numbers are in **boldface**, followed by a colon; the number after the colon refers to the page. An asterisk (*) indicates a place where an alteration to the ASPR text is suggested, or a reconstruction offered.

## OLD ICELANDIC

## OLD SAXON

## OLD ENGLISH

# INDEX OF AUTHORITIES

Some authorities are also listed in the Index of Subjects. Page numbers may also refer to footnotes on the given pages.

# INDEX OF SUBJECTS

Page numbers may also refer to footnotes on the given pages.

286, 294–98, 305, 343, 345

Meter: different from prose rhythms, 27–28; Indo-European, 201, 206; insufficiencies in current understanding of, 25–30; Middle English alliterative, 257

*Meters of Boethius, The:* authorship, 62; date, 3; dialect, 49; innovative or inept technique of, 32, 35–36, 251–52, 282

Metrical history: defined, 1; limits to current studies of, 60

Middle English evidence (*see also titles of individual texts*), 253–54, 264–65, 283–93 (passim), 316

Minot, L., 134

*mi*-verbs. *See* Athematic verbs

Monasteries: as site of verse production, 324, 343, 345–46; movement between, 338; ninth-century decline, 53

Monosyllabic and dissyllabic stems in West Germanic distinguished, 72–73

Morphological conditioning in phonology, 124, 176, 272, 384

Morphological suture. *See* Analogy

Names, Old English (*see also* Biblical names), 321–22; conservative spellings of, 317–18; in Latin verse, 170, 190–91; meter altered to accommodate, 210, 221, 230, 322; stress on the second elements of, 178–79, 190–91, 208–10, 229, 234, 261

Nasal consonants: mutation of /a/ before, 44; rounding of /a/ before, 43

Naturalness in linguistic explanation, 10

Noncontraction: in late Anglian texts, 117–21; in late West Saxon, 103–4, 116–17, 410; of vowels, 188, 392

Norman Conquest, 266–68, 287

Northumbrian, Northern and Southern, 361

Norwegian, 67

Nouns: *a*-stems and *wa*-stems, 420, 421; feminine stems in \*-*iþu*, 173; genitive plural of *a*-stems, 245–46; inflections, 419–23; *i*-stems, 243–47,

382, 383, 419–21; *ja*-stems, 173, 288, 420; *n*-stems, 389, 422–23; *ō*-stems, *jō*-stems, and *wō*-stems, 381–82, 384, 419–20; *r*-stems, 76, 86–87; *u*-stems, 379, 382–83, 397

Numbers, 195, 206, 225

Numismatics. *See* Coins

Objectivity, 6–8, 17–19

Offa, king of Mercia, 42, 296, 344

Old Frisian, 122, 389

Old High German, enclisis in, 271; inflections, 419–22

Old Saxon: caesura in, 222–23; inflections, 419–22; rule of the coda in, 210–211

Onset, defined, 201

Orm, *The Ormulum*, 147, 174, 191, 197, 198–99, 203, 229, 253, 335

Orosius, Old English, 134, 293, 294, 314, 319

Orthographic linguistic criteria (*cf.* Structural linguistic criteria), 122–23, 133–34, 275–76, 283–318, 350, 394–414 (passim)

Orthography: conservative, conventional, 360; letter-forms, 353

*Owl and the Nightingale, The*, 191, 253–54, 266

Paradigm regularization. *See* Analogy

Parallelism, 213–14

Parasiting (*see also* Anaptyxis), 29, 38, 48, 67–91, 121, 125, 212, 236, 348, 376, 396–414 (passim); as an areal change in West Germanic, 87; date, 377, 379; orthographic treatment of, 74, 90–91

Paris Psalter, 319; dialect features of the metrical portion, 410–14; metrical Psalms, metrical innovations of, 73, 216, 323, 339–40, 410; Saxonization of metrical portion, 339, 411–14

*Pastoral Care, The*, 134, 200, 271, 294–97 (passim), 304, 314, 319, 328

*Pearl*, 134, 311

*Phoenix, The*, 393, 402–404

*Piers Plowman*, 310

University of Pennsylvania Press
MIDDLE AGES SERIES
Edward Peters, General Editor

F. R. P. Akehurst, trans. *The* Coutumes de Beauvaisis *of Philippe de Beaumanoir.* 1992

Peter L. Allen. *The Art of Love: Amatory Fiction from Ovid to the* Romance of the Rose. 1992

David Anderson. *Before the Knight's Tale: Imitation of Classical Epic in Boccaccio's* Teseida. 1988

Benjamin Arnold. *Count and Bishop in Medieval Germany: A Study of Regional Power, 1100–1350.* 1991

Mark C. Bartusis. *The Late Byzantine Army: Arms and Society, 1204–1453.* 1992

J. M. W. Bean. *From Lord to Patron: Lordship in Late Medieval England.* 1990

Uta-Renate Blumenthal. *The Investiture Controversy: Church and Monarchy from the Ninth to the Twelfth Century.* 1988

Daniel Bornstein, trans. *Dino Compagni's* Chronicle *of Florence.* 1986

Betsy Bowden. *Chaucer Aloud: The Varieties of Textual Interpretation.* 1987

James William Brodman. *Ransoming Captives in Crusader Spain: The Order of Merced on the Christian-Islamic Frontier.* 1986

Maureen Barry McCann Boulton. *The Song in the Story: Lyric Insertions in French Narrative Fiction, 1200–1400.* 1993.

Kevin Brownlee and Sylvia Huot, eds. *Rethinking the* Romance of the Rose: *Text, Image, Reception.* 1992

Otto Brunner (Howard Kaminsky and James Van Horn Melton, eds. and trans.). *Land and Lordship: Structures of Governance in Medieval Austria.* 1992

Robert I. Burns, S.J., ed. *Emperor of Culture: Alfonso X the Learned of Castile and His Thirteenth-Century Renaissance.* 1990

David Burr. *Olivi and Franciscan Poverty: The Origins of the* Usus Pauper *Controversy.* 1989

Thomas Cable. *The English Alliterative Tradition.* 1991

Anthony K. Cassell and Victoria Kirkham, eds. and trans. *Diana's Hunt/Caccia di Diana: Boccaccio's First Fiction.* 1991

Brigitte Cazelles. *The Lady as Saint: A Collection of French Hagiographic Romances of the Thirteenth Century.* 1991

Karen Cherewatuk and Ulrike Wiethaus. *Dear Sister: Medieval Women and the Epistolary Genre.* 1993

Anne L. Clark. *Elisabeth of Schönau: A Twelfth-Century Visionary.* 1992

Willene B. Clark and Meradith T. McMunn, eds. *Beasts and Birds of the Middle Ages: The Bestiary and Its Legacy.* 1989

Richard C. Dales. *The Scientific Achievement of the Middle Ages.* 1973

Charles T. Davis. *Dante's Italy and Other Essays*. 1984

Nancy Edwards. *The Archaeology of Early Medieval Ireland*. 1990

Margaret J. Ehrhart. *The Judgment of the Trojan Prince Paris in Medieval Literature*. 1987

Richard K. Emmerson and Ronald B. Herzman. *The Apocalyptic Imagination in Medieval Literature*. 1992

Felipe Fernández-Armesto. *Before Columbus: Exploration and Colonization from the Mediterranean to the Atlantic, 1229–1492*. 1987

Katherine Fischer Drew, trans. *The Burgundian Code*. 1972

Katherine Fischer Drew, trans. *The Laws of the Salian Franks*. 1991

Katherine Fischer Drew, trans. *The Lombard Laws*. 1973

R. D. Fulk. *A History of Old English Meter*. 1992

Patrick J. Geary. *Aristocracy in Provence: The Rhône Basin at the Dawn of the Carolingian Age*. 1985

Peter Heath. *Allegory and Philosophy in Avicenna (Ibn Sînâ), with a Translation of the Book of the Prophet Muḥammad's Ascent to Heaven*. 1992

J. N. Hillgarth, ed. *Christianity and Paganism, 350–750: The Conversion of Western Europe*. 1986

Richard C. Hoffmann. *Land, Liberties, and Lordship in a Late Medieval Countryside: Agrarian Structures and Change in the Duchy of Wrocław*. 1990

Robert Hollander. *Boccaccio's Last Fiction: Il Corbaccio*. 1988

Edward B. Irving, Jr. *Rereading* Beowulf. 1989

C. Stephen Jaeger. *The Origins of Courtliness: Civilizing Trends and the Formation of Courtly Ideals, 939–1210*. 1985

William Chester Jordan. *The French Monarchy and the Jews: From Philip Augustus to the Last Capetians*. 1989

William Chester Jordan. *From Servitude to Freedom: Manumission in the Sénonais in the Thirteenth Century*. 1986

Ellen E. Kittell. *From* Ad Hoc *to Routine: A Case Study in Medieval Bureaucracy*. 1991

Alan C. Kors and Edward Peters, eds. *Witchcraft in Europe, 1100–1700: A Documentary History*. 1972

Barbara M. Kreutz. *Before the Normans: Southern Italy in the Ninth and Tenth Centuries*. 1992

E. Ann Matter. *The Voice of My Beloved: The Song of Songs in Western Medieval Christianity*. 1990

María Rosa Menocal. *The Arabic Role in Medieval Literary History*. 1987

A. J. Minnis. *Medieval Theory of Authorship*. 1988

Lawrence Nees. *A Tainted Mantle: Hercules and the Classical Tradition at the Carolingian Court*. 1991

Lynn H. Nelson, trans. *The Chronicle of San Juan de la Peña: A Fourteenth-Century Official History of the Crown of Aragon*. 1991

Charlotte A. Newman. *The Anglo-Norman Nobility in the Reign of Henry I: The Second Generation*. 1988

Joseph F. O'Callaghan. *The Cortes of Castile-León, 1188–1350*. 1989

William D. Paden, ed. *The Voice of the Trobairitz: Perspectives on the Women Trou-*
*badours.* 1989

Edward Peters. *The Magician, the Witch, and the Law.* 1982

Edward Peters, ed. *Christian Society and the Crusades, 1198–1229: Sources in Trans-*
*lation, including The Capture of Damietta by Oliver of Paderborn.* 1971

Edward Peters, ed. *The First Crusade:* The Chronicle of Fulcher of Chartres *and Other*
*Source Materials.* 1971

Edward Peters, ed. *Heresy and Authority in Medieval Europe.* 1980

James M. Powell. *Albertanus of Brescia: The Pursuit of Happiness in the Early*
*Thirteenth Century.* 1992

James M. Powell. *Anatomy of a Crusade, 1213–1221.* 1986

Michael Resler, trans. Erec *by Hartmann von Aue.* 1987

Pierre Riché (Michael Idomir Allen, trans.). *The Carolingians: A Family Who Forged*
*Europe.* 1993

Pierre Riché (Jo Ann McNamara, trans.). *Daily Life in the World of Charlemagne.* 1978

Jonathan Riley-Smith. *The First Crusade and the Idea of Crusading.* 1986

Joel T. Rosenthal. *Patriarchy and Families of Privilege in Fifteenth-Century England.*
1991

Steven D. Sargent, ed. and trans. *On the Threshold of Exact Science: Selected Writings*
*of Anneliese Maier on Late Medieval Natural Philosophy.* 1982

Sarah Stanbury. *Seeing the* Gawain-*Poet: Description and the Act of Perception.* 1992

Thomas C. Stillinger. *The Song of Troilus: Lyric Authority in the Medieval Book.* 1992

Susan Mosher Stuard. *A State of Deference: Ragusa/Dubrovnik in the Medieval Cen-*
*turies.* 1992

Susan Mosher Stuard, ed. *Women in Medieval History and Historiography.* 1987

Susan Mosher Stuard, ed. *Women in Medieval Society.* 1976

Jonathan Sumption. *The Hundred Years War: Trial by Battle.* 1992

Ronald E. Surtz. *The Guitar of God: Gender, Power, and Authority in the Visionary*
*World of Mother Juana de la Cruz (1481–1534).* 1990

Patricia Terry, trans. *Poems of the Elder Edda.* 1990

Hugh M. Thomas. *Vassals, Heiresses, Crusaders, and Thugs: The Gentry of Angevin*
*Yorkshire, 1154–1216.* 1993

Frank Tobin. *Meister Eckhart: Thought and Language.* 1986

Ralph V. Turner. *Men Raised from the Dust: Administrative Service and Upward*
*Mobility in Angevin England.* 1988

Harry Turtledove, trans. *The* Chronicle *of Theophanes: An English Translation of* Anni
Mundi *6095–6305 (A.D. 602–813).* 1982

Mary F. Wack. Lovesickness in the Middle Ages: The Viaticum *and Its Commentaries.*
1990

Benedicta Ward. *Miracles and the Medieval Mind: Theory, Record, and Event, 1000–*
*1215.* 1982

Suzanne Fonay Wemple. *Women in Frankish Society: Marriage and the Cloister, 500–*
*900.* 1981

Jan M. Ziolkowski. *Talking Animals: Medieval Latin Beast Poetry, 750–1150.* 1993